READINGS IN CONSUMER BEHAVIOR:
INDIVIDUALS, GROUPS, AND ORGANIZATIONS

THEORIES IN MARKETING SERIES

READINGS IN CONSUMER BEHAVIOR: INDIVIDUALS, GROUPS, AND ORGANIZATIONS

Edited by

MELANIE WALLENDORF
University of Michigan

GERALD ZALTMAN
University of Pittsburgh

JOHN WILEY & SONS

New York   Chichester   Brisbane   Toronto

Library of Congress Cataloging in Publication Data:

Main entry under title:

The Consumer behavior of individuals and organizations.

1. Consumers—United States—Addresses, essays,
lectures. 2. Consumer protection—United States—
Addresses, essays, lectures. I. Wallendorf, Melanie.
II. Zaltman, Gerald.

HC110.C6C559   658.8'34   78-13228
ISBN 0-471-03021-X

Printed in the United States of America

10 9 8 7 6 5 4 3 2 1

THIS BOOK IS DEDICATED TO

The Valles: (M.W.)

To Valerie for her understanding,
To Ron for asking the questions, and
To Demian for being open.

and

Franklin B. Evans (G.Z.)

who introduced me to the behavioral
sciences and the role of constructive
iconoclasm in furthering knowledge.

ABOUT THE AUTHORS

Melanie Wallendorf is an assistant professor of marketing at the University of Michigan. She received her M.A. in sociology in 1977 and her Ph.D. in marketing in 1979 from the University of Pittsburgh. Professor Wallendorf's interests center on the social aspects of consumer behavior and the social research methodologies that can be used for empirically exploring this area. Specifically, her interests include such topics as the diffusion of innovations, social roles, the structure of exchange transactions, consumer satisfaction/dissatisfaction and complaining behavior, and consumerism.

Gerald Zaltman holds a Ph.D. degree in sociology from the Johns Hopkins University and an M.B.A. degree in marketing from the University of Chicago. He is currently the Albert Wesley Frey Distinguished Professor of Marketing, University of Pittsburgh. He previously taught marketing at Northwestern University where he was the A. Montgomery Ward Professor of Marketing. Professor Zaltman is very active as a researcher and as a consultant to numerous firms and government agencies in the United States and abroad. His special interests focus on the responses of individual consumers and organizations to new products and services and the development of product management strategy. He is author, coauthor, or editor of numerous books and monographs, including *Consumer Behavior: Basic Findings and Management Implications; Industrial Buyer Behavior; Metatheory and Consumer Research; Marketing, Society, and Conflict; Marketing Research Fundamentals and Dynamics; Cases in Marketing Research; Innovations and Organizations; Strategies for Planned Change; Dynamic Educational Change;* and *Marketing: Theoretical Perspectives on an Applied Social Science.* Professor Zaltman is a frequent contributor to professional journals and conferences, and is a past member of the Board of Directors of the Association for Consumer Research. He is on the Editorial Board of numerous journals in the management and social science areas.

PREFACE

This collection of readings introduces the reader to a sample of the best research in the consumer behavior area. Most readings are presented primarily because of the importance of their findings. Other readings are presented because they are examples of sound research methodology or because they address important issues. Some readings address important but generally neglected topics.

This reader was developed to supplement existing consumer behavior textbooks by providing a detailed look at particular issues or particularly rich and important studies. The readings are current in that they represent not only recent work for the most part, but the best extant statements on various topics. In making selections, we had one inflexible criterion; that is, readings had to be meaningful to students who had no substantial prior background in consumer behavior. It is the intention of the authors that the book be used to provide examples of the way in which our knowledge of consumer behavior is built and tested.

Melanie Wallendorf
Gerald Zaltman

ACKNOWLEDGMENTS

First and foremost, we wish to thank the authors of each of the 42 articles for giving us permission to reprint their work. In particular, we wish to thank John Cipkala, John D. Eveland, and Everett Rogers who wrote articles especially for this volume. In addition, we would like to express our appreciation to the journals that gave us permission to reprint articles.

We would also like to thank students in our consumer behavior class who were helpful in earmarking areas of consumer behavior that they wanted to know more about and what aspects of consumer behavior research they found difficult to understand. Their comments guided us in selecting articles for inclusion in this book, as well as in writing the introductory remarks for each article.

Several people have reviewed this book at various stages. In particular, we benefitted from the suggestions of Richard M. Durand of the University of Alabama and Helmut Becker of the University of Portland.

Finally, we wish to express our appreciation to five people whose assistance was of utmost importance in the physical preparation of the manuscript, Chris Cameron, Shirley Dunham, Linda Graf, Beverly Penn, and Arlene Wycich. Their good humor as well as their efficiency has been very helpful.

Of course, we share full responsibility for any errors or omissions.

M.W.
G.Z.

CONTENTS

SECTION 1:   THE FIELD OF CONSUMER BEHAVIOR

SECTION 2:   SOCIETAL BASES OF CONSUMER BEHAVIOR

SECTION 3: THE CONSUMER BEHAVIOR OF FAMILIES AND ORGANIZATIONS

SECTION 8: ATTRIBUTION

SECTION 9: NEEDS AND MOTIVATION IN CONSUMER BEHAVIOR

SECTION 10: PERSONALITY

SECTION 11: LEARNING AND INFORMATION PROCESSING

SECTION 12: CONSUMER PROTECTION

SECTION 13: INNOVATIONS AND CONSUMER BEHAVIOR

SECTION 14: CONSUMER RESEARCH

INDEX

READINGS IN CONSUMER BEHAVIOR: INDIVIDUALS, GROUPS, AND ORGANIZATIONS

SECTION 1

THE FIELD OF CONSUMER BEHAVIOR

The field of consumer behavior is one of the most exciting areas of study in marketing today. Perhaps no other field is characterized by such rapid growth and diversity. Marketers and economists have been joined by anthropologists, psychologists, sociologists, lawyers and political scientists in trying to understand, influence, and predict the behavior of consumers. Government policy makers, business executives and citizen action agencies are all vitally concerned with the behavior of consumers. The term "consumers" no longer refers only to private individuals buying and using products and services offered by commercial agencies. Organizations are also recognized as consumers. Mothers on welfare, students enrolled in schools, and patients in psychotherapy are viewed as consumers as well. Understanding consumers is the cornerstone of not only marketing but of a responsive society meeting the needs of its citizens.

Despite a blossoming literature and a growing diversity of interests and backgrounds among researchers active in the field, some particular patterns are evident which should be noted. These patterns refer to both current and emerging trends.

1. The study of consumer behavior is becoming much more rigorous. The incidence of well-conceptualized, well-designed, and well-analyzed research is increasing. From this type of research a sound knowledge base is beginning to develop.
2. There is an increasing focus on the public policy implications of consumer behavior research, particularly on matters pertaining to how consumers process information, such as product ingredients.

1

3. Psychology and social psychology are the disciplines which have had the greatest influence. This is due largely to the greater acceptance in these disciplines of consumer behavior as an important context in which to study human behavior.
4. However, in the past few years there has been a substantial renewal of interest in the sociology of consumer behavior by both sociologists and those interested in sociological phenomena.
5. Consumerism has become a major and enduring social institution which has not only triggered public policy concern but enhanced concern with providing consumer education. Thus, the audience for consumer research studies has broadened greatly beyond marketing managers to include people in governmental agencies, citizen interest groups, educational institutions, and private not-for-profit social welfare agencies.
6. Research on attitudes and purchase intentions is perhaps the single most widely studied phenomena with information-processing issues a close second. However, other topics seem to be on the ascent, including interpersonal processes of social exchange which involve power relationships, influence attempts and negotiation, the buying behavior of organizations, and the impact on consumers of their social roles.

The above observations are only a sample of many which might be offered to the reader. Three articles are selected for this section that will expand the reader's sense of the field. One is authored by a marketing-oriented researcher, the second by a psychologically-oriented researcher, and the third by two sociologically-oriented consumer behavior experts. Each of these articles is introduced below.

"THE FUTURE OF BUYER BEHAVIOR THEORY"

This paper was originally prepared for presentation at the third annual conference of the Association for Consumer Research. This is a professional association of people from many disciplines and from many different types of organizations—business firms, government agencies, and universities.

The purpose of the paper is to offer predictions about future developments in the area of buyer behavior theory. However, before these predictions are made, Sheth presents a brief history of the consumer behavior field. In this history, he emphasizes basic subject areas which were explored in each time period as well as the development of new methods for doing research on these subject areas. In addition, he pinpoints the contributions from other disciplines, such as experimental psychology, social psychology, sociology, economics, and management science. The key point of this section is for the reader to develop an understanding of the stages of development the field of consumer behavior has gone through.

The sections of the paper following the discussion of history deal with buyer behavior theory in the future. The insight of the paper derives from Sheth's ability to decide which present events are indicators of future trends. Again, these predictions discuss subject areas (e.g., standardized tests and measurement procedures), as well as theory construction processes (e.g., theory evaluation criteria). It is just as important to look for the groups into which Sheth's predictions fall as to understand his specific predictions. Most importantly, the predictions made in the paper must be synthesized in one's imagination so there is a clear picture of what the field of consumer behavior will be in the future. Notice that many of the subject areas mentioned by Sheth (e.g., social class, role orientations, perceptions) are the subjects of other articles in this volume. Thus, this article is general; the specifics of buyer behavior are dealt with in other articles.

"CONSUMER PSYCHOLOGY AS A SOCIAL PSYCHOLOGICAL SPHERE OF ACTION"

Jacob Jacoby is one of the people interested in consumer behavior who is truly interdisciplinary. That is, he considers himself a consumer psychologist and places equal emphasis on both terms. The ideas in the following article were originally delivered as his presidential address to the Division of Consumer Psychology of the American Psychological Association. Thus, the audience consisted of people whose primary professional identification was, in most cases, psychology. Some of them were, perhaps, not very familiar with the marketing literature on consumer behavior; others were. Jacoby's purpose in this paper then is to address these people as psychologists and persuade them to become more involved in the psychology of consumer behavior. In particular, he is encouraging social psychologists to also be consumer psychologists.

Social psychology is a subdiscipline of psychology which studies the mental processes of people as social beings. Social psychology also studies the behavior of individuals as it is affected by social interactions and their social context. Consumer behavior, then, since it consists of behavior and mental processes occurring in a social context, can be studied from a social psychological perspective. This is what Jacoby means when he asserts that consumer psychology can be derived from social psychology. The definitions of consumer behavior and consumer psychology given in the article are concise and sound; they help clarify exactly how these subject areas fit with social psychology.

The Jacoby article, through its psychological approach, serves as a reminder that the study of consumer behavior relies heavily on work in other behavioral sciences. Many times this is referred to as consumer behavior "borrowing from" other disciplines. This article points out that the benefits from interdisciplinary work do not flow only one way. Consumer behavior is, perhaps, ready to "pay back" some of its debts from "borrowing" by offering a good research context for other fields. Jacoby describes 10 benefits that social psychologists can receive by becoming more involved in consumer research.

"TOWARD A SOCIOLOGY OF CONSUMPTION"

Since consumer behavior is an interdisciplinary field, different views on the same basic phenomena can be put forth. The fact that they are different does not mean that any of them are wrong. In fact, one reason the field is so exciting is because there is such a diversity of perspectives. Nicosia and Mayer use a sociological approach to the study of consumption. Their article is not meant to deny the importance of the social psychological ideas of Jacoby in the previous article or any of the ideas contributed by economists, physiological psychologists, anthropologists, or political scientists. Each of these approaches is needed to fully understand consumer behavior.

This article makes a case for studying consumption in a society as a social indicator, as well as the effect of the society on individual consumer behavior. Nicosia and Mayer cover four main concepts and their relationships to each other. These four concepts are: (1) values, (2) institutions, (3) institutionalized norms, and (4) consumption activities. The basic relationships explored are shown in the following diagram:

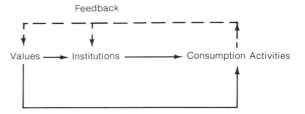

The authors do an excellent job of defining these terms in the first section of the article. The reader is advised to read this section closely. Like the definition used by Jacoby in the previous article, the definition of consumption activities is broader than is usually reflected in consumer behavior studies. Such studies usually only cover the acquisition phase of consumer behavior.

The authors have a particularly thought-provoking section exploring issues of causality. They ask: What causes what? Do changes in cultural values lead to increasing briefness of women's swimwear; or does the wearing of brief bathing suits produce changes in cultural values? The point is that it is not so easy to determine which of two events occurring at about the same time caused the other. We can know that the two are correlated, but not know if there is a causal link.

In the next major section, the relationships between these concepts are discussed. The research orientation of the authors and their audience (readers of the *Journal of Consumer Research*) is evident; however, the research questions are also posed in the light of the answers they can provide for government officials and corporate managers.

There is one point in the section on institutional arrangements and norms which needs further comment. In this section, the argument is put forth that since such a plurality of consumption institutions exists, there will be few norms governing the buying, use, and disposal of goods. The justification given is that there will be little consistency in the other persons present in different situations, and thus norms will not be enforced. At this point, the editors would like to raise a few points for the readers.

By definition a norm is a culturally accepted and enforced rule which applies in several similar situations and institutions. For example, the norm of not requesting help from sales clerks unless you are actually looking for an item (that is, only when you are not "just looking") applies in many types of retail establishments. It applies even though the people encountered in the various retail establishments (e.g., sales clerks) are different. By its nature, a norm applies even when the actors in the situation change. Thus, it appears that the lack of norms referred to by Nicosia and Mayer applies only to norms enforced by particular individuals, such as family members. Since people spend less time in family activities, the family members are less able to communicate and enforce norms. However, this does not mean that norms about other consumer activities do not exist.

THE FUTURE OF BUYER BEHAVIOR THEORY

JAGDISH N. SHETH

The motivational force behind writing this paper can only be the need for venturesomeness. This need was aroused partly by the speculative nature of the topic itself, which is to predict the future of buyer behavior theory, and partly by the deft encouragement of the session chairman, Jerry Zaltman. I am quite certain that some of my colleagues will disagree with things I foresee in buyer behavior theory, while others are likely to approve my assertions about the future of buyer behavior theory. Like a good forecaster let me simply say that "I may be mistaken but I am never wrong."

Future predictions typically entail the utilization of the Bayes theorem in some way because essentially prognosis implies revising the prior probability based on the assessment of some symptoms currently manifested in the phenomenon to be forecasted. Future predictions are also typically hazardous to one's welfare in any discipline because often the prior probabilities are no better than random probabilities due to relatively short histories of the disciplines, and because the assessment of contemporary symptoms is very difficult due to the rapid and complex changes the discipline may be undergoing. Buyer behavior theory may very well present these problems.

My objective in this paper accordingly is to estimate the prior probability by very briefly reviewing the historical perspective of the buyer behavior discipline and then focus on a number of current events which are likely to determine both the velocity and the direction of buyer behavior theory. I shall focus on changes in structure and content of the theory which are likely to arise during the current decade and, so to speak, go out on a limb in my speculative tree.

A BRIEF HISTORICAL PERSPECTIVE OF BUYER BEHAVIOR

In the last quarter of a century, in my opinion, we have come a long way from the dark ages of strictly sporadic and random research in buyer behavior. The cumulative research effort in buyer

Source: Jagdish N. Sheth, "The Future of Buyer Behavior Theory," *Proceedings 3rd Annual Conference,* 1972, Association for Consumer Research, pp. 562–575.

behavior, both academic and professional, theoretical and empirical, or published and unpublished, is indeed impressive as can be gauged from several recent reviews (Guest, 1962; Howard, 1965; Twedt, 1965; Burk, 1967; Sheth, 1967; and Perloff, 1968). A closer examination of these reviews clearly indicates that we can identify four distinct phases of differential thoughts and emphases in the discipline.

The Empirical-Inductive Phase

The decades of the thirties and forties seemed to be dominated by strictly empirical research mostly conducted by or for the industry's marketing decisions and their impact in the marketplace. Furthermore, the major emphasis tended toward gauging the effects of distribution, advertising and promotion decisions.

Among the several distinct characteristics of this phase, we may list (1) dominance of economic theory of the firm and especially the concepts of monopolistic competition, marginal utility analysis, and welfare economics; (2) macro market analysis at the aggregate level or at best at some predefined segmented level; and (3) emphasis on market's behavior responses as opposed to psychological responses.

The only exception to the above characterization of this phase of the buyer behavior discipline seemed to be the acceptance of motivation research in which both the concepts and the methods of clinical psychology were widely applied to the understanding of buyer behavior.

The Formative Phase

The decade of the fifties must be regarded as the formative years of buyer behavior in which several major elements cemented the foundation of buyer behavior theory.

The first such element was the shift from measurement of aggregate to individual buyer behavior. Two different groups of scholars simultaneously contributed toward bringing about this change. The first was the Lazarsfeld School of Sociologists interested in measuring total change in voting behavior based on longitudinal panels which led to the establishment of household consumer panels in buyer behavior. The second was the Katona School of Economic Psychologists interested in building better indicators of economic growth based on the micro data of household acquisitions and inventories of durable appliances.

The availability of data on household purchase behavior eventually led to the interest in developing quantitative measures of brand or store loyalty and switching behaviors which in turn brought the utilization of stochastic processes such as Markov chains.

A second major element of the fifties was the growing interest in providing explanations for buyer behavior differences based on the *social* environment of the consumer. This led to the borrowing of the concepts of social stratification, reference groups, role orientations and opinion leadership. The major discipline relied upon, therefore, tended to be sociology and economic anthropology. Even though the theorizing was unsystematic and less refined in these attempts, they should be regarded as the pioneering efforts in search for causal explanations from disciplines other than the economic theory.

The third distinct element was the initial introduction to formal model building of buyer responses to marketing stimuli based on the optimization theory of operations research and econometrics (see Bass, et al., 1961 for examples). Simultaneously, the utility theorists in economics were also formalizing Samuelson's revealed preference theory of consumption. The combined effect was the introduction of deductive formal model building based on normative axioms and assumptions. This was further facilitated by the feasibility of building complex simulation models with the use of the computer. Given the infant stage of buyer behavior theory development, it is quite surprising to observe that management science was adopted in buyer behavior so early in the game. It is, therefore, not at all surprising that most efforts at normative-deductive model building met with failures and premature rejection. As we shall see later, this fact has had tremendous implications for the future of buyer behavior theory.

It must be pointed out that all through these formative years, the empirical research on buyer behavior continued to accelerate independently due to the availability of micro data and the computer facilities to analyze them.

The Middle-Range Theory Phase

The first half of the sixties can best be described as the identification stage. Buyer behavior began to be understood for its own sake rather than from the point of view of the marketer or the government or some other entity with vested interests. In my opinion, this can be directly attributed to the intensive borrowing of theories and concepts from those branches of behavioral sciences which had emerged as "pure" disciplines themselves. This included experimental psychology with emphasis on learning and perception, social psychology with emphasis on cognitive consistency, and rural sociology with emphasis on adoption processes of innovative products, practices and services. For further discussion I must refer you to the excellent review provided by Burk (1967).

The intensive borrowing from the behavioral sciences by numerous researchers, each one interested in some aspect of buyer behavior and predisposed or trained in some branch of behavioral sciences, resulted in the development of well-identified middle-range theories of buyer behavior. Any examples must include Howard's learning theory, Bauer's perceived risk theory, and several researchers developing theories based on Festinger's cognitive dissonance, Lewin's field theory, opinion leadership, and innovativeness and even on several personality theories. As I pointed out elsewhere (Sheth, 1967), the outstanding characteristic of this borrowing phase was the *partial explanations* each theory provided to the otherwise complex phenomenon of buyer behavior, especially the one related to the problem-solving and habitual buying decisions. Not very surprisingly, other types of buyer behaviors were neglected in these middle-range theories including unplanned impulsive behavior, novelty-seeking and situationally-anchored behaviors because very little theorizing was offered by the behavioral sciences in these areas.

Even though the bulk of this era concentrated on building middle-range theories, the efforts to build formal models based on optimization theory including linear programming, on stochastic processes including Bernoulli and Markovian processes, and on heuristics and other Monte Carlo type techniques continued. In fact, the early sixties can be regarded as the golden era of management science in buyer behavior as evidenced from Massy, Montgomery and Morrison (1970).

The Integrative-Comprehensive Theory Phase

The last half of the sixties and early years of the seventies are best identified with the emergence of comprehensive theories of buyer behavior. This basically entailed integrating several middle-range theories which had come to be accepted as well as putting together empirical research not identified with any theory in buyer behavior (Nicosia, 1966; Howard and Sheth, 1969; Andreasen, 1965; Engel, Kollat, and Blackwell, 1968; Sheth, 1971; Sheth, 1972). In my opinion, the integrative-comprehensive theory building brought three factors in the development of the discipline. First, it emphasized the limitations of direct borrowing of theories from behavioral sciences without first adapting them to the complexity of buyer behavior. Furthermore, it established a precedent in reversing the process of borrowing by first conceptualizing the buyer behavior phenomenon and then searching for as many constructs as can be logically found in behavioral and social sciences. Second, and perhaps most important, the integrative-comprehensive theories brought to bear in buyer behavior the self confidence of independently building theories of buyer behavior in place of simply applying a social science theory to the buyer behavior area with or without modifications. This must be regarded as the genesis for the emergence of buyer behavior as a discipline in itself rather than simply a problem area which can be explained by some social science discipline. Finally, they provided insights into building complex but realistic formal models of buyer behavior which may have contributed toward changing the traditional course of model building in terms of starting with simple, unrealistic assumptions and relaxing them to make them realistic as was true, for example, in utility theory (Katona, 1953).

During this phase, two other developments in buyer behavior theory are worth noting. The first was discarding the deductive-normative model building approach based on operations research methods in favor of statistical inductive model building with the use of multivariate analysis of large scale survey data. The second development was the broadening of marketing and buyer behavior horizons to nontraditional areas such as population control, nutrition, and public service delivery systems under the pioneering efforts of Kotler and Zaltman.

Assessment of History and Contemporary Signals

From the above brief historical review, it is my contention that buyer behavior theory is a far cry from random thinking. Within a very short period of time, we seem to have firmly laid the foundation for building a distinct discipline of buyer behavior which will neither be a subsystem of marketing nor that of any of the other older social sciences. An even more pleasant observation is that we seem to have achieved more with respect to richness of thinking, comprehensiveness of theorizing, and testing of theories in naturalistic and realistic settings than many of the older behavioral science disciplines in their comparative periods of development. And why should it not be that way? Unless the newer disciplines learn to

avoid the trial-and-error learning of older disciplines similar to the experiences of developing nations, there is very little hope of uplifting ourselves from becoming strict problem-solvers for the government or the industry. In summary, then, it is safe to predict that buyer behavior theory has nothing but a bright future.

However, an assessment of a number of contemporary events also indicates that the velocity of growth will not only be more rapid and diffused but is likely to significantly change the course of the growth curve. Rather than listing my assessment of these events and then forecasting the future directions of buyer behavior theory, I plan to devote the rest of the paper in detailing the major dimensions of future direction of the theory and link them to my assessment of contemporary events. The future developments are described in terms of the following categories: (1) structural changes in buyer behavior theory, (2) broadening the horizons of relevance and applications of buyer behavior principles, and (3) active interest of other disciplines to borrow from buyer behavior theory.

STRUCTURAL CHANGES IN BUYER BEHAVIOR THEORY

In the Bayesian crystal urn, I foresee four types of structural changes in the development of buyer behavior theory during the decade of the seventies. They are (1) establishing criteria to evaluate the relevance of different theories of buyer behavior, (2) constructing tests and scales to measure widely accepted hypothetical constructs in buyer behavior theory, (3) building complex formal but highly realistic and inductive models based on comprehensive theories of buyer behavior and, (4) theoretical and empirical research on nonpurposeful buyer behavior hopefully leading to a comprehensive theory.

Criteria for Evaluating Theories of Buyer Behavior

Although we have developed several theories of buyer behavior in both middle-range and comprehensive categories, surprisingly we have so far failed to develop widely accepted criteria with which to evaluate their usefulness or even relevance to buyer behavior. To be sure, existing theories are differentially accepted and diffused, but this seems to be based on tenuous factors such as the degree of face validity or predictive validity, the reputation of the author, the prestige of the institution, and ability to generate more research funds and commensurately more publicizing of the theory. In view of the fact that even greater number of researchers are likely to contribute in the coming years, I think the discipline is likely to experience personal rivalries and showmanship among competing authors unless some evaluative criteria are developed and accepted. I foresee three different types of criteria emerging within the next five years in order to minimize the personal rivalry and showmanship mentioned above.

The first type of criteria seems already to be emerging in the form of the development of a meta theory of buyer behavior (Zaltman, Pinson, & Angelmar, 1973). In other words, theories of buyer behavior are likely to be critically examined, compared, and contrasted based on some fundamental judgments of philosophy of science. This type of criteria is strictly discipline-oriented and tends to emphasize the evaluation of the *process* of theorizing.

The second type of criteria, on the other hand, is likely to be pragmatic by being based on the usefulness of a theory of buyer behavior to solve specific problems. The emphasis in this type of evaluation is likely to be on the capability of a theory to enable the problem solver to achieve his own goals. What are the entities who are likely to increasingly utilize buyer behavior theories to help solve their problems? Obviously, the public policy makers, the business managers and consumer advocates seem the most likely entities. To the extent that each entity differs in its own perspective and activity, we are likely to see very different ways by which each entity is likely to put buyer behavior theories to its own use. For example, the research based on buyer behavior theories is likely to be very specific, ad hoc and symptomatic in the case of consumer advocates since typically they have tended to be issue-oriented. The public policy makers, on the other hand, are more likely to utilize comprehensive theories to conduct research on an exhaustive and systematic basis to search for the root causes of problematic symptoms pointed out by the consumer advocates. At least this is my hope. Finally, the marketing management is certainly likely to favor comprehensive theories of buyer behavior to understand and monitor market behavior simply because past experience has given enough evidence that middle-range theories are not satisfactory.

The final type of criteria is likely to emerge from the efforts to generalize a theory to diverse and nontraditional areas of buyer behavior. The greater the ability of a theory to extend itself with a minimum number of modifications to the unexplored areas of buyer behavior such as a search for information process or to nontraditional areas such as product utility and value formation, the greater is likely to be its popularity and diffusion. However, the diffusion of the theory is likely to be evaluated in terms of specific criteria similar to the criteria in statistics for parameter estimation procedures.

It is my hope that with the development of agreed-upon criteria in buyer behavior, we will see greater rigor and deductive logic in future theories of buyer behavior.

Standardized Measurement of Buyer Behavior

Even though we are still striving to develop better theories of buyer behavior, I think we have a consensus on several hypothetical constructs in buyer behavior. These include the constructs of brand and store loyalty, behavioral intentions or buyer plans, predispositions toward choice alternatives, and perceptual biases in selective exposure and processing of information just to name a few. In addition, there seems to be a basic understanding that individual differences in buyer behavior are likely to be determined by constructs such as the life cycle, life style, socioeconomic status and role orientation differences among consumers. Secondly, we have recently tended to follow the psychometric tradition of data analysis, especially with the use of multivariate methods, which has brought to our attention the need for better and isomorphic measures of the above mentioned constructs which we strive to relate to one another in order to describe and explain buyer behavior.

I, therefore, foresee major research effort in buyer behavior channeled toward developing standardized scales for many of the constructs in buyer behavior mentioned above. I also think that this research effort is likely to be heavily influenced by the psychometric theories of scaling. Several important implications emerge from this forecast. First, we are likely to become more skeptical of the *direct use* of standardized scales and tests developed for comparable constructs in behavioral sciences. For example, in the area of attitudes, it is more likely that we will question the measurement procedures proposed in expectancy-value models in social psychology. Thus, we are likely to separate theories from measurement as we continue to borrow from the behavioral and social sciences. Second, the buyer behavior theory is very likely to become more mathematical and formal due to the research thrust in measurement and development of tests for the constructs. Finally, the development of standardized tests is likely to augment the empirical research in the unexplored areas of buyer behavior because research efforts will tend to be routinized as is true today in some branches of psychology.

Quantitative Modeling of Buyer Behavior

In the distant future, I foresee the reemergence of quantitative model building in buyer behavior. In other words, it will be quite some time before good mathematical models of buyer behavior are likely to emerge. Furthermore, the model building effort is likely to be distinctly different from what has been historically attempted in marketing. First, the models are likely to be problem-oriented instead of technique-oriented. Thus, by definition, they will be empirical in nature summarizing the efforts to research a problem area with the use of existing theories of buyer behavior. For example, a number of researchers are currently applying various theories of buyer behavior to understand how advertising works, how public delivery systems can be made more efficient in health, education and welfare, and how future transportation and communication needs can be fully met without endangering the environment. Second, the models are likely to utilize several statistical techniques in some sort of sequential multistage process rather than try to fit the empirical problem into a single technique such as mathematical programming of multidimensional scaling. Finally, the quantitative models of buyer behavior will be more positive rather than normative. In other words, we are more likely to see predictive models of buyer behavior and less likely to see control models. Accordingly, the model building effort will coincide with testing and continuous updating. Furthermore, the adaptive control concepts are likely to be at the core of the updating process. In short, Bayesian philosophy is likely to dominate the model building effort replacing the search for optimality.

I also think that a number of researchers will attempt to decompose agreed-upon comprehensive theories of buyer behavior into smaller theories and develop models for them. We have already seen some efforts in this direction in regard to information processing and attitude structure subsystems of buyer behavior.

Research on Nonpurposeful Behavior

Based on the historical review, it is fair to state that we have so far concentrated on habitual, purposeful and problem-solving buyer behavior. Furthermore, we have developed several fairly comprehensive theories to explain it. However, the nonpurposeful behavior has received relatively little attention in the past, and it is, therefore, likely to emerge as the major substantive area of empirical research and theory building. By nonpurposeful behavior, I am primarily referring to curiosity, novelty seeking and exploratory behavior as well as cue-triggered impulsive buyer behavior. Some theorizing on this aspect of buyer behavior based on Berlyne's theory was recently developed by several researchers (Howard and Sheth, 1969; Hansen, 1972; Venkatesan, 1972). However, considerable work still remains to be done especially in terms of gathering empirical data before a good systematic theory of nonpurposeful behavior can be developed.

It seems inevitable but to speculate that any comprehensive theory of nonpurposeful behavior will be extremely difficult to build and when built, it will more heavily depend on the typology of situational influences surrounding the nonpurposeful behavior than on the personal attributes of the buyer.

BROADENING THE HORIZONS OF BUYER BEHAVIOR

Simultaneously with the structural changes in buyer behavior theory, I foresee rapid applications of buyer behavior concepts to three broadly-defined substantive problem areas. These are (1) cross-cultural buyer behavior research required by the emergence of multinational corporations, (2) public policy research on marketing institutions and practices required by increased concern in consumer welfare on the part of regulatory agencies, and (3) extension of buyer behavior to non-traditional areas of societal problems directly attributed to the mass consumption nature of our society. I expect the bulk of applied research in buyer behavior will be limited to these problem areas in the coming decade.

Cross-Cultural Buyer Behavior

I foresee extensive applied research in buyer behavior across different cultures simply because of the increased multinational characterization of most large business corporations. With the maturity of many foreign markets, the multinational corporations have become sensitive to the marketing-orientation in their efforts to diffuse products and services on a worldwide basis. The need to understand the impact of cultures on buyer behavior is obvious. In fact, it is surprising to observe how little attention has been paid to assessing cultural influences on buyer behavior despite the fact that the United States is recognized to be the melting pot of diverse ethnical groups.

I think research on cross-cultural buyer behavior is likely to go through the same stages as buyer behavior theory itself has gone through. First, there will be clusterings of studies most idealized to some industries and some countries. Given the pattern of multinational business expansion, it is logical to presume that cross-cultural studies will be concentrated in European markets and with respect to nondurable consumer goods. Second, we should expect the development of several middle-range theories of cross-cultural buyer behavior based on the research in the first stage. Furthermore, the middle-range theories will be generated by the marketing practitioners and not by the academicians due to substantial costs involved in cross-cultural research. Of course, the academic scholars are likely to be instrumental in guiding the marketing practice's efforts to build middle-range theories. Finally, I foresee the eventual emergence of several comprehensive theories of buyer behavior. These will mostly constitute efforts to integrate both diverse middle-range theories and existing empirical research in cross-cultural buyer behavior. Furthermore, I also think that there will be virtually no differences between cross-cultural theories and domestic theories of buyer behavior in their structure.

Public Policy Research

It is but inevitable to foresee rapid applications of buyer behavior theories for the purpose of better regulation of marketing practices and institutions. Perhaps the single most important factor for this observation is the singular inadequacy of the traditional concepts of micro economic theories to properly guide the function of regulation. A related reason is the divorce of marketing from economics during the past two decades. A second major factor is the increased pragmatism recently exhibited by the regulatory agencies such as the FTC and the FDA. This has brought home the need for empirical research on buyer behavior at the micro level both before and after major regulatory decisions, for example, the policy of corrective advertising, in order to ensure that desired consequences follow from them. Finally, the recent emergence of consumerism is likely to encourage the public policy makers to conduct fundamental research on buyer behavior in the hopes of producing good legislative policies.

The bulk of research in buyer behavior for public policy is likely to be problem-oriented, and most of the problems are likely to emerge from the negative side effects of mass marketing and mass consumption, for example, mass media effects on the citizen's values.

Buyer Behavior Research on Social and Environmental Problems

Perhaps the most critical applications of buyer behavior theories are likely to emerge from the research on social and environmental problems. We have already witnessed some utilization of marketing and buyer behavior concepts to social problems of less developed economies, for example, population explosion and malnutrition. However, the societal and environmental problems directly related to mass consumption and mass production are closer to home for most people working in consumer behavior. These problem areas include environmental and social pollution, welfare of minorities, and delivery of public services such as education and health. The greater social consciousness in solving these problems fortunately seems to be transcending the vested interests of the components of our mass production and mass consumption system so that research in these areas will tend to be nonpartisan.

In addition to the broadening of the horizons of buyer behavior, I foresee two subtle and indirect benefits arising from the research on social and environmental problems. The first is the separation of buyer behavior theory from marketing theory. In other words, I foresee emergence of greater respectability of buyer behavior theory by its extension to socially relevant issues. It is surprising, on reflection, to see how much psychology has suffered from the crisis of relevance because it emerged as a discipline in those areas of research which were not considered relevant or essential to mass consumption societies.

The second benefit is the rapid cross-fertilization of philosophy, theory and methodology between natural sciences and buyer behavior theory. I think it is simply inevitable that we will be working together with researchers from hard sciences such as physics, mechanics and biochemistry in search of solutions to social and environmental problems. Thus, rather than borrowing from the other social sciences, it is likely that we will be borrowing the philosophy and methodology from the hard sciences. To me, this appears to be an unique opportunity for buyer behavior theory to elevate itself to a more mature level.

BORROWING FROM BUYER BEHAVIOR THEORY

Historically, we have borrowed a great deal from other disciplines to build buyer behavior theory. However, I think within a decade, it is very likely that other disciplines will be actively interested in buyer behavior and consequently borrow from it a set of concepts and research tools. Implicit in this prediction is my conviction that we either already have or will very soon have richness of thinking, variety of methodology and respectability of the discipline to motivate other disciplines to search for relevant concepts and methods from buyer behavior. It is interesting, therefore, to speculate which disciplines are likely to borrow what from buyer behavior theory. I have described below three types of borrowing activities: (1) less mature disciplines of social science borrowing the methodology of research in buyer behavior, (2) older social sciences borrowing concepts and theories of buyer behavior, and (3) hard sciences borrowing both the theory and methodology of buyer behavior discipline.

Less Mature Social Sciences

Relative to some mature social sciences such as macroeconomics and experimental psychology, the buyer behavior discipline looks less mature. By the same token, there are many other social sciences which are even less mature than buyer behavior. I include political science, parts of sociology, history, religion, home economics, law, and public health in the category of less mature disciplines in social sciences. Just as we have borrowed from psychology and economics, I believe these disciplines are likely to borrow from us. In fact, this is already evident from the recent trend of citing marketing and buyer behavior references in these disciplines.

The less mature social sciences are likely to borrow the research methods identified and routinely utilized in buyer behavior. This includes longitudinal panels, cost-oriented sampling procedures, the survey methods of data collection, and the use of multivariate methods. In addition, there is always the possibility of utilizing marketing strategies and tactics to diffuse radical innovations in each of those disciplines.

Mature Social Sciences

Some of my colleagues may not agree with me, but I think many of the traditional social sciences to which we owe so much are likely to at first participate in understanding buyer behavior, and eventually to borrow from it. My prediction is based upon two facts. First, these traditional disciplines are currently facing the crisis of relevance because foundations of their theory and research have been based on less critical areas of human behavior. I include experimental psychology, social psychology and small group theory among others who have encountered this crisis in recent years. Second, many of the traditional disciplines have built formal models of behavior which have tended to be unrealistic or have become obsolete due to unprecedented technological change in our society in the last thirty years. I include the utility theory, micro theory of the firm and allied areas of economics and decision making as illustrative of this type of social sciences. In their search for societally relevant and useful problem areas, and to build realistic theories to help solve them the probability is extremely high that buyer behavior will become the center of attention because social problems of a mass consumption society tend to be directly reflected in it.

Due to the problem-solving interests of these traditional social sciences, I believe the traditional disciplines are likely to be more interested in the theoretical concepts and substantive findings than in the research methodology of buyer behavior. This also looks plausible in view of the fact that the traditional disciplines tend to be rich in methodology. I think buyer behavior has a lot to offer to the utility theory in economics from its thinking on choice behavior anchored to cognitive-evaluative structures. Similarly, I think we have a lot to offer to social psychology both in theory and research methodology in terms of conducting complex longitudinal studies of attitude change and brand choice behavior in naturalistic settings. Third, the growing literature and theory on diffusion of innovations in buyer behavior may well enable rural sociology to rethink diffusion theory. Finally, the recent emergence of efforts to build test batteries to measure life styles in buyer behavior is likely to significantly alter the thrust of personality tests in clinical psychology.

Although most of the borrowing from buyer behavior by the traditional social sciences is likely to be with respect to concepts and substantive findings, there are certain areas of research methodology which may also be useful to them.

These include the survey research aspects entailed in the design and execution of large scale studies in naturalistic settings.

Hard Sciences

By hard sciences, I mean natural sciences and engineering based on physics, mechanics, chemistry and biochemistry. The hard sciences have reached a level of maturity in their own disciplines to an extent whereby it is inevitable for them to broaden their horizons. I expect them, therefore, to concern themselves with the problem of *social consequences* arising from technology and depletion of natural resources. This includes, for example, areas of pollution of resources, urban planning, and the like. Recently, we have witnessed research undertakings by the hard sciences in those areas of social concern which typically have been the domain of social scientists. It seems inevitable, therefore, that sooner or later, the hard sciences are likely to be exposed to, and interested in buyer behavior. When that happens, it is equally inevitable that they will extensively borrow both the substantive findings and research methodology, because the newer research areas will force them to examine alternative theories and methodology. For it is generally conceded that the concepts of hard sciences may only be analogously related to social problems.

CONCLUSIONS AND DISCUSSIONS

In this paper, I have attempted to speculate on the future of buyer behavior theory. My speculations were limited to forecasting major directions which it is likely to take in the coming decade. These predictions were based on reviewing historical perspectives of buyer behavior theory and taking into account the contemporary events. I have suggested that four major changes are likely to occur in the structure of buyer behavior theory. They are (1) development of criteria to evaluate theories of buyer behavior, (2) construction of standardized tests and scales to measure buyer behavior constructs, (3) complex model building in an inductive manner with the use of several statistical procedures, and (4) research emphasis on nonpurposeful behavior. Second, I have suggested three major ways by which buyer behavior theory is likely to broaden its horizons, namely (1) development of cross-cultural theories of buyer behavior, (2) research and theories of buyer behavior for public policy purposes, and (3) research on social and environmental problems created by mass consumption societies. Third, I have predicted that a number of other disciplines will actively engage in buyer behavior and, therefore, substantially borrow research methodology and theory typically identified with buyer behavior theory. Specifically, I have suggested that (1) less mature social sciences such as political science, law, education and public health will borrow research methodology, (2) more mature and older social sciences are likely to borrow the concepts and theories from buyer behavior in their efforts to become more relevant and realistic disciplines, and (3) some natural sciences will borrow both methodology and theory from buyer behavior in the process of broadening their horizons to understand social consequences of technology.

Despite the bright predictions for the future of buyer behavior theory, I think there are some identifiable ailments in today's theories of buyer behavior which may impede the achievement of these predictions. First, most theories look upon buyer behavior as the consequence of some form of the decision-making process, and thus implicitly concede that buyer behavior consists of only goal-directed behavior. This may very well restrict the horizons to which buyer behavior theory can be broadened. Second, a large number of theories of buyer behavior often examine the buyer decision process from the point of view of marketing. While marketing management has made the greatest use of findings and concepts of buyer behavior, there is no reason why others from different viewpoints cannot utilize the same concepts and findings. Not only has this tendency made buyer behavior theory somewhat myopic, it has produced a terminology and vocabulary for buyer behavior which impedes its extension to nontraditional areas. Third, it seems that most theories of buyer behavior tend to overemphasize the process leading up to behavior and underemphasize the buying behavior or the antecedent and subsequent events which surround the behavior. Unless we consciously strive to remove these ailments, buyer behavior theory may take a longer time to gain respectability across disciplines.

REFERENCES

Andreasen, A. R. (1965), "Attitudes and Customer Behavior: A Decision Model," in L. E. Preston, ed., *New Research in Marketing,* Berkeley: University of California, 1–16.

Bass, F. M. et al. (1961), *Mathematical Models and Methods in Marketing,* Homewood, Ill.: Irwin.

Burk, M. C. (1967), "Survey of Interpretations of Consumer Behavior by Social Scientists in the Postwar Period," *Journal of Farm Economics,* 49, 1–31.

Engel, J. F.; Kollat, D. T.; and Blackwell, R. D. (1968), *Consumer Behavior,* New York: Holt, Rinehart & Winston.

Guest, L. (1962), "Consumer Analysis," *Annual Review of Psychology,* 13, 315–44.

Hansen, F. (1972), *Consumer Choice Behavior,* New York: Free Press.

Howard, J. A. (1965), *Marketing Theory,* Boston: Allyn and Bacon.

Howard, J. A., and Sheth, J. N. (1969), *The Theory of Buyer Behavior,* New York: Wiley.

Katona, G. (1953), "Rational Behavior and Economic Behavior," *Psychological Bulletin,* 60, 307–18.

Massy, W. F.; Montgomery, D. B.; and Morrison, D. G. (1970), *Stochastic Models of Buying Behavior,* Cambridge, Mass.: MIT Press.

Nicosia, F. M. (1966), *Consumer Decision Processes,* Englewood Cliffs, N. J.: Prentice-Hall.

Perloff, R. (1968), "Consumer Analysis," *Annual Review of Psychology,* 19, 437–66.

Sheth, J. N. (1967), "A Review of Buyer Behavior," *Management Science,* 13, B718–B756.

Sheth, J. N. (1971), "A Theory of Family Buying Decisions," in P. Pellemans, ed., *Insights in Consumer and Market Behavior,* Namur: Namur University, 32–49.

Sheth, J. N. (1972), "A Theory of Industrial Buying Decisions," *Faculty Working Paper No. 61,* Urbana: College of Commerce, University of Illinois.

Twedt, D. W. (1965), "Consumer Psychology," *Annual Review of Psychology,* 16, 265–94.

Venkatesan, M. (1972), "Novelty Seeking," *Working Paper,* University of Iowa.

Zaltman, G.; Pinson, C. and Angelmar, R. (1973), *Metatheory and Consumer Behavior Research,* New York: Holt, Rinehart, and Winston.

CONSUMER PSYCHOLOGY AS A SOCIAL PSYCHOLOGICAL SPHERE OF ACTION

JACOB JACOBY

This article is based upon the presidential address delivered to the Division of Consumer Psychology (Division 23) at the meeting of the American Psychological Association, New Orleans, September 1974, and originally entitled "Consumer Psychology: The Legitimate Child of Social Psychology?"

Source: Jacob Jacoby, "Consumer Psychology as a Social Psychological Sphere of Action," *American Psychologist,* Vol. 30, October, 1975, pp. 977–987.

Five years ago, few consumer or social psychologists would have paused to reflect on the relationship between consumer and social psychology. Although consumer psychologists did borrow concepts and methods from social psychology, they were probably less in quantity and kind than were borrowed from numerous other subdisciplines of psychology. In fact, psychologists who were aware of consumer psychology tended to consider it a variant of industrial psychology, because most people who identified themselves as consumer psychologists had, up to that time, been trained as traditional industrial psychologists. As for social psychologists, many were not even aware of consumer psychology's existence five years ago, and those who were aware probably cared little about the occasional borrowing of concepts. In short, the question of a relationship between consumer and social psychology was rarely entertained.

Today, things are quite different. Even if they have not articulated it to others or even to themselves, most consumer psychologists cannot help but notice that the overwhelming majority of the material published in the consumer psychological literature is decidedly social psychological in nature. For example, since 1970 almost *every* single issue of the *Journal of Marketing Research* has contained at least 5 social psychological articles and sometimes as many as 10 or more.

Articles have examined personality, attitudes, attitude change, role expectations and behavior, decision making, information processing, reference groups, group influence, informal (opinion) leadership, interpersonal communication, attribution theory, and persuasive communications, to cite just a few. The *Journal of Advertising Research,* the consumer behavior articles appearing in the *Journal of Applied Psychology,* and recent Division 23 programs at the annual APA conventions all evidence the same trend. Finally, at least half the articles in the inaugural (June 1974) issue of the *Journal of Consumer Research* are essentially social psychological in nature.

17

The intended audience for this entire article is actually not consumer psychologists but social psychologists who may have been enticed by its title. My primary purpose is to indicate why and how attention to consumer behavior provides numerous exciting possibilities for the enrichment and further development of social psychology as a scientific discipline. Hopefully, this will stimulate greater interest and empirical involvement in consumer psychological issues by social psychologists than is currently the case—to the benefit of both consumer and social psychology.

RECENT TRENDS IN CONSUMER BEHAVIOR RESEARCH

Extrapolating from numerous personal conversations with traditional social psychologists, it is apparent that most of them have little, if any, idea of what consumer psychology is, while many who think they do often possess distorted or erroneous images. These distortions usually stem from circumstances prevailing during an earlier era when, except perhaps for the work of George Katona (1951, 1953, 1960, 1963) and his colleagues, consumer psychology was essentially a psychological subdiscipline in the service of business. This is definitely no longer so.

As early as the mid-1960s, Perloff (1963, 1964, 1968), Krugman (1968), and others were calling attention to a shift in focus from attention to the consumer qua purchaser to attention to the consumer qua consumer. This shift was being manifested along two separate but compatible dimensions. First, some consumer psychologists began conducting research primarily in the service of consumers and directed toward safeguarding their rights and looking after their welfare. For example, work by Friedman (1966, 1967, 1968) was introduced and published as part of the records of both the U.S. House and U.S. Senate Hearings on the Fair Packaging and Labeling Bill. This work, and the testimony of people like Perloff, served as a cornerstone in the early consumer protection ac-

tivities of the Federal Trade Commission and the Food and Drug Administration. Second, some consumer psychologists actually eschewed immediately applied questions altogether and began considering consumer behavior as an aspect of human behavior worthy of study in its own right. In large measure, this second path involved the development and incorporation of theory (cf. Engel, Kollat, & Blackwell, 1968, 1973; Howard & Sheth, 1969, Nicosia, 1966; Ward & Robertson, 1973), particularly social psychological theory, and the examination of consumer behavior from a social psychological perspective.

If consumer psychology is no longer solely an applied discipline operating primarily in the service of big business, then just what is it? Of greater importance to social psychologists, why is it to their advantage to acquire a working familiarity with and perhaps even become actively involved in consumer psychology?

CONSUMER BEHAVIOR AND CONSUMER PSYCHOLOGY

Any definition of consumer psychology requires that it be distinguished from and predicated upon a prior definition of consumer behavior. One definition that is evolving (Jacoby, 1971, in press-a, in press-b; Jacoby, Note 1) holds that consumer behavior is the acquisition, consumption, and disposition of goods, services, time, and ideas by living units (e.g., individuals, families, firms). As such, it represents classes of behaviors directed toward specific aspects of the environment. It encompasses much more than just the purchase of products and/or services by humans. For example, acquisition occurs in a wide variety of ways, only one subcategory of which entails the exchange of money. To illustrate, the sensuous young lady

1. Jacoby, J. *Toward a definition of consumer psychology: One psychologist's views.* Paper presented at the meeting of the American Psychological Association, Washington, D. C., September 1969.

dispensing favors to her 50-year-old "uncle" in return for a mink coat, a luxury apartment, and a vacation on the Riviera is, among other things, engaging in a very old form of consumer behavior. In fact, the chimpanzee who works for tokens and then exchanges them either for a banana or an opportunity to look through a window into another room is also engaging in consumer behavior (cf. Cowles, 1937; Wolfe, 1936). Although some may see in this the need for large-scale graduate programs in comparative-consumer psychology, I delimit my attention here to human consumer behavior.

Moreover, consumer behavior also includes the interaction between man and his acquisitions, specifically, how man goes about using and consuming that which he has acquired. Like acquisition, consumption is a complex process having many facets. Among other things, it may be immediate, delayed, or extended through time, and the object of consumption may be entirely consumed (e.g., a cookie) or may remain in complete or partial form after consumption has ceased (e.g., a candy bar wrapper, an old shirt, an auto that is beyond repair). In the latter event, the consumer must eventually become involved in the process of attending to the object that has outlived its original function, at least insofar as he is concerned. This involves a decision-making process regarding whether to throw the object in the trash, give it away, sell it, rent it, convert it to another purpose, etc., and then acting on the basis of this decision. Finally, the acquisition, consumption, or disposition of one item often requires the acquisition, consumption, or disposition of another item (e.g., buying a car usually requires that we purchase auto insurance; using a car requires that we purchase gasoline; selling a car usually requires that a new vehicle be acquired, or a new mode of transportation be employed). Thus, consumer behavior often assumes complex overlays of decision making and choice behavior. Moreover, it takes place not in a vacuum but in the social context of everyday life, where it has the potential to be influenced by numerous social factors such as peer-group influence, informal (word-of-mouth) communications, and formal (mass-media advertising) communications.

Consumer behavior exists and would continue to exist even if no discipline chose to make it the object of study. However, as one might expect of such a ubiquitous and frequently occurring phenomenon, a wide variety of disciplines (e.g., economics, agricultural economics, home economics, journalism, law, architecture, marketing, sociology, finance, political science, industrial engineering, food sciences, to cite but a very few) attempt to bring their unique concepts and methods to bear on the study of selected aspects of consumer behavior. The shared frame of reference adopted by many of these disciplines is that man qua consumer is an information-processing, problem-solving, decision-making, choice-making entity, and that these elements are reflected throughout the acquisition, consumption, and disposition processes. However, many of these disciplines have historically tended to focus only on limited aspects of consumer behavior. For example, marketing has been principally concerned with the acquisition process, particularly insofar as this involves the purchase of goods and services. Home economics has been traditionally interested in postpurchase consumption activities, although this emphasis has been changing.

Consumer psychology may be defined as that branch of psychology which seeks, through the utilization of distinctively psychological concepts and methods, to understand the dynamics underlying and determining consumer behavior, including the factors that influence such behavior. Consideration of the published literature of consumer psychology circa 1974 suggests that, though it still maintains an applied orientation, it also possesses a theoretical orientation that is decidedly social psychological in character. In fact, some consumer psychologists consider themselves to be social psychologists who simply delimit their attention to the consumer domain.

THE DEVELOPING SOCIAL PSYCHOLOGICAL INTEREST IN CONSUMER RESEARCH

Not surprisingly, one of the very first consumer psychologists was none other than Kurt Lewin, who, "more than any other single figure, . . . stands as the source of experimental social psychology . . . [and is] the intellectual father of many of the senior leaders of the discipline" (Smith, 1972, p. 95). During World War II, when the United States was experiencing shortages in its supply of traditional cuts of beef and other meats, Lewin's (1943, 1958) classic studies on the relationship of public versus private commitment to subsequent behavior helped both government and industry to make internal meats (e.g., brains, livers, and kidneys) more palatable to the American consumer.

Of course, Lewin was a full-time social psychologist and only a part-time consumer psychologist. More recently, other full-time social psychologists have, in various ways, also evidenced involvement in consumer behavior and consumer behavior research.

Indeed, it appears as if an increasing number of social psychologists are finding it meaningful—either in their research, their writings, or in advisory and consulting roles—to occasionally become involved with consumer psychological research.

Regarding research in particular, examination of the basic social psychological literature reveals an increasing number of instances in which consumer choice settings have served as the vehicle for examining basic, theoretically derived social psychological propositions. In some instances, the choice of a consumer setting is more accidental than intentional, but the effect is often the same, namely, a contribution is simultaneously made to both social and consumer psychology. It is our contention that greater emphasis on intentional, as opposed to accidental, involvement by social psychologists would result in considerable benefit accruing to both psychological subdomains.

REASONS FOR GREATER SOCIAL PSYCHOLOGICAL ATTENTION TO CONSUMER RESEARCH

Why should social psychologists become more cognizant of and perhaps even active in consumer psychological research? What can it do for them and for social psychology as a whole? At least 10 answers can be provided to these questions.

The first and perhaps most basic reason for social psychologists to become knowledgeable regarding consumer research is the heuristic potential it offers for contributing to the ddvelopment and extension of social psychology itself. In general, when social psychological principles and methods are applied to consumer problems, they are often applied in novel ways and in a variety of contexts. This stretching often provides new and richer meaning to the constructs or methods being stretched. Moreover, reflection on applied problems is frequently capable of illuminating significant gaps in basic social psychological knowledge. As one example, the social psychological literature on persuasive communications employing the source-message-medium-receiver paradigm displays considerable attention to source credibility and receiver personality. Somewhat surprisingly, the personality of the persuasive *source* has been empirically and conceptually ignored. This omission readily surfaces when one considers the fact that sales people are real-world persuasive sources and many firms daily confront the problem of identifying, hiring, and developing such persuasive sources. Another and more profound omission is the almost complete lack of social psychological attention devoted to media effects.

Second, social psychology is essentially a basic discipline, and the validity of its propositions will eventually have to be established in specific, real-world contexts. Because of the universal and frequently occurring nature of consumer behavior, this context seems to provide excellent opportunities for examining the validity of social psychological constructs. Stated somewhat differently, if you are really interested in theory, the best place to test it is in the field. Although the social psychologist's laboratory generally provides a superb setting for rigorously testing explicit theoretically derived hypotheses, the natural environment provides the ultimate setting in which to establish both the construct validity and generality of these findings (Campbell and Stanley, 1963). As Hovland (1959) pointed out in a classic paper, our neat and tidy laboratory findings are often completely reversed when we consider them in the field. If social psychology is not to delude itself and become a captive of the ivory tower, it must engage in reality testing in the field, and the consumer behavior context provides an excellent setting for such kinds of research.

Third, in addition to construct validation, consider the opportunities for consensual validation. Scientists are almost invariably excited and delighted if and when they find that their theories, constructs, and findings are supported by parallel theories, constructs, and findings developed independently by others operating within the boundaries of different content domains. The three dominant components of source credibility identified in academic investigations, namely, competence, trustworthiness, and dynamism (cf. Berlo, Lemert, and Mertz, 1970), find direct parallels in the applied literature on salesmanship, where it is generally stressed that good salesmen must have high product knowledge, empathy so as to engender trust, and enthusiasm. The great number of such parallels would probably surprise most social psychologists.

Fourth, engaging in consumer research provides social psychologists with numerous opportunities for working with relatively clean, real, and, from the perspective of the subject, meaningful dependent measures. For example, purchase—a fundamental, real, and meaningful form of human behavior—represents one such relatively clean dependent variable. The phrase "Put your money where your mouth is" pithily describes the layman's intuitive understanding of the relationship between attitude (particularly attitude strength) and behavior. Nearly two decades ago, the clamor

within personality psychology for it to redirect some of its one-sided attention to the abnormal personality so as to consider the more prevalent healthy personality became overpowering. Isn't it about time that social psychology experienced a similar broadening of focus by studying real attitudes held by people in the real world?

Consider, for example, the person who replies "Crest" in response to questions regarding what his favorite brand of toothpaste was and which brand he was predisposed to purchase the next time he needed toothpaste. Moreover, we observe his behavior over the subsequent 12 months and find that he repeatedly and almost invariably does purchase Crest toothpaste in preference to the many other available brands of toothpaste. Doesn't this reflect all the elements inherent in the attitude-behavior relationship? Wouldn't it be a social psychological question having considerable theoretical merit to consider how this attitude developed; how, why, and under which circumstances it relates to behavior; and how, why, and under which circumstances it could be changed? Wouldn't it also be interesting for social psychologists to be able to consider the manifestation of such attitude-behavior relationships longitudinally, as in a series of purchase trials, rather than having to rely on single, cross-sectional indicants? Think of the added reliability and implications for validity that multiple measures of purchase behavior over time have for establishing the significance of attitudes as an explanatory and predictive construct.

Toothpaste has intentionally been used in this example because some social psychologists are likely to contend that it reflects a trivial attitude object. But is it any more trivial than, say, attitudes toward vivisection (Lana, 1961) or any other attitude the subject happens to develop on the spot in response to an experimenter's questionnaire item (cf. Bogart, 1967)? The fact that a large number of people use toothpaste an average of twice a day, often the first thing in the morning and the last thing at night, probably purchase toothpaste once a month or so, and over the years actually spend a small fortune on toothpaste, suggests that attitudes toward different brands of toothpaste may not be all that trivial. But even if it were trivial, at least it is real—and that is more than can be said for the risky-shift phenomenon that engaged the attention and creative efforts of too many social psychologists for far too long. How many other risky-shift phenomena do we social psychologists still have rattling around in our closets?

Steiner (1972) suggests that the most flagrant abuse of human subjects, and that which gives psychological research a bad name, is the waste of subject time and energy incurred when subjects participate in trivial research. I submit that much contemporary social psychological research immerses subjects in just such trivial and seemingly meaningless research, and it is just these kinds of antagonized subjects who are most likely to subvert the data and generate the wide variety of artifactual findings we seem to be obtaining.

A basic argument being made here is that in purchase behavior we have individuals acting and reacting to a virtual cornucopia of real-world attitude objects, with these reaction tendencies often being modified over time as a function of past experience, formal (mass-media) communications, informal (word-of-mouth) communications, and a wide variety of other factors and inputs. As Kelman (1974) so ably points out, "Attitude remains a viable and potentially powerful concept *as long as we place it firmly in a context of action*" (p. 311, italics added). "Not only is attitude an integral part of action, but action is an integral part of the development, testing, and crystallization of attitudes" (p. 324). Consumer behavior provides one such meaningful and easily accessible field of action. Moreover, numerous other basic social psychological concepts find expression in this field of action and are being given considerable attention in contemporary consumer psychological research. These include object perception, social perception, the attribution process, judgmental processes, decision and choice processes, information processing, social influence, persuasive communications, norms and conformity, leadership, social roles, socialization and social learning, personality and other individual difference factors, and risk perception and risk taking.

A fifth reason for social psychological involvement in consumer research is that, in attempting to understand consumer behavior, one is often forced to think in relatively broad terms. This occasionally leads to seeing relationships that might not have been noted had this broader perspective not been forced upon us. It also tends to make us more aware of possible pitfalls and the limitation of our research than is often the case. Finally, we live in a multivariate world. Bivariate and trivariate social psychological studies, regardless of how many levels of each variable are employed, typically consider negligible (perhaps even insignificant) proportions of the variance in human decision making and behavior. Broader perspectives might at least assist in identifying which of the many variables that we can study in bivariate and trivariate designs should receive our earliest and concentrated attention.

Sixth, considerable concern has recently been expressed (Fried, Gumpper, & Allen, 1973; Higbee & Wells, 1972; McGuire, 1967, 1973; Proshansky, 1972; Ring, 1967; Smith, 1972; Singer & Glass, Note 2) about the narrow mold into which most social psychological research can be placed. One needs only nine words to describe the current state of affairs obtaining in the vast majority of contemporary social psychological research. These are: Method? Experimentation. Situation? Laboratory. Subjects? College students. Analysis? ANOVA. Consumer behavior research provides excellent opportunities for contemporary social psychology to extend its research options.

Lest I be misunderstood, let me clearly state that I am not finding fault with doing experimental lab-

2. Singer, J. E., & Glass, D. C. *Social psychology in the 1970's: From experimentation to policy.* Paper presented at the meeting of the Society for Experimental Social Psychology, Minneapolis, October 1970.

oratory research using college sophomores as subjects and employing analysis of variance designs to analyze the results. I, myself, live in a house partially made of glass (e.g., Jacoby, Olson, and Haddock, 1971; Jacoby, Speller, and Kohn, 1974; Szybillo and Jacoby, 1974a, 1974b). Rather, my objection is to doing *only* this type of research. The content and setting of consumer behavior provides a viable and attractive alternative for social psychologists to the social psychology of volunteer college sophomores (cf. Rosenthal and Rosnow, 1969, p. 110).

Seventh, I contend that consumer psychology provides numerous exciting opportunities for socially relevant research that would yield major benefits to society at large. In summarizing a recent study involving 2,340 psychology graduate students and 500 faculty members in graduate departments of psychology, Lipsey (1974) writes:

> The issue that generated the most heat was social relevance, the demand that psychology involve itself constructively in the widespread social problems that beset society. A large majority of both students and faculty felt that the discipline should be contributing to the solution of social problems, and an equally large majority felt that at present it was making no important contribution. (p. 553)

In contrast, consider some of the challenging opportunities for social psychological research that consumer behavior provides. As examples, what are the effects of advertising on children? In this time of growing scarcity and ecological concern, how can we generate anticonsumption (or reduced consumption) attitudes and behavior? How can we apply knowledge regarding the adoption and diffusion of commercial products, services, and ideas to stimulating the acceptance of birth control or modern agricultural practices in underdeveloped countries? Can we develop techniques for resisting persuasion and teach people— particularly the elderly, the disadvantaged, and children—how to apply them? Numerous other socially relevant examples abound. To show that these are not isolated examples of consumer psy-

chology's attention to meaningful social problems, consider some of the Division 23 symposia presented at the 1974 APA Convention. Included in a list of these titles are: Consumer Issues in Health Care; Improving Product Safety Through Consumer Education; The Role of Consumer Psychology in Matters of Corporate Social Responsibility; The Psychology of Inflation; Psychological Methods and Planning a Better Transportation Environment; and Consumer Product Labeling: Can You Tell a Book by Its Cover? (which considered the manner in which consumers process and are affected by package information and what various federal agencies, such as the Federal Trade Commission, can do to assist the consumer in this task).

An eighth reason for social psychologists to adopt a more consumer-research-oriented posture is that, in this era of tight federal money for basic research, the purse strings are opening up for social qua consumer research. As one example, I can cite my own recent large-scale grant from the National Science Foundation to continue work on consumer information acquisition and processing. The findings from this series of investigations are already being provided to the Federal Trade Commission, the Food and Drug Administration, the Department of Agriculture, and other appropriate governmental agencies to assist them in developing consumer-beneficent regulations regarding the content, organization, and display of information on product packages.

A ninth reason for social psychologists to consider devoting some attention to the issues and research problems found in consumer psychology is that, if they do not apply their concepts and methods in this domain, they can be assured that others will. There are important social ramifications couched in this reason. Most social psychologically oriented consumer research conducted thus far has been conducted by nonpsychologists. Not unexpectedly, a large proportion of the early work was of rather poor quality. Yet, many important decisions, some affecting each and every one of us as consumers, have been made by government and industry alike on the basis of such data—*because they were the only data available.* Although most of the more recent consumer research involving social psychological variables and concepts tends to be substantially better—indeed, often of comparable quality to articles appearing in the *Journal of Personality and Social Psychology* and the *Journal of Experimental Social Psychology*—it still remains true that social psychologists, by not entering the arena to study consumer behavior, are abdicating an important responsibility and leaving a void for others to enter and apply (or sometimes misapply) social psychological concepts and methods. Social psychology has much to offer, yet social psychologists are contributing little.

Tenth, at a time when job opportunities for new social psychology PhDs seem to be decreasing, job opportunities for students having course work and research experience bearing on consumer behavior are opening up in universities, government, and industry faster than they can be filled. Relatedly, the rates of remuneration for social-consumer psychologists tend to be higher than that for traditional social psychologists, and opportunities always exist for supplementing one's income through consulting (Jacoby, Note 3). Although many such consulting opportunities exist with large consumer product firms, not all consulting is focused on assisting marketers and advertisers. A substantial number of challenging opportunities are to be found elsewhere. As one example, I can cite my own involvement with the Food and Drug Administration in which a paradigm for assessing misleading prescription drug advertising is being developed (Jacoby & Small, in press).

Like most any other form of social psychology, consumer psychology is just plain fun and exciting. However, there are several reasons why this

3. Jacoby, J. *The roles, value, and training of a consultant.* Paper presented at the Meeting of the American Psychological Association, New Orleans, September 1974.

excitement is magnified in consumer psychology. First, the field is really just in its infancy, with more than 50% of the published empirical research appearing since 1968. Second, consumer behavior research is basically interdisciplinary. As one reflection of this, the most dynamic and fastest growing scholarly organization in the consumer field, the 5-year-old Association for Consumer Research, has an overwhelmingly interdisciplinary constituency. Consider also the fact that the new *Journal of Consumer Research* is cosponsored by 10 different professional organizations. Third, consumer psychological researchers not only interact with others from a variety of academic disciplines but very often with researchers and public policymakers in government and industry as well. Such interactions usually tend to be stimulating experiences and generate the feeling that one is functioning "where it's at" and having at least a modicum of impact on what's happening out there in the real world. It is a true "field of action."

SOCIAL PSYCHOLOGY'S LEWINIAN HERITAGE AND ACTION RESEARCH

Let me return in closing to Kurt Lewin's classic study of public versus private commitment, because it embodies much of what I believe the interaction between social and consumer psychology is capable of being and reflects a research orientation and model which I, as a social-consumer psychologist, would dearly love to see rekindled in contemporary social psychology. Lewin (1946) called this orientation "action research." Basically, this is "research done in an actual problem context and which would be socially useful as well as theoretically meaningful" (Proshansky, 1972, p. 211).

As several other social psychologists have recently noted, contemporary social psychology has, for the greater part, dwelled far afield from Lewin's nuclear model. Indeed, it has become increasingly obvious that a "pervasive prejudice against applied research exists among academic psychologists" (Gergen, 1973, p. 317). Yet, "for Lewin, basic and applied research, laboratory and field research, were complementary, not opposed" (Smith, 1972, p. 95). It has been my purpose to indicate that consumer psychology provides a set of challenging opportunities and an

appropriate environment with which to rekindle this model and reactivate Lewin's seminal social psychological values. I hope that this article stimulates a few of my social psychological brethren to consider following in Lewin's consumer psychological footsteps. It is certain that we and our discipline would all profit substantially thereby.

REFERENCES

Berlo, D. K.; Lemert, J. B.; and Mertz, R. J. (1970), "Evaluating the Acceptability of Message Sources," *Public Opinion Quarterly,* 33, 563–76.

Bogart, L. (1967), "No Opinion, Don't Know, and Maybe No Answer," *Public Opinion Quarterly,* 31, 331–45.

Campbell, D. T., and Stanley, J. (1963), "Experimental and Quasi-experimental Designs for Research on Teaching," in N. L. Gage, ed., *Handbook of Research on Teaching,* Chicago: Rand McNally.

Cowles, J. T., (1937), "Food Tokens as Incentives for Learning by Chimpanzees," *Comparative Psycho-Monographs,* 4(5).

Engel, J. F.; Kollat, D. T.; and Blackwell, R. D. (1968), *Consumer Behavior,* (1st ed.), New York: Holt, Rinehart & Winston.

Engel, J. F.; Kollat, D. T.; and Blackwell, R. D. (1973), *Consumer Behavior,* (2nd ed.), New York: Holt, Rinehart & Winston.

Fried, S. B.; Gumpper, D. C.; and Allen, J. C. (1973), "Ten Years of Social Psychology: Is There a Growing Commitment to Field Research?" *American Psychologist,* 28, 155–56.

Friedman, M. P. (1966), "Consumer Confusion in the Selection of Supermarket Products," *Journal of Applied Psychology,* 50, 529–34.

Friedman, M. P. (1967), "Quality and Price Considerations in Rational Consumer Decision Making," *Journal of Consumer Affairs,* 1, 13–23.

Friedman, M. P. (1968), "Short-term Effects of Truth-in-lending Legislation on Consumer Behavior," *Proceedings of the 76th Annual Convention of the American Psychological Association,* 3, 667–68.

Gergen, K. J. (1973), "Social Psychology as History," *Journal of Personality and Social Psychology,* 26, 309–20.

Higbee, K. L., and Wells, M. G. (1972), "Some Research Trends in Social Psychology during the 1960s," *American Psychologist,* 963–66.

Hovland, C. I. (1959), "Reconciling Conflicting Results Derived from Experimental and Survey Studies of Attitude Change," *American Psychologist,* 14, 8–17.

Howard, J. H., and Sheth, J. N. (1969), *The Theory of Buyer Behavior,* New York: Wiley.

Jacoby, J. (1971), "Training Consumer Psychologists: The Purdue University Program," *Professional Psychology,* 2, 300–302.

Jacoby, J. (in press (a)), "Consumer and Industrial Psychology: Prospects for Theory Corroboration and Mutual Contribution," in M. D. Dunnette, ed., *The Handbook of Industrial and Organizational Psychology,* Chicago: Rand McNally.

Jacoby, J. (in press (b)), "Consumer Psychology: An Octennium," *Annual Review of Psychology.*

Jacoby, J.; Olson, J. C.; and Haddock, R. A. (1971). "Price, Brand Name, and Product Composition Characteristics as Determinants of Perceived Quality," *Journal of Applied Psychology,* 55, 570–79.

Jacoby, J., and Small, C. B. (in press), "The FDA Approach to Defining Misleading Advertising," *Journal of Marketing.*

Jacoby, J.; Speller, D. E.; and Kohn, C. A. (1974), "Brand Choice Behavior as a Function of Information Load," *Journal of Marketing Research,* 11, 63–69.

Katona, G. (1951), *Psychological Analysis of Economic Behavior,* New York: McGraw-Hill.

Katona, G. (1953), "Rational Behavior and Economic Behavior," *Psychological Review,* 60, 307–18.

Katona, G. (1960), *The Powerful Consumer,* New York: McGraw-Hill.

Katona, G. (1963), "The Relationship between Psychology and Economics," in S. Koch, ed., *Psychology: A Study of Science* (Vol. 6), New York: McGraw-Hill.

Kelman, H. C. (1974), "Attitudes Are Alive and Well and Gainfully Employed in the Sphere of Action," *American Psychologist, 29,* 310–24.

Krugman, H. E., (1968), "Consumer Behavior," in *International Encyclopedia of the Social Sciences,* New York: Macmillan and the Free Press.

Lana, R. E. (1961), "Familiarity and the Order of Persuasive Communications," *Journal of Abnormal and Social Psychology, 62,* 573–77.

Lewin, K. (1943), "Forces behind Food Habits and Methods of Change," *National Research Council Bulletin, 18,* 35–65.

Lewin, K. (1946), "Action Research and Minority Problems," *Journal of Social Issues, 2,* 34—46.

Lewin, K. (1958), "Group Decision and Social Change," in E. E. Maccoby, T. M. Newcomb, and E. L. Hartley, eds., *Readings in Social Psychology,* New York: Holt, Rinehart & Winston.

Lipsey, M. W. (1974), "Research and Relevance: A Survey of Graduate Students and Faculty in Psychology," *American Psychologist, 29,* 541–53.

McGuire, W. J. (1967), "Some Impending Reorientations in Social Psychology. Some Thoughts Provoked by Kenneth Ring," *Journal of Experimental Social Psychology, 3,* 124–39.

McGuire, W. J. (1973), "The Yin and Yang of Progress in Social Psychology: Seven Koan," *Journal of Personality and Social Psychology, 26,* 446–56.

Nicosia, F. M. (1966), *Consumer Decision Processes,* Englewood Cliffs, N. J.: Prentice-Hall.

Perloff, R. (1963), "Roles of Consumer and Psychology in Consumer Psychology," *Psychological Reports, 13,* 931–33.

Perloff, R. (1964), "The Work of the Industrial Psychologist in Relation to Consumers and the Public," *Business and Society, 4,* 23–24.

Perloff, R. (1968), "Consumer Analysis," *Annual Review of Psychology, 19,* 437–66.

Proshansky, H. M. (1972), "For What Are We Training Our Graduate Students?" *American Psychologist, 27,* 205–12.

Ring, K. (1967), "Experimental Social Psychology: Some Sober Questions about Some Frivolous Values," *Journal of Experimental Social Psychology, 3,* 113–23.

Rosenthal, R., and Rosnow, R. L. (1969), "The Volunteer Subject," in R. Rosenthal and R. L. Rosnow, eds., *Artifact in Behavioral Research,* New York: Academic Press.

Smith, M. B. (1972), "Is Experimental Social Psychology Advancing?" *Journal of Experimental Social Psychology, 8,* 86–96.

Steiner, I. D. (1972), "The Evils of Research: Or What My Mother Didn't Tell Me about the Sins of Academia," *American Psychologist, 27,* 766–68.

Szybillo, G. J. and Jacoby, J. (1974a), "Effects of Different Levels of Integration on Advertising Preference and Intention to Purchase," *Journal of Applied Psychology, 59,* 274–80.

Szybillo, G. J., and Jacoby, J. (1974b), "Intrinsic versus Extrinsic Cues as Determinants of Perceived Product Quality," *Journal of Applied Psychology, 59,* 74–78.

Ward, S., and Robertson, T. S. (1973), *Consumer Behavior: Theoretical Sources,* Englewood Cliffs, N. J.: Prentice-Hall.

Wolfe, J. B. (1936), "Effectiveness of Token-rewards for Chimpanzees," *Comparative Psychological Monographs, 12*(5).

TOWARD A SOCIOLOGY OF CONSUMPTION

FRANCESCO M. NICOSIA AND ROBERT N. MAYER

Source: Francesco M. Nicosia and Robert N. Mayer, "Toward a Sociology of Consumption," *Journal of Consumer Research,* Vol. 3, September, 1976, pp. 65–75.

INTRODUCTORY REMARKS

It should not be too controverisal to assert that consumer research, as we know it today, was born about two decades ago. We would probably also agree that consumer research is focused primarily on the study of the decision process of an *individual,* although the economic and social events that interact with the psychological attributes of an individual are also frequently included in consumer research.

In the early 1960s, some of us noted that the study of a *society's* consumption might also be useful (e.g., Glock and Nicosia, 1964). So far, however, only a few scholars have considered the consumption of a society (e.g., Bauer, 1966; Felson, 1975; Katona, Strumpel, and Zahn, 1971; Mayer, 1975; Nicosia and Glock, 1968; Nicosia and Witkowski, 1975; Smelser, 1963; Zaltman and Bagozzi, 1975). Even the vast literature on the so-called social indicators has practically ignored a society's consumption as a fundamental social indicator, especially in affluent, post-industrial societies (see, for example, the annotated bibliography by Wilcox et al., 1972).

This lack of attention to a society's consumption is surprising because macroeconomics has shown some of the advantages of studying production and consumption at the societal level rather than at the level of the single firm or the single household. In particular, the conceptual and empirical studies of the "consumption function" in macroeconomics have helped both the private and the public sectors in formulating and implementing policies.

Neither sociologists nor consumer researchers, however, have accepted the challenge of studying a society's consumption in relation to other societal characteristics, despite its potential as a social indicator. Understanding some of a society's characteristics could provide a consumer researcher with the context necessary to help the study of individual consumer choices. For example, understanding the effect of cultural values concerning achievement and the use of time is at least as important as understanding whether consumers process information in an additive or multiplicative manner.

Understanding the interactions among consumption and other societal characteristics would also contribute to the study of consumerism, the social responsibilities of marketing, the involvement of governments in providing consumer information (Mayer and Nicosia, 1974), and the roles of the mass communication systems—including advertising—in a society (Nicosia, 1974a).

More important, such understanding is a necessary input into the difficult decisions of social managers—legislatures, regulatory agencies, and courts—concerning long-term and crucial problems. For instance, it is an understatement to assert that many public policy decisions on management of human and natural resources may affect not only consumption but also institutions, norms, and, eventually, cultural values (Pirages and Ehrlich, 1974). This is true for all societies, regardless of their stage of evolution.

The experiences of societies now struggling to grow past a state of survival imply very difficult decisions for social managers. They must contend with consumption aspirations and activities unknown even half a century ago. The social and economic processes that led to the development of Western societies no longer seem to work. In particular, the visibility of consumption styles in Western societies affects both the kind and the intensity of consumption in developing societies, so that the old cycle of ''saving-investment-production and *then* consumption'' no longer seems applicable to these societies.

In affluent, post-industrial societies, social management of consumption faces different dilemmas. The recent history of these societies has been an evolution from solving problems of quantity—that is, the delivery of standards of living—to assuring quality of life. The meaning of this evolution for consumers has been the growing expectation that aesthetic as well as functional needs could be fulfilled. Spiraling aspirations to quantity and quality

went hand in hand until the energy crunch, stagflation, and unemployment entered the picture. In this new climate, quality is beginning to be perceived not as the handmaiden of quantity but rather as its enemy. To satisfy needs for quantities of goods, we sacrifice qualities of the environment: building a pipeline in Alaska and postponing clean air standards.

Society and consumers had thought that quantity and quality were complementary. Now they are learning that there are conflicts; they are facing trade-offs, and, knowingly or not, they are assuming historical and moral responsibility. What kind of knowledge do social managers have for dealing with this situation? We doubt that either *existing* concepts or *data* are sufficient.

These remarks are only an initial indication of why we propose to focus on society rather than on the individual consumer (or types of consumers). We shall unfold our arguments gradually—in particular, specifying a *few* characteristics (cultural values, institutions and their norms, and consumption) and their possible relationships—for very little has been dared in this direction.

In the next section of this article we begin the review of the literature in order to define some of the constructs that we believe are basic to a sociology of consumption. We continue the review in the following section, and by using the chosen constructs, work toward the specification of new research directions, hoping to lay the groundwork for future empirical research. In essence, we are proposing a prospectus for basic and applied research, thereby delineating a sociology of consumption and its potential contributions.

THE DOMAIN OF A SOCIOLOGY OF CONSUMPTION

The development of empirically based knowledge depends on a process of measuring the words central to the inquiry at hand. To appreciate our efforts, recall that the first step of this process involves mapping of a word's daily meanings. The next step is explication—that is, choosing a number of dimensions, given a research purpose. Thus, a word defined in the space of the chosen dimensions can now be considered a *construct*. The next step involves choices of indicators, measuring instruments, and measurement. The end result is usually a numerical representation of a word.

In the social sciences, even the first step of this process presents major difficulties because a word's daily connotations are many and confusing. Even key words in social science literature may be vague, for they have not yet been translated into clearly defined constructs. This initial difficulty applies particularly to the literature that we have reviewed.

In this section, we choose cultural values, social institutions and their norms, and consumption activities as central to our domain of inquiry. We then discuss the problems of dimensionalizing these words.

Definition of "Cultural Value"

To transform the term "cultural value" into a measurable construct is more difficult than is the case with either "social institution" or "consumption activities." There is agreement that the term implies *widely held beliefs* as well as a *general guide* for some set of activities. Beyond these, however, many issues have not been settled. We should mention a few that we have found relevant.

To begin with, a cultural value by definition has as its referent an entire population, e.g., all U.S. citizens. The literature has not addressed, however, the problem of how widely held a value must be. Must it be held by a majority or only a plurality of the population? Without an answer to this question, the distinction between cultural values and the frequently used term "subcultural" values is neither conceptually nor operationally clear.

Another unsettled issue is the relationship between the intensity with which a value is held and that value's impact on behavior. An additional issue is that for some authors a cultural value must

be considered both desirable *and* essential by a population, while for others it must be desirable but not necessarily essential. An implication for a sociology of consumption is that, for example, if a society believes it *only* desirable that everyone have food, clothing, and shelter, one would expect to see private charitable institutions but not a government welfare apparatus.

A further issue involves the origins and consequences of cultural values. As an example of the ambiguity one faces, recall that the increasing briefness of women's bathing suits over the past 40 years is generally attributed to changes in morality, but to what extent did such fashion changes reinforce or even cause these changes in morality?

We do not intend to resolve these debates. For our purposes, we shall use cultural values in the sense that (a) they are widely held beliefs, (b) they affirm what is desirable, and (c) they have some impact on activities. Some examples of cultural values that might characterize a contemporary society and perhaps bear on its consumption are success through individual achievement, freedom of choice, egalitarianism, active use of time, orientation toward the future (e.g., progress, security), and active mastery of the physical environment.

We must deal with one final difficulty. In the literature, the terms "cultural value" and "norm" are associated but not clearly distinguished. For the purpose of understanding society and its consumption, we find it useful to draw a distinction between the two terms by locating norms in the context of social institutions.

Definition of "Institution"

Understanding society is often based on the study of its organization, namely, its institutions. The term "institution" has different meanings in the literature. Confronted with this variety, we view an institution as a set of specific *activities* performed by specific *people* in specific *places* through *time*. What is important in defining a particular institution is its unique *pattern* of interaction among activities, people, and places through time. Consider, for example, the nuclear and the extended family. They are two different institutions because their patterns of activities, people, and places through time differ.

An institution creates *norms* directing specific activities. For example, when two people marry, norms guiding their financial activities emerge (Ferber and Lee, 1974). Furthermore, norms maintain the pattern of interaction characteristic of a particular institution.

To be viable, an institution must find ways to apply its norms. The primary ways are the creation and implementation of specific *rewards* and *sanctions*. In a work institution, the norm "be productive" may be supported by the reward of wages proportional to productivity and by the sanction of fines for employees found to be intoxicated. Of course, the nature of rewards and sanctions does not need to be financial.

Success in implementing norms depends on at least two facilitating conditions: *communication* and *visibility*. Communication here includes both its amount and content, as well as its channels (e.g., purely visual, mass media, and word of mouth). For example, a story in a company's newsletter for its employees describing how a worker's idea led to both increased productivity and his promotion is an attempt to reinforce the norm "take initiative."

Visibility is usually associated with communication. The aspect that must be emphasized here, however, is the possible influence on a person of knowing that his actions are visible to others. To illustrate, if the norm "do not throw garbage in the street" prevails in a community, it may be adhered to more fully if people live in sight of each other. In fact, even the perception of being visible was found to be associated with energy conservation behavior (Warren and Clifford, 1975).

At the very least, institutional norms are *bounded* by cultural values. To illustrate, the cultural value "freedom of choice" prevents a private firm from specifying where its employees will live. In addition, some norms *interpret* cultural values into clearer criteria for the performance of specific

activities in an institution. For instance, in an American business firm, the cultural value "achieve individual success" is interpreted by norms such as "work hard," "be punctual," and "take reasonable risks." The same cultural value may be translated into different norms in another society. Thus, in a French firm, being successful entails retention of one's own property and the minimization of risk (Landes, 1951; Pitts, 1963).

In searching for norms bearing on *consumption activities,* we should not consider only such institutions as the family, restaurants, department stores, and sports arenas. Work, educational, and religious institutions also create norms bearing on clothes, cars, food, and entertainment.

The important research questions for our purposes, then, are the following:

1. Which institutions create which norms bearing on which consumption activities?

2. How are these norms bounded by cultural values, and how do they interpret cultural values?

Definition of "Consumption Activities"
Conceptual and empirical research implies a classification of activities, with each class concerned with a kind of behavior—e.g., political, occupational, educational, religious. Consumption activities, however, have been either ignored or lumped into the broad class of leisure activities.

We have also found that much social science literature describes some societies as "postindustrial," "materialistic," "service-oriented," or "affluent." Although these adjectives may describe many classes of activities, they seem to stress that consumption activities are relatively more important in distinguishing such societies from those referred to as "pastoral," "developing," or "industrial." An obvious case is the recent value-oriented literature exemplified by the popular writings of Galbraith and Kaysen. Yet, curiously enough, there are practically no attempts to study, systematically and comprehensively, a modern society's consumption activities and their possible correlates.

We distinguish three classes of consumption activities: buying, using, and disposing. Why these three instead of some others? What about searching for information? The specific activities implied by information search (e.g., reading ads, asking friends, window shopping) may be performed in the buying, using and disposing of goods. Thus, for the moment, we conceive of information search as a class of activities subordinate (but not hierarchically) to the three we propose.

There remains the problem of operationalizing the term "consumption activity" (Nicosia and Glock, 1968). We can begin with the long-term use and relative success of macroeconomic research on a society's consumption expenditures, which shows that *dollars spent* must be part of the explication, at least for some problems faced by public policy makers.

It is also clear that consumption activities imply goods; thus, the *specific basket of goods* (bought, used, and disposed) is also a salient dimension. The construction, early uses, and refinements of the cost-of-living index are proof of this. One refinement, now routinely implemented, is the computation of the cost of living for different "typical" baskets, each for a different level of income and for a different geographical area. To the extent that there is a tendency toward an increasing number of typical baskets, a primary contribution of a sociology of consumption is to observe such pluralism and begin analyses not only of the demographic and economic correlates of each typical basket but also of the social processes (involving cultural values, institutions, and norms) that may govern this pluralism.

We should illustrate further the importance of explicating consumption activities not only in terms of dollar expenditures but also in terms of the content of the baskets. Assume that three typical baskets involve the same dollar expenditure for "entertainment." Yet, in one case, the specific entertainment goods are mostly spectator sports events. The second basket includes mostly records, art supplies, and books, while the third consists mostly of outdoor activities such as swimming or backpacking. These differences, and particularly the distribution of people over these three baskets, have implications for resource management and preservation of environmental quality. For instance, the first basket involves transportation and the use of energy, the disposal of food and drink containers, and so on, plus long-term commitments by society to build and operate highways, parking lots, and stadiums.

The explication of consumption activities in terms of baskets is important for understanding the functioning of an institution. Suppose we observe that, within the same family, some members are more committed to spectator sports, others to intellectual entertainment, and others to outdoor pleasures. If this pluralism occurs in an increasing number of families, it may affect the families' abilities to formulate and implement coherent patterns of norms guiding consumption activities.

In addition to dollars spent and goods purchased, *time* should be included in any operational definition of consumption activities. Each activity implies time, but more important, different goods imply different amounts of time allocated to buying, using, and disposing.

It may well be that time is the crucial dimension, since its supply is fixed. The interdependence among all kinds of activities because of the fixed supply of time has strong implications for the study of a society's consumption. How does a society cope with a fixed amount of time available (Nicosia, 1974b)? Whatever social mechanisms lead to greater allocation of time to consumption activities, a net consequence is that some other activities will necessarily receive less time. It is here that cultural values, institutions, and norms may confer meaning to time and thus guide the allocation of time to different activities.

Summary

The domain of a sociology of consumption concerns the study of three classes of variables: cultural values, institutions and their norms, and consumption activities. It also includes the study of the possible interrelationships between these classes of variables—for example, (1) from cultural values to institutions and then to consumption activities, (2) from cultural values directly to consumption activities, and (3) possible feedbacks from consumption activities to institutions and/or cultural values.

We have very little theoretical and empirical knowledge of the processes that govern a society's consumption. In the next section, we shall develop some points of departure for building such knowledge. We shall use as much evidence as exists that is possibly relevant, and, as is always the case in a new venture, we shall make a number of reasonable—common-sense, if you will—speculations.

THE NATURE AND DYNAMICS OF CONSUMPTION IN AFFLUENT SOCIETIES

In reviewing the concepts basic to our inquiry, the emphasis was on the development of operational definitions. In this section, we discuss some new research directions. This is a rather ambiguous undertaking, with few, if any, guides.

Our discussion of consumption and its underlying social processes will be organized around three research directions:

1. What are the institutional arrangements—that is, the social organization—of consumption activities in affluent societies?
2. How do cultural values relate to the social organization of consumption activities?
3. How do changes in a society's consumption activities relate to broader social change in cultural values and nonconsumptional institutions, norms, and activities?

Institutional Arrangements of Consumption Activities in Affluent Societies

To understand the social organization of any activity, we must examine the number and types of institutions in which the activity occurs. If we look

at an affluent society, we observe that one type of activity primarily occurs in one type of institution—for example, work activities usually occur in work institutions, educational activities in educational institutions. Where do consumption activities take place?

In searching for an answer, let us appreciate the historical background of this association of type of activity with type of institution. In pastoral and agrarian societies, by and large, the institution of the family (or the clan, the immediate community) tended to be the locus of most activities (e.g., production, consumption, education and socialization, procreation, religion, and self-government). During the feudal period, too, the family remained the locus of most of these activities, with the exception of those taken on by the church and the centralized state.

With the advent of industrialization in Western societies, several activities became increasingly organized into specialized institutions outside the family. For example, production moved to the factories; education and increasingly socialization became the job of schools; political-legal activities and the control of deviance were performed by the state through its legislatures, police, and growing court system; and medical care was dispensed in hospitals and, recently, also in outpatient clinics and HMOs.

During this industrialization the family was still the main focus of consumption activities, but as affluence spread throughout society, consumption activities also began to move out of the family. It appears, however, that the movement of consumption activities out of the family differs from that of work, education, and other activities. The identification of these differences poses new research questions. What happened to the consumption activities of buying, using, and disposing?

Buying activities. In agrarian times, buying activities were rare, relegated to ceremonial visits with other families and tribes or to occasional journeys to the village market, for the family tended to be self-sufficient. As production activities became specialized and moved out of the family, however, buying activities increased and moved outside of the family. As production specialized further, industrializing Western societies had to develop ways of facilitating the buying activities of its members. Thus, we have the growth and differentiation of retailing institutions with which consumers can interact directly and of backup institutions such as warehousing, financing, and wholesaling, all attempting to search and match points of original supplies with points of final use (Nicosia, 1962).

The impact of this evolution in retailing institutions is that any consumer faces at least two kinds of choices. First, for most products, a consumer can choose among different types of stores. For example, car engine oil can be purchased in gasoline stations, hardware stores, auto parts stores, and even supermarkets (Nicosia and Mayer, 1973). Secondly, within each type of store, a consumer can also choose one particular store. These two choices are always discretionary and, in principle, at least, they are made for each purchase. These characteristics distinguish buying activities from most nonconsumption activities because work, educational, religious, and other activities, tend to be performed in a particular institution for relatively long periods of time.

The significance of this difference is that norms concerning buying activities cannot be strongly enforced. The exposure to a large number of consumption institutions, combined with the briefness of the stay in each, makes it difficult for norms to be communicated. Furthermore, the ability not to return to any particular consumption institution makes it difficult to enforce its norms through rewards and sanctions.

To the extent that buying activities are performed in a large number of retail institutions, the less likely it is that norms will be consistent for each consumer. To the extent that these institutions are incapable of communicating and enforcing their norms, the more likely it is that the only norm applying to buying activities is "the customer is always right"—as if buying activities were not subject to norms!

Use activities. Use activities may also be gradually moving out of the family in ways different from nonconsumption activities. As in buying activities, one sees an increasing number of use-oriented institutions (e.g., for food, entertainment, and transportation).[1] Here again, consumers choose not only among types (e.g., restaurant, coffee shop, or fast-food outlet) but also within types of use-institution (e.g., McDonald's, Jack in the Box, or Burger King). Moreover, consumers' participation in each institution is brief and changing, with potential implications for the operation of norms similar to those in the case of buying activities.

Use activities are further distinguished by their frequent occurrence in nonconsumption institutions, e.g., at factories, hospitals, schools, and homes of friends. This exposure to a range of institutional types wider than that of buying activities makes it even more problematic that any set of norms can guide use activities.

To what extent, then, are consumers exposed to many differing, often competing, and even contradictory sets of norms? Take, for example, the child who eats dinner at home with his parents one night, with the babysitter the next night, at a restaurant the next night, and at the home of a friend the night after that (not to mention the diversity of norms governing the conduct at different restaurants and in different homes of friends). This type of social organization of use activities should

---

[1]The $64 billion food service industry, for example, has become the third largest consumer industry, behind the $100 billion retail food business and the $93 billion auto business. The food service industry, moreover, is first in number of outlets (half a million) and in employment (4.7 percent of the labor force) ("America's Eating-out Splurge," 1975, p. 43). At the level of the household, the 1972-73 U.S. Consumer Expenditure Survey showed that 27 percent of the food budget (excluding alcoholic beverages) of the average U.S. family was spent away from home. And a recent report by the Bank of America suggests that by 1980 consumers may be eating half of their meals away from home.

bear on the socialization of future consumers and on the fate of cultural values such as frugality, cleanliness, and religiosity.[2] Only the analysis of the social organization of use activities leads to the posing of these new questions and, eventually, to the collection of appropriate data.

Disposal activities.   Unlike virtually all other activities, disposal activities have remained within the family, but only to the extent that use activities are also performed there. The single corollary in terms of social organization is the birth of the disposal service institution, now practically a legal requirement. Here too, however, it is difficult for norms to emerge and guide disposal activities because of the relative invisibility of these activities and lack of communication concerning them. The content of the garbage can is not made public unless a neighborhood dog intervenes, and the subject is unlikely to come up in daily conversation.

The social organization of disposal activities has begun to change with the timid appearance of public and private recycling efforts. Recent resource management problems emphasize disposal activities, for they bear on the availability of scarce resources and the maintenance of a livable environment. Optimal solutions to these problems require finding the social organization of disposal activities that is most capable of generating and enforcing norms guiding consumers—a fundamental research direction.

Future directions for research.   Let us identify the research area that emerges from our understanding of what has happened to the social organization of consumption during industrialization and affluence. Like other activities, buying and use activities have also gradually moved out of the family institution and thus have become less likely to be governed by norms administered by it.

[2]A pertinent question in this regard is whether anyone has measured changes in the frequency of the traditional family supper, with the members gathering each night at the same time, and all beginning the meal with a prayer.

However, the administration of norms concerning types of nonconsumption activities has been largely absorbed by the corresponding types of nonconsumption institutions. We argue that this has not happened for consumption activities. Instead, they are increasingly dispersed in both consumption and nonconsumption institutions; consumers are thus increasingly exposed to a multiplicity of potentially conflicting norms, none of which can be strongly enforced.

So far, we have stressed only one set of changes that may cause consumers to experience either an overload or an absence of normative regulation. There is an additional set of changes in the very structure of the modern affluent family that further diminishes the ability of the family to administer norms bearing on consumption activities. Some of these changes are well documented: trends in family formation, changes in divorce rates and frequency per person, and the explosion of married women in the work force. By suggesting that these changes affect the family's ability to guide consumption activities, we offer to empirical researchers in these areas a theoretical way to contribute to the synthesis of knowledge of consumer behavior.

Future research should focus on the following themes: changes in the social organization of consumption activities, changes in the family structure, and the consequences of both for private and social management.

Cultural Values and the Social Organization of Consumption Activities

In the previous subsection, we discussed research directions concerning consumption activities, institutions, and norms. Further directions emerge from considering the roles of cultural values in the consumption of affluent societies.

A first research problem is one of identifying which cultural values, if any, are relevant.

The identification of cultural values relevant to consumption poses methodological challenges to future research. There is little empirical work and experience to rely on.

A second research problem concerns the identification of the *social processes* by which cultural values relate to institutions, norms, and activities. There are many such processes in principle; we shall mention a few.

One possibility is that some cultural values can guide some consumption activities directly rather than through intervening social mechanisms. Little research has addressed this possibility, but applicable findings suggest the absence of a direct relationship (e.g., Heberlein and Black, 1974). In fact, current understanding of society indicates that cultural values relate to activities primarily through institutions and their norms.

As mentioned earlier, activities are related to cultural values through institutions in two ways. First, activities may be guided by institutional norms that are bounded by cultural values. For example, consumption institutions such as restaurants have been generating the norm "any attire is acceptable." Yet, nudity is not acceptable, for the norm is bounded by cultural values concerning morality. Second, activities may be guided by norms that interpret cultural values in clear ways. For instance, the norm "save some of your monthly income" interprets cultural values stressing the importance of the future.

The institutions mediating cultural values and consumption activities may be either consumptional, as in these examples, or nonconsumptionable. As an example of norms interpreting cultural values, some educational institutions may interpret the value "freedom of choice" by generating the norm "select your own course of study," with implications for the consumption not only of books but also of records, films, musical instruments, and pocket calculators (and, ultimately, future consumptional styles).

Another social process comprehends a class of feedbacks. Changes in consumption activities may feed back into institutions and their norms. For instance, as affluence spreads and eating in restaurants becomes more common, the adherence to and enforcement of religious dietary norms become more difficult. This state of affairs may force religious institutions to change these norms, or may ultimately change the nature and extent of member participation.

Changes in consumption activities may also feed back directly into cultural values. Opposition to the purchase and use of alcohol, drugs, and pornographic films *assumes the empirical possibility of this feedback.*

So far, we have suggested some of the basic processes that may underlie change in a society's consumption. Empirical research is needed to establish the presence and relative magnitude of these processes. Our discussion has also shown that changes in a society's consumption are part of and interact with social change in general. We thus expect that there are complex processes at work, all of which still require conceptualization. In the following subsection, we shall develop some conceptualizations of more complex processes on the basis of already available evidence.

Changes in a Society's Consumption Activities and Broader Social Change

The relationships between changes in a society's consumption activities and social change in general are the result of numerous and complex social processes. We shall conceptualize one case of social change in which consumption activities may be seen both as results and as causes. In our example, cultural values are "deflected" into consumption activities. Deflection processes can be expected to occur when certain nonconsumption institutions no longer interpret and translate a particular cultural value into activity-specific norms.

The deflection process that we shall map out considers (1) the cultural values of success through individual achievement and of frugality; (2) the institutions of the firm and of the labor union, and their norms; and (3) work and consumption activities. We shall then discuss the interactions among these variables by considering the following questions: What happens when an institution no longer interprets a certain cultural value? Will new institutions emerge capable of interpreting that value, will the value die, or will members of society search for new activities in which to express that cultural value? What are the effects of these possible adjustments on consumption activities?

We begin with the cultural value of getting ahead, i.e., "success through individual achievement." Throughout industrialization, the institutional locus for achieving success was the productive sector, and institutional norms specified how an individual could in fact strive for success (e.g., be punctual, come to work alert, show dedication, meet quotas).

Two of the changes in the character of productive activities and institutions that accompanied industrialization had implications for individual achievement. First, increasing specialization and scale of organizations meant a decreasing objective probability of getting ahead, and certainly of reaching the top, in industry. A second change was the birth of the labor union. This latter change has had an impact on working conditions, job security, recruitment and training. However, we want to note its impact on the success ethic. In this regard, labor unions make it increasingly difficult for the worker to distinguish himself and to be rewarded on the basis of his *individual* effort and achievement. The collective bargaining of the union presupposes that rewards are won for a group rather than for specific individuals. Furthermore, unions seek to have job advancement and promotion based on seniority rather than on performance-related attributes of individuals.

If production and labor institutions no longer constitute the primary mechanism by which the cultural value of getting ahead can realistically and feasibly be pursued, what adjustments are likely to occur? Will the cultural value of individual success lose its force? Some counterculture movements may be seen as evidence of this. A second adjustment is also possible—the deflection of the success ethic into consumption activities.

Chinoy (1952) observed this deflection in his study of auto workers. He found that the workers redefined getting ahead in terms of owning certain goods and that this allowed them to continue to believe in the reality of upward mobility. Thus, for Chinoy the major consequence of this deflection process was that consumption activities sustained the success ethic.

We might add that the possible consequences of this process for other values should also be explored. For instance, to what extent does sustaining the success ethic through consumption activities undermine the values of frugality and orientation toward the future? Can this strengthen the societal desirability for egalitarianism to imply not only equal opportunities but also equal economic results? Are we thus observing the birth of the cultural value "the right to consume" beyond the survival level?

An affluent society provides the facilitating conditions for the deflection of the success ethic into the realm of consumption. These conditions include increases in discretionary income *and* time and the reduced physical demands of most jobs, all of which provide the means for pursuing personal achievement in leisure activities and through the acquisition of status-conferring goods. The explosion in hobbies and do-it-yourself activities that began in the 1950s can probably be seen in this light. We may similarly interpret the increase in interest in quasi-cultural activities, from trips to Europe to pottery and jewelry making, which are capable of bestowing distinction on those who experience, rather than own, them.

Finally, this deflection of getting ahead finds expression in the intensity, pace, and efficiency orientation with which some people pursue supposedly relaxing activities, e.g., traveling, entertaining friends, even camping and backpacking. These observations also suggest the possible displacement of another cultural value from the productive sphere, namely, the prescription to derive a high yield from one's use of time and never to waste it (Linder, 1970).

Are there larger socioeconomic consequences of this pursuit of success, achievement, and personal distinction through consumption activities?

Does this deflection contribute to an increasing number of consumption styles and a pluralism of market baskets (i.e., the goods, activities, and time implied by one's consumption activities)? The traditional explanations for the increasing differentiation among consumers are differences in income, occupation, education, and psychological predispositions. The presence of deflection processes is an additional explanation to be explored empirically.

Our discussion of the deflection of the success ethic from the sphere of production to that of consumption is only one example of a class of possible deflection processes. We have just mentioned that a similar analysis could be done on cultural prescriptions concerning the use of time. We may add that, in industrializing societies, the value "freedom of choice" was supposed to apply in a variety of institutional spheres. However, developments such as centralization of government and technological complexity have left consumption as the primary area in which a person can exercise some freedom of choice.

In this section, we have suggested research directions for understanding the nature and dynamics of consumption in affluent societies. By using concepts basic to a sociology of consumption, we have explored and often reinterpreted changes in consumption and its related social processes.

Our approach to the study of consumption in affluent societies suggests these research areas:

1. Identification of cultural values, institutions, and norms which are related to consumption activities.

2. Identification of processes of social change which underlie changes in a society's consumption.

We have shown that these areas are points of departure for the specification of testable hypotheses.

We have argued that comprehensive and systematic study of consumption in affluent societies poses research questions that are intrinsically interesting and potentially useful to private and social managers. Our interest in the development of a sociology of consumption goes beyond that of posing new basic and applied research questions. We are asking whether Western history is reaching a crucial point in its evolution. For most of its history, mankind related to its environment by "the sweat of its brow," and its morality was largely based on fear. By trial and error, through victories and defeats, much of humanity has freed itself from toil and reached the opportunity to choose a new kind of morality. It may choose to worship God not out of fear and to organize itself primarily for the satisfaction of social, psychological, and, ultimately, aesthetic and ethical wants (Nicosia, 1966, p. 6).

REFERENCES

"America's Eating-out Splurge," (Oct. 27, 1975), *Business Week,* 2404, 42–46.

Bauer, R. A., ed. (1966), *Social Indicators,* Cambridge: M.I.T. Press.

Chinoy, E. (March 1952), "The Tradition of Opportunity and the Aspirations of Automobile Workers," *American Journal of Sociology,* 57, 453–59.

"Egalitarianism: Threat to a Free Market," (December 1, 1975), *Business Week,* 2409, 62–65.

Felson, M. (1975), "The Differentiation of Material Life Styles: 1925–1966," Working paper, Department of Sociology, University of Illinois at Urbana-Champaign.

Ferber, R., and Lee, L. C. (June 1974), "Husband-Wife Influence in Family Purchasing Behavior," *Journal of Consumer Research,* 1, 43–50.

Glock, C. Y., and Nicosia, F. M. (July, 1964), "Uses of Sociology in Studying 'Consumption' Behavior," *Journal of Marketing,* 28, 51–54.

Heberlein, T. A., and Black, J. S. (August, 1974), "The Land Ethic in Action: Personal Norms, Beliefs, and the Purchase of Lead Free Gasoline," Paper presented at the Annual Meetings of the Rural Sociological Society, Montreal.

Katona, G.; Strumpel, B.; and Zahn, E. (1971), *Aspirations and Affluence: Comparative Studies in the United States and Western Europe,* New York: McGraw-Hill.

Landes, D. S. (1951), "French Business and the Businessman: A Social and Cultural Analysis," in E. M. Earle, ed., *Modern France: Problems of the Third and Fourth Republics,* Princeton, N.J.: Princeton University Press, 334–53.

Linder, S. B. (1970), *The Harried Leisure Class,* New York: Columbia University Press.

Mayer, R. (1975), "Consumer Consciousness and Social Change," Paper presented at the 70th Annual Meeting of the American Sociological Association, San Francisco, August.

———, and Nicosia, F. M. (1974), "Technology, the Consumer, and Information Flows," Vol. 4 in F. M. Nicosia, et al., *Technological Change, Product Proliferation, and Consumer Decision Processes,* Washington, D.C.: National Science Foundation.

Nicosia, F. M. (October 1962), "Marketing and Alderson's Functionalism," *Journal of Business,* 35, 403–13.

———. (1966), *Consumer Decision Processes: Marketing and Advertising Implications,* Englewood Cliffs, N. J.: Prentice-Hall.

———. (1974a), *Advertising, Management, and Society: A Business Point of View,* New York: McGraw-Hill.

———. (1974b), "Summary Report. Technology and Consumers: Individual and Social Choices," Vol. 1 in F. M. Nicosia, et al., *Technological Change, Product Proliferation, and Consumer Decision Processes,* Washington, D.C.: National Science Foundation.

———, and Glock, C. Y. (1968), "Marketing and Affluence: A Research Prospectus," in R. L. King, ed., *Marketing and the New Science of Planning.* Proceedings of the Fall Conference of the American Marketing Association, August, 1968, Chicago: American Marketing Association, 510–27.

———, and Mayer, R. N. (1973), "Changing a Car's Engine Oil at Home: A Consumer Survey," A report for the U.S. Environmental Protection Agency, Consumer Research Program, University of California, Berkeley.

———, and Witkowski, T. H. (1975), "The Need for a Sociology of Consumption," in G. Zaltman and B. Sternthal, eds., *Broadening the Concept of Consumer Behavior,* Atlanta: Association for Consumer Research, 8–24.

Pirages, D. C., and Ehrlich, P. R. 1974), *Ark II: Social Response to Environmental Imperatives,* New York; Viking.

Pitts, J. R. (1963), "Continuity and Change in Bourgeois France," in S. Hoffmann, et al., eds., *In Search of France,* Cambridge: Harvard University Press, 235–304.

Smelser, N. J. (1963), *The Sociology of Economic Life,* Englewood Cliffs, N. J.: Prentice-Hall.

Warren, D. I., and Clifford, D. L., (August, 1975), "Local Neighborhood Social Structure and Response to the Energy Crisis of 1973–74," Paper presented at the 70th Annual Meeting of the American Sociological Association, San Francisco.

Wilcox, L. D.; Brooks, R. M.,; Beal, G. M.; and Klonglan, G. E. (1972), *Social Indicators and Societal Monitoring: An Annotated Bibliography,* San Francisco: Jossey-Bass.

Zaltman, G., and Bagozzi, R. P. (August, 1975), "Structural Analysis and the Sociology of Consumption," Paper presented at the 70th Annual Meeting of the American Sociological Association, San Francisco.

SECTION 2

SOCIETAL BASES OF CONSUMER BEHAVIOR

Consumers live in large social systems. Examples of large social systems include cultural groups such as Polish, Chinese, or Jewish cultural groups living in the United States; nations such as Sweden, Germany or Colombia; particular social classes; or a city or town. Cultural groups may influence food preferences; a nation, through its regulatory system and system of services, may influence the price of imported goods and the cost and availability of medical services; a social class may influence the socialization process of a child, what this child's attitudes are toward spending, and the child's aspiration for owning particular products; a city or town may influence whether shoppers will find stores open on Sundays or are able to purchase alcoholic beverages in that community.

The reader will realize that consumers live in, and thus are influenced by, many different large-scale social systems simultaneously. Each of these social systems influences consumer behavior in different ways. A town may influence whether or not adult education classes on consumerism are available, whether through its zoning laws a particular home improvement will be allowed, and whether a particular type of business will be allowed to locate in an area near where many consumers live. A town council may also influence the type of recreational and entertainment facilities available, e.g., whether a theater will be permitted to show ''X'' rated films.

The influences of culture and social class on consumers are much more familiar to the reader and are the areas where most consumer studies concerned with large-scale social systems have focused. This is reflected by articles in this section. Before introducing these articles a few observations should be made.

1. The impact of large-scale social systems on consumer behavior is vast. The impact of such systems as culture, class, nation and community may, collectively, be the single most important force influencing consumer behavior. In every respect these systems shape not only what institutions exist, but also the very way in which their members perceive the world.

2. Despite the vastness of this influence few studies exist which describe and explain this influence, with the exception of those studies pertaining to social class. One reason for this is that the influence process is difficult to study. It is difficult to separate the influence of a culture from the influence of other social systems. It is especially difficult to separate the influence of several cultures from each other when a consumer participates in or is touched by more than one of them.

3. Understanding social-system influences on consumers is especially important for marketers whose products are distributed broadly, e.g., to different countries or to different regions of a given country. Social systems represent one of the first bases for segmenting markets because they are the most general dimension along which groups of people are differentiated from each other.

4. Public policy makers and consumer educators should realize that their regulatory efforts and educational programs apply to diverse groups. This is often not considered in designing an educational program or in formulating a trade regulation. Instead, the audience or market for these programs is frequently assumed to be homogeneous.

"SELECTING THE SUPERIOR SEGMENTATION CORRELATE"

Since the late 1950s, social class has been considered an important determinant of consumer behavior. Social class is a set of attitudes, beliefs, and values that people acquire during the process of socialization and exhibit in their daily living. Social class affects such diverse things as attitudes toward minority groups, type of education and occupation selected, neighborhood lived in, risk-taking propensity, concern with national politics, willingness to accept deferred gratification, and image of the ideal mate.

In their article, Hisrich and Peters consider the question of how social class is related to consumer behavior. Several studies have tested the relationship between social class and purchase of particular products, and have had mixed results. The Hisrich and Peters study is an attempt to pull these findings together. They have used four segmentation variables (income, social class, age, and family life cycle) to help understand use or nonuse of several entertainment activities, as well as frequency of use of these activities. The indexes used for social class and for family life cycle are explained in the article.

A useful way for the reader to note the findings would be to construct a table in which the rows are the four segmentation variables and the columns are the two entertainment activity variables. The cells can then be filled in with the findings concerning the correlation between the two variables.

After constructing the table, it is necessary to go one step further. Here the reader should try to answer the following questions: Why is social class more strongly correlated with frequency of use of entertainment activities than with use vs. nonuse of the activities? Why does social class affect consumer behavior? How does income affect consumer behavior? What other factors (not included in the study) may be stronger correlates of use vs. nonuse of various entertainment activities?

"FAMILY BUYING DECISIONS: A CROSS-CULTURAL PERSPECTIVE"

There are two basic types of comparisons which are of interest in the article by Donald Hempel. There are comparisons of husbands with their wives and comparisons of spouses in the United States with spouses in England. Many research studies have been done on husband-wife comparisons (see Hempel's list of references), but very few marketing studies have been cross-cultural. This seems to have been left to the comparative cultural anthropologists. Comparisons in the Hempel study include the following:

Intra-cultural Comparisons

U.S. husbands with U.S. wives
English husbands with English wives
English husbands on one buying decision
(e.g., neighborhood) with English husbands
on another buying decision (e.g., style
of house)
English husbands on one decision process
(e.g., initiation) with English husbands on
another decision process (e.g., information
seeking)

Cross-cultural Comparisons

U.S. husbands with English husbands
U.S. wives with English wives

These comparisons were made for several stages in the decision process (initiation, information seeking, purchase decision), for five different buying decisions (neighborhood, style of house, etc.), for consensus about roles, and for overall role structure.

It is important to remember that the study measures perceptions, not actual behavior. Thus, the reports of role structures are the ways the people *believe* they made the decision, which is perhaps not how they *did* make the decision. Yet, since they are the actors in the situation, it is necessary to see the process through their *eyes* rather than through the biases of the researcher. It is consumers' own perceptions which will guide their actions; thus, this is the focus of the study.

The basic finding is that sex differences are greater than are cultural differences. That is, intra-cultural comparisons of two spouses showed greater differences than did cross-cultural comparisons. For example, English husbands and U.S. husbands were more alike than were U.S. husbands and U.S. wives.

One other interesting feature of the Hempel article is its discussion of response bias. The research notes that spouses are likely to report joint or shared decision making if they are interviewed together. However, if they are interviewed separately, they are each likely to report that one person was dominant. For example, husbands and wives interviewed together report shared initiation of the decision process. Husbands interviewed alone report that they initiated the decision process. Thus, response bias exists: the same couple, interviewed in two different ways, might give two different responses. This report of response bias by Hempel gives many insights into the problems of researching family decision processes.

"CROSS-NATIONAL COMPARISONS AND CONSUMER STEREOTYPES: A CASE STUDY OF WORKING AND NON-WORKING WIVES IN THE U.S. AND FRANCE"

The article by Susan Douglas is interesting from several perspectives: anthropologically, methodologically, and philosophically. The anthropological question which is asked concerns a comparison of comparisons. Basically, it asks: Are women from one country more alike than women in similar life situations in different countries? The individual comparisons which are compared with each other are:

1. U.S. working wives and French working wives;
2. U.S. nonworking wives and French nonworking wives;
3. U.S. working wives and U.S. nonworking wives;
4. French working wives and French nonworking wives.

The question raised is, which of these pairs are most alike in their attitudes and behaviors? The apparent answer is that wives from the same country are more alike than are wives from different countries who are in a similar life situation. In other words, the two groups in comparison 3 are more alike than are the two groups in comparison 1.

Methodologically, there are two interesting points to note about the article. Considerable care was taken to match the samples on socioeconomic status and background characteristics. This is a common sampling procedure which is done to make conclusions more valid. First, two groups which are different in some way (e.g., national origin) are matched on certain variables (e.g., age, income, number of children). Then the researcher sees if there is a difference between the groups on another variable (e.g., food shopping behavior). If there is a difference, the researcher can be more certain that it is due to a "main effect" (national origin in this case), rather than the matched variables. In other words, the observed difference in food shopping behavior is due to national origin rather than background variables.

The other methodological feature to note is the description of attitude scale construction. This description is in the body of the article under "Research Analysis" and in footnote 3. The attitude scales shown in Table 2 were constructed for this research using factor analysis. This procedure indicates the underlying variables in a set of measures (see Cipkala, in Section 14).

A philosopher of science would also point out some interesting features of the Douglas article. Once the finding of intra-cultural similarity is reported, Douglas explores several explanations which could all account for this phenomenon. An effort is made to come to a conclusion about which explanation is best. Douglas thus explains the intra-cultural similarity as resulting from a similar retail environment. Behavior is constrained by what products are available in the culture. Thus, she concludes that the behavioral similarity is not due so much to similarity of the women as it is to similarity of their retail environment. However, Douglas still leaves the possibilities open by indicating that the environment (that is, product availability) must derive in some part from a preference on the part of the women. The important point is that Douglas is thorough in exploring alternative explanations for one phenomenon.

The explanation is less complete in the discussion of the relationship between attitudes and purchase behavior. For instance, no indication is given as to *why* optimism is correlated with use of convenience products. Correlations do not imply causation, and neither do they imply that a full explanation has been accomplished.

SELECTING THE SUPERIOR SEGMENTATION CORRELATE

**ROBERT D. HISRICH
AND
MICHAEL P. PETERS**

Source: Robert D. Hisrich and Michael P. Peters, "Selecting the Superior Segmentation Correlate," *Journal of Marketing*, Vol. 38, July, 1974, pp. 60–63.

Recently a series of articles in the *Journal of Marketing* questioned the use of social class as a correlate of buyer behavior. One of these studies found that income was superior to social class as a correlate of commercial bank credit card usage (Mathews and Slocum, 1969; Slocum and Mathews, 1970). Two others in this series reported similar findings regarding the significance of these two variables in the consumer decision process. In the first of these two studies, income was found to be superior to social class in explaining purchases of a wide variety of consumer packaged goods (Myers, et al., 1971). The second study found income to be a superior correlate to social class in the purchase of home furnishings, appliances, and ready-to-wear products as well as some services (Myers and Mount, 1973).

ISSUES IN SELECTING A SEGMENTATION VARIABLE

These recent studies provide substantial insight into the problem of overemphasizing the relevance of social class as a means of segmenting a given market. However, a number of observations common to most research in this area should be noted before any major conclusion is drawn. For example, Myers, Stanton, and Haug's basis for determining the use of any packaged consumer good was whether or not a respondent had the product on hand (Myers, et al., 1971). The basis used by Myers and Mount to determine the dependent variable was whether a respondent had purchased a particular item or service within the year prior to the date of the interview (Myers and Mount, 1973). In neither study, however, was any indication made as to how often the items were purchased.

The issue of frequency of use of any product needs further exploration since it appears to be quite relevant to the identification of market segmentation criteria. There are many types of convenience goods that consumers across a broad spectrum would be very likely to buy or use *at least once.* Thus, actual use of these products would not appear to be affected by such independent variables as social class and life cycle. However, the frequency of use of these types of products may vary as a function of such factors.

It is also important to recognize that a substantial amount of previous research has found statistically significant differences between social class and a variety of purchase activities (Martineau, 1958; Warner, 1949; Coleman, 1960; Levy, 1966). It would be presumptuous to discount a priori all of the research without careful analysis of the full impact of social class across a wide variety of buyer behavior activities. The fact that social class is not a significant segmentation variable in the purchase of consumer packaged goods does not necessarily discount its importance as a possible segmentation variable in the purchase of other products or services. In other words, a practitioner should be cautious in selecting a segmentation variable for his particular product on the basis of that variable's usefulness in another market/product context. Choice of the variables to be significant in the decision-making process for the product and market under consideration should be based on a careful consideration of the *nature* of the product or service as well as the *frequency of use* of the product or service.

Family life cycle as a correlate of buyer behavior may be considered a criterion for segmentation in much the same manner as social class. Previous research indicated that family life cycle was a useful segmentation variable for such activities as housing purchases, finances, and the purchase of certain packaged consumer goods (Clark, 1955). This variable has also been significant in "explaining" certain shopping factors such as sources of shopper information, shopping frequency, browsing, and shopping location (Rich and Jain, 1968). As income appears to represent a superior proxy for social class, perhaps age may represent a superior proxy for family life cycle.

The present study examines the significance of each of four commonly used segmentation variables (income, social class, age, and family life cycle) as a correlate of two aspects of purchase behavior: (1) the choice of an entertainment activity during the past year, and (2) the frequency of use of a number of entertainment activities. In addition, the significance of these variables across several entertainment activities is examined to ascertain the best correlate for this general purchase decision.

METHODOLOGY

The data in this study were collected by interviewing 158 families, randomly selected from a large New England city, on their use of fourteen specific activities. In each household either the wife, the husband, or both were interviewed depending on their availability at the time. This did not present any problem because either could satisfactorily describe which types of entertainment activities and how often they were used by the husband or wife. Doubt or disagreement regarding these activities did not occur in any of the interviews.

Social class, one of the independent variables, was measured using Warner's Index of Status Characteristics (Warner, 1949). This method, widely used by social scientists, measures four variables: occupation, source of income, house type, and dwelling area. Ratings are multiplied by a weight and the product then summed to obtain the social class score. These scores were then used to obtain the following six social classes: upper upper, lower upper, upper middle, lower middle, upper lower, and lower lower.

To measure life cycle, the procedure used by Rich and Jain was followed, giving four categories: under 40 without children, under 40 with children, 40 and over without children in household, and 40 and over with children in the household (Rich and Jain, 1968). It was felt that using 40 as a dividing point would be appropriate since it gives some indication as to whether there are preschool children at home, which necessitates the need for babysitters and thus makes it more difficult to go out as often.

Each family included in the sample was queried to determine whether they used any of the selected entertainment activities during the past year. They were also asked to indicate on the average how often they used activities by selecting one of the six frequency-of-use descriptions ranging from about once a year to more than once a week. Income and age data were also obtained during the interview. Social class, income, life cycle, and age were then correlated first with actual use of any of the entertainment activities, and then with the frequency of use of these activities, to determine whether the significance of the variable was strongly affected by frequency of use as well as which variable provided the highest correlation.

RESULTS

The analysis of the data obtained from this research is grouped into three areas: (1) correlations of the dependent variable (selecting an entertainment activity) with the independent variables (income, social class, age, and stage in the life cycle); (2) correlations of the frequency of use of each entertainment activity with each of the independent variables; and (3) multiple correlation coefficients for each independent variable across all entertainment activities.

Use or Nonuse of an Entertainment Activity

In Table 1, it can be seen that income and life cycle are the most significant correlates in use or nonuse of an entertainment activity, while social class appears to be the weakest.

The data on use/nonuse show that high income affects a respondent's choice of movies, skiing, and golfing. Bowling as an activity is positively correlated with age and stage in the life cycle, but negatively correlated with social class. Older, lower-income respondents in the later stages of their life cycle traveled in-state for pleasure (40 miles or more). This finding, however, points out

the weakness of using simple use or nonuse of an entertainment activity as the dependent variable. For example, it would be more meaningful to determine the correlation of these variables with *how often* the respondents traveled for pleasure. Also noted in the selection correlations of Table 1 is that older, lower-class respondents in the later stages of their life cycle dined at inexpensive restaurants. Again, the importance of this finding is tenuous since it may be expected to find many people dining at one of these restaurants at least once. It is apparent that the significance of the use/nonuse findings in Table 1 was weakened by the absence of information on how often respondents participated in these activities.

Frequency of Use of Entertainment Activities

The results for frequency of use in Table 1 indicate that the significance of each independent variable as a superior segmentation correlate was affected by the frequency of use in comparison to the use or nonuse of a particular entertainment activity. In fact, social class becomes a somewhat superior correlate to income, and the number of significant correlation coefficients of age and life cycle declines.

A number of general observations from the frequency data are particularly noteworthy. Older respondents in the later stages of their life cycle bowled most often. The frequency with which respondents attended movies was positively correlated with social class and negatively correlated with age and life cycle. For skiing, the correlation coefficients were negative, indicating that respondents belonging to lower social classes skied most often. It may be recalled that the selection of skiing as an entertainment activity was significantly correlated with income; however, this relationship disappeared when skiing frequency was considered as the dependent variable.

Golf, on the other hand, did appear to have some hierarchical appeal, since the higher-class respondents reported playing golf most often.

Table 1 Correlation coefficients for the use/nonuse and frequency of use of an entertainment activity

Entertainment Activity	Use/Nonuse				Frequency of Use			
	Income	Social Class	Age	Life Cycle	Income	Social Class	Age	Life Cycle
Bowl	−.08	−.15[b]	.28[a]	.38[a]	.12	−.04	.35[b]	.25[b]
Movies	.25[b]	.01	.38[a]	.46[a]	−.14	.35[a]	−.44[a]	−.49[a]
Ski	.18[b]	−.02	.27[a]	.36[a]	−.05	−.25[b]	−.08	−.07
Golf	.43[a]	.06	−.08	.04	.06	.32[b]	.15	.15
In-state travel	−.20[a]	−.02	.26[a]	.25[a]	.09	.06	.14	.05
Out-of-state travel	−.24[a]	.10	−.07	.06	.13	−.05	−.03	−.07
Foreign travel	.14	.09	−.01	.01	—[c]	—[c]	—[c]	—[c]
Dine at expensive restaurant	.27[a]	.02	.08	.17[b]	.12	.23[a]	.13	.17[b]
Dine at moderately priced restaurant	−.22[a]	−.03	.17[b]	.20[a]	.19[b]	−.12	.17[b]	.08
Dine at inexpensive restaurant	−.14	−.16[b]	.25[b]	.31[a]	.10	−.25[a]	−.07	−.07
Nightclubs	.12	.08	−.32[a]	.41[a]	.28[a]	.11	−.42[a]	−.34[a]
Cocktail parties	−.23[a]	.03	.03	.16[b]	.15	−.02	.05	.01
Professional athletic events	−.32[a]	.01	.21	.33[a]	−.13	.07	−.09	−.12
College/high school athletic events	−.25[a]	−.06	.11	.17[b]	.35[a]	.23[b]	−.12	−.22[b]

[a]Significant at .01 level or better.
[b]Significant at .05 level or better.
[c]Foreign travel was excluded from this part of the analysis because it rarely occurs more than once a year.

Similarly, upper-class respondents in the later stages of the life cycle also dined at expensive restaurants most often. Yet the frequency of dining at inexpensive restaurants was negatively correlated with social class. It can also be seen that higher-income respondents who were younger in age and in the earlier stages of their life cycle attended nightclubs most often.

The frequency of use of any product or service appears to add an important dimension to the arguments being made with regard to selecting the superior segmentation variable. Before any future attempts are made to discount the relative significance of any variable such as social class, it will be necessary to secure additional evidence regarding the effect of any of these variables on the frequency of use of a wide variety of products. This evidence will be particularly important to marketers in determining and defining their market segments. Indeed, marketing managers may be more interested in those variables that are significantly related to the frequency of use of their products, since it is conceivable that a consumer could use or try a product at least once during the course of a year.

Multiple Correlation Coefficients

One question remains: What is the overall superior correlate in the choice of an entertainment activity? To answer this question, the multiple correlation coefficient (R) was calculated for each of the four variables across all entertainment activities for both the use/nonuse situation and the frequency of use.

The multiple correlation coefficients appeared to substantiate the results found in Table 1. Income and stage in the life cycle were more highly related to *use* of all the entertainment activities than age and social class. Social class had the weakest association, with an R value of .28. However, when the multiple correlation coefficients were calculated for the *frequency of use* of all entertainment activities, all four variables showed strong associations. Social class was highly related, with an R value of .75, which was a significant change from its R value for the mere use situation. The R value for stage in the life cycle changed only slightly in the frequency-of-use situation, from .63 to .71.

It appears from the multiple correlation coefficients that any of these variables would provide a meaningful basis for market segmentation with respect to frequency of use. In this regard, it is important to note the changes in the R values from the use to the frequency-of-use situation. These changes indicate the importance of frequency of use as a basis for determining the relative significance of any segmentation variable.

CONCLUSIONS

This study provides important evidence on the relative significance of certain segmentation variables used as correlates of buyer behavior. The doubt expressed in previous research regarding weak associations of social class to product or service usage may be unwarranted, since these studies based their findings on use or nonuse of a product or service rather than on *how often* that product or service was used.

Two conclusions from this study appear to be of particular importance. First, a variable significant in one market/product context may not be signifi-cant in another. Possible segmentation variables need to be tested in each individual market/product context to ascertain the superior correlate or correlates. Second, the practitioner, at least in the instance of many consumer goods and services, should be more concerned with the frequency of use of his product or service in determining the segmentation variable(s).

REFERENCES

Clark, Lincoln, ed. (1955), *The Life Cycle and Consumer Behavior,* Vol. 2, New York: New York University Press.

Coleman, Richard P. (1960), "The Significance of Social Stratification in Selling," in Martin L. Bell, ed., *Marketing: A Maturing Discipline,* Chicago: American Marketing Association.

Levy, Sidney J. (1966), "Social Class and Consumer Behavior," in *On Knowing the Consumer,* Joseph W. Newman, ed., New York: John Wiley & Sons, 146–60.

Martineau, Pierre (1958), "Social Classes and Spending Behavior," *Journal of Marketing,* 23, October, 121–30.

Mathews, H. Lee, and Slocum, John W., Jr. (1969), "Social Class and Commercial Bank Credit Card Usage," *Journal of Marketing,* 33, January, 71–79.

Myers, James H.; Stanton, Roger R.; and Haug, Arne F. (1971), "Correlates of Buyer Behavior: Social Class vs. Income," *Journal of Marketing,* 35, October, 8–15.

Myers, James H., and Mount, John F. (1973), "More on Social Class vs. Income as Correlates of Buying Behavior," *Journal of Marketing,* 37, April, 71–73.

Rich, Stuart U., and Jain, Subhash C. (1968), "Social Class and Life Cycle as Predictors of Shopping Behavior," *Journal of Marketing Research,* 5, February, 41–49.

Slocum, John W., Jr., and Mathews, H. Lee (1970), "Social Class and Income as Indicators of Consumer Credit Behavior," *Journal of Marketing,* 34, April, 69–74.

Warner, W. Lloyd (1949), *Social Class in America,* New York: Harper & Row.

FAMILY BUYING DECISIONS: A CROSS-CULTURAL PERSPECTIVE

DONALD J. HEMPEL

Source: Donald J. Hempel, "Family Buying Decisions: A Cross-Cultural Perspective," *Journal of Marketing Research,* Vol. 11, August, 1974, pp. 295–302.

INTRODUCTION

Despite widespread recognition of the household as the basic decision-making unit in consumer markets, family decision processes have received relatively little attention in marketing research (Frank, et al., 1972; Robertson, 1971). The continuing interests of other behavioral disciplines in family decision making have been more evident, but the output has been less comparable in the types of decisions considered (Blood, 1958; Blood and Wolfe, 1960; Bott, 1957; Foote, 1961; Heer, 1963; Heer, 1962; Herbst, 1954; Kenkel, 1964; Kenkel and Hoffman, 1956; Komarovsky, 1961; Lu, 1959; Olson and Rabunsky, 1972; Safilios-Rothschild, 1970; Safilios-Rothschild, 1969; Turk and Bell, 1972).

CONCEPTUAL APPROACH AND METHODOLOGY

Husband-wife interaction in family decisions was measured here with a series of questions about the relative importance of each spouse in specific decisions at different stages in the house-buying process. Two different measures of husband-wife roles were contained in separate self-administered questionnaires. The husband was asked to identify who was "mainly responsible" for selected decisions, while the wife was asked to indicate the "relative influence" of each spouse in these buying decisions.

The responses of each spouse were scored by assigning a value of 1 when the wife's role was perceived as dominant, 2 for joint decisions, and 3 when the husband's role was dominant. An overall index of perceived dominance was computed for each spouse by adding the scores for five major purchase decisions concerning choice of neighborhood, style of house, when to buy, acceptable price, and mortgage source. The family role structure was classified into one of four categories on the basis of the following decision patterns:

49

Family role structure	Relevant decision pattern	Range of dominance index
Husband dominant	Husband dominates or shares all five decisions	12 to 15
Wife dominant	Wife dominates or shares all decisions	5 to 9
Syncratic	At least three of the five decisions are joint and dominance is balanced	10 to 11
Autonomic	Not more than two of the five decisions are joint but dominance is balanced	10 to 11

Data

The data were obtained from two surveys of recent home buyers conducted during the summers of 1968 and 1971. The first sample involved 206 families from Hartford, Connecticut and 8 adjacent towns. The 1971 study included 317 households from 7 towns in the Preston-Lancaster area of Northwest England. Both investigations incorporated probability samples of households who purchased either a new or previously occupied house and recorded their ownership during the first six months of the study year.

Extensive personal interviews were conducted with the husband and/or wife in each of the 523 sample households. The interviews were followed by a request that two self-administered questionnaires be completed separately by each spouse[1]

---

[1]There is considerable evidence that most husbands and wives completed their mail questionnaires independently. This behavior was encouraged by the interviewer and reinforced by a cover letter. The mail questionnaire data indicate significant husband-wife differences on items which are likely to be reconciled through discussion (e.g., reasons for buying). The respondents for this study are mainly from socioeconomic groups in which independence of husband-wife responses is likely to be relatively high.

and returned by mail.[2] Identical data collection instruments were used in both studies, except for some minor adaptations to English word usage in the 1971 study. Details concerning the research design and the three questionnaires used in Connecticut have been published elsewhere (Herbst, 1970).

FINDINGS

The Initiator Role

Who initiates the house-buying decision process? Previous studies generally indicate that joint decision making is lower at this stage of the decision process, with the husband usually playing the dominant role (Hansen, 1972; Sheth, 1971). This pattern was confirmed in Connecticut where husband-initiated moves exceeded shared decisions by a small margin. In Northwest England, however, more than one-half of the respondents identified this as a joint decision. The cultural differences are statistically significant ($\chi^2 = 42.4, p < .001$):

Who was primarily responsible for the decision to move?	Connecticut (N = 200)	Northwest England (N = 285)
Husband	37%	25%
Wife	27	23
Both (joint)	32	52
Other (children/ relatives)	5	1

Source: Personal interviews

The possibility of response bias was checked by examining the relationship between the sex of the respondent(s) and the designated initiator. There was a tendency among those Connecticut re-

---

[2]Because of nonreturns, the bases for the analysis of the mail questionnaire data were reduced to 159 (77%) and 211 (67%) for Connecticut and Northwest England respectively. Incomplete responses account for further reductions in the effective sample size for some measures.

spondents who were interviewed alone to identify their spouse as the primary initiator, but the differences were not significant ($\chi^2 = 5.0$, $p < .25$). In contrast, those English respondents who were interviewed in their spouse's absence were significantly more likely to designate themselves as responsible for the decision to move ($\chi^2 = 10.5$, $p < .05$). The proportion of shared initiator roles in both countries was highest where spouses were interviewed jointly, and lowest where the husband was interviewed alone. This apparent respondent bias may account for the greater emphasis on shared decisions in England, since 61% of the English interviews included both spouses, whereas both husband and wife were present in only 28% of the Connecticut interviews. Fortunately, separate information from husband and wife mail questionnaires was available to supplement the interview data.

Information-Seeking Roles

Who performs the task of obtaining and evaluating information? Several studies have indicated that this task is usually shared, with some concentration on areas of relative expertise (Hansen, 1972; Sheth, 1971). The data clearly support the hypothesis of joint information-gathering roles, with remarkable consistency across cultural settings.

How was the task of obtaining and evaluating information distributed?	Connecticut (N = 188)	Northwest England (N = 277)
Mainly husband	14%	18%
Mainly wife	30	28
Shared (joint)	56	54

Source: Personal interviews

There is some indication of a response bias which favors the respondent. Both husbands and wives were more likely to name themselves as mainly responsible for the information gathering

when they were interviewed alone. These differences were statistically significant for Connecticut ($\chi^2 = 9.8$, $p < .05$), but not for England ($\chi^2 = 4.4$, $p < .40$). The conditional probability that the information-seeking role would be reported as shared by Connecticut respondents was 0.41 when husbands were interviewed alone, 0.54 when wives were interviewed alone, and 0.67 when both were respondents. These differences may reflect market segments where the availability of husband/wife as respondents is related to individual needs for ego enhancement, and where these needs are manifested in self-designating responses. For example, the husband's needs for self-assertion may be greater among households in which he is more likely to be home alone.

Purchase Decision Roles

The role performance perceived by husbands and wives in each of five major purchase decisions is summarized in Table 1. Each matrix shows the percentage distribution of husband and wife responses across the nine possible combinations which can be formed from the decision patterns of each household. The addition of row entries in the marginal brackets indicates the relative frequency of the roles perceived by husbands, while column marginals reveal the distribution of wives' responses. Results of chi-square tests of the sexual differences in each country and of the cultural differences for each sex are also presented.

Joint decision making predominates in both cultures, but the extent of mutual involvement varies by decision area. Almost three of every four households reported that the neighborhood and style decisions were shared, whereas less than one-half of the families perceived the choice of mortgage source to be a shared decision. Both sexes perceived more sharing of decision roles in England than in Connecticut. In general, the evidence suggests that some role specialization does exist in both countries, with wives concentrating on the social-expressive decisions and husbands

Table 1 Cross-cultural comparisons of role differentiation perceived by husbands and wives in house-buying decisions

Buying decision		Connecticut (N = 145)				N.W. England (N = 183)				Husband vs. Wife	Connecticut vs. England
		WW	WJ	WH		WW	WJ	WH			
Neighborhood	HW	4	11	1	(16)	HW	7	7	1	(15)	C: 6.66	H: 3.56
	HJ	6	66	6	(78)	HJ	7	65	2	(74)	E: 42.20[a]	W: 1.19
	HH	1	4	1	(6)	HH	2	7	2	(11)		
		(11)	(81)	(8)			(16)	(79)	(5)			
Style of house	HW	7	16	1	(24)	HW	3	14	0	(17)	C: 18.81[a]	H: 5.11
	HJ	7	60	2	(69)	HJ	7	64	3	(74)	E: 12.24[c]	W: 2.16
	HH	1	4	2	(7)	HH	2	6	1	(9)		
		(15)	(80)	(5)			(12)	(84)	(4)			
When to purchase	HW	4	3	1	(8)	HW	1	5	1	(7)	C: 38.15[a]	H: 2.41
	HJ	6	45	10	(61)	HJ	1	57	10	(68)	E: 10.11[c]	W: 21.80[a]
	HH	2	13	16	(31)	HH	2	17	6	(25)		
		(12)	(61)	(27)			(4)	(79)	(17)			
Acceptable price	HW	0	1	1	(2)	HW	2	2	1	(5)	C: 7.65	H: 1.59
	HJ	4	36	17	(57)	HJ	2	51	8	(61)	E: 40.31[a]	W: 10.70[b]
	HH	1	20	20	(41)	HH	2	18	14	(34)		
		(5)	(57)	(38)			(6)	(71)	(23)			
Where to apply for mortgage	HW	1	1	0	(2)	HW	1	6	0	(7)	C: 42.94[a]	H: 4.89
	HJ	4	24	6	(34)	HJ	4	35	8	(44)	E: 38.16[a]	W: 7.16[c]
	HH	1	21	42	(64)	HH	1	17	31	(49)		
		(6)	(46)	(48)			(3)	(58)	(39)			

a = The frequency differences in the contingency tables on which these decision matrices are based were statistically significant at the .001 level;
b = .01 level;
c = .05 level.
HW = husband perceived wife as dominant; HJ = husband perceived joint decision; HH = husband perceived self as dominant; WW = wife perceived self as dominant; WJ = wife perceived joint decision; WH = wife perceived husband as dominant.
Data Source: Mail questionnaires.

being involved in the financial-instrumental decisions.

Sexual differences in role perceptions were generally greater than the international differences. Wives were more likely than husbands to perceive a joint role in all five purchase decisions, but the differences were greatest for decisions regarding mortgage source and style of house. There was a tendency for both spouses to perceive themselves as more influential than reported by their mates, especially for the mortgage decision.

There was much greater cultural similarity in the role performance reported by husbands than in those reported by wives. A chi-square test indicated no significant cultural differences for husbands. In contrast, the decisions about when to buy, price, and mortgage were much more likely to be reported as joint decisions by English wives.

Role Consensus

The extent of husband-wife agreement in role perceptions is shown by the percentages along the main diagonals of the decision matrices in Table 1. These data, reflecting intrafamily comparisons, indicate a high level of role consensus for all five decisions in both cultures. The proportion of couples who agree on individual decisions is remarkably similar across cultures and decision areas:

	Percentage of husband-wife agreement	
Decision	*Connecticut (N = 145)*	*Northwest England (N = 183)*
Neighborhood	71%	74%
Style of house	69	68
When to buy	65	64
Acceptable price	56	67
Mortgage source	67	67

Source: Mail questionnaires

Most of the sexual differences in role perceptions involve discrepancies of only one scale point in the decision scores, and they are symmetrically distributed in terms of which spouse was favored.

A high level of consensus on specific decisions does not necessarily indicate high perceptual congruency in the family decision process as a whole. The extent of agreement across the set of five decisions was measured by aggregating the number of decisions on which there was intrafamily consensus. Complete husband-wife agreement on role performance was limited to approximately one-sixth of the Connecticut families and one-fourth of the English households. These response distributions reflect a pattern of compensating role allocations in which attribution of importance to oneself on some decisions is offset by designation of one's spouse as more important on other decisions. The cultural differences are not statistically significant ($\chi^2 = 5.55, p < .25$).

Extent of husband-wife agreement (Number of decisions)	*Percent of households*	
	Connecticut (N = 145)	*Northwest England (N = 183)*
All five decisions	17%	27%
Four	32	27
Three	26	26
Two	17	13
One	4	3
None	4	4

Source: Mail questionnaires

Role Structure

Despite some serious questions about the validity and reliability of a general dominance measure (Davis, 1971; Olson and Rabunsky, 1972), it is desirable to characterize family buying decisions in terms of an overall decision pattern. If a decision typology can be established to represent greater homogeneity among households in family information processing and influence, then it may be useful as a basis for market segmentation. Table 2

Table 2   Cross-cultural comparison of family role structure perceived by husbands and wives

Role structure category	Percent distribution by market area and respondent			
	Connecticut		Northwest England	
	Husband's perceptions	Wife's perceptions	Husband's perceptions	Wife's perceptions
Husband domi-nant	33%	31%	32%	20%
Wife dominant	12	15	7	11
Syncratic	38	42	50	62
Autonomic	17	11	11	7
	(N = 157)	(N = 150)	(N = 185)	(N = 182)

Chi Square Test of Cultural Differences: Husbands: $\chi^2 = 7.21$, $p < .10$
                                                                  Wives: $\chi^2 = 13.00$, $p < .01$
Data Source: Mail questionnaires

shows the frequency distributions which result from the classification of households into role structure categories.

These role patterns indicate that house buying can best be characterized as a cooperative venture in which joint decision making predominates, notwithstanding a number of perceptual differences. Wives were more likely than husbands to perceive syncratic role structures—especially in England. English respondents of both sexes were more likely to report syncratic decision patterns. This was partially offset by more frequent cases of shared responsibility through autonomous decision making in Connecticut. The infrequency of an entirely joint decision-making pattern is indicated by the fact that the total set of five decisions were *mutually* perceived as joint decisions in less than one tenth (7%) of the Connecticut families, and in only 19% of the English households.

According to husbands' reports, his role was dominant in one of *every* three families. English wives were significantly less likely (20%) to perceive a decision pattern dominated by the husband's influence. Husbands in both countries were more likely to indicate a pattern of com-

plementary role specialization (autonomic) than a wife-dominated role structure; the relative frequency of these role classifications was reversed for wives. Generally, the cultural differences in the role structure distributions were statistically significant for wives but not for husbands.

The extent of husband-wife agreement in the decision patterns was almost identical (62%) in both cultures. There was *complete* agreement in the wife-dominated cases. Couples characterized by a syncratic role structure were in agreement in 72% of the Connecticut households and in 80% of the English families. Consensus in the husband-dominated cases was found in 54% of the Connecticut families and 44% of the English households. The lowest levels of agreement occurred in the households classified as autonomic.

Role Interdependency

Does knowledge about role performance at one stage of the buying process facilitate prediction of roles at other stages? The data presented in Table 3 indicate that the information-gathering responsibility was significantly greater for the spouse who initiated the decision to move, especially when this

Table 3 Relationship between the initiator and information-seeking roles in house-buying decisions

Responsibility for decision to move	Percentage distribution of responsibility for obtaining and evaluating information				
	Husband	Wife	Joint	Total	n
Connecticut					
Husband	21%	16%	63%	100%	67
Wife	6	47	47	100	49
Joint	10	29	61	100	70
$(\chi^2 = 16.0, p < .01)$					
Northwest England					
Husband	35%	20%	45%	100%	66
Wife	14	46	40	100	63
Joint	13	23	64	100	134
$(\chi^2 = 28.5, p < .001)$					

Data Source: Personal interviews

was the wife. The continuity of role allocations across these two stages was greatest for those households who shared responsibility for the initial decision of the buying process.

The correlation among specific decision scores indicates the interdependency of role allocations perceived by each spouse. In general, the correlation among individual decision scores for each spouse was surprisingly low (almost two-thirds of the correlation matrix entries were less than .15). The apparent independence of the initiator and information-seeking roles from the purchase decision roles was particularly notable.

Table 4 shows the extent to which the role performance perceived for any single decision is related to the spouse's perceptions of roles over the set of five purchase decisions. It is apparent from these rank-order correlations that this specific-general association is considerably greater than the relationship between individual decisions. Part of this correlation is an artifact resulting from the fact that the individual decision scores are incorporated in the overall measures, but the relative

magnitude of the coefficients are still useful as measures of role interrelationships.

The value of individual decisions as predictors of family role structure is generally greater for the instrumental decisions about when to purchase, price, and mortgage. The best single predictor for Connecticut families was the decision when to purchase. In England, the associations between the role structure and the price and mortgage decisions were more significant. The husband's dominance of the purchase decisions was positively correlated with the initiator role in Connecticut, and with the information-seeking role in England.

Conflicts in Family Decisions

Unresolved differences of opinion between husband and wife can delay the purchase and limit sales opportunity. If the areas of intrafamily conflict can be identified, then communications can be directed toward helping the couple to reach agreement or compromise. Thus, knowledge which enables one to anticipate conflict areas can

Table 4   Correlations (Spearman rank-order) between husband-wife influence in specific decisions and overall role structure

Decisions by respondent and country	Role structure classification				Dominance index
	Husband dominant	Wife dominant	Syncratic	Autonomic	
Neighborhood					
Conn-Husbands	.27	.03	−.03	.13	.38
Wives	.32	−.28	.12	.15	.38
NWE-Husband	.40	−.11	−.05	.22	.51
Wives	.28	−.35	.07	−.27	.35
Style					
Conn-Husbands	.39	−.07	.18	.10	.40
Wives	.24	−.35	.21	−.10	.33
NWE-Husbands	.39	−.01	−.10	.22	.53
Wives	.11	−.28	.24	−.25	.15
When to purchase					
Conn-Husbands	.59	−.28	−.27	.54	.69
Wives	.61	−.47	−.23	.07	.70
NWE-Husbands	.51	−.07	−.39	.49	.51
Wives	.48	−.23	−.32	.11	.54
Acceptable price					
Conn-Husbands	.39	−.09	−.47	.50	.50
Wives	.46	−.40	−.38	.07	.60
NWE-Husbands	.55	−.23	−.43	.58	.63
Wives	.58	−.23	−.49	.18	.62
Mortgage source					
Conn-Husbands	.42	−.23	−.39	.52	.60
Wives	.51	−.46	−.28	.19	.70
NWE-Husbands	.59	−.15	−.55	.65	.71
Wives	.51	−.30	−.35	.12	.70
Initiator role					
Conn-Husbands	.19	−.15	−.03	.17	.23
Wives	.13	−.17	.11	−.06	.16
NWE-Husbands	.14	−.01	−.09	.12	.12
Wives	.02	−.04	−.05	−.07	.10
Information-seeking role					
Conn-Husbands	.03	−.15	.03	.05	.05
Wives	.11	−.16	.04	.06	.12
NWE-Husbands	.24	−.05	−.13	.20	.26
Wives	.12	−.05	−.09	−.10	.20

Data Source: Mail questionnaires and personal interviews.

help to increase buyer satisfaction as well as market efficiency.

Respondents were asked what type of husband-wife conflicts arose in the home-buying process, and how these differences were resolved. Only 29% of the Connecticut households and 32% of the English families reported any major disagreements. These areas of conflict were distributed as follows:

	Percent of respondents who reported conflicts	
Source of disagreement	Connecticut (N = 55)	Northwest England (N = 102)
Location	24%	20%
Special house features (e.g., fireplace, garage)	24	17
Price	15	12
Style	11	13
Floor plan	7	18
Age of house	4	5
When to purchase	2	2
Other	14	14

Source: Personal interviews

Disagreements were most likely to be resolved in the wife's favor in both Connecticut (42% vs. 39% in favor of husband) and in England (36% vs. 28% in favor of husband). English respondents were more likely to report a compromise solution to the disagreement (36% vs. 19% for Connecticut). The role structure perceived by either spouse was not significantly related to the pattern of conflict resolution.

DISCUSSION

This investigation reveals a surprisingly high degree of cross-cultural similarity in household decision-making processes. In most instances, the differences between the roles perceived by husbands and wives within the same cultural setting were greater than the differences between cultures for either sex. The evidence clearly supports the contention that accurate and reliable insights into family buying decisions cannot be obtained from responses of the husband or wife alone. If it is necessary to restrict inquiry to a single respondent, then variations in the extent of agreement across different market segments should be considered.

It may be feasible for those who are interested only in specific decisions or stages of the decision process to use information about role performance as a basis for market segmentation. In contrast to the purchase of many other products, there is a tendency for the husband to be more involved than the wife as the initiator of the home-buying process. The relative involvement of each spouse is reversed for the search task. Role performance in the purchase decisions appears to depend upon the type and nature of decisions—husbands were more involved in decisions concerning mortgage, price, and when to buy, while wives were more involved in decisions regarding neighborhood and house style. These role distributions were very similar in both cultures, although the husband's involvement generally was slightly lower in Northwest England.

There is need for more information about the interdependency among family roles at different stages of the buying decision process. Available evidence indicates that the goals, preferences, and perceptions of individuals often are translated into buying behavior through a family role structure that varies by type of product and household characteristics. Studies of house-buying decisions can contribute some unique insights into these role structures, because they represent a product class in which there is a very high interest and involvement of family members. The extent of joint decision making, the degree of consensus in role perceptions, and the conflict resolution patterns reflected in this decision process may provide useful base points for developing buyer behavior.

REFERENCES

Alderson, Wroe (1957), *Marketing Behavior and Executive Action,* Homewood, Ill.: Richard D. Irwin.

Blood, Robert O. (February 1958), "New Approach in Family Research: Observational Methods," *Marriage & Family Living,* 20, 47–52.

———, and Wolfe, Donald M. (1960), *Husbands and Wives: The Dynamics of Married Living,* Chicago: The Free Press.

Bott, E. (1957), *Family and Social Network,* London: Tavistock Publications.

Brown, G. H. (1961), "The Automobile Buying Decision Within the Family," in N. N. Foote, ed., *Household Decision-Making,* New York: New York University Press, 193–99.

Davis, H. L. (August 1971), "Measurement of Husband-Wife Influence in Consumer Purchase Decisions," *Journal of Marketing Research,* 8, 305–12.

———, (May 1970), "Dimensions of Marital Roles in Consumer Decision Making," *Journal of Marketing Research,* 7, 168–77.

Ferber, Robert (January 1955), "On the Reliability of Purchase Influence Studies," *Journal of Marketing,* 19, 225–32.

Foote, Nelson N. (1961), *Household Decision-Making,* New York: New York University Press.

Frank, Ronald E.; Massy, William F.; and Wind, Yoram (1972), *Market Segmentation,* Englewood Cliffs, N.J.: Prentice-Hall.

Fry, Joseph N., and Siller, Frederick H. (August, 1970), "A Comparison of Housewife Decision Making in Two Social Classes," *Journal of Marketing Research,* 7, 333–37.

Granbois, Donald H. (1972), "Decision Processes in Major Durable Goods," in G. Fisk, ed., *New Essays in Marketing Theory,* Boston: Allyn and Bacon.

——— (1971), "A Multi-Level Approach to Family Role Structure Research," *Proceedings,* Second Annual Conference, Association for Consumer Research, 99–107.

———, and Willett, Ronald P. (February, 1970), "Equivalence of Family Role Measures Based on Husband and Wife Data," *Journal of Marriage and the Family,* 32, 68–72.

——— (1963), "The Role of Communication in the Family Decision-Making Process," in S. A. Greyser,

ed., *Toward Scientific Marketing,* Chicago: American Marketing Association, 44–57.

Hansen, Flemming (1972). *Consumer Choice Behavior: A Cognitive Theory,* New York: The Free Press.

Heer, David M. (May 1963), "The Measurement and Bases of Family Power: An Overview," *Marriage and Family Living,* 23, 133–39.

——— (February, 1962), "Husband and Wife Perceptions of Family Power Structure," *Marriage and Family Living,* 24, 65–67.

Hempel, Donald J. "A Cross-Cultural Analysis of Husband-Wife Roles in House Purchase Decisions," *Proceedings,* Third Annual Conference, Association for Consumer Research, 816–29.

Herbst, P. G. (1954), "Conceptual Framework for Studying the Family," in O. A. Oeser and S. B. Hammond, eds., *Social Structure and Personality in a City,* New York: Macmillan.

——— (1970), *A Comparative Study of the Home Buying Process in Two Connecticut Housing Markets,* Storrs, Conn.: Center for Real Estate and Urban Economic Studies, The University of Connecticut.

Jaffee, Laurence J., and Senft, Henry (1966), "The Roles of Husbands and Wives in Purchasing Decisions," in Lee Adler and Irving Crespi, eds., *Attitude Research at Sea,* Chicago: American Marketing Association, 1966.

Kelly, R. F., and Egan, M. B. (1969), "Husband and Wife Interaction in a Consumer Decision Process," in P. R. McDonald, ed., *Marketing Involvement in Society and the Economy,* Chicago: American Marketing Association, 250–58.

Kenkel, William F. (1964), "Husband-Wife Interaction in Decision Making and Decision Choices," in Martin M. Grossak, ed., *Understanding Consumer Behavior,* Boston: Christopher Publishing, 275–85.

———, and Hoffman, D. K. (November, 1956), "Real and Conceived Roles in Family Decision Making," *Marriage and Family Living,* 18, 211–16.

Komarovsky, M. (1961), "Class Differences in Family Decision Making on Expenditures," in N. N. Foote, ed., *Household Decision-Making,* New York: New York University Press, 255–65.

——— (September 19, 1958), "Family Buying Decisions: Who Makes Them, Who Influences Them?'' *Printer's Ink,* 22–28.

Lu, Yi-Chuang (July, 1952), ''Predicting Roles in Marriage,'' *American Journal of Sociology,* 58, 51–52.

Olson, David H., and Rabunsky, Carolyn (May 1972), ''Validity of Four Measures of Family Power,'' *Journal of Marriage and the Family,* 34, 225–34.

Nuckols, Robert C., and Mayer, C. S. (February, 1970), ''Can Independent Responses be Obtained from Various Members in a Mail Panel Household?'' *Journal of Marketing Research,* 7, 90–94.

Robertson, Thomas S. (1971), *Innovative Behavior and Communication,* New York: Holt, Rinehart and Winston.

Safilios-Rothschild, C. (November, 1970), ''A Study of Family Power Structure: A Review of 1960–1969,'' *Journal of Marriage and Family,* 32, 539–52.

———— (May 1969), ''Family Sociology or Wives' Family Sociology? A Cross-Cultural Examination of Decision-Making,'' *Journal of Marriage and the Family,* 31, 290–301.

Sharp, Harry, and Mott, Paul (October, 1956), ''Consumer Decisions in the Metropolitan Family,'' *Journal of Marketing,* 21, 149–56.

Sheth, Jagdish N. (1971), ''A Theory of Family Buying Decisions,'' in Paul Pellemans, ed., *Insights in Consumer and Market Behavior,* Namur, Belgium: Namur University, 31–49.

Turk, James L., and Bell, Norman W. (May 1972), ''Measuring Power in Families,'' *Journal of Marriage and the Family,* 34, 215–22.

Wolgast, Elizabeth H. (October, 1958), ''Do Husbands or Wives Make the Purchasing Decisions?'' *Journal of Marketing,* 23, 151–58.

Woodside, Arch G. (1972), ''Dominance and Conflict in Family Purchasing Decisions,'' *Proceedings,* Third Annual Conference, Association for Consumer Research, 650–59.

Zober, Martin (1966), ''Determinants of Husband-Wife Buying Roles,'' in S. Britt, ed., *Consumer Behavior and the Behavioral Sciences,* New York: Wiley, 244–45.

CROSS-NATIONAL COMPARISONS AND CONSUMER STEREOTYPES: A CASE STUDY OF WORKING AND NON-WORKING WIVES IN THE U.S. AND FRANCE

SUSAN P. DOUGLAS

Source: Susan P. Douglas, "Cross-National Comparisons and Consumer Stereotypes: A Case Study of Working and Non-Working Wives in the U.S. and France," *Journal of Consumer Research,* Vol. 3, June, 1976, pp. 12–20.

INTRODUCTION

Cross-national comparisons of purchase and consumption behavior often focus on examining overall differences and similarities between countries. In many cases these result in the perpetuation of stereotypes such as those proposed by Dichter (1962): "one out of every three Frenchmen brushes his teeth, four out of five Germans change their shirts but once a week."

These generalizations not only tend to emphasize differences rather than similarities *between* countries but also to minimize the importance of differences in behavior patterns *within* a country.

Such a limited approach appears to be little justified from either a theoretical or management standpoint. In the first place, the findings of various sociological and marketing studies (Frank, Massy and Wind, 1972; Engel, Kollat and Blackwell, 1968) reveal the existence of considerable heterogeneity in response patterns within countries; these variations are evident in social class, life-style and geographic location, as well as in personality, interests and purchase behavior. Thus membership in a common culture or society does not necessarily imply similar response patterns, and consequently "national" consumer stereotypes are unlikely to be particularly meaningful or useful.

In addition, management is typically more interested in finding similarities with other countries rather than differences. Often a primary objective in investigating markets overseas is to assess whether production skills or marketing expertise developed in one country can be exploited on a wider scale, by marketing similar products or to similar market segments in other countries (Wind, 1967).

According to the underlying rationale in segmentation, members of a segment should have response patterns which are closer to each other than to those of members of other segments. Transposing this to the international context, the feasibility of utilizing cross-national bases of segmentation depends on whether the behavior patterns of a customer subgroup in one country are more similar to those of the same group in another country than to other customers in their own country. This requires examination of the relative importance of *between* as opposed to *within* country differences in consumer behavior. The pilot study described in this paper was intended to provide an illustrative example examining this issue based on a comparison of purchase behavior for grocery products and women's clothing of working and non-working wives in the U.S. and France.

The primary objective of this study was thus to assess whether working wives facing similar problems in the two countries, such as constraints on the time available for shopping, would tend to adopt similar purchasing strategies, different from those of their non-working counterparts, or whether differences in behavior patterns between the two countries would tend to be greater.

In addition two other questions were considered. First, whether behavior patterns would be similar across product classes. For example, would working and non-working wives tend to have different behavior patterns for grocery products, but similar patterns for purchasing clothing, or *vice versa*? Second, whether differences and similarities in attitudes would be more significant than in relation to behavioral patterns. Would, for example, working wives in the two countries have similar and perhaps more liberated attitudes toward female roles than non-working wives, or would differences in role perceptions between the two national samples tend to be greater?

THE DATA BASE AND RESEARCH METHODOLOGY

The Data Base

The data base for the study consisted of a questionnaire administered by personal interview to 98

wives in France and in the U.S.A.[1] All the respondents had been married for at least two years and were between the ages of 25 and 50. Half had held full-time jobs for at least eighteen months, while the other half were not gainfully employed outside the home. The jobs held by the working wives covered a wide range of occupations including lawyers, doctors and researchers as well as secretaries, waitresses and sales clerks. In each country the sample was selected by a quota procedure, and both working and non-working groups were stratified by age, income and number of children. As far as possible the working wives were drawn from similar occupational categories in each country and the non-working wives from families of similar socioeconomic status based on husband's occupation and family income. The objective was thus to obtain four groups which were "matched" in terms of background characteristics rather than groups representative of the working and non-working wife populations in each country. Although this structure and the small sample size restricts the extent to which the results can be generalized on a wider basis, it helps to isolate the effect of the wife's employment and to control for the impact of differences in other background characteristics between the working and non-working wife groups or between countries, on behavior and attitudes, which might otherwise obscure the analysis.

The questionnaire covered four key areas: grocery purchase behavior, women's clothing purchases, attitudes to various female roles, and family background characteristics. In relation to grocery purchases respondents were asked to indicate the frequency of purchasing 10 convenience or time-saving products and services;[2] and

---

[1] Initially 106 wives were interviewed in the U.S., and 102 in France. However the MANOVA analysis required equal cell sizes, and hence the sample size was reduced to 49 working and 49 non-working wives in each country.

[2] Products and services were defined as "convenience" insofar as they enabled women to economize on time devoted to the performance of meal preparation and other household tasks.

were also questioned on shopping patterns such as store choice and loyalty, and husband involvement in shopping activities. Similarly, in relation to women's clothing purchases, respondents were asked various questions concerning the type of store visited, the role of the husband in selecting clothes, as well as the relative importance of seven sources of information for new clothing styles. Attitudes towards four aspects of a woman's role were also examined: a) involvement in home and family, b) cooking, shopping and other household tasks, c) self-perceptions and concepts, and d) social interaction. The background characteristics included some describing the home, as well as various standard family socioeconomic and demographic characteristics such as income, age and education of husband and wife.

Research Analysis

The principal analytic technique was multivariate analysis of covariance (Cooley and Lohnes, 1971, Green and Tull, 1975), a generalization of the classical ANOVA model to cases involving more than one criterion variable. In this study a 2×2 factorial design (country × working/non-working) was used to examine variance due to country, the wife's employment, and the interaction between the two variables (Figure 1).

Five sets of criterion variables were examined by means of separate MANOVA analyses; four of these sets related to purchases of grocery products and women's clothing as shown in Table 1, and

Table 1 The purchasing behavior variables

A. — Grocery purchase behavior

The ten convenience products and services	The grocery shopping variables
Takeout dinners	Frequency of grocery shopping
Instant desserts	Frequency of shopping in large supermarket
Canned main dishes	Frequency of shopping in neighborhood supermarket
Baked goods	
Frozen main dishes	Frequency of buying in corner grocery store
Cold cuts	
Laundry services	Frequency of shopping market
Paper plates and cups	
Aerosol carpet cleaner	Husband accompanies grocery shopping
Instant dusting spray	Husband shops for occasional items
	Husband does major grocery shopping

B. — Clothing purchase behavior

The clothing shopping variables	Fashion information sources
Frequency of buying clothing	Fashion magazines
Buys in dept. stores	Newspaper advertising
Buys in specialty stores	Other friends & neighbors
Buys in general & chain stores	Family & relatives
Buys in discount stores	Store personnel and displays
Store loyalty	T.V. and radio
Accompanied by husband	What I see in the street
Husband helps to choose clothes	
Amt. spent on clothes this fall	

		Employment	
		Working	Non-working
Country	U.S.	49	49
	France	49	49

Figure 1 The Factorial Design

the fifth consisted of ten attitudinal scales (Table 2). These scales were developed from a series of factor analyses of the attitudinal variables (Figure 2).[3] The use of the multivariate procedure took into consideration possible intercorrelation between variables within each criterion set, such as the use of different convenience products, or shopping in different types of stores. Each criterion set was first adjusted for a number of socioeconomic and demographic covariates. This step ensured that significant differences in the criterion variables observed between the two national samples or between the employed and nonemployed women would not merely reflect differences in their background characteristics. The four sets of purchase variables were then adjusted for the ten attitudinal variables, to assess whether these might account for the observed differences in purchase behavior.

RESEARCH RESULTS

Purchasing Behavior Patterns

Examination of the purchasing behavior patterns of U.S. and French working and non-working wives shows that differences between the two national samples are more significant than between working and non-working wives for all four sets of variables (Table 3), even after adjustment for the socioeconomic and demographic variables. Thus at first glance the results appear to confirm traditional views about cultural stereotypes and the

---

[3]The attitudinal data, which consisted of 70 statements rated on a 6 point Likert scale, was divided into four subsets, relating to the four aspects of a woman's role. Each subset was first factor-analyzed separately for each national sample. Highly similar underlying factor structures were identified in both cases. Consequently, joint analyses (across countries) were conducted for each of the four attitudinal subsets. Ten attitude scales were then constructed, using for each scale the three statements with the highest loadings on the first two or three factors identified in each of the four analyses. In each case the two or three factors accounted for 60–80% of the variance. For further discussion of the rationale underlying this procedure see Douglas and Le Maire (1974).

Table 2 The statements comprising the ten attitude scales (factor loadings for statements from the joint factor analysis)

Female role perceptions
- A woman's place is in the home .88
- Politics are a man's affair .87
- I do not think women with young children should work 65

Price consciousness
- I find myself checking prices even for small items .90
- I am very careful about the amount of money I spend .71
- I shop a lot for specials .63

Pride in home
- I am uncomfortable when my house is not completely clean .76
- A house should be cleaned and dusted at least twice a week .66
- I take a great deal of pride in my home .53

Opinion leadership
- I am more interested in food products than most people .73
- I am generally the first of my friends to buy a new product .68
- People often ask me for my advice about products and brands .64

Cooking
- I collect cooking recipes .81
- I love to bake cakes and frequently do .65
- The kitchen is my favorite room .62

Personal shopper
- I prefer to shop in stores where sales people are friendly .74
- I like to shop in a store where I feel at home .69
- One should support local shopkeepers .64

News and reading interest
- I spend a lot of time reading .85
- I keep up-to-date on the latest news .54

Fashion interest
- I keep up-to-date with the latest changes in fashion .83
- I invariably buy the latest fashion .79
- An important part of my life is dressing smartly .65

Personal influence
- I often listen to friends' advice about where to shop .67
- Before I do something, I often consider how my friends would react to it .60
- I like to wait and see how other people like new brands before I try them .59

Optimism
- In spite of all my efforts, I don't seem to be getting anywhere .81
- I wish I knew how to relax .72
- What I am doing with my life will not make a lasting contribution to the world .63

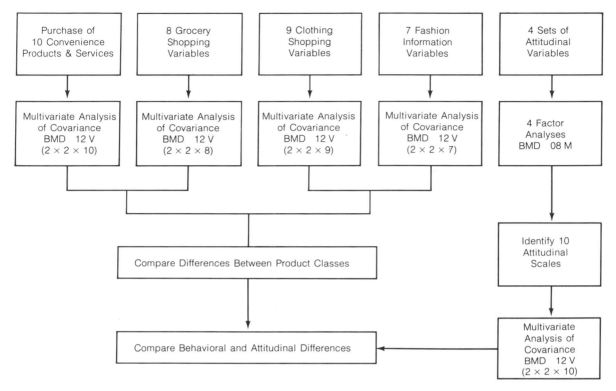

Figure 2 Flow Chart of Analysis

importance of differences in purchasing patterns between countries. A closer examination of the results via the univariate ANOVA reveals however, that these differences are largely due to the retail environment.

Grocery Purchase Behavior. The main differences between the two national samples in grocery shopping occur in the type of store in which they shop (Table 4). U.S. wives tend to shop more in large supermarkets and less in neighborhood supermarkets and corner stores than French housewives, but then large supermarkets are more common in the U.S. and equally, small traditional stores less common, than in France. U.S. husbands also seem more likely to purchase occasional grocery items than French husbands,

though not necessarily to do major grocery shopping.

As far as the use of convenience products and services is concerned, as one might expect, U.S. housewives tend in general to be heavier users than French wives (Table 5). However, the differences are most marked in relation to products and services such as take-out dinners, packaged cold-cuts, paper plates and cups which are typically widely available in the U.S. though not in France. Not all French grocery outlets, particularly small neighborhood stores, stock such items. On the other hand, the more common convenience products, such as instant desserts and canned main dishes, which are found in most stores in both France and the U.S. appear to be used with similar frequency in both countries.

Table 3 Summary table of the multivariate analyses of covariance for the purchasing and attitudinal variables (with 10 socioeconomic and demographic covariates)

(Approximate F Statistics)

Source of Variance	Purchasing Variables				Attitudinal
	8 grocery shopping charac- teristics	10 con- venience product services	9 clothing shopping charac- teristics	Rating of 7 fashion info. sources	Ratings on 10 attitudinal scales
U.S. vs. France	18.94*	11.52*	5.36*	6.51*	3.38*
Working vs. non-working wives	2.20*	1.35	1.57	1.19	2.06*
Interaction	2.87*	1.36	1.28	0.53	0.92
Covariates					
No. of Children	4.61*	0.66	3.28*	2.25*	0.94
Wife's Age	0.83	1.88	2.57*	1.43	1.22
Daily Help	1.01	0.68	0.52	1.78	2.66*
Wife's Education	1.44	2.65*	0.63	0.78	4.25*
No. of Cars	1.63	0.95	1.41	0.96	1.23
Husband's Occupation	1.07	2.47*	0.68	1.90	0.99
Husband's Education	0.23	0.65	0.50	2.03	2.63*
Income	1.23	2.27*	2.68*	2.17	2.18*
No. of Rooms in Home	1.86	1.20	1.79	0.44	1.20
Live in Apartment	1.13	0.95	1.12	0.18	1.01

*Significant at the .05 level.

The univariate analysis thus suggests that the differences observed are predominantly a reflection of differences in the retail environment in the two countries rather than in consumer preferences. The high proportion of small independent grocery retailers in France perpetuates the typical pattern of fragmented purchasing, and is an important factor contributing to the lag between France and the U.S. in the adoption of new products and services. It is, however, also possible to argue in the reverse sense that the differences in the retail environment reflect underlying differences in consumer attitudes and preferences in the two countries. Contrary to expectations, working and non-working wives did not have substantially different purchasing behavior. Since working wives typically have more limited time available for shopping and other household chores and have to perform these tasks at specific times such as in the evening or at the weekend, it seems reasonable to anticipate that they will organize shopping activities differently from non-working wives, and look for products and services which will enable them to save time in household tasks. In this respect the findings confirm those of other studies which indicate that working wives tend to shop less frequently, and make greater use of husbands in shopping activities than non-working wives

Table 4 Summary univariate analysis of variance for grocery shopping variables

	(F Statistics)		
	U.S. vs. France[1]	Working vs. Non-working[2]	Inter-action
Frequency of shopping market	72.93*	7.29*	15.18*
Frequency of shopping in large supermarket	*67.90**	*0.24*	0.00
Frequency of shopping in neighborhood supermarket	12.67*	4.83*	0.99
Husband shops for occasional items	*6.08**	0.35	0.98
Frequency of shopping in corner grocery store	5.78*	1.66	1.74
Husband accompanies grocery shopping	*1.91*	*2.36*	1.53
Frequency of grocery shopping	1.63	2.63	4.29*
Husband does major grocery shopping	0.03	*4.58**	1.00

*Statistically significant at the .05 level.
[1]Figures in italics indicate that the mean for the U.S. sample was higher than for the French sample.
[2]Figures in italics indicate that the mean for working wives was higher than for non-working wives.

(Anderson, 1972). However, working wives do not appear to make greater use of convenience products and services than non-working wives. No significant differences were observed in relation to any of the ten products.

The results of the covariance analysis shown in Table 3 suggest that differences between countries and between working and non-working wives are not substantially affected by socioeconomic and demographic differences. Grocery shopping, particularly the frequency of shopping, is related to the number of children. Equally the heavier use of convenience products and services in the U.S. appears in part to be a reflection of higher socio-economic status. However, the covariate adjustment is minor, and does not affect the main conclusions.

Women's Clothing. Similar patterns, though less marked, emerge in relation to women's clothing purchases, where again there were significant differences between the two countries though not between working and non-working wives. As in the case of grocery shopping the major differences occur in the type of store where they shop, and again appear to reflect the greater prevalence of small specialty stores in France (Table 6). U.S. wives tend to shop more frequently in department and discount stores as opposed to the boutiques typically frequented by French women.

Once adjustment had been made for differences in income and stage in life-cycle, no significant differences emerged between working and non-working wives in clothing purchase in either the univariate or the multivariate analyses. Equally the only significant difference in fashion information sources was, as hypothesized, a somewhat greater reliance by working wives on in-store sources of information.

Table 5 Summary univariate analysis of variance for convenience products & services

	(F Statistics)		
	U.S. vs. France[1]	Working vs. Non-working[2]	Inter-action
Cold cuts	*34.29**	0.25	1.38
Laundry services	24.74*	*1.09*	1.66
Paper plates and cups	*21.90**	0.15	1.00
Aerosol carpet cleaner	*9.21**	*3.30*	8.27*
Takeout dinner	*7.57**	3.21	0.13
Baked goods	7.06*	0.57	0.14
Instant dusting spray	*4.07**	0.02	6.34*
Canned main dishes	0.91	*1.69*	0.06
Frozen main dishes	0.50	*0.97*	0.15
Instant ready-to-serve desserts	0.23	0.02	0.03

*Statistically significant at the .05 level.
[1]Figures in italics indicate that the mean for the U.S. sample was higher than for the French sample.
[2]Figures in italics indicate that the mean for working wives was higher than for non-working wives.

Table 6 Summary univariate analysis of covariance for clothing variables

	(F Statistics)		
	U.S. vs. France[1]	Working vs. Non-working[2]	Inter-action
Buys in dept. stores	16.27*	2.03	1.42
Buys in specialty stores	14.17*	0.97	0.41
Buys in discount stores	12.18*	0.00	0.26
Husband helps to choose clothes	1.37	0.04	0.01
Store loyalty	1.12	2.10	4.40*
Accompanied by husband	0.21	2.19	1.25
Frequency of buying clothing	0.19	0.94	0.20
Buys in general & chain stores	0.03	2.27	0.43
Amt. spent on clothes this fall	0.00	1.53	0.00

*Statistically significant at the .05 level.
[1]Figures in italics indicate that the mean for the U.S. sample was higher than for the French sample.
[2]Figures in italics indicate that the mean for working wives was higher than for non-working wives.

Thus, in all cases differences between countries appear to dominate differences between working and non-working wives. Consequently there is little indication to suggest that a strategy of cross-national segmentation focusing on working vs. non-working wife families is likely to be appropriate either for grocery products or women's clothing. This conclusion does, however, appear in many respects to result from the lack of differences between working and non-working wives in both countries and hence does not necessarily imply that national differences will automatically be more important in relation to other customer sub-groups, especially if marked differences are observed between groups within countries.

Role Perceptions and Attitudes

Examination of attitudes towards female roles again reveals greater differences between coun-

tries than between working and non-working wives, though this time the gap between the significance of the U.S. vs. France and working vs. non-working results is considerably smaller. A more detailed analysis of the ten attitudinal scales for the American and French samples (Table 7) suggests that traditional attitudes towards a woman's role in society are not necessarily associated with traditional attitudes towards homemaking roles. As might be expected, differences in cultural norms prevalent in the U.S. and in French society lead U.S. wives to hold more liberated attitudes. Somewhat surprisingly, however, these views do not seem to carry over in relation to attitudes toward other female and homemaker roles. One might expect liberated views to be associated with less interest in traditional homemaking activities such as cooking and shopping. Yet, despite their more liberated role perceptions, U.S. wives appear to be more price conscious, more interested in cooking and are more inclined to be personalizing shoppers than French wives. In comparing attitudes of working

Table 7 Summary of the univariate analysis of covariance for the attitude scales

	(F Statistics)		
	U.S. vs. France[1]	Working vs. Non-working[2]	Inter-action
Female role perceptions	14.1*	19.1*	1.7
Opinion leadership	14.0*	0.0	0.0
Personalized shopping	7.6*	0.7	0.6
Price consciousness	7.5*	3.0	0.2
Cooking interest	7.5*	3.4	4.4*
Optimism	5.4*	1.5	0.3
News & reading interest	2.7	0.2	0.9
Fashion interest	2.2	1.1	0.3
Personal influence	2.0	0.0	2.0
Pride in home	0.4	8.9*	0.2

*Statistically significant at the .05 level.
[1]Figures in italics indicate that the mean for the U.S. sample was higher than for the French sample.
[2]Figures in italics indicate that the mean for working wives was higher than for non-working wives.

Table 8 Summary table of the multivariate analyses of covariance for the purchasing variables (with 10 attitudinal scale covariates)

	(Approximate F Statistics)			
	Purchasing Variables			
Source of Variance	*10 convenience products services*	*8 grocery shopping characteristics*	*9 clothing shopping characteristics*	*Rating of 7 fashion info. sources*
U.S. vs. France	13.4*	34.5*	8.4*	6.8*
Working vs. non-working wives	1.7	3.2*	1.3	1.2
Interaction	0.9	3.2*	1.4	0.5
Covariates:				
Female role perceptions	0.7	0.4	0.6	1.0
Pride in home	1.0	1.5	1.6	1.7
Cooking interest	0.8	0.5	1.5	0.9
News and reading interest	1.2	1.4	1.1	1.2
Personal influence	0.8	1.7	0.5	3.2*
Price consciousness	1.4	1.4	2.1*	1.3
Opinion leadership	2.1*	0.8	0.4	2.7*
Personal shopper	0.8	1.7	1.2	3.2*
Fashion interest	1.0	0.5	7.7*	8.5*
Optimism	1.5	2.5*	0.6	0.8

*Significant at the .05 level.

and non-working wives, the most important differences also occur in relation to female role perceptions where it comes as little surprise to find that working wives have more liberated attitudes than non-working wives. Consistently, working wives also appear to be less house-proud. French working wives are also less interested in cooking than non-working wives, though the reverse is true in the U.S. case.

In relation to the use of convenience products and grocery shopping, only one attitudinal covariate—optimism—is significant, and chiefly affects the tendency to shop in large or neighborhood supermarkets. In relation to shopping for clothes, however, interest in fashion results in a higher frequency of shopping for clothes, coupled with higher expenditure on clothes, and a greater tendency to shop in specialty stores. Fashion interest also appears to be associated with a tendency to rely on personal sources of information, particularly friends. Opinion leadership, susceptibility to personal influence, and personalizing shopping attitudes also affect sources of fashion information.

CONCLUSIONS

Although clearly the illustrative character of the study and the small sample size do not permit any definitive conclusions, the findings nonetheless suggest a number of tentative observations and guidelines for further research.

1) Differences between the two countries overwhelmingly dominate differences between working and non-working wives.

2) The significance of differences observed both between countries and between the two subgroups varies with the product class, and is greater in relation to grocery products than clothing. This implies that the relative importance of national and sub-group differences is likely to vary from one product group to another.

3) Behavior patterns appear to differ more in the two countries than attitudes.

4) Retail environmental factors seem to play a key role in shaping and conditioning behavior patterns. Consequently, apparent differences in behavior patterns between countries may in many respects merely reflect current market conditions such as the availability of different products and services or the number of supermarkets or small, traditional retailers. Consequently, low usage frequency, for example, of convenience products or services does not necessarily imply absence of a market. If widespread distribution of such products or services is obtained, behavior patterns may well change accordingly.

In brief, while cross-national differences are, on the surface, greater than within country differences between working and non-working wives, a closer examination shows that observed differences probably reflect differences in the retail environment rather than in underlying attitudes and preferences. Consequently, focus on apparent differences in behavior between national samples may tend to be misleading, especially where this leads to negative conclusions concerning the feasibility of influencing or changing these patterns. Since, however, the impact of retail environmental factors was not explicitly examined, such conclusions can only be regarded as tentative.

In conducting further research in this area, a number of recommendations emerge from the experience of this pilot study. In the first place, further investigation of the role of retail environmental factors in influencing customer response patterns seems desirable. This might, for example, examine whether differences in the availability of various products, or in retail structure, are a root cause of variance in purchase behavior between countries. For example, a comparison of behavior patterns of shoppers frequenting various types of stores in the two countries, or a comparison of behavior relating to products which are equally available rather than those which differ in availability in the two countries would seem appropriate. Attention should, however, be focused on comparisons relative to specific product classes, or groups of products.

Secondly, examination of appropriate research procedures in making cross-national comparisons of attitudinal variables is needed. Although relatively little bias appears to be introduced by using equivalent measurement instruments and procedures to examine behavioral variables, it is not clear that such an assumption can be made in relation to attitudes. A more detailed investigation of the effect of using different measurement and analytical procedures on research findings is therefore needed. In particular, attention should be directed at assessing how adequately equivalent concepts such as innovativeness or opinion-leadership are measured by the same measurement instrument in different national contexts; how far the exclusive use of concepts and measures for which equivalents are available in each country tends to bias findings; and to what extent country-specific concepts should be included, and if so, how they should be integrated into the comparison.

Thirdly, the approach based on the use of "matched" groups in each country seems a promising one. In this particular case, the conclusions concerning the relative importance of cross-national differences appear largely to result from the lack of differences between working and non-working wives. Use of a similar procedure investigating other customer groupings where more marked differences are observed within countries could prove highly illuminating. In any event, whether in relation specifically to marketing or other aspects of social behavior, comparisons of similar groups in different countries appear to provide an instructive way of examining the role of national environmental factors influencing behavior patterns, and isolating their impact and interaction with other variables such as socio-economic, demographic and attitudinal characteristics.

REFERENCES

Anderson, B. (August, 1972), "Working vs. Non-Working Women: A Comparison of Shopping Behavior," *Proceedings of the AMA Fall Conference.*

Cooley, W. M., and Lohnes, Paul R. (1971), *Multivariate Data Analysis,* New York: John Wiley & Sons.

Dichter, E. (July-August, 1962), "The World Customer," *Harvard Business Review,* 40.

Douglas, S. P., and Le Maire, Patrick (September, 1974), "Improving the Quality and Efficiency of Life-Style Research," *Proceedings of the XXIII ESOMAR Congress.*

Engel, J. F.; Kollat, D. T.; and Blackwell, P. (1968), *Consumer Behavior,* New York: Holt, Rinehart and Winston, Inc.

Frank, R. E.; Massy, W. F.; and Wind, Yoram (1972), *Market Segmentation,* Englewood Cliffs, N.J.: Prentice-Hall.

Green, P. E., and Tull, Donald S. (1975), *Research for Marketing Decisions,* 3rd ed. Englewood Cliffs, N.J.: Prentice-Hall.

Triandis, M. (1972), *The Analysis of Subjective Culture,* New York: John Wiley & Sons.

Wind, Y. (Winter, 1967), "Cross Cultural Analysis of Consumer Behavior," in R. Meyer, ed., *Changing Marketing Systems.* Proceedings of the American Marketing Association Conference.

THE CONSUMER BEHAVIOR OF FAMILIES AND ORGANIZATIONS

There are two types of formal organizations which are central to consumer behavior. One is the family. Although the family is not often referred to as a formal organization, it is a legally constituted group. The second type of formal organization is the type we usually associate with a business firm, although nonbusiness organizations are also formalized through the law. Families as consuming groups have received considerable attention by consumer behavior researchers. Other organizations have received far less attention as consumers, although this is changing now as consumer behavior researchers begin to view the term *consumer* broadly.

The family and other organizations are especially interesting because they highlight the fact that there is often a division of labor in the overall consumption process. This division of labor is important to marketers and consumer educators. An organization or a family usually assigns different activities to different members. This may be done very explicitly, as is likely in the case of a business firm, or it may be done without any real awareness of a division of responsibility occurring. In a given instance of buying and consuming the following responsibilities are assigned:

1. Gatekeeping. Someone in the family or firm determines whether or not information about a product or a supplier is passed along to other members of the group. A mother learning of a new restaurant determines whether or not her family also hears about it, and therefore whether the family has a chance to try it.

2. Opinion leadership. Someone in the group provides information about the desirability of a restaurant, for example, or the quality of industrial cable provided by a particular supplier.
3. Decision making. The task of deciding to actually try a restaurant, or sign a contract with a supplier, is made by an individual or subgroup.
4. Implementor. This task of carrying out a decision may be made by the mother in the case of the restaurant or by a purchasing agent in the case of industrial cable.
5. User. The user is the person or group which consumes the product. It may be the entire family or those not on a diet or it may be the production department of a firm.

One single person may perform more than one task or responsibility although it is not likely that this number would exceed more than two or three. Who assumes which responsibilities will very likely differ from product to product. This is especially true for families and somewhat less true in business and public organizations. There will also be some variation across different families and firms for a given product. For example, in one family the husband may be the decision maker for a restaurant, while in another family the children may be the dominant decision makers. In one firm the purchasing agent's role may be limited to soliciting bids from suppliers, while in another firm the purchasing agent may have a major role in selecting the supplier.

We shall turn now to a consideration of some other dynamics among families and firms as consumer units.

"PERCEPTION OF MARITAL ROLES IN DECISION PROCESSES"

Although much of the work in consumer behavior involves individual buyer behavior, it is quite likely that most consumer behavior phenomena involve interaction with other people. This would include family purchases (whether decided upon jointly or by one person acting as an agent for others), as well as organizational buying. Davis and Rigaux report findings on husband-wife decision processes. They are interested in how the roles of the two people vary over the different phases of the decision process (problem recognition, internal and external search, and final decision). They are also interested in the agreement between the husband's and wife's perceptions of who played what roles during the different phases.

Davis and Rigaux are careful to specify how their research was conducted and how this limits the conclusions they can draw. For instance, students conducted the interviewing by selecting respondents who were accessible to them. The bias of this convenience sample is evident in the demographic description of the sample which appears at the end of the section on methodology. The age groups reflect large proportions of respondents who are near the age of the students or who are approximately the age of college students' parents. Thus, it appears that the students interviewed their married friends, their parents, and perhaps some friends of their parents. In addition, it appears that their selections represent an upscale bias. That is, the respondents tend to be well educated and in upper-income brackets.

Notice also the large amount of information gathered from each respondent. Each person was asked about decision roles for the three stages in the decision process for 25 different decisions. This means each person answered 25×3 or 75 questions about roles in decision-making processes.

A two-dimensional chart is needed to display the results. If the husband says he is dominant (score of 1) and the wife says she is dominant (score of 3), their average score is $(1 + 3)/2 = 2$. This answer implies that their decision making is joint and therefore is in one of the middle two sections of the chart. The second dimension (the horizontal axis in the three figures) is needed to accurately describe the findings. The horizontal axis indicates what proportion of the families actually report joint decision making.

The three figures, when studied closely, provide substantial information. Figure 1 averages the role patterns over all three stages in the decision process. Thus, a point on this chart is the average of the role patterns in the three successive stages of the decision process. Figure 2 shows changes in the role patterns from the problem recognition stage to the internal and external search stage. Similarly, Figure 3 shows changes in the role patterns from the search stage to the final decision stage. These figures show that it is most likely that roles will become more specialized in moving from the problem recognition stage to the search stage (that is, either the husband or the wife will become dominant), and the role pattern will become more joint in moving to the final decision stage.

With respect to the findings on husband-wife agreement, a cautionary note is in order. Aggregate findings indicate a high level of agreement between husbands and wives. However, when comparing individual husbands with their own wives, on the average, only 68 percent of the couples are in agreement. The managerial implications of this finding are discussed in a very interesting way.

"GIFT DECISIONS BY KIDS AND PARENTS"

Unfortunately, many studies of family consumer decision processes are actually studies of husband-wife interactions only. The effects of children on consumer behavior patterns are ignored too often. Caron and Ward investigated the effect of children's requests for Chirstmas gifts on the gifts actually chosen by the parents. Note that there are multiple roles which apply in this situation. The child is the user of the product, but the parent is the purchaser. Due to this decision, the child is then an influencer in the parent's decision process.

Figure 1 in the article gives an explicit model of the relationships between variables which are studied. In addition to these variables, social class and age are studied for their relation to purchase processes. However, only middle and upper social classes are sampled; the article's results thus cannot be used to make generalizations about child influence patterns in lower-class families.

The Caron and Ward article presents several findings which raise new questions about family decision processes. Why are older children more likely than younger children to use the mass media as a source of product information? Caron and Ward suggest that over time children may learn to use the media as an information source. Why do upper-class children prefer competitive and interactive toys? Why do middle-class children receive more gifts? Caron and Ward suggest that the differences might be due to different value orientations.

Although these suggested explanations sound plausible, they can only be validated through additional research. The suggested explanations are not the findings of the research. This is a problem whenever research investigates differences between groups of people (e.g., social classes or age groups). This points out that much research discovers what relationships exist, but researchers must then construct explanations about why these relationships hold. The statistical analyses in research reports give a sense of how valid and reliable the findings are. Only additional research can validate explanations about why certain differences between groups of people exist.

"EXPLORING ENVIRONMENTAL INFLUENCES IN ORGANIZATIONAL BUYING"

Until recently, industrial purchasers were assumed to act as strictly rational problem solvers. However, in the past few years, consumer behavior researchers have become increasingly aware that industrial purchasers are humans attempting to make choices which fit their understanding of the situation. In this respect, they are no less subject to the kinds of behavioral influences which have been associated with ultimate consumer behavior. Secondly, industrial buying, like much ultimate consumer buying, is done in a group setting. One person or a small set of people are charged with the responsibility of making purchases of products which will be used by others from the group. The basic process is the same whether the purchaser is a purchasing agent, a buying center, or a family shopper, and whether users are workers on a production line or children eating cereal for breakfast.

Grønhaug's article suggests a way that industrial buyers may be segmented. Because of different environmental situations, organizational buying may be conducted differently. Specifically, Grønhaug describes two types of organizational environment situations—product dependent and product independent. This differentiation is based on the extent to which the survival of the firm is dependent on the exchange of produced items or services for fees.

Appendix A at the end of the article lists the variables studied. The appendix also provides information about how these variables were measured (operational definitions) and the type of scales used in answering the questions. Particularly interesting are the findings reported in Table 1. These findings indicate that persons at particular levels in the organization are more or less likely to play certain roles in the purchase process. An interesting exercise is to try to answer the question, "What might this suggest about who would play these same roles in a family purchase process?" Consider parents, older children, and younger children.

The basic point of the Grønhaug article is that given different environmental situations, industrial buyers map their environments and make choices differently.

PERCEPTION OF MARITAL ROLES IN DECISION PROCESSES

**HARRY L. DAVIS
AND
BENNY P. RIGAUX**

The literature on marital roles in family consumption behavior reveals an interesting trend away from highly simplified notions of role differentiation in decision-making. Raising doubts about unidimensional theories of marital roles (Burgess and Locke, 1960; Parsons and Bales, 1955) are data showing substantial specialization within families by decision area or product category (Blood and Wolfe, 1960; Sharp and Mott, 1956; Wolgast, 1958). Other studies, either because of their commercial orientation or concern with identifying other bases for role differentiation, indicate that marital roles differ within purchase categories depending upon which product characteristic is selected (Starch, 1958; Davis, 1970). Thus, for example, Davis (1970) found that roles in several decisions, related either to furniture or automobile purchases, were differentiated for each on the basis of product-related decisions on the one hand, and scheduling or resource allocation decisions on the other.

In comparison with these studies of decision roles for the choice of product characteristics (brand, store, price, color), there is much less data concerning marital roles at different phases of the decision-making process. While there is considerable research on group problem-solving and decision-making, it is difficult to generalize the results to the internal dynamics of families. For example, economists have measured the length and character of consumer purchase plans but, to our knowledge, not in terms of the roles played by each spouse in initiating, searching, or evaluating alternatives. Sociological work on group problem-solving, while rich in data and theoretical constructs, is based to a very large extent on the behavior of short-lived, *ad hoc* groups (Bales and Strodtbeck, 1951; Kelley and Thibaut, 1969). The difficulty of generalizing findings from such studies to family units which have prescribed roles, permanence, and recurrent decision situations is obvious. The relevant marketing literature also has shortcomings. With few exceptions, researchers either oversimplify their conceptualization of the decision-making process (who discussed the pur-

Source: Harry L. Davis and Benny P. Rigaux, "Perception of Marital Roles in Decision Processes," *Journal of Consumer Research,* Vol. 1, June, 1974, pp. 51–62.

chase and who then bought it), or construct very detailed models of the decision-making process either lacking any empirical validation or limited to a small number of product categories (Time Inc., 1967; Gredal, 1966; Jaffe and Senft, 1966; Scott, 1970).

In order to broaden understanding of role differentiation in family economic decisions, this article is addressed to two related questions:

1. Do marital roles in consumer decision-making differ by phase of the process?
2. To what extent do husbands and wives agree in their perception of roles at various phases of the decision process?

Answers to these questions will be useful to a large number of researchers sharing an interest in consumer behavior. Marketing researchers continue to explore alternative bases for segmenting markets. Information about the roles played by husbands and wives throughout the decision-making process is relevant in assessing the wisdom of continuing to rely upon the housewife in marketing research (Frank, Massy, and Wind, 1972), and the feasibility of using marital roles in addition to sex roles as a basis for market segmentation. The results are also interesting for any organization—private or public—interested in communicating with the appropriate decision-maker(s) in the family or obtaining valid data about household preferences, intentions, or behavior.

METHODOLOGY

Data useful for examining marital roles in economic decisions were gathered in a project for a marketing research course during the 1971 fall term at the Catholic University of Louvain, Belgium (Rigaux, et al., 1972). A questionnaire was separately administered to each spouse in 73 households[1] selected by students for their ac-

cessibility. Among other tasks, the respondents had to fill in a two-way table, in which 25 household purchasing decisions were listed as row elements[2] and three phases of the decision process[3] as column elements. These decisions were selected so as to be representative of that larger group having economic consequences for families. For each item, the respondent had to indicate the major influence (Husband = 1; Joint = 2; Wife = 3) in the different phases.

The use of a three phase decision process (that is, problem recognition, internal and external search, and final decision) differs somewhat from the classic conceptualization (Dewey, 1910) which includes a phase of alternative evaluation. We have chosen to eliminate this phase because it is so intimately related to the search process. Even with the three phases we have chosen, subjects may view the distinction among phases as somewhat artificial for the following reasons: 1) the consumer need not be, and indeed, probably is not aware that he passes through these phases; 2) this, like any other process conceptualization, has some time dimension; and, finally, 3) all phases do not always occur (Engel, Kollat and Blackwell, 1973, pp. 47, 59–62). Nevertheless, as emphasized by Brim et al., (1962, p. 11), "it is this type of formal analysis of the basic phases of the process which permits one to see the similar nature of all decision problems."

One other aspect of the methodology used in this study deserves comment. Similar to many other studies of family roles in decision-making, we have made use of direct questions about the relative influence of each spouse. Direct questions of this sort assume, according to Kenkel (1961), that individuals 1) know the relative amount of influence they have; 2) are willing to admit it to themselves and others; and 3) are able to recall

---

[1]The modest size of this sample is not uncommon in marital role studies. See, for example, Starch (1958), Davis (1970), and Scott (1970).

[2]The specific decisions can be found in Table 2.

[3](1) Problem recognition: who is the first in the household to recognize the need?
(2) Search for information: who provides and collects information about possible alternatives?
(3) Final decision: who makes the final choice?

with accuracy how influence was distributed in some past decision-making session. While these assumptions are undoubtedly questionable, we feel, as do others, that direct questions about specific decisions represent the best "interim approach" for identifying roles (Engel, Kollat, and Blackwell, 1973, p. 203). This solution seems even more appropriate in this study since independent data from husbands and wives within the same families allow one to assess the validity of these scales measuring relative influence (Davis, 1971).

Since we have used a convenience sample, it is perhaps useful to describe it in terms of several demographic characteristics. The households range in age from the twenties up to the sixties, with 36 percent in their twenties and 26 percent in their fifties. Twenty-five percent have no children; 47 percent, one or two children; and 28 percent, three or more. The respondents are fairly well educated—54 percent of the wives and 56 percent of the husbands had completed a high school program. Among them, 13 percent and 24 percent have a university degree. Thirty-four percent of the households have a working wife. The sample is definitely urban—59 percent live in one of the five largest Belgian cities. Finally, the level of income is also rather high, according to Belgian living standards: fifty-two percent of the households have an annual income higher than 7,500 U.S. dollars.

FINDINGS

A Framework for Classifying Decisions
In order to avoid a lengthy presentation of numerical results where the interrelations among decisions are not easy to seize, we employ a diagram that displays all decisions simultaneously. Each decision is positioned in terms of two axes. The first is a scale of the relative influence between husband and wife. Given the coding that was used in this study, average relative influence for a decision when aggregated over families can range

along a continuum from 1 (if all respondents report husband dominance) to 3 (if all respondents report wife dominance). The mean score of a decision along this axis does not, however, reflect the extent of role specialization in those families. For example, a mean of 2 could imply either a complete lack of specialization where all couples decide jointly, or a complete specialization where the decision is wife dominant in 50 percent of the families and husband dominant in the remaining 50 percent. Indeed, any percentage of families making the decision jointly combined with an even split between husband dominant and wife dominant cases would also yield a mean of 2. Notice that ambiguity about the extent of role specialization only arises when one wants to aggregate influence scores for two families or more. Thus, the second axis is a scale of the extent of role specialization as measured by the percentage of families reporting that a decision is jointly made.

Figure 1 shows the position of the twenty-five decisions with reference to these two axes. The location of each decision is, for this illustration, based upon an average across the three stages of the decision process and across the 146 respondents (73 households). The two lines which converge at the point 2, 100 percent, limit the feasibility region to a triangle since the axes are obviously not independent.

This framework was originally suggested by Wolfe (1959) for distinguishing among families having different role structures. Our representation differs from his only in that we have plotted decisions rather than families. Wolfe divided the feasibility triangle into four patterns of influence according to a classification proposed by Herbst (1952). Tracing these same boundaries in Figure 1 leads to four decision areas. Decisions for which the mean relative influence is 1.5 or less are defined as "husband dominant" while those with means of 2.5 or greater are "wife dominant." In both of these areas, the proportion of families that decide jointly is by definition less than 50 percent.

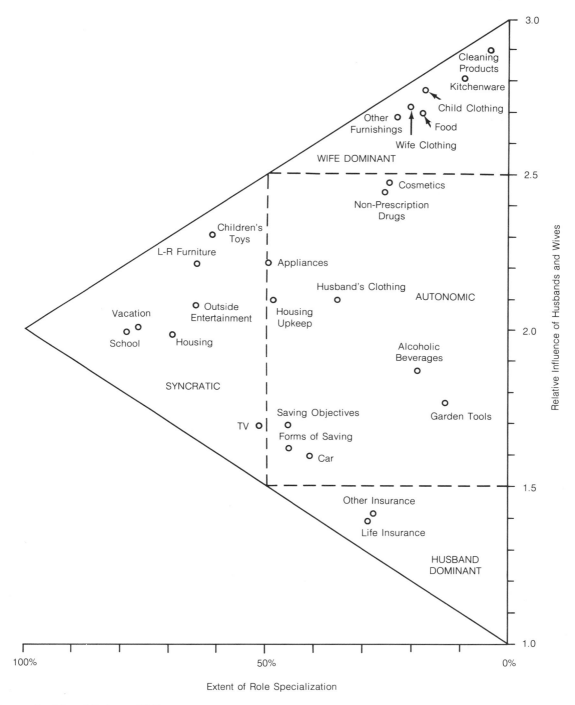

Figure 1 Marital Roles in 25 Decisions

Decisions with mean relative influence between 1.5 and 2.5 fall into either a "syncratic" or "autonomic" pattern. If more than 50 percent of the families make a decision jointly, it is classified as syncratic. If this percentage is less than 50 percent, the decision is classified as autonomic. Husband dominant and wife dominant families reach a majority for this latter type of decision. The figure also shows the 25 decisions are distributed widely throughout the feasibility triangle. The actual range along the relative influence axis is from 1.37 for life insurance to 2.91 for household cleaning products. The actual range along the second axis is from a low of 6 percent of the families who decide jointly in the case of household cleaning products to a high of 78 percent of the families in the case of vacations. The presence of decisions in all four areas of the triangle is a necessary condition if we want to generalize our results about the variation in roles at different stages of the decision process.

Differences in Roles by Decision Phase

We turn now to the central issue of this paper and consider the stability of relative influence and extent of specialization between Phase 1 (problem recognition), Phase 2 (search for information), and Phase 3 (final decision).

A gross measure of the stability or change of decisions among stages is simply the influence pattern in which they appear. For this reason, Table 1 classifies the 25 decisions at each stage according to this criterion. Although there is little difference in the proportion of decisions falling into the four patterns between problem recognition and search and evaluation, there is a significant change in the final stage. Thirteen of the decisions are classified as syncratic for the final decision as compared with only six or seven in the earlier stages. A corresponding change is apparent for the autonomic patterns in the final stage (five decisions as compared to ten and nine).

Continuing the same analysis at the level of individual decisions, one observes that 16 of the 25

Table 1 Patterns of influence at three stages of the decision process

Pattern of influence	Phase		
	Problem recognition	Search for information	Final decision
Husband Dominant	2	3	2
Autonomic	10	9	5
Syncratic	7	6	13
Wife Dominant	6	7	5

decisions (64 percent) remain in the same pattern of influence throughout all phases of the decision process. Life and other insurance remain husband dominant while decisions regarding kitchenware, household cleaning products, wife's and children's clothes as well as food and nonalcoholic beverages stay wife dominant. The syncratic pattern characterizes decisions about housing, living room furniture, children's toys and school, concerts, movies and theater, as well as the family vacation for all three stages. Three decisions—garden tools, alcoholic beverages, and nonprescription drugs—remain in the autonomic pattern. Five of the nine decisions that change patterns at least once over the three phases move from autonomic in the first two phases to syncratic for the final decision. These include housing upkeep, household appliances, the husband's clothing, and the objectives and forms of saving. Of the four decisions, the purchase of a car is the most varied, moving from autonomic for problem recognition, to husband dominant for the search and evaluation of alternatives, and finally, to syncratic for the final decision.

While an analysis based upon the pattern of influence gives a general impression of the change in marital roles throughout the decision process, the criterion is such that much information is lost. A decision's position could change rather dramatically along the dimension of relative influence as well as in terms of joint decision-making and still remain within the same pattern of influence. A much smaller change along either dimension, on the other hand, can produce a shift in patterns if the decisions happen to lie close to the boundaries. In order to view more precisely the change between stages, we will consider separately relative influence and the extent of joint decision-making.

Relative influence changes very little among the three phases if one examines the average across all 25 decisions for each stage (2.19, 2.15, and 2.06 respectively). Notice that the movement between the second and third stage in the direction of husband influence is somewhat greater than that between the first two stages. This trend becomes much more evident if the same analysis is made for the individual products between the first and third stage. Wives' influence in the stage of problem recognition is greater than their influence in making the final decision for 20 of the 25 decisions. Interestingly, the five decisions for which wives' influence is greater in the final stage are those which are the most husband influenced—that is, garden tools, car, life and other insurance and forms of saving. Thus, rather than a slight increase in the husband's influence throughout the decision process, there appears to be a "regression toward the mean" in making the final decision. The fact that this is concealed in the averages for each stage is due to an "oversampling" of decisions in the region of wife dominance.

The same analysis along the axis of joint decision-making reveals a very noticeable increase in the percentage of shared decisions between the second and third stage—that is, an average for all 25 decisions at each stage of 38 percent, 32 percent, and 51 percent respectively. All 25 decisions become less specialized between the stages of search and evaluation and final decision, while all except housing become less specialized between the first and third stage. At this global level of analysis it appears that the change toward greater jointness of decision-making in the last phase is relatively more pronounced than the change in the balance of influence between husband and wife.

Figures 2 and 3 summarize the change along both of these axes from stage 1 to 2 and from 2 to 3 respectively. These figures illustrate in a very graphic way the conclusions described above. In Figure 2, most of the arrows (20 out of 25) point to the right, suggesting more specialization in the stage of search and evaluation. At the same time, no overall pattern is evident with respect to change in the relative influence of husband and wife. The arrows in Figure 3, on the other hand, all point to the left or in the direction of less specialization, and there is a corresponding movement along the axis of relative influence toward the center. Thus, in the third stage we see a movement of the decisions further into or toward the syncratic region.

The artificiality of separating the decision process into three distinct phases, as was earlier discussed, would have been reinforced had respondents reported similar roles at each phase. However, the analysis has shown that husbands and wives did distinguish between the stages in assessing their roles, thus providing some face validity to this conceptualization.

Similarity of Roles Perceived by Husbands and Wives

While the preceding results are interesting, we have not up to this point taken advantage of the fact that data were collected from both husband and wife within the same families. Analyzing the data at this level provides a way of assessing the validity of the above findings. Moreover, it will lead to insights about the more practical issue of which spouse to interview in family research studies.

Previous research has shown few consistent differences between responses of husbands as a group compared with wives (Wilkening and Morrison, 1963; Davis, 1970; Granbois and Willett, 1970). On the other hand, when intrafamily com-

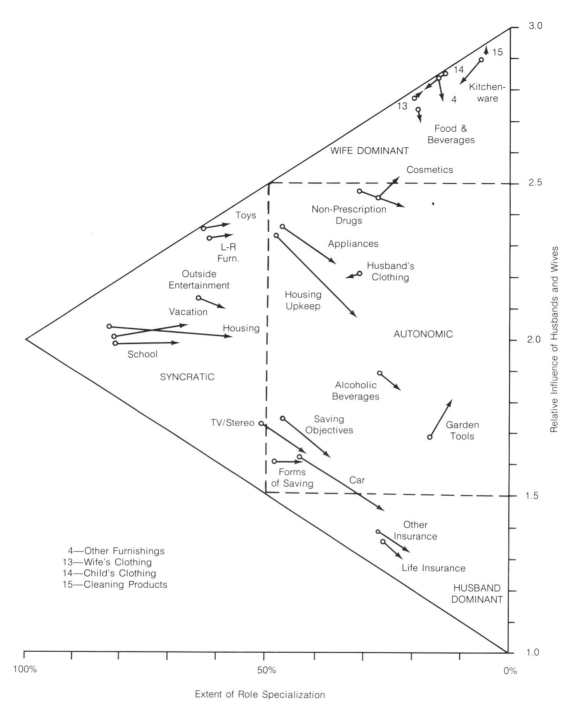

Figure 2 Changes in Marital Roles Between Phase 1 and Phase 2

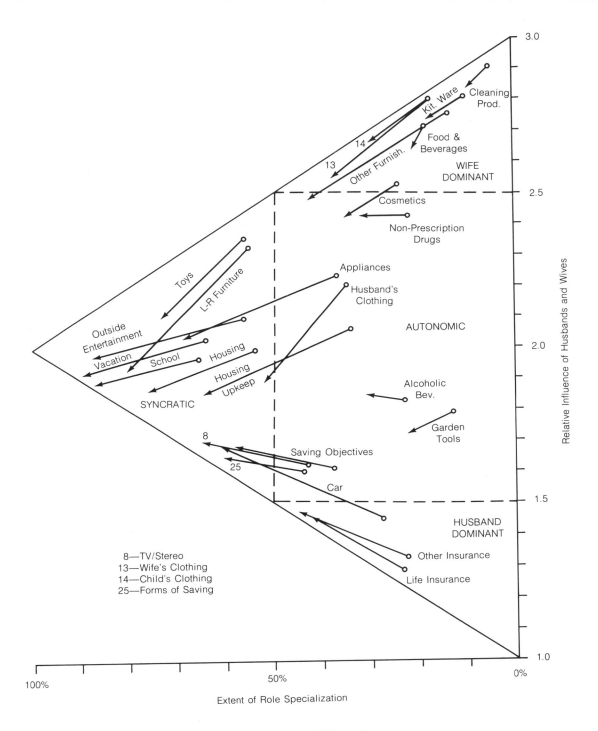

Figure 3   Changes in Marital Roles Between Phase 2 and Phase 3

parisons of direct questions are made, considerable disagreement is often evident (Scanzoni, 1965; Davis, 1971). While the level of agreement is generally greater than chance, a common finding is that from 10 percent to 50 percent of couples disagree about the influence of one spouse relative to the other for any given decision. The size of this percentage seems to vary with the specificity of questions and, not surprisingly, with the number of possible response categories.

Our data, in general, support the previous research. The location of each decision (averaged across the three phases) along the two dimensions of relative influence and specialization is very close when comparing husbands' and wives' responses in the aggregate. Only three of the 25 decisions are classified according to different influence types and these three happen to lie close to the frontiers dividing the triangle into four regions.[4] Moreover, the differences between husbands and wives in their *average* scores on relative influence (2.153 versus 2.156) and the extent of shared decision-making (39 percent versus 40 percent) are very small. A lack of discrepancy is also found when comparing husbands' and wives' responses at each phase.

Thus, the results shown in Figures 2 and 3 are altered only slightly by splitting the sample into two halves. Both husbands and wives perceive roles as becoming more specialized between the phase of problem identification and information search while less specialized for the final decision.

These data, of course, do not provide any information about the extent to which a husband and wife from the same family agree in role perception. In order to examine this more detailed aspect of consensus, 75 intrafamily comparisons were made—one for each decision at each of the three phases (see Table 2).

[4]Nonprescription drugs and cosmetics and toiletries are classified as autonomic with the husbands' data but as wife dominant with the wives'. Household appliances appear as syncratic with the wives' data, autonomic with the husbands'.

The percentage of couples who agree about their roles averages 68 percent across all of the 25 decisions and phases. There is a range around this mean figure from 57 percent to 88 percent. Generally, those decisions with the highest consensus are very skewed in terms of relative influence (kitchenware or household cleaning products) or have the majority of respondents in the "joint" category (children's school and program of study). In contrast, those decisions having the lowest consensus (household appliances, husband's clothing, and car) are found in the center of the triangle—the region which includes decisions having very flat or bimodal distributions. While variability in role consensus is evident for different decisions, little variability is apparent among the three phases of the decision process. The average levels of consensus for each of the three phases (69 percent, 68 percent, and 68 percent) are essentially the same.

Looking now at those couples who do not agree in their perception of roles in a decision, it is possible to see whether or not any systematic bias exists. We will define two types of nonconsensus in order to facilitate the presentation of results. Nonconsensus can result from *modesty*—either or both spouses overestimating the other's influence in a decision or underestimating their own influence. Nonconsensus can also be the result of *vanity*—either or both spouses overestimating their own influence in a decision or underestimating the other's influence. If role perception regarding influence in a decision is not systematically biased, we should expect to find a relatively equal percentage of couples who are "modest" and those who are "vain."

If one examines for each stage the number of decisions for which the difference between the modesty and vanity column is at least five percentage points, the overwhelming majority of these indicate vanity (10 out of 13 in problem recognition, 14 out of 14 in search for information, and 10 out of 12 for the final decision). The vanity bias is somewhat more pronounced in the phase

Table 2 Extent of husband-wife agreement about roles in 25 decisions (in percentages)

	Problem Recognition			Search for Information			Final Decision		
	Mod-esty	Con-sensus	Vanity	Mod-esty	Con-sensus	Vanity	Mod-esty	Con-sensus	Vanity
1. Housing (location, purchase price or rent)	7	81	12	20	60	20	11	82	7
2. Housing upkeep (repairs, improvements)	20	63	17	17	59	24	24	62	14
3. Living-room furniture	24	57	19	17	69	14	14	80	6
4. Other furnishings (rugs, drapes)	8	80	12	9	82	9	28	49	23
5. Kitchenware	9	86	5	7	83	10	14	72	14
6. Household appliances excluding T.V.	27	55	18	22	54	24	16	63	21
7. Garden tools	10	74	16	9	71	20	17	61	22
8. T.V., Hi-Fi, tape recorder	17	59	24	17	62	21	18	59	23
9. Car	24	53	23	18	58	24	19	64	17
10. Food and non-alcoholic beverages	14	71	15	15	68	17	14	67	19
11. Alcoholic beverages	11	55	34	14	62	24	15	63	22
12. Husband's clothes	22	64	14	25	52	23	24	54	22
13. Wife's clothes	15	70	15	9	74	17	14	72	14
14. Child(ren)'s clothes	7	86	7	10	83	7	17	63	20
15. Household cleaning products	5	91	4	2	90	8	5	82	13
16. Cosmetics and toiletries	15	60	25	10	61	29	17	59	24
17. Child(ren)'s toys for birthdays and holidays	15	70	15	22	59	19	18	60	22
18. Life insurance	8	79	13	5	81	14	18	68	14
19. Other insurance	9	72	19	7	80	13	18	60	22
20. Nonprescription drugs and first-aid items	13	64	23	4	70	26	9	68	23
21. Child(ren)'s school and program of study	8	72	20	7	70	23	7	83	10
22. Concerts, movies, theater	21	58	21	17	56	27	14	76	10
23. Family vacation	18	64	18	14	61	25	5	88	7
24. Saving objectives	16	64	20	15	60	25	9	69	22
25. Forms of saving (stocks, saving accounts, bonds)	10	73	17	16	64	20	11	70	19
Average	14	69	17	13	68	19	15	68	17

of information search than in the other two phases.

It is interesting to note that these results agree with those reported by Hempel (1972) concerning marital roles in five house-buying decisions. At the same time, however, other studies in both the U.S. and Canada show a strong modesty bias in selected automobile and furniture purchase decisions (Davis, 1970, 1972; Scott, 1970).

Changes in Role Specialization

Marital roles were found to vary throughout three phases of the decision process. While no noticeable differences were apparent in average relative influence, the phase of information search was characterized by considerably more role specialization than either of the other two phases for almost all of the products studied.

Several explanations for this finding can be advanced. Differences in the degree of role specialization may reflect characteristics of the task. That is, the act of setting in motion a consumer decision may often require legitimization by the other spouse. In a similar way, the final decision, if shared, reduces the risk of either spouse having made a bad decision. The task of information seeking, in contrast, may call for an appropriate division of labor based, for example, on the availability of one spouse relative to the other or the competence as well as vested interest of one party. An explanation for this finding could also be found in the fact that information search is likely to elicit specific behaviors while the phases of problem recognition and final decision are not associated with concrete activities. Faced with a certain ambiguity regarding their respective roles in these two phases, respondents may be inclined to select the joint category. Finally, it is possible that social desirability accounts for some of the movement toward the syncratic region when respondents were asked who made the final decision.

Whatever the explanation is, our results clearly have practical implications for those involved in consumer behavior studies. For example, let us develop some issues related to communication. The mere classification of a decision into one of the four types of influence (see Figure 1), already suggests the need for various communication strategies. When a decision is either husband or wife dominant, messages have to be designed in reference to a particular spouse. In the case of a syncratic decision, the message has to be tailored for the couple as an entity showing, for example, group decisions and activities, or the way in which the purchase of a particular brand or service can resolve certain decision conflicts within the family. What is often overlooked is that for decisions in or near the autonomic range a different strategy is required. Remember that decisions in this area are *within families* most often wife dominant or husband dominant. Thus, what might appear to be one audience to a communicator in terms of the relative influence of husbands and wives, is in reality two audiences. So, in the case of advertising for alcoholic beverages, it will be more justifiable to develop two campaigns—one stressing husband-oriented appeals and the other wife-oriented apeals—rather than to employ one campaign that tries to "mix" the two. The latter campaign will be inappropriate, in the case of alcohol, for 75 percent of the decision units.

More subtle implications stem from the changes in role specialization which were observed throughout the decision process. Again in terms of the message content, we would argue that the most common approach in communication strategy is to assume that an individual moves through several steps leading to action. While our analysis has shown that this model may be appropriate for decisions always in the regions of wife dominance and husband dominance (only 7 of the 25 decisions in this study), it cannot be generalized without modifications to the other regions. What is perhaps more interesting than trying to adapt an individual-based model to a group situation, is to model directly group-based phenomena in decision-making such as bargaining, coercion, persuasion, or problem-solving.

Implications for the timing of messages require additional information about the length of the decision span from problem recognition to final decision. If this span were for most family decisions a question of hours or days, our results would have less meaning since so little opportunity for role differentiation would exist. In fact, however, the decision span, reported by both husbands and wives is in terms of months for 12 of the 25 decisions.[5] In light of this time opportunity, consider, for example, any organization that wants to encourage families to take winter vacations and is aware that the average decision span lasts four months. With the information contained in Figures 2 and 3, a "joint" campaign would be appropriate during September stressing the idea of taking a vacation rather than consuming other forms of leisure, followed by "individual" campaigns (directed to husbands and wives separately) during October which describe alternative vacation plans, and finally, a "joint" campaign during November and December which tries to convince couples that "now is the time to make the final decision."

Level of Role Consensus

The analysis of role consensus revealed a high level of agreement in comparing responses of husbands and wives in the aggregate. In contrast, the level of consensus within families, although higher than chance, was nevertheless lower than one might assume if comparing husbands' and wives' responses as groups. Differences in the level of consensus for specific decisions seemed to be related to the distribution of responses across

categories as well as a systematic bias toward "vanity."

The methodological implications of these findings for researchers who want to collect data about household economic behavior relate to both interviewing and question construction. Depending upon the objectives and budget of a research project, the use of either husband or wife would be appropriate if the analysis was limited to gross descriptions of marital decision roles. As soon as the researcher tries to explain differences in role structure among families, however, the level of consensus within families becomes critical. For example, in terms of the decisions showing the highest level of consensus (household cleaning products), 12 percent of the families would be classified as having a different role structure depending upon whether the husband or wife had been interviewed. *Forty-three percent* of the families would be classified differently in the case of the two decisions (husband's clothes and household appliances) with the lowest level of consensus.

Our analysis of role consensus once again has implications for the content of communication. We earlier described that intrafamily consensus was lowest for those decisions having the greatest variance in roles. This suggests the need to distinguish between families with high and low consensus even if the overall distribution of relative influence is the same. To illustrate, consider a decision for which families are equally divided into husband dominant and syncratic types. If both spouses within all families agree about this role structure, messages should reach their targets even if the initial recipient is not the appropriate decision unit. Either the husband or wife will be likely to pass on the information received to the other person since a particular role structure is mutually accepted. If, on the other hand, couples disagree internally as to whether a decision is husband dominant or joint, messages are likely to be diverted from their targets.

---

[5]These include in order of decreasing length of the decision process: housing, living room furniture, car, TV/stereo, children's school, life insurance, family vacation, housing upkeep, household appliances, forms of savings, other insurance, and saving objectives. These results are from data included in another part of the same data bank (see Rigaux, in process).

In conclusion, these two major findings suggest that marital roles are differentiated according to various phases in the decision process, as well as to consumption categories. Recalling that earlier research has shown role differences by product characteristics, it would seem that a fuller understanding of household economic behavior will require data in which these three bases of role differentiation can be studied simultaneously.

REFERENCES

Bales, R. F., and Strodtbeck, F. L. (October, 1951), "Phases in Group Problem-Solving," *Journal of Abnormal and Social Psychology,* 46, 485–95.

Blood, R. O., Jr. and Wolfe, D. M. (1960), *Husbands and Wives, The Dynamics of Married Living,* Glencoe, Ill.: The Free Press of Glencoe.

Brim, O.; Glass, D. C.; and Lavin, D. E., and Goodman, N. (1962), *Personality and Decision Processes,* Stanford, Calif.: Stanford University Press.

Burgess, E. W., and Locke, H. J. (1960), *The Family,* New York: American Book Company.

Davis, H. L. (May, 1970), "Dimensions of Marital Roles in Consumer Decision-Making," *Journal of Marketing Research,* 7, 168–77.

Davis, H. L. (August, 1971), "Measurement of Husband-Wife Influence in Consumer Purchase Decisions," *Journal of Marketing Research,* 7, 305–12.

———(1972), "Determinants of Marital Roles in a Consumer Purchase Decision," unpublished paper, Brussels: European Institute for Advanced Studies in Management.

Dewey, J. (1910), *How We Think,* New York: D. C. Heath and Co.

Engel, J. F.; Kollat, D. T.; and Blackwell, R. D. (1973), *Consumer Behavior,* 2nd ed. New York: Holt, Rinehart and Winston, Inc.

Ferber, R. (December, 1954), "The Role of Planning in Consumer Purchases of Durable Goods," *American Economic Review,* 44, 854–74.

Frank, R. E.; Massy, W. F.; and Wind, Y. (1972), *Market Segmentation,* Englewood Cliffs, N. J.: Prentice-Hall, Inc.

Granbois, D. H., and Willett, R. P. (February, 1970), "Equivalence of Family Role Measures Based on Husband and Wife Data," *Journal of Marriage and the Family,* 32, 68–72.

Gredal, K. (1966), "Purchasing Behavior of Households," in M. Kjaer-Hansen, ed., *Readings in the Danish Theory of Marketing,* Amsterdam: North-Holland.

Hempel, D. J. (1972), "A Cross-Cultural Analysis of Husband-Wife Roles in House Purchase Decisions," in M. Venkatesan, ed., *Proceedings,* Association for Consumer Research, Chicago: ACR.

Herbst, P. G. (February, 1952), "The Measurement of Family Relationships," *Human Relations,* 5, 3–35.

Houthakker, H. S. (1961), "An Economist's Approach to the Study of Spending," in N. N. Foote, ed., *Household Decision-Making,* Consumer Behavior Series, Vol. 4, New York: New York University Press.

Jaffe, L. J., and Senft, H. (1966), "The Roles of Husbands and Wives in Purchasing Decisions," in L. Adler and I. Crespi, eds., *Attitude Research at Sea,* Chicago: American Marketing Association.

Kelley, H. H. and Thibaut, J. W. (1969), "Group Problem Solving," in G. Lindzey and E. Aronson, eds., *The Handbook of Social Psychology,* Vol. 4, 2nd ed., Reading, Mass.: Addison-Wesley Publishing Co.

Kenkel, W. F. (1961), "Family Interaction in Decision-Making on Spending," in N. N. Foote, ed., *Household Decision-Making,* Consumer Behavior Series, Vol. 4, New York: New York University Press.

Parsons, T., and Bales, R. F. (1955), *Family Socialization and Interaction Process,* Glencoe, Ill.: The Free Press.

Rigaux, B., et al. (1972), "Enquête sur la prise de décisions économiques au sein des menages: document de synthèse," CESAM Working Paper 21-0572, Université Catholique de Louvain.

———, "La prise de décisions économiques au sein de la famille." Ph.D. dissertation in process, Université Catholique de Louvain.

Scanzoni, J. (Fall, 1965), "A Note on the Sufficiency of Wife Responses in Family Research," *Pacific Sociological Review,* 8, 109–15.

Sharp, H., and Mott, P. (October, 1956), "Consumer

Decisions in the Metropolitan Family,'' *Journal of Marketing,* 21, 149–56.

Silverman, W., and Hill, R. (May, 1967), ''Task Allocation in Marriage in the United States and Belgium,'' *Journal of Marriage and the Family,* 29, 353–59.

Starch, D. and staff (1958), ''Male vs. Female: Influence on the Purchase of Selected Products as Revealed by an Exploratory Depth Interview Study with Husbands and Wives,'' New York: Fawcett Publications.

Time Inc. (1967), ''Family Decision-Making,'' Research Report 1428.

Wilkening, E. A., and Morrison, D. E. (August, 1963), ''A Comparison of Husband and Wife Responses Concerning Who Makes Farm and Home Decisions,'' *Marriage and Family Living,* 25, 349–51.

Wolfe, D. M. (1959), ''Power and Authority in the Family,'' in D. Cartwright, *Studies in Social Power,* Ann Arbor: University of Michigan Press.

Wolgast, E. H. (October, 1958), ''Do Husbands or Wives Make The Purchasing Decisions?'' *Journal of Marketing,* 23, pp. 151–58.

GIFT DECISIONS BY KIDS AND PARENTS

ANDRE CARON
AND
SCOTT WARD

Consumer groups, government officials, and marketers have debated the possibly deleterious effects of television advertising on pre-teenage children. While the issues are complex, perhaps the single fact with which all the involved parties can agree is that research is needed as a basis for valid and effective government or industry regulation.

One major issue concerns children's ability to process information in television advertising. Critics imply that a wide range of techniques in television commercials render children unable to effectively process information—that is, to fairly evaluate information about products and brands and to make decisions based on this information. Younger children, and perhaps especially children from disadvantaged family backgrounds, are thought to be particularly limited in their information-processing abilities and, consequently, may be more "vulnerable" to advertising's persuasive influences.

Defenders of advertising to children, on the other hand, imply that even if children make poor consumer choices due to their limited ability to process information in advertising, such consequences are rarely lasting. They may even be beneficial, since children will be less likely to repeat the error.

A related issue concerns the effects of television advertising on family life—for example, does television advertising cause children to influence their parents to buy various products for them? And are some families (especially low-income families) less able to cope effectively with these influence attempts than other kinds of families?

Previous research has shown that the frequency of children's in-family purchase influence attempts varies with the child's age and with the particular product. Children are more likely to influence their parents to purchase products which are frequently consumed by them (e.g., breakfast cereal) and which are of particular interest to them (e.g., toys for younger children, records for older children). The frequency of children's purchase influence at-

Source: Andre Caron and Scott Ward, "Gift Decisions by Kids and Parents," *Journal of Advertising Research,* Vol. 15, August, 1975, pp. 15–20.

tempts generally decreases among older children, but parental acceding to such attempts increases with age. A modest correlation (.18, p < .05) has been found between frequency of children's asking for products and patterns of intra-family conflict (Ward and Wackman, 1972).

It is not possible to isolate effectively the singular influence of television advertising on children's attempts to influence parental purchasing, since the products children most want are those which are most advertised. However, it is possible to examine differences in these patterns of intra-family influence among families in different social classes—a question not addressed in previous research.

PILOT STUDY

This reports initial analyses of an extensive research project. The study examines certain aspects of the relative influences of mass media and interpersonal sources on children's product desires and parental decision-making regarding their children's product desires. In the study, these desires were explored in the setting of children expressing their wants for Christmas gifts, expressed to mothers or in a letter to Santa. An attempt was made to trace children's desires for Christmas gifts from the initial idea to influencing parents to purchase the product, to parental responses—initial verbal response (e.g., "yes," "no," "maybe") and ultimate behavioral response (buying or not).

The various relationships investigated in the overall study are displayed in Figure 1.

METHODOLOGY

Data were gathered from a total of 84 mother-child pairs from an initial random sample of third graders (n = 54) and fifth graders (n = 52) in Montreal. Samples were drawn from two different socioeconomic areas: middle-class (average family income $9,000) and upper-class (average family income $14,500). Essentially we were interested in understanding where children get ideas for things they request, what kinds of things they request, and what kind of reception their request is likely to get inside the family.

The procedures were as follows: Approximately four weeks before Christmas, children were asked to write a letter to Santa, telling him what they wanted for Christmas. Information sources were ascertained by asking children to tell where they got the idea for each gift they requested of Santa.

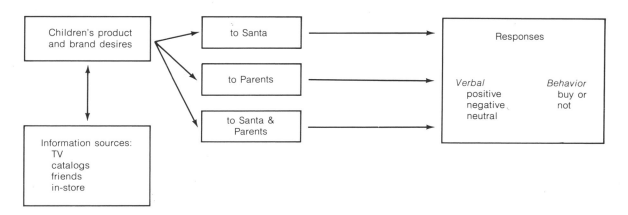

Figure 1   Model of Relationships Investigated in Study

Meanwhile, mothers were trained to unobtrusively record each Christmas gift request during a seven-day period and to note their verbal response (if any) to the child. Also during this period we conducted a content analysis of television commercials directed to children in these age groups. Following the Christmas vacation, we ascertained the specific gifts which children received.

FINDINGS

Mothers registered a total of 360 requests during the seven-day period. From letters to Santa written outside the home, we tabulated requests made exclusively to Santa (total requests = 677). By comparing letters to Santa with requests to mothers, we found 117 common requests made both to mothers and to Santa.

Children requested much the same kinds of items (to Santa, parents, or both) regardless of age or social class. Most requested were non-interactive toys (23 per cent of all requests). These are toys such as dolls, models, etc., which children normally play with alone, or at least do not require others in order to enjoy them. Second most requested were sports items (18 per cent), followed by competition toys (e.g., slot-racing sets, 14 per cent) and clothing (13 per cent).

Regarding information sources about the gifts requested, children most often cited television as the source of gift ideas, closely followed by friends (Table 1). Minor variations to these patterns were observed by social class and by sex, but older children were considerably more likely to cite television as the idea source and considerably less likely to cite friends than were younger children. Older children were also more likely to cite catalogs. These findings suggested that older children have learned to use a variety of mass media as sources of product ideas. This age-related finding was similar to patterns found for kindergarten, third, and fifth grade children when they were asked how they would find out about new products (Ward and Wackman, 1973).

Gift Requests

Data in Table 2 show that younger children asked for more gifts than older children; however, their

Table 1   Sources of gift ideas*

| Information Source | Total | Grade | | Middle-class | Upper-class | Sex | |
		3	5			M	F
Television	27%	23%	31%	26%	27%	28%	25%
Catalog	19	14	24	17	21	22	15
Store	22	21	22	24	18	15	29
Friends	26	34	17	27	24	27	24
Other	7	8	6	6	10	8	7
Total	100%	100%	100%	100%	100%	100%	100%
n =	(320)	(172)	(148)	(186)	(134)	(180)	(140)

*Cell entries are percentages of all requests cited in letter to Santa, in response to the question: "Where did you get the idea that you wanted (*each item requested*)?"

Table 2 Summary of mean number of gift requests, receipts, and proportion of requests to parents, and/or Santa, by social class and grade

	Middle-class n = 45	Upper-class n = 39	Grade 3	Grade 5
Total requests (mean)	8.7	7.3	8.5	7.5
Gifts received (mean)	5.7	4.7	5.0	5.5
Requested (Santa or Parent) and received (mean)	2.7	2.5	2.6	2.6
Received without requesting (mean)	3.0	2.2	2.4	2.9
% Requests to Parents only	32%	41%	38%	34%
% Requests to Santa only	54	37	48	45
% Requests to Santa and Parents	14	22	14	21

conversion rate (i.e., receiving specifically-requested gifts) was not as high as that for older children. More important were the social class differences. Middle-class children requested more gifts than upper-class children, and they directed more requests to Santa only than did upper-class children. Middle-class children in the sample fantasized more than upper-class children, or were perhaps more intimidated at the prospect of directing purchase influence attempts at their parents; they preferred to cast their lot with Santa instead. On the other hand, they received more gifts, requested or not, although the conversion rate of requests to gifts was very similar in both economic groups (all proportions considered).

Types of Gift Requests

Data in Table 3 show significant differences in the type of gift requested by children of different social class groups. Middle-class children prefer non-interactive toys, followed by sport items; upper-class children request more competition games, toys, clothing, and sport items. Our data also showed significant age differences ($p < .008$) with younger children requesting overall more non-interactive toys (27 per cent), and older children

preferring more sport items (20.7 per cent). Sex differences were not found to be significant.

Parents' Responses to Requests

When children asked for specific items as Christmas gifts, parents most often responded verbally in neutral terms (e.g., "we'll see"). This finding was reasonably consistent, regardless of the specific item asked for, although requests for clothing, books, and records were somewhat more likely to elicit positive verbal responses. Data in Table 4 show few age differences, although middle-class parents were slightly more likely to respond negatively than were upper-class parents. Differences in the total number of requests (middle-class requesting more) might be explained by the fact that upper-class children received more positive responses and less negative ones.

Total Gifts Received Whether or Not Requested by the Child

In terms of gifts received, data in Table 5 indicate that both groups (middle- and upper-class) receive mostly what they requested—that is, non-interactive toys for the middle-class children and

Table 3   Total requests by type of gift and by social class

Types of items	% Middle-class	n =	% Upper-class	n =
Non-interactive Toys	27.4	(107)	15.7	(45)
Creative Games/Toys	10.5	(41)	9.4	(27)
Competition Games/Toys	10.2	(40)	18.5	(53)
Sport Item	18.9	(74)	17.5	(50)
Clothing	10.0	(39)	17.5	(50)
Books & Records	7.4	(29)	9.4	(27)
Others	15.6	(61)	11.9	(34)
Total	100.0	(391)	100.0	(286)

$X^2 = 28.13$ d.f. = 6, $p < .001$

competition games/toys for the upper-class children. Percentages of items requested are repeated from Table 3 to compare kinds of gifts received and frequency of requests for each gift item. Significant differences for age ($p < .01$) show younger children received mostly non-interactive toys (23 per cent) and competition games/toys (15.4 per cent), while older children receive more creative games/toys (21 per cent) and clothing (17 per cent). Not unexpectedly, girls received different items than did boys; clothing (17.4 per cent) and "other" (i.e., jewelry, musical instruments, etc.) were most likely to be given to girls; non-interactive toys (19 per cent) and competition

games/toys (17.1 per cent) were received in the most part by boys. Further data analysis indicates that approximately 50 per cent of the gifts received had not been explicitly requested either in the letter to Santa Claus or to the parents. The majority of these unsolicited gifts were of the following nature: creative games/toys (22.9 per cent), competition games (17 per cent), others (16.6 per cent), and clothing (14.8 per cent). No significant differences were found for social class or for age; differences for sex ($p < .004$) were similar to those previously indicated.

Table 4   Parents' verbal responses to children's overt gift requests

	Grade		Social class	
	3	5	Middle	Upper
Positive	32%	32%	29	35%
Negative	19	21	22	18
Neutral	48	47	48	47
	100%	100%	100%	100%
n =	(182)	(160)	(170)	(172)
	X^2 = n.s.		X^2 = n.s.	

Fulfillment of Gift Requests

Data in Table 6 show the percentage of requests which were and were not fulfilled. For example, 28 per cent of middle-class children's requests were fulfilled (i.e., the specific gift requested was received); thus, 72 per cent were not. The percentage of specific gift requests that were received is somewhat higher for upper-class children. For both groups of children, requests made to both Santa and parents ("common requests" in Table 6) were most likely to be fulfilled. This finding probably reflects the intensity of children's desires. That is, there may have been qualitative differences in the requests of children, and the more

Table 5 Total gifts requested and total received (requested or not)* by type of gift and by social class

	Middle [n = 45]				Upper [n = 39]			
	Requested		Received requested or not		Requested		Received requested or not	
Types of Items	%	n	%	n	%	n	%	n
Non-interactive Toys	27.4	(107)	21.5	(55)	15.7	(45)	11.4	(21)
Creative Games/Toys	10.5	(41)	18.4	(47)	9.4	(27)	15.3	(28)
Competition Games/Toys	10.2	(40)	10.5	(27)	18.5	(53)	22.3	(41)
Sports Items	18.9	(74)	11.7	(30)	17.5	(50)	13.0	(24)
Clothing	10.0	(39)	14.1	(36)	17.5	(50)	15.8	(29)
Books & Records	7.4	(29)	6.6	(17)	9.4	(27)	9.2	(17)
Other	15.6	(61)	17.2	(44)	11.9	(34)	13.0	(24)
Total	100	(391)	100	(256)	100	(286)	100	(184)

*$X^2 = 18.93$ d.f. = 6   p = < .0043

intense desires may have been reflected in the child's asking both Santa and his parents for the particular item.

Data in Table 7 examine patterns of parental yielding to children's purchase influence attempts by item requested and by social class. Middle-class families are shown to be somewhat more likely to yield to requests for non-interactive toys; however, upper-class parents are more likely to yield to requests for sports items, clothing, books, and records, and slightly more likely to yield to requests for creative games. Again, the context of these data should be kept in mind: while middle-class children made more requests, they were more likely to get "neutral" verbal reactions from their parents and slightly less likely to get positive reactions when compared to upper-class children. In any case, the proportion yielding is quite similar for the two social class groups.

CONCLUSION

Interpretations of these data are highly speculative, as the sample was small. However, this study could be a prototype for larger-scale work, which would permit more definitive conclusions about the relative influences of mass media advertising on children and how children's desires for advertised products are handled in the family environment.

Table 6 Percentage of gift requests fulfilled by parents, by recipients of gift request, social class, and grade

Recipients of gift request	Social class		Grade	
	Middle	Upper	3	5
Parents Only	28%*	34%	33%	30%
Common	51	52	53	50
Santa Only	27	23	21	32
Total	31	34	30	35
N =	(120)	(97)	(110)	(107)

*Should be read: "Among middle-class children, 28% of specific gift requests made to parents were fulfilled—the specifically requested item was received."

Table 7   Purchase requests and parental acceding by gift items and social class

Items	Middle Class						Upper Class				
	Asked		Asked and received		% Acceding		Asked		Asked and received		% Acceding
	%	n	%	n		%	n	%	n	
Non-Interactive Toys	27.4*	107	33.3	40	37.3	15.7	45	11.3	11	24.4
Creative Games/ Toys	10.5	41	11.7	14	34.1	9.4	27	10.3	10	37.0
Competition Games/Toys	10.2	40	9.2	11	27.5	12.5	63	19.6	19	30.2
Sports Items	18.9	74	15.0	18	24.3	17.5	50	16.5	16	32.0
Clothing	10.0	39	10.8	13	33.3	17.5	50	19.6	19	38.0
Books & Records	7.4	29	5.0	6	20.7	9.4	27	9.3	9	33.3
Others	15.6	61	15.0	18	29.5	11.9	34	13.4	13	38.2
Total	100.0	391	100.0	120	30.6	100.0	286	100.0	97	33.9

*To be read: "Of all gifts children requested, 27.4% of requests were for non-interactive toys. Of all gift requests which were fulfilled, 33.3% were requests for non-interactive toys. Of all requests for non-interactive toys, parents acceded 37.3% of the time."

The data do suggest that the family environment is indeed a mediator of television advertising's effects. In fact, the differences in children's product desires and parents' patterns of responding to requests for particular types of toys may reflect fundamental value orientations of parents and children. Middle-class children exhibited less interest in competition toys than did upper-class children; parents of upper-class children were more likely to buy competition toys for their children. While care must be taken in interpreting the data on this point, it seems reasonable to conclude that both middle- and upper-class children were exposed to roughly the same level of advertising for competition games/toys. However, the two groups of children were apparently differentially interested in receiving them, perhaps reflecting dif-

ferent value orientations already formed by third and fifth grade.

The fact that parents mediate gift requests, regardless of social class, is seen in the data. For example, middle-class parents are less likely to respond to requests for sporting goods than are parents of upper-class children. This may reflect high cost, or it may reflect the fact that middle-class children may already possess many sporting goods items. In any case, middle- and upper-class parents selectively yield to purchase requests. Also reflective of different family environments are the different numbers of requests. Middle-class children did indeed make more gift requests than upper-class children. A number of explanations could be advanced for this finding—e.g., norms in upper-class homes mediate against frequent asking for products; upper-class children receive more positive responses to their requests, so the need to repeat them is not great.

A final, highly suggestive finding in the study is that children cite a variety of sources for gift (product) ideas. It is particularly interesting to note that fifth grade children are more likely to cite television as a source of gift ideas than are third grade children. This finding is consistent with larger scale research (Ward and Wackman, 1973), and it suggests that older children learn to use television as a source of product information. Younger children are more bound to their perceptual environment, and are more likely to find out about products by actually seeing them in stores.

Some further analyses will be done on these data in an effort to relate content of commercials—including stylistic variables—and patterns of interpersonal relationships, as determined by sociometric data, to children's product desires and subsequent parental behavior.

Aside from the small sample sizes, an obviously limiting factor is that the differences between our age and social class groupings are not large. The income variations are not that great, and neither are the age differences. High proportions of third and fifth graders are probably in the concrete operational stage of development, although at different ends of the developmental continuum. Consequently, our age-related differences are not great.

REFERENCES

Ward, Scott, and Wackman, D. (August, 1972), "Children's Purchase Influence Attempts and Parental Yielding," *Journal of Marketing Research,* 9, 316–19.

Ward, Scott, and Wackman, D. (1973), "Effects of Television Advertising on Consumer Socialization," Marketing Science Institute Research Report, Cambridge, Mass.

EXPLORING ENVIRONMENTAL INFLUENCES IN ORGANIZATIONAL BUYING

KJELL GRØNHAUG

Source: Kjell Grønhaug, "Exploring Environmental Influences in Organizational Buying," *Journal of Marketing Research,* Vol. 13, August, 1976, pp. 225–229.

INTRODUCTION

To understand and predict organizational behavior in buying situations, several authors have stressed the importance of including variables related to the organization and its environment. However, review of the literature reveals with few exceptions (Grønhaug, 1975a; Grønhaug, 1975b; Hakansson, 1975) little empirical support for the assumed importance of such variables in organizational buying.

Frame of Reference

Today it is common to view the organization as an open system (for overview see Azumi and Hage, 1972) continuously interacting with its unstable environment (Emery and Trist, 1965; Terreberry, 1962). Most organizations must produce output, which must be exchanged (Levine and White, 1961) in order to get input for continued survival (Thompson, 1967). No doubt, however, the degree of output dependence varies across organizations. For the sake of simplicity, the following dichotomy is introduced: (1) product *dependent* versus (2) product *in*dependent organizations.

The first type are organizations for which survival mainly depends on the exchange of output. Business organizations operating in competitive markets are an example. For other organizations, where an important part of the income (budget) is distributed by regulatory groups, the output-income relationship is less clear. Of course, such organizations also are dependent on output, not at least in order to get support from the regulatory group(s)! However, it seems reasonable to assume that the two types of organization are apt to stress different parts of the environment, so that product dependent more than product independent organizations will emphasize markets rather than a regulatory group(s). Because of the link between input (i.e. purchase) and output, and the efforts directed toward the market(s) (Kotler and Levy, 1973), perceived variations in environmental influences may have an impact on how the two types of organizations perform activities to cope with their buying problems. Perceived variations in environmental influences may result in different ways of organizing the purchasing activities (Galbraith, 1974), besides influencing purchase goals and decision strategies employed (Emery and Trist, 1965).

THE STUDY

The organizational buying situation studied involved the decision to purchase a minicomputer by a variety of both business and nonbusiness organizations, classified as product dependent and product independent organizations, respectively.

A variety of organizational characteristics were described and data on how the various organizations handled a complex buying situation (purchase of a minicomputer) were gathered. The reasons for this data collection strategy were to ensure a base for comparison and to map a buying situation sufficiently complex that search and various members of the organizations might be involved (Robinson, et al., 1967).

A list of last year's buyers was obtained from a company holding a considerable market share. Two separate samples were used, one for the pilot study and one for the main study.

Pilot Study
From the list of buyers, the 19 local buyers in Bergen, the second largest town in Norway, were considered to constitute a subsample. All 19 buyers were contacted and 15 agreed to participate. In a "snowball" approach, data about various internal and external conditions (including organizational structure, buying influences, use of information, etc.) were gathered by means of semistructured personal interviews. It was found to be very easy to trace the persons involved in the buying process. Furthermore, information from various members of the organization showed consistency, which indicated face validity of the observations. In previous studies, however, difficulties in tracing the persons involved in the buying process and in assessing their influence have been

stressed (Harding, 1966; Walsh, 1961). This apparent inconsistency with previous research is probably due to the fact that here an *actual* buying decision was mapped whereas in most previous studies, *relative* influence was assessed.

Main Study
A questionnaire containing an instruction was mailed to the 160 (179 minus 19) buyers not previously contacted. One followup letter was sent, and "motivating" telephone calls were made. Usable answers were received from 48 organizations, a response rate of 30%. No differences were found between early and late respondents. Furthermore, comparison of the results from the pilot study and the main study showed no differences.

The variables, their measurements, and assumptions about scales are reported in Appendix A. Twenty organizations were classified as product dependent and 28 as product independent. Furthermore, 21 of the purchases were classified as "new task" and 27 as "modified rebuy." Ordinary product-moment correlations, partial correlations, and tests of differences were used to analyze the data. Also cross-tabulations performed in the bivariate analysis yielded approximately the same results as the zero-ordered correlation coefficients (not reported here). The nominal scaled variable "type of organization" was transformed into two dummy variables (product dependent and product independent organizations), each assigned the values 0, 1 and treated as a special case of interval scaled variable (Blalock, 1970, p. 499). Other nominal scaled variables also were transformed in this way. Furthermore, because of the explorative nature of the research, all tests reported are two-tailed.

FINDINGS

Organizational Characteristics
The organizations studied were considerably varied in size, ranging from less than 20 to more than 500 employees. Comparison of the two types of organization by structural characteristics such as

number of departments, number of levels, relative portion of managers, education of top manager, and size showed no significant differences.

However, when environmental variables were considered, differences were found in perceived competition ($r = .43$, $p < .001$) and perceived organizational slack ($r = -.31$, $p < .10$).[1] These results indicate that product dependent organizations are more apt to perceive competition than are product independent organizations. Also, product dependent organizations perceive *fewer* budgetary limitations than do their independent counterparts (the negative sign of the correlation coefficient is due to the coding: $1 =$ budgetary limitations, $0 =$ budgetary limitations not perceived). A possible explanation for this result may be that product dependent organizations either possess or perceive greater possibilities to influence relevant environmental elements than do product independent organizations.

The use of a separate department for purchasing was found to correlate positively with organizational size ($r = .53$, $p < .001$). However (also controlling for size), a positive correlation was found between product dependent organization and the use of a separate purchasing department ($r = .31$, $p < .03$). Furthermore, in organizations without a purchasing department, product dependent more than product independent organizations were found to have a "specialist" in charge of this activity ($r = .32$, $p < .03$). These findings demonstrate a relationship between organizational size and departmentalization. The results also indicate that purchasing is more frequent, and is connected with less task uncertainty (Tyler, 1973), in product dependent than in product independent organizations.

Organizational Decision Making

In performance of the buying activities, several roles are played. Furthermore, if one perceives the organization as a hierarchical structure, the per-

sons playing the various roles may hold different positions in this structure. Distinguishing between various organizational *levels* yielded the findings shown in Table 1.

From the table it is evident that top and middle management personnel primarily play the key roles in this context and, as is often assumed, that several persons may be involved in organizational buying. Comparisons between product dependent and product independent organizations with regard to distributions of roles by organizational levels showed *no* differences.[2]

Buying Motives

Examination of the underlying buying motives yielded the results shown in Table 2.

Product dependent more than product independent organizations stress internal need ($p < .10$) and new products on the market (n.s.), whereas product independent more than product dependent organizations are apt to stress support from regulatory authorities. In other words, the results stress differences in conception of environmental influences for the two types of organizations.

Search

The buyer may make use of a variety of information sources. It was found that, before the purchase,

    67% contacted more than one supplier,
    67% solicited bids,
    85% read brochures,
    46% read advertisements, and
    58% asked other users for advice.

On the average each organization made use of 3.2 of the foregoing sources, a result which indicates intensive search in the buying situation investigated.

Furthermore, decreasing prepurchase activities were demonstrated for "modified rebuy" in com-

---

[1] The results reported are for product dependent organizations. The same numerical results, but with opposite signs, emerged for product independent organizations.

[2] Both organizational size and buyclass may influence these results. However, almost no differences were found between the two types of organization with regard to these variables.

Table 1 Overlap between organizational positions and roles as initiator, decision-maker, and influencer

Organizational level	Role		
	Initiator	Decider	Influencer
Top	35.4%	50.0%	16.7%
Top + middle	—	27.1	—
Middle	52.1	12.5	18.8
Other	—	—	29.2
No answer	12.5	10.4	35.4[a]
Total	100%	100%	100%
n =	(48)	(48)	(48)

[a]No other influence 25.8%, no answer 10.4%.

parison with "new task" buying situations (the following results are for "modified rebuy"):

contact with suppliers ($r = -.09$, n.s.),
bids solicited ($r = -.18$, n.s.),
brochures ($r = -.13$, n.s.),
advertisements ($r = -.20$, $p < .10$), and
advice seeking ($r = -.23$, $p < .10$).

These results indicate that organizational learning may take place (Cyert and March, 1963), and are in accordance with both previous hypotheses (Howard and Sheth, 1969) and findings (Hakansson, 1975).

Comparison of the use of various sources of

Table 2 Buying motives in product dependent and product independent organizations

Buying motive	Organization		
	Product dependent	Product independent	Total
Received money from/budgets accepted by regulatory groups	10.0%	28.6%	20.8%
Internal need	70.0	46.4	56.3
New product	20.0	10.7	14.6
n =	(20)	(28)	(48)

information in the two types of organizations gave the results in Table 3. Even though the correlations all are modest, an interesting *pattern* emerges. Product dependent more than product independent organizations solicit bids, read brochures, and study advertisements, whereas product independent more than product dependent organizations are apt to contact suppliers and to seek advice from other organizations that previously bought such a product. A closer look at the various sources used gives the impression that product dependent more than product independent organizations make use of "formalized" sources of information. This pattern may be due partly to differences in purchasing professionalization, but perhaps also to variations in the competitive environment influencing the perceived social restrictions.

Buying Criteria and Strategies

When making a buying decision, the buyer may use various criteria in pursuing his buying goal(s). Product dependent more than product independent organizations used service as a criterion ($r = .20$, $p < .10$), whereas a weak negative correlation was found for price deductions ($r = -.04$, n.s.). These results probably are due to differences in organizational perception (March and Olsen,

Table 3 Use of various sources of information in product dependent organizations

Variable	r^a	s.l.
Contact with suppliers	−.21	$p < .10$
Bids solicited	.17	n.s.
Brochures	.11	n.s.
Advertisements	.09	n.s.
Advice seeking from previous buyers	−.11	n.s.

[a]Second-ordered partial correlations controlled for buyclass and organizational size. Because of modest overlap between type of organization and buyclass, and organizational size (cfr. footnote 2), only very small numerical differences between the zero-ordered and the second-ordered partial correlations were observed (cfr. Emery and Trist, 1965).

Appendix A Variables, operational definitions, and assumption about scales

Variable	Operational definition	Scale
1. *Type of organization*	Business and nonbusiness classified as product dependent and product independent organizations.	Nominal
2. *Structure*		
Size	"How many persons are employed in this organization?"	Ratio
Relative portion of managers	Based on listing and counting of management, and computing managers/employees.	Ratio
Number of departments	Based on listing and counting the number of	Ratio
Number of levels	a. departments.	Ratio
Education of top man	b. levels.	Ratio
	Requested by direct question. Converted into years of education (after public school).	
3. *Environment*		
Competition	Based on a description of perceived competitors, i.e. organizations offering approximately the same output on the market.	Nominal
Perceived slack	Based on determining the perceived scarcity in budgets.	Nominal
4. *Purchasing*		
Purchasing department	"Does the organization have a purchasing department?"	Nominal
"Purchasing specialist"	"Does the same person(s) usually take care of purchasing in this organization?"	Nominal
5. *The buying center*		
Initiator	"Who (position/title) initiated this purchase?"	Nominal
Decision-maker	"Who (title/position) took part in the buying process?" "Who made the final decision?"	Nominal
6. *The purchase*		
Buying motive	"What initiated/caused this purchase?"	Nominal
Buyclass	"Was this type of product bought for the first time?" If "yes" the past history was mapped. (No previous purchase = new task; previous purchase = modified rebuy.)	Nominal
Perceived risk		
Importance	"How important was it to you to make the best purchase?" (Very important,. . .)	Interval
Uncertainty	"How certain would you be that a computer in the same price range not previously on the market would be as good as the one you bought?" (Very certain,. . .)	Interval
Venturesomeness	"Would you buy such a computer?"	Nominal
Buying goals	"What was assessed in the purchase?" (Probe: quality, guarantees, price deduction, relationship with supplier,. . .)	Nominal
Information		
Suppliers	"Did you contact supplier other than the one that was chosen?" If yes, "Who?"	Nominal/ratio
Bids	"Did you solicit bids?"	Nominal
Brochures	"Did you study brochures?"	Nominal
Advertisements	"Did you read advertisements?"	Nominal
Advice seeking	"Did you contact other users to get advice?"	Nominal

1975). Because of the perceived weaker link between output and income as well as more restricted resources in product independent organizations, these seem to be more apt than their product dependent counterparts to focus on the procurement per se rather than the long-term consequences. Furthermore, though *no* differences in perceived risk as measured in terms of both perceived importance ($r = -.01$, n.s.) and hypothetical certainty ($r = -.05$, n.s.) were found between the two types of organizations, a *higher* degree of venturesomeness was demonstrated in product independent than in product dependent organizations ($r = -.26$, $p < .05$). This result to some degree may be due to less focus on long-term consequences related to the purchase in product independent than in product dependent organizations.

CONCLUSIONS

The taxonomy of product dependent versus product independent organizations was used as a basis for classification and comparisons. The results to some extent demonstrate differences in buying behavior due to variations in environmental influences. However, a more detailed mapping of the environment, taking into account such factors as organization task environment and market power, would yield more precise descriptions of variations in buying behavior.

A very natural question is, "What are the managerial implications—if any?" The "fixed" structure for handling purchase activities in product dependent companies indicates that the identification of buying influences and responsibilities is easier for a marketer approaching a product dependent buyer. However, because of the higher degree of professionalization in purchasing in such companies, other requirements are imposed on the marketer confronted with a product dependent buyer. Furthermore, variations in buying motives, goals pursued, and information sources used should be of importance to the marketer tailoring his marketing strategies (Wind and Cardozo, 1974).

REFERENCES

Azumi, K., and Hage, J. (1972), *Organizational Systems,* Lexington: D.C. Heath and Company.

Blalock, H. M. (1970), *Social Statistics,* New York: McGraw-Hill Book Co.

Cyert, R. M., and March, J. G. (1963), *A Behavioral Theory of the Firm,* Englewood Cliffs, N.J.: Prentice-Hall, Inc.

Emery, F. E., and Trist, E. L. (1965), "The Causal Texture of Organizational Environment," *Human Relations,* 18, 21–32.

Galbraith, J. R. (May 1974), "Organization Design: An Information Processing View," *Interfaces,* 4, 28–36.

Grønhaug, K. (1975a), "Search Behavior in Organizational Buying," *Industrial Marketing Management,* 4, 15–23.

———(1975b), "Autonomous vs. Joint Decisions in Organizational Buying," *Industrial Marketing Management,* 4, 265–71.

Hakansson, H. (1975), "Studies in Industrial Purchasing with Specific Reference to Determinants of Communication Patterns," *Acta Universitatis,* 9.

Harding, M. (September 1966), "Who Really Makes the Purchasing Decision?" *Industrial Marketing,* 76–81.

Howard, J. A., and Sheth, J. N. (1969), *The Theory of Buyer Behavior,* New York: John Wiley and Sons, Inc.

Kotler, P., and Levy, S. (January 1973), "Buying is Marketing Too!" *Journal of Marketing,* 3, 54–59.

Levine, S., and White, P. E. (March 1961), "Exchange as a Conceptual Framework for the Study of Interorganizational Relationships," *Administrative Science Quarterly,* 5, 583–601.

March, J. G., and Olsen, J. P. (1975), "The Uncertainty of the Past: Organizational Learning under Ambiguity," *European Journal of Political Research,* 3, 145–71.

Robinson, P. J.; Faris, C. W.; and Wind, Y. (1967),

Industrial Buying and Creative Marketing, Boston: Allyn & Bacon, Inc.

Terreberry, S. (March 1962), "The Evolution of Organizational Environments," *Administrative Science Quarterly,* 12, 590–613.

Thompson, J. D. (1967), *Organizations in Action,* New York: McGraw-Hill Book Co., Inc.

Tyler, W. B. (September 1973), "Measuring Organizational Specialization: The Concept of Role Variety," *Administrative Science Quarterly,* 18, 383–92.

Walsh, C. H. (October, 1961), "Reaching Those 'Hidden' Buying Influences," *Industrial Marketing,* 164–70.

Wind, Y., and Cardozo, R., (March, 1974), "Industrial Market Segmentation," *Industrial Marketing Management,* 3, 153–64.

GROUPS AND NORMS IN CONSUMER BEHAVIOR

Consumers participate in numerous groups within the larger social systems to which they belong. The preceding section discussed two particular formal groups, the family and a firm or work group. Both of these latter groups are groups to which the consumer belongs. Such groups are called *affiliative groups*. Other groups to which consumers do not belong still influence their behavior because they would like to join these groups. These groups are called *aspiration groups*. There are still other groups consumers may not wish to join but which somehow influence their behavior because they want to show that they do *not* belong. These groups are called *dissociative groups*. All three types of groups are called *reference groups:* they are groups consumers may think about and hence may be influenced by when forming an attitude or behaving in a certain way. The reader will probably encounter these terms when studying consumer behavior and the terminology is introduced for this reason.

An illustration of these groups might be helpful. Consider a teenager choosing new clothing. Two important affiliative groups would be the teenager's family and immediate circle of friends. The family may influence what is purchased by controlling the amount of financial resources provided to the teenager. The friendship group may influence how much of the wardrobe is comprised of very informal leisure clothes as opposed to dressier items. The style of clothes displayed by an in-group in the teenager's school may also influence clothing selection. By choosing clothing compatible with the style displayed by this group to which the teenager doesn't belong (we'll assume), the teenager may feel the chances of acceptance by this group are increased. This in-group is an aspiration group. A dissociative group may be a group which is thought of negatively or positively, and membership in that group is not desired. The dress behavior of a disliked group may serve as clear clues to the teenager about what clothing behavior to avoid.

Consumers need not interact regularly with a group for it to be influential in their buying behavior. Nor is it necessary for face-to-face interaction to ever occur for a group to be influential. Examples include movie stars, leaders of a consumer advocate group, or a legislative subcommittee holding a hearing on food quality. There are many ways in which groups are influential regardless of their type (e.g., affiliative group versus dissociative) or the degree of interaction and face-to-face contact. Groups influence such phenomena as:

1. Product preferences,
2. Brand preferences,
3. Deliberate avoidance of products and brands,
4. The allocation of income across product categories,
5. Price sensitivity,
6. Store patronage,
7. Sensitivity and susceptibility to nonprice promotional activities such as advertising and cents-off coupons, and
8. How consumers process information.

It is one thing to know what kind of groups may influence consumers and what attitudes and behaviors can be influenced by social groups. It is another matter to know how and why groups influence consumers. In addressing this latter issue we shall consider only groups to which consumers belong. Individual consumers have goals which are often best achieved in collaboration with other people usually seeking the same goals or compatible goals. Individuals in the group reward a group member to the extent that the group member contributes toward the achievement of the collective goals of the group. Similarly, individuals are punished if they detract from the achievement of group goals.

Through the application of rewards and punishments, certain behaviors emerge that are important for achieving goals. These behaviors represent what the group as a whole believes are appropriate behaviors. Such collective evaluations of behavior in terms of what is appropriate are called *norms*. Some norms reflect the values and goals of the group. These are called *expressive norms*. A purchasing agent who is constantly seeking information about new technological developments by reading the relevant literature in his or her area and attending professional meetings and trade shows reflects the firm's goals of being a leader in the field and being up-to-date. The purchasing agent's information-gathering behavior is expressive of what the firm values. The purchasing agent seeking the best price-quality combination for a component part from a supplier is following the firm's goal of obtaining profit while maintaining a reputation for quality products. This price-quality concern is an instrumental norm encouraged by the firm for all its members, perhaps especially those in the purchasing department.

Thus norms are specifications of behaviors which group members are expected to show or approximate. The task of the marketing manager is to identify these norms and to establish in the mind of the consumer just how a particular product fits with important norms, and also how a product may help the consumer conform to these norms. This brings us back to the earlier discussion of the various influences groups have on consumers. The influence of a group, say a family, on a teenager's price sensitivity may be exerted by the family rewarding the teenager for being frugal and punishing the teenager for being extravagant. A salesperson serving this particular teenager might want to know that the family group in this example has a norm about frugality. Thus each of the phenomena identified earlier as being influenced by groups is really influenced by the norms of groups. Group norms prescribe appropriate behaviors for each of those phenomena.

"SOCIALLY DISTANT REFERENCE GROUPS AND CONSUMER ASPIRATIONS"

Reference groups are groups to which a person looks in forming attitudes toward products and in choosing what actions to take. To have an effect, the reference group or members of it need not be physically present when the action is taken. In other words, consumers can carry around in their heads ideas of what the reference group would approve. Reference groups then can have an effect due not only to their actual presence, but also to their internalized presence.

Cocanougher and Bruce treat reference groups which are socially distant. That is, they are discussing groups with which the person does not have regular interaction. Thus, the group serves a comparative function. Their prediction is that consumers will act in ways which they believe are similar to the expectations of groups to which they would like to belong. They find that consumers are more likely to behave in this way when their attitudes toward group members and their activities are positive.

"NORMS: THE PROBLEM OF DEFINITION AND CLASSIFICATION"

Norms are frequently referred to by sociologists, but little work has been done in this area by consumer behavior researchers. Yet norms govern much of the behavior related to the purchase and consumption of products and services. Norms, in the form of laws, specify the way a buyer and seller must interact in conducting their exchange. Norms also specify which products or services one should or should not purchase. For instance, purchasing pornographic material violates a norm, unlike purchasing or using bath soap. Yet there are people who engage in each of these activities. Therefore, norms are not always followed. Finally, norms specify how a person should go about choosing something to purchase. For instance, it is commonly believed that one should make price comparisons as well as read package information. Again, however, not all consumers follow the mandates of the norm.

Gibbs' article provides a typology which can be used for classifying and understanding norms. The article was originally written for a sociology journal, so the examples are not always drawn from consumer settings. A useful exercise for the reader would be to think of consumer examples for the categories in the typology. This will demonstrate which categories of norms are particularly relevant to consumer behavior. However, in this exercise one must be cautious and not overuse the concept of norms. Not all regularities in behavior occur because of the existence of a norm. Thus, Gibbs' definition of exactly what a norm is must be followed closely.

SOCIALLY DISTANT REFERENCE GROUPS AND CONSUMER ASPIRATIONS

A. BENTON COCANOUGHER
AND
GRADY D. BRUCE

Several specific effects of various social groups on consumer behavior have been studied. Venkatesan demonstrated experimentally that individuals' product choices may be affected by conformity and reactance in small face-to-face groups (Venkatesan, 1968). Stafford (1966) and Witt (1969) found that small primary groups influence certain brand choice decisions, and Bourne suggested that the purchase of certain types and brands of products may be influenced by a person's reference group (1965). However, there is a significant gap in knowledge about the effects of the socially distant reference group on consumer behavior.[1]

CONCEPTUAL FRAMEWORK

Theorists disagree about the functions reference groups perform in influencing individual attitudes, values, and behavior. However, Kelley identified two primary functions which incorporate most reference group theorists' viewpoints: the normative and comparative functions (1965). The normative function is the setting and enforcing of standards for the individual, and most previous research has explored the efficacy of small groups in enforcing such group norms on interacting individuals.

The comparative function is the group's capacity to serve as a point of comparison against which an individual can evaluate himself and others. That is, a group can influence an individual to the extent that the attitudes, values, and behavior of its members represent standards which he voluntarily uses in making judgments and evaluations. Unlike the normative influence, which requires at least enough interaction to enable the group to evaluate the extent of the individual's conformity to group norms, comparative influence depends only upon the influence recipient being attracted to group members or activities (Hollander, 1967).

Source: A. Benton Cocanougher and Grady D. Bruce, "Socially Distant Reference Groups and Consumer Aspirations," *Journal of Marketing*, Vol. 36, April, 1972, pp. 12–19.

[1] "Socially distant" is used in this context to describe that relationship between the potential influence recipient and the reference group characterized by the absence of regular interaction.

This research was designed to investigate the relationship between an individual's choice of a socially distant aspiration group and the development of his aspirations as a consumer. Thus it is concerned with the comparative function: the influence on purchase aspirations of the individual's perceptions of the behavior of a group to which he is attracted, but with which he has little or no interaction. Since, as previously stated, attraction may exist along two dimensions, a two-part proposition was tested: the amount of influence exerted by the aspiration reference group will be related to the individual's expressed attitudes toward: (1) group members and (2) their activities.

METHODOLOGY

Subjects for the study were 114 male undergraduate students at The University of Texas at Austin, and the socially distant reference group used was business executives. This reference group was deemed especially appropriate with student subjects since it represents a potential career and since most students have some perception of the behavior and activities of this group. Student subjects were from business and nonbusiness classes in order to get a wide range of expressed attraction to the business executive group.

The working hypotheses were:

1. The amount of influence exerted by the business executive group will be related to subjects' expressed attitudes toward a career in business, with those subjects having the most favorable attitudes being the most influenced.

2. The amount of influence exerted by the business executive group will be related to subjects' attitudes toward business executives, with those subjects having the most favorable attitudes being the most influenced.

The Remmers short-form adaptation of the Miller Attitude Toward Any Occupation Test was employed to evaluate the subjects' attitudes toward business careers (Shaw and Wright, 1967). This is a Thurstone equal-appearing interval scale test with 17 statements; reliabilities ranging from .71 to .92 have been reported.

A semantic differential test was used to measure subjects' attitudes toward business executives. Pretesting and subsequent revisions helped identify those adjectives offering the most appropriate and discriminating choices to the subjects in this study. The eight adjective pairs finally used in a seven-point scale were: interesting-uninteresting, honest-hypocritical, skillful-unskillful, selfish-unselfish, fair-biased, cruel-kind, sincere-insincere, and ethical-unethical. Eight other pairs of adjectives were used as buffer items. The test score for each subject was derived by summing the scale values for the appropriate eight items.

Operationalizing the dependent variable (reference group influence as measured in terms of consumer product aspirations) presented a problem. However, since a number of recent marketing studies have demonstrated the adaptability of Q-methodology to problems of this nature, that technique was used in this study (Sommers, 1964; Sommers and Bruce, 1968). Basically, Q-methodology involves the use of a forced choice method whereby a subject is provided with a number of items and asked to use them to describe his actual-self, ideal-self, or some defined "other." When two or more such sorts are made under different sets of instruction, such as one sort for self and one sort for other, the resulting arrays can be correlated to determine the effect of different conditions of instruction on the test items (Sommers, 1964).

In this application of the technique, every subject was given two decks of 38 cards each, each card with the name of a consumer product imprinted on the front. The two decks were identical, except for color: one was blue, the other green. The different colors were used to help respondents distinguish between the different frames of reference called for in the sorting instructions.

The subjects were first instructed to sort the blue deck according to whether or not the product shown on a card was representative of what he would ideally like to have five years after graduation. All 38 cards were rank ordered from most to least descriptive of a futuristic ideal-self. Then subjects were instructed to perform the same task with the green deck, except that with this deck the products should be used to describe their perception of the products used by a typical business executive, again from the most to least descriptive.

The two independent sorts performed by each subject were then subjected to correlation analysis to determine the degree of congruency between his ideal-self and his perception of a typical business executive. These *r*-values were calculated by correlating sets of Q-sorts (Hilden, 1954). The *r*-values thus derived were operationally defined as indicating the degree of influence which the business executive reference group exerted on the subject's development of ideal-self.

A pretest was conducted to select products to be used by subjects to describe their future ideal-self and a typical business executive. One hundred and six male students in an introductory marketing course were given a list of 76 relatively common consumer products and asked to indicate those which they felt were most characteristic of the following individuals: (1) self, (2) best friend, (3) father, (4) male social worker, (5) attorney, (6) truck driver, (7) male "hippie," and (8) male business executive. These rankings were tabulated and analyzed to select products highly descriptive of either self or a business executive.

In addition, an effort was made to select the products with strong business executive identification so that the same products were not equally descriptive of other occupational types or significant others. This step was taken to reduce the likelihood of a subject's displaying a high degree of congruency between ideal-self and his perception of business executives which is, in reality, merely a reflection of influence exerted by a reference group other than business executives. The

Table 1   Q-sort products

Lincoln Continental	*Sports Illustrated*	Buick Riviera
Stereo equipment	Electric shoe polisher	*Newsweek*
Mercedes sports car	Camping equipment	Corvette
Cardigan sweater	*Playboy*	Lawn furniture
Theatre tickets	Portable radio	Tennis racquet
Reclining chair	Sport coat	Bar B-Q grill
King-size bed	Hair spray	*Time*
Fireplace	Loafer shoes	Golf clubs
Attache case	Manicure set	Tuxedo
Cadillac	Swim suit	Dress shoes
Hair brush	Rifle	Fishing rod
Camera	Pipe (smoking)	Mustang
Speedboat	Dark suit	

38 products listed in Table 1 were those chosen as best meeting this criterion.

ANALYSIS AND FINDINGS

Since the basic premise upon which the working hypotheses were analyzed is that the degree of congruency between the two Q-sort rankings is a measure of the reference group's influence on the subject, correlation coefficients were calculated for each subject's Q-rankings. These were transformed to z-values, which were the criterion variables used in correlation and covariance analysis with the predictors: attitudes toward a career in business and attitudes toward business executives.[2]

---

[2]One additional evaluation of the subjects' Q-sorts consisted of correlating the average business executive ranking for those subjects in the upper quartile of both attraction variables with the average business executive ranking for those subjects in the lower quartile of both attraction variables. The resulting *r* of .80 indicates that even those subjects feeling widely divergent attraction to the group had similar perceptions of group norms.

The variable of attraction to group activities, or the measure of attitudes toward a career in business, correlated with group influence at $r = .53$, significant at $p < .0001$. Attitudes toward business executives, the measure of attraction to group members, correlated with group influence at $r = .45$, also significant at $p < .0001$ (see Table 2). Thus, both working hypotheses were clearly supported.

In order to evaluate the predictive power of total attraction to the reference group, multiple correlation analysis was performed using both independent variables. Covariance analysis revealed that the resulting multiple R of .57 was significantly greater than the correlation obtained when using only attitudes toward a career in business or attitudes toward business executives at $p = .0075$ and $p = .0001$, respectively. This suggests the advisability of using both predictors (or *total* attraction to reference group) to explain variations in an individual's choice of a socially distant reference group.

Table 2   Correlation models

Model number	Independent variable	Correlation coefficient	Coefficient of determination
I	Attitudes toward career	.53[a]	.28
II	Attitudes toward executives	.45[a]	.20
III	Both attraction variables	.57[a]	.32

[a] $p < .0001$.

IMPLICATIONS

The use of "distant others"—for example, cultural heroes, such as movie stars, athletes, and the like—in all forms of advertising is a clear illustration of the basic assumption in marketing that there is a relationship between an individual's attraction to a socially distant reference group and the amount of influence the group exerts. Indeed, any marketing communication which urges consumers to act in terms of the behavior of a referent individual or group with whom the consumer has no regular personal interaction would appear to be based on the assumption that such distant referents can influence the consumer's product aspirations or formulation of his ideal-self-image. Yet despite the prevailing acceptance of such an influence, little empirical support has been generated, because most previous reference group research has concentrated on small face-to-face groups where interaction is on a regular, routine basis or where it has been experimentally induced.

Although exploratory in nature, the findings of this study may be suggestive in a number of contexts. First, since market segments represent relatively homogeneous groupings of individuals, it may be possible to identify similarities among individuals within a segment with regard to the distant referents they find most attractive. Along this same line, it may even prove useful to formulate new classifications of market segments based on potentially influential distant referents. Such a segmentation would be useful in advertising and, perhaps, product development.

Second, individuals do have negative reference groups whose norms they seek to avoid adopting as their own (Kassarjian and Robertson, 1968). Therefore, it may be necessary to recognize that the use of any referent group in advertising necessarily repels some individuals who may be potential consumers.

REFERENCES

Bourne, Francis S. (1965), "Group Influence in Marketing and Public Relations," in James U. McNeal, ed., *Dimensions of Consumer Behavior,* New York: Appleton-Century-Crofts, 137–46.

Hilden, Arnold H. (1954), "Manual for Q-Sort and Random Sets of Personal Concepts," Unpublished paper, Washington University.

Hollander, Edwin P. (1967), "Conformity, Status, and Idiosyncrasy Credit," in Edwin P. Hollander and Raymond G. Hunt, eds., *Current Perspectives in Social Psychology,* New York: Oxford Press, 465–75.

Kassarjian, Harold H., and Robertson, Thomas S., eds. (1968), *Perspectives in Consumer Behavior,* Glenview, Ill.: Scott, Foresman, 274–75.

Kelley, Harold H. (1965), "Two Functions of Reference Groups," in Harold Proshansky and Bernard Siedenberg, eds., *Basic Studies in Social Psychology,* New York: Holt, Rinehart and Winston, 210–14.

Shaw, Marvin E., and Wright, Jack M., eds. (1967), *Scales for the Measurement of Attitudes,* New York: McGraw-Hill, 129–31.

Sommers, Montrose S. (Fall, 1964), "The Use of Product Symbolism to Differentiate Social Strata," *University of Houston Business Review,* 11, 28–29.

———, and Bruce, Grady D. (December, 1968), "Blacks, Whites and Products: Relative Deprivation and Reference Group Behavior," *Social Science Quarterly,* 49, 631–42.

Stafford, James E. (February, 1966), "Effects of Group Influence on Consumer Brand Preferences," *Journal of Marketing Research,* 3, 68–74.

Venkatesan, M. (1968), "Consumer Behavior: Conformity and Independence," in Harold H. Kassarjian and Thomas S. Robertson, eds., *Perspectives in Consumer Behavior,* Glenview, Ill.: Scott, Foresman, 306–12.

Witt, Robert E. (November, 1969), "Informal Social Group Influence on Consumer Brand Choice," *Journal of Marketing Research,* 6, 473–76.

NORMS: THE PROBLEM OF DEFINITION AND CLASSIFICATION

JACK P. GIBBS

Sociological literature reveals three shortcomings in the conceptual treatment of norms: (1) a lack of agreement in generic definitions, (2) no adequate classificatory scheme for distinguishing types of norms, and (3) no consistent distinction between attributes of norms that are true by definition and those that are contingent (i.e., attributes which vary from one norm to the next and therefore are not relevant for a generic definition of norms). This paper considers the three problems and offers a solution for each.

LACK OF AGREEMENT IN DEFINITION

The following definitions of norms illustrate differences and certain points of agreement among sociologists.

Bierstedt: "A norm, then, is a rule or a standard that governs our conduct in the social situations in which we participate. It is a societal expectation. It is a standard to which we are expected to conform whether we actually do so or not." (Bierstedt, 1963)

Broom and Selznick: "All societies have rules or norms specifying appropriate and inappropriate behavior, and individuals are rewarded or punished as they conform to or deviate from the rules. The norms are blueprints for behavior, setting limits within which individuals may seek alternate ways to achieve their goals. Norms are based on cultural values, which are justified by moral standards, reasoning, or aesthetic judgment." (Broom and Selznick, 1963)

Homans: "A norm is a statement made by a number of members of a group, not necessarily by all of them, that the members ought to behave in a certain way in certain circumstances." (Homans, 1961)

Johnson: "A norm is an abstract pattern, held in the mind, that sets certain limits for behavior. An 'operative' norm is one that is not merely entertained in the mind but is considered worthy of

Source: Jack P. Gibbs, "Norms: The Problem of Definition and Classification," *American Journal of Sociology,* Vol. 70, March, 1965, pp. 586–594.

following in actual behavior; thus one feels that one ought to conform to it. This feeling means that one 'accepts' the norm." (Johnson, 1960)

Morris: "Norms are generally accepted, sanctioned prescriptions for, or prohibitions against, others' behavior, belief, or feeling, i.e., what others ought to do, believe, feel—or else. Norms must be shared prescriptions. . . . Norms always include sanctions." (Morris, 1956)

Newcomb: "The term 'norm,' unfortunately, has several meanings. We shall use it, however, only in the sense of 'more or less fixed frame of reference,' whether of quantitive or qualitative nature." (Newcomb, 1958)

Williams: "Norms . . . are rules of conduct; they specify what should and should not be done by various kinds of social actors in various kinds of situations . . . The term 'cultural norm' refers to a specific prescription of the course that action should (is supposed to) follow in a given situation. . . . For a whole group or society, probably the best index to an institutional norm is the occurrence of severe penalties for violation. Such penalties are truly institutional, however, only if supported by an effective consensus of the society. (Williams, 1960)

In a survey of the conceptual treatment of norms some ten years ago, Rommetveit observed that there are three distinct uses of the term: (1) to indicate uniformities in behavior, (2) to designate a particular shared "frame of reference," and (3) to express the existence of social obligation or pressure (Rommetveit, 1955). Inspection of the above definitions reveals only two points of agreement. First, none of them suggests that a norm is simply a uniformity in behavior. Second, with the exception of the definition offered by Newcomb, none of the definitions identifies a norm as a shared frame of reference in a strictly psychological sense. However, beyond these two points there is very little agreement among the definitions. Further, most of the definitions are ambiguous in that they leave various questions

concerning the character of norms unanswered. For example, must a norm in fact govern conduct; or, stated otherwise, how much deviation is allowed before the standard is no longer a norm? Also, must norms be supported by, or otherwise consistent with, collective values, in the sense that most persons find them just and acceptable? If so, are the military laws which govern an occupied country to be excluded from the category of norms?

The reference to military laws leads to a consideration of sanctions as a normative element. But observe that some of the above definitions mention sanctions, while others do not. Moreover, the definitions which do refer to sanctions leave three important questions unanswered: (1) Does the content of the sanction enter into the definition of norms? (2) Must the sanction be administered in a particular way? (3) Must the sanction actually be administered in a large proportion of cases or is it only necessary that an attempt be made to administer it?

Differences in the above definitions and the ambiguous quality of some of them stem primarily from the fact that there are several distinct types of norms.[1] One treatment of the concept may differ from another because the two are actually concerned with different types of norms; and, when the definition is truly generic, it is typically ambiguous because it is not set forth in the context of a typology which makes all of the attributes of norms explicit.

The latest survey of the conceptual treatment of norms, that conducted by Dohrenwend, implicitly recognizes various types in setting forth a generic

[1]The heterogeneous character of norms evidently prompts some observers to focus on types of norms and to eschew a generic definition. Kingsley Davis, for example, offers a systematic analysis of several commonly recognized types of norms (folkways, mores, customary law, enacted law, custom, morality, etc.), but does not set forth a formal and explicit definition which applies to norms generally (*Human Society* [New York: Macmillan Co., 1949], chap. iii).

definition: "A social norm is a rule which, over a period of time, proves binding on the overt behavior of each individual in an aggregate of two or more individuals. It is marked by the following characteristics: (1) Being a rule, it has content known to at least one member of the social aggregate. (2) Being a binding rule, it regulates the behavior of any given individual in the social aggregate by virtue of *(a)* his having internalized the rule; *(b)* external sanction in support of the rule applied to him by one or more of the other individuals in the social aggregate; *(c)* external sanctions in support of the rule applied to him by an authority outside the social aggregate; or any combination of these circumstances." (Dohrenwend, 1959)

The above definition of norms is commendable, in that it is precise but at the same time so general that other definitions can be subsumed under it. However, the definition suggests that the members of a social aggregate must actually conform to a certain standard of conduct before that standard is a norm. Some other conceptual treatments (see, e.g., Bierstedt's definition) do not agree. Furthermore, if we identify norms in terms of behavior, it is tautological to speak of the former as influencing or controlling the latter. The position is taken here that the degree of conformity to norms is a contingent but not a definitional attribute. Finally, in ascribing multiple attributes to norms, Dohrenwend's treatment suggests but does not produce a typology of norms.

DEFINITIONAL ATTRIBUTES

A norm in the generic sense (i.e., encompassing all the various types of norms) involves: (1) a collective evaluation of behavior in terms of what it *ought* to be; (2) a collective expectation as to what behavior *will be;* and/or (3) particular *reactions* to behavior, including attempts to apply sanctions or otherwise induce a particular kind of conduct. Virtually all conceptions of norms can be subsumed

under this generic definition, and it further has the virtue of encompassing all of the attributes which distinguish types of norms.

Collective Evaluations

Perhaps the most commonly recognized characteristic of a norm is a shared belief that persons *ought* or *ought not* to act in a certain way. An emphasis on such an evaluation as an attribute of norms is in some respects closely associated with a particular sociological perspective (Durkheim and Parsons in particular), because it implies the existence of shared values. However, while a collective evaluation of an act may be the attribute of some types of norms (e.g., mores), this is not so for all types. Rules imposed on a group by an external authority (e.g., some prison regulations as they apply to convicts) or simply "unpopular" laws do not have the support of shared values; but, nonetheless, it would be most questionable to label them as non-normative. Further, collective evaluations do not characterize what are often regarded as customs. Thus, as an example, the typical American probably expects his fellow countrymen to drink coffee; but in most cases it is a matter of extreme indifference to him whether or not they do so, certainly in the sense of *ought* or *should*.

While mores are virtually excluded from urban societies, such is not the case for morals. In the present typology, morals are sanctioned norms; but the sanctions may be administered by anyone rather than persons in a particular status, and the means of administering the sanction or the sanction itself exclude the use of force. However, as in the case of mores, while morals represent collective beliefs as to what conduct should be, they may or may not correspond to what people actually expect conduct to be.

When mores or morals are supported by collective beliefs *and* are consistent with expectations concerning behavior, the term *collective* is an appropriate designation. On the other hand, if they are supported by collective beliefs but are not consistent with expectations as to actual conduct, the appropriate term is *problematic*.

SUMMARY AND CONCLUSION

Although the concept is central to the social sciences, norms have not been treated in a truly systematic manner, and particularly so with regard to the construction of typologies. The present analysis suggests three definitional attributes of norms: collective evaluations, collective expectations, and reactions to behavior.

An analysis of the three normative attributes in terms of substruction and their property-space arrangement reveals nineteen distinct types of norms. The typology enables us to identify most of the commonly recognized kinds of norms and, at the same time, to designate certain kinds which have not been treated conceptually or empirically.

REFERENCES

Bierstedt, Robert (1963), *The Social Order,* 2nd ed., New York: McGraw-Hill Book Co., 222.

Bodenheimer, Edgar (1962), *Jurisprudence,* Cambridge, Mass.: Harvard University Press.

Broom, Leonard, and Selznick, Philip (1963), *Sociology,* 3rd ed., New York: Harper and Row, 68.

Dohrenwend, Bruce P. (August, 1959), "Egoism, Altruism, Anomie, and Fatalism: A Conceptual Analysis of Durkheim's Types," *American Sociological Review,* XXIV, 470.

Hart, H. L. A. (1961), *The Concept of Law,* Oxford: Clarendon Press.

Hoebel, E. Adamson (1954), *The Law of Primitive Man,* Cambridge, Mass.: Harvard University Press, esp. chap. ii.

Homans, George C. (1961), *Social Behavior: Its Elementary Forms,* New York: Harcourt, Brace & Co., 46.

Johnson, Harry M. (1960), *Sociology,* New York: Harcourt, Brace & Co., 8.

Morris, Richard T. (October, 1956), "A Typology of Norms," *American Sociological Review,* XXI, 610.

Newcomb, Theodore M. (1958), *Social Psychology,* New York: Henry Holt and Co., 266.

Rheinstein, Max, ed. (1954), *Max Weber on Law in Economy and Society,* Cambridge, Mass.: Harvard University Press.

Rommetveit, Ragnar (1955), *Social Norms and Roles,* Minneapolis: University of Minnesota Press, 18–26.

Sorokin, Pitirim A. (1947), *Society, Culture, and Personality,* New York: Harper & Bros., 71–85.

Williams, Robin M. (1960), *American Society,* 2nd ed., New York: Alfred A. Knopf, 24–25 and 30.

SOCIAL INTERACTION AND SOCIAL ROLES IN CONSUMER BEHAVIOR

Social groups often have a division of labor among their members to facilitate the achievement of group goals. Section 4 discussed the existence of norms which specify behaviors appropriate for achieving these goals. Often these norms apply differentially. They may be more relevant to some people in a group and less relevant to other people, depending on the division of labor. Thus some people in a group for whom a norm is especially relevant are expected to behave somewhat differently. These expectations actually apply to any person who has a particular position assigned by the division of labor in a group. This position is called a *role*. A role is a set of expected behaviors for individuals who occupy a certain position as they interact with other people. The interaction may involve many people from diverse groups.

While it is important to determine what groups affect consumers and through what norms, it is also important to understand what roles individuals occupy. Knowing that social roles are important helps identify the set of norms which are most important in a group. If we know that a mother is the most important role in a family with regard to the use of credit cards for nonbusiness reasons, then to understand household credit card usage we would want to study social norms pertaining to mothers' usage of credit cards.

It is important to remember that roles are social in nature; they involve a relationship between two or more individuals. Thus the role of mother really refers to relationships between mothers and children and probably mothers and fathers as well. The behavior of a mother will vary as a result of interaction with various children as the mother encounters their expectations and their efforts to influence her, and as she expresses her own expectations and influence efforts. Moreover, the role relationship between a mother and child may be influenced by the relationship the mother has with the father, by a school teacher, and by friends who have children.

Similarly, the behavior of a purchasing agent is a result of expectations held by other people, such as salespeople from other firms, and various individuals in the company, such as the production manager and vice-president for finance. The expectations of these various people may actually create conflict for the purchasing agent. The production manager may demand high-quality materials while the financial officer demands purchasing at the lowest cost possible.

Many products and services are purchased as a symbolic expression of a role relationship. An engagement ring expresses the formation of a new role relationship. A gold watch given at a retirement ceremony expresses a change in another role relationship. Other products and services are required for the performance of a role. Medical equipment for medical personnel is an example of this. Food served to a dinner guest would be another illustration. The reader may well imagine numerous other situations where the purchase and use of products and services directly pertains to a role relationship.

Identical roles in different settings may vary. This is important to the marketer. A purchasing agent in one firm may have much less influence on a purchase decision than his or her counterpart in a competing firm. Similarly, the role of parent may vary substantially from culture to culture or even over time within the same family. Thus variation in roles exists and must be considered in the formulation of marketing strategy. One reading in this section is concerned with a very important type of variation, that which occurs as a result of deepening involvement in a social role. Two other readings examine interaction between two of the most basic roles in social life: buyer-seller.

"THE DYNAMICS OF ROLE ACQUISITION"

Different positions in society have different expectations attached to them. People occupying these positions then are expected to think, feel, and act in certain ways. Expectations that are associated with certain positions are called *role expectations* by sociologists. Thornton and Nardi discuss the ways people learn and begin to fulfill these role expectations as they take on new positions.

The basic idea of the article is that people go through four stages (anticipatory, formal, informal, and personal) in acquiring roles. In these stages, the person interacts with the role expectations; that is, the role changes the person and the person changes the role. To understand these changes one must focus on the definitions of concepts in the second section and on the five dimensions which characterize role acquisition stages (source of information, content of information, type of expectation, degree of consensus, and individuals' reactions). Thus, in reading the article one should try to imagine a table where the four stages of role acquisition are across the top of the page and the five dimensions are along the left side. In the cells are the characteristics of that particular stage.

This analysis can be carried one step further in trying to relate this scheme to consumer behavior. The article was originally written for a sociology journal, but it does combine sociological as well as psychological ideas. No examples are given, however, of role acquisition as it relates to consumption-related activities.

First of all, we can note that somehow children learn how to shop and how to consume. Thus, they acquire the shopper/consumer role. What would occur in each of the stages in acquiring this role? How do parents, teachers, and friends convey the formal and informal expectations attached to this role? How do people personalize the role?

Secondly, the purchase or consumption of particular products is often linked to role transitions. For instance, in becoming a parent one often purchases many products (baby clothes and furniture, carpeting, a station wagon or second car, a larger home, fencing around a yard, etc.). At what stage do these purchases occur and how do they reflect changes in the five dimensions? What are some other roles for which the process of role acquisition implies the purchase or use of products?

At this point, the reader should take the ideas obtained in the article one step further. This step involves deriving implications for actions which should be taken by marketing managers and government policy makers. For instance, the notion that having a child means that one should have a crib is characteristic of the anticipatory stage which occurs before one actually becomes a parent. However, some parents may not purchase a crib until some time after the child is born. Even though two couples may be purchasing the same item, their purchase process and the features of the crib which they consider important will be different depending upon whether they can draw information from their experience with their child or whether they must rely on stereotypes about parenthood. A similar difference can be noted in college freshmen furnishing their dormitory rooms. Those who attempt to purchase furnishings before going away to school invariably overestimate the amount of space available. Those who make these purchases after arriving on campus are more likely to realize their space limitations.

"BUYER-SELLER INTERACTION: A CONCEPTUAL FRAMEWORK"

Many people see consumer behavior as essentially a dyadic process. That is, they take the view that the behavior of a consumer depends upon the way in which the consumer interacts with the seller. Just as baking chocolate tastes very different after it is mixed with sugar, so the behavior of the buyer must be understood in the context of the behavior of the seller with whom the buyer interacts. The presence of one member affects the other. This interaction approach is in contrast to more traditional approaches to consumer behavior. These approaches considered the behavior of the consumer as emanating only from his or her attitudes, personality, and learning processes.

Sheth takes an interaction approach in this article. His basic idea is that the outcome of an interaction is dependent upon the fit between the buyer and the seller. Specifically, the content of their expectations may or may not fit, and their styles of communication may or may not fit. Figure 1 in the article details the different possible combinations, their antecedents, and their outcomes. Because this figure contains the basic ideas of the article, it should be examined closely.

Five different types of product expectations are given: functional, social-organizational, situational, emotional, and curiosity utilities. One interesting point made in the article is that organizations as buyers as well as individual consumers are concerned with all five types of utility. This emphasizes the point made repeatedly in this book that in many ways organizational buyers and individual consumers are similar.

It is purported that the buyer and seller will probably not match on their expectations about these five types of utility. If they are approximately equal in power, it is likely that they will negotiate a mutually acceptable arrangement. However, if they are power unequals, it is more likely that the less powerful person will move toward the more powerful person. Thus, the behavior of each person is dependent upon the power relations between the two parties and their expectations about the five types of utilities.

This interactional approach does not negate the importance of individual factors as determinants of behavior. In fact, personality is seen as a key variable in determining which of the three styles of interaction (task-oriented, interaction-oriented, self-oriented) a person will prefer. Thus, the final section, which is on determinant factors, explains where a person's interaction style preferences and expectations about the product come from.

While reading the article, an interesting exercise for the reader would be to use the information presented to analyze a recent purchase. That is, the following questions should be addressed: What were the buyer's original expectations on the five types of utility? How did these match with the seller's offerings? Were any adjustments of expectations/offerings made? What does this imply about the power relations? What were the relevant styles of communication? Can any of the expectations or styles be traced to the three determinant factors?

This exercise will enable the reader to evaluate the explanatory power of the conceptual framework. Perhaps it applies more readily in certain kinds of situations. Perhaps it enables the buyer to understand the outcomes as they derive from the interaction process.

"AN EXPERIMENTAL ANALYSIS OF A SALESMAN'S EXPERT AND REFERENT BASES OF SOCIAL POWER IN THE BUYER-SELLER DYAD"

Power is an interactional concept. Power is not a characteristic that one person can have. Instead, power arises from a differential control of resources in a relationship. French and Raven propose that power can arise from five bases. These five bases of power are:

(1) Reward power: the ability of one person to give positive benefits to another;

(2) Coercive power: the ability of one person to give negative benefits or punishments to another;

(3) Legitimate power: the ability of one person to have another accept his or her influence due to the influenced person's internalized norms of authority and respect for certain positions;

(4) Referent power: the ability of one person to have another accept his or her influence due to the influenced person's feeling of identity or similarity to the influencer;

(5) Expert power: the ability of one person to have another accept his or her influence due to the influenced person's perception of the influencer as highly knowledgeable.

The Busch and Wilson article examines only the effects of these latter two bases of power.

The research methodology employed is somewhat complicated. Since it is necessary to understand what tests were performed in order to understand the results, the methodology will be briefly explained here. The research is experimental; in other words, an attempt was made to construct a certain type of situation. Then the effects of this situation on the respondents were measured. There were four treatment or experimental groups as shown in the diagram below:

		Salesperson's Referent Power	
		High	Low
Salesperson's Expert Power	High	1	2
	Low	3	4

In addition, there was a control group which had no experimental treatment. This is known as a 2 x 2 factorial design with control group. Thus, there were two independent variables (that is, variables whose levels were manipulated by the experimenters): expert power and referent power. The dependent variables (that is, the variables which were checked to see if the independent variables had an effect) were: trust (both a global attitude and a message-specific attitude), behavior (including behavioral intention and a behavioroid measure), and range of power base. The hypotheses then can all be fit into the format: the higher the (independent variable), the greater the (dependent variable). For instance, Hypothesis 1 can be reworded: the higher the referent power of the salesperson, the greater the perceived trust. The reader should try to reword the other hypotheses to make certain there is a clear understanding of the hypothesized relationships between the independent and the dependent variables.

Mention is made in the article of internal validity and manipulation checks. Through the manipulation checks, Busch and Wilson tried to determine whether or not the respondents had experienced the situation in the same way as the researchers had tried to construct it. For example, the manipulation checks were used to see if those people in the high expert power, low referent power condition had really felt that the salesperson was high in expertise, but not very similar to themselves. It is fortunate that there was a manipulation check because the researchers' intentions had not been actualized. Persons in cells 2 and 3 in the above figure were not significantly different in their perceptions of the referent power of the salesperson. These people's responses were therefore reassigned to the cells based on the way the person had interpreted the situation, rather than based on the way the researchers thought they had constructed the situation.

One of the strengths of experimental research is that one can make causal statements about the relationships between independent and dependent variables. For instance, from this study one can infer that "an increase in salesperson expert power will produce an increase in the consumer's perceived trust of the salesperson." However, since the experimental conditions were not established for referent power and the responses had to be reassigned to cells based on actual perceptions, causal statements cannot be made about this independent variable. This is what is meant when the researchers say that they can only make correlational rather than causal statements about referent power.

One final point must be added about the research results. Note that behavioral intentions and behavioroid measures often produce different results. In other words, when asked questions like "If you were in the market for life insurance, would you be willing to discuss it with this salesperson?," many respondents answered yes. However, when asked to indicate whether or not they were willing to talk by putting their name, address, and telephone number on a postcard, many respondents did not indicate willingness. Why are these two measures of behavior different? Two explanations are possible. First, respondents might be willing to talk, but are not presently in the market. If this were the case, they would answer yes to the hypothetical question, but not fill out the postcard. Second, respondents frequently try to give researchers the response that they think the researchers want. Therefore, if respondents thought that the researchers wanted them to feel that they would talk to the salesperson if they were in the market for life insurance, they may have reported this feeling. However, when it came down to actually giving their name, address, and phone number to the salesperson, the respondents may have been less willing to comply with what they thought the researchers wanted. When there was a cost to be borne by the respondents, they may have been less willing to comply. Either of the two explanations is possible.

THE DYNAMICS OF ROLE ACQUISITION[1]

**RUSSELL THORNTON
AND
PETER M. NARDI**

Several conceptions of how individuals acquire social roles may be found in the literature of the social and psychological disciplines. The traditional approach to role acquisition views it as synonymous with the acquisition of a new position in a social system. Role acquisition is thus considered a one-step event whereby individuals assume new social positions and conform immediately to the expectations consequently directed at them (see Linton, 1936; Sherif, 1936).

In more recent works, role acquisition is viewed frequently as a developmental process. Often this process is only implied, usually by asserting that psychological phenomena become important at some time during the acquisition of a new role (see Becker, et al., 1961; Dornbusch, 1955; Goffman, 1961; Olesen and Whittaker, 1968; Zurcher, 1967). Some works, however, contain discussions of explicitly defined stages of role acquisition. These works give great importance to the psychological aspects of the process and tend to emphasize the interaction between individuals and roles (see Bourne, 1967; Cogswell, 1967; Gordon, 1972; Hall, 1948; Sherlock and Morris, 1967; Simpson, 1967).

Some problems are evident in all of these perspectives, however. Each seems to underestimate the degree of interaction between person and role during the process of acquisition. The emphasis is placed clearly on the ways in which social situations impose rights and duties on individuals and the ways individuals conform passively to that imposition. The first view, for example, regards individuals as mere recipients of

[1]Several of the ideas presented in this paper originated while the senior author was a research sociologist at the 1970 Summer Research Institute of the American College Testing Program. Gratitude is extended to Robert E. Herriott, director of that institute, as well as to the American College Testing Program. Other ideas were developed under grant OEG-3-71-0114 from the U.S. Office of Education to the senior author during 1971–72; this support is gratefully acknowledged. Appreciation is extended also to Neal Gross, Charles Wright, Bruce Cooper, and several anonymous reviewers for insightful comments on earlier drafts of the paper.

Source: Russell Thornton and Peter M. Nardi, "The Dynamics of Role Acquisition," *American Journal of Sociology,* Vol. 80, January, 1975, pp. 870–885.

expectations and role acquisition as merely a performance in accord with these expectations. That people do not always conform to roles but in fact modify them is not taken into account. To a lesser degree, the same problem is evident in the implicit developmental analyses, with their perfunctory acknowledgment of interaction between individuals and social situations. Each of the works cited asserts that interaction occurs during role acquisition and may change over time, but then tends to ignore it. The imposition of external requirements is emphasized, with the implicit changes being those made in conforming to a role. The more explicit developmental analyses take cognizance of interaction and incorporate it clearly into the acquisition process, but here again the emphasis is on persons modifying themselves to fit their roles, not on how they may modify roles to fit themselves. The explicit stages of role acquisition are those individuals go through in conforming to and psychologically accepting new roles.

There are two partial consequences of these views of role acquisition. First, its complexity is deemphasized. Neither the various types of expectations which may be directed at people in new positions nor their content and requirements and the degree of consensus on them is taken into account. Second, these conceptualizations afford little possibility of explaining variations in the acquisition and performance of the same type of role by different individuals.

The model of role acquisition presented here develops out of these previous writings and research and represents an endeavor to overcome some of their shortcomings. In order to enhance the model's applicability, a general formulation is developed, capable of being applied (with perhaps varying degrees of accuracy) to virtually any role which may be acquired rather than restricted to a particular type of role. Even though it is general, the formulation allows for the examination of variations in the acquisition of different types of roles and of the same type of role by different persons. The temporal dimension consists of four stages—anticipatory, formal, informal, and personal—whereby individuals move from passively accepting roles to actively engaging in and shaping them. The crucial variables around which each stage is formed consist of the source, content, and form of expectations encountered at different points in time, the degree of consensus on the content of the expectations, and individuals' reactions to them.

SPECIFYING SOME CONCEPTS

As a prelude to the actual formulation of the stages of role acquisition, it is necessary to set forth and clarify some concepts. For our purposes, we define a role as a set of expectations impinging on an incumbent of a social position (see Gross, Mason, and McEachern, 1958, p. 60). There are several possible sources of these expectations. First, they may be generalized; that is, they may come from "society at large," for example, the various components of the mass media, the legal system or other codified sources, and people in general. Next, they may, in Merton's terms, come from members of the role set; in other words, "that complement of role-relationships in which persons are involved by virtue of occupying a particular social status" (1957, p. 110). Within the role set, two sources may be distinguished: people enacting the same role as the incumbent (similar-role others) and people enacting reciprocal roles (reciprocal-role others). Finally, the incumbent may be a source of expectations for his own role enactment.

The content of expectations may be behavioral, attitudinal, or cognitive; that is, they may refer to the ways in which an incumbent of a social position should behave, to the particular attitudes and values appropriate to him, or to the knowledge and skills he should have.[2] The form the expecta-

---

[2]Israel (1966) distinguishes between the technical-instrumental aspects of a role, comprising the knowledge and skills necessary to carry out the tasks, and the expressive-ideological aspects, comprising the attitudes, values, and ideals related

tions take may be either overt or covert. In other words, they may be presented in an explicit, formal manner, or they may be implicit in the social structure as part of its informal properties. Hence role acquisition involves, in part, an increasing awareness of implicit as well as explicit expectations encompassing attitudes and values, and knowledge and skills in addition to behavior. These expectations coming from the four sources we have identified may also be described in terms of the degree of consensus concerning them. Two types of consensus may be distinguished: first, consensus or dissensus within a source; second, consensus or dissensus between any two sources. Also, consensus or dissensus may be actual or only supposed by the person in question.

Now that selected features of the expectations comprised in a role have been described, the three possible reactions to them can be delineated. The first is *social adjustment,* the adequate meeting of role expectations and performance in accordance with them. The second is *psychological adjustment,* the achievement of congruity between individual psychological needs and desires and the role. Neither social nor psychological adjustment is a matter of strict conformity to role expectations, though a high degree of conformity may be present, and often is. Individuals may, however, modify their roles to fit themselves and/or develop their own private meanings for role enactment. These processes, too, constitute adjustment. A third and final reaction, *adaptation,* occurs if the role is internalized and assimilated so that in a sense, person and role become inseparable. Social and psychological adjustment may lead to adaptation but do not necessarily do so: they provide only the conditions whereby it is possible.

FOUR STAGES OF ROLE ACQUISITION

In our formulation, the acquisition of a role entails progression through four stages—anticipatory, formal, informal, and personal. Each stage is characterized by the type of expectations which predominate and to which individuals consequently give most attention. Each stage involves interaction between individuals and external expectations, including individuals' attempts to influence the expectations of others as well as others' attempts to influence individuals. (The nature of the interaction changes during role acquisition, as we have indicated: individuals are more passive in early stages, more active in later ones.) A role is not fully acquired until an individual has anticipated it, learned anticipatory, formal, and informal expectations comprised in it, formulated his own expectations, reacted to and reconciled these various expectations, and accepted the final outcome.[3]

Anticipatory Stage

The first stage of role acquisition is the period prior to incumbency in a social position during which individuals generally encounter a variety of relevant expectations.

Perhaps the most important single source of role conceptions at this phase is what we have referred to collectively as generalized sources, an important example being the mass media.[4] Other sources of role conceptions (or expectations) are,

---

to carrying out the technical-instrumental tasks; and Silber, et al. (1961) demonstrate that coping with the anticipation of college involves both behavioral and attitudinal changes and adjustment. These references parallel our behavioral-attitudinal-cognitive dimension.

[3]It could be argued (albeit in general terms only) that the extent to which any role is enacted appropriately and convincingly is dependent on a balance and regulation of expectations coming from various others and the self. If this is so, more effective performance of a particular role would seem to come from meeting all expectations adequately, rather than some more than adequately and others less than adequately. (Effectiveness is, of course, a social evaluation rather than an absolute standard and is defined in terms of others' evaluations.) The development of one's ability to achieve balance and regulation can be seen as an outcome of the role-acquisition process.

[4]Ample support for this view seems to exist. For example, Gershon (1966, p. 49) asserts that the mass media constitute

of course, also present. Specific roles may be learned about from role incumbents themselves, as in the case of a child's contact with adults or a future physician's contact with the family doctor, or from future reciprocal-role others, as in the case of a future physician learning about physicians from patients. Obviously, from these contacts one formulates his own conceptions of what the role will be like. Nevertheless, the first view of a role typically comes primarily from generalized sources.

Seemingly because of the predominance of these sources of role information, individuals are usually presented with a very generalized and stereotyped conception of roles during this period.[5] It is generalized in the sense that only certain features of the role are presented and many others ignored. Consequently role conceptions formed in this phase are often incomplete.[6] The conception presented is stereotyped in that

idealized expectations tend to be emphasized. Future role enactors are exposed to behavioral, attitudinal, and cognitive features of roles at this time, either overtly or covertly. However, the specific features evident during this stage tend to be those the enactment of the role *should* involve, rather than those it actually involves. Perhaps because of this a fairly high degree of consensus is usually perceived during the anticipatory stage. Also, individuals tend to fantasize somewhat about future roles, viewing them as more consensual than they are. We assert, then, that there is relatively little dissensus on the ideal level for most roles, particularly with respect to what is perceived by the future incumbent.

Social and psychological adjustment to a role begins during this first period. Individuals develop images of what they feel will be expected of them and start to prepare themselves psychologically for what they expect the roles will be like. This anticipation is usually colored by what individuals want and need: therefore there tends to be a relative degree of congruity between individuals and their conceptions of future roles at this point. However, because it is influenced in this way, because it is idealized, and because individuals fantasize about future roles, anticipation may not be congruent with what will actually be experienced.

Although the anticipatory stage of socialization is generally considered functional for subsequent adjustment to acquired roles, research indicates that adjustment is in fact dependent on the degree of accuracy of what is conveyed and perceived. Thus the degree of congruity between what individuals learn to anticipate and what they subsequently experience will likely determine how quick and smooth the process of adjustment will be. Given our earlier comments about the conceptions of roles conveyed during anticipatory socialization, this stage would seem as likely to be dysfunctional as functional.[7]

---

[5]This appears to be a common conclusion of the few studies undertaken to investigate the communication of roles by the mass media. De Fleur concludes his examination of the portrayal of occupational roles on television thus: "Television content that deals with occupational roles can be characterized as selective, unreal, stereotyped, and misleading. . . . Television tends to make use of stereotyped beliefs and conceptions, and to focus upon atypical, dramatic, or deviant aspects of others" (1964, p. 74).

[6]They also tend to be ambiguous. For example, Feldman and Newcomb (1969, p. 71) report that much of the literature on preconceptions of college shows that "young men and women about to enter college seem to have only a hazy picture about life that lies ahead of them for the next four years." In the entire process of professional socialization, viewed as an extended period of anticipatory socialization, there exists a similar uncertainty about future roles. Sibley (1963, pp. 104–5) finds that first-year graduate students in sociology do not have a clear conception of the roles for which they are being prepared; and Lortie (1959, p. 366) concludes that law students leave ". . . law school with only a hazy and incomplete conception of what lawyer's work consists of."

[a social structure ". . . through which symbolic anticipatory socialization can occur." And Sarbin and Allen (1968, p. 546) argue: "Through the mass media of television, movies, newspapers, and books, as well as through contact with other persons, the individual acquires information about a great many roles which in the future he may be required to learn more thoroughly and to enact himself."]

[7]Support is found in a statement by Schramm, Lyle, and Parker: "There is no doubt that television's picture of the world includes an abnormally high proportion of sexy

Formal Stage

In the second phase of role acquisition the individual, now in a social position, experiences the role as an incumbent and shifts from viewing it from an outside perspective to viewing it from inside. In contrast to the anticipatory stage, when expectations arising from society at large predominate, expectations now arise characteristically from members of the role set (both others enacting the same role and others enacting strictly reciprocal roles) and from the incumbent himself, whose expectations for his performance are formed at least partially in response to those of others.

For social roles embedded in organizational structures, the expectations encountered during the formal phase pertain frequently to the organizationally defined rights and duties inherent in the position and usually codified by the social system in which it is located (see Sarbin and Allen, 1968, p. 499).[8] We refer to these as formalized expectations because they are often stated in formal, written terms; for example, in job descriptions and handbooks for new employees.

Also characteristic of the role expectations encountered now is that they are directed typically toward everyone occupying a particular social position. They are often a set of ''must'' behaviors, generally related to the goals of the system in which the particular position is located.[9] (Because of this, they cannot be left to chance; hence their explicit presentation.) Here we have the Hippocratic oath governing physician-patient relationships, the legal obligations of one spouse to another or of a parent to a child, and the employee's duties for an organization. These expectations may also be thought of as idealized, in much the same way as those encountered during the anticipatory stage.

Though formalized expectations tend to refer to the expected behavior and knowledge and skills of role enactors rather than to their attitudes or orientations toward a role and its enactment, attitudinal elements may be present. These may take the form of allegiance to certain others (e.g., ''the customer is always right''), specific emotions to be displayed (e.g., ''salesperson must exude warmth, not sarcasm''), and sometimes certain likes and dislikes (e.g., ''Conservative party members must dislike Communists''). Nevertheless, formalized expectations are set apart from those of the following stage by their emphasis on expected behavior and abilities, not attitudes.

A final characteristic of the expectations presented during the formal stage is their fairly high degree of consensus, particularly *within* each of the four sources we have identified. For example, we would expect that at this stage most people in reciprocal roles would agree in general on what an incumbent's role enactment should be. We would also expect a certain amount of consensus *between* sources. Typically, there seems to be little disparity at this rather abstract level among the expectations of society in general, others with reciprocal roles, others with similar roles, and even the individual himself. Such consensus would seem to exist because of the idealized nature of formalized expectations, which are not necessarily experienced in the everyday enactment of a role. Few would argue against the Hippocratic oath or the legal obligations of parents to children.

The reaction to what is encountered during this phase tends to be one of conformity. It occurs because of the relatively high degree of consensus and because individuals are only beginning psychologically to feel out the situation and what it may hold in store for them. In terms of the

---

women, violent acts, and extra-legal solutions to legal problems . . . inadequate fathers, of get-rich-quick careers, and of crooked police and judges. . . . If this is the case . . . then obviously this is not a positive contribution to socializing . . . [the child] . . . , and may require some very hard adjustments later'' (1961, p. 155).

[8]Levinson (1959, p. 177) speaks of these as the external forces derived from the ''organizational matrix,'' composed of pressure from authority, impending sanctions, and situational demands.

[9]As Berlo (1960, p. 141) describes them: ''The set of 'must' behaviors goes with the role. It is independent of the person occupying that role. . . . *These behaviors are independent of people; they are fixed by the system.*''

adjustment-adaptation feature of our scheme, people may be seen as postponing their own modes of meeting role expectations until they have become more familiar with them. They tend to adjust socially by meeting the requirements rather than modifying them, partly because formal requirements are open to little modification and partly because they are merely getting a feel for the role at this time. Psychologically, adjustment occurs through postponement of reactions to roles and situations, often by playing at roles rather than truly enacting them (see Turner, 1956). It is only later that one's personal reactions to the role become established and real adjustment and adaptation occur.

Informal Stage

In addition to the anticipatory and formalized role expectations of the two stages discussed above, the process of role acquisition involves encounters with unofficial or informal expectations and ways of doing things. These can occur in formal contexts because of the frequent need to modify or circumvent formal requirements as well as to deal with problems or areas of concern not covered directly by them. On occasion informal expectations are in direct contradiction to formal ones.[10] It is through informal systems that a new secretary knows how long a coffee break she may take, a college professor knows what unofficial restrictions there may be on what he wears to class, and any new employee learns when company rules may be bent.

These informal features of the new role are not usually conveyed by the system itself. They are not included in such formalized statements as job descriptions or handbooks for new employees: rather they arise and are transmitted through interaction of individuals. Peer groups, work groups,

cliques, car pools, and people encountered in daily activities are important sources of informal expectations. As with formalized expectations, both people enacting similar roles and those enacting reciprocal roles are primary sources, but at this stage role colleagues probably become more important in this regard than people with strictly reciprocal roles. Also, during this phase the personal expectations generally held in abeyance earlier become important. Upon encountering the informal nature of roles, individuals begin to place greater weight on their own role expectations.

In this stage there tends to be less consensus among the various expectations encountered than in the prior stage. Various groups and individuals tend to present differing informal expectations, which may be in opposition to formally expressed ones as well as to those a role incumbent is beginning to develop and those he learned during the anticipatory phase. Dissensus occurs both within and between the various sources of expectations.

In many instances informal expectations do not refer to the "musts" of role performance, as do formalized ones, but to the "mays," for they are not fixed in any explicit and rigid sense (Berlo, 1960, p. 141). They provide for flexibility within roles, for spontaneity allowable without losing sight of a role's function for the system in which it is located. Often, however, informal expectations can be quite imperative, and the sanctions attached to them can be more severe than those attached to formal expectations.

Like anticipatory and formal expectations, informal ones may be either explicit or implicit and may refer to behavior, attitudes, knowledge, and skills; but they tend to be implicit and to refer to the attitudinal and cognitive features of role performance. Although groups and individuals often present explicitly informal norms and ways of doing things, it is really through everyday interaction that a neophyte learns the obscure nuances and subtleties of the enactment of a new role. Likewise, some of the attitudinal components of role enactment may be explicitly stated, but most

---

[10]As De Fleur, D'Antonio, and De Fleur (1971, p. 75) assert, "In general the development of an informal structure in an association . . . results in the reinterpretation of roles that are theoretically fixed. . . ."

are not, and even an explicit statement is likely to be of only a general nature.

As Parsons has observed, roles allow for a certain range of variability, and it is this which enables actors with different personalities to enact the same role (see Parsons, 1951, pp. 234–35; Parsons and Shils, 1951, p. 24). Such leeway also provides a means of achieving adjustments to roles, and the informal stage of role acquisition is the period during which the final phases of adjustment begin (though in our view they are not fully accomplished until the succeeding stage). Because many informal expectations refer to "mays" rather than "musts" and because of the high degree of dissensus concerning them, an individual now has an opportunity to start shaping a role to fit himself, his past experiences and future objectives, and to work out an individual style of role performance. Final social adjustment thus commences, and one begins to finalize his own techniques of handling the social requirements of the role. Psychological adjustment as well begins in earnest at this point. Through the freedom allowed, one can start to formulate his own meanings for a role and its performance. In fact, as will become clearer in the discussion of the following stage, effective role performance typically requires this.

Personal Stage

For many years role theory has been characterized by attempts to explain variation and style within roles without the insights of personality theory. The results have not been adequate. In recent years it has been realized that any strong analysis of role performance has to include a psychological dimension. The individual cannot be ignored, for his personality, past experiences, unique abilities and skills, and culturally defined values and beliefs all affect how he enacts his roles.

Neglecting the individual in the role-acquisition process seems even more serious, since, as we view it, it is in part a process whereby individuals

and social roles, personalities and social structures become fused.

Our view is that as anticipatory, formal, and informal expectations are encountered, personal role expectations develop and are transmitted to others with whom one is in contact. Role acquisition thus comes to involve individuals imposing their own expectations and conceptions on roles and modifying role expectations according to their own unique personalities.[11] Because this cannot fully occur until the various types of expectations have been experienced, we consider it the final step in role acquisition.[12]

Whereas the informal stage tends to be characterized by role dissensus, a relative degree of role consensus now begins to reappear. Individuals are usually able to influence the expectations others hold for them and to achieve some degree of consensus among others' expectations and between those and their own; in other words, they impose their own style (usually a modified style) on their role performance and others accept it in large measure. This is important for social and psychological adjustment as well as for adaptation. Social adjustment tends to occur through the modifica-

---

[11]Getzels (1963, p. 311) speaks of need-dispositions which influence a person's perceptions and his reactions to the social world and asserts that "in order to understand the behavior of *specific* role-incumbents in *specific* institutions, we must know both the role expectations and the need-dispositions involved. Generally, it is only after this modification has been accomplished that appropriate and convincing role enactment will occur." This is what Sarbin and Allen (1968, p. 524) call self-role congruence: ". . . when self characteristics are congruent with role requirements, role enactment is more effective, proper, and appropriate than when role and self are incongruent."

[12]Goffman's essay on "role distance" anticipates our treatment of the personal dimension. He writes for example: "It is right here, in manifestations of role distance, that the individual's personal style is to be found. And it is argued in this paper that role distance is almost as much subject to role analysis as are the core tasks of roles themselves" (1961, p. 152). He further emphasizes (p. 130) that this showing of distance from a role occurs once the individual has been "validated" in the role (i.e., when he has conformed to the prescriptive aspects of it and has proved his competency and sincerity).

tion of a role rather than through earlier conformity to it. If one is able to relate his psychological needs to the (modified) requirements of the new role, then we may say that he has adjusted psychologically to it, in contrast to his earlier postponement of a psychological reaction. In terms of the distinction between adjustment and adaptation made earlier, adaptation (in the form of internalization of the role) may now occur. It probably will occur if adjustment has been successful in terms of what the person requires of his role and what it requires of him.

It is not enough, then, to view individuals as simply carrying out formal and informal expectations in new roles. They also seek to impose personal conceptions and needs and to reconcile these with the demands of the situation. Incongruence of self and role often results in perfunctory role enactment and in problems of social and psychological adjustment.[13] This in itself exemplifies the importance of including the personal phase in any discussion of role acquisition. Equally important, "role" is generally considered as the concept whereby the person and the social structure are linked (and thus as a point of reference for both sociology and psychology); this linkage can only be understood finally in terms of the mutual transformation of person and role.

An Overview

The formulation of role acquisition presented in this paper combines some loose ends from the literature into an interdisciplinary schema that we

---

[13]The individual might respond to such a situation by changing his personal value system to conform to the structural demands, by changing the social structure itself, by relinquishing the role, due to choice or force, or by meeting the formal and informal expectations with indifference and receiving little satisfaction from his role (Levision, 1959, p. 179). Conceivably, he could also formulate his own private meanings for his role enactment, meanings entirely different from those incorporated in the role.

feel describes clearly and succinctly how individuals acquire social roles. This synthesis is affected largely by emphasizing that learning new roles and adjusting to them are continuous, dynamic processes involving a personal dimension. Our view is that role acquisition is not a one-step process, and that norms, values, attitudes, information, and behavior are not simply conveyed and assimilated in a vacuum during that process. Centrally involved are individuals with specific (though changeable) personality characteristics who encounter a diverse series of expectations regarding their behavior, attitudes, and knowledge at different points in time.

People first develop preconceptions from exposure to anticipatory expectations presented by the mass media and by others enacting the type of role anticipated and strictly reciprocal roles. Once neophytes enter social positions, the process of learning and reacting to more formalized expectations begins. Initial success is partly dependent on the closeness of the anticipatory experiences to these actual ones. Overt and covert, behavioral, attitudinal, and cognitive, formal expectations typically are ones necessary for the achievement of the objectives of the system in which the role is located and are fixed by it.

Roles allow, however, for leeway and spontaneity, as has been noted on several occasions, and this latitude is provided to a certain degree through informal expectations learned after exposure to more formalized ones. Informal features are often derived from small group interactions among individuals of the system and are not made explicit. It is not really until the formal and informal expectations have been encountered that the final processes of adjustment begin. It is then that individuals, now familiar with new positions and their requirements, modify and mold roles around personality characteristics and the demands of other roles and achieve some balance among conflicting expectations.

REFERENCES

Becker, Howard S.; Geer, Blanche; Hughes, Everett C.; and Strauss, Anselm L. (1961), *Boys in White,* Chicago: University of Chicago Press.

Berlo, David (1960), *The Process of Communication,* New York: Holt, Rinehart & Winston.

Bourne, Peter (May 1967), "Psychosocial Phenomena in Basic Training," *Psychiatry* 30, 187–96.

Cogswell, Betty (Winter, 1967), "Rehabilitation of the Paraplegic: Processes of Socialization," *Sociological Inquiry* 37, 11–26.

De Fleur, Melvin (Spring, 1964), "Occupational Roles as Portrayed on Television," *Public Opinion Quarterly* 28, 57–74.

———; D. Antonio, William; and De Fleur, Lois (1971), *Sociology: Man in Society,* Chicago: Scott, Foresman.

Dornbusch, Sanford (May, 1955), "The Military Academy as an Assimilating Institution," *Social Forces* 33, 316–21.

Feldman, Kenneth, and Newcomb, Theodore (1969), *The Impact of College on Students,* Vol. 1, San Francisco: Jossey-Bass.

Gershon, Walter (September, 1966), "Mass Media Socialization Behavior: Negro-White Differences," *Social Forces* 45, 40–50.

Getzels, Jacob (1963), "Conflict and Role Behavior in the Educational Setting," in W. W. Charters and N. L. Gage, eds., *Readings in the Social Psychology of Education,* Boston: Allyn and Bacon, 309–18.

Goffman, Irving (1961), *Encounters,* Indianapolis: Bobbs-Merrill.

Gordon, Chad (1972), "Role and Value Development across the Life Cycle," in J. A. Jackson, ed., *Role* London: Cambridge University Press, 65–105.

Gross, Neal; Mason, Ward; and McEachern, Alexander (1958), *Explorations in Role Analysis,* New York: Wiley.

Hall, Oswald (March, 1948), "The Stages of a Medical Career," *American Journal of Sociology* 53, 327–36.

Israel, Joachim (1966), "Problems of Role-Learning," in Joseph Berger, Morris Zeldich, and Bo Anderson, eds., *Sociological Theories in Progress,* Vol. 1, Boston: Houghton Mifflin, 199–212.

Levinson, Daniel (March, 1959), "Role, Personality, and Social Structure in the Organizational Setting," *Journal of Abnormal and Social Psychology* 58, 170–80.

Linton, Ralph (1936), *The Study of Man,* New York: Appleton-Century.

Lortie, Dan (Fall, 1959), "Laymen to Laymen: Law School, Careers, and Professional Socialization," *Harvard Educational Review* 29, 352–69.

Merton, Robert (June, 1957) "The Role-Set: Problems in Sociological Theory," *British Journal of Sociology,* 8, 106–20.

Olesen, Virginia and Elvi Whittaker (1968), *The Silent Dialogue: A Study in the Social Psychology of Professional Socialization,* San Francisco: Jossey-Bass.

Parsons, Talcott (1951), *The Social System,* New York: Free Press.

———, and Shils, Edward A., eds. (1951), *Toward a General Theory of Action,* Cambridge, Mass.: Harvard University Press.

Sanford, Nevitt (1962), "Higher Education as a Field of Study," in *The American College,* New York: Wiley, 31–73.

Sarbin, Theodore and Allen, Vernon (1968), "Role Theory," in Gardner Lindsey and Elliott Aronson, eds., *The Handbook of Social Psychology,* Vol. 1, Reading, Mass.: Addison-Wesley, 488–567.

Schramm, Wilbur; Lyle, Jack; and Parker, Edwin (1961), *Television in the Lives of Our Children,* Palo Alto, Calif.: Stanford University Press.

Sherif, Muzafer (1936), *The Psychology of Social Norms,* New York: Harper.

Sherlock, Basil, and Morris, Richard (Winter, 1967), "The Evolution of the Professional: A Paradigm," *Sociological Inquiry* 37, 27–46.

Sibley, Elbridge (1963), *The Education of Sociologists in the United States,* New York: Russell Sage Foundation.

Silber, Earle; Hamburg, David; Caelho, George; Murphy, Elizabeth; Rosenberg, Morris; and Pearlin, Leonard (October 1961), "Adaptive Behavior in Competent Adolescents," *Archives of General Psychiatry* 5, 62–73.

Simpson, Ida Harper (Winter 1967), "Patterns of Socialization into Professions: The Case of Student Nurses," *Sociological Inquiry* 37, 47–54.

Turner, Ralph (September, 1956), "Role-Taking, Role Standpoint, and Reference Group Behavior," *American Journal of Sociology* 61, 316–28.

Zurcher, Louis A. (Winter, 1967), "The Naval Recruit Training Center: A Study of Role Assimilation in a Total Institution," *Sociological Inquiry* 37, 85–95.

BUYER-SELLER INTERACTION: A CONCEPTUAL FRAMEWORK

JAGDISH N. SHETH

This paper attempts to provide a comprehensive conceptualization of the buyer-seller interaction process as it occurs in traditional broadened contexts. The basic postulate underlying the conceptualization is that the quality of interaction is a function of the compatibility between the buyer and the seller with respect to both the style and the content of communication. After defining the dimensionalities of style and content, a number of personal, organizational and product-specific factors are described as determinants of style and content of communication in the buyer-seller interaction process.

A review of the literature in the area of buyer-seller interaction process points out at least three dimensions of the state of the art (see Evans, 1963; Davis and Silk, 1972; Hulbert and Capon, 1972; O'Shaughnessy, 1972; and Webster, 1968, for summaries and reviews of the knowledge in the area). First, the extent of empirical research on the buyer-seller interaction process is relatively sparse suggesting little interest in this area, at least among the academic researchers. While there is considerable talk about the mysteries of the super-salesman and some good research in the area of selection and training of sales representatives in industrial marketing, the vital linkage of the buyer-seller interaction process remains yet to be systematically researched.

Second, whatever empirical research one finds in the area is highly sporadic and ad hoc. Most of it consists of attempts to extend specific hypotheses borrowed from the behavioral sciences to describe and explain the process of buyer-seller interaction. Consequently, the area of buyer-seller interaction is replete with numerous hypotheses, interesting observations and a considerable degree of contradictory or unrelated research findings.

Third, there is a conspicuous absence of any comprehensive conceptualization or theory of buyer-seller interaction. It seems no one has as yet attempted to go beyond reviewing the literature in order to sort out existing evidence and to reconcile inconsistent or contradictory findings by offering a comprehensive or holistic perspective to the problem area.

Source: Jagdish N. Sheth, "Buyer-Seller Interaction: A Conceptual Framework" in Gerald Zaltman and Brian Sternthal (eds.) *Broadening the Concept of Consumer Behavior,* 1975, The Association for Consumer Research, pp. 131–140.

A comprehensive perspective of the buyer-seller interaction process seems timely and can serve several useful functions. It will encourage more systematic and realistic research which takes into account many interdependent phenomena relevant to understanding the buyer-seller interaction process; it will probably point out new areas of research by providing insights which can only come from a comprehensive perspective; finally it is likely to discourage research in what may prove to be irrelevant or less useful to subareas.

OVERVIEW

The conceptual framework suggested in this paper is comprehensive and abstract enough to include buyer-seller interactions in both household and organizational marketing. It is capable of explaining the process of buyer-seller interaction which takes place at the retail outlets for consumer goods as well as between sales representatives and purchasing agents of formal organizations. It is also comprehensive enough to include all types of buyer-seller interactions. These can be interpersonal (face-to-face), written or even telecommunication in nature. It is surprising to note how written and telecommunication buyer-seller interactions have been ignored in past research activities.

The basic postulate underlying the conceptual framework summarized in Figure 1 is that whether a specific buyer-seller interaction will or will not work is a function of two distinct dimensions of interaction. The first dimension is the *content of communication* representing the substantive aspects of the purposes for which the two parties have gotten together. It entails suggesting, offering, promoting or negotiating a set of product-specific utilities and their expectations.

While the dimensions of product-specific utilities will be described in detail later in the paper, it is sufficient to note here that often the expectations offered by the seller and desired by the buyer for a specific product or service do not match resulting in failure of the interaction transaction to be consummated successfully and satisfactorily.

A second dimension of buyer-seller interaction determination is the *style of communication*. It represents the format, ritual or mannerism which the buyer and the seller adopt in their interaction. The style of interaction reflects the highly individualistic preferences and normative expectations of the buyer and the seller about the process of interaction itself. Much of the search for the super-salesman is often localized in identifying the style of interaction of highly successful salesmen in organizational marketing.

The buyer-seller interaction process itself is treated as a transaction which can have multiple effects or consequences. Comparable to the impact of advertising (Sheth, 1974), the buyer-seller interaction is presumed to perform any of the following five functions: (a) increase awareness of each other's expectations about the product or service; (b) remind each other of past satisfactory transactions and their behavioral outcomes; (c) reinforce each other's behavior related to the sale of the product or service; (d) precipitate behavioral actions on each other's part by intensifying expectations; and (e) persuade each other to change their respective expectations.

Whatever the objective, a satisfactory interaction transaction between the buyer and the seller will occur if and only if they are compatible with respect to *both* the content and style of communication. In all other situations, the interaction transaction is presumed to be less than ideal. In Figure 1, a two by two classification of interaction transaction is provided as a very simple framework to understand the impact of incompatibility with respect to style and content of communication. For example, if the buyer and the seller are compatible with respect to style but not with respect to content of communication, it is argued that while a dialogue will continue between the two parties, the actual sale may not be consummated due to difference in product expectations. Either the interaction process will be terminated or negotiations will take place to change each other's product expectations. On the other hand, if the buyer and the seller are compatible with respect to content but not the style of communication, it is argued that either the process will be terminated or even if the sale is consummated there will be negative feelings about each other's style or manner of interaction resulting in an unsatisfactory transaction. Finally, when both the style and the content are incompatible between the buyer and the seller, not only will there be no transaction culminating in a sale, but there are likely to be negative side effects of complaints, bad word of mouth about each other, and distrust of each other.

Both the style and content of buyer-seller communication are determined by a number of personal, organizational and product-related factors. For example, the personal life styles and backgrounds will often determine the style of communication the buyer or the seller chooses to engage in. Similarly, organizational training and orientation will also mold the buyer or the seller with respect to the style of communication he is expected to engage in. Finally, the content of communication is likely to be determined by product-related variables such as market motivations, buyer and seller plans and technology or competitive structure of industry.

CONTENT OF COMMUNICATION

While it is obvious that any incompatibility with respect to what the buyer wants and what the seller offers in a product or service will be detrimental to consummating a sale, it is more interesting and useful to identify dimensions and sources of content incompatibility. Based on a recent model of individual choice behavior (Sheth, 1975), it is proposed that underlying buyer-seller expectations about a product or service, there lies a five dimensional utility space. The five dimensions represent different types of product-related utilities which the buyer desires and the seller offers to each other. Each type of utility is briefly described below:

1. Functional Utility. It represents a product's utility which is strictly limited to its performance

and which defines the purpose of its existence and classification as a type of good or service. For example, the functional utility associated with an instant breakfast can be described in terms of taste, convenience, nutrition and calories. Similarly, the functional utility associated with a passenger car tire can be defined in terms of mileage, blow out protection, traction, handling and ride. The functional utility is often measured in terms of a person's expectations on a number of product-anchored attributes or evaluative criteria.

2. Social-Organizational Utility. Sometimes a product or service acquires social-organizational connotations or imageries independent of its performance or functional utility. For example, cigarettes are often consumed due to their social imagery even though they may be functionally harmful. Certain products are, therefore, used for their prestige and not so much their performance. The existence of social-organizational utility in a product or service is also prevalent in organizational buyer behavior especially with respect to those products and services which are directly associated with the organization man. This is not surprising in view of the fact that there exists an organizational stratification of people working in organizations comparable to social stratification of households based on organization structure, hierarchy, and power distribution.

3. Situational Utility. It represents a product's utility which is *derived* from the existence of a set of situations or circumstances. The product or service has no intrinsic or independent utility and will not be offered or bought without the presence of circumstances which create its need. The situational utility is often strong among those products or services which are consumed on an ad hoc basis rather than on a continuous basis. For example, the utilization of the services of the priest for a marriage ceremony or the lawyer for divorce proceedings tends to be nonrepetitive by and large. Similarly a housewife may buy a product or service as a gift item due to a very specific situation

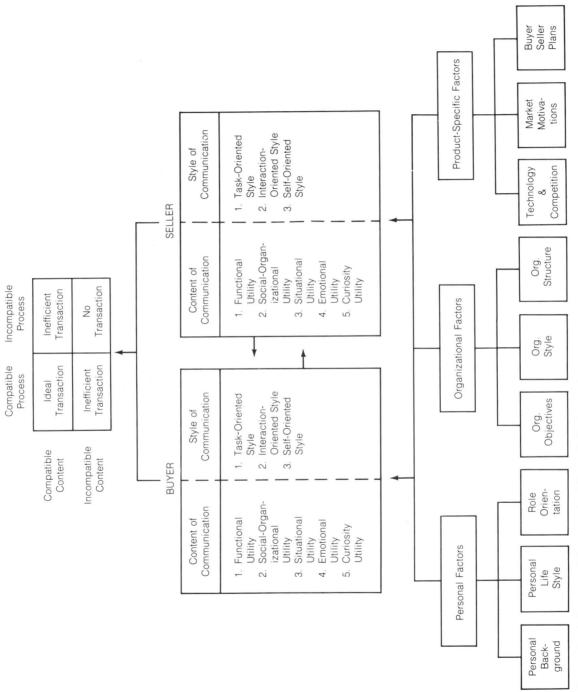

Figure 1 A Conceptual Framework of Buyer-Seller Interaction

or occasion such as graduation or marriage. Organizations often tend to use the services of professionals on an ad hoc basis because of a specific project. Many of the capital expenditure items and highly specialized professional skills have a greater degree of situational utility in them. It is extremely important to identify situations and activities which add to the utility of the product or service.

4. Emotional Utility. Sometimes a product or service evokes strong emotive feelings such as respect, anger, fear, love, hate or aesthetics due to its association with some other objects, events, individuals or organizations. The strong emotive feelings are therefore generalized to the product or service resulting in a different type of utility or disutility. For example, some Jewish buyers tend to refrain from buying German products because of strong emotional feelings they arouse as reminders of the German Nazi movement. Similarly, many Hindus refrain from eating beef due to strong emotive feelings anchored in religious tenets. While one would expect less prevalence of emotive utility in organizational products or services than in household products or services, this is not borne out by empirical research. Organizations also tend to manifest emotive behavior as is evidenced in international trade and cross-national negotiations.

5. Curiosity Utility. The fifth type of utility often present in both household and organizational products or services is related to novelty, curiosity and exploratory needs among individuals. Based on the assumption that man constantly seeks out new, different things due to either satiation with existing behavior or due to boredom inherent in highly repetitive tasks, certain *new* products or services acquire additional utilities which are not intrinsic to their performance. These products or services are both offered and sought largely due to their novelty and to satisfy a person's curiosity arousal. They have a very short life cycle and often degenerate as fads or fashions.

Each product or service has a vector of the five types of utilities described above. Furthermore, both the buyer and the seller will have certain expectations about the product or service on these five types of utilities. It is not at all uncommon both in household and organizational marketing to learn that the specific utility expectations of the buyer and the seller do not match resulting in some form of incompatibility with respect to content of interaction.

The degree of incompatibility can be measured by performing a dimensional analysis of the vectors of buyer-seller expectations. For example, we can locate the vectors of buyer and seller expectations in a five dimensional space, and measure the degree of incompatibility as a function of the distance between the buyer and the seller points located in the space. The greater the distance between the buyer and the seller points in space, the greater the incompatibility with respect to the content of communication.

The distance between the buyer and the seller will determine to what extent they are matched with respect to content of communication. Since the buyer in a free enterprise system has the economic buying power, it is presumed that the seller will often adapt or change his offerings in such a way as to minimize the distance. However, it is often not true in reality because the seller also attempts to change the location of buyer expectations in the space by persuasive communication strategies or sales tactics.

Who will make the adjustment is clearly a function of who has the greater power in the buyer-seller relationship. While the buyer has the economic power, the seller often has greater technical expertise to offset the buyer's power. As a very broad generalization, it is likely that in a buyer's market, the seller is more likely to change in the long run. In the seller's market, it is more likely that the buyer will change or adapt. In all other cases, tactics of persuasion, negotiations and bargaining are likely to emerge as consequences of the buyer-seller interaction.

STYLE OF COMMUNICATION

The vast literature on group dynamics and inter-personal relationships in small groups (Bass, 1960; Heider, 1958; Homans, 1961), provides an excellent source to discuss the concept of style of interaction. The style of interaction is presumed to be three dimensional. The specific dimensions are described below:

1. Task-Oriented Style. This style of interaction is highly goal oriented and purposeful. The individual is most interested in the efficiency with which the task at hand can be performed so as to minimize cost, effort and time. Any activity during the interaction process which is either not task-oriented or inefficient is less tolerated by the individual who prefers the task-oriented style. The buyer or the seller who prefers this style of interaction often tends to be mechanistic in his approach to other people.

2. Interaction-Oriented Style. The buyer or the seller who prefers this style of interaction believes in personalizing and socializing as an essential part of the interaction process. In fact, preference for this style of interaction is often manifested at the loss or ignoring of the task at hand. The buyer or the seller motivated by the interaction-oriented style is often compulsive in first establishing a personal relationship with the other person and only then getting involved in the specific content of interaction.

3. Self-Oriented Style. This style reflects a person's preoccupation with himself in an interaction situation. He is more concerned about his own welfare and tends to have less empathy for the other person. He is often unable to take the other person's perspective and views all aspects of interaction from his own selfish point of view. The concepts of self-preservation, self-survival and self-emulation tend to dominate this style of interaction.

It is also not uncommon to find situations in which the buyer and the seller are incompatible with respect to style of interaction. Given a three-dimensional vector of style of interaction, it is possible to measure the extent of incompatibility. The greater the distance between the buyer and the seller points in the style space, the more incompatible they will be with respect to style of interaction.

Unlike content of interaction, it is more difficult to change or adapt with respect to style of interaction. This is largely because the style orientations of individuals are often deep rooted in personality variables, early socialization processes and personal life styles. It is, therefore, difficult to discuss who should make changes in what situation in the buyer-seller interaction process. If the style of interaction is highly incompatible between the buyer and the seller, it is probably best to terminate interaction and attempt to link the right types of sellers with the buyers in the interaction process.

DETERMINANT FACTORS

Both the style and the content of buyer-seller interaction are determined by a set of exogenous factors. These are classified into three categories: (a) personal factors anchored to the individuals involved in the interaction; (b) organizational factors anchored to the respective organizations the buyer and the seller belong to (even in household marketing, we believe there are organizational factors not only associated with the seller but also with the buyer insofar as a typical household has some organizational structure, no matter how implicit it may be); and (c) product-related factors anchored to market motivations, competitive structure and buyer-seller plans. We will briefly describe some of the more salient variables in each category.

1. Personal Factors. The personal factors are likely to determine the style of interaction each individual prefers. The first one is the demographic, socioeconomic and organizational background of the individual. These include physical characteristics such as sex, race, height, and weight, as well as both generalized education and special skills acquired by the individual. A second specific variable is the individual's life style. It reflects the molding of the individual over time as a function of socialization and personality development. The third specific variable is the role orientation of the individual with respect to the interaction process. It includes expectations and performance of specific roles on the part of the salesman such as a consultant, order taker, informer, and persuader.

2. Organizational Factors. Organizational factors often determine the style and the content of interaction. The organization often recruits, selects, trains and prepares the buyer or the seller with respect to both the content and style of communication. The organizational factors which account for variability among organizations in their degree of controlling the content and style of interaction are organization objectives, organization style and structure. The content will be heavily influenced by organization objectives and to some extent by organization structure.

3. Product-Specific Factors. The product-specific factors are more likely to determine the content rather than the style of interaction. While there are many specific factors one can include in the list, we will isolate three specific factors which seem more relevant and interesting. The first factor, of course, relates to market motivations. It refers to the generalized needs, wants and desires customers have for which the specific product is more or less relevant. The second factor relates to

buyer and seller plans. The buyer has certain plans in his mind about the specific use he is likely to make of the product. Similarly, the seller has certain plans with respect to market differentiation and customer segmentation. The product expectations of the buyer and the seller are likely to be heavily determined by their respective plans. The third factor is anchored to the supply side of the product. It refers to the technological and competitive leadership the seller has in that product category. The product expectations and utilities especially in regard to functional, situational and curiosity utilities are more likely to be determined by technology and competition prevalent in the industry.

The three types of determinants of style and content of interaction are extremely relevant to isolate individual differences among buyers and sellers, product differences for the same buyer or seller, and organizational differences for the same product. They essentially serve the function of reducing all the buyer-seller interactions to a common base by partialling out the effects of personal, organizational and product differences.

CONCLUSION

This paper develops a comprehensive conceptualization of the buyer-seller interaction process based on the presumption that whether or not there will be a satisfactory interaction will depend on whether the buyer's and the seller's style as well as content of interaction match. To the extent they do not match, the interaction is likely to be either terminated or will entail negative side effects.

REFERENCES

Bass, M. (1960), *Leadership, Psychology and Organizational Behavior,* New York: Harper & Brothers.

Davis, H. L., and Silk, A. J. (Winter, 1972), "Interaction and Influence Process in Personal Selling," *Sloan Management Review,* 13, 54–56.

Evans, F. B. (May, 1963), "Selling as a Dyadic Relationship—A New Approach," *The American Behavioral Scientist,* 6, 76–79.

Heider, F. (1958), *The Psychology of Interpersonal Relations,* New York: John Wiley & Sons.

Homans, G. (1961), *Social Behavior: Its Elementary Forms,* New York: Harcourt, Brace & World.

Hulbert, J., and Capon, N. (February, 1972), "Interpersonal Communication in Marketing: An Overview," *Journal of Marketing Research,* 9, 27–34.

O'Shaughnessy, J. (Winter, 1971–72), "Selling as an Interpersonal Influence Process," *Journal of Retailing,* 47, 32–46.

Sheth, J. N. (January, 1974), "Measurement of Advertising Effectiveness: Some Theoretical Considerations," *Journal of Advertising,* 3, 6–11.

Sheth, J. N. (June 11, 1975), "Toward a Model of Individual Choice Behavior," paper presented at the ESOMAR Seminar on Modeling.

Webster, F. E., Jr. (July, 1968), "Interpersonal Communication and Salesman Effectiveness," *Journal of Marketing,* 32, 7–13.

AN EXPERIMENTAL ANALYSIS OF A SALESMAN'S EXPERT AND REFERENT BASES OF SOCIAL POWER IN THE BUYER-SELLER DYAD

PAUL BUSCH
AND
DAVID T. WILSON

Source: Paul Busch and David T. Wilson, "An Experimental Analysis of a Salesman's Expert and Referent Bases of Social Power in the Buyer-Seller Dyad," *Journal of Marketing Research,* Vol. 13, February, 1976, pp. 3–11.

INTRODUCTION

This study's purpose is to analyze the effects of differential levels of a salesman's expert and referent social power bases on the customer. French and Raven's (1959) bases of social power and the literature on interpersonal communications, e.g., Hovland, et al. (1953) are the main theoretical frameworks for specifying hypotheses.

THEORETICAL BACKGROUND

Social Power
According to the most generally accepted definition, social power is the ability of one person or group to cause another person or group to change in the direction intended by the influencer (Bither and Busch, 1972; Kornberg and Perry, 1966).

One major recurring misconception is that power is an attribute or possession of an individual or group. Several theoreticians (Dahl, 1957; El-Ansary and Stern, 1972; Kornberg and Perry, 1966; Nagel, 1968; Schopler, 1965) have stressed the importance of conceptualizing power not as an attribute but as a relationship among persons.

Although there are many specific power bases (French and Raven, 1959), expert and referent bases of social power are the primary concern in this study.

1. Expert power is based on the influencee's perception that the influencer has valuable knowledge, information, or skills in a relevant area. Expertise is a source of influence that must emanate from the participant in the dyad and cannot be delegated by a third party. It seems that at least a threshold level of a salesman's expertise must be demonstrated to establish a sound interpersonal selling relationship.

2. Referent power is based on the perceived attraction of members in the dyad to one another. The source of this power may arise from friendship, identification with a successful model, or feelings of a shared identity

(Gemmill and Wilemon, 1972). Studies in marketing suggest that perceived similarities in personal goals, interests, or values are sources that increase the effectiveness of this power base (Evans, 1963; Wilson, et al., 1972).

PERSONAL SELLING RESEARCH

The context of this social power research is personal selling. Several marketing scholars (Cotham, 1970; Engel, et al., 1973; Evans, 1963) have indicated that research on personal selling can be classified into two major categories: (1) the traditional approach emphasizing the salesman and his performance characteristics relevant to some criterion of sales performance, and (2) the emerging perspective which focuses on the customer-salesman interaction. The present study used both approaches to varying degrees.

RESEARCH DESIGN AND PROCEDURE

Subjects
Subjects were 187 (148 experimental and 39 control group) male junior level students enrolled in the College of Business Administration at the Pennsylvania State University. Juniors instead of seniors were selected because juniors have interests comparable to those of seniors and are in the same age group, but have not been contaminated for research purposes by the life insurance salesman's intensive selling efforts aimed at seniors. The selection of subjects was sound from the standpoint of external validity because college upperclassmen are an important market segment for life insurance.

The experimental procedure involved two separate meetings with each subject.

Meeting One
The first contact with subjects was made in the classroom and lasted approximately 20 minutes. The subjects were (1) recruited, (2) provided with

a statement of the study's objectives, and (3) given Byrne's (1971) Survey of Attitude questionnaire.

Meeting Two
The objectives of meeting two were to (1) administer the experimental treatments to the subjects, (2) measure the impact of these treatments on the dependent variables, and (3) assess the presence of demand characteristics in the study. The meeting lasted approximately one hour and ended with a question and answer period, debriefing, and three dollar payment to each subject.

One hundred forty-eight subjects were recruited and processed through the entire experiment. Of this group, 16 were eliminated because their responses to a postexperimental questionnaire indicated a suspicion of the study's method and purpose. Removal of the suspicious subjects eliminated the potential response bias of subjects who responded to their perceptions of the researchers' expectations rather than to the experimental stimulus.

A control group of 39 subjects completed a questionnaire and were paid one dollar for about 20 minutes of their time.

Independent Variables

Referent power. Referent power was based on the subject's perceived attraction to the salesman.

The differential levels of referent power involved manipulation of the perceived attitudinal similarity between the salesman and the subject. The methodology was adapted from the procedures established by Byrne (1961). The specific steps are described hereafter.

1. At the initial recruiting meeting subjects completed a 26 item questionnaire called the Survey of Attitudes. This instrument measured the subjects' feelings on a variety of topics ranging from fraternities and sororities to premarital sexual relations.
2. On the basis of the completed questionnaires, subjects were assigned randomly to

the high referent or low referent treatment conditions.

3. During the experimental sessions, subjects were presented with another Survey of Attitudes questionnaire ostensibly completed by the salesman.

4. In the *high referent condition,* the salesman's responses were made similar to the subjects' responses on 84.6 percent (22/26) of the attitude items. On a six point scale, similarity was defined as a response always one scale point away from the subject's response.

5. In the *low referent condition,* the salesman's responses were made dissimilar to the subjects' responses on 76.9 percent (20/26) of the attitude items. Dissimilarity was defined as a response always three scale points away from the subject's response. The number of similar and dissimilar responses was determined by pretesting designed to eliminate subjects' suspicions of the experimental manipulation.

6. After the measurement of the dependent variables, the subjects were given a questionnaire requiring judgments about the salesman. The measure of attraction was the sum of the last two items on the scale.

Expert power. One issue in creating differential levels of salesman expertise was to avoid the situation in which the low expert salesman is rejected as incompetent. It seemed reasonable to assume that a salesman perceived as totally incompetent would be rejected despite any other desirable characteristics he might have. Therefore, to create conditions for an externally valid test of the hypotheses it became necessary to present the salesman identified herein as a low expert to be "about average" in terms of his knowledge of life insurance. The high expert salesman was presented as being clearly "above average" or excellent on the various dimensions of expertise: (1) years of experience in selling life insurance,

(2) years of formal education, (3) amount of specialized and advanced training in the life insurance field, (4) success measured by number of times sales quotas were met or exceeded, (5) ability to communicate verbally, and (6) ratings of knowledgeability made by peers, superiors, and customers. The salesman was compared to a hypothetical national average on each of the dimensions.

Dependent Variables

Trust. Trust was measured as the sum of four Likert type scales. Subjects responded to the following: "I feel that the life insurance salesman being studied here is: dependable, reliable, trustworthy, reputable." The approach was adopted from a study which measured trust (Wilding and Bauer, 1968). Two attitude measures were developed.

Global attitude. One measure of attitude was the subject's general or global affective feelings toward the attitude object, in this case life insurance. This measure recognized that a single message cannot direct arguments at every dimension of a product which an individual finds relevant. The purpose of the global measure is to assess the extent to which the influence of the sales message is transferred into affect toward the product in its entirety (Wright, 1971).

Message specific attitude. Another measure of attitude reflected the position that the most meaningful assessment of marketing influence focuses on the message specific content.

Behavioral measures. Two measures of the subjects' behavior pertinent to the attitude object of life insurance were administered.

Behavioral intention. One behavioral measure required subjects to indicate their willingness to meet with the salesman to discuss life insurance. Subjects were asked to assume that they were in the market for life insurance when making their responses.

This hypothetical approach reduced reluctance to meet with the salesman on the part of subjects who already owned or were marginally interested in life insurance. Control group subjects were asked if they would be interested in discussing life insurance with an agent.

Behavioroid measure. Subjects completed a postcard with their name, address, and telephone number. An indication of the subject's behavioral commitment to learn more about life insurance was determined by having subjects indicate their level of interest in life insurance. The specific levels of interest included (1) no interest at all, (2) would like to receive information in the mail, (3) would talk with the agent over the phone, and (4) would meet with the agent in person. These four levels of interest constituted the *behavioroid* measure for this study.

Range. Range refers to the number and type of influencee's responses or behaviors over which the influencer has control (Nagel, 1968). The operational definition of range involved three steps. First, subjects indicated the probability that they would accept the advice or agree with the salesman's opinion on several topics: (1) the importance of a college education, (2) the importance of fresh air and exercise, (3) the means of adjusting to and handling stressful situations, and (4) the selection of worthwhile novels. These topics were selected from a list of 56 items and represented four points on a continuum from high to low importance (Byrne, 1971). The second step required subjects to rank the importance of these issues. Third, calculation of the range score involved multiplying the probability of accepting advice on a given topic by the rank importance scores. These four products were summed for each subject to arrive at a total range score.

Videotaped sales message. To approximate the conditions of an actual buyer-seller interaction, a videotaped sales message was presented which lasted approximately 14 minutes. The message was informative rather than persuasive. It explained life insurance, its role in a well-planned financial program, and why a college student should consider buying a policy. The salesman making the presentation was a very successful local life insurance agent. The use of professional agents guaranteed the technical accuracy of the presentation and enhanced its credibility.

ANALYSIS

Internal Validity: Manipulation Checks on Expert and Referent Variables

The basic research design required the establishment of four experimental conditions involving high and low levels of the salesman's expert and referent power bases. The issue of internal validity (Campbell and Stanley, 1966) demands that these independent variables be analyzed to ascertain whether the various treatment conditions were established during the experimental sessions.

Expert power: manipulation check for internal validity. To verify the expert manipulation's effectiveness, subjects responded on a nine point scale with end points labeled "slightly below average" and "definitely above average" to the statement: "I feel that the knowledge and competence of the salesman who is being studied here is." An ANOVA strongly supports the efficacy of the experimental manipulation. The mean score for the high condition was 7.17 and for the low condition it was 4.33 ($F = 117.41$, d.f. = 1, 128, $p = .0001$). These scores are significantly different and fall on opposite sides of the scale's midpoint.

Referent power: manipulation check for internal validity. To assess the referent power manipulation, subjects responded to two questions: (1) how much they would like the salesman if they met him, and (2) would they enjoy working with him in a research experiment. This two item response has a reported split half reliability of .85 (Byrne and Nelson, 1965).

ANOVA results indicated a main effect for referent power ($F = 12.384$, d.f. = 1, 128, $p = .001$). However, a comparison of the high referent-low expert condition with the low referent-high expert condition indicates that the mean attraction score for the former is 9.45 and for the latter is 9.40. The difference between these means is in the intended direction, but it is trivial.

Internal analysis: referent power. A perusal of ANOVA results indicated that hypothesized effects of the referent power base did not materialize. One explanation is that the referent power's manipulation may have been caused by additional information which may have had a significant impact on the subjects' liking for the salesman.

To obtain a fairer test of the referent power hypotheses, an internal analysis of the data was performed (Aronson and Carlsmith, 1968). An internal analysis is appropriate when an experimenter has assigned subjects randomly, but the effects of his independent variable are not powerful enough to make a discernible difference between his conditions. The internal analysis involved two steps. First, subjects were reassigned to treatment groups on the basis of their manipulation check scores for the attraction measure. Subjects who scored nine or below on the attraction measure were reclassified into the low referent condition even though they originally had been assigned randomly to the high referent condition. Those who scored 10 or above on the 14 point attraction scale were reassigned to the high referent condition. To preserve the strong expert manipulation, the reassignment of subjects on their attraction scores was done within each level of expert power. The second step in the internal analysis was to analyze the data with the reassigned subjects.

The major consequence of the reassignment of subjects on the basis of their attraction scores is that no causal statements can be made regarding the influence of referent power. The reassignment of subjects changes the research design from an experimental paradigm to a correlational one (Aronson and Carlsmith, 1968).

For some dependent variables, two separate ANOVAs were performed. One assessed the influence of the expert power base on the dependent variable. For this analysis, subjects were assigned to treatment groups on a random basis. Therefore, causal statements are made in interpreting the impact of the expert power base. Another ANOVA was performed to assess the relationship between the referent power base and the dependent variables. Because the assignment of subjects to treatment groups was done on a nonrandom basis, correlational rather than cause and effect interpretations are made regarding the impact of the salesman's referent base.

The basic research design was a 2×2 factorial. Analysis of variance procedures were used throughout the study.

Hypotheses and Results

H₁: A salesman in a high referent power relationship with a customer is perceived as more trustworthy than is a low referent salesman.

The theoretical justification of this hypothesis is found in the literature on interpersonal communications. A communicator who is similar to his audience on some dimension, in this case attitudinally similar, is expected by the audience to be more sincere. The audience assumes that the communicator feels a commonality with them and is concerned about their welfare (Mills and Jellison, 1968).

Table 1 contains the mean perceived trustworthiness scores and Table 2 provides a summary of the ANOVA. The analysis indicates a main effect for referent power ($F = 12.567$, d.f. = 1, 128,

Table 1 Mean scores for dependent variables listed by treatment condition

Dependent variables	High expert High referent	High expert Low referent	Low expert High referent	Low expert Low referent
Trust	14.30 (n = 43)	13.00 (n = 27)	11.81 (n = 27)	9.91 (n = 35)
Attitude specific	4.60 (n = 43)	4.48 (n = 27)	4.40 (n = 27)	3.54 (n = 35)
Attitude global[a]	36.65 (n = 35)	34.80 (n = 35)	35.61 (n = 31)	34.67 (n = 31)
Behavioral intention	5.25 (n = 43)	4.25 (n = 35)	4.66 (n = 27)	3.28 (n = 35)
Behavioroid measure	2.00 (n = 43)	1.74 (n = 27)	1.81 (n = 27)	1.82 (n = 35)
Behavioral intention[a]	5.08 (n = 35)	4.57 (n = 35)	3.93 (n = 31)	3.83 (n = 31)
Behavioroid measure[a]	1.91 (n = 35)	1.94 (n = 35)	1.77 (n = 31)	1.80 (n = 31)
Range	61.06 (n = 43)	57.59 (n = 27)	55.62 (n = 27)	49.37 (n = 35)

[a]Represents cell means for original random assignment of subjects to treatment groups. All other cell means are based on internal analysis of data.

$p = .0009$). The results provide strong support for the hypothesis that a high referent or attitudinally similar salesman is perceived as more trustworthy than a low referent salesman.

> H_2: A salesman in a high referent power relationship with a customer is more effective in producing an intended attitude change than is a low referent salesman.

The basis of this hypothesis is a group of studies in the communication literature (Brock, 1965; Burnstein, et al., 1961; Weiss, 1957). The studies found that people are more persuaded by a communicator who is similar to themselves.

The present study extends the previous research by analyzing the impact of attitude similarity between a buyer and seller on the customer's agreement with the salesman's arguments. The statistical analysis produced a significant main ef-

fect for referent power ($F = 6.19$, d.f. = 1, 128, $p = .014$). Thus, the hypothesis that a high referent salesman is more persuasive than a low referent salesman is supported.

The impact of the salesman's expert and referent social power bases on a global measure in comparison with a message specific measure of attitude was assessed. The basic hypothesis is that one persuasive message about a product as familiar as life insurance produces an insignificant amount of change in the respondent's general affective feelings toward the product.

The results indicated that neither the salesman's level of expertise nor level of referent power had an impact on the respondents' general affective feelings toward life insurance. A comparison of the experimental and control groups by Dunnett's (1955) test also yielded no differences. Therefore, as expected, one message about a product as familiar as life insurance is not likely to have an appreciable impact on one's overall affective feeling toward the product.

> H$_3$: A salesman in a high referent power relationship with a customer is more effective in producing the intended behavioral changes in a customer than is a low referent salesman.

The hypothesis is theoretically important because it concerns the impact of the salesman's power base on a customer's behavior.

The results in Table 2 indicate that referent power did produce a strong significant main effect ($F = 21.342$, d.f. $= 1$, 128, $p = .0001$) on the behavioral intention, e.g., willingness to meet with the salesman. Consequently, support was found for the hypothesis that a high referent salesman has a favorable influence on the behavioral dimension of attitude.

The ANOVA of the behavioroid scores (level of interest in life insurance) reported in Table 2 indicated that neither the expert ($F = 1.244$, d.f. $= 1$, 128, $p = .267$) nor the referent ($F = .0235$ d.f. $= 1$, 128, $p = .629$) the power base made a significant difference.

The findings provide only partial support for the theoretical proposition that a high referent salesman is more effective in generating the intended behavioral changes in customers than is a low referent salesman. The results highlight the importance of multiple dependent measures and the varying conclusions which may be reached depending upon the degree of the subject's involvement when responding to dependent measures.

> H$_4$: A salesman in a high expert power relationship with a customer is more effective in producing the intended behavioral changes in a customer than the salesman who is in a low expert power relationship.

The objective of this hypothesis is to extend the domain of social power theory to the marketing context of buyer-seller relationships. The dependent variables heretofore referred to as behavioral intention and behavioroid scores were used. The results presented are based on the original random assignment of subjects to the treatment groups.

The results of the analysis reported in Table 2 indicate a main effect of expert power on behavioral intention scores ($F = 11.68$, d.f. $= 1$, 128, $p = .001$). These findings provide sound support for the hypothesis that a high expert salesman is more effective than a low expert in producing the intended behavioral response in potential customers.

The impact of the expert power base on the behavioroid scores was assessed. The analysis of variance results indicate no main effect for the expert power base ($F = .414$, d.f. $= 1$, 128, $p = .237$).

The main theoretical finding was that only partial support was provided for the proposition that a high expert salesman is more effective than a low expert salesman in producing the intended behavioral responses in potential customers (McGuire, 1969). Methodologically, the results demonstrate that care must be taken to develop meaningful operationalizations of dependent variables. The results show that conclusions can differ considerably, depending upon the specific operational definitions of dependent variables.

Control and experimental group contrasts were made by Dunnett's (1955) procedure. The results of the analysis for the behavioral intention variable are reported in Table 3. With the exception of the contrast between the high expert-high referent group and the control group, the differences are significant at the .05 level. With the behavioroid scores as the dependent variable, none of the contrasts were significantly different at the $\alpha = .05$ level (see Table 3).

The results of the behavioroid analysis (Table 3) are readily interpretable in terms of the subjects' commitment to their responses. The behavioroid measure was much more involving and required the subjects to make a behavioral commitment by providing their names, addresses, and telephone numbers to the life insurance salesman. Signifi-

Table 2 ANOVA results for each dependent variable

Dependent variable	Source	d.f.	MS	F	p
Trust	Expert (A)	1	246.70	38.051	0.0001
	Referent (B)	1	81.47	12.567	0.0009
	A × B	1	2.84	0.438	0.5162
	Error	128	6.48		
Attitude specific	Expert (A)	1	9.47	8.291	0.005
	Referent (B)	1	7.07	6.192	0.014
	A × B	1	4.35	3.814	0.053
	Error	128	1.14		
Attitude global[a]	Expert (A)	1	11.19	0.385	0.536
	Referent (B)	1	66.93	2.302	0.132
	A × B	1	6.98	0.240	0.625
	Error	128	29.07		
Behavioral intention	Expert (A)	1	18.85	9.125	0.003
	Referent (B)	1	44.10	21.342	0.000
	A × B	1	1.17	0.567	0.453
	Error	128	2.06		
Behavioroid measure	Expert (A)	1	0.54	1.244	0.267
	Referent (B)	1	0.10	0.235	0.629
	A × B	1	0.59	1.345	0.248
	Error	128	0.43		
Behavioral intention[a]	Expert (A)	1	29.14	11.681	0.001
	Referent (B)	1	3.34	1.333	0.249
	A × B	1	1.43	0.575	0.450
	Error	128	2.49		
Behavioroid measure[a]	Expert (A)	1	0.62	1.414	0.237
	Referent (B)	1	0.03	0.068	0.794
	A × B	1	0.00	0.000	0.987
	Error	128	0.44		
Range	Expert (A)	1	1448.77	11.907	0.001
	Referent (B)	1	728.39	5.987	0.016
	A × B	1	61.22	0.503	0.479
	Error	128	121.67		

[a]Represents ANOVA results for original random assignment of subjects to treatment groups. All other tests are based on internal analysis of data.

Table 3 Contrast of experimental group means and control group means with behavioral intention and behavioroid measures as dependent variables

Treatment groups	Behavioral intention			Behavioroid measure		
	Mean value	Difference between group mean & control group mean	.05 Dunnett value	Mean value	Difference between group mean & control group mean	.05 Dunnett value
High expert— high referent	5.255	− .514[a]	±.9027	2.000	0.103[a]	±.4423
Low expert— high referent	4.666	− 1.103[b]	±.9027	1.740	−.157[a]	±.4423
Low referent— high expert	4.259	− 1.510[b]	±.9027	1.814	−.083[a]	±.4423
Low referent— low expert	3.285	− 2.484[b]	±.9027	1.828	−.069[a]	±.4423
Control	5.769			1.897		

[a]Not significant.
[b]$p < .05$.

cantly different results and conclusions are drawn from the analyses of the behavioral intention and behavioroid scores. Methodologically, the main conclusion is that multiple measures of dependent variables which require varying respondent involvement should be made and analyzed in experimental marketing research.

> H₅: A salesman in a high referent power relationship with a customer is able to exert influence over that customer across a broader range of circumstances than is a low referent salesman.

The source of this hypothesis is the social power base theory of French and Raven (1959). The mean range scores are reported in Table 1 and the analysis of variance is reported in Table 2. The results of the analysis indicate a main effect due to the referent power base ($F = 5.987$, d.f. = 1, 128, $p = .016$). These findings support the hypothesis that a high referent salesman exerts influence across a broader range of behaviors than does a low referent salesman.

A major benefit of the present research design is

that it permitted a comparison of the relative and interactive effects of the referent and expert power bases. For the range variable, the expert power base also produced a significant main effect (Table 2, $F = 11.907$, d.f. = 1, 128, $p = .001$). This finding is in conflict with social power base theory stating that expert power is limited or constrained to those areas in which the influencer has expertise (Collins and Raven, 1969). An explanation for this finding may be the "halo effect," i.e., the expertise in one area may generalize to other areas. In other words, an individual may be an expert on one topic but others may attribute to him expertise in other areas. The interaction of the referent and expert power bases did not approach significance ($F = .503$, d.f. = 1, 128, $p = .479$).

MANAGERIAL IMPLICATIONS

The development of the customer's trust is one of the major challenges confronting the salesman (Stryker, 1967). The findings indicate that the stronger the expert and referent power bases the more trustworthy the salesman was perceived to be by the customer. Expert power was more important than referent power as a factor affecting trust. By the criterion of explained variance (Hayes and Winkler, 1971) as a measure of importance, expert power accounted for 20.7% of the variance in trust whereas referent power explained only 6.4%. A salesman's expertise appears to be more important than his referent power in gaining the customer's trust. Therefore, sales training programs should be designed to increase the strength of the expert power base. Salesmen should make thoughtful efforts to communicate information about their expertise to the customer.

The findings indicate that a high referent salesman had a wider range of influence than did a low referent salesman. In other words, greater referent power enabled the salesman to exert influence in a large number of situations or circumstances. The range of situations which the salesman tries to influence is represented by the variety of products and services he sells. Therefore, the development of a referent power base would be particularly important for a salesman selling a great variety of products or services. A salesman who continually uses rewards, such as gratification of a customer's ego, entertainment, and "favor-doing" for customers, eventually may develop a referent power base of influence over the customer. This is particularly important in industrial selling where long-term buyer-seller relationships are common.

With regard to the measurement and assessment of marketing communication effectiveness, two aspects of the present research are of interest to marketing management. A specific measure of the subjects' attitudes toward the content of a life insurance message indicated that the salesman's expert and referent power bases had the intended effect on attitude. However, these same power bases had no significant impact on the subjects' general or global attitudes (affect) toward life insurance. A noninvolving behavioral measure requiring subjects to respond to a hypothetical situation indicated that high levels of a salesman's expert and referent power bases produced the intended change. However, a more involving behavioral measure, which required subjects to provide their names, addresses, and telephone numbers to enable a salesman to contact them in the future, demonstrated that the expert and referent power bases were not effective in producing the desired behavioral changes.

The major conclusion is that the specificity versus generality of measurement and the degree of respondent involvement dramatically affect the responses that subjects make in experimental research. Consequently, researchers and decision makers should be aware of these issues and make provisions for them when assessing marketing communication goals.

REFERENCES

Aronson, E., and Carlsmith, J. M. (1968), "Experimentation in Social Psychology," in G. Lindzey and E. Aronson, eds., *Handbook of Social Psychology,* Vol. 2, Reading, Mass.: Addison-Wesley.

Bither, S. W., and Busch, P. S. (1972), "Social Power: A Perspective for Viewing the Buyer-Seller Dyad in Industrial Marketing," Working Series in Marketing Research, College of Business Administration, Pennsylvania State University, Paper No. 17.

Brock, T. C. (June 1965), "Communicator-Recipient Similarity and Decision Change," *Journal of Personality and Social Psychology,* 1, 650–54.

Burnstein, E.; Stotland, E.; and Zander, A. (1961), "Similarity to a Model and Self-Evaluation," *Journal of Abnormal and Social Psychology,* 62, (March), 257–64.

Byrne, D. (1961), "Interpersonal Attraction and Attitude Similarity," *Journal of Abnormal Social Psychology,* 62 (May), 713–15.

———, ed. (1971), *The Attraction Paradigm,* New York: Academic Press.

——— and Nelson, D. (1965), "Attraction as a Linear Function of Proportion of Positive Reinforcements," *Journal of Personality and Social Psychology,* 1 (June), 659–63.

Campbell, D. T., and Stanley, J. C., eds. (1966), *Experimental and Quasi-Experimental Designs for Research,* Chicago: Rand McNally and Co.

Collins, B. E., and Raven, B. H. (1969), "Group Structure: Attraction, Coalitions, Communication, and Power," in G. Lindzey and E. Aronson, eds., *Handbook of Social Psychology,* Vol. 4, Reading, Mass.: Addison-Wesley.

Cotham, J. C., III (1970), "Selecting Salesmen: Approaches and Problems," *MSU Business Topics,* 18 (Winter), 64–72.

Dahl, R. A. (1957), "The Concept of Power," *Behavioral Science* 2 (July), 201–18.

Dunnett, C. W. (1955), "A Multiple Comparison Procedure for Comparing Several Treatments with a Control," *Journal of the American Statistical Association,* 50 (October), 1096–121.

El-Ansary, A. I. and Stern, L. W. (1972), "Power Measurement in the Distribution Channel," *Journal of Marketing Research,* 9 (February), 47–52.

Engel, J. F.; Kollat, D. T.; and Blackwell, R. D., eds. (1973), *Consumer Behavior,* 2nd ed., New York: Holt, Rinehart, and Winston, Inc.

Evans, R. B. (1963), "Selling as a Dyadic Relationship—a New Approach," *American Behavioral Scientist,* 6 (May), 76–79.

French, J. R. P., Jr., and Snyder, R. (1959), "Leadership and Interpersonal Power," in D. Cartwright, ed., *Studies in Social Power,* Ann Arbor: University of Michigan Press.

——— and Raven, B. (1959), "The Bases of Social Power," in D. Cartwright, ed., *Studies in Social Power,* Ann Arbor: University of Michigan Press.

Gemmill, G. R., and Wilemon, D. L. (1972), "The Product Manager as an Influence Agent," *Journal of Marketing,* 36 (January), 26–30.

Hayes, W. L., and Winkler, R. L., eds. (1971), *Statistics: Probability Inference and Decision,* New York: Holt, Rinehart, and Winston, Inc.

Hovland, C. I.; Janis, I. L.; and H. H. Kelley, eds., *Communication and Persuasion,* New Haven, Conn.: Yale University Press, 1953.

Kornberg, A., and Perry, S. D. (1966), "Conceptual Models of Power and Their Applicability to Empirical Research in Politics," *Political Science,* 18 (March), 52–70.

McGuire, W. J. (1969), "The Nature of Attitudes and Attitude Change," in G. Lindzey and E. Aronson, Eds., *Handbook of Social Psychology,* Vol. 3, Reading, Mass.: Addison-Wesley, 136–314.

Mills, J., and Jellison, J. M. (1968), "Effect on Opinion Change of Similarity Between the Communicator and the Audience He Addressed," *Journal of Personality and Social Psychology,* 9 (June), 153–56.

Nagel, J. H. (1968), "Some Questions About the Concept of Power," *Behavioral Science,* 13 (March), 129–37.

Schopler, J. (1965), "Social Power," in L. Berkowitz, ed., *Advances in Experimental Social Psychology,* Vol. 2, New York: Academic Press.

Stryker, P., ed. (1967), *The Incomparable Salesman—A Study of the Dollar Round Table, Including the Greatest Salesman in the Business World,* New York: McGraw-Hill Book Company.

Weiss, W. (1957), "Opinion Congruence with a Negative Source on One Issue as a Factor Influencing Agreement on Another Issue," *Journal of Abnormal and Social Psychology,* 54, 180–86.

Wilding, J., and Bauer, R. A. (1968), "Consumer Goals and Reactions to a Communication Source," *Journal of Marketing Research,* 5 (February), 73–77.

Wilson, D. T.; Mathews, H. L.; and Monoky, J. F., Jr., eds. (1972), *Attitudes as a Predictor of Behavior in a Buyer-Seller Bargaining Situation: An Experimental Approach,* Working Series in Marketing Research, Report No. 15, Pennsylvania State University.

Wright, P. L. (1971), "Factors Affecting the Role of Cognitive Processes in the Advertising Influence Process," unpublished doctoral dissertation, Pennsylvania State University.

SECTION 6

COMMUNICATION PROCESSES IN CONSUMER BEHAVIOR

Role relationships and the implied interactions are maintained through communication. Communication is the process of establishing a commonness of thought between two or more persons. It is, in effect, the "glue" of social interaction. Without communication, interaction could not occur and hence buyer-seller relationships could not develop.

The communication process involves five key factors. First, there is the *source* of a communication. An important issue in the study of consumer behavior concerns the credibility of various sources of information. Does a communication about a product have more of an impact on consumers when the source of the communication is an acknowledged expert rather than when it comes from a trusted friend who is not an expert? Second, it is necessary to consider the particular *message* being conveyed. Should the message be of a threatening nature, i.e., should it stress the bad consequences of not using a particular product or brand? Should the message be highly persuasive or should it merely try to convey information without interpretation or evaluation? A third consideration involves the *channel* of communication. What channel is most likely to catch the attention of consumers for a particular product? Are some channels such as informal word-of-mouth discussions better than more formal channels such as newspapers for disseminating information about a new product? Channels such as print, broadcast, and interpersonal media may vary greatly in their possible persuasive effects, their speed in disseminating information, their ability to overcome biases among consumers, and the number and type of people reached. A fourth important consideration in communication is the *receiver* or the intended audience. Here research has focused on the relative susceptibility to influence of consumers with different personalities, levels of formal education, and perceptions of themselves and others. A final consideration concerns *destination* effects. What happens after a communication is received? How is it remembered by the consumer? If the communication changes consumers' attitudes, will those attitudes fade quickly, especially if competitive advertising occurs?

It is important to consider key communication roles as they may occur in formal groups. There appear to be four key communication roles in any type of group. One role has been mentioned in Section 3 of this reader, that of the *gatekeeper*. The gatekeeper may or may not belong to a particular group. The gatekeeper serves to prevent too much information from entering a group by filtering communications. Too much information can cause an overload and result in a breakdown in the channels of communication. For example, if a consumer receives too much information, there may be a tendency to "turn off" that channel altogether. A second role, that of *liaison,* integrates and interconnects various parts of an organization or different informal groups. The liaison role is thus very important for rapidly disseminating information from a gatekeeper. The *opinion leader* is the person who helps evaluate the reliability of communications. The opinion leader is able to informally influence the attitudes and behaviors of others more or less frequently. Finally, the *cosmopolite* role relates a social system to its environment. The cosmopolite person is often in contact with sources of information outside the group, but also belongs to the group. This is what differentiates the cosmopolite from a gatekeeper who may not belong to the group for which he or she serves as gatekeeper. Also a gatekeeper is likely to function with respect to only one type of channel or one type of product. A cosmopolite, on the other hand, is likely to be in contact with diverse channels dealing with diverse topics.

"A CONTROLLED STUDY OF THE EFFECT OF TELEVISION MESSAGES ON SAFETY BELT USE"

One of the most common misperceptions about consumer behavior relates to the persuasive effect of television advertisements. Most people overestimate the power of a television advertising campaign. In particular, even the best-designed campaign is likely to have little or no impact if it is attempting to persuade people to do something they do not want to do. It is one thing to encourage a person to try a new brand of soap when that person already uses and has a positive attitude toward soap in general. It is quite another thing to try to persuade people to change a negative attitude into a positive attitude and thereby change their action patterns.

These contentions are well illustrated by the Robertson article. The researchers followed practices which are usually suggested for those planning communication messages. The content and basic message of the ads were based on preliminary research to determine differences between seat belt users and nonusers. An advertising agency with experience in these types of campaigns was employed. The context of the ads was matched to that of the programs in which they were embedded. A fairly large amount of prime time slots were used for the messages. The length of the campaign was long enough (nine months) to assume that effects should be manifested. The ads were well done and received several awards. One of the editors of this volume (Melanie Wallendorf) has viewed the ads. They have a very strong impact: a naive guess might easily be that they would produce a 70 percent increase in seat belt use. Viewer involvement is high and the emotional reactions (particularly to the "girl at the window" ad) are strong. The emotions evoked include sympathy, fear, horror, regret, anger, and resolution to act differently. Not all of the messages, of course, can be classified as high-fear appeals.

Yet, these ads still had no effect on seat belt use. How can one know that this experimental result accurately reflects people's actual responses to the ads? This question can only be answered by examining the research methodology.

The research methodology used in this study is very strong. Actual behavior was observed rather than relying on self-claimed use of seat belts. Observations were made before the message campaign, continuously during the campaign, and after the campaign. This made it possible to determine whether or not there was a change in behavior. The people observed did not know they were being observed and therefore they could not adjust their behavior to make it congruent with the research purposes. The observers did not know whether or not particular people were in the treatment group (cable A) or the control group (cable B). Therefore, they could not manufacture results congruent with the research hypotheses. The importance of the use of a control group is demonstrated by this article. Without the control group, the researchers would have concluded that belt use decreased as a result of the television messages. However, since the control group also showed this decline, their conclusion is that the messages had no effect.

The researchers thus conclude that certain strategies will not change behavior in certain situations. In particular, they advocate the use of passive approaches. These are strategies which bring about change without relying on action on the part of the protected persons. The passive alternative to seat belts (which are an active strategy) is air bags or other passive restraint systems. Other consumer-related examples include required nutritional levels in foods rather than nutritional labels, and fixed finance charges rather than finance charge disclosures. Thus, in addition to demonstrating the persuasive potential (or rather, persuasive failure) of television messages in certain situations, this article offers strategy recommendations for successful change programs.

"WORD-OF-MOUTH PROCESSES IN THE DIFFUSION OF A MAJOR TECHNOLOGICAL INNOVATION"

When most people think of communication processes which are relevant to consumer behavior, they immediately think of advertising. Yet another source of information about products is through a person's friends. In fact, word-of-mouth communication processes have been found to be particularly important in the diffusion of innovations. That is, people seem to rely very heavily on their friends and acquaintances for information about new products, services, and brands. The innovation need not be new in an absolute sense, but rather can be considered an innovation if it is perceived to be new by the person.

Most of the research on word-of-mouth communication processes in the diffusion of innovations has been done in the context of ultimate consumers considering new products. The Czepiel article is interesting because it explores these communication processes in the context of industrial buying decisions. First, Czepiel establishes that, in fact, word-of-mouth processes do operate in this context. Secondly, he extends previous work by ascertaining the pattern of this communication process. The following hypothesis is supported: The greater the similarity of the sizes of the firms and of the types of business of the firms, the more likely it is that they will communicate with each other about technological innovations. However, status within the industry also plays a role. Low-status firms may contact a high-status firm for information, but it is unlikely that the reverse process will occur.

One of the strengths of the Czepiel article is that it sometimes answers a particular question or addresses a particular hypothesis by doing several kinds of analysis. This establishes *convergent validity* for the findings. If the same result is obtained in several different ways, we are more confident of it being true. For example, the third hypothesis (that early adopters are more likely to be opinion leaders) is addressed in Figures 4 and 5. Different bits of information were used to construct each figure, but each figure provides a test of the hypothesis.

"ANTI-DRUG ABUSE COMMERCIALS"

In any communication message there are many elements which can be varied—time length, message approach (humor, fear), level of complexity, number of actors, and credibility of source. Feingold and Knapp examine the differential effects of varying three particular elements: high vs. low threat, explicit vs. implicit conclusions, and monologue vs. dialogue. Therefore, there are three variables, each of which has two levels. This is called a $2 \times 2 \times 2$ factorial experimental design, as shown below:

	Threat				
	High		Low		(Variable C)
	Monologue	Dialogue	Monologue	Dialogue	(Variable A)
Explicit	1	2	5	6	
Implicit	3	4	7	8	

Conclusions (Variable B)

There were eight experimental conditions. In each condition, the group had a pretest, six exposures to the ads, and a post-test questionnaire after each two exposures (three post-tests in all). The sequence was as follows:

Pretest → 2 exposures → Post-test → 2 exposures
→ Post-test → 2 exposures → Post-test questionnaire

In addition, two control groups were used. Control group A had a pretest and the three questionnaires, but no exposure to messsages. The data from this group provide information about history (effects of particular events which occur between measurements, e.g., between pretest and the first questionnaire) and about maturation (individual processes which occur due to the passage of time, e.g., growing older). Control group B had two exposures and one post-test questionnaire. Data from this group can be compared with the experimental groups to see if the experimental groups responded differently because they took a pretest questionnaire before they saw any messages. In other words, this comparison checks to see if, because they took a pretest, they became aware of the purposes of the study, and therefore listened more carefully to messages about drug abuse or thought more about the topic. Additional evidence that this did not occur is derived from the subjects after the experiment was completed. In a discussion period (which is called a debriefing), subjects are probed about whether they knew the purposes of the study. Then they are slowly brought to a full understanding of how and why the study was conducted. In this study, none of the subjects reported that they had known the purposes of the research.

None of the three experimental variables showed highly statistically significant results ($p < .08$ for the explicit vs. implicit conclusions variable is not really highly significant). Thus, the between-group comparisons were not very productive. However, within the groups there was a main effect. The attitudes shifted between the pretest and the second and third post-test. However, the shift was toward less negative attitudes toward drugs. In other words, the effect of the anti-drug abuse commercials was to move subjects from having a negative attitude toward having a *less* negative attitude. The implications of this boomerang effect are discussed in the article.

The importance of this article is to note the well-planned methodology for studying the effects of communication programs.

A CONTROLLED STUDY OF THE EFFECT OF TELEVISION MESSAGES ON SAFETY BELT USE

LEON S. ROBERTSON, PhD
ALBERT B. KELLEY
BRIAN O'NEILL
CHARLES W. WIXOM
RICHARD S. EISWIRTH
WILLIAM HADDON, Jr., MD

Source: Leon S. Robertson, Albert B. Kelley, Brian O'Neill, Charles W. Wixom, Richard S. Eiswirth, and William Haddon, Jr., "A Controlled Study of the Effect of Television Messages on Safety Belt Use," *American Journal of Public Health,* Vol. 64, November, 1974, p. 1074.

INTRODUCTION

The use of safety belts in automobiles greatly reduces the probability of death and injury in crashes (Tourin and Garrett, 1960; Bohlin, 1967; Campbell, 1968; Levine and Campbell, 1971). As a result of legislation in several states, lap belts have been standard equipment in at least the front outboard seating positions of 1964 and later models of American made cars (Seat Belt Accidents, 1965). Authorized by the National Traffic and Motor Vehicle Safety Act of 1966, the Secretary of Transportation issued a federal motor vehicle standard, effective January 1, 1968, which requires lap and upper torso belts in front outboard seating positions except in convertibles and lap belts in all other seating for folding auxiliary jump seats, side-facing seats, and rear-facing seats of automobiles manufactured for sale in the U.S. (Standard Number 208, 1967).

However, the availability of safety belts does not guarantee their use. In October, 1970, a study was conducted which included actual observation of drivers in their automobiles. In a metropolitan area, only 7 percent of drivers of 1968 and later models were using lap and upper torso belts and an additional 16 percent were using lap belts only. Lap and upper torso belts were used by 1 percent of drivers of 1968 and later models in smaller cities and 9 percent of such drivers used lap belts only (Robertson, O'Neill, and Wixom, 1972). Belts even when present, were used less often in earlier models. In spite of a number of campaigns urging safety belt use, the proportion of vehicle occupants using them is so low that much of the reduction in death and injury that should be achieved by their use is not being realized.

Campaigns promoting the use of safety belts have been based on inadequate knowledge of the factors contributing to lack of use. If the campaigns have been evaluated at all in terms of effectiveness, the evaluations have been faulty in design and execution (Haskins, 1969; Haskins, 1970).

161

In the present work, we have avoided some of the problems of previous studies and have tried to design and implement as definitive a study as present knowledge and technology allow. First, a survey was conducted of actually observed safety belt users and nonusers to determine the factors which distinguished the two groups (Robertson, et al., 1972). Second, television messages based partially on the preliminary study were developed and produced. These messages were then shown on one cable of a dual cable television system designed for marketing studies. The second cable as well as noncable groups allows comparison with groups not exposed to the messages to determine the effect of the messages relative to the effect of other factors which may influence belt use. The messages were shown for 9 consecutive months. For 1 month before and throughout the campaign, drivers were observed as to safety belt use and were matched through license plate numbers to the households on a given cable. In addition to being controlled, the study was "double blind," that is, the television viewers did not know that they were being studied and the observers did not know the purpose of the study or that the persons being observed were in experimental or control groups.

THE TELEVISION MESSAGES

The preliminary survey consisted of interviews with actually observed safety belt users and a random sample of nonusers observed at the same sites and times. The higher the respondent's education, the greater the likelihood that he was observed wearing safety belts. Those who rated safety belts as relatively more comfortable and convenient, those who said that they did not smoke while driving, and those who had a friend or relative injured, but not killed, in an automobile crash were also more likely to use belts. Furthermore, these factors were additive, that is, the presence of each factor increased the probability of

use independent of the other factors (Robertson, et al., 1972).

The finding that a friend's injury, but not death, increased the probability of use indicates the likelihood that fear of being disfigured or disabled is more conscious and motivational in the use of safety belts than fear of death in a crash. Thus, we decided to emphasize the efficacy of safety belts in decreasing the probability of disfigurement and disability.

We were more wary of the comfort and convenience factor. Realizing that the safety belts in many automobiles are uncomfortable and inconvenient because of poor design, we did not want to reinforce the tendency not to use belts because of this factor. Smoking while driving and education probably reflect a number of differences in personal characteristics such as risk-taking behavior and self-esteem. Since we do not believe that these characteristics are readily manipulable by television messages, these factors were not considered in the creation of the messages. Techniques which are said in the industry to be successful in product marketing—for example, physician endorsement and a family responsibility theme—were employed in addition to the disfigurement-disability theme.

The television messages were written and produced in collaboration with an advertising agency which had a record of success in advertising commercial products as well as experience with public service material. Six basic messages were eventually developed and filmed. The following are brief descriptions of these messages:

1. A father (Figure 1) is shown lifting his teenaged son from a wheelchair into a car. As they ride along, safety belts obviously fastened, the father's thoughts are voiced off-camera intermixed with the son's on-camera expressions of excitement at going to a football game. The father expresses guilt for not having encouraged his son to use safety belts before the crash in which he was in-

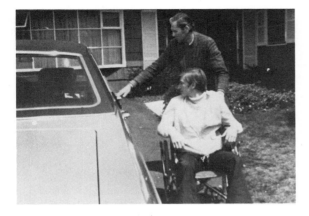

Figure 1   Father and Son Advertising Message

jured. The analogy to the protection that the son wore when he played football is drawn.

2. A teenaged girl (Figure 2) is shown sitting in a rocking chair looking out a window. She says, "I'm not sick or anything. I could go out more but since the car crash, I just don't. . . . The crash wasn't Dad's fault. I go for walks with my father after dark . . . that way I don't get, you know, stared at." She turns enough to reveal a large scar on what was the hidden side of her face. She continues, "It doesn't hurt anymore." An announcer says off-camera, "Car crashes kill two ways: right away and little by little. Wear your safety belts and live!"

3. A woman whose face cannot be seen (Figure 3) is shown in front of a mirror applying makeup. A full face picture on her dressing table shows her as a beautiful woman. Her husband enters the scene and suggests that they go to a party. She asks him not to look at her without makeup as she turns to reveal a scarred face. An off-camera announcer describes a crash in which the wife was driving slowly and carefully. The announcer continues, as the picture on the table is shown, "Terry would still look like this if she had been wearing safety belts." Safety belts are shown through a shattered windshield. Announcer: "It's much easier to wear safety belts than to hear your husband say . . ." Husband: "Honey, I love you anyway."

4. A father and mother (Figure 4) are shown riding in the front seat of a car, their 8-year-old daughter seated between them. The father must brake hard to avoid another car entering from a side road. The daughter bumps her head as she is thrown into the dashboard and begins to cry. A policeman walks up to the car and the father angrily says: "Did you see what that guy just did? That jerk. I had to jam on my brakes. My little girl hit her head." The policeman asks

Figure 2   Girl at the Window Advertising Message

the father why the child wasn't wearing safety belts. Over the father's protestations about the other driver, the policeman emphasizes the father's responsibility to protect his child. The scene closes with the policeman walking away saying: "When are people gonna learn?" and the announcer following with: "It doesn't take brains to wear safety belts. But it sure is stupid not to."

5. Two physicians and a nurse (Figure 5) are shown ordering coffee. The nurse asks: "Trouble?" A doctor replies: "Another guy driving home not wearing his safety belts." Nurse: "Gonna live?" Doctor: "Guess you could call it living." Nurse: "You've had a lot of car crash cases lately." Doctor: "Yeah, and I'm getting sick of it. They've got safety belts in the cars. Why . . . why in the name of God don't they put 'em on?" Waitress: "Do safety belts really make a difference?" The doctor shows her how a thermometer case can be hit and the thermometer inside not broken, but it shatters when hit out of the case. The waitress expresses further doubt and the doctor says: "How many times do you have to tell 'em?"

6. A car is shown in a driveway (Figure 6). From a puff of smoke steps a witch who announces: "Ha, ha, ha. I'm the Wicked Car Witch. Your Mommy and Daddy cannot see me but I make them drive without their safety belts. That's how they get hurt in car crashes." The mother gets into the car and the witch hides some belts in the seat and tangles others. A Good Car Fairy appears and says: "Children! I am the Good Car Fairy. When your Mommy and Daddy get in the car, say 'Mommy! Daddy! If you love me, wear your safety belts!'" The Wicked Witch and the Good Fairy argue as the father enters the car. A little girl calls from the porch: "Mommy! Daddy! Wear your safety belts." The parents fasten the belts, the

Figure 3 Woman at the Mirror Advertising Message

Figure 4 Family and Policeman Advertising Message

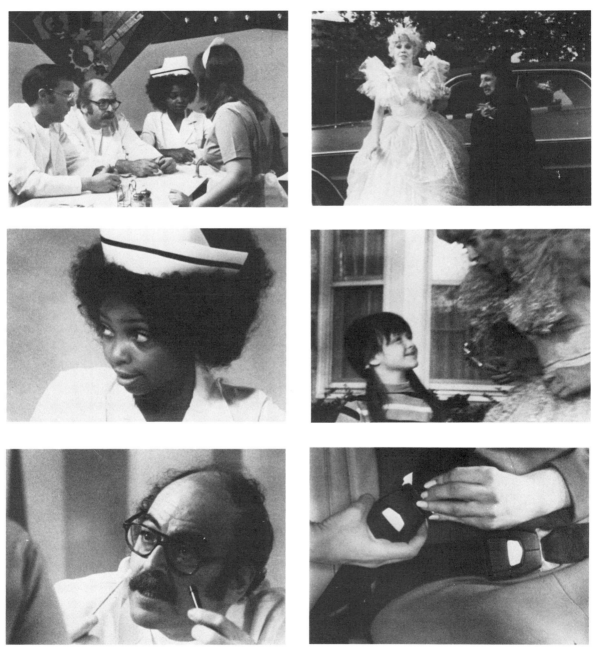

Figure 5 Physicians and Nurse Advertising Message

Figure 6 Witch and Fairy: Children's Advertising Message

Wicked Witch disappears in a puff of smoke, and the Good Fairy again admonishes the children to urge their parents to demonstrate their love by wearing their safety belts.

By industry standards, the messages were of high quality. The "father and son" was judged the best among 30 entries in the public service category of the TV-Radio Advertisers Club of Philadelphia. The "teenaged girl at the window" was among the 10 finalists of 400 entries in the public service category of the Advertising Club of New York. It was also chosen as a finalist among the public service entries in the American TV and Radio Commercials Festival and National Print Advertising Competition. An informal opinion was obtained from the Director of the National Association of Broadcasters Code Authority that the messages were in compliance with the code.

The messages were not shown indiscriminately. Each was placed on or adjacent to a program likely to have an audience to whom the message would most likely appeal. For example, the witch was shown on network children's programs, the father and son on National Football League games, and the scarred faces on popular "soap operas." No attempt was made to control what was shown in addition to our messages. For example, a number of automobile manufacturers had "tag lines" urging safety belt use at the end of their commercials throughout the study period. Of course, these additional messages were shown to both experimental and control groups and were thus constant for both audiences.

STUDY DESIGN

The messages were shown on one cable of a dual cable television system designed for marketing studies (Brown and Gatty, 1969). Located in a county of 230,000 people (1970 census), the two cables feed television signals to 13,800 households. There were 6,400 of these households on Cable A, on which our messages were shown, and 7,400 on Cable B, which was, in this case, the control cable. Each cable contains the full range of channels available from local stations as well as special movie and weather channels.

The two cables are distributed in a checkerboard fashion among blocks of homes in the community that have chosen to pay for the improved signal which the cable provides. Although the assignment of households to one or another cable was not strictly random, the various marketing studies done in the community have found no significant differences between the two in demographic characteristics, ownership of automobiles and other consumer goods, and pretest purchasing behavior for a large number of products (Adler and Kuehn, 1969).

In all, 14 observation sites were chosen. Using maps of the cable distribution among the streets and traffic flow maps obtained from the local traffic engineer, we chose observation sites at points which maximized the likelihood of observing automobiles from the neighborhoods where the cables were installed. Observers were assigned to a particular site for a given number of hours on a given day. No deviation from the observation sites was allowed. From May 10 through October 15, the observers were rotated among the sites daily. Observation periods were 7 a.m. to 10 a.m., 10 a.m. to 1 p.m., 1 p.m. to 4 p.m., and 4 p.m. to 7 p.m. Because of shortened daylight, the periods were changed to 8 a.m. to 12:30 p.m. and 12:30 p.m. to 5 p.m. after October 15. Half of the sites allowed observation of cars going into the center of the city and were observed during morning hours. The remaining sites, situated so as to observe drivers leaving the center of the city, were observed during afternoon hours. A morning and an afternoon site each was observed each weekday in the May to October 15 period. Observations were also obtained on Saturdays and Sundays but on a separate rotation among the sites. After October 15, only one site per day was observed, alternating morning and afternoon sites every other weekday. Thus, 14 weekdays were required to observe all of the sites in each time period in a given rotation during both summer and winter months. The sites remained constant and the observers were rotated among them in the same order throughout the study.

The observers were hardly noticed by persons being observed. The occasional motorist or pedestrian who stopped and asked, "What are you doing?" was satisfied with the answer "Taking a traffic survey."

Observing the driver only, observers stood at designated sites on the opposite side from the driver of an approaching automobile. The driver's sex, racial appearance, and approximate age were tape recorded as the vehicle approached the observer. The driver's use or nonuse of lap and lap-and-shoulder belts was observed as the automobile passed the observer. The automobile license number was then obtained as the automobile moved away.

The license plate numbers were matched with owner's names and addresses using the files of the state department of motor vehicles. The names and addresses were then matched to the file specifying which cable was assigned to given households. In those cases where the household was not on a cable, the household was specified as to whether or not it was in the same county as the cable groups.

Thus, there are four groups for comparison: Cable A households where the messages were shown, Cable B households which constitute a control group, noncable households in the same county as the cable households, and out-of-county households.

The messages were shown for 9 months on Cable A exclusively. Table 1 presents the distribution of the messages by time of day over the 9-month period, June 7, 1971, through March 5, 1972. For the first few months, the messages were shown mainly in daytime hours. In the late fall and winter, more "prime" evening time became available through the courtesy of insurance companies and other advertisers who were willing to have public service advertising in lieu of their scheduled commercials on Cable A. These arrangements were made with the parent companies so that local affiliates of the companies were unaware of the experiment. The local television station managers were aware of the campaign, as they are of all tests on the experimental cable system. Since

Table 1 Number of safety belt messages shown by month and time of day

	1971							1972		
Times	June	July	August	September	October	November	December	January	February	Total
Sign-on—noon										
No.	30	31	40	53	32	32	12	14	33	277
%	21*	28	29	48	30	33	17	19	34	
12:01—6:00 p.m.										
No.	105	68	78	43	50	25	26	41	43	479
%	73	62	57	39	48	26	38	55	45	
6:01 p.m.—signoff										
No.	8	11	19	15	23	40	31	20	20	187
%	6	10	14	13	22	41	45	27	21	
Total	143	110	137	111	105	97	69	75	96	943

*Percentages are based on the total number of messages in a given month.

their stations receive extra income for some of the tests, it is in their interest not to reveal the experimental nature of the cable system to the population in the city. Special arrangements were made with the station managers to forward complaints to us—which were anticipated because of the strong themes—but none occurred.

There were fewer exposures in the later months because a greater number of people can be reached by fewer exposures in prime time. We estimate on the basis of ratings of the audience of the programs on which the messages were shown that the average television viewer saw one or another of the messages two to three times per week. Of course, high frequency viewers saw the messages more often and low frequency viewers saw them less often than the average. In total, the campaign was equivalent to the type of major advertising effort which companies use to promote a new product. If this campaign had been sponsored on a national basis, it would have cost approximately $7,000,000.

RESULTS

The campaign had no measured effect whatsoever on safety belt use. Table 2 shows the percentage of observed male drivers using lap or lap-and-shoulder belts for each of the time periods necessary to observe drivers at all of the designated sites.

There is no significant difference between drivers from households on the experimental cable and drivers from households on the control cable

Table 2 Percentage of male drivers using safety belts in experimental, control, and nonstudy groups

Dates	Experimental cable A		Control cable B		No cable, same county		No cable, out of county	
	% use	No. observed	% use	No. observed	% use	No. observed	% use	No. observed
Preexperimental	15	461	16	552	14	4343	14	1672
5/28–6/16	14	372	14	469	13	3840	12	1521
6/17–7/6	13	338	15	511	14	3706	9	1551
7/7–7/26	8	370	11	456	11	3825	9	1764
7/27–8/13	11	332	11	465	11	3785	8	1641
8/16–9/2	12	356	10	442	9	3458	8	1455
9/3–9/22	7	312	9	439	8	3367	7	1861
9/23–10/12	7	343	6	372	7	3322	5	1776
10/13–10/29	13	199	8	287	12	2005	7	1151
11/1–11/16	9	304	10	428	8	3207	8	1725
11/17–11/30*	9	124	10	164	10	1301	9	723
12/13–12/30	5	274	7	278	5	3271	5	1704
12/31–1/18	5	382	4	447	5	4154	4	2091
1/19–2/7	6	355	5	457	4	4497	6	2544
2/8–2/25	5	408	5	564	4	5139	4	2903
2/28–3/16	4	308	4	478	5	4270	4	2889
3/17–3/31	5	297	6	371	5	3474	4	2400

*Some sites missing due to observer illness.

in any of the observation periods. Also, there is no difference in use between those on the cables and other drivers observed at the same sites whether from in or out of the county. The same conclusion must be reached when the data for females are viewed in Table 3.

There is a downward drift in safety belt use from the spring through the winter months, more remarkable among male than female drivers. However, this decline occurs in the control and noncable groups as much as in the experimental group. Therefore, it cannot be argued that the messages had a deleterious effect on safety belt use. Some unknown factor or factors contributed to a decreased use of safety belts in the winter months in all of the groups studied. The overall use rates were significantly lower for black persons (3 per cent) than for whites (10 per cent) as found in

earlier studies (Council, 1969). Age differences were not statistically significant.

DISCUSSION

It must be concluded that the television campaign did not affect the use of safety belts. The decrease in belt use observed during the study occurred in the control and noncable groups as well as the group exposed to the campaign. It is clear that safety belt use did not increase during that campaign. The observed reduction in safety belt use in winter could be a result of other factors. For example, belt systems (which are at present in the U.S. usually designed without inertia reels, long known devices that allow free movement until an impact occurs) are often rated as inconvenient

Table 3   Percentage of female drivers using safety belts in experimental, control, and nonstudy groups

Dates	Experimental cable A		Control cable B		No cable, same county		No cable, out of county	
	% use	No. observed	% use	No. observed	% use	No. observed	% use	No. observed
Pre-experimental	15	273	13	374	17	2760	15	772
5/28–6/16	13	238	16	301	14	2310	6	639
6/17–7/6	12	240	13	276	13	2139	11	685
7/7–7/26	13	197	11	273	13	2193	11	769
7/27–8/13	13	226	12	277	11	2105	13	753
8/16–9/2	12	187	10	273	11	1933	11	641
9/3–9/22	12	150	13	288	8	1948	10	696
9/23–10/12	10	206	8	259	7	1935	5	724
10/13–10/29	13	118	10	173	12	1136	12	455
11/1–11/16	16	192	14	324	11	2029	10	717
11/17–11/30*	14	74	15	103	14	743	12	227
12/13–12/30	8	196	8	232	7	1933	6	720
12/31–1/18	7	248	8	342	10	2494	9	1088
1/19–2/7	12	259	8	368	8	2731	8	1130
2/8–2/25	7	272	5	354	7	2727	6	1318
2/28–3/16	8	232	7	336	7	2565	7	1333
3/17–3/31	10	170	7	222	7	2006	7	1114

*Some sites missing due to observer illness.

(Robertson, et al., 1972). Having to adjust them to fit over bulky winter clothing could deter some persons from using them in winter.

The failure of these campaigns to increase safety belt use adds evidence to the argument that approaches directed toward changing behavior are inefficient and often ineffective means of reducing highway losses (Klein and Waller, 1970). "Passive" approaches, i.e., those which reduce the frequency or severity of damage to people and property, or both, irrespective of voluntary action on their part (Haddon and Goddard, 1962), show greater promise toward reducing the deaths and injuries in crashes, as they have historically in closely analogous public health situations. Some passive devices, e.g., energy-absorbing steering columns and windshields that perform like firenets, have been required by federal standards since 1968 and have been shown to produce large reductions in fatalities and injuries (Levine and Campbell, 1971; Haddon, 1972).

Arguments against passive approaches are often based on the reasoning that human behavior produces the losses in energy-damaged people and property and, therefore, human behavior must be changed to prevent them. The fallacy in this argument is the assumption that "causes" must be attacked in order of their contribution to the "effect" to be prevented or ameliorated (Haddon, 1970). In illustration, some epidemics are the result of high rates of interpersonal contact which facilitate transmittal of infectious organisms from one person to another. Yet as a group their control has typically been far more successful when based on immunization rather than on attempts to modify the frequency of interpersonal interaction.

Other than the act of driving itself, there is no known behavioral act that is a necessary condition for automobile crashes. In contrast, no injury whatsoever can occur to either humans or vehicles in automobile crashes unless mechanical energy is transferred in amounts and at rates which exceed the limits the human or vehicle structure can tolerate. A number of strategies are available to control the energy transfer and reduce the losses which occur when energy transfer is not properly controlled (Haddon, 1970). These range from preventing vehicles from being placed in motion to emergency medical care and later rehabilitation. Safety belts are one means of energy control, but, as presently designed, they require action on the part of the exposed individual each time he is exposed. It should be obvious that passive approaches are more likely to be successful. However, there seems to be an inherent bias in the U.S. culture against public health strategies which bypass a voluntary individual decision by the person to be protected. The controversy over the fluoridation of drinking water to reduce the incidence of tooth decay should be a sufficient example (Sapolsky, 1968), one that has paralleled earlier controversies such as those related to pasteurization of milk and chlorination of water.

Perhaps because of such a bias, rather than choose the most logical strategy or mix of strategies at the outset, persons responsible for the implementation of injury control programs frequently try a series of methods from the least to the most obtrusive forms of behavior modification.

The apparent failure of a number of mass media safety belt campaigns to increase use beyond precampaign levels may not mean that it is impossible to create a campaign which will increase safety belt use. However, the evidence on lack of effect of past efforts is sufficiently strong that the burden of proof of substantial further gains in belt usage resulting from such campaigns is on those who advocate use of mass media to promote use of safety belts.

REFERENCES

Adler, J., and Kuehn, A. A. (1969), "How Advertising Works in Market Experiments," Fifteenth Annual Conference of the Advertising Research Foundation.

Bohlin, N. I. (1967), "A Statistical Analysis of 28,000 Accident Cases with Emphasis on Occupant Restraint Value," Eleventh Stapp Car Crash Conference Proceedings, 299–309.

Brown, N., and Gatty, R. (1969), "Designing Experiments with TV Advertising Laboratories," Proceedings of the Business and Economic Statistics Section, American Statistical Association, 120–29.

Campbell, B. J. (1968), "Seat Belts and Injury Reduction in 1967," University of North Carolina Highway Safety Research Center, Chapel Hill.

Council, F. M. (1969), "Seat Belts: A Follow-up Study of Their Use under Normal Driving Conditions," University of North Carolina Highway Safety Research Center, Chapel Hill.

Haddon, W., Jr., and Goddard, J. L. (1962), "An Analysis of Highway Safety Strategies in Passenger Car Design and Highway Safety," Association for the Aid of Crippled Children and Consumers Union of the U. S., New York.

———. (1972), "A Logical Framework for Categorizing Highway Safety Phenomena and Activity," *Journal of Trauma*, 12, 193–207.

———. (1970), "On the Escape of Tigers: An Ecologic Note," *American Journal of Public Health*, 60, 2229–234.

Haskins, J. B. (1969), "Effects of Safety Communication Campaigns: A Review of the Research Evidence," *Journal of Safety Research*, 1, 58–66.

———. (1970), "Evaluative Research on the Effects of Mass Communication Safety Campaigns: A Methodological Critique," *Journal of Safety Research*, 2, 86–96.

Klein, D., and Waller, J. A. (1970), "Culpability and Deterrence in Highway Crashes," U.S. Government Printing Office, Washington, D.C.

Levine, D. N., and Campbell, B. J. (1971), "Effectiveness of Lap Seat Belts and the Energy Absorbing Steering System in the Reduction of Injuries," University of North Carolina Highway Safety Research Center, Chapel Hill.

Robertson, L. S.; O'Neill, B.; and Wixom, C. W. (1972), "Factors Associated with Observed Safety Belt Use," *Journal of Health and Social Behavior*, 13, 18–24.

Sapolsky, H. M. (1968), "Science, Voters, and the Flouridation Controversy," *Science*, 162, 427–33.

Seat Belt Accidents (1965), *American Jurisprudence*, Rochester, N.Y.: Lawyers Cooperative Publishing Co., 355.

Standard Number 208; Occupant Crash Protection. Federal Register. 32: 2415, 1967.

Tourin, B., and Garrett, J. W. (1960), "Safety Belt Effectiveness in Rural California Automobile Accidents," Automotive Crash Injury Research of Cornell University (now Cornell Aeronautical Laboratory, Inc.), Buffalo.

Westland, J. G. (1971), "Progress of Victorian Seat Belt Legislation to 30th September, 1971," Road Safety and Traffic Authority, Victoria, Australia.

WORD-OF-MOUTH PROCESSES IN THE DIFFUSION OF A MAJOR TECHNOLOGICAL INNOVATION

JOHN A. CZEPIEL

Source: John A. Czepiel, "Word-of-Mouth Processes in the Diffusion of a Major Technological Innovation," *Journal of Marketing Research,* Vol. 11, May, 1974, pp. 172–180.

INTRODUCTION

The question of the prevalence and impact of word-of-mouth communications in industrial buying decisions in general, and in the diffusion of innovations in industrial settings specifically, has been the subject of conflicting views (Allvine, 1968; Martilla, 1971; Ozanne and Churchill, 1971; Webster, 1967; Webster, 1970). The approach of Rogers (1967) and of Rogers and Shoemaker (1971), which views diffusion as a social process, has long appealed to those interested in industrial innovation diffusion (Ozanne and Churchill, 1968; Webster, 1967; Webster, 1971), as it has to those in the consumer sphere (Robertson, 1971). In Rogers' terms, "the diffusion process consists of (1) a new idea, (2) individual A who knows about the innovation, and (3) individual B who does not yet know about the innovation. The social relationship of A and B has a great deal to say about the conditions under which A will tell B about the innovation and the results of this telling" (Rogers, 1962).

Several factors, however, have seemingly prevented the application of this approach to diffusion in industrial settings. First is that the obvious importance of the economic factors caused by the large absolute size of innovation decisions tends to make the economic factors salient and gives rise to group decision making. None of the diffusion studies so far has focused on groups as adopting units or on the diffusion of major innovations. Second, and more important, there seems to be a lack of evidence to support the basic notion of the existence of a viable social system in industrial markets. As Webster has noted, without this evidence the most significant part of the definition of the diffusion process is missing (Webster, 1971). In addition, such barriers as the very nature of economic competition, potential legal restraints on collusive activity, and geographical dispersion are all cited as mitigating against informal interfirm communication. Finally, it has been noted that industrial marketers provide buyers with more complete information than in other markets and thereby reduce the need for informal product-related interfirm communication (Webster, 1970).

On the other hand, experience in different industrial markets seemed to indicate otherwise. Meetings of technical societies and trade associations indicate a rather high level of personal familiarity among the group of competitors in attendance. Conversations with industrial salesmen underline the importance to them of recommendations from friend to friend within an industry. Finally, while infrequent, it is not unusual for competitors actually to make social calls on each other.

HYPOTHESES

The study was designed to test hypotheses concerning the diffusion process in industrial markets. Those to be discussed are:
1. There exist informal communications networks and interactions within the industry sufficient to term it a community.
2. The pattern of these networks will be related to the similarity in the firms' size and type of business.
3. Early adopters will have greater opinion leadership with respect to the new idea than later adopters.
4. Centrality in informal opinion/advice networks will be associated with early adoption.

All of these hypotheses are related to the overall perspective of the study—that diffusion in industrial markets can be studied as a social process. The first two concern the existence and structure of a functioning informal social system. Opinion leadership is hypothesized to be a result of early adoption, and the fourth hypothesis is concerned with centrality (the extent to which others in the social system seek the advice of a firm and its relation to the time of adoption which has been found in similar studies in other settings (Coleman, et al., 1966; Robertson, 1971).

SELECTION OF THE INNOVATION

Three criteria determined the industry setting and the selection of the innovation: (1) the industry must be one comprised of business organizations in economic competition; (2) the innovation must be both major and a "true" (discontinuous) innovation; and (3) the innovation must require, both in absolute and relative terms, a substantial economic investment. The study chose as its vehicle the diffusion of the continuous casting process in the steel industry.

In economic terms, the innovation was a major one. The minimum investment decision studied was in the neighborhood of $1 million and ranged up to 8 and even 9 figures. By any objective criteria, whether absolute or relative, the decision to adopt continuous casting was of major proportions.

THE STUDY

Thirty-two firms were identified as having adopted the innovation in the 1960–1972 period. Of these 32 firms, 5 were "Mini-Mills" which started in business with the innovation as an integral part of their production system after the initial introduction of the innovation. For these firms, continuous casting was not considered to be an innovation by their own admission (several were contacted) in terms of the definition of innovation used in the study. It defined an innovation as "any idea, practice, or material artifact perceived to be new by the relevant adopting unit" (Zaltman and Stiff, 1973).

Of the 26 remaining firms, 2 were used extensively in pilot testing, a third was deleted because of an incomplete interview, 5 more refused interviews, and 18 were fully interviewed and entered into analysis. This represented two-thirds of the qualified universe. On the basis of such external factors as size, time of adoption, and width of product line, no significant differences were observed between responding and nonresponding firms.

By letter and phone call, interviews were secured with those managerial and technical people who were directly involved in making the initial recommendation to use continuous casting. Of the 61 persons identified by the firms as having participated in the "group which made the recommendation" to adopt the innovation, about half (some 31) were actually interviewed. An additional 30 persons were identified by the firms as having been involved in the decision process in an "ex officio" capacity.

It should be noted these groups made the recommendation to such higher authority as was necessary to approve such an expenditure. Generally speaking, they were special decision groups constructed for this project and whose recommendations were made to a board of directors either directly or through a vice-president or president. The individual members of such a group frequently had their own supporting staff. Looked at in this manner, it can be seen that many more than the 91 indicated above were involved in the decision process. In this respect, the sample, while covering a good proportion of the significant decision makers, did not cover a substantial proportion of the entire and more broadly defined decision group.

The *time of adoption* was based on the date the decision was made to adopt the innovation, not the date of its installation which followed by as much as two years. Conceptually, of course, the decision point is the important one, while installation is often times affected by production delays and the like.

THE INTERVIEW

The interview itself was highly structured with both open-ended and scaled items, although the latter predominated.

The findings reported here are based on a series of three lengthy sociometric questions concerning various information sources and their frequency of use. After a series of introductory questions, some discussing suppliers, respondents were asked (1) if, in their initial search process, they had contacted any other sources for information concerning the innovation. If they indicated they had contacted other competitive firms, they were handed a list of industry firms and asked to specify those from which they had sought information. Following that, respondents were asked (2) whether, if following their decision to adopt the innovation, any firms had contacted them for information concerning the innovation and, again, to specify which. Finally, a third question asked (3) whether the respondents had regular opinion/advice relationships with any specific firms. Following this series of questions they were also asked about the frequency of these contacts, both inward and outward bound from the firm.

It should be noted that, because of the relatively large proportion of the universe interviewed, much of the data obtained in questions (1) and (2) above could be cross-checked within the sample. This check showed the data to be highly consistent. For example, of those responses to question (1) which could be checked by other firms' responses to question (2), 70% (45 out of 65) were confirmed. It should be noted that these confirmations of information seeking were not necessarily of specific individual contacts. While some such contacts were confirmed by name, more generally this confirmation should be construed to mean that someone in firm A contacted someone in firm B. These confirmations may have involved different individuals in the firms involved.

FINDINGS

The analysis proceeded in the order of the hypotheses stated above. That is, it sought through the sociometric data to find out if there is an informal society within the industry. If so, how is it organized and used and what are its effects on the diffusion process?

Society

How does one determine that a social group or community exists? This was the problem faced in the analysis of the sociometric data.

From the literature, however, four concepts or criteria were established as guidelines. First, the organizations must have informal communications channels linking them together by which the industry can be termed *connected* in the graph theoretic sense (Alba, undated). Second, these interconnections must be *dense* in that their incidence should resemble those of known social groupings. Third, these interconnections must be shown to be other than random. That is, the overall pattern should be explained by reason of similarity or geographical proximity among the connected firms as are patterns in known social groupings. Finally, the frequency-of-use data must indicate that the networks are used on some regular basis.

The initial analysis proceeded through the construction of sociograms based on the general opinion/advice nominations received in response to the third question previously listed. Reciprocated relationships were first identified in the data matrix (a zero/one square matrix indicating the existence and direction of an opinion/advice relationship) and graphed. Next, the additional relationships were included until all respondents and even nonrespondents were included in the final graph. Figures 1 and 2 depict this increasing expansion of the sociogram. A single-headed arrow, such as that between firms 18 and 17, indicates that the respondent in firm 18 "nominated" (regularly sought general opinion and advice from) firm 17. Double-headed arrows, such as that between 17 and 09, indicate that respondents in both firms indicated they regularly went to the other firm for opinion and advice.

Insofar as the criteria above are concerned, inspection of Figure 2, which includes nonrespondents, shows that with one exception the network or graph can be termed *connected*. Of the 32 firms which adopted the innovation, 31 are linked to at least one other firm and most to many. It should be noted that, because not all decision makers and all firms were interviewed, these graphs may understate the true extent of the complete communications network operating.

For the density criterion, two computed indices were used. One was the Proctor and Loomis measure of group expansiveness and the other an index created by the author for the purpose. Proctor and Loomis's expansiveness measure is the average of the sum of all the choices made by all group members. It gives the average number of other firms with which each firm is in direct contact. The second measure involves the computation of the average and the range of the path "lengths" connecting each member to every other.[1] In one sense this is a measure of density and efficiency both. It yields the average number of intermediary firms necessary to link, in communication, any two firms in the network. These measures were computed for both the lowest portion of Figure 1 and Figure 2 and are presented in Table 1. While there are available no outside criteria for comparison, both measures indicate that, on the average, industry members have regular opinion/advice relationships with between two and three other firms in the industry (Proctor & Loomis's "E") and that a message can travel between any two firms in the industry through a little over one intermediary firm ("D").

Insofar as the patterning of the interconnections is concerned, two methodologies were used. The first was through analysis of the directed graph for

[1]Computed as follows: $d = \sum_{i=1}^{n} (x_i/n - 1)/n$, where x = the sum of the path lengths necessary to link firm i to every other firm. For example, in the case of perfect communications with each firm in direct contact with every other, this measure (d) would equal 1 and the maximum path length would also equal 1.

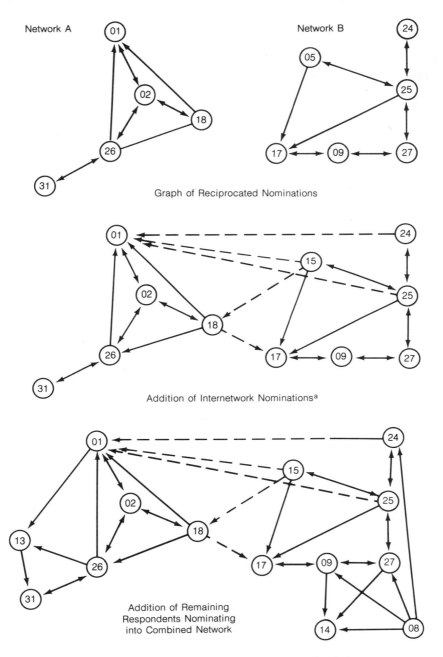

Graph of Reciprocated Nominations

Addition of Internetwork Nominations[a]

Addition of Remaining
Respondents Nominating
into Combined Network

[a]Internetwork nominations shown by broken lines for clarity.

Figure 1 Analysis of Group Structure by Expansion of the Directed Graph

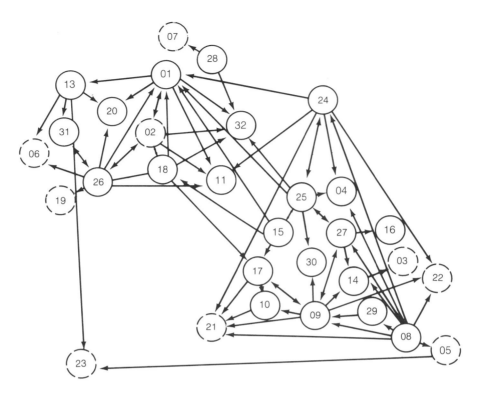

Note: Broken circles indicates nonrespondent firms.

Figure 2   Complete Directed Graph Including Respondent and Nonrespondent Firms

the existence of subgoups and the second through matrix manipulation. This latter technique involved the rearrangement of the initial nomination matrix so as to minimize the square of the perpendicular deviations from the diagonal of the matrix.

Table 1   Table of indices computed

	Figure 1	Figure 2
Proctor & Loomis's E	2.6	2.5
Density-efficiency (d)	2.2	2.6
Average range for individual firms	1.6–2.8	1.9–4.1
Longest path (number of links)	5	6
Firms linked longest path	(14↔31)	(5↔7)

The rearranged matrix will then show as clusters (subgroups) those firms who choose each other frequently. It was hypothesized that such subgroups, if found by either method, would be based on the size and nature of the firms included in each of the subgroups.

The analysis of the directed graph was based on the reciprocal communications networks shown at the top of Figure 1. The stepwise expansion of the directed graph was important in that it allowed the structure of the group to be identified at an early stage and traced throughout the analysis. An examination of Figures 1 and 2, for example, shows that the two subgroups initially identified through reciprocal opinion/advice nominations (the naming of each other as opinion/advice sources) maintained their separate identities throughout. If Figure 2 with all 32 firms had been the only directed graph created, the analysis would have been far more difficult. This stepwise analysis of the directed graphs also highlighted the importance of intragroup and intergroup nominations. Examination of the lowest part of Figure 1 and Figure 2, for example, will show that intragroup nominations far outnumber intergroup nominations in both. Accordingly, most firms can be readily classified as to which subgroups they belong. Analysis of data on the firms involved showed that those belonging to Network A are all "Big Steel" firms including the six largest firms in the industry. Those in Network B, on the other hand, are almost without exception classified as "Mini-Mills" and many belonged to a trade association of small firms to which no firms in Network A belonged. Also, firms in Network B are substantially smaller than those in Network A. A test of the difference in sales volume between the members of the two networks, using Student's *t*, showed the difference to be significant beyond the .01 level.

Most interesting and intriguing is the strong evidence of a difference in status between the two groups. In the lowest part of Figure 1, which includes only those firms interviewed and responding to the opinion/advice question, five intergroup nominations were made (24 → 01; 15 → 01; 15 → 18; 25 → 01; and 18 → 17). Four of these nominations are directed *from* Network B (Mini-Mills) *to* Network A (Big Steel), whereas only one nomination is made by a member of Network A to Network B. As has recently been noted, this difference is potentially significant (Rogers and Bohwmik, 1970). It is hypothesized that Big Steel has more status than the Mini-Mills on the basis of this differential in the frequency of intergroup nominations. Lower status individuals initiate conversations with higher status individuals more frequently than the reverse occurs. This is clearly the case here.

Figure 3 shows the result of the matrix manipulation technique suggested by Forsythe and Katz

for the data contained in Figure 2.[2] It can be seen that this technique confirms the previous analysis by separating the two clusters. The existence of overlap, however, does reduce the clarity of the separation. In fact, the matrix seems to indicate that firms 15, 17, 24, and 25 might be considered a sociometric clique in themselves, perhaps as a "bridge" or even an intermediate status group. The matrix manipulation approach does, of course, have an advantage in that it allows for less subjective interpretation on the part of the researcher.[3] The data and the algorithm in this method determine the rearrangement of the rows and columns in the matrix whereas in the graphical form of the analysis, the researcher has considerable latitude in the placement of the respondents in the graph.

The data on the *frequency* of the use of these informal channels indicated that they were more than infrequent although not a daily occurrence for the average decision maker. Direct informal interpersonal contacts among decision makers in different firms occurred about 5 times a month, on the average, or in other words about weekly. With respect to the innovation adoption decision itself, measured separately, respondents reported contacts with an average of 5.5 other firms. Some of these other firms were contacted on many occasions for this particular purpose. Observational data collected during the interviews confirmed the above data. One respondent, for example, exchanged several phone calls with colleagues in other firms during the course of the two-hour interview. This was not an uncommon occurrence.

Based on the evidence and criteria mentioned earlier, it has been demonstrated that the decision makers involved in this study could indeed be

---

[2]The algorithm and computer school program for this analysis were written by Michael Wagner, Graduate School of Business Administration, New York University.

[3]This form of the analysis is helpful in answering the question posed by one researcher using sociometric methods: "Would I have reached the same overview had I not 'known' the participants' names?" (Levine, 1972).

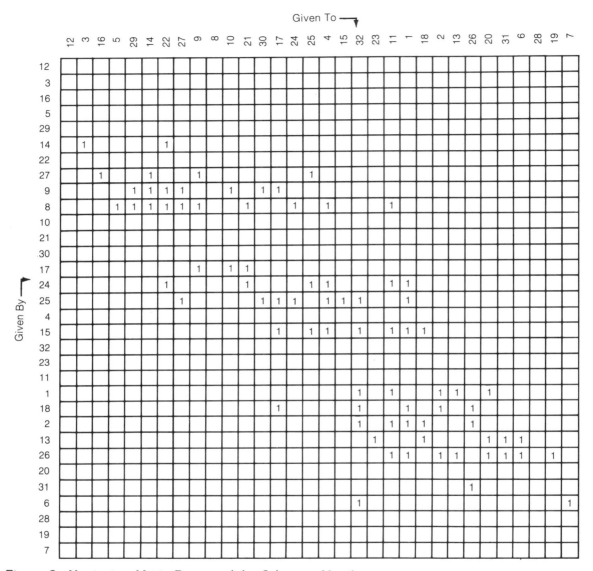

Figure 3   Nomination Matrix Rearranged for Sub-group Identification

studied as and termed a society or community as hypothesized. The communications channels were many and dense; they were shown to have a regularity in their pattern based on firm size and type of business hypothesized, and were shown to have occurred with some level of frequency which indicated them to be more than isolated instances.

Opinion Leadership

The third hypothesis stated that early adopters would exhibit greater opinion leadership with respect to the innovation. The data were generated through analysis of the first and second sociometric questions noted earlier. Early adopting firms were each contacted by an average of 19.5 firms about the innovation, 15.0 of which had not yet adopted the innovation. Later adopters reported that an average of 10.7 firms had contacted them concerning the innovation; however, most of these contacts were from earlier adopters, an average of only 3.2 coming from firms which were to adopt later. The differences between earlier and later adopters on both comparisons, total contacts, and contacts by firms which had not yet adopted are significant beyond the .05 level using Student's *t*.[4]

From these data it is clear that opinion leadership with respect to the innovation is greater among early adopters than among later adopters as hypothesized. Figure 4 shows the amount of interfirm information seeking conducted by firms arranged by year of adoption. This figure clearly shows the importance of interfirm contact in the diffusion process. When these who-contacted-who data are plotted by time of adoption, as shown in Figure 5, the hypothesis that early adopters have opinion leadership with respect to continuous casting stands out more clearly. Aside from the few instances of information seeking among concurrently adopting firms, all information seeking concerning the innovation was directed to earlier adopters. Given both forms of the analysis, it can be seen that the hypothesis that opinion leadership with respect to innovation is greater among earlier adopters is upheld.

It was of interest to know the basis for these information-seeking contacts. Respondents were asked if the contact was arranged (1) by suppliers, (2) through friendship relationships, or (3) on the basis of colleague relationships.[5]

Table 2 shows there to be no discernible difference in the proportion of the source of information

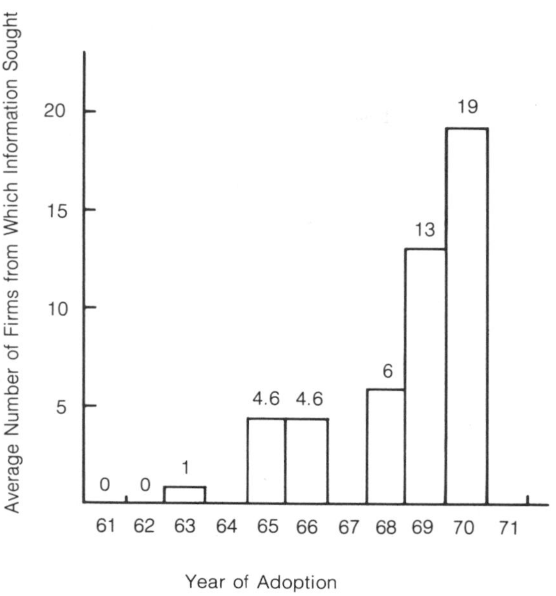

Figure 4 Average Amount of Interfirm Information Seeking by Year of Adoption

seeking between the adopter categories. It is interesting to note, however, the small incidence of supplier arranged interfirm contacts. The importance of friendship relationships in the diffusion process, however, is rather clearly evident.

Centrality
Hypothesis 4, of course, flows from all previous discussion. Does centrality in opinion/advice networks lead to earlier adoption? Table 3 compares those firms termed high on centrality (based on the number of opinion/advice nominations received) with those termed low. It can be seen that while the relationship is in the expected direction, the level of significance is not acceptable.

DISCUSSION

The major premise of this study was that diffusion in industrial societies could be studied as a behavioral process. The study in an overall sense supported this initial premise. The most significant

---

[4]Of the 18 firms in the analysis, the first 7 to adopt were designated early adopters for this analysis.

[5]It should be noted that the steel industry has established a formal procedure for initiating a visit from one firm to another. Formal requests are channeled through the V. P. for Operations in each firm. The participants, however, are more likely to initiate the formal process, if, through a friendship relationship, the visit has already been "approved."

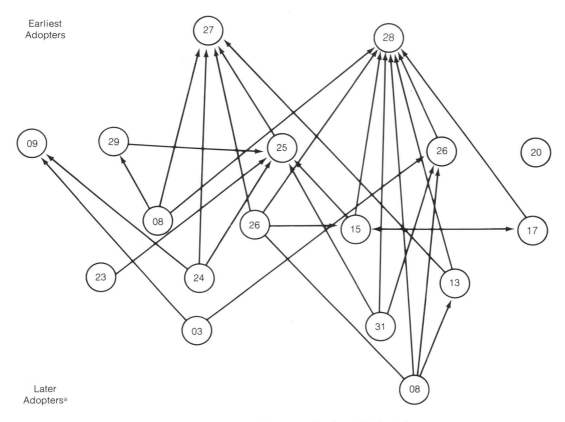

Earliest
Adopters

Later
Adopters[a]

[a]Scale is ordinal; however, all firms adopting in same year are in same row. One firm omitted for clarity.

Figure 5   Self-Reported Usage of Interfirm Communications in the Diffusion of Continuous Casting by Time of Adoption

Table 2   Source of interfirm contacts by adopter category

	Early adopters	Later adopters
Source of contact	n = 7	n = 11
Friendship relationship	6 (.40)[a]	53 (.46)
Colleague relationship	5 (.33)	44 (.38)
By suppliers	4 (.26)	18 (.15)
Total	15 (.99)[b]	115 (.99)[b]

[a]Percentage in parentheses.
[b]Do not total 100% due to rounding.

findings were those concerning the existence of a functioning informal community linking together the firms. Given the barriers to this informal interaction, that it exists at all, let alone with the fairly complex structure found to exist, is extremely important.

The active use of friendship relationships in information seeking concerning the innovation not only reinforces the societal findings but makes real the concept of diffusion as a social process in the industry.

While no objective measures of the impact of this communication activity were collected, it is

Table 3 Time of adoption by centrality

Variable	Number firms in group	Mean time of adoption	t-value	d.f.	l-tail probability
Number opinion/advice nominations received					
High	11	64.7273	−.45	16	.331
Low	7	65.2857			

possible to assess this factor. Table 3 indicates that 130 firms were contacted at least once by the firms in the study in the diffusion process. One could argue that if this activity was not important in some sense, it would not have been performed to this extent. A second indication of impact is provided by respondents' comments. One such was a statement, ''We watch what firm X does. We talk to them and find out how it might work for us. We generally do the things they do.'' The president of one smaller company, on the other hand, mentioned that he told the president of another firm that the innovation was not economically suited to the other's operation. It might be noted that this other firm had not yet adopted the innovation. Together, such comments and the frequency-of-use data seem to indicate some more than minimal degree of impact of the communications.

Several things should be noted to put this research in proper perspective. Since the study was concerned with one specific innovation in one specific industry, it could be termed a microanalytic case study with its attendant limitations on generalization to other contexts. In addition, hypotheses were formulated about the existence of a social system and adopters' places within that social system in the industry and its effect on the time of adoption. The main focus, therefore, was on the group of adopters.

The study was also concerned with investigating contact between firms. Actual communication, of course, can only occur between individuals. As was noted earlier, while some of the data confirmed specific individual to individual relationships between firms, for the most part the linkages on which this analysis are based were more general. Because of differences in function and managerial level of those interviewed, the resulting networks may represent a combination of several different communication networks which were in existence.

REFERENCES

Alba, Richard D. (undated), ''A Graph Theoretic Definition of a Sociometric Clique,'' unpublished paper, Bureau of Applied Social Research, Columbia University.

Allvine, Fred C. (1968), ''Diffusion of a Competitive Innovation,'' *Proceedings,* National Conference, American Marketing Association, 341–51.

Coleman, James S.; Katz, Elihu; and Menzel, Herbert (1966), *Medical Innovation: A Diffusion Study,* Indianapolis: Bobbs-Merrill.

Levine, Joel H. (February, 1972), ''The Sphere of Influence,'' *American Sociological Review,* 37, 14–27.

Martilla, John A. (May 1971), ''Word-of-Mouth Communication in the Industrial Adoption Process,'' *Journal of Marketing Research,* 8, 173–78.

Ozanne, Urban B., and Churchill, Gilbert A. (1968), ''Adoption Research: Information Sources in the Industrial Purchasing Decision,'' *Proceedings,* National Conference, American Marketing Association, 352–59.

———. (August, 1971), ''Five Dimensions of the Industrial Adoption Process,'' *Journal of Marketing Research,* 8, 322–28.

Proctor, C. H., and Loomis, C. P. (1951), ''Analysis of

Sociometric Data," in Marie Johada, M. Deutsch, and S. W. Cook, eds., *Research Methods and Social Relations, Part II,* New York: Holt, Rinehart and Winston, 561–85.

Robertson, Thomas S. (1971), *Innovative Behavior and Communication,* New York: Holt, Rinehart and Winston.

Rogers, Everett M. (1962), *The Diffusion of Innovations,* New York: The Free Press.

———, and Bohwmik, 'Dilit R. (Winter, 1970), "Homophily-Heterophily: Relational Concepts for Communication Research," *Public Opinion Quarterly,* 34, 523–38.

———, and Shoemaker, F. Floyd (1971), *Communication of Innovations: A Cross Cultural Approach,* New York: The Free Press.

Webster, Frederick E., Jr. (1967), "Diffusion of Innovations: A Literature Review with Special Reference to Industrial Markets," unpublished working paper, Dartmouth College.

———. (May, 1970), "Informal Communication in Industrial Markets," *Journal of Marketing Research,* 7, 186–89.

———. (1971), "Communication and Diffusion Processes in Industrial Markets," paper presented at the American Marketing Association Workshop on Industrial Buying Behavior, University of California, Berkeley.

Zaltman, Gerald, and Stiff, Ronald (1973), "Theories of Diffusion," in Scott Ward and Thomas S. Robertson, eds., *Consumer Behavior: Theoretical Sources,* Englewood Cliffs, N.J.: Prentice-Hall, 416–68.

ANTI-DRUG ABUSE COMMERCIALS

**PAUL C. FEINGOLD
AND
MARK L. KNAPP**

Vast sums of money have been expended by federal, state, and local governments, ad agencies, and public minded groups to produce advertising designed to convince people—primarily the young—to avoid "harmful" drugs. Yet there is little research to indicate whether these anti-drug messages are producing the desired results.

In one study, five groups of businessmen listened to a speech on drug abuse, but no significant impact was found upon their attitudes toward drug abuse (Derry, 1969). Ner Littner, a specialist in child psychology, noted the possibility of a boomerang effect:

> Without question some of these anti-drug commercials could have the opposite effect. Scare techniques—if they are not tuned out by children who have learned to listen selectively—can intrigue the child and become a format of action. They've learned that a lot of don'ts aren't as dangerous as parents have led them to believe (Nelson, 1970).

The purpose of our research was to test the effects of anti-drug messages by manipulating certain persuasive variables in a field setting.

The messages used in this study were limited to two kinds of drugs, amphetamines and barbiturates. The research questions were derived from an analysis of numerous anti-drug messages gathered from television and radio stations, the National Clearinghouse for Drug Abuse Information, drug companies, pharmacies, and advertising agencies. Three variables appeared to be prevalent in the messages: (1) the threat of serious vs. minimal harm; (2) explicit vs. implicit conclusions; and (3) presentation as a monologue or a dialogue.

1. The first research question was concerned with the desirability of anti-drug messages predicting serious harm or minimal harm. We formulated the following question for research: Is an anti-amphetamine/anti-barbiturate persuasive message containing a threat of serious harm delivered in a radio commercial context more effective in producing attitude change than an anti-ampheta-

Source: Paul C. Feingold and Mark L. Knapp, "Anti-Drug Abuse Commercials," *Journal of Communication,* Winter, 1977, pp. 20–28.

185

mine/anti-barbiturate persuasive message delivered in a radio commercial context containing a threat of minimal harm?

2. Research concerning the use of conclusions suggests that informed audiences and audiences with above average intelligence may not require an explicit conclusion to be persuaded. Uninformed audiences and less intelligent individuals may need an explicit conclusion for attitude change to occur (Fine, 1957; Hovland, Janis, and Kelly, 1953; Hovland and Mandell, 1952; Walster and Festinger, 1962).

   Since the research on explicit vs. implicit conclusion drawing did not adequately answer the question for an audience of *varied intelligence levels,* the following research question was developed: Is an anti-amphetamine/anti-barbiturate persuasive message with an explicit conclusion delivered in a radio commercial context significantly more effective in producing attitude change than the same message with an implicit conclusion?

3. Some evidence on "overheard" communication indicates that a person who overhears a dialogue will be influenced in the direction of the communication if he is predisposed to agree with the communication (Brock and Becker, 1965; Thistlethwaite, et al., 1955). In these studies, the sources of the communication were presumably viewed by the recipients as having no intent to persuade. Therefore, the recipients supposedly did not erect the defensive mechanisms they might have had they believed the communicator was trying to influence them. No research could be found that compared the different effects of messages heard in the form of a monologue with those heard in the form of a dialogue. Hence, the following research question was framed: Is a persuasive anti-amphetamine/anti-barbiturate message presented as a dialogue and delivered in a radio

commercial context significantly more effective in producing attitude change than the same message heard as a monologue?

To answer these questions, we tested students in ten sophomore and junior high school English classes. The classes[1] were left intact and were randomly assigned to eight treatment groups (see Figure 1) and two control groups A and B.[2] The messages used in the experiment were designed to be similar to actual sixty-second anti-drug commercials, constructed to insure consistency, and randomly varied according to the treatment condition.

Fifteen high school students not known to any of the participants but similar in age and background to them read the messages before they were recorded. They were asked to rewrite the messages or criticize them and to discuss their reactions. The final messages utilized the students' suggestions. Content validity was established for all messages by testing them on one group of high school students and another group of graduate students and professors.

The following descriptions indicate how we presented each variable.

Threat of serious harm. Statements that grave consequences (death, loss of mental abilities, hospitalization, prison, etc.) befall people who excessively use amphetamines or barbiturates.

Threat of minimal harm. Statements that some harm (nervous for a number of days, loss of privileges, disappoint parents if caught, etc.) might befall people who excessively use amphetamines or barbiturates.

Explicit conclusions. A statement at the end of the message that summarizes its main theme and

---

[1]The high school students used as subjects in this study were randomly assigned to different classes by the school registrar.

[2]Control group A was not exposed to any treatment and was used to control for history and maturation effects. Control group B heard the first two treatments and was administered a posttest; this group was used as a check for pretest sensitization.

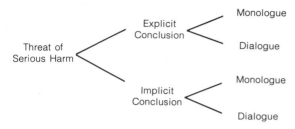

Figure 1 Variable Matrix

states the action desired. For instance, "Using amphetamines and barbiturates can lead to serious trouble, if you're using them—stop now—before it's too late."

Implicit conclusions. Omission of any statement at the end of the message designed to summarize its main theme or state the action desired.

Monologue. An oral message utilizing one speaker talking to radio listeners.

Dialogue. An oral message utilizing two speakers conversing together (but presented in the context of this research, as a "packaged" message directed to a high school audience).

High school students not associated with the students being tested recorded the messages. We decided to use peer voices because many studies indicate that an individual may be influenced by a persuasive message coming from a similar source (Brock, 1965; Katz and Lazarsfeld, 1955; McGuire, 1969; Purdue Opinion Panel, 1971).

The data were gathered over a three-week period. The experimenters met with each group twice each week during a scheduled class hour. The groups were exposed to an audio tape of a radio program lasting fourteen minutes. Embedded in the radio program was the appropriate message for that group.

The groups were told that they would be participating in a study on the effects of different types of radio programming on high school students. All they would have to do was to listen closely to a short tape of a radio program and fill out a questionnaire designed to measure attitudes toward

the program format, the music, the disc jockey, and two of the commercials.[3]

The format for each radio program remained constant: one record, one commercial, one record, two commercials, one record, one commercial, one record. Non-relevant commercials were chosen randomly from a collection of radio commercials that were played regularly over the radio. All groups heard the same segment except that the appropriate commercials were inserted according to the treatment assigned to a particular group. The order of presentation of commercials was randomly changed each time a new program was heard. The musical selections were chosen from the "top 40."

Control group A was given a slightly modified version, as they did not actually hear a radio program.[4] The times remained constant, but a new questionnaire was constructed by randomly rearranging each item each time a questionnaire was to be administered. Only five of the scales were actually used to measure attitudes toward drugs. The rest of the scales were concerned with the program format, the music, the announcer, and one of the unrelated commercials.

The five scales used to measure attitudes toward amphetamines/barbiturates were chosen after sixty naive subjects were asked to respond to twenty-eight five-interval, Likert-type scales designed to measure attitudes toward amphetamines/barbiturates. To test for differences within each scale, each of the student's responses was totalled and a t-test was computed by comparing each item from the highest fifteen scores with each item from the lowest fifteen scores. Those items that were significantly ($p < .01$) different from

---

[3]In post-hoc interviews with fifty of the original subjects, none indicated that they had any reason to suspect the stated purpose of the study.

[4]The same scales were used in both instruments. However, fifteen new scales were constructed for the control group to add credibility to the instrument. None of the new scales was designed to measure attitudes toward amphetamines/barbiturates. The addition of extra scales helped to disguise the real purpose of the study.

each other were marked for consideration. To test for dimensionality, a correlation matrix and a principal components factor analysis were computed using the responses of all sixty students.

After all three statistical computations were made, three pools of possible scales remained (one for each computation). Those scales that could be found in each of the three different pools were combined into another pool from which the five scales used in the measuring instrument were chosen.

A 2×2×2×4 mixed analysis of variance was performed in order to ascertain if there was a significant difference between the groups and within the groups. When a significant F ratio was indicated, a Newman-Keuls sequential range test was performed to test for significance between pairs of means.

Three one-way analyses of variance were performed to test for statistically significant differences between: (1) the pretests of all treatment groups and control group A pretest; (2) first posttests of all treatment groups and the posttest for control group B; and (3) pretest and all subsequent tests for control group A. None of these analyses was statistically significant. This suggests that the results obtained were primarily due to the messages used in the experiment.

The first of the three research questions asked whether an anti-amphetamine/anti-barbiturate persuasive message containing a *threat of serious harm* was more effective in producing attitude change than a message containing a *threat of minimal harm*. In terms of this study, a threat of serious harm was *not* significantly more effective (see Table 1).

The second question asked whether a persuasive anti-amphetamine/anti-barbiturate message with an *explicit conclusion* was significantly more effective in producing attitude change than the same message with an *implicit conclusion*. It appeared that an anti-amphetamine/anti-barbiturate persuasive message containing an explicit conclusion tended to be more effective ($p < .0840$, Table 1).

The last question asked whether an anti-amphetamine/anti-barbiturate message presented as a *dialogue* was significantly more effective in producing attitude change than the same message presented as a *monologue*. The dialogue was *not* significantly more effective ($p < .2522$, Table 1).

For this study, a significant within-group main effect ($p < .003$) was found. A Newman-Keuls sequential range test indicated that there was no significant shift between the pretest and the first posttest but that there was a significant shift between the pretest and the second and third posttest ($p < .01$).

Table 1 2×2×2×4 analysis of variance between and within groups

Source	MS	df	F Ratio	p
TOTAL	26.899	591		
Between	32.948	147		
A	41.597	1	1.3142	.2522
B	93.490	1	2.9538	.0804
C	34.764	1	1.0984	.2967
AB	43.100	1	1.3617	.2436
AC	175.517	1	5.5454	.0188*
BC	11.742	1	.3710	.5506
ABC	12.032	1	.3801	.5457
(E)	31.651	140		
Within	24.896	444		
D	119.546	3	4.8688	.0028**
AD	17.826	3	.7260	.5402
BD	4.148	3	.1689	.0169*
CD	12.579	3	.5123	.6784
ABD	18.504	3	.7536	.5237
ACD	.8737	3	.3558	.7879
BCD	23.962	3	.9759	.5946
ABCD	25.039	3	1.0198	.3846
(E)	24.554	420		

*$p < .05$
**$p < .01$

Note: A—Type of presentation—Monologue/Dialogue
B—Type of conclusion—Implicit/Explicit
C—Type of appeal—Threat serious harm/Threat minimal harm
D—Within group over time

There are two things worth noting when considering the within-group main effects. First, there was a significant shift in a direction opposite to the one advocated in the messages. After repeated exposure to messages designed to engender or reinforce negative attitudes toward amphetamines/barbiturates, the groups significantly shifted from generally negative attitudes to significantly less negative attitudes.

Second, the significant shift was not indicated between the pretest and the first posttest, but was indicated between the pretest and the second and third posttests. A traditional study, designed without repeated measures, might not have shown these significant within-group main effects. After hearing the messages six times in three weeks, the attitudes of the exposed groups significantly shifted to a less negative attitude toward amphetamines/barbiturates than prior to exposure.

A number of explanations about possible causes of a boomerang effect are offered by Hovland, Janis, and Kelley (1953):

1. A boomerang effect may be caused when no good arguments are contained in a message delivered by a source with perceived low-credibility (p. 36).
2. The boomerang effect may occur when the persuasive message is too far removed from the receiver's position, causing a negative effect (p. 286).
3. A boomerang effect may occur when a sender uses counternorm communications. By describing the norms in order to argue against them, the sender may add to the receiver's knowledge of the norms and, thereby, heighten the conformity (p. 142).
4. A boomerang effect may occur when the audience members anticipate that the conclusions to be drawn by a source having perceived low-credibility will be counter to their interests (p. 36).
5. The boomerang effect may occur when, after being influenced by a sender, the receiver becomes sharply aware that he is deviating from the group norm (p. 164).
6. The boomerang effect may occur when communication induces aggression and unalleviated emotional arousal (p. 63).

Other explanations may be derived from Hovland, *et al.* For example, the groups might have accepted the messages and perceived the source as being credible but rejected the messages within the context of the total situation (Scheidel, 1967). That is, the significant boomerang effect might have been a product of a reaction against the whole anti-drug movement. This reaction might then have become a perceived group norm causing some of the subjects in the groups to shift their attitudes in order to conform to the group norm.

In March of 1973 the National Commission on Marijuana and Drug Abuse made many recommendations to then President Nixon based on a two year study of the problem. Among the recommendations, the commission urged a freeze on dissemination of anti-drug literature, most of which they claimed is factually wrong, and may *"merely stimulate youthful interest in drugs."*

The fact that the exposed groups significantly shifted from a negative attitude toward amphetamines/barbiturates toward a less negative attitude suggests that well-intentioned campaigns and agencies may be unwittingly "nudging" (if not pushing) drugs through their drug abuse information programs.

REFERENCES

Brock, T. C. (1965), "Communication-Recipient Similarity and Decision Change," *Journal of Personality and Social Psychology,* 1, 650–54.

————, and Becker, L. A. (1965), "Ineffectiveness of 'Overheard' Counter Propaganda," *Journal of Personality and Social Psychology,* 2, 654–60.

Derry, J. O. (1969), "The Effects of a Public Relation Speech on Five Chicago Audiences," unpublished master's thesis, University of Wisconsin, Milwaukee.

Fine, B. (1957), "Conclusion-Drawing, Communicator Credibility and Anxiety as Factors in Opinion Change," *Journal of Abnormal and Social Psychology,* 54, 369–74.

Hovland, C. I.; Janis, I. L.; and Kelley, H. H. (1953), *Communication and Persuasion,* New Haven: Yale University Press.

———, and Mandell, W. (1952), "An Experimental Comparison of Conclusion Drawing by the Communicator and by the Audience," *Journal of Abnormal and Social Psychology,* 47, 581–88.

Katz, E., and Lazarsfeld, P. F. (1955), *Personal Influence,* Glencoe, Ill.: Free Press.

McGuire, W. J. (1969), "The Nature of Attitudes and Attitude Change," in G. Lindzey and E. Aronson, eds., *The Handbook of Social Psychology,* Vol. 4, (2nd ed.) Reading, Mass.: Addison-Wesley.

Nelson, R. (1970), "Dragon Slayers on an Ominous Crusade," *Marketing Communication,* 9, 20–24.

Purdue Opinion Panel (April, 1971), *Drugs and Narcotics: The Role of the School in Prevention and Remediation,* Measurement and Research Center Report 91, Purdue University.

Scheidel, T. M. (1967), *Persuasive Speaking,* Glenview, Ill.: Scott, Foresman.

Thistlethwaite, D.; de Hann, H.; and Kamenetsky, J. (1955), "The Effects of 'Directive' and 'Non-Directive' Communication Procedures on Attitudes," *Journal of Abnormal and Social Psychology,* 51, 107–13.

Walster, E., and Festinger, L. (1962), "The Effectiveness of 'Overheard' Persuasive Communication," *Journal of Abnormal and Social Psychology,* 65, 395–402.

ATTITUDES AND CONSUMER BEHAVIOR

Attitudes are learned predispositions to respond to some object in a consistent way. The response may be favorable or unfavorable. These learned predispositions are important because they influence intentions to behave in various ways. These intentions in turn influence behavior. However, the causal linkages among attitudes, intentions, and behavior are not unfailing. Many factors may prevent attitudes from being expressed in stated intentions or in behavior. A consumer may have a favorable attitude toward a retail outlet but never really intend to shop there because it is a very expensive store. The consumer may develop an intention to visit that store when it is conducting a sale but may be ill or without adequate transportation on the day of the sale. The factors which may prevent consumers from converting their attitudes into intentions and buying behavior are very numerous and frequent. Hence it is not surprising that researchers in marketing and other contexts have found that attitudes have a very low correlation with behavior.

Nevertheless, there are many reasons for studying consumer attitudes. Several are noted below.

1. Attitudes are sometimes expressed in behavior.
2. The attitudes of consumers may affect their openness to information about products and services.
3. The attitudes of opinion leaders are important even when they are nonbuyers since they may influence the attitudes of people who are able to buy. Attitudes of parents may influence the socialization of their children, for example.

4. The certainty of attitudes appears to affect their impact on behavior. Thus, knowing what degree of certainty consumers possess about their attitudes can suggest to the marketer whether those attitudes may be relied on in promotional efforts.

5. The certainty of attitudes is a clue about the importance the marketer should place on variables other than attitudes. These other variables may be consumers' abilities to behave in certain ways and the role of other people.

6. Studying consumer attitudes may provide clues to opportunities for developing new products and for improving present products by uncovering product attributes consumers do not like.

7. The study of attitudes, especially how attitudes change, may help evaluate the impact of advertising, particularly advertising directed to creating awareness of a new or forthcoming product.

The literature on consumer attitudes is very large. Most textbooks devote at least one entire chapter to this topic. The four articles selected in this section are representative of some of the more frequently appearing issues or topics related to attitudes.

"DO ATTITUDE CHANGES PRECEDE BEHAVIOR CHANGE?"

The role of attitudes in affecting behavior is one which has received much academic as well as everyday attention. We can all think of a time when we heard a teacher telling a misbehaving youth, "I don't like your attitude!" Everyone understood that this meant that the teacher didn't like the youth's behavior, and that the teacher thought that a change in the youth's attitude would produce a change in the youth's behavior.

In many cases, it does appear that attitude changes produce behavior changes. For instance, potential voters who are originally indifferent about a campaign may develop positive attitudes toward one candidate. It is expected then that these voters will cast their ballots for the candidate. Similarly, many advertising campaigns are designed with the goal of improving the attitude consumers have toward the product. The idea is that this improved attitude will lead to increased sales.

Pinson and Roberto point out, however, that just because attitudes precede behavior in some cases does not mean that this is always the case. For example, a friend may encourage a person to try a new food which is being served. When the person asks what the food is, the friend may say, "Don't worry about that—just try it!" What the friend is actually saying is: "Don't try to label the item so you can connect previously formed attitudes with it. Consume it and then form an attitude toward it." The friend is supporting a sequence which is different from the sequence usually proposed in stages of adoption. The proposed sequence is trial (limited behavior); then attitude formation; then complete awareness. This final stage occurs when the friend finally tells the person what the food is.

Attribution theorists (see the section following this one) are very interested in attitude changes which follow behavioral changes. For instance, in self-attributions the foot-in-the-door technique relies on attitude changes which follow behavioral changes. In this situation, a person who initially agrees to do some task will later agree to do a much larger task which would not be accepted if it were not for the initial small request. The process which occurs between the two behaviors is a change in attitude. The sequence is outlined below:

(1) Person is asked to do a small task;

(2) Person agrees; [Behavior$_1$]

(3) Person asks, "Why did I do that?";

(4) Person explains the action, "I must believe that this is a worthwhile activity."; [Attitude Change]

(5) Person is asked to do a larger related task;

(6) Person agrees. [Behavior$_2$]

This frequently studied and frequently used phenomenon is based on the fact that attitude change can either precede or follow behavioral change.

Pinson and Roberto make one other key point. They mention a problem which is encountered in comparing different studies of the attitude-behavior link. Many of these studies use the same terminology (e.g., attitude, behavioral intention, behavior), but very different measurement techniques. This makes it seem that the various studies are referring to the same thing, when in fact, they are not. Therefore, in reading articles on the effect of attitudes on consumer behavior, one must always check to see how the concepts have been measured.

"THE ROLE OF CONFIDENCE IN UNDERSTANDING AND PREDICTING BUYERS' ATTITUDES AND PURCHASE INTENTIONS"

Many different models of attitude structure have been proposed. The Bennett and Harrell article explores the role of two types of confidence with regard to the Fishbein Behavioral Intentions model (also called the extended Fishbein model). The two types of confidence are the buyer's confidence in the brand and the buyer's confidence in his or her own ability to evaluate the brand.

The specific hypotheses tested are explicitly stated in the article, so they will not be restated here. These are further explained in the methodology section by describing the measures of the predictor and criterion variables. Criterion variables are those which a researcher is interested in explaining. In an experimental study, criterion variables are called the dependent variables. Predictor variables are those which are used to explain variations in the criterion variables. In experimental studies, predictor variables are called independent variables. The researcher is not concerned with explaining where variation in the predictor variables comes from. Instead, this variation is taken as given. The variation in the predictor variables is used to explain the sources or correlates of variation in the criterion variables.

Bennett and Harrell's third hypothesis is interesting because it illustrates the effect of a moderating variable. This relationship can be put in an "if-then" format:

CASE 1: If the buyer's confidence in his or her ability to evaluate brands is *high,* then the buyer will have *well-developed attitudes* toward the brands.

CASE 2: If the buyer's confidence in his or her ability to evaluate brands is *low,* then the buyer will have *poorly developed attitudes* toward the brands.

When attitudes are well developed (as in case 1), attitudes will be a good predictor of behavioral intentions (as in the Fishbein model). When attitudes are poorly developed (as in case 2), attitudes will be a poor predictor of behavioral intentions. Thus, the effect of moderating variables is:

If moderating variable = X, then criterion variable = A.
If moderating variable = Y, then criterion variable = B.
where: moderating variable can take on only two values, X and Y, and criterion variable can take on only two values, A and B.

One element of the discussion is missing in the article and must be provided by the reader. Bennett and Harrell do not discuss the following questions: For which types of products will consumers likely have high confidence in their ability to judge? What characteristics of some consumers would lead them to have high confidence in their ability to judge certain types of products? Answering these questions will help the reader see possible managerial implications of this research finding.

"TOWARD UNDERSTANDING ATTITUDE STRUCTURE: A STUDY OF THE COMPLEMENTARITY OF MULTI-ATTRIBUTE ATTITUDE MODELS"

Many models of attitude structure have been proposed. These include various weighted and unweighted forms of a linear compensatory model (such as Fishbein's attitude-toward-the-object model, Fishbein's extended behavioral intentions model, Rosenberg's model, Talarzyk's model), conjunctive models, disjunctive models, maximin models, maximax models, and lexicographic models. (The five models used in the Bruno and Wildt article are described there. Readers should pay particular attention to these descriptions.) The problem with there being such a plethora of proposed models is that many people begin wondering which is the "best" model. Therefore, several research investigations have been conducted which have attempted to discover which model's predictions are closest to actual consumer preferences.

The main point of the Bruno and Wildt article is that this type of research oversimplifies the nature of the subject matter—namely, choice processes. One model cannot be the "best" predictor of attitude and change processes. Instead, Bruno and Wildt suggest that each of the models is one pure type of attitude structure. However, actual people often combine elements of several different models in making their choices. For instance, a consumer may use a process which resembles a maximin model to eliminate from consideration those brands which do not meet a certain standard on a certain criterion (e.g., laundry detergents which are not biodegradable are eliminated from consideration). This same consumer may then use a process resembling a weighted linear compensatory model to evaluate the remaining brands. Thus, people's actual attitude formation and choice processes are mixtures of the models which have been proposed.

In reading the Bruno and Wildt article, it is not important to try to remember how prevalent the various model combinations were in choices of the industrial product. It is very likely that the relative use of different combinations of models varies by product, by individual, and by purchase situation. Therefore, it is not so important to know that 52% of the sample used elements of both the maximin and the linear compensatory model in choosing which brand of an industrial product to purchase. The important point is that a large percentage of people used elements from several models.

Readers may better understand the concept of model complementarity if they use it to explore their own choice processes. Purchases which are easily related to those models include toothpaste, laundry detergent, breakfast cereal, calculators, and automobiles. The first questions to be asked are: How do I go about deciding which brands or makes to consider? How do I decide which brand or make to choose? Finally: Which of the five models (possibly more than one) seem to describe the various considerations which went into the choice?

"THE PROCESS OF ATTITUDE ACQUISITION: THE VALUE OF A DEVELOPMENTAL APPROACH TO CONSUMER ATTITUDE RESEARCH"

Most of the studies of consumer attitudes deal with the structure of attitudes (as in the Bruno and Wildt article) or with strategies for changing attitudes. The Olson and Mitchell paper, however, describes how attitudes are acquired or formed.

The first part of the paper describes the advantages of focusing on the attitude acquisition process. The second part of the paper details a theory of attitude acquisition. The reader should pay particularly close attention to this second section.

Two responses to a stimulus object are described: (1) concept labeling responses, and (2) evaluative responses. Concept labeling involves learning a name for a stimulus and associating that name with the stimulus. Evaluative responses (or attitudes) involve associating a positive or negative evaluation with the stimulus. Both types of responses are acquired and over time become bonded together so that the mention of the name of the stimulus (e.g., ice cream) calls to mind its properties (e.g., cold, creamy, moist) as well as the evaluation of it (e.g., delicious; favorable attitude).

Both concept labels and evaluations or attitudes can be acquired in two ways: (1) through direct conditioning, and (2) through mediated generalization. The paper explains these two processes in the text and through the figures. In both concept label acquisition and attitude acquisition for most products, mediated generalization occurs more frequently than direct conditioning. The reader should closely study the explanations of concept formation through mediated generalization and attitude acquisition through mediated generalization. The reader should also note in the summary of the paper the brief discussion of how the use of the attitude acquisition theory can improve consumer attitude research.

As a check on their understanding of the paper, readers should consider a situation in which a consumer first hears of a new product category, say electronic television games. Using the terminology and concepts discussed in the paper, describe the process the consumer might go through in acquiring an attitude toward this product.

DO ATTITUDE CHANGES PRECEDE BEHAVIOR CHANGE?

CHRISTIAN PINSON AND EDUARDO L. ROBERTO

Source: Christian Pinson and Eduardo L. Roberto, "Do Attitude Changes Precede Behavior Change?," *Journal of Advertising Research,* Vol. 4, August, 1973, pp. 33–38.

The question of whether attitude change comes before or after behavior change has been a raging controversy for many years in consumer behavior research and in the social sciences, and the subject has served as a central theme in three consecutive attitude research conferences of the American Marketing Association.

Studies linking attitude and behavior change have not gone any further than those by social psychologists in clarifying the real connection between the two variables. There is a group of consumer behaviorists who maintain that a necessary connection between attitude change and behavior change exists, or, more specifically, that behavior change must be somehow generated by an attitude change. Contesting this view is another group which holds the position that an attitude change is not necessary for behavior to change. Those who favor this position suggest that the only attitude change often observed comes from an antecedent behavior change.

The following article presents an analysis of some of the theoretical and empirical arguments exchanged by these two groups. In this analysis, the propositions developed are that: (1) the theoretical basis of the controversy suffers from the fallacy of division, and (2) that the empirical arguments exchanged are obscured by terminological and methodological ambiguities, failure to take account of third factors, and the unbounded nature of the proposition empirically tested.

The belief that attitude change and behavior change are strongly related is intuitively accepted as obvious on the basis of indirect evidence from many studies showing high correlations between measures of attitudes and behavior (Bauer, 1966).

The major issue here concerns the presumption that, in a logical sense, there cannot be behavior change without attitude change. As Robertson (1971) more specifically states: "It is difficult to conceive of a change in behavior occurring without some prior change within the organism." Supporters of this view allow only one exception—the case of "coercion." For example, Roper (1966) found that ". . . some attitude change must precede behavioral change barring the circumstances of coercion. Some internal change must precede a new external act assuming that that act is voluntary." Fothergill (1968) takes the same stand: "The natural feeling of those in the advertising business that attitude changes must precede changes in behavior must be tautologically true unless, for example, people buy things which, at least at the time of purchase, they dislike." There is the problem here of deciding what situations should be defined as coercive, but more importantly the logical basis of these statements must be questioned.

THE FALLACY OF DIVISION

Some interesting insights are gained by representing the preceding reasoning in the following syllogistic arguments: Some internal change must precede a new external act; attitude change is an internal change and behavior change is a new external act; therefore, some attitude change must precede behavior change.

While the premise is reasonable, the conclusion is not because the argument is logically fallacious.

The invalid argument involved here is what logicians call the "fallacy of division." This is found in the faulty transition from the premise that something holds true for some whole to the conclusion that the same holds true for a part of that whole (Mackie, 1967). In the present context of the attitude/behavior debate, this transition is readily seen. While it may be true that some internal change must precede a new external act, it does not necessarily follow that some attitude change must precede a behavior change, even if attitude change is a form of internal change and even if behavior change is also a form of an external act.

The real question is that of identifying the internal change. There are many plausible forms of internal changes that one can elect as possible explanatory variables. Is it, for example, a motivational variable, an opinion variable, or some other psychological factor? All too readily internal change is interpreted to be attitude change without seriously considering and screening the plausibility of these alternative internal variables.

Some may counterargue that there is not, in fact, a fallacy of division. It may be contended that the concept of attitude is broad enough to encompass any internal change. This position is best stated by Robertson (1971): "The concept of attitude as originally introduced into psychology was so broad as to refer to any intervening state of the organism that preceded and presumably accounted for a change in behavior."

The above understanding of the concept of attitude cannot be challenged on logical or theoretical grounds. After all, any definition of attitude is valid in a theoretical context. What is at stake, however, is the soundness of the controversy. If attitude is conceived as subsuming all hypothetical mediators, then there is no reason for dispute since the argument that there cannot be behavior change without attitude change is then true by definition. This holds even in the case of coercion. The conception of attitude as the set of behavior mediators must be opposed not on theoretical or logical grounds but on practical ones.

EMPIRICAL ARGUMENTS

For a proper, empirically grounded evaluation of the controversy, it is important to have studies dealing directly with the relationship between changes rather than between levels. Studies of change constitute the relevant evidence in the controversy.

In the consumer behavior literature, there is no shortage of studies dealing with the relationship between levels of attitude and behavior, although several do exist.

Achenbaum (1968) presented data derived from a three-wave study of 4,000 women regarding their purchase behavior and attitudes toward

19 brands of packaged products. His conclusion was:

> If attitudes shift upward among non-users from June to September, the likelihood of their becoming users from September to December increases. . . . As attitudes from June to September dropped . . . the chances of a non-user becoming a user dropped too. . . . The situation is much the same among users. (Thus) . . . there is a direct relationship—a predictive one if you wish—between attitude changes and purchase behavior.

Assael and Day (1968) reported finding support for the proposition that "changes in attitudes are more closely related to subsequent behavior change, than are changes in awareness (and) that attitude change precedes rather than follows a behavioral change." Support came from the results of their analysis of time series data using a set of regression equations. The data came from Bristol-Myers' 14-month survey of brand attitude, awareness, and reported usage of deodorants and analgesics, and the Nestle Company's two-and-a-half year survey on the same variables for instant coffee.

Challenging the results of the foregoing studies are researchers who are skeptical about the empirical connection between attitude change and behavior change. The studies of Appel (1966) and Atkin (1962) represent this opposing view.

Appel reported an advertising experiment where attitude change supposedly was found not to precede a change in sales. His analysis concluded that, "The relationship between attitude and behavior is not nearly so simple as has been assumed." Atkin came to a similar interpretation after analyzing the results of a study on store patronage. He found that attitudes toward various stores changed only after shoppers bought there.

In his review of attitude research in England, Fothergill (1968) stated, "Changes in the attitude variables follow changes in the usage variable." In support of this proposition, he invoked evidence from data collected from some 250,000 interviews conducted by the British Market Research Bureau,

Ltd. over a five-year period (Bird and Ehrenberg, 1965; 1966).

Conflicting interpretations in the studies just reviewed prompt a closer look. Doing so reveals that major sources of disagreement of results are in the variations of terminological usages and in the measurement techniques. Achenbaum, for example, measured attitude toward a brand as the position that a person takes on a five-point rating scale from excellent to poor. Assael and Day indicated that the Bristol-Myers survey measured brand attitudes by respondent agreement with a series of statements derived from advertising themes and product characteristics, while the Nestle survey derived measures of attitudes from statements based on the relative perception of each brand. Fothergill considered "intentions to buy" and "top of the mind awareness" of a product as measures of generalized attitude.

This kind of situation is, of course, not peculiar. Use of terms with associated alternative meanings pervades the whole of social sciences. The confusing use of ambiguous terms in attitude research has even been noted by some attitude researchers themselves. For instance, Crespi (1966) comments:

> One difficulty is the inconsistencies in the use of terminology and of techniques of measurement. These inconsistencies can easily lead to a situation in which people think they are talking about the same thing when they are not, so that they think their findings are in conflict when they are merely different.

The different definitions of attitude can always be justified on the grounds that they merely represent what is judged by each investigator to be the most useful measure of the concept for his purposes. After all, an attitude is a hypothetical construct. By definition, it can have no true expression nor a valid measure. However, it must be realized that the ambiguity of the concept of attitude greatly reduces the possibility of a given proposition's confirmation or refutation. As a consequence, the consumer behavior studies reviewed are semantically inconsistent, thereby obstructing the possibility of reaching an agreement among different observers on the meaning of the empirical evidence they obtain.

RIVAL HYPOTHESES

It is also worthwhile noting that an observed absence or presence of a relationship between an attitude change and a behavior change does not necessarily mean that the two variables are unrelated or truly related. The way attitude change and behavior change co-vary may, in the first place, be highly contextual as suggested by Campbell (1963), McGuire (1969), and Wicker (1969).

Moreover, several intervening variables exist which may have a suppressing or multiplier effect on the empirical connection between attitude change and behavior change. First, the threats to internal and external validity developed by Campbell and Stanley (1963) constitute a set of potential factors that can affect the degree of empirically discernible relationships between attitude and behavior change. A partial treatment of this in the marketing context is found in Lipstein (1968).

A second factor is the degree to which the consumer perceives the connection between his attitude change and the possibility of changing his future behavior. Researchers mistakenly may assume the existence of a linkage when in fact, insofar as the consumer is concerned, there are no such ties.

A third factor is the cost of behaving relative to the cost of the act at an earlier point in time, or relative to those of other alternative forms of behaving. Krugman (1965), for example, suggested that when the individual is highly involved with an object the precedence of attitude over behavior holds. When there is low involvement, behavior precedes attitude change.

Lipstein cited "the degree of economic risk which the consumer incurs in buying a product" and "the degree of anxiety surrounding a product category" as being the important cost contingencies. He went on to say that "Attitude change does

in fact precede purchase in the case of big ticket items."

From the attitude consistency school comes a fourth factor: the degree of interrelationships among different attitudes that may individually influence the same behavior. A fifth factor is the presence or absence of opportunities to perform the behavior expected. Howard and Sheth (1969) discussed this factor under the name of "inhibitory factors" and included under its rubric such variables as time pressure, lack of availability, financial constraint, and momentary price change.

Finally, a sixth factor resides in the time gap between the attitude change and the expected behavior change. The foregoing intervening factors will have a higher probability of exerting their influence as this time gap increases. As Day (1972) explained, "There is a strong likelihood that unforeseen circumstances may intervene between the attitude measurement and the actual behavior."

The implication is clear. The important question is not whether attitude precedes behavior change but rather under what conditions does attitude change precede behavior change.

EMPIRICAL TESTING

A closer look at the studies reviewed indicates still another source of ambiguity in the current controversy. Explicating this source requires reference back to the studies that have sought to test the proposition that attitude change precedes behavior change.

Logicians call this an unbounded universal general proposition. This means that all types of attitude and behavior change that have taken place in the past, are taking place at present, and will occur in the future. What is crucial to note is that, from a philosophy of science viewpoint, this proposition can never be confirmed because of its high level of spatial and temporal universality. However, a single negative instance could suffice to falsify it. This means that the proposition is refutable but unconfirmable.

In order to be refutable and confirmable, the proposition should be bounded. This means that instead of working with the proposition "attitude change precedes behavior change," we should work with its more restricted form of "all cases in x universe are such that attitude change precedes behavior change." As a research requirement, this may be attained by working with and paying more attention to singular cases under varying contexts.

REFERENCES

Achenbaum, Alvin A. (1968), "Relevant Measures of Consumer Attitudes," cited in J. Fothergill, "Do Attitudes Change Before Behavior?" *Proceedings of ESOMAR Congress,* Opatija, 875–900.

Appel, V. (1966), "Attitude Change: Another Dubious Method for Measuring Advertising Effectiveness," in Lee Adler and Irving Crespi, eds., *Attitude Research at Sea,* Chicago: American Marketing Association, 141–52.

Assael, H., and Day, George (1968), "Attitudes and Awareness as Predictors of Market Share," *Journal of Advertising Research,* Vol. 8, No. 4, 3–10.

Atkin, K. (1962), "Advertising and Store Patronage," *Journal of Advertising Research,* Vol. 2, No. 4, 18–23.

Bauer, Raymond (1966), "Attitudes, Verbal Behavior and Other Behavior," in Lee Adler and Irving Crespi, eds., *Attitudes Research at Sea,* Chicago: American Marketing Association, 3–14.

Bird, M., and Ehrenberg, A. S. C. (1965), "Intentions-to-Buy and Claimed Brand Usages," a paper presented at the 9th ESOMAR-WAPOR Congress.

——— (1966), "Non-Awareness and Non-Usage," a paper presented at the ESOMAR Seminar, Deauville.

Campbell, Donald T. (1963), "Social Attitudes and Other Acquired Behavioral Dispositions," in S. Koch, ed., *Psychology: A Study of a Science,* Vol. 6, New York: McGraw-Hill, 94–172.

———, and Stanley, J. C. (1963), "Experimental and Quasi-Experimental Designs for Research in Teaching," in N. L. Gage, ed., *Handbook of Research on Teaching,* Chicago: Rand McNally, 171–246.

Crespi, Irving (1966), "The Challenge to Attitude Research," in Lee Adler and Irving Crespi, eds., *Attitude Research at Sea,* Chicago: American Marketing Association, 187–89.

Day, George (1972), "Theories of Attitude Structure and Change," in Scott Ward and T. Robertson, eds., *Consumer Behavior: Theoretical Sources,* Englewood Cliffs, N. J.: Prentice-Hall.

Fothergill, Jack (1968), "Do Attitudes Change Before Behavior?" *Proceedings of the ESOMAR Congress,* Opatija, 875–900.

Howard, John A. And Sheth, Jagdish N. (1969), *The Theory of Buyer Behavior,* New York: John Wiley and Sons.

Krugman, Herbert (Fall, 1965), "The Impact of Television Advertising: Learning without Involvement," *Public Opinion Quarterly,* Vol. 30, 583–96.

Lipstein, Benjamin. "Anxiety, Risk, and Uncertainty in Advertising Effectiveness Measurements," in Lee Adler and Irving Crespi, eds., *Attitude Research on the Rocks,* Chicago: American Marketing Association, 1968, pp. 11–27.

Mackie, J. L. (1967), "Fallacies," in Paul Edwards, ed., *The Encyclopedia of Philosophy,* New York: Macmillan Co., 172–73.

McGuire, W. J. (1969), "The Nature of Attitude and Attitude Change," in G. Lindzey and E. Aronson, eds., *The Handbook of Social Psychology,* 2nd ed., Reading, Mass.: Addison-Wesley, 136–314.

Mueller, E. (1957), "Effects of Consumer Attitudes on Purchases," *The American Economic Review,* Vol. 47, 946–65.

Robertson, Thomas S. (1971), *Innovative Behavior and Communication,* New York: Holt, Rinehart and Winston, 66–67.

Roper, Burns (1966), "The Importance of Attitudes, the Difficulty of Measurement," in J. S. Wright and J. Goldstucker, eds., *New Ideas for Successful Marketing,* Chicago: American Marketing Association.

Wicker, Allan, (1969), "Attitudes versus Actions: The Relationship of Verbal and Overt Behavioral Responses to Attitude Objects," *The Journal of Social Issues,* Vol. 25, 41–78.

THE ROLE OF CONFIDENCE IN UNDERSTANDING AND PREDICTING BUYERS' ATTITUDES AND PURCHASE INTENTIONS

PETER D. BENNETT
GILBERT D. HARRELL

Source: Peter D. Bennett and Gilbert D. Harrell, "The Role of Confidence in Understanding and Predicting Buyers' Attitudes and Purchase Intentions," *Journal of Consumer Research*, Vol. 2, September, 1975, pp. 110–117.

The research reported here is rooted in a number of theoretical and empirical propositions about the role of a psychological construct which we shall label "confidence" in the formation of buyers' attitudes toward brands and their reported intention to buy brands. Most researchers agree that overt purchase behavior toward brands of products is largely a function of the buyer's intention to purchase (alternatively called behavioral intention or brand preference), which in turn is largely a function of the buyer's attitudes toward the brands in the product class in question. These relationships are not clearcut because of intervening factors—either situational factors (Sheth, 1970) or constructs such as the confidence construct.

In the consumer behavior literature, the confidence construct is used in two theoretically different ways (sometimes in the same work). It may refer to the buyer's overall confidence in the brand, for example, ". . . the degree of certainty the buyer perceives toward a brand." (Howard and Sheth, 1969, p. 35) Alternatively, it may refer to the buyer's confidence in his ability to judge or evaluate attributes of the brands.

This research is designed to evaluate both meanings for confidence.

The researchers concluded that the most appropriate and the most accurate method of operationalizing the constructs was Fishbein's (1967) Behavioral Intentions model. This paradigm is an extension of a group of "expectancy × value" or "multi-attribute" models.

Of special importance is that the concern is with the individual's attitude toward the *act* of performing a behavior and not his attitude toward the *object*. Second, the model requires that the attitude be measured toward a highly *specific* situation. Third, the attitude toward the act in question is a function of the individual's beliefs about the possible outcomes of performing the act and his evaluation of those beliefs. Finally, the later model includes the influence of significant others through the addition of the normative factors. In terms of buyer behavior, the model appears as follows:

$$B \approx BI = \left[\sum_{i=1}^{n} B_i a_i \right] W_1 + [NB \cdot Mc]W_2 \quad (1)$$

where: B = behavior regarding a specific brand;
BI = behavioral intention regarding a specific brand in a specific situation;
B_i = beliefs about the consequences or outcomes from performing the behavior;
a_i = the evaluative aspects of the consequences;
NB = the normative beliefs;
Mc = the motivation to comply with norms;
W_i = beta weights (standardized partial correlation coefficients) derived from multiple regression; and
n = the number of relevant consequences of the behavioral act.

Without alteration, the model provides no measure of the confidence constructs. Confidence was measured in two different ways. First, subjects were asked to express their overall confidence in the brands (C_o) and, second, their confidence (c_i) in their judgments about each separate belief (B_i). These procedures are more completely spelled out in the discussion of methodology.

HYPOTHESES

Two separate research questions were faced: (1) the relationship between the buyer's overall confidence *in the brand* and his behavioral intention toward the brand, and (2) how a buyer's confidence *in his system of brand beliefs* influences the way those beliefs relate to his expressed behavioral intention, and presumably to his actual purchase behavior. The first hypothesis addresses

the first of these questions, while hypotheses two and three address the second.

H₁: The buyer's overall confidence in a brand is positively related to his intention to behave toward the brand.

The rationale for this hypothesis is anchored in both theoretical and empirical conclusions in the literature.

There have been two empirical tests of this relationship. In a study of store choice, using methodologies derived from Assimilation/Contrast Theory (Sherif, Sherif and Nebergall, 1965), San Agustin (1972) found a positive relationship between a global measure of housewives' confidence in a set of supermarkets and their reported intention to shop at those stores. Ostlund (1973) evaluated the hypothesized relationship with six "relatively inexpensive" and "new" consumer products (again with housewives) and found strong support for the positive relationship for all six products.

H₂: When subjects' belief statements (B_i) are weighted by a measure of their confidence in those beliefs (c_i), the Fishbein model will provide a superior prediction of their behavioral intentions.

This hypothesis is further clarified by stating that model [2] below will perform better, in terms of correlation coefficients, than model [3].

$$BI = \int_{i=1}^{n} B_i c_i a_i + NB \cdot c_{NB} \cdot Mc \quad (2)$$

$$BI = \int_{i=1}^{n} B_i a_i + NB \cdot Mc \quad (3)$$

where: c_i = confidence in responses to belief statements;
c_{NB} = confidence in response to normative belief;

$f = \sum$ as in the Fishbein model, or it becomes an operator symbolizing the extended disaggregative form in which each $B_i c_i a_i$ or each $B_i a_i$ provides a separate independent variable in the multiple regression equation.

H_3: When used as a moderator variable, confidence will improve the predictive power of the Fishbein behavioral intention model.

For clarification, this hypothesis states that if the buyers are segmented on the basis of their confidence in their beliefs, model [3] will perform better for those who are *high* in that confidence than for those who are *low* in confidence.

Hypotheses two and three are in one sense compatible and in another competitive. On the one hand, they both suggest an improvement in the predictive power of the Fishbein model through the inclusion of a measure of buyers' confidence in their ability to judge brand attributes. They disagree as to the *form* of the confidence relationship. The researchers had no *a priori* expectations as to which (or both) of these forms would appear most appropriate. Rather, as stated previously, the second research question was addressed to how a buyer's confidence in his system of brand-beliefs influences his expressed intention, and presumably his actual purchase behavior. Hypothesis two appears to be a logical extension of the expectancy × value model to an expectancy × value × confidence model.

This final hypothesis is an obvious alternative to the multiplicative weighting scheme. Based on more recent theoretical argument and empirical evidence, this alternative explanation clearly deserved to be tested in the consumer behavior domain.

In a study concurrent with but unrelated to this one, and in a different domain (student attitudes toward campus politics), Warland and Sample (1973) found empirical evidence for this position:

For those who were confident in their Likert responses, the relationships between attitude and several criterion variables were stronger than for the aggregate sample. For those who were not confident of their responses, correlations between the criterion variables and the attitude measure were considerably weaker than for the entire sample. (p. 174)

In a study more directly related to consumer behavior, Day (1970) found evidence that confidence may be an important moderator variable in the measurement of brand attitudes. He used both income and confidence in judgments about brands to segment his sample. When confidence was used alone as a moderator, the spread of adjusted R^2 between high and low confidence groups was .45 for high and .13 for low confidence subjects. When income and confidence were both used, the spread increased to .54 for high versus .04 for low. He concludes that income plays a role as an *intensifier* of the differences between groups. His tentative conclusions are that income might be a proxy for a more basic moderator (e.g., buying style) or that it might represent another dimension of confidence (Day, 1970, pp. 138–139).

METHODOLOGY

The setting of this research was that of physicians' prescribing behavior. The subjects in the study were 93 private practicing physicians located in eleven cities, primarily in the Eastern half of the United States.[1] The subject of the study was the physicians' prescribing behavior related to the available brands of a class of ethical drugs used to treat a single disease (diabetes mellitus) in adults.

---

[1] In addition to the data collected from this sample in personal interviews, similar data were collected from 52 matched physicians in a mail survey, which was used for purposes of cross-validating the multiple regression results from the main sample. In all the analyses, the multiple regression tests held up very well under well-accepted methods of cross-validation (McNemar, 1969).

Pretest Procedures

As previously stated, the Fishbein behavioral intentions model requires both (1) a highly specific situation in which the respondent is asked to state his attitudes toward a specific behavioral act, and (2) a set of salient beliefs about the consequences of outcomes of performing that act. Four focused group interviews were conducted with both internists and general practitioners to develop a description of a "most typical case" of maturity-onset diabetes and a list of salient beliefs about the outcomes of prescribing the available five brands of the drug used to treat this illness, through content analysis of the taped interviews.

Predictor Variables

A questionnaire was developed and pretested which provided measures of the criterion and predictor variables necessary for the Fishbein model. Eleven salient belief statements (B_i) resulted from the pretest and were measured on seven-point probability scales of the form:

"Brand A" Adequately Lowers Blood Sugar

Extremely	Extremely
Improbable	Probable

Subjects were then asked to ". . . indicate on the second scale the level of confidence you have in your answer to the first part."

Extremely	Extremely
Low	High
Confidence	Confidence

This measure was used to operationalize the confidence variable (c_i) for each belief about each brand it represents an extension of the Fishbein model.

For each of the beliefs (B_i), but for all brands collectively, subjects were asked their evaluation of the desirability (a_i) of each belief, that is, whether the outcome from prescribing the drug was negative or positive. These measures took the form:

Adequately Lowers Blood Sugar

Extremely	Extremely
Negative	Positive
(undesirable)	(desirable)

The normative factors *(NB* and *Mc)* were also measured on seven point scales. They took the forms indicated below:

> Assume you have talked with other respected physicians you know with regard to this patient's condition. In light of your discussions, what do you think most of them would recommend for you to do? Please estimate the probability that they would recommend for you to prescribe each of the agents.

"Brand A"

Extremely	Extremely
Improbable	Probable

"In general, do you care if your drug choice in this situation is similar to the choice of colleagues?"

Don't care at all	Care a great deal

As with each of the belief statements (B_i), the respondents were asked to indicate their confidence in their judgments as to what other respected physicians would recommend that they do on a scale identical to the confidence scale shown above (c_i). This scale is labeled c_{NB}. In addition, they were asked to state the overall confidence they would have in using each drug (C_o) again on a scale identical to that for c_i above, with the following stimulus: "This question attempts to measure the overall confidence you would have in using each drug. Overall, how confident are you in your use of each drug?"

Criterion Variables

The measure for behavioral intention *(BI)* is the principal variable used in the tests of the hypotheses. The sample of physicians was presented with a patient description including such information as age, sex, symptoms and results of laboratory tests. The description was based on the four focused group interviews and was intended to be an example of the most typical case of maturity-onset diabetes faced by most physicians, and was a clear candidate for treatment with the class of drugs in question.

The physicians were presented with a probability statement: "Please give your drug preference for treating this patient. That is, when a similar prescribing situation occurs, what is the probability that you would prescribe each drug?"

"Brand A"

Extremely   Extremely
Improbable   Probable

_____

The subjects were therefore asked to force-rank the five brands from (1) most preferred to (5) least preferred. Ties were not allowed.

RESULTS

The first hypothesis was tested with the simple correlation between the two variables, Behavioral Intention *(BI)* and Overall Confidence (C_o) in using the brand. Table 1 contains the results of that analysis.

It would appear that the direct relationship between overall confidence and behavioral intention which is suggested by Howard and Sheth (1969, p. 145) is well supported. It can be concluded that the overall confidence the buyer feels toward the brand is directly related to his intention to use the brand. Therefore, hypothesis one is retained.

The second hypothesis was subjected to two tests. The first utilized the model as suggested by Fishbein (1967), where all beliefs are summed, and the second utilized the disaggregated form of the model so commonly used and supported in the consumer behavior literature (Wilkie and Pessemier, 1973). The results of both tests are included in Table 2.

Table 1 Simple correlations between behavioral intention *(BI)* and overall confidence (C_o)
$(n = 93)$

Brand	r	p<
A	.59	.001
B	.55	.001
C	.57	.001
D	.64	.001
E	.62	.001

As is evident without tests of significance, the improvements in the multiple correlations from including the confidence construct in a multiplicative manner (that is, using the c_i to weight the B_i) does not improve the performance of the models. While correlation coefficients were higher for four of the five brands, the differences are too small to reject the null hypothesis. We therefore reject the second hypothesis.

The third hypothesis is the foundation for an alternative to the *form* of the relationships used in the second hypothesis. It suggests that confidence performs as a moderator variable. Those subjects who are highly confident in their responses to belief statements comprising their attitude toward a specific act are presumed to have developed attitudes, while those low in confidence have poorly developed or undeveloped attitudes toward the act. If such is the case, attitudes should be better predictors of behavioral intention for the former than for the latter.

All tests of this hypothesis involved partitioning the sample of respondents based on the sum of their confidence scores $(\Sigma c_i + c_{NB})$ for each brand separately. A median split was used, placing those 46 physicians with the highest confidence scores in one category and those 47 with the lowest scores in the other.

Cross-Sectional Analysis

Cross-sectional analyses were conducted on both the summative and disaggregative forms of the

Table 2 Comparisons of the relationships between behavioral intention and the summative and disaggregative versions of the expectancy/value model including and excluding confidence constructs
($n = 93$)

	Summative Model			Disaggregative Model	
Brand	Excluding Confidence Constructs R	Including Confidence Constructs R	Brand	Excluding Confidence Constructs R	Including Confidence Constructs R
A	.42	.43	A	.53	.54
B	.41	.43	B	.43	.44
C	.45	.46	C	.48	.50
D	.46	.48	D	.48	.50
E	.54	.53	E	.60	.58

model. Results of those analyses are included in Table 3. While there is no appropriate test for the statistical significance of the differences evident in Table 3, it is clear that in nearly all cases, the models explain a greater amount of the variance in behavioral intention for high than for low confident subjects. While it is not possible to state a significance level (e.g., .05), the researchers accept these results to suggest support for the third hypothesis. Confidence in their ability to judge their beliefs about the outcomes of purchase appears to act as a moderator variable as hypothesized.

Individual Level Analysis

Bass and Wilkie (1973, p. 10) have raised questions about the use of cross-sectional analysis in similar cases where respondents' uses of scales may differ. They propose that individual level analysis may be more appropriate. In addition to the subjects' actual preference rankings, preference rankings were predicted for each subject based on the summative form of the behavioral

Table 3 Comparisons of the relationships between behavioral intention and the summative and disaggregative versions of the expectancy/value model for subjects high and low in confidence

	Summative Model			Disaggregative Model	
Brand	High Confidence ($n = 46$) R	Low Confidence ($n = 47$) R	Brand	High Confidence ($n = 46$) R	Low Confidence ($n = 47$) R
A	.52	.47	A	.62	.56
B	.51	.10	B	.58	.35
C	.53	.29	C	.54	.47
D	.58	.19	D	.61	.37
E	.43	.50	E	.65	.58

Table 4 Predicted and actual ranked preferences for brands—high confidence subjects
($n = 46$)

		Actual Rank Preference					
		1	2	3	4	5	Totals*
	1	.63	.17	.12	.04	.04	1.00
	2	.20	.41	.19	.14	.05	.99
Predicted Rank Preference	3	.11	.22	.29	.28	.09	.99
	4	.03	.11	.23	.38	.25	1.00
	5	.03	.07	.18	.16	.57	1.01
	Totals	1.00	.99	1.01	1.00	1.00	

45% on the diagonal.
79% on or only one off diagonal.
*Some totals may not add to 1.00 because of rounding.

intentions model. Tables 4 and 5 represent the resulting "confusions matrices" for high and low confident subjects respectively.

Again, there is no appropriate test of statistical significance for these results. For those subjects high in confidence, the predicted and actual rankings were identical in 45 percent of the cases. That figure was 36 percent for the low-confidence subjects. When including rankings that were either identical or only one rank off (plus or minus), the figures are 79 percent for high and 73.5 percent for low confidence subjects.

In summary, these results appear to suggest that buyers' confidence in their ability to judge brand attributes acts as a moderator variable in the relationship between attitudes and behavioral inten-

Table 5 Predicted and actual ranked preferences for brands—low confidence subjects
($n = 47$)

		Actual Rank Preferences					
		1	2	3	4	5	Totals*
	1	.44	.25	.14	.07	.11	1.01
	2	.27	.32	.22	.05	.11	.97
Predicted Rank Preference	3	.11	.22	.23	.27	.17	1.00
	4	.08	.16	.24	.37	.15	1.00
	5	.10	.04	.19	.21	.45	.99
	Totals*	1.00	.99	1.02	.97	.99	

36% on the diagonal.
73.5% on or only one off the diagonal.
*Some totals may not add to 1.00 because of rounding.

tion. Therefore, while it deserves further empirical testing, hypothesis three is retained.

SUMMARY AND IMPLICATIONS

The research reported here was designed to answer two questions regarding the role of confidence in the buyer behavior process. The evidence appears to support the first of these, that buyers' confidence in brands of a product class is related to their stated intention to use the brands, and presumably to their actual purchase behavior. While this research provides empirical support for that proposition, it is probably of minor significance. Indeed, it could be argued that the proposition itself approaches being a tautology.

The more important issue concerns the role of buyers' confidence in their beliefs about brands in the buyer behavior process. The evidence fails to support the proposition that confidence combines in an expectancy × value schema in a multiplicative weighting form of expectancy × value × confidence. It appears instead that confidence in judgments about brands acts as a moderator variable. That is, the expectancy × value model is more accurate for those individuals who are highly confident than for those who are less confident in their evaluations.

There would appear to be two implications of this research. For attitude *theory*, there is support for the role of involvement in the formation of attitudes as suggested by the Sherifs (1965) and in attitude stability as suggested by Day (1970). The *methodological* implication follows directly. It is likely that our attempts to measure buyers' attitudes are perhaps confounded if the sample of subjects includes individuals with poorly developed attitudes (or "non-attitudes") along with those with well developed attitudes. This would appear to be especially true for products or brands which are new or different, when a sizeable number of individuals may not have well developed attitudes. The inclusion of a measure of confidence may be advisable in many instances.

REFERENCES

Bass, Frank M., and Wilkie, William L. (February, 1973), "A Comparative Analysis of Attitudinal Predictions of Brand Preference," Purdue Working Paper No. 398.

Day, George S. (1970), *Buyer Attitudes and Brand Choice Behavior,* New York: The Free Press.

Fishbein, Martin (1967), "Attitude and the Prediction of Behavior," in M. Fishbein, ed., *Attitude Theory and Measurement,* New York: John Wiley and Sons, 447–92.

Howard, John A. (1973), "Confidence as a Validated Construct," in John A. Howard and Lyman E. Ostlund, eds., *Buyer Behavior: Theoretical and Empirical Foundations,* New York: Alfred A. Knopf, 426–33.

————, and Sheth, Jagdish N. (1969), *The Theory of Buyer Behavior,* New York: John Wiley and Sons.

McNemar, Quinn (1969), *Psychological Statistics,* New York: John Wiley and Sons.

Ostlund, Lyman E. (1973), "Product Specific Self-Confidence Related to Buying Intentions," in John A. Howard and Lyman E. Ostlund, eds., *Buyer Behavior: Theoretical and Empirical Foundations,* New York: Alfred A. Knopf, 434–42.

San Agustin, Andres A. (1972), "An Empirical Investigation of Attitude, Confidence, and Commitment in the Theory of Buyer Behavior," unpublished Ph.D. dissertation, The Pennsylvania State University.

Sherif, C. W.; Sherif, M.; and Nebergall, R. E. (1965), *Attitude and Attitude Change,* Philadelphia: W. B. Saunders Company.

Sheth, Jagdish N. (April, 1970), "An Investigation of Relationships Among Evaluative Beliefs, Affect, Behavioral Intention and Behavior," Urbana, University of Illinois Working Paper.

Warland, Rex H. and Sample, John (Summer, 1973), "Response Certainty as a Moderator Variable in Attitude Measurement," *Rural Sociology,* 38, 174–86

Wilkie, William L., and Pessemier, Edgar A. (November, 1973), "Issues in Marketing's Use of Multi-Attribute Attitude Models," *Journal of Marketing Research,* 10, 428–41.

TOWARD UNDERSTANDING ATTITUDE STRUCTURE: A STUDY OF THE COMPLEMENTARITY OF MULTI-ATTRIBUTE ATTITUDE MODELS

ALBERT V. BRUNO
ALBERT R. WILDT

Source: Albert V. Bruno and Albert R. Wildt, "Toward Understanding Attitude Structure: A Study of the Complementarity of Multi-Attribute Attitude Models," *Journal of Consumer Research,* Vol. 2, September, 1975, pp. 137–145.

INTRODUCTION

A plethora of articles has emerged recently which are concerned with developing multi-attribute attitude models to assist in evaluating attitude formation and structure. A 1973 discussion of the literature by Wilkie and Pessemier reviewed forty-two such articles. Since then the number has increased exponentially. The unifying feature of most of these articles, regardless of whether the models trace their origins to information processing/ decision making settings or to attitudinal/ preference formation and structure settings, is the focus upon "goodness of fit" as the evaluation criterion. There has been a tendency to assume that the greater the predictive ability of the model (as measured by some "goodness of fit" criterion), the better the model. In addition, most authors tend to treat alternative forms of these models as competitors. The resolution of this competition often results in one particular model being designated as superior even though it demonstrates only marginally superior "goodness of fit."

Clearly, prediction is an important output of these types of models since the prediction of brand preference is an intermediate step to successful predictions of brand choice. However, good prediction should not be a sufficient condition for determining the efficacy of a model. The appropriate perspective has been suggested by Day (1972, p. 279). "Most research on attitudes has emphasized either their explanatory or predictive power, although the utility of the construct depends on achieving both." Given the marketing manager's ability to modify the real and perceived characteristics of his brands, it is desirable that research be directed toward gaining an understanding of which characteristics are determinant of consumer brand preference and choice decisions. Ideally, researchers in this area should consider both explanatory and predictive objectives when evaluating the models which they employ.

Unfortunately, this statement of appropriate research objectives is more easily stated than achieved. One of the major obstacles has been the conceptual difficulty associated with evaluating and comparing multi-attribute attitude models on both explanatory and predictive objectives simultaneously. To appraise successfully the efficacy of multi-attribute models in achieving both objectives has been especially difficult since the satisfaction of "goodness of fit" criteria has multiple explanations in behavior. Einhorn has suggested at least one reason why this is true. "Even if a model is highly accurate in describing the judgmental process, it does not necessarily mean that the process has actually worked in exactly the way the model has specified" (Einhorn, 1970, p. 229).

Given the validity of the preceding discussion, it is unlikely that means will be devised to infer directly "explanation of behavior" from the results of these types of analyses. However, indirect means to better interpretations do exist. This paper presents one such method.

The problem under consideration is characterized by uncertainty as to the correct model specification. The collected data provide information concerning the fit, or lack of fit of each model under consideration. By selecting one model, the researcher is in fact defining a subspace which contains all possible explanations consistent with the selected model. (It may be more appropriate to state that the subspace contains all explanations which are not in conflict with the selected model.) However, if the researcher were to dispense with the model selection and instead utilize all information available to him, he might be able to define a much smaller, or more restrictive subspace, containing a smaller number of explanations which are simultaneously consistent with information on the fit, or lack of fit, to all models. Viewed in this light, the procedure of selecting a single model appears to represent an inefficient utilization of information. The approach outlined above provides an indirect means to better interpretations and should be useful in gaining insight into the phenomena under investigation.

This paper is concerned with the development of a procedure for collectively utilizing alternate model formulations in a manner which provides potentially useful managerial information about the underlying attitude structure. We will call this collective procedure complementarity. The remainder of the paper is devoted to the explanation and illustration of the complementarity of multi-attribute attitude models within the context of attitude structure. It should be noted, however, that the complementarity approach described here is not limited to the study of attitude structure. It is applicable to a variety of situations in which "goodness of fit" measures are used to compare and evaluate alternate model forms. In this particular case we address the topic of attitude structure due to the nature of the data used to illustrate the concept.

DESCRIPTION OF DATA

The data for this research were gathered in a large survey conducted recently for an industrial product: capital equipment ranging in price from $6,000 to $20,000 and in expected life from 3 to 15 years. Respondents were asked to rate the importance of five attributes in the consumer's preference for the capital equipment. Five-point scales were used ranging from extremely important to not important. In addition, brands within the product category were evaluated on each of the five attributes. The attributes considered were: convenience of operation, dependability, operating cost, productivity, and availability and quality of service.

For the product category under consideration, 9 brands were evaluated by 281 respondents on each of the attributes previously mentioned. Overall preference for the particular brands of capital equipment was operationally measured as follows: which brand would be your first, second and third choice?

THE COMPUTATIONAL MODELS

To illustrate adequately the complementarity approach it is desirable to have a number of alternative models which are capable of describing attitude structure. It is this requirement, in conjunction with the limitations of the readily available data, which prompts the consideration of five attitudinal models.[1] Two of these models are the often used linear compensatory model and the linear compensatory model with weighted components. The remaining three models, which we refer to as the maximin model, the maximax model and the power model, were adapted from the information processing/decision setting. Essentially, these three models describe attitude structures which are respectively consistent with the conjunctive, disjunctive and lexicographic models of information processing.[2] These three models are non-linear and noncompensatory. The operational definitions of the five models are discussed below.

Linear Compensatory Model With Weighted Components (W)

The mathematical formulation of the linear compensatory model with weighted components is:

$$A_{ij} = \sum_{k=1}^{K} C_{ik} B_{ijk}$$

where: A_{ij} = individual i's attitude toward brand j,
B_{ijk} = individual i's evaluation of brand j on a specific attribute k, and
C_{ik} = individual i's importance of attribute k.

---

[1]Since this paper seeks only to illustrate the complementarity concept, the selection of models for initial consideration is not emphasized. However for the analyst, the step of selecting the models which are to be included in the analysis is most important, especially since this selection will have a direct bearing on the results. Therefore, it is incumbent upon the analyst to specify a set of models which, when taken collectively, provide useful managerial insights regarding the particular problem under investigation.

[2]The maximin and maximax models are more similar to the minimax and maximax models used by Wright (1975) than to the conjunctive and disjunctive models since no cut-off points (minimum or maximum standards) are assumed as is usually the case with conjunctive and disjunctive models. It should also be noted that the models employed here result in a ranking of brands rather than the choice of a single brand.

This model is compensatory in that low evaluations on one attribute may be compensated for by high evaluations on other attributes. Stimuli are ranked by scores which are determined by the weighted sum of stimuli evaluations on all attributes. This model was originally applied in a brand preference setting by Bass and Talarzyk (1972).

Linear Compensatory Model (L)

The linear compensatory model is mathematically defined as:

$$A_{ij} = \sum_{k=1}^{K} B_{ijk}$$

This model is compensatory. Stimuli are ranked by attitude scores which are determined by the summation of ratings on all attributes. This model weights all attributes equally.

Maximin Model (I)

The maximin model is a minimum evaluation model. Brands are eliminated from consideration if they don't meet minimum standards (evaluations) on a set of attributes. This model is non-compensatory in nature and does not consider importance ratings. The implications of the maximin model are that for a brand to be acceptable it must exceed the minimum acceptable evaluation on all attributes; thus models of this type are referred to as minimum evaluation or gate keeping models.

For our operationalization of this model we desire the end results to be a ranking rather than a partition. Also we are unaware of the minimum acceptable evaluation for each respondent. These considerations lead to an operational model in which brand preference ordering is accomplished by examining the minimum attribute rating of each brand. The brand with the maximum minimum attribute evaluation is ranked first. In case of ties, the brands are compared on the second lowest attribute rating.

Maximax Model (A)

The maximax model is a maximum evaluation model. The model is noncompensatory and the brand preference rankings are based on the highest attribute evaluation regardless of the ratings on other attributes. In case of ties, the stimuli are compared on the second highest evaluation and if necessary successive attribute evaluations are utilized. This model does not consider importance ratings.

Power Model (P)

The power model specifies that the attributes are ordered by importance. Brand preference orderings are based on the evaluations of the brands on the most important attribute(s). In case of ties, the next most important attribute is considered. The process of considering successive attributes continues until ties are resolved. This model is noncompensatory.

Summary Remarks Concerning Computational Models

It is not the purpose of this paper to propose or promote alternative non-linear, noncompensatory models for the study of attitude structure. But rather, it is felt that the nature and usefulness of the complementarity approach is best illustrated through the use of a number of alternative models. The two linear compensatory models used in this study were selected because of their widespread use as demonstrated by the marketing literature. The three non-linear, noncompensatory models were selected because they are consistent with certain often-used information processing models. They also possess some conceptual appeal and possibly offer certain promise for modeling attitude structure.

PREDICTIVE RESULTS

The predictive power of the five attitudinal models is examined by comparing the relative frequency

Table 1 Confusion matrices: conditional probability of brand's actual rank given brand's predicted rank[a] (N = 281)

Model	Actual Rank	Predicted Rank		
		1	2	3
Maximin (I)	1	.39	.21	.07
	2	.17	.24	.13
	3	.05	.10	.19
Maximax (A)	1	.66	.23	.07
	2	.21	.41	.23
	3	.07	.16	.33
Power (P)	1	.56	.25	.06
	2	.20	.42	.19
	3	.06	.13	.37
Linear Compensatory With Weighted Components (W)	1	.67	.23	.06
	2	.20	.42	.20
	3	.06	.15	.35
Linear Compensatory (L)	1	.68	.22	.06
	2	.20	.42	.21
	3	.06	.16	.34

[a]Ties in predicted rank have been resolved by using market share as the criterion for establishing the probabilities. Columns do not sum to one due to truncation of the table.

with which each model predicts the individual preference orderings of the respondents. The bases of comparison are directly elicited preference orderings supplied by each respondent. The results are presented in Table 1.

With the notable exception of the maximin model, all models performed well. The maximin model was able to predict correctly only 39 percent of the first brand preferences whereas the other four models were successful in predicting first brand preference for at least 65 percent of the respondents. Also, the main diagonal is dominant for all models, indicating a strong ability to predict the preference orderings for the first three choices.

Table 2 summarizes the ability of the five models to cumulatively predict preference orderings.

Table 2 Cumulative prediction: probability of model correctly predicting the rank order of the first R preferences[a]

(N = 281)

Prediction	Model Designation				
	I	A	P	W	L
First Preference	.39	.66	.65	.67	.68
First and Second Preference	.20	.38	.39	.39	.39
First, Second and Third Preference	.09[b]	.21	.22	.22	.21

[a]The footnote in Table 1 also applies here.
[b]READ: The probability of the maximin model successfully predicting the first, second *and* third brand preferences is .09.

If one wished to be consistent with most of the previous research conducted in this area, it would now be the time to compare and evaluate each model and select the "winner." If we were forced into this position the authors might well vote for the linear compensatory model. This choice could be preferred on both the grounds of the simplicity of the model formulation and the already wide acceptance which this model enjoys. However, we view this process of selecting one model in deference to the others, in the absence of conclusive evidence, to be an inefficient procedure. An alternative to this procedure is presented below.

MODEL COMPLEMENTARITY: THE CONCEPT

The discussion above served to delineate the ability of the five multi-attribute models to "predict" brand preference orderings. For predictive purposes it appears that all models, with the exception of the maximin, perform rather well. However, this fact taken by itself may not be of much value since the different models imply different attitude structures, which have differing implica-

tions. Therefore, we may conclude that four models maintain a reasonable degree of accord with the data, but we also may be at a loss to utilize this information in a decision context.

At this point in the discussion it may be helpful to make explicit two facts relative to an individual's attitude structure.

1. The attitude structure of each individual need not be the same. This implies that one model may simulate the attitude structure of individual A reasonably well, while at the same time, being a very poor representation for individual B.

2. The attitude structure of a given individual may not conform to any of the proposed models. If this condition exists, the models we have used may or may not simulate preference orderings for the specific situation under consideration. But in either case we feel that the researcher has information which should not be discarded.

It is the authors' position that these facts are not adequately taken into account by the previous research in this area. As a partial remedy of this situation the complementarity approach is introduced.

To extend the potential usefulness of the predictive results, it will be helpful to examine the complementarity of the models. In this discussion, complementarity will be defined as the extent to which the models overlap in their simulation of a respondent's brand preference ordering. The rationale behind this approach pertains to the unique/common contribution which each of the models offers to our understanding of the underlying attitude structure. If a number of models are equally successful in simulating a respondent's preference orderings, this indicates the existence of conditions which result in that common prediction. Conversely, if only one model successfully simulates a respondent's preference orderings while the other models fail, this too indicates the presence of certain conditions unique to this situation. In general, the joint consideration of the success and/or failure of a number of models should

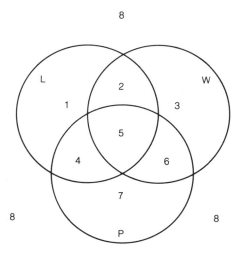

Figure 1 Venn Diagram Illustrating Model Complementarity for the Linear Compensatory Model (L), Linear Compensatory Model with Weighted Components (W) and Power Model (P)

be expected to result in a more restrictive description of attitude structure than one resulting from the consideration of only a single model with no consideration given to other models.

To illustrate this concept it may be useful to refer to the Venn diagram of Figure 1. For purposes of illustration only three models are represented in Figure 1: the linear compensatory model (L), the linear compensatory model with weighted components (W), and the power model (P). As represented in the diagram, the attitude structure of an individual respondent may be simulated by any one of the three models separately or in combination or by none of the models. Of particular importance is the fact that the models are not disjoint. That is, any two or all three models could conceivably simulate the observed attitude structure. The diagram depicts the circular areas, corresponding to each of the three models, as being composed of four distinct elements. Each of these elements implies certain limitations or restrictions for the attitude structure. For example, area 4 in Figure 1 implies that brands with successively higher preference ratings have larger values

for the sum of attribute evaluations *and* that for attributes of greatest importance have higher relative evaluations *and* do not have successively larger values for the weighted sum of attribute evaluations. This last condition indicates that some brands under consideration have lower relative evaluations on some attributes of moderate importance and have higher relative evaluations on some attributes of low importance. To select arbitrarily one model as representative of the attitude structure for a respondent who is in fact represented by the intersection of two or more models would be discarding useful information and might well lead to inefficient decision making.

Up to this point the discussion has centered on the individual respondent. It is necessary, however, to consider the aggregation of respondents if implications for marketing decisions are desired. Most research in this area revolves about the selection of one model (with different parameters) for all respondents. It is the authors' position that respondent attitude structure is person-situation specific and therefore it is desirable to allow for differing models of structure over respondents. By approaching the problem of attitude structure from the viewpoint of a family of models (the complementarity approach) rather than a single model we do allow for respondent differences if they exist.

MODEL COMPLEMENTARITY: AN ILLUSTRATION

The initial step in studying the complementarity of the five attitudinal models is to take each possible combination of models and determine the degree of groupwise overlap in the model predictions of brand preference orderings. Table 3 contains a summary of model complementarity for the first and second preference predictions for each of the 281 respondents.[3] Note that the models range in

[3]An arbitrary decision was made to utilize the first *and* second brand preferences of each respondent rather than all three. The decision was motivated by illustrative requirements.

Table 3 Summary of model complementarity for first and second brand preferences predictions (ties included)

(N = 281)

	Overlap	
Models	No. of Respondents	Percentage of Data Base
IA	140	49.8
IP	135	48.0
IL	147	52.3
IW	140	49.8
AP[a]	224	79.7
AL	240	85.4
AW	235	83.6
PL	232	82.6
PW	260	92.5
LW	247	87.9
IAP	128	45.6
IAL	140	49.8
IAW	133	47.3
IPL	132	47.0
IPW	134	47.7
ILW	138	49.1
APL	214	76.2
APW	223	79.4
ALW	225	80.1
PLW	232	82.6
IAPL	128	45.6
IAPW	128	45.6
IALW	133	47.3
IPLW	132	47.0
APLW	214	76.2
IAPLW	128	45.6

CODE

    I = Maximin
    A = Maximax
    P = Power
    L = Linear Compensatory
    W = Linear Compensatory with
            Weighted Components

[a]READ: The maximax and power models produced identical first and second brand preference predictions (ties included) for 224 of the 281 respondents.

overlap of predicted preferences from 45.6 percent of the sample (overlap among all five models) to 92.5 percent of the sample (overlap between the power model and linear compensatory model with weighted components).

An alternative method of examining the complementarity of predicted preference would be to group respondents according to the agreement or disagreement of preference rankings derived from all five models. For example, those respondents for whom the power and linear compensatory models result in the same preference ranking and the other three models each result in a different preference ranking would be grouped together. One may suspect that this procedure would result in too large a number of groups to be meaningful. But for the specific example under consideration, it was found that to accommodate all 281 respondents required only 27 groups and 81 percent of all respondents were contained in only 3 groups.[4] These results may be derived from the information in Table 3.

Since the two methods discussed above simply compare models on the similarity of preference prediction among models, it may be logical to suspect that the same information can be obtained by examining the pair-wise correlations of the predicted preferences among models. This information is provided in Table 4.

From Table 4, one could conclude that the pair-wise correlations parallel the degree of overlap among models. Slight discrepancies do exist, however. For example, the WP and WL correlations are .95 and .98 respectively while the model overlaps are 92.5 and 87.9 percent respectively. This illustrates even the lack of a monotonic relationship between the two measures. It should be noted that in the general case there is no guarantee that any consistent relationship will exist between the model overlap and correlation measures. The basic difference between the two

[4]The three groups and corresponding percentages of respondents are: IAPLW (45.6), APLW (30.6) and PLW (5.0).

Table 4 Correlation matrix for the five models[a]

	Model Designation			
Model	I	A	P	L
Maximin (I)	—			
Maximax (A)	.39	—		
Power (P)	.40	.86	—	
Linear (L)	.46	.93	.92	—
Linear Weighted (W)	.45	.91	.95	.98

[a]Correlations are based on the predicted brand rankings assigned by each model. It was necessary to use ranks since the algorithms used for the non-linear models result in non-metric evaluative scores. This also has the effect of normalizing over respondents.

measures is best seen at the individual level. For a single respondent model overlap is a binary measure, i.e., either model predictions overlap or they don't, whereas correlations measure the degree of linear association between two preference orderings. As a result, one could conceive of a number of situations having identical model overlap but with very different correlation coefficients. Also, since the correlation coefficient provides a pairwise measure of association, it becomes much less useful when considering overlap among three or more models.

To expand the complementarity concept to a more meaningful level, the directly elicited preference orderings are introduced. Each respondent was asked to indicate the first, second, and third brand preferences. A disaggregate comparison was made of the extent to which the five models successfully duplicated these directly elicited preference rankings[5] for each of the 281 respondents. Ties are excluded from consideration since an unambiguous level of success will enhance interpretation. The results of this analysis appear in Table 5.

[5]To be consistent with the initial portion of the illustration only the first and second brand preferences were considered.

Table 5 Summary of model complementarity for first and second brand preference predictions and directly elicited preference orderings (N = 281)

Models	Percent of respondents excluding ties for which *first* and *second* brand preference orderings are successfully predicted by models specified[a]
Maximin (I)	12.2%
Maximax (A)	32.5
Power (P)	33.8
Linear Compensatory (L)	31.6
Linear Compensatory with Weighted Components (W)	33.8
IAPW	12.5
IAP	12.4
IAW	12.9
APW	30.6[b]
IPW	12.9
IA	12.2
IP	12.8
IW	13.3
AP	30.3
AW	31.4
PW	33.2
LW	31.8

[a]For a specific combination of models this analysis excludes those respondents who had two or more brands tied on either the first or second preference ranking on any of the models specifically considered. This can result in different bases for different combinations of models.

[b]READ: The maximax, power, and weighted linear compensatory models successfully predicted the first and second brand preference orderings of the same group of respondents which represents 30.6% of the data base, excluding ties. Note that the complementarity of the models will be *understated* since ties are not considered.

A closer examination of the complementarity of the various models can best be achieved through the use of Venn diagrams. For example, in Figure 2 the Venn diagram portrays the complementarity in the prediction of preference ranking of the max-

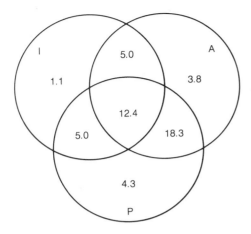

Figure 2   Venn Diagram Portraying the Complementarity of the Maximin (I), Maximax (A), and Power (P) Models[a]

[a]The percentages reported here are based on that subset of respondents for whom none of the three models result in ties in preference rankings. The entries represent the percentage of this subset corresponding to each overlap category. These percentages are not directly obtainable from Table 5 (except for the three-way overlap) because those tabulated values are computed using a variable base of comparison.

imin, maximax, and power models. The three models jointly predict the first and second preference rankings of 12.4 percent of the non-tie respondents. For the three models to jointly simulate the preference orderings of these respondents, it would be necessary for the first and second preferred brands to have extremely high ratings on at least one attribute, extremely low ratings on no attributes and relatively high ratings on those attributes considered to be the most important by each of these respondents.

Perhaps an illustration would better explain the procedure for making this determination. Suppose that a hypothetical respondent provided the responses which appear in Table 6. For this given response pattern the maximin model will rank Brand C as most preferred brand as long as the minimum attribute rating for Brand C is the high-

est of any of the minimum attribute ratings for all other brands. The maximax model will rank Brand B as most preferred brand because its score of 5 on attribute 1 is the highest score assigned to any attribute for any brand by the hypothetical respondent. Finally, the power model ranks Brand B as the most preferred brand because Brand B enjoys the highest rating on the most important attribute. The reader should note that for this hypothetical respondent, the first, second, and third brand preferences are predicted identically by both the maximax and power model. This situation prevails because the hypothetical respondent awarded the highest overall attribute score to Brand B and this evaluation was on attribute 1 which was rated the most important attribute by the respondent. The complementarity approach makes possible this type of insight within the context of large scale analysis.

An examination of the complementarity aspects of the maximax model, the power model and the linear compensatory model with weighted components yield somewhat different results. Refer to

Table 6   Illustration for hypothetical respondent

Evaluation of Brands on Attributes
(1 = unfavorable, 5 = favorable)

Attribute Designation	Importance Rating	Evaluation of Brand		
		A	B	C
1	5	1	5	4
2	3	3	2	3
3	3	3	2	3

Preference Rankings of Brands by Model

Model Designation	Preference Rankings		
	1	2	3
Maximin (I)	C	B	A
Maximax (A)	B	C	A
Power (P)	B	C	A

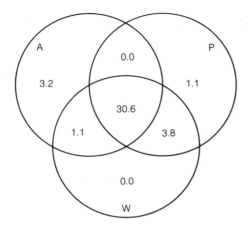

Figure 3 Venn Diagram Portraying the Complementarity of the Maximax (A), Power (P), and Weighted Linear Compensatory (W) Models[a]

[a]The footnote in Figure 2 also applies here.

Figure 3 for a diagram of the complementarity among these models. The models jointly predict the first and second brand preference orderings of 30.6 percent of the non-tie respondents. For the three models to perform similarly, it is probable that the brand attributes which have the highest ratings overall are also those that are considered relatively important by each of these respondents. This situation would exist because the maximax model utilizes the highest attribute ratings of each respondent to predict the respondent's most preferred brands. Since the power model utilizes the attribute ratings for the most important attributes, the two conditions must exist simultaneously for the two models to simulate preference orderings identically for these respondents. For the linear compensatory model with weighted components also to yield comparable results, the aggregation of the products of the brand attributes and importance scores for the higher ratings must compensate for the lower scores generated by multiplying less important attributes times brand ratings. Of the respondents (39.8 percent of total, excluding ties) whose first and second brand preferences were successfully predicted by some combination of all three models, 8.1 percent were predicted uniquely by the maximax model. It would appear that, for this small but unique set of respondents, attitude structure is a function of the highest brand attribute ratings independent of importance ratings.

In general, a number of other observations emerge. The first and second brand preference orderings of 31.6 percent and 33.8 percent of the respondents were simulated by the linear compensatory model and linear compensatory model with weighted components respectively. However, when the joint predictive nature of the two models is examined, it can be seen that the two models overlap in predicting the preference orderings to such a degree that the linear compensatory model with weighted components duplicates the predictions of the unweighted model for *all* of its successful predictions, excluding ties. It should be noted that this information does not provide a base which leads to the rejection of one of the models. Rather, it specifies in further detail the attitude structure for this significant group of respondents as a structure which is consistent with both models.

Another observation relates to the extent to which the models uniquely simulate the first and second brand preference orderings of the 281 respondents. Two or more of the models are equally successful in simulating the preference rankings for those respondents whose rankings are successfully simulated. The maximax model, power model, and the linear compensatory model with weighted components perform similarly in this product category/brand/buyer situation because the most preferred brands are earning the highest scores and higher attribute scores compensate for lower attribute scores on less important attributes. The maximax model contributes the highest number of uniquely successful simulations. The maximin model is the poorest performer, both in terms of absolute number of successful simulations and because of the extent of its overlap with other models. This conclusion applies only to our operational definition of the maximin form. It should be observed that other models could and possibly should be conceived since a modest percentage of the first and second brand preference orderings of the respondents were successfully predicted under the most efficient combination of models. Although the results reported above were impressive given the difficulty of the task (first *and* second preference, ties excluded), quantum jumps in improvement could certainly become possible through more creative model development and improved measurement techniques.

SUMMARY

In this paper, the usefulness of several multi-attribute attitudinal models of attitude structure is examined in the context of an industrial market environment. The predictive ability of selected non-linear models and the most commonly used forms of linear models was compared using confusion matrices and cumulative prediction tables. As an alternative to the traditional approach of selecting one model as representative of the entire population, the concept of complementarity was introduced. The complementarity approach focuses on respondent by respondent comparisons, allowing for different segments of the population to be represented by different models and utilizing information provided by all models under consideration to describe the attitude structure of each respondent. Those readers who are dissatisfied that we did not conclude by selecting a "best" model should recognize that there may be no "best" model. In addition, we feel that this type of selection process has been overemphasized.

The complementarity approach illustrated in this paper emerges as a useful tool for researchers. The procedure has several advantages over the more traditional approach which considers only one model formulation as being representative of an entire population. The complementarity procedure:

1. Recognizes the individuality of consumers and/or consumer segments by not presuming that one model is representative of all consumers. By recognizing the need for allowing different groups of consumers to be represented by different models, we are able to obtain more information concerning the population. A logical extension of this would be to use the different attitude structure models as a basis for market segmentation.

2. Allows for a more detailed or restrictive description of attitude structures. Conditional upon the failure of the traditional approach to adequately indicate a single appropriate model, multi-attribute models should be viewed as a family of inter-related techniques which provide useful information as a group. The use of several models simultaneously will provide a richer picture of the attitude structure under consideration.

3. Is potentially more useful from a managerial viewpoint. By allowing for heterogeneity over consumers, the complementarity approach appears to represent the market place more realistically. By providing a more detailed description of attitude structure, this approach should enable the manager to evaluate more effectively alternate courses of action.

REFERENCES

Bass, Frank M., and Talarzyk, W. Wayne (February, 1972), "An Attitude Model for the Study of Brand Preference," *Journal of Marketing Research,* 9, 93–96.

Day, George S. (August, 1972), "Evaluating Models of Attitude Structure," *Journal of Marketing Research,* 9, 279–86.

Einhorn, Hillel J. (1970), "The Use of Nonlinear, Noncompensatory Models in Decision Making," *Psychological Bulletin,* 221–30.

Wilkie, William L., and Pessemier, Edgar A. (November, 1973), "Issues in Marketing's Use of Multi-Attribute Attitude Models," *Journal of Marketing Research,* 10, 428–41.

Wright, Peter (February, 1975), "Consumer Choice Strategies: Simplifying Vs. Optimizing," *Journal of Marketing Research,* 12, 60–67.

THE PROCESS OF ATTITUDE ACQUISITION: THE VALUE OF A DEVELOPMENTAL APPROACH TO CONSUMER ATTITUDE RESEARCH

JERRY C. OLSON
AND
ANDREW A. MITCHELL

Source: Jerry C. Olson and Andrew A. Mitchell, "The Process of Attitude Acquisition: The Value of a Developmental Approach to Consumer Attitude Research," *Advances in Consumer Research*, Vol. 2, 1975, pp. 249–264.

Over the last 40 or 50 years in psychology and at least over the last decade in marketing, immense efforts have been devoted to the study of attitudes and attitude-related phenomena such as attitude change. In particular, consumer researchers, beginning perhaps with Hansen (1969), have become enamoured with attitudes, especially with attitude models of the expectancy-value variety.

Given the widespread use of the attitude construct in consumer behavior research, it is surprising to find few (if any) explicit discussions of the antecedent conditions and dynamic processes underlying attitude formation. On the contrary, much attitude research is cross-sectional and treats attitude as given, a variable to be measured and related to other concepts such as behavioral intention, purchase, or information search. Those studies which have examined the attitude construct in an experimental and/or longitudinal fashion generally have not explicitly discussed the factors and processes which *cause* attitudes, but rather seem to suggest that attitudes rather "magically" occur upon, for example, exposure to an advertising communication or after some purchase/use experience.

We contend that consumer researchers have ignored a critical phase in their research on attitudes and now need to "back-track" to that point and conduct several important studies. Specifically, we believe that consumer behaviorists should devote substantial research attention to the process by which attitudes are formed or acquired, a process which underlies the important phenomena of attitude structure and attitude change. Thus, when attitude models are used in our research, we should identify and validate the *processes* by which the *components* of that model are acquired by the consumer. Even if empirical validations are not conducted, we should at least force ourselves to logically describe in conceptual terms the acquisition processes involved in our attitude models.

Such theoretical and empirical attention to the attitude acquisition process could have a variety of benefits. For example, by forcing researchers to be more precise in their conceptual thinking, confusing and conflicting terminology would be clarified. Thus, our hypothetical concepts would be developed to fit the underlying theory rather than the researcher's problem area or purpose.

Another benefit derived from concentrating upon the attitude acquisition process would be to aid and encourage the formulation of an explicit, clear attitude construct and of a formal conceptualization of attitude structure. Such theoretical developments would in turn encourage researchers to validate these notions, the success of which would provide investigators with a firmer conceptual base.

Moreover, an explanation of attitude formation would be useful in developing an explanation of the attitude change process. With an explicit conceptualization of *how* attitudes change, communications research would be on firmer theoretical ground than in the past, and perhaps findings of a generalizable nature could at last be developed. Also, with a theoretical base from which to work, advertising researchers may be more willing to study difficult phenomena such as image advertising or nonverbal communication.

Finally, an explication of the process of attitude acquisition would provide a firmer and less ambiguous relationship between information processing phenomena and attitude structure. Indeed, it seems clear that attitude development occurs through information processing. What researchers need now is a description, in theoretical terms, of the *process* by which one incorporates information and acquires an attitude.

In order to stimulate research and hopefully begin to achieve some of the above-stated benefits, the following section presents a conceptual model of the attitude acquisition process based upon behavioristic learning theory. This model was chosen for its parsimony, the precision of its concepts, the amount of past research it has generated (especially in the psychology literature), and simply because it is the only model of which we are aware. Although we have made several minor conceptual modifications to this model of attitude acquisition, essentially the following discussion is a summary of the work of others (as referenced).

THE PROCESS OF ATTITUDE DEVELOPMENT, FORMATION, OR ACQUISITION

Although seemingly ignored by most marketing researchers and social psychologists, a substantial body of conceptual and empirical work in psychology has addressed the issue of attitude[1] acquisition in terms more specific than the typical lipservice that "attitudes are learned through experience." The usual theoretical perspective of this research is drawn from behavioristic learning theory[2] and, consequently, relies heavily upon the basic learning mechanisms of classical and instrumental or operant conditioning (as well as the more complex mechanisms of generalization) for explanations of the attitudinal acquisition process.

Doob (1947), who was perhaps the first to apply learning theory principles to the attitude formation process, considered attitude to be ". . . (1) an implicit response, (2) which is both (a) anticipatory and (b) mediating in reference to

---

[1] In this paper, attitude is considered to be a unidimensional evaluative construct, equivalent to affect (liking) toward, or an evaluative judgment (good-bad) of, a stimulus object. This view is consistent with most of the behavioristically oriented researchers who are concerned with attitude formation, for example, Doob (1947), Eisman (1955), Staats and Staats (1958), and Fishbein (1967). However, it should be noted that the tripartite conceptualization of attitude, with affective, cognitive, and conative components, has numerous apostles and certain unique advantages (cf. Triandis, 1971) as well as disadvantages, particularly operational problems (Fishbein, 1967).

[2] Van De Geer and Jaspars (1966) have termed this theoretical perspective the neobehavioristic approach to cognition.

patterns of overt responses, (3) which is evoked (a) by a variety of stimulus patterns (b) as a result of previous learning or of gradients of generalization and discrimination, (4) which is itself cue- and drive-producing, (5) and which is considered socially significant in the individual's society." Generally, later theorists maintained the essence of Doob's conceptualization while frequently emphasizing, after Allport (1935), that the implicit (i.e., internal) attitudinal response is of an evaluative nature (cf. Rhine, 1958; Staats and Staats, 1958). Our interest, of course, is with the *process* by which a subject acquires that implicit evaluative response called attitude.

Before examining the specific learning processes by which one acquires a particular attitude toward a stimulus object, it should be noted that the conceptual perspective of the present paper is grounded in the theoretical positions of Osgood (e.g., Osgood, Suci, and Tannenbaum, 1957) and Fishbein (cf. 1967), among others, in that *all* stimulus objects are considered to have associated with them two implicit, mediating responses (see Figure 1). That is, a stimulus object elicits two internal responses from a subject. One of these mediating responses represents the identification or categorization of the stimulus object and is often termed a concept-labeling response, while the other internal response is the attitudinal, affective or evaluative response. This attitudinal response may be positive or negative in varying degrees of intensity or, in the case of novel, unfamiliar stimuli,

the evaluative response may be neutral. The critical aspect of this theoretical notion is that the elicitation of the evaluative attitude response (either positive, negative, or neutral) is "automatic" upon exposure to and identification/categorization of the stimulus object (see Fishbein, 1967, for a more detailed presentation and justification of this position).

To summarize, note in Figure 1 that a stimulus object elicits two internal, mediating responses, one a concept-labeling response and the other an evaluative, attitude response. Furthermore, over time, through classical conditioning, the labeling and evaluative responses become conditioned to, and are elicited by, one another. Note, however, that this theoretical position merely states that persons have attitudes (in the form of evaluative responses) to all discriminable stimuli, but does not account for the acquisition of a specific attitude— i.e., one with a particular degree of positive or negative direction. Before discussing that acquisition process, let us first examine the processes by which one may acquire the concept-labeling response to a stimulus object.

Concept Formation Through Direct Conditioning

Before an attitudinal evaluative response to a stimulus object can be acquired, one must first be able to discriminate, identify, and categorize that stimulus. These latter abilities are developed as one comes to recognize that a set of specific stimuli "belong together" or form a discriminable stimulus pattern, and thus are given a specific meaning,[3] typically in the form of an internal labeling response. Such learning has been termed concept formation (cf. Rhine, 1958). For instance, in our culture a stimulus object with four legs, a back, and a seat is usually recognized as a chair while a four-legged, backless object with a seat is com-

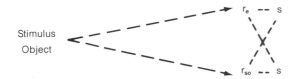

Figure 1 A stimulus object elicits two implicit responses, an evaluative response with associated stimulus properties (r_e—s) and a labeling response with cue properties (r_{so}—s), both of which become conditioned to, and tend to elicit, one another.

[3]Note that this process of assigning meaning to stimulus patterns is essentially equivalent to the formation of chunks in information processing (cf. Newell & Simon, 1972; Olson, 1974, p. 34).

monly labeled a stool. The process of learning such concepts (i.e., attributing meaning to stimuli) takes place over a period of time and is a function of both classical conditioning and reinforcement contingencies. For instance, parents may continually point out and verbally identify objects for their children and, moreover, may provide positive reinforcement when the child demonstrates concept learning by making the correct overt, verbal labeling response. Thus, as depicted in Figure 2, first-order concept formation may be conceptualized as the acquisition of an implicit response to a stimulus or set of stimuli (cf. Osgood, 1952). The response is typically considered to be an internal, labeling response with associated cue (stimulus) properties which may in turn mediate (or guide) other internal or overt responses.

Concept Formation Through Mediated Generalization

It is perhaps more realistic conceptually, especially for multi-attribute brands and other complex marketing stimuli, to discuss a somewhat more complicated concept formation process based upon the principle of mediated or secondary generalization (e.g., Cofer and Foley, 1942; Eisman, 1955). This more involved type of concept acquisition is essentially analogous to direct conditioning. However, instead of external, physical stimuli coming

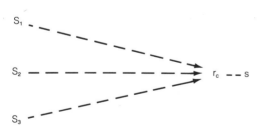

Figure 2 First-order concept formation occurs when a specific pattern of stimuli (S_1, S_2, and S_3) comes to elicit, through classical and/or instrumental conditioning, an implicit labeling response (r_c) which possesses certain cue properties (s), and which may mediate other responses.

to elicit an internal, labeling response, in this case the concept labeling response is a generalization of previously learned, internal, concept responses. Since the generalized, higher-order labeling response is a function of other internal, mediating responses, the process is termed secondary or mediated generalization.

To illustrate secondary generalization of a concept labeling response, consider in Figure 3 a relatively complex stimulus object such as a product brand X which possesses three discriminable attributes A, B, and C (e.g., price of $4.98, red color, large package size). Each of these three attributes is, in fact, an array of stimuli which, through previous conditioning, has come to elicit its own concept labeling response and, of course, its own implicit evaluative response (see Figure 2). If the three attributes A, B, and C are frequently experienced together, i.e., contiguously as they would be if they were stable characteristics of a brand, the three labeling responses and their respective stimuli (i.e., r_a—s, r_b—s, and r_c—s) may come to be associated with and thus elicit a secondary, generalized, internal labeling response (r_x—s) which represents the meaning of the overall stimulus object, brand X. Usually this internal labeling response will be the brand name. Of course, concept formation through mediated generalization is facilitated by both classical conditioning (frequent exposure to brand X) and reinforcement contingencies (rewards or punishments for overt, verbal labeling responses or other overt behaviors).

Acquisition of the Evaluative, Attitudinal Response

Now let us turn our attention to the process by which one acquires a specific attitude response to a stimulus object (i.e., an evaluative response with a particular degree of positive or negative intensity). The attitude acquisition process may occur in essentially two ways: (a) through direct conditioning of the evaluative response by classical or reinforcement conditioning mechanisms, or

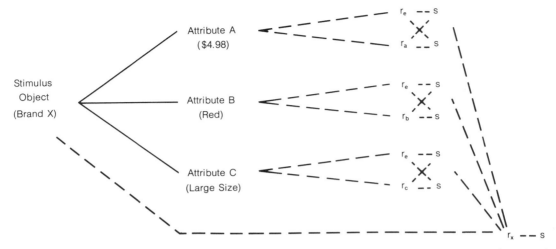

Figure 3 Formation of a second-order concept response (r_x—s) to a stimulus object by secondary, mediated generalization of the set of first-order labeling responses (r_a—s, etc.) associated with the attributes of the stimulus object (X).

(b) through more indirect conditioning of the evaluation response by mediated generalization mechanisms, in addition to classical and instrumental conditioning influences.

Attitude Acquisition Through Direct Conditioning. A particular evaluative response to a stimulus object may be acquired directly through classical conditioning mechanisms (cf. Staats and Staats, 1958). For example, a positive attitude toward brand X may be established by repeatedly and contiguously presenting a subject with brand X and another stimulus which elicits the desired evaluative response either innately (e.g., food) or through previous conditioning (e.g., colorful sunsets). Conversely, a negative evaluative response could be conditioned to brand X by repeatedly pairing it with a stimulus which elicits the desired negative response (e.g., electric shock, Bandura and Rosenthal, 1966).

Alternatively, attitude responses may also be acquired through reinforcement mechanisms. For example, by rewarding overt, verbal evaluations of a positive nature (e.g., Eisman, 1955), a posi-tive, internal, evaluative response may be conditioned.

Attitude Acquisition Through Mediated Generalization. For multi-attribute stimuli of major interest to consumer researchers, the usual process by which a particular evaluative response is acquired may be considered to be "higher-order" conditioning based upon the principle of mediated generalization, in addition to classical and operant conditioning mechanisms. To illustrate that process, consider the acquisition of a specific attitude (of a particular direction and intensity) toward a product brand, X (see Figure 4).

Suppose that brand X has three attributes or characteristics (A, B, and C) associated with it, each of which elicits its own unique, previously learned labeling and evaluative responses (e.g., r_a—s and r_e—s). The reader may recall from the discussion above that a second-order concept labeling response (r_x—s) to brand X is acquired through the process of secondary, mediated generalization (and perhaps also classical and reinforcement conditioning). By a similar process of

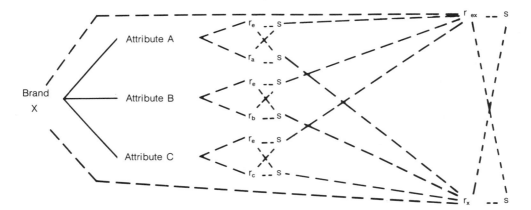

Figure 4   Brand X has three characteristics or attributes (A, B, and C), each with previously-acquired labeling and evaluative responses. The overall evaluative response to brand X (r_{ex}—s) is a function, through generalization, of the combination of the separate evaluative responses to the attributes associated with brand X. Moreover, through exposure to and experiences with brand X, (i.e., classical and instrumental conditioning, respectively), brand X may come to elicit the generalized overall evaluative and labeling responses directly.

mediated generalization, an overall evaluative response may be acquired toward brand X. That is, the evaluative attitudinal response to brand X (r_{ex}—s) is generalized from, or derived from, the various mediating evaluative responses associated with the attributes comprising brand X (see Figure 4). Thus, through the mechanisms of mediated generalization, and perhaps classical and reinforcement conditioning as well, a consumer acquires a particular evaluative response, an attitude, toward brand X.

The notion that the overall, evaluative, attitudinal response to a stimulus object is a generalization from specific evaluative responses to the attributes (or concepts) which are associated with that stimulus object is a basic theoretical position of many attitude researchers (e.g., Osgood and Tannnenbaum, 1955; Peak, 1955; Rosenberg, 1956; Fishbein, 1963), although some do not explicitly recognize this basic assumption (e.g., Thurstone, 1928). Not only does this notion make good logical sense, but it has also received indirect empirical validation (e.g., Fishbein and Hunter, 1964), although the specific form of the mediated generalization (i.e., the combination of evaluative responses) is not agreed upon (see Anderson and Fishbein, 1965, for a "test" of two alternative combination forms).

However, irrespective of the generalization/combination procedure favored (additive, averaging, differentially weighted, etc.), we believe that it is extremely important, conceptually and operationally, to remind ourselves of the basic theoretical premise that the formation of a specific attitude toward a complex stimulus object is a function of the combined evaluative responses to the attributes of that stimulus object.

SUMMARY

In this paper, we have argued for an examination of the *processes* underlying *acquisition* of a specific attitude. The model presented and advocated here is derived from the behavioristic learning theory approach to attitude formation (see Doob, 1947; Fishbein, 1967; Staats, 1967). This model makes the following basic points. (a) The hypothetical construct of attitude is most usefully considered as a unidimensional evaluation or affect. (b) Any stimulus object automatically elicits two implicit responses, (1) a concept labeling response, and (2) an evaluative response, both of which possess stimulus properties capable of eliciting other implicit or overt responses. (c) These implicit responses may be acquired either through the mechanisms of classical conditioning, instrumental conditioning, or mediated generalization, or some combination thereof.

We believe that a close examination of the attitude construct from a development process perspective, such as that provided by the present model, will enrich consumer attitude research, in the following ways. (a) Researchers will be forced to be more precise, conceptually and operationally, in their use of attitude and attitude-related constructs. (b) The process approach will encourage the development of models of attitude structure, such as expectancy-value models, which are theoretically consistent with these acquisition concepts (or with some other conceptualization of attitude formation). (c) Theoretically based attitude models encourage researchers to more directly test the basic notions (now explicitly stated) which underlie the model, thus yielding validated frameworks. (d) Attitude models which are based upon a validated developmental process may be more easily used to structure and predict a variety of attitude-related phenomena (e.g., attitude change, non-verbal communication effects).

REFERENCES

Allport, G. W. (1935), "Attitudes," in C. Murchison, ed., *Handbook of Social Psychology,* Worchester, Mass.: Clark University Press, pp. 798–884.

Anderson, L. R., and Fishbein, M. (1965), "Prediction of Attitude from the Number, Strength, and Evaluative Aspect of Beliefs About the Attitude Object: A Comparison of Summation and Congruity Theories," *Journal of Personality and Social Psychology,* 3, 379–91.

Bandura, A., and Rosenthal, T. L. (1966), "Vicarious Classical Conditioning as a Function of Arousal Level," *Journal of Personality and Social Psychology,* 3, 54–62.

Cofer, C. N., and Foley, J. P. (1942), "Mediated Generalization and the Interpretation of Verbal Behavior: I. Prolegomena," *Psychological Review,* 49, 513–40.

Doob, L. W. (1947), "The Behavior of Attitudes," *Psychological Review,* 54, 135–56.

Eisman, B. S. (1955), "Attitude Formation: The Development of a Color Preference Response Through Mediated Generalization," *Journal of Abnormal and Social Psychology,* 50, 321–26.

Fishbein, M. (1963), "An Investigation of the Relationships Between Beliefs About an Object and the Attitude Toward That Object," *Human Relations,* 16, 233–40.

Fishbein, M. (1967), "A Behavior Theory Approach to the Relations Between Beliefs About an Object and the Attitude Towards the Object," in M. Fishbein, ed., *Readings in Attitude Theory and Measurement,* New York: Wiley, 389–400.

Fishbein, M., and Hunter R., (1964), "Summation Versus Balance in Attitude Organization and Change," *Journal of Abnormal and Social Psychology,* 69, 505–10.

Hansen, F. (1969), "Consumer Choice Behavior: An Experimental Approach," *Journal of Marketing Research,* 6, 436–43.

Newell, A., and Simon, H. A. (1972), *Human Problem Solving,* Englewood Cliffs, N.J.: Prentice-Hall.

Olson, J. C. (1974), "Cue Properties of Price: Literature Review and Theoretical Considerations," *Working Series in Marketing Research,* College of Business Administration, Pennsylvania State University, Paper No. 20.

Osgood, C. E. (1952), "The Nature and Measurement of Meaning," *Psychological Bulletin,* 49, 197–237.

Osgood, C. E.; Suci, G. J.; and Tannenbaum, P. H. (1957), *The Measurement of Meaning,* Urbana, Ill.:

University of Illinois Press.

Osgood, C. E., and Tannenbaum, P. H. (1955), "The Principle of Congruity in the Prediction of Attitude Change," *Psychological Review, 62,* 42–55.

Peak, H. (1955), "Attitude and Motivation," in M. Jones, ed., *Nebraska Symposium on Motivation,* Lincoln: University of Nebraska Press.

Rhine, R. J. (1958), "A Concept-Formation Approach to Attitude Acquisition," *Psychological Review, 65,* 362–70.

Rosenberg, M. J. (1956), "Cognitive Structure and Attitudinal Affect," *Journal of Abnormal and Social Psychology, 53,* 72–75.

Staats, A. W. (1967), "An Outline of an Integrated Learning Theory of Attitude Formation and Function," in M. Fishbein, ed., *Readings in Attitude Theory and Measurement,* New York: Wiley, 373–76.

Staats, A. W., and Staats, C. K. (1958), "Effect of Number of Trials on the Language Conditioning of Meaning," *Journal of General Psychology, 61,* 211–23.

Thurstone, L. L. (1928), "Attitudes Can be Measured," *Journal of Sociology, 33,* 529–54.

Triandis, H. C. (1971), *Attitude and Attitude Change,* New York: Wiley.

SECTION 8

ATTRIBUTION

Why do consumers prefer one store over another? Why do consumers consistently select one brand of food item when many alternatives are available? Why do consumers blame retailers more than manufacturers for product failures? In these actions consumers are making inferences, that is, they are making attributions about the causes of events related to their consumption. For example, consumers may attribute the satisfaction they experience by going to a particular store to the friendliness and helpfulness of the sales personnel. This attribution leads them to return to the store. The satisfaction they experience involving the store is not perceived to be simply an accident but rather a "caused" event. They know or believe that the store executives deliberately hired sales personnel with those traits. Thus the consumer expects such traits among all sales personnel in that store.

Understanding the processes whereby attributions are made is central to understanding consumer behavior. Attribution theorists see people as actively trying to understand their world by forming explanations for events and behavior that they encounter. That is, people are seen as everyday scientists who try to understand *why* certain events took place. In other words, people attribute meanings and conditions to objects and events. For example, a person may notice a Boy Scout helping a little old lady across the street. The person is likely to attribute this to a disposition of the Boy Scout—that is, his helpfulness. However, a more cynical observer might attribute the Boy Scout's behavior to a desire to make a fast, easy dollar. Attribution theory explains the process that the observer will go through in developing an explanation. The theory also addresses itself to the probability of the occurrence of various types of attributions based on the context in which the observation occurs.

In order to fully understand attribution theory, one must put aside the notion that there exists an objective reality. Attribution theorists deal only with people's perceptions and explanations of their experiences. To exist in any form for people, the world must be internalized, perceived, and experienced, which necessarily means that individual understandings and explanations will be created.

The relevance of attribution theory for consumer behavior is quite high. A few short examples will demonstrate this. Consumers viewing ads or listening to friends talk about products will attribute various intentions to the communicator (e.g., intention to persuade, to inform, or to deceive). After purchasing a product, consumers will sometimes have dissatisfactions about their experience with the product. They will attribute this to intentions of the manufacturer, the retailer, the salesperson, the advertiser, or to their own shopping pattern. Agencies which handle consumer complaints must make attributions about who or what is the cause of the complaint.

The two articles in this section discuss two different attempts to study how consumers' attributions are related to their behavior. Each discusses consumer attributions in a different context.

"CHILDREN AND COMMERCIAL PERSUASION: AN ATTRIBUTION THEORY ANALYSIS"

One way that attribution theory can be applied to consumer behavior is in the area of mass communications. Consumers attribute intentions and qualities to advertisers. The Robertson and Rossiter study examines the attributions made by children about advertisers' intentions. Specifically, the study attempts to determine the antecedents and the effects of various attributions of intent. The two types of attributions and their hypothesized antecedents and consequences are listed in Table 1. The research hypotheses test whether or not these antecedents and consequences are associated with either of the two types of attributions.

The Robertson and Rossiter study is based on a set of stages of cognitive development which were postulated by Jean Piaget, a Swiss psychologist. The Robertson and Rossiter article makes reference to Piaget's work, but never explicitly describes Piaget's stages of cognitive development. These will be briefly highlighted here.

    (1) Sensorimotor stage (birth to age two): development of an understanding of self/environment distinction, the connection between sensory experiences and motor activities, and object constancy (object exists even when it is out of sight).

(2) Preoperational thought stage (age two to seven): develop ability to use symbols to represent parts of the environment (e.g., through language).

(3) Concrete operations stage (age seven to eleven): develop ability to solve problems using reason, and ability to construct hierarchical orders of objects.

(4) Formal operations stage (begins around age eleven): develop ability to understand and apply abstract ideas, and can understand hypothetical relationships.

The implications of Piaget's stages for a study such as the one by Robertson and Rossiter are important. Children can make certain types of attributions of intent only if they have the cognitive ability to reason in this way. This is not saying that some children are too unintelligent to see the real intentions of advertisers. Rather, according to Piaget, making attributions of this kind is a task which is beyond the present cognitive abilities of some younger children. As children become older and pass through successive stages of cognitive development, they will be more likely to attribute persuasive intentions to advertisers. This idea, developed from Piaget's theory, is borne out in the test conducted by Robertson and Rossiter.

However, a cautionary note is in order concerning conclusions which can be drawn from the Robertson and Rossiter study. This is a cross-sectional rather than a longitudinal study. That is, students from the first, third, and fifth grades were interviewed at one point in time rather than interviewing the same students when they were in the first grade, then later when they were in the third grade, and then in the fifth grade. The latter type of study, involving a four-year time span, is called a longitudinal study.

In a cross-sectional study of the type conducted by Robertson and Rossiter, only correlational conclusions can be drawn. We can say that the likelihood of a child making an attribution of persuasive intent is positively correlated with age. However, we cannot conclude, solely on the basis of the Robertson and Rossiter study, that increases in age *cause* increases in the likelihood of attributions of persuasive intent. A longitudinal study is necessary before such a conclusion can be drawn. In this particular case, information about Piaget's longitudinal studies can be combined with Robertson and Rossiter's findings to support the conclusion that age is a causal factor.

"INTERPERSONAL INFLUENCE ON CONSUMER BEHAVIOR: AN ATTRIBUTION THEORY APPROACH"

People are evaluated by others partially on the basis of the products which they choose to purchase. That is, a person may observe a friend who has purchased a particular item, say a very expensive wine, and infer something about the purchaser's personality. However, the inferences which are drawn may differ. It may be inferred that the purchaser is a very knowledgeable connoisseur of wines or that the purchaser is a lavish fool for wasting money in this way.

The Calder and Burnkrant article describes some research which examined these kinds of product-based inferences. They draw from the literature in social psychology on attribution processes. Basically they were trying to understand which variables affect whether or not strong attributions will be made about a consumer's personality based on purchases of certain products. The paradigm within which their research is conducted is shown in Figure 1 in the article.

There are two types of attributions which can be made following an event. These are internal and external attributions. Internal attributions are inferences made about the disposition or personality of an actor in a situation. External attributions occur when the causes of an event are inferred to be something other than the actor. If we see a person put up an umbrella when the sky is only hazy, we can make several attributions. We can infer that the person is either crazy or cautious. These are internal attributions. Alternatively, we can infer that the person has put up the umbrella because someone else said to do this, or because it has begun raining very lightly. These are external attributions. The Calder and Burnkrant article is concerned only with internal attributions.

There are several independent variables which are studied to see if they affect the types of attributions which are made. These are reviewed here for purposes of clarification. There are four independent variables, each of which has two levels. This is what is meant in the article by a 2x2x2x2 design. These four variables and their two levels are listed below:

a. Social desirability: high (Revlon) and low (Walgreens)
b. Choice: high (four dissimilar brands) and low (two similar brands)
c. Use context: public (evening out with friends) or private (lounge at work)
d. Product: mascara or deodorant.

Combining these, there are 16 possible combinations. These are shown in Table 2 in the article. Each questionnaire contained one possibility. The reader is cautioned to note the small sample sizes in each cell (also shown in Table 2). Small cell sizes are undesirable because the smaller the cell size, the greater the possibility of large deviations from the population values which are estimated by the sample values.

Two dependent variables were studied. The first dependent variable is the inferred or attributed personality traits. One problem with this study is that the design forced the subjects to make attributions about personality traits. This may have forced some subjects to make certain kinds of attributions which they otherwise would not have made.

Since 27 traits were studied, the researchers realized that if they checked to see if the independent variables were related to each of these traits in a statistically significant way, they could expect some relationships to be discovered by chance. Therefore, they combined the traits into two factors by using factor analysis. These two factors were labeled social evaluation and personal effectiveness. Seven of the individual traits were included in the final analyses because they did not fit into these two factors. On any of the traits, an extreme personality trait evaluation in either direction indicates an internal attribution.

The second dependent variable is confidence. This variable reflects how certain the respondent is that the inferred trait is in fact an accurate description of the consumer.

In reading the *Results* section of this article, the reader may wish to make a table with 16 cells representing the possible combinations of independent variables. Then, as results are described they can be filled in the cells in words. Then before reading the *Discussion* section, the reader should try to develop some explanations of why these results might have been obtained. A reading of the *Discussion* section will then indicate why the authors feel these were the results. Whether or not the reader's explanation corresponds to that of the authors, the attempt to move from description to explanation is an instructive exercise.

CHILDREN AND COMMERCIAL PERSUASION: AN ATTRIBUTION THEORY ANALYSIS

THOMAS S. ROBERTSON AND JOHN R. ROSSITER

This study was prompted by the question of the extent to which children are capable of understanding the purposes of television commercials and the effects of such understanding on attitudes and purchase requests. In conceptualizing these problems into a research structure, it appeared that attribution theory would provide the most relevant and meaningful theoretical perspective.

Attribution theory concerns the processes by which individuals interpret events in their subjective environment. It is a theory of perception which takes the point of view of the lay observer, as he sorts and interprets incoming information and infers causality, rather than the analytic framework of the scientific observer (Heider, 1958). As such, attribution theory has been termed a "naive psychology." Its value is its focus on *subjectively operative causal processes*—the "real" factors from the actor's vantage point—which determine his perception, thought, and action.

The central idea of attribution theory is that an individual is motivated "to attain a cognitive mastery of the causal structure of his environment" (Kelley, 1967, p. 193). The individual attempts to make sense out of his environment by the attribution of causal relationships. This process of causal attribution, according to Piaget (1970), begins at a very young age and much of the child's subsequent development is toward a more sophisticated and discriminating sense of causality.

THE RESEARCH PROBLEM

The present study, then, investigates a particular class of causal perceptions—children's attributions about the intent of television commercials. Essentially, we are dealing with the child's inferences as to what the communicator intends. In order to attribute a motive of intent, the child must first presumably be capable of: discerning commercials as discrete from regular programming, recognizing a sponsor as the source of the commercial message, and perceiving the idea of an intended audi-

Source: Thomas S. Robertson and John R. Rossiter, "Children and Commercial Persuasion: An Attribution Theory Analysis," *The Journal of Consumer Research,* Vol. 1, June, 1974, pp. 13–20.

ence for the message. Furthermore, it would appear that full comprehension of the purposive intent of commercials would be evidenced by the child's ability in: understanding the symbolic nature of product, character and contextual representation in commercials and discriminating, by example, between products as advertised and products as experienced.

In the pilot study for this research project, open-ended interviews revealed that children exhibited two basic forms of attributional intent—"assistive" and "persuasive"—and that these were not necessarily independent. A child might see only assistive intent (for example, "commercials tell you about things") or only persuasive intent (for example, "commercials try to make you buy things"), or some combination of both. A similar duality has been observed in previous research with children (Ward, 1972) and adults (Bower, 1973).

The case in which the child simultaneously attributes assistive and persuasive intent to commercials is interesting. Extant attribution theory, in fact, offers contrary predictions as to the relative weight of "positive" and "negative" factors when jointly perceived. Kelley (1971, p. 12) suggests that positive or "facilitative" factors will outweigh negative or "inhibitory" factors, whereas Kanouse and Hanson (1971, p. 56) suggest the opposite—that negative factors will be dominant. The assistive-persuasive intent dichotomy allows us to test these alternative predictions.

Hypotheses

The primary concern is what attributions (as to commercial intent) children hold and what factors account for these attributions. We are further concerned with the ramifications of these attributions in attitudinal and response tendency outcomes.

Hypothesis 1: Developmental Factors Related to Intent. Ability to perceive intent in commercials (either assistive or persuasive) will be positively associated with (a) the child's age, (b) the presence of older siblings, (c) the educational level of his parents,

(d) the child's level of interaction with his parents, and (e) the child's peer integration.

Prior research on the development of children's attributions toward television advertising has focused primarily on age as the explanatory variable. More recently, however, Ward and Wackman (1974) have used Piagetian concepts in an attempt to explain age-related differences in children's reactions to commercials. In general, the existing research indicates that the older the child, then the greater his awareness, understanding, and discernment of television commercials. It should be noted that age, as such, is a surrogate for both level of cognitive development and cumulative level of exposure to television advertising. It is assumed that some minimum level of exposure to commercials is a prerequisite in the development of valid attributions. In the absence of longitudinal research, of course, it is extremely difficult to sort out developmental and experiential factors in age-related effects.

The initial hypothesis, therefore, also takes into account the child's level of social support, postulating that development of the concepts of assistive or persuasive intent will be fostered by the presence of older siblings, higher levels of parental education, higher levels of interaction with parents, and higher levels of peer integration. Because the child is informationally dependent upon other people—parents, peers, and siblings in particular—in their relative absence he will be slower to develop a valid attributional set (Kelley, 1967; Festinger, 1954).

Hypothesis 2: Cognitive Factors Which Would Logically Precede Attribution of Intent. Ability to recognize assistive or persuasive intent in television commercials is dependent upon the child's making a number of prior cognitive distinctions: (a) discrimination between programming and commercials; (b) recognition of an external source; (c) perception of an intended audience; (d) awareness of the symbolic nature of commercials; and (e) experience of discrepancies between the product as advertised and the actual product.

These factors would logically appear to precede the development of valid attributions of commercial intent. Given the cross-sectional nature of the research, however, we are not truly testing a development process but rather examining the incidence of these cognitive distinctions by age level and the relationship to intent. Operationalization of these cognitive factors is shown in Table 1 (variables 3-7).

Attribution of intent must, by necessity, be preceded by discrimination as to what a commercial is. A pilot study by Blatt, Spencer and Ward (1971) suggests that discrimination between commercials and programming may be absent in some children, even by first grade.

Increasing perceptual ability logically requires that the child be able to recognize the existence of an "other" whose perspective he may be able to adopt (Mead, 1934). Flavell (1970) notes that "perspective," or alternative source perception, is only partly accomplished in early school years and that children at Piaget's pre-operational stage have difficulty in "taking the role of another." The development of attribution as to the assistive or persuasive intent of commercials would seem to proceed, in part, as a function of external source perception.

Perception of an implied audience as the target of the advertiser's message would seem to be a further attributional prerequisite. We might posit that the child advances from a lack of audience perception to the egocentric view that all commercials are directed at him. Later he realizes that commercials are directed to his peers as well as himself and later still he realizes that commercials are directed to a general audience. Finally, the child recognizes that commercials are directed at specific segments of the general audience, of which he may not always be a part.

As regards perception of symbolic representation, we again posit a developing sequence. The child initially shows no recognition of the symbolic nature of commercials. He then proceeds to an implicit recognition of the distinction between images and reality without clear articulation of the representation devices used to enhance the presentation of the product. Lastly, the child becomes aware of the symbolic devices used in many commercials, for example, idealized settings for product display or dramatized character emotions.

Personal experience of discrepancies between products as advertised and products in actuality is the final variable hypothesized to precede attribution of intent in commercials. This variable is operationally dichotomized because the child either has or has not experienced specific commercial-product discrepancies.

Hypothesis 3: Consequences of Perceived Intent. Given that an attribution of intent is made, assistive intent attribution will be positively related, and persuasive intent negatively related, to: (a) belief and trust in television commercials, (b) liking of commercials, and (c) consumption motivation, that is, desire for the advertised products. As a corollary: persuasive intent will outweigh assistive intent in cases where both attributions are made.

The present hypothesis differs from the first hypothesis in that it considers not just the emergence of attributions, per se, but the "directionality" of their consequences. Our expectation is that recognition of the persuasive purpose of commercials will reduce their influence on the child, while recognition of assistive intent will increase their influence.

These would seem to be logical predictions. Although the available research evidence is indirect, it indicates that as children grow older they exhibit more cynical attitudes toward commercials, and make fewer consumption requests (Ward, 1972; Wells, 1965). In the present research we are postulating that attribution of intent is an important mediating factor in this process.

Furthermore, previous research has tended to conceptualize persuasiveness as though it were part of a perceptual continuum which ranges from the favorable perceptions of young children to the cynical outlook of older children. Our pilot study indicated, however, that children can hold dual

Table 1 Measurement components

Variables	Code values	Questionnaire items
Attributions		
1. Assistive Intent	1— No assistive intent perceived 2— Recognition of assistive intent	
2. Persuasive Intent	1— No persuasive intent perceived 2— Recognition of persuasive intent	
Antecedents		
3. Discrimination Between Programs and Commercials	1— No discrimination 2— No confusion but discreteness not explicit 3— Explicit discrimination	Variables 1 to 7 were assessed independently based on responses to the following questions:
4. Recognition of Source	1— No source perceived 2— Ambiguous source reference 3— Clear source reference	What is a television commercial? Why are commercials shown on television?
5. Perception of Audience	1— No audience perceived 2— Personal audience 3— Peer audience 4— General audience 5— Segmented audience	What do commercials try to get you to do?
6. Awareness of Symbolic Nature of Commercials	1— No symbol-reference distinction 2— Implicit distinction 3— Explicit perception of representational techniques	
7. Perception of Discrepancy Between Message and Product	1— No discrepancy experienced 2— Discrepancy experienced	
Consequences		
8. Trust in Commercials	1— Disbelieves all commercials 2— Believes some only or disbelieves some 3— Believes all commercials	Do you believe what television commercials tell you?
9. Liking of Commercials	1— Dislikes all commercials 2— Likes some only or dislikes some 3— Likes all commercials	Do you like television commercials?
10. Consumption Motivation	1— Wants some peer-oriented products 2— Wants all peer-oriented products, with some limitations, e.g., price 3— Wants all advertised products	Do you want every toy or game that you see advertised on television?

perceptions, just as adults recognize both the informative functions of advertising and the inherent selling motives (Bauer and Greyser, 1968; Bower, 1973).

In the dual attribution situation, our prediction is that persuasive intent attribution will outweigh assistive intent attribution in determining commercial believability, liking, and consumption motivation (Kanouse and Hanson, 1971).

RESEARCH DESIGN

Sample

Respondents for this study were 289 primary school boys in three grades, ranging from upper-lower to upper-middle social class. The grades represented are first, third, and fifth. The sample was selected from five schools within the Philadelphia area Catholic school system in which we interviewed the entire set of boys at each grade level, or, in the case of one large school, the entire set of boys within one class at each grade level. Because only two parents refused permission to have their children participate in the study, cooperation was almost universal.

Data

The data analyzed here are from the second of four waves of interviews with these children and their parents as part of a broader study of the consumer behavior of children. By the second interview rapport had been well established for the introduction of open-ended questions.

We established procedures to give the child every opportunity to reflect his view of reality: ". . . the kind of interview which lets the interviewer see the world the way the respondent sees it requires sympathetic cultivation. The child's world is a different world, and patience is the price of admission" (Wells, 1965, p. 6).

Measurement

The measurement components are exhibited in Table 1 for those variables for which judgment

was necessary in coding. For those variables not exhibited, such as age and presence of older siblings, standard closed-end measures were used. Parent-child interaction was based on frequency for a sequence of interaction events, as reported by the child, and peer integration was based on the child's designation by other students in the sample as a "best friend."

An obvious issue when interviewing children is whether results are affected by children's differential abilities to articulate. This is a point worthy of elaboration since the measurement components (Table 1) are open-ended and could differentially favor children with superior verbal facility. The child was, however, given ample opportunity to express his ideas and, in fact, interviews with first graders took significantly longer to complete than interviews with fifth graders—an average of 30 minutes versus 20 minutes.

Analysis

Two statistical procedures were employed to test the three main hypotheses. Because the dependent variables involved discrete categorical measurement, nonparametric tests were indicated. The separate effects of the independent variables were examined by computing the relevant Kendall bivariate correlation coefficients (τ).[1] The combined operation of independent variables within each hypothesis set was assessed by performing stepwise multivariate discriminant analyses.

RESULTS

An overview of results is provided in Table 2 indicating the data patterns by grade level for the main research variables. These results show clear developmental trends toward increasingly sophisticated cognitions and less positive attitudinal structures. The single exception to the grade-related

---

[1]Kendall's tau coefficient is usually preferred to Spearman's when a relatively large proportion of tied ranks is involved, as with the present data.

Table 2 Overview of results by grade level[a]

Variables	First grade	Third grade	Fifth grade
Attributions			
Assistive Intent	51.7%	68.3%	55.3%
Persuasive Intent	52.7	87.1	99.0
Antecedents[b]			
Discrimination Between Programming and Commercials	73.5	90.1	100.0
Recognition of Source	48.2	81.2	94.7
Perception of Audience	50.0	73.7	88.3
Awareness of Symbolic Nature of Commercials	43.2	71.3	93.7
Perception of Discrepancies Between Message and Product	12.5	48.0	78.7
Consequences			
Trusts All Commercials	64.8	30.4	7.4
Likes All Commercials	68.5	55.9	25.3
Wants All Products Advertised	53.3	26.7	6.4

[a]Percentages are based on minimum response rates of 85 first graders, 95 third graders, and 94 fifth graders. Total sample size varied from 276 to 289 due to deletion of responses that did not attain modal agreement in coding.
[b]Percentages for antecedent variables are based on minimum levels of concept acquisition (see Table 1).

pattern is assistive intent attribution which reaches a maximum among third graders.

Hypothesis #1: Developmental Factors

Children's attribution of persuasive intent to commercials is very much related to age and parental education. That is, those children who see commercials as designed to induce purchases are older and have parents of higher educational levels than those children who do not perceive persuasive intent (Table 3). The child's interaction level with his parents, the presence or absence of older siblings, and his level of peer integration are all unrelated to his ability to perceive persuasive intent. The discriminant equation based on this hypothesis shows age to be the most significant factor. The level of correct prediction for the overall discriminant function is 75 percent versus a chance prediction of 50 percent.

In comparison, the only factor associated with the child's holding assistive intent attributions is the absence of older siblings; that is, the child who sees advertising as designed to assist tends to be the oldest or only child in the home.

It is interesting that age correlates so well with perception of persuasive intent yet is unrelated to assistive intent. Apparently, attribution of assistive intent is not inconsistent with a concurrent attribution of persuasive intent. Persuasive intent, as would clearly be surmised, is a higher order of attributional sophistication and is dependent upon maturational development and, by implication, cumulative exposure to television commercials.

The lack of relationship for either form of intent with parent-child interaction might suggest that this is too general a measure and that it would be necessary to focus on interaction directly relevant to consumption values and decision rules. Alterna-

Table 3 Developmental factors related to intent (hypothesis #1): Kendall τ correlations and discriminant weights

Developmental factors	Assistive intent		Persuasive intent	
	Kendall τ	Discriminant weights	Kendall τ	Discriminant weights
Age	.05	.27	.41[a]	.94
Parental Education	.03	.40	.19[a]	.32
Parent-Child Interaction	.04	.74	.02	.08
Presence of Older Siblings	−.13[a]	−1.02	−.06	−.30
Peer Integration	.03	.23	.02	.09
Percentage Correctly Classified (vs. 50% Chance Level)		59%		75%
Significance of F Value		NS		.01

[a]Correlation significant at .001 level.

tively, it might suggest that parents are not particularly involved in the consumer education of their children. Similarly, the peer integration measure may have been too general, or again, peers may not provide particularly relevant reality checks as to the intent of commercials since they themselves are similarly naive.

Hypothesis #2: Cognitive Factors Likely to Precede Attribution of Intent

Focusing on the attribution of *persuasive intent,* the hypothesized results are borne out uniformly by the correlation data at a .001 level of significance (one-tailed test) and the discriminant function correctly classifies 73 percent of the cases (Table 4). This suggests that those children who are capable of recognizing commercials as persuasive messages meet a set of (hypothesized) antecedent criteria: (1) they can distinguish commercials from programming; (2) they recognize the existence of an external source or commercial sponsor; (3) they perceive the idea of an intended audience; (4) they are aware of the symbolic nature of commercials; and (5) they cite instances of negative discrepancies where the product did not meet their expectations based on the commercial message.

Analysis of the results for *assistive intent* (Table 4) indicates that only two of the hypothesized variables achieve significant correlations. Bivariate relationships indicate that assistive intent attribution is predicated only on the ability to understand basic source and receiver concepts. The discriminant function, furthermore, is fairly weak, correctly classifying only 61 percent of the cases, versus a chance level of 50 percent.

Hypothesis #3: Consequences of Intent

In this hypothesis we are looking at the effects of children's attributions of commercial intent on their levels of trust, liking, and consumption motivation. Thus, the two intent measures are now used as the independent variables in examining impact upon attitude structures. From Table 5 some rather interesting results emerge, consistent with this hypothesis.

First of all, the correlational results indicate that children holding assistive intent attributions tend to trust commercials more, whereas children seeing persuasive intent place less trust in them. Similarly, if a child sees commercials as assistive, he tends to like them, while persuasive attribution connotes dislike.

Finally, ability to recognize either type of intent

Table 4   Cognitive factors likely to precede attribution of intent (hypothesis #2): Kendall τ correlations and discriminant weights

Cognitive antecedent factors	Assistive intent		Persuasive intent	
	Kendall τ	Discriminant weights	Kendall τ	Discriminant weights
• Discrimination Between Program and Commercials	.04	*	.18[a]	−.21
• Recognition of Source	.10[b]	.21	.42[a]	−.06
• Perception of Audience	.16[a]	−.62	.37[a]	.58
• Awareness of Symbolic Nature of Commercials	.06	−.75	.45[a]	1.23
• Perception of Negative Discrepancies Between Message and Product	.01	1.15	.43[a]	−.81
Percentage Correctly Classified (vs. 50% Chance Level)		61%		73%
Significance of F Value		.01		.01

[a]Correlation significant at .001 level.
[b]Correlation significant at .01 level.
*Variable did not pass tolerance level for inclusion.

Table 5   Consequences of intent (hypothesis #3): Kendall τ correlations and discriminant weights

Intent	Trust in commercials		Liking of commercials		Consumption motivation	
	Kendall τ	Discriminant weights	Kendall τ	Discriminant weights	Kendall τ	Discriminant weights
Assistive Intent	.16[a]	.13	.08[c]	.01	−.05	.07
Persuasive Intent	−.16[a]	−1.00	−.12[a]	1.00	−.32[a]	−.99
Percentage Correctly Classified (vs. 33% Chance Level)		58%		38%		49%
Significance of F Value		.01		.05		.01

[a]Correlation significant at .001 level.
[b]Correlation significant at .01 level.
[c]Correlation significant at .05 level.

has negative consequences for consumption motivation. In the case of assistive intent this is contrary to our predicted direction, although the effect of assistive attribution on motivation is near zero ($-.05$). However, a highly significant ($p < .001$) relationship holds, as predicted, between persuasive intent recognition and diminished desire for advertised products.

Moreover, when both types of intent are considered *in combination,* persuasive intent is clearly the dominantly weighted factor. This is evidenced by the discriminant functions in Table 5 which combine assistive intent and persuasive intent as predictors of trust, liking and consumption motivation. Persuasive intent carries at least seven times the weight of assistive intent according to the standardized coefficients. This result is consistent with Kanouse and Hanson's (1971) general hypothesis that individuals will weigh negative factors more heavily than positive factors in evaluative situations.

In sum, the data suggest that the development of persuasive intent attribution, regardless of "offsetting" assistive attribution, acts as a cognitive defense for the child against persuasion. Advertising, as Banks (1973) suggests, does not always have a "silver bullet" effect. Cognitive defense is reflected in a more skeptical, less accepting reception of television commercials, and, in particular, in less intention to respond to the advertising message. Persuasive intent attribution is almost universally operative by fifth grade.

Nevertheless, possible limitations of the present research should be indicated. The study does not examine sex differences since the sample was limited to boys. It is possible that girls may have somewhat different processes of attributional development. Furthermore, the study was confined to children within the Catholic school system. This control was imposed after a pilot study, conducted by Rossiter at a public Philadelphia school representing a mix of religions, found that differential beliefs and gift-giving practices associated with Christmas and Chanukah tended to complicate interview content and measurement.

Finally, our analysis centers on television commercials as a generalized concept. Children's ability to recognize persuasive intent in commercials should not be taken as implying immunity to all commercials; clearly, individual commercials may be highly persuasive for children, just as for adults. Attribution of persuasive intent merely signifies that the child has acquired the general capability to recognize commercial persuasion.

CONCLUSIONS

Our conclusions can be stated as a series of tentative propositions.

Proposition 1.   Although children are capable of perceiving both the informative and the persuasive characteristics of commercials, recognition of persuasive intent is the main determinant of the child's attitudinal response set to television advertising.

Proposition 2.   Although attribution of persuasive intent can be advanced in homes with high parental education ("enriched environment"), it is primarily age-dependent. Age, as a variable, reflects not only maturational factors but also cumulative experience with commercial messages.

Proposition 3.   The development of persuasive intent attributions acts as a cognitive defense to persuasion. The child who is able to discern persuasive intent is less influenced by advertising in that he is less trusting, likes commercials less, and tends to make fewer consumption requests.

Proposition 4.   Alternatively, younger children who lack persuasive intent attributions are more persuasible.

Proposition 5.   The cognitive antecedents to attribution of persuasive intent are program-message discrimination, sponsor perception, audience perception, awareness of symbolic representation, and awareness of possible message-product discrepancies.

IMPLICATIONS

The logical social policy question emerging from this research is whether younger children are deserving of some form of special protection from the effects of advertising. This might seem to be a natural conclusion since first graders appear to be quite persuasible; roughly two-thirds of them indicate that they trust all commercials and like all commercials and roughly one-half claim to want all products that they see advertised. Alternatively, it can be indicated that these percentages decline dramatically among third and fifth graders and the argument can be advanced that exposure to advertising is a necessary prerequisite for the development of cognitive defenses against advertising's persuasive effects.

REFERENCES

Banks, S. (May, 1973), "Advertising and Children," a talk presented to the American Marketing Association Advertising and Public Interest Workshop, Washington, D.C.

Bauer, R. A., and Greyser, S. A. (1968), *Advertising in America,* Boston, Mass.: Division of Research, Harvard Business School.

Blatt, J.; Spencer, L.; and Ward, S. (1971), "A Cognitive Development Study of Children's Reactions to Television Advertising," in *Effects of Television Advertising on Children and Adolescents,* Cambridge, Mass.: Marketing Science Institute.

Bower, R. T. (1973), *Television and the Public,* New York: Holt, Rinehart and Winston.

Festinger, L. (May, 1954), "A Theory of Social Comparison Processes," *Human Relations,* 7, 404–17.

Flavell, J. H. (1970), "Concept Development," in P. H. Mussen, *Carmichael's Manual of Child Psychology,* 3rd ed., Vol. 1, New York: John Wiley and Sons.

Heider, F. (1958), *The Psychology of Interpersonal Relations,* New York: John Wiley and Sons.

Kanouse, D. E., and Hanson, L. R. (1971), "Negativity in Evaluations," in E. E. Jones, et al., eds., *Attribution: Perceiving the Causes of Behavior,* Morristown, N.J.: General Learning Press.

Kelley, H. H. (1971), "Attribution in Social Interaction," in E. E. Jones, et al., eds., *Attribution: Perceiving the Causes of Behavior,* Morristown, N.J.: General Learning Press.

Kelley, H. H. (1967), "Attribution Theory in Social Psychology," in D. Levine, ed., *Nebraska Symposium on Motivation,* Lincoln: University of Nebraska Press.

Mead, G. H. (1934), *Mind, Self and Society,* C. W. Morris, ed., Chicago: University of Chicago Press.

Piaget, J. (1970), "Piaget's Theory," in P. H. Mussen, *Carmichael's Manual of Child Psychology,* 3rd ed., Vol. 1, New York: John Wiley and Sons.

Ward, S. (April, 1972), "Children's Reactions to Commercials," *Journal of Advertising Research,* 12, 37–45.

————, and Wackman, D. B. (1974), "Children's Information Processing of Television Advertising," in G. Kline and P. Clark, eds., *New Models for Communication Research,* Beverly Hills, Calif.: Sage Publishing, 81–119.

Wells, W. D. (June, 1965), "Communicating with Children," *Journal of Advertising Research,* 5, 2–14.

INTERPERSONAL INFLUENCE ON CONSUMER BEHAVIOR: AN ATTRIBUTION THEORY APPROACH

BOBBY J. CALDER
ROBERT E. BURNKRANT

Source: Bobby J. Calder and Robert E. Burnkrant, "Interpersonal Influence on Consumer Behavior: An Attribution Theory Approach," *Journal of Consumer Research*, Vol. 4, 1977, pp. 229–38.

Interpersonal influence is widely recognized as a major determinant of consumer behavior. It is typically considered at the sociological level of group membership (social class, subcultures, etc.). Psychological studies at the individual process level have been less common.

None of these provides an integrative psychological approach to interpersonal influence. Each attacks a different aspect of the problem. A more general approach is needed—an approach that (1) conceptualizes the consumer as a social actor linked to others through a variety of role relationships, all of which are specific sources of influence as well as indirect normative influence, and (2) accounts for influence in psychological terms applicable to both the consumer and the influencer. This paper develops such an approach using attribution theory.

"Attribution" is a psychological construct referring to the cognitive processes through which an individual infers the cause of an actor's behavior. Studies of attribution have relied heavily on two theoretical perspectives, one due to Kelley (1967, 1971, 1972) and the other to Jones and Davis (1965). Both perspectives dwell on conditions which determine whether a behavior is attributed to internal, personal causes or to external forces. In general, individuals are biased toward internal attributions. That is, they tend to see the dispositions (traits, preferences, etc.) of an actor as causing the actor's behavior.

Internal attributions are not automatic, however. Individuals consider external factors as alternative explanations. Kelley suggests an "analysis of variance" analogy. An individual analyzes the covariation between observed behaviors and a possible dispositional cause. There are four dimensions of possible covariation. One dimension is the "distinctiveness" of the behavior. If an observer tends to attribute a certain disposition to everyone (low distinctiveness), a self-attribution external explanation is ruled out, and an internal attribution to the actor is plausible. The plausibility of an internal attribution also increases if there is "consistency" over time and place in the observations of the actor's behavior. Such consistency eliminates possible confounds with nonpersonal factors. Finally, the plausibility of an internal attribution increases if there is a consensus among other people that a behavior reflects a disposition. Thus, to the extent that an actor's behavior exhibits distinctiveness and consistency over time, place, and the reactions of others, it is accepted as evidence of a personal disposition. Otherwise, the behavior is discounted and attributed to external factors.

Jones and Davis' perspective is formulated somewhat differently. They pose the question of how an observer can be sure that the language he uses to describe an actor's behavior is also descriptive of the personal dispositions of the actor. Their term for the match between observed behaviors and inferred dispositions is "correspondence." The problem for the observer is whether the actor's dispositions correspond to the observer's description of the actor's behavior. Jones and Davis explicitly include the "effects" produced by a behavior as well as the behavior itself in their analysis. Correspondence depends on the number of "noncommon effects" produced by a choice act.

The theory postulates that observers construe behavior as a choice between either explicit or implicit alternatives. A chosen alternative is associated with a set of observed effects; each of the unchosen alternatives is associated with a set of hypothetical consequences which would have been the effects had it been chosen. The chosen alternative may or may not have effects in common with the unchosen alternatives. Noncommon effects indicate the basis of choice more clearly than do common effects. Common effects reflect external, situational constraints. To the extent that a choice results in noncommon rather than common effects, it yields a stronger inference of correspondence. Moreover, the inference is stronger the fewer the number of noncommon effects, for a few noncommon effects indicate the actor's intentions more precisely than a larger number.

Jones and Davis also hold that correspondent inference depends on the "assumed social desirability" of effects. If most people would not have preferred a chosen alternative, the effects of that choice should be more descriptive of the uniquely personal characteristics of the actor than of external factors. "To learn that a man makes the conventional choice is to learn only that he is like most other men" (Jones and Davis 1965, p. 227). The lower the social desirability of a chosen alternative, the stronger is the inference of correspondence.

Most social psychological research has treated the concept of correspondent inference as equivalent to that of a strong internal attribution. Internal attributions are typically measured by asking observers to rate the extent to which an actor possesses a disposition, e.g., rating the actor's honesty on a semantic differential scale. Confidence ratings are sometimes used, more in keeping with the notion of correspondence, to assess the overall strength of internal attribution.

Attribution theories, as we shall see, are by no means fully developed. Even so, our position is that these ideas suggest a general approach to interpersonal influence. In purchasing and using products, the consumer is a social actor whose behavior is largely open to observation by others. The consumer's behavior is informational input for the attribution processes of observers. Observers infer the consumer's personal dispositions from his or her behavior. Our argument is that attributions underlie interpersonal influence. Attributions amount to judgments about the consumer. These judgments shape the observer's actions with respect to the consumer. The observer's actions may directly affect the consumer's behavior. Attributions thus provide a psychological basis, or reason, for the actions of influencers, something that is missing from "group pressure" studies.

Influence of a more indirect kind is accomplished if the consumer is sensitive to the attributions others make, or to those he expects them to make, or to those "generalized others" might make, and he acts so as to produce the attributions he desires. That is, the consumer engages in behaviors which he believes will lead observers to make attributions which he considers desirable. Conceptualizing such indirect influence as operating through perceived product attributes is potentially misleading. The influence does not stem from the product itself but from the consumer's beliefs about the attributions others make from observing his behavior.

We propose a paradigm for research rather than a full-blown model. This paradigm is diagrammed in Figure 1. The research reported in this paper deals with a fundamental aspect of this paradigm, shown as Relationship (1) in Figure 1. This is the functioning of the attribution process itself: how an observer infers personal dispositions from a consumer's behavior. In order to pursue the full paradigm, it is necessary, as a first step, to investigate this relationship, to explore the applicability of existing attribution theory to observations of consumer behavior.

There are, however, two other aspects of the full paradigm (see Figure 1). One is the accuracy of the consumer's knowledge of the attributions observers make from his behavior. We refer to this as the consumer's attributional sensitivity.[1] The other aspect of the full paradigm is how the consumer's attributional sensitivity affects his own subsequent behavior.

Let us further consider how people make internal attributions from observing consumer behavior—the fundamental aspect of the proposed influence paradigm. The basic principle emerging from Kelley's and Jones and Davis' work is that *a person is more likely to attribute an internal disposition or personal characteristic to an actor when there are no plausible external, alternative explanations for an act.* This "discounting principle" may be further operationalized in terms

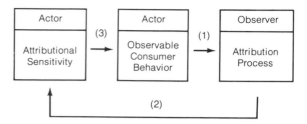

Figure 1 An Attribution Paradigm for the Study of Influence

of two variables which we believe are especially significant for the consumer context. The first variable is suggested by Jones and Davis' hypothesis that the strength of an internal attribution varies inversely with the assumed social desirability of a choice. If most other people would not have made the choice, the actor is less likely to have been forced into the choice by external constraints. In Kelley's terms, the choice is highly distinctive if most people would not have made it. Applied to the context of consumer behavior, assumed social desirability is closely linked to brand advertising. One of the major purposes of advertising is to generate a consumer franchise for a brand, to create the impression that a brand is prestigious and widely purchased. With the cosmetic products used in this study, a heavily advertised manufacturer's brand (Revlon) should be perceived as more widely desired than a private-label manufacturer's brand (Walgreens).[2] Observing the purchase of the Walgreen brand may thus be expected to lead to stronger internal attributions than the purchase of the Revlon brand.

The second variable operationalizes the discounting principle in terms of the structure of the choice situation observed. A high-choice situation is one in which an actor selects from a variety of different alternatives; a low-choice situation is one in which he selects from fewer, more similar alter-

---

[1] It is of interest to note that recent work in the social psychology literature has examined how accurate observers are in inferring the dispositions of actors (e.g., Calder, Ross, and Insko, 1973), but there has been no work on the problem posed here—how sensitive actors are in their knowledge of observer attributions.

[2] The greater social desirability of the Revlon over the Walgreen brand name is an assumption of this research. While this assumption was suggested by preliminary interviews before the study, we have no pilot data to support it.

natives. In the high-choice situation, the actor is less constrained by the alternatives present. The chosen alternative is likely to be associated with noncommon effects. In the low-choice situation, the alternatives are likely to have common effects. The high-choice situation implicitly indicates distinctiveness. This logic implies that internal attributions are stronger under high choice than low choice.[3]

It may be argued, however, that an actor's consideration of only a few alternatives in a low-choice situation indicates a prior choice, a choice of these alternatives from a wider consideration class or evoked set. Accordingly, both the prior choice of the alternative set and the terminal choice act may provide a basis for attributions. This argument is particularly applicable to consumer choices which frequently entail shopping decisions as well as purchasing decisions. An actor who shops at a store providing a low-choice situation when there are different, alternative stores available, has indeed made two choices, in which case an observer might not construe the overall situation as one of low choice. An observer might take into account both choices in making attributions about the actor.

It should be noted that Jones and Davis explicitly contend that prior choices have no effect on attributions.

> If we observe that a man leaves his chair, crosses the room, closes the door, and the room becomes less noisy, a correspondent inference would be that he intended to cut down the noise. One might ask whether the inference that the man intended to reach the door is not also a correspondent inference since "reaching the door" is an effect of crossing the room. But the subordinate parts of a meaningful action sequence do not have to be confused with the effects of an action. In this case, the perceiver is likely to "organize" the action in his mind as beginning with the decision to leave the chair and ending with the closing of the door. It is the effects of the terminal act in a meaningful sequence, then, that provide the grist for our theory. (Jones and Davis 1965, p. 225)

While the effects of prior choices have not been empirically ruled out, most attribution theory research does support the prediction of stronger internal attributions under high rather than low choice (cf. Calder, Ross, and Insko, 1973). This study tests this prediction in a consumer context in which prior choices may be more salient than in previous research. If prior choice is salient, low choice may well yield stronger attributions than high choice.

The present study thus seeks to demonstrate that people make attributions from observing consumer behavior in accordance with the discounting principle. In addition to whether the product chosen was a Walgreen or Revlon brand and whether the situation was one of high or low choice, two other variables were included to explore the generality of the discounting principle. One variable was the product usage situation. Belk's (1974) research suggests the importance of different situations for consumer behavior. He conceives of the situation as everything which exists at a point in time that is not a property of the product or the consumer. He defines the situation in terms of observable aggregate effects that are susceptible to external verification without reference to any psychological state. This objective approach is employed here to examine how different situations modify attributions made about a consumer. The two situations investigated differ, at a minimum, in the extent to which the use of the chosen product is public and involving, or more private and less involving.

This situational difference seems particularly relevant to attribution theory, though existing

---

[3]This logic assumes that the low-choice situation results in no noncommon effects. According to Jones and Davis' theory, low choice would result in a stronger attribution than high choice if there were some noncommon effects but fewer than under high choice. While this does not seem the more likely possibility in this case, and for this reason the high-choice prediction is stated here, it illustrates the difficulty of developing attribution theory predictions. Note that the high-choice prediction is bolstered by Kelley's (1967) distinctiveness hypothesis.

theories do not make clear predictions. Certainly, public involvement is more likely to reflect external constraints, thereby hindering attributions. Sometimes, however, a publicly involving situation of use also conveys stronger behavioral evidence of commitment to the choice, which might lead to a stronger attribution than would private usage. In any event, the two situations are less important for theoretical prediction than for assessing the cross-situational generality of the two discounting variables. For this, it is only required that the situations differ in a way that might be expected to affect attributions.

The other variable included for generality was the product itself. Two cosmetic products, mascara and deodorant, were employed. They were selected because usage of mascara is more observable and conspicuous than usage of deodorant. As with the situation of use variable, it is of interest to determine whether attributions are made in a parallel manner for objectively different products.

METHOD

Subjects
One hundred twenty-four female subjects participated in this study. They were students at the University of Illinois at Urbana-Champaign enrolled in home economics courses. The study was conducted during the scheduled sessions of five classes. No communication was allowed between subjects, and subjects in each class received all the experimental treatments.

Independent Variables
The independent variables were manipulated by asking subjects to take the role of observers while reading written scenarios portraying a consumer's behavior. The choice situation varied according to whether the consumer chose a brand of a given product from two similar brands (low choice) or from four, more dissimilar brands (high choice). Also varied was whether the consumer chose a

heavily advertised manufacturer's brand (Revlon) or a private-label brand (Walgreens). In the low-choice condition, the consumer chose Revlon after considering Revlon and Max Factor or chose Walgreens after considering Walgreens and K-Mart. In the high-choice condition, the consumer chose Revlon after considering Revlon, Max Factor, Walgreens, and K-Mart or chose Walgreens after considering all four brands.

The two variables included for generality were manipulated by changing the situation of use and the product described in the scenarios. The situation of use was either to wear on an evening out with people the consumer considered important (public and involving use) or to keep in the lounge at the consumer's place of work (more private and less involving use). The product was either mascara or deodorant.

Procedure
These variables were manipulated in a $2 \times 2 \times 2 \times 2$ between-subjects factorial design. Each subject received a description of a typical consumer situation that could well face a young woman similar to herself. The specific description read as follows:

> A young woman about 20 years old is going to college and working part-time in a medium-sized midwestern city. She works in a small office with one other female employee. The woman shops fairly regularly at one of the larger local shopping centers. There are two women's specialty shops, a Walgreens, and a K-Mart that she goes to. On one such occasion, one of the items she intends to buy is deodorant [mascara]. As she has noted on her shopping list, she wants the deodorant [mascara] for everyday use. In fact, she would like to keep it in her compartment in the women's lounge at work to freshen up occasionally [for a special occasion. In fact, she has been invited out to dinner with several people whom she likes and for whom she is especially anxious to be at her best].

> On this particular trip, the woman looks at the following brands of deodorant [mascara] displayed at the cosmetic counters in these stores: Revlon

deodorant [mascara], Max Factor deodorant [mascara], Walgreen deodorant [mascara], and K-Mart deodorant [mascara]. These are the only brands she considers buying on this trip. [In the low-choice condition, only two brands were provided: either Revlon and Max Factor or Walgreens and K-Mart.]

After looking at these brands, the woman chooses the Walgreen [Revlon] deodorant [mascara] to keep in the women's lounge at work for her private use [to wear out to dinner with her friends].

Subjects were contacted in the normal classroom environment. After being introduced by the instructor, the researchers informed the subjects that they would be given a brief questionnaire in which a typical consumer situation would be followed by a series of questions about the person described in that situation.

Each questionnaire contained one of the sixteen possible descriptions. The questionnaires were distributed to subjects in each classroom so that descriptions were assigned at random. After reading the brief description of the consumer situation, subjects were asked to evaluate the shopper's personality. They were instructed to "think back to the person described on the previous page and try to determine the personality traits she might have."

Dependent Variables

Consistent with previous attribution research, two types of dependent variables were assessed— semantic differential ratings of the consumer on twenty-seven personality traits and a rating on a ten-point scale of confidence in these personality ratings. An internal attribution, the extent to which the consumer is seen to have a given disposition, is indicated by the extremity of the trait ratings. Both positive and negative extremes on the bipolar adjectives indicate strong internal attributions. The confidence ratings measure the overall extent to which observers believe that their attributions correspond to the actor's actual internal dispositions. Higher confidence ratings indicate that ob-

servers are more sure that they learned something about the consumer.

The personality traits were selected to represent a broad spectrum. The two discounting variables are predicted to affect all traits which are perceived as potential causes of the consumer's behavior. In the absence of any theory about which traits might be relevant as potential causes, it was necessary to select traits on a representative basis. Null-hypothesis results, as usual, are uninformative: the absence of experimental effects could be due to inadequacy of the discounting principle or to failure to include appropriate traits. The existence of the predicted effects for the selected traits, however, provides evidence for the discounting principle.

RESULTS

Since the personality traits were selected on a representative basis, it would be capitalizing on chance to analyze the effects of the independent variables for each trait separately. It was thus necessary to determine the interrelationships among traits. To do this, a within-cells correlation matrix was computed for the twenty-seven personality trait ratings. The correlation between each pair of elements in such a matrix is adjusted to remove treatment effects. The within-cells correlation matrix thus reflects the general structure of the subjects' attributions without being affected by the independent variables. To uncover this structure, the matrix was submitted to a principal-components analysis.

Two factors clearly emerged from this analysis (Table 1). Limiting a factor pattern to those variables with more than 25 percent of their variation involved in a pattern (a loading greater than .50), reveals in Table 1 that the variables composing Factor 1 might be labeled "social evaluation" and those for Factor 2 "personal effectiveness." Scores on these variables were summed to yield two derived dependent variables, one for each factor. The remaining analyses were conducted

Table 1 Factor matrix for personality ratings[a]

Variable	Orthogonally rotated factors[b]	
	1	2
Rugged/delicate[c]	(.59)	−.06
Unattractive/attractive	(.77)	.18
Low status/high status	(.73)	−.07
Inferior/superior	(.66)	.18
Insincere/sincere	.22	.41
Unsociable/sociable	(.70)	.18
Insecure/secure	.41	.37
Introvert/extrovert	(.68)	.14
Masculine/feminine	(.73)	.16
Foolish/wise	.45	(.58)
Worthless/valuable	.48	(.64)
Unhappy/happy	(.69)	.50
Awkward/graceful	(.73)	.39
Submissive/dominating	.37	.49
Unpopular/popular	(.70)	.50
Extravagant/economical	−.20	(.77)
Immature/mature	.30	(.74)
Unsuccessul/successful	(.55)	(.58)
Uninformed/informed	.32	(.72)
Dull/interesting	.50	(.66)
Conformist/nonconformist	−.13	(.65)
Cautious/impulsive	.41	.04
Critical/tolerant	.30	.37
Frivolous/serious	−.15	(.63)
Quiet/talkative	.43	.42
Sloppy/neat	(.65)	.35
Ungenerous/generous	.49	.48
Percent Total Variance	55.7	44.3

[a]Loadings greater than an absolute value of .50 are shown in parentheses.
[b]Varimax rotation.
[c]The order of the adjectives represents the order in which they were scored from one to seven (for some the order was reversed on the questionnaire).
NOTE: These results are based on a principal components/ principal axis factor analysis of the within-cells correlation matrix. The factors are not affected by the experimental treatment conditions.

for the summed (raw score) social evaluation and personal effectiveness variables and the seven separate personality traits not included in either factor. Table 2 presents the means for all but two of these variables.

An exact least-squares analysis of variance was performed on each of the variables in Table 2. As shown in Table 3, there was a highly significant main effect for Walgreens versus Revlon and a significant product by Walgreens-Revlon by public-private use interaction for the social evaluation dependent variable. In general, subjects' social evaluation attributions were more positive with Revlon than Walgreens. (Note that 44 is the objective midpoint of this scale.) The triple interaction, however, adds further information and is displayed in Figure 2. For the mascara product, there is a sharper increase in social evaluation from Walgreens to Revlon with private use than with public use. On the other hand, for the deodorant product, there is a sharper increase with public use. Subjects infer a more positive social evaluation from the choice of Revlon, especially for the private use of mascara and the public use of deodorant.

The analysis of variance for the personal effectiveness variable revealed a significant product by Walgreens-Revlon interaction. The form of this interaction is quite simple (see Figure 3): There is no difference between Walgreens and Revlon for mascara but a large difference for deodorant. Attributions of personal effectiveness lie at the objective midpoint of the scale for mascara. For Walgreens deodorant, however, personal effectiveness is rated positively. For the Revlon deodorant, it is rated negatively. Apparently, subjects felt the consumer to be wiser, more informed, etc., for buying the Walgreen brand deodorant and not so wise for buying the Revlon brand deodorant, while the brand made no difference for mascara in terms of personal effectiveness.

The mean confidence ratings of subjects in their personality attributions are shown in Table 2 and

Table 2 Means for personality factors, separate traits, and confidence

	Mascara							
	Low choice				High choice			
Variable	Walgreens		Revlon		Walgreens		Revlon	
	Private	Public	Private	Public	Private	Public	Private	Public
Social evaluation[a]	40.89	49.29	59.89	58.13	48.71	56.00	58.13	53.57
Personal effectiveness[b]	31.89	37.43	38.00	10.67	36.86	40.43	34.88	35.57
Insincere/sincere	5.44	3.86	4.33	3.00	4.57	5.71	5.25	3.57
Cautious/impulsive	3.33	4,14	4.78	4.25	4.57	4.00	4.50	4.29
Critical/tolerant	2.89	2.57	4.00	3.38	2.57	2.71	3.38	3.57
Quiet/talkative	3.00	3.57	4.56	4.50	3.14	3.86	4.00	4.14
Ungenerous/generous	3.00	3.71	4.22	4.00	3.57	5.00	4.00	5.43
Confidence	3.11	4.00	4.44	4.50	3.86	3.14	4.88	4.14
n	9	7	9	8	7	7	8	7

	Deodorant							
	Low choice				High choice			
Variable	Walgreens		Revlon		Walgreens		Revlon	
	Private	Public	Private	Public	Private	Public	Private	Public
Social evaluation[a]	51.50	48.12	60.14	56.89	52.63	43.43	58.12	59.57
Personal effectiveness[b]	41.38	38.50	35.71	34.56	44.25	35.14	30.62	34.28
Insincere/sincere	6.88	6.00	7.43	5.56	5.12	6.14	2.88	5.29
Cautious/impulsive	5.00	3.75	3.86	3.89	5.75	4.86	3.75	4.43
Critical/tolerant	2.75	2.25	4.00	3.58	2.25	2.71	3.88	4.14
Quiet/talkative	4.00	2.13	4.29	3.89	4.00	4.14	3.00	4.00
Ungenerous/generous	4.25	4.00	4.14	4.44	3.25	3.43	3.88	4.43
Confidence	4.12	4.00	4.14	4.67	4.37	3.57	3.12	4.71
n	8	8	7	9	8	7	8	7

[a]Average of eleven semantic differentials from Factor 1.
[b]Average of nine semantic differentials from Factor 2.

the analysis of variance in Table 3. There were two significant interactions, a choice by private-public use effect ($F = 4.13$, $p < .045$) and a choice by product effect ($F = 4.65, p < .033$) (see Figure 4). Subjects were more confident under low choice and private use and under high choice and public use. Similarly, subjects were more confident under low choice and the deodorant product and under high choice and the mascara product. As indicated by Figure 4, a high-choice purchase is clearly more revealing for mascara and a low-choice purchase for a private-use situation.

Table 3 Analyses of variance for personality factors and confidence

Source[a]	Social evaluation F's	Personal effectiveness F's	Confidence F's
Product (P)	<1	<1	4.95[b]
Choice (C)	<1	<1	<1
Walgreens-Revlon (WR)	22.60[c]	2.84	2.65
Public-private use (U)	<1	<1	<1
P × C	<1	<1	4.65[b]
P × WR	<1	4.46[b]	<1
P × U	2.28	2.52	1.08
C × WR	1.26	2.56	<1
C × U	<1	<1	4.13[b]
WR × U	<1	<1	<1
P × C × WR	2.35	<1	<1
P × C × U	<1	<1	<1
P × WR × U	4.12[b]	2.61	<1
C × WR × U	<1	<1	<1
P × C × WR × U	<1	<1	1.75

[a]Each source has one degree of freedom.
[b]Significant at .05 level.
[c]Significant at .01 level.

DISCUSSION

The major results for the personality traits can be summarized as follows. The Revlon brand implied more positive social evaluation than the Walgreen brand, this effect being even greater for the private use of mascara and the public use of deodorant. In contrast, for the deodorant purchase, the Revlon brand indicated less personal effectiveness than the Walgreen brand. (Personal effectiveness was not affected for the mascara product.) Thus, purchase of the Revlon deodorant implied a socially popular but not especially competent person. In addition, the Revlon brand led to greater attributions of sincerity and generosity, except for the private use of deodorant. Buying the Revlon brand suggested that the consumer was more talkative, more impulsive, and, under low choice, less critical. Again, the Revlon brand implied the consumer was socially positive but not very thoughtful.

Whereas brand was the central factor affecting personality attributions, the strength of subjects' general propensity to make internal attributions, as reflected by their confidence ratings, depended mainly on choice. For private use, the low-choice situation led to greater confidence. For mascara, the high-choice situation generated more confidence.

What do these results mean for the applicability of attribution theory to the consumer context? Recall that the private-label Walgreen brand was expected to lead to stronger internal attributions than the Revlon brand on the basis of its lower assumed social desirability and higher distinctiveness. To the contrary, however, the Revlon brand yielded the stronger attributions across both situations of use and both products. (Except for the deodorant product, these attributions were in the positive direction.) This unpredicted finding casts doubt on the adequacy of existing attribution theory. The discounting principle, or at least

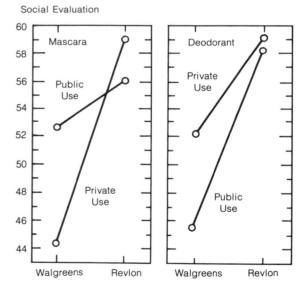

Figure 2 Mean Social-Evaluation Scores for the Product by Walgreens-Revlon by Private-Public Situation of Use Interaction

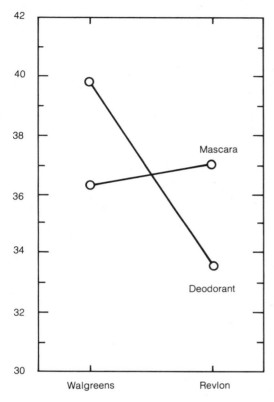

Figure 3 Mean Personal Effectiveness Scores for the Product by Walgreens-Revlon Interaction

common operationalizations of it, is not sufficient as an explanation of how attributions are made.

The Revlon versus Walgreens result suggests what is lacking. Attribution theorists have failed to consider fully the differential significance of choices for observers. Observers may expect some choices to be more revealing than others because actors implicitly or explicitly attach special importance to them. A special case of such importance is when an actor is thought to engage in a behavior at least partly for the reason of expressing, i.e., revealing, himself. It should be noted that Jones and Davis predict more corre-

spondent inferences as the worth (hedonic relevance) of a choice increases. This is another special case of the choice's perceived importance to the actor. In general, observers may believe that a choice which is important to an actor, for any reason, is more closely linked to specific intentions of the actor than one which is unimportant. For these significant choices, observers may pay less attention to plausible external, situational explanations, thereby not conforming to the discounting principle.

The consumer context provides a likely setting for variations in the significance of choices. In terms of our results, the choice of a Revlon brand may have indicated to the observers that the purchase was important to the consumer. The greater social desirability of the Revlon brand implies that the consumer choosing it must be more concerned about the product than one who buys the Walgreen brand. The significance of the Revlon

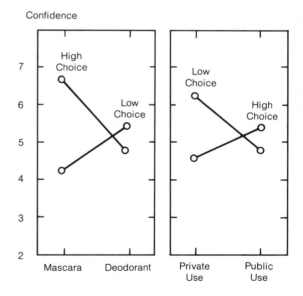

Figure 4 Mean Confidence in Attributions for the Choice by Product Interaction (Left) and the Choice by Private-Public Situation of Use Interaction (Right)

choice would explain the stronger internal attributions with Revlon than Walgreens.

Further evidence regarding the discounting principle comes from the choice variable. Choice affected the global confidence ratings rather than, with one exception, the specific trait attributions. Most interesting is that the effects of choice depended on both the situation of use and the product. Confidence was not always higher in the high-choice situation. This result may reflect the prior choice problem discussed earlier. With the private-use situation and deodorant product, the purchase might have seemed more routinized to the observers under low than high choice, indicating a history of prior choices. Observers may have interpreted the low choice-private use and low choice-deodorant conditions as actually reflecting a higher degree of choice than the corresponding high-choice conditions. This would explain the stronger internal attributions under low choice.

The results involving the situation of use and product variables confirm the desirability of investigating attributions in different settings. Both of these variables affected the degree to which Revlon yielded stronger attributions than Walgreens. Evidently, the situation of use can have either of the effects postulated: with mascara, public use may have indicated external constraints while, with deodorant, public use may have indicated a stronger behavioral commitment. As discussed previously, these variables may also have altered observers' interpretations of the choice variable.

The present results are useful in two ways. For one, they attest to the need for an attribution approach to interpersonal influence. Most interesting in this regard is the finding that the Revlon brand implied a socially positive but not very competent consumer. Suppose that our observers were linked to our hypothetical consumer through actual role relationships. Their influence would depend on the consumer's attributional sensitivity (Figure 1). Assuming that the observers' behavior reflected their attributions, if the consumer were

most sensitive to social evaluation attributions, the observers' influence would be to support the Revlon choice. But, if the consumer were most sensitive to personal effectiveness attributions, the observers' influence would be to undermine the Revlon deodorant choice. *Interpersonal influence is only to be accounted for in terms of the psychological processes which underlie it.*

This study illustrates the importance of understanding the variables which affect observers' internal attributions and the consumer's sensitivity to them. If subsequent research confirms that heavily advertised brands engender stronger internal attributions, the marketers of such brands would want to increase their attention to interpersonal influence in their advertising strategies. They would particularly want to counteract negative internal attributions such as the personal effectiveness attribution associated in this study with the use of Revlon deodorant.

The present results are also useful in suggesting the need for extending existing attribution theory. Although attribution theory is presently one of the most active areas of social psychological thinking, almost all of this work is guided by the discounting principle. Our results, however, indicate that the discounting principle is not sufficient to explain attributions made in a consumer context. It appears necessary, at a minimum, to consider the importance observers believe consumers attach to a choice (the significance of the choice) and the assumptions observers make about prior choices.

Attribution theorists have, in general, neglected people's expectations about the meaning of observed behaviors. In addition to discounting, it is necessary to consider the role of "typicality" in making attributions (Calder 1974a, 1974b, 1977). Typicality refers to the observer's intuitive beliefs about the internal characteristics that are usually associated with a given behavior. To make an internal attribution, apart from discounting situational causes of the behavior, an observer must believe that certain characteristics are typical of the behavior. The choice of Revlon must mean something to an observer. We have suggested that it means that the particular product is important to the consumer. However, the choice of Revlon may imply other characteristics which are thought to be typical of Revlon users as well.

Just as it is plausible that choosing Walgreens may mean that the particular product is not important to the consumer, it may be that the choice of Walgreens means less in general. Observers may have weaker beliefs about the characteristics typical of choosing Walgreens than about those typical of choosing Revlon. Although nonpersonal influences can be discounted more easily with the choice of Walgreens, this may be outweighed by the stronger beliefs about the characteristics typi-

cal of the Revlon choice. Thus, the present findings of stronger attributions with Revlon than Walgreens may depend more on typicality than discounting.

In developing an attribution approach to interpersonal influence, it will be necessary to clarify the roles of discounting and typicality. While both are probably important in the attribution process, for consumer behavior, the question boils down to which kind of choices yield stronger attributions: choices for which nonpersonal causes can be discounted or choices for which people have strong beliefs about the internal characteristics typical of the choice?

REFERENCES

Belk, R. W. (1974), "An Exploratory Assessment of Situational Effects on Buyer Behavior," *Journal of Marketing Research,* 11, 15–63.

Calder, B. (1974a), "Informational Cues and Attributions Based on Role Behavior," *Journal of Experimental Social Psychology,* 10, 121–25.

———— (1974b), "An Analysis of the Jones, Davis, and Gergen Attribution Paradigm," *Representative Research in Social Psychology,* 5, 55–59.

———— (1977), "An Attribution Theory of Leadership," in B. Staw and G. Salancik, eds., *New Directions in Organizational Behavior,* Chicago: St. Clair Press.

————; Ross, M.; and Insko, C. (1973), "Attitude Change and Attitude Attribution: Effects of Incentive, Choice, and Consequence," *Journal of Personality and Social Psychology,* 25, 84–99.

Jones, E., and Davis, K. (1965), "From Acts to Disposition: The Attribution Process in Person Perception," in L. Berkowitz, ed., *Advances in Experimental Social Psychology,* Vol. 2, New York: Academic Press.

Kelley, H. (1967), "Attribution in Social Psychology," *Nebraska Symposium on Motivation,* 15, 192–238.

———— (1971), *Attribution in Social Interaction,* New York: General Learning Press.

———— (1972), *Causal Schemata and the Attribution Process,* Morristown, N.J.: General Learning Press.

Witt, Robert E. (1966), "Informal Social Group Influence on Consumer Brand Preferences," *Journal of Marketing Research,* 6, 473–77.

NEEDS AND MOTIVATION IN CONSUMER BEHAVIOR

Any effort to understand consumer behavior must consider consumer needs and motivations. In many instances consumer needs and motivations are the fuel for the buying process. Needs might be thought of as discrepancies consumers experience between an actual and a desired state of being. The larger this discrepancy, the greater the likelihood of a behavior such as making a purchase to reduce or satisfy the felt need. Commonly discussed needs are needs for social contact and belonging, identity, power, satisfaction, security, sex, sleep, and stimulation. The force which leads a person to act in a particular way in response to a need is called motivation. Motivations may assume a variety of forms. They can be physiological or social, internal or external to the consumer, conscious or unconscious, and instinctual or learned.

Elderly consumers living alone may experience a discrepancy between their actual present state of involvement with other people and a desired state of much greater involvement. This discrepancy creates a social and psychological need for social contact and motivates these individuals toward extended interaction with people they meet, especially visitors to their homes. Thus elderly people are believed to buy more products from unsolicited door-to-door salespersons and telephone salespersons because the caller at the door or on the telephone provides desired social contact which the consumer rewards by making a purchase. The need for social contact motivates the consumer to engage in the sales transaction process.

There are several different perspectives about needs and motivations. A classical construct of needs frequently used in the consumer behavior literature is Abraham Maslow's hierarchy of needs. Maslow suggested that needs are arranged in a hierarchy. As needs lower in the hierarchy are satisfied, people shift to higher-order needs. Maslow's ordering or hierarchy is presented below:

1. Physiological needs
2. Safety needs
3. The need for belonging
4. The need for esteem
5. The need for self-actualization

Maslow has suggested that the proportion of our needs which are unsatisfied increases as one moves from physiological needs to self-actualization needs. In a developed society consumers may thus display more motivation for satisfying needs for esteem and self-actualization. This suggests that marketplace motivations among consumers may be more sociological and psychological than physiological, and more learned than instinctual. Consumers experiencing a strong need for belonging may follow a consumption pattern that is approved of by the group or set of people they want to be accepted by. This consumption pattern may be more extravagant or lavish than is actually necessary for the consumers' physical well-being. The motivation in this case is the force which caused the consumers to satisfy the need for belonging through lavish consumption rather than through an alternative action. Needs, then, can tell us what it is that consumers are satisfying, while motivations can explain the particular way in which these needs are satisfied. For example, our extravagant consumers seeking approval could have joined a monastic order or, more plausibly, become active as volunteers in a number of charitable or community service groups.

"REDUCE NEW PRODUCT FAILURES: MEASURE NEEDS AS WELL AS PURCHASE INTEREST"

The basis of the marketing concept is consumer needs. The marketing concept dictates that managers should begin their marketing efforts by determining existing unmet consumer needs. Products and marketing plans should then be developed in such a way as to meet these needs.

In spite of the centrality of the concept of needs, few efforts are made to actually measure and determine what consumers' needs are. Part of the problem is that consumers find it difficult to answer unguided, unfocused questions about their needs. They seem to be much better at answering questions about whether or not they would purchase a particular item. Since questions about purchase intentions are easier for consumers to answer, they are used more frequently than are questions about consumers' needs. It is, therefore, assumed that purchase intentions reflect underlying needs.

The main conclusion of the Tauber article, however, is that an indication of intentions to purchase does not necessarily imply the existence of unmet consumer needs. Tauber reports that those consumers who said a certain product would fulfill an unmet need were very likely to also report an intention to purchase the product. This finding would seem to support the assumption that measures of intentions can serve as surrogates for measures of unmet needs. However, Tauber's analysis continues and disconfirms this assumption. Tauber finds that some consumers who said the product would *not* fulfill an unmet need also reported an intention to purchase the product. These consumers, Tauber suggests, may be one-time purchasers who are drawn to the product out of curiosity. Consumers who purchase because of an unmet need, on the other hand, are more likely to continue purchasing the product.

These two groups, then, comprise two different segments for the product. Carrying this idea beyond the Tauber article, several questions can be raised. How could marketing strategies be designed for each segment? Specifically, what promotional themes could be used? How would promotional media, distribution channels, and product design be managed for the two segments? How might these two types of people (curiosity-seekers and need-fulfillers) be reflected in curves of the diffusion of innovations and curves of sales over the product life cycle?

"A MOTIVATIONAL MODEL OF INFORMATION PROCESSING INTENSITY"

In the past several years, many government regulations have been passed that require the disclosure of certain types of information to consumers. In addition, due to the ever-increasing number of new products which are introduced, commercial messages about products are so widespread as to practically bombard consumers with product information. Yet, in the face of this information explosion, it appears that consumers pay attention to and use only a very small proportion of those bits of information with which they have contact.

Information processing models describe what people do with information once they have decided to use it. Yet these models leave open to question how the selective choices of which information to use are made. The Burnkrant article uses the concept of motivation to describe this selective processing.

As with many other behaviors, the processing of information can be seen as a motivated behavior. Consumers use information when they are motivated to do so. But what does it mean to be motivated to do something? This question is the subject of the Burnkrant article.

Burnkrant describes a general model of motivation and then shows how it can be used in the specific case of information processing behavior. This general model states that motivation is the multiplicative product of three components: need, value, and belief. With respect to information-processing behavior, need refers to the need for information to reduce uncertainty to a desired level. The value of the information resides in its ability to meet the desired goal (e.g., reducing uncertainty). The final component is one's belief that a particular piece of information will satisfy the need.

Since consumers use so few of the bits of product information that they encounter, it can be concluded that this is due to a low motivation to process the information. But what is the source of the low motivation to process the information? It may be that different components (i.e., need, value, belief) are responsible for low usage of different types of information. Which component(s) is (are) probably responsible for low motivation to process much of the information contained in commercial messages? For the information which is required by law to be disclosed, for instance, on product packages? What could be done in each of these cases to bring about higher rates of usage of the information provided?

REDUCE NEW PRODUCT FAILURES: MEASURE NEEDS AS WELL AS PURCHASE INTEREST

EDWARD M. TAUBER

Source: Edward M. Tauber, "Reduce New Product Failures: Measure Needs as Well as Purchase Interest." *Journal of Marketing,* Vol. 37, July, 1973, pp. 61–70.

It is the contention of this article that concept testing as presently conducted is partially to blame for the high failure rate of new products. In particular, the testing procedure may be misleading companies to introduce products with limited chance of success and to avoid some products for which solid potential markets exist. These errors are not due to technical problems in the testing but rather to a failure of research to reflect the basic philosophy and criteria for introducing new products.

TRIAL OR ADOPTION

According to consumer sovereignty, a fundamental principle of economics, consumers determine with their dollar votes what will be produced over the long run. The marketing correlate to this principle is the marketing concept, which advocates that firms begin with consumer needs and work backwards to develop products that fill these unmet needs (Levitt, 1960). This concept is related to the idea that a product must have a significant point of difference to be successful, and it specifies that the point of difference must be in filling unmet consumer needs. This is obviously not necessarily the same as offering unique product features.

Traditionally, concept testing measures whether a new product idea generates interest in the market, although according to the marketing concept it should measure whether the product fills unmet needs. Another way of looking at this issue is that present concept research attempts to predict the number of persons who will try the product, when it should predict how many will adopt the product.

Adoption "is the acceptance and continued use of a product. . . . Purchase of a product is a necessary but not sufficient condition for adoption, since adoption includes a sense of product commitment, involving acceptance and use over time" (Robertson, 1971). The conditions that are necessary to move a person from trial to adoption are: (1) the product must perform in use in a satisfac-

263

tory manner, and (2) it must solve a problem or meet a need. The first condition is probed with product usage tests; the second condition should be probed in the concept phase.

Present concept test methodology closely parallels the Lavidge-Steiner hierarchy-of-effects adoption model, which postulates that consumers move up a series of steps before purchase (Lavidge and Steiner, 1961; Palda, 1966).

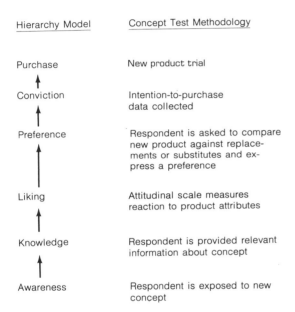

Hierarchy Model | Concept Test Methodology

Purchase — New product trial

Conviction — Intention-to-purchase data collected

Preference — Respondent is asked to compare new product against replacements or substitutes and express a preference

Liking — Attitudinal scale measures reaction to product attributes

Knowledge — Respondent is provided relevant information about concept

Awareness — Respondent is exposed to new concept

However, this hierarchy model does not result in adoption but only in initial trial. The addition of the two necessary conditions for adoption would complete the steps.

Adoption

↑

Need fulfillment/problem solution

↑

Satisfactory product performance

↑

Purchase

An assumption here is that trial may occur with low-price, frequently purchased items (e.g., food) without expectation of need fulfillment, but long-run adoption will not. For higher-priced, infrequently purchased items (e.g., durables) expected need fulfillment may be a necessary condition for trial as well as repeat purchase.

The implication for concept testing is that we should move away from measuring only interest, attitudes, preferences, or buying intentions and attempt to quantify the extent to which a product fills *significant unmet needs*. While concept testing cannot quantify repeat purchasing, it may be able to identify those need segments which are assumed to have a higher predisposition to adoption.

IS CONSUMER INTEREST THE SAME AS CONSUMER NEED?

The marketing concept implies that a new product that solves a problem or fills a significant unmet need for a substantial segment of the population has a higher probability of achieving adoption and, therefore, market success than one which does not. The question raised in this study is whether a product which generates buying interest, creates favorable attitudes, and scores well in present concept tests is necessarily perceived as solving problems or unfilled needs for consumers. To answer this question, an experiment was conducted with eight new product ideas which a major food company was considering.

The open-end questioning of consumers as to what problems or needs they have has never met with much success. However, it was thought that if consumers were presented with specific new product ideas, they could answer whether the products solved any problems or needs they had.

The study entailed two concept tests—four ideas per test—using a sequential monadic design with orders of presentation rotated to minimize order effects. Each idea was presented in the form of a concise written statement describing the major features, attributes, and benefits with a minimum of "sell." A convenience sample of 400 women in the greater Los Angeles area was surveyed by professional interviewers with a questionnaire containing the standard questions with one exception: a question sequence was inserted to determine whether the products would fill unmet needs for any portion of the sample.

1. Does this product solve a problem or need you or other members of your family now have that *isn't* being satisfied by products now on the market?

If yes:

2. What is the problem or need? _____

_____

3. Is this a very important need?
   somewhat important need?
   slightly important need?

An initial split-sample test which asked this series of questions both before and after the intention-to-buy scale revealed no differences in response. The intention-to-buy scale used was the traditional five-point format:

Definitely would buy.
Probably would buy.
Might or might not buy.
Probably would not buy.
Definitely would not buy.

FINDINGS

The results of this study are shown in Tables 1 and 2. Needs appear to be an important determinant of purchase intent, since virtually all repondents who claimed that a product solved a problem or unmet need had a positive intention to purchase

Table 1 Products

	A	B	C	D	E	F	G	H
	Intention-to-buy the products							
Definitely buy	26%	20%	23%	13%	24%	17%	14%	11%
Probably buy	45	42	37	47	27	29	30	11
Total positive purchase intention (sum of Definitely and Probably)	71	62	60	60	51	46	44	22
	Solves a problem or unfilled need[a]							
	45%	37%	18%	19%	27%	37%	10%	19%
	Of those with positive purchase intention, the percentage who report product solves a problem or unfilled need							
	63%	59%	30%	31%	53%	79%	26%	86%
	Of those who report product solves a problem or unfilled need, the importance of that problem or need							
Very important	22%	38%	26%	27%	22%	35%	60%	63%
Somewhat important	60	47	46	32	41	46	10	32
Slightly important	18	15	28	41	37	19	30	5

[a] All respondents who reported product solves a problem or unfilled need had a positive purchase intention.

Table 2   Intention-to-buy[a]

Solves a problem or unfilled need	Definitely buy	Probably buy	Might or might not/probably not/definitely not buy
YES	69%	37%	0%
NO	31	63	100
	100%	100%	100%

[a] Relationship of need and purchase intention based on 2000 observations from the eight products.

(said they would either definitely or probably buy). Likewise, of those with strong purchase conviction (definitely buy), 69% felt the product solved a problem or need (Table 2).

However, as Table 2 reveals, a considerable number of respondents who expressed purchase interest did not believe the product solved a problem or unmet need. In open-end questioning of why these people would buy, most answered "I like to try new products," "would just like to try it," "curiosity," "sounds good," "variety," and so on. Thus, the typical overstatement of purchase intent may be simply those with curiosity to try but little expectation of adopting.

Purchase intent is a poor surrogate measure of the number of people who feel a product solves a problem or unfilled need, because some products and categories attract more curiosity triers than others. This is evident in Table 1: of those with positive purchase intention, the percentage who report the product solves a problem or unfilled need varies widely from product to product.

Because purchase intent is not a good indicator of perceived need fulfillment, present market research may deceive us into introducing products with limited chance of long term success. Product concept C in this study, a fancy dessert product,

generated broad trial interest but is unlikely to achieve a high adoption level because it fails to fill unmet needs for most of those intending to buy. Product F was positioned to compete in a narrow market segment and thus received moderate purchase intent. Nevertheless, it solved an unmet need for 37% of the sample, the vast majority of those having purchase conviction. Product H would have been rejected immediately on the basis of its purchase intention scores, yet a segment exists that reports the product solves important needs for them and it could, therefore, represent a viable business. In effect, the testing procedure proposed here, based on the marketing concept, results in a type of need segmentation determined by self-report from respondents.

In the free-response question "What is the problem or need?" respondents gave a surprising variety of answers about any one product. Since the concept statements mentioned certain differentiating benefits or problem-solving properties (e.g., it will not spoil for three weeks), usually the majority of answers played back these needs. In a few instances, problem-solving features of which management had not been aware were mentioned.

IMPLICATIONS

The results of this study indicate that *consumer interest is not the same as consumer needs* (since the number of curiosity triers varies from product to product). Thus, present concept testing, as a screening device, can be faulty since broad interest does not always mean a product has market validity, i.e., offers a reason for consumer adoption.

Although at present these results must be accepted on face validity, it is compelling to believe that those who report the product solves a problem or fills an unmet need will be more likely to adopt than those with curiosity to try. This is the major premise of the marketing concept.

REFERENCES

Lavidge, Robert J., and Steiner, Gary A. (October, 1961), "Model for Predictive Measurements of Advertising Effectiveness," *Journal of Marketing,* Vol. 25, 59–62.

Levitt, Theodore (July–August, 1960), "Marketing Myopia," *Harvard Business Review,* Vol. 38, 55–68.

Palda, Kristian S. (February, 1966), "The Hypothesis of a Hierarchy of Effects: A Partial Evaluation," *Journal of Marketing Research,* Vol. 3, 13–24.

Robertson, Thomas S. (1971), *Innovative Behavior and Communication,* New York: Holt, Rinehart and Winston, Inc., 56–57.

A MOTIVATIONAL MODEL OF INFORMATION PROCESSING INTENSITY

ROBERT E. BURNKRANT

Source: Robert E. Burnkrant, "A Motivational Model of Information Processing Intensity," *Journal of Consumer Research,* Vol. 3, June, 1976, pp. 21–30.

Information processing theorizing has sought to specify the mechanism by which information is taken in and interpreted (e.g., Newell, Shaw, and Simon, 1958; Reitman, 1965; Norman, 1968). This work has generally assumed a level of motivation sufficient to move the person into an information processing cognitive state. As such, it appears to minimize the motivational and information selection issues in order to grapple with how and what occurs during or as a function of information processing.

The motivational model presented here treats information processing as another act of behavior and, hence, ties information processing to more general work on motivated behavior. It focuses on the issue of approach/avoidance of information and the implications of this approach/avoidance for attitude change. It seeks to account for the intensity of this cognitive behavior and specify the implications of this intensity for attitude change.

Many of the issues (i.e., advertisements and other communications) which people confront in their daily lives are presented in situations or at times when the recipients' motivation to process the messages is quite low. Krugman (1965) alluded to this in his discussion of what he called "learning without involvement." Under such circumstances one would expect little belief change even if the message and recipient characteristics are such that belief change would be expected in the event of active processing.

The model of information processing intensity to be presented here will be developed directly from theory and research in motivation. The following section presents aspects of this theory and research. It will provide the theoretical basis for the information processing model to be developed in the subsequent section. The final section of the paper will treat evidence supporting the information processing model and consider implications of the model for future research.

Motivation may be regarded as a complex integrative process which accounts for all those contemporaneous influences which determine the action, vigor and persistence of behavior (Atkinson, 1964). Although motivational theory and research may be viewed as falling into either an expectancy × value or a drive × habit school of thought, the orientation to be followed here is that of the expectancy × value tradition (cf. Atkinson, 1964).

The emergence of expectancy × value theory is perhaps best identified with the work of two researchers—Edward Tolman and Kurt Lewin. While both psychologists developed specific theories with many striking similarities, Tolman's work, following his behaviorist orientation, is more precisely and operationally defined than is Lewin's (Atkinson, 1964). More recent formulations (e.g., Atkinson, 1964; Atkinson and Feather, 1966; Weiner, 1972), however, have provided further specification using a system of constructs similar to those developed by Tolman. We shall follow Tolman's theorizing for the basic framework of the model turning to later formulations and more recent evidence for further elaboration.

Three types of mediating variables may be identified as representing the distinguishing aspects of Tolman's theory. Tolman has identified these constructs in their general form as need, belief, and value (e.g., Tolman, 1951).[1] The level of these constructs at a point in time is said to determine the magnitude of a performance tendency which immediately precedes and is directly related to overt performance (Tolman, 1951; Atkinson, 1964). Tolman viewed the strength of the tendency to obtain a particular type of food, for example, as being directly related to performance in obtaining that type of food (i.e., the time required to reach the food in the goal box of a maze). The same principles employed to develop a tendency to obtain a particular type of food could be applied to develop a tendency to process a particular type of message. The strength of this tendency would then be directly related to the intensity of the processing engaged in with respect to that message.

Need or Motive

According to Tolman (1951), the total set of needs which, for the organism, are active at a given point in time comprise his need system. Each need within the need system is seen as a readiness to approach a class of goal objects believed to be instrumental in the satisfaction of that need and to avoid other classes of objects believed to be irrelevant or detrimental to the satisfaction of that need.[2]

Tolman operationally defined need as "the propensity of an individual to perform a characteristic type of consummatory response" (1949, p. 362). The response is defined in terms of the goal which satisfies it. To take a classic example, the need for food may be defined in terms of the propensity for eating. This observed readiness of the organism to approach and consume food objects and to avoid nonfood objects provides a basis for inferring that the organism has an aroused need for food.

An activated need or motive (whether for food or for information) is said to call up a belief-value matrix within the organism (e.g., Tolman, 1951). This belief-value matrix is a representation of that part of the individual's cognitive structure which is believed to be relevant to the satisfaction of the aroused need. More specifically, the matrix is said to contain images of those objects which the individual has learned, through past experience, are relevant to his satisfaction of the aroused need.

---

[1]Tolman distinguishes between the general form of these constructs and their specific representations which he labels need-push, expectancy and valence, respectively (e.g., Tolman, 1951).

[2]The one exception to the directive nature of needs is a general need which Tolman calls the "libido need." This libido need is seen as a general multiplier of all the specific needs acting at a given point in time and is said to vary across individuals and over time within individuals (Tolman, 1951).

Value

Associated with each object in the matrix is a value, "that is, goodness or badness deposited on the various cells of the matrix" (Tolman, 1951, p. 293). For instance, if a person is hungry, "given types of food are represented as having different degrees of positive values insofar as they are 'believed' to lead on successfully to hunger gratification and away from hunger deprivation" (Tolman, 1951, p. 293). Similarly, if a person has an aroused need for information, given types of informational stimuli would be "represented as having different degrees of positive values insofar as they are 'believed' to lead on successfully" to the satisfaction of the need for information.

The readiness for a specific type of object from among a class of objects is treated as a function of not only the degree of need arousal for an object of that general class but also the value of the specific type of object within that class as a satisfier of the aroused need.

Belief or Expectancy

A complete representation of a model capable of accounting for behavior requires, in addition to need and valued objects, a construct representative of the associative link between the performance of a behavior with respect to those objects and the satisfaction of the need. This link is provided by what Tolman calls "means-end beliefs" (Tolman, 1951) or "means-end readiness" (Tolman, 1932).

A means-end belief, therefore, may be said to account for the expectation that performing a particular behavior with respect to a particular object will lead to goal attainment. For instance, it may be said to account for the expectation that processing a particular informational stimulus will lead to the attainment of information relevant to that which is needed. The strength of this belief may be operationalized in terms of the probability that an individual would assign to the occurrence of the association (Tolman, 1959; Hilgard and Bower, 1966).

MOTIVATION TO PROCESS INFORMATION

As a general theory of motivation, the previously discussed framework is applicable to the determination of the tendency to perform any specific behavior. Since cognitively processing information may be viewed as a behavior, the strength of the tendency to perform this behavior should be determinable through the appropriate application of this model.

Need for Information

The strength of the tendency to process information may be viewed, therefore, as being determined by three constructs. The first construct to be considered is the relevant need confronting the individual and directing his behavior. In order to determine the appropriate need, it is necessary to infer the goal toward which the behavior is being directed (Tolman, 1951; MacCorquodale and Meehl, 1954; Schroder, Driver, and Streufert, 1967). The goal toward which the organism strives on a particular occasion may be inferred from an assessment of the organism's behavior on that occasion.

All behavior directed at seeking out and processing information seems to have one characteristic in common: that the acquisition and processing of the information leads to a change in uncertainty. Furthermore, it appears that after some amount of uncertainty change takes place, the individual ceases to perform behavior directed at further changing his uncertainty (e.g., Berlyne, 1960; Berlyne, 1965).

We may postulate that an individual processes information to satisfy a need for uncertainty change. The need for uncertainty change may be viewed as a psychological state of readiness for informational stimuli or a class of informational stimuli. It may be more concise, however, to refer to the need simply as the need for information.

Expectancy

The remaining constructs comprising the tendency to process a particular stimulus display are specifiable in terms of the goal identified as motivating the organism. As noted earlier, the construct expectancy accounts for the cognitive association between the performance of a particular response (i.e., processing a particular message) and the expected consequence in terms of goal attainment. Its strength is accounted for in terms of likelihood or probability. Therefore, the expectancy appropriate to the tendency to process a particular message is the cognitive association between processing that particular message and the attainment of information relevant to that which is needed. If the association is perceived as being very likely or very probable, the expectancy would be considered to be strong.

Value

The value construct represents the object-specific (message-specific) aspect of incentive to act. As such, it is meant to account for the value of the particular message as a source of information relevant to that which is needed. It is measured in terms of the goodness or badness of the given message as a source of the type of information needed. If the message is perceived as being a very good source of the type of information needed, its value would be considered to be very high.

Model of Information Processing

It is suggested here that the need for information combines multiplicatively with the appropriate expectancy and value to yield a tendency to process a particular message. The proposed motivational model of information processing, therefore, may be represented as follows:

$$M \times E \times V = B_{TP} \cong B_p,$$

where:

1. M is the need for information on some topic.

2. E is the expectancy that processing a particular stimulus display will lead to exposure to information relevant to M.

3. V is the value of the particular stimulus display as a source of information relevant to M.

4. B_{TP} is the behavioral tendency to process the stimulus display.

5. B_p is the processing behavior.

TESTABLE IMPLICATIONS OF THE MODEL

The tendency to process a message should be directly related to the intensity of the processing behavior engaged in with respect to that message.

An increase in any one or more of the constructs making up the tendency to process a message, leaving all else constant, will produce an increase in the tendency to process that message. Therefore, one may infer a manipulation of the tendency to process a message from evidence supporting the manipulation of the constructs which comprise this tendency. The attainment of a direct relationship between each of the constructs which comprise the tendency and belief change would provide support for the contention that message processing intensity is a determinant of belief change.

The functional form by which motive, expectancy and value combine to yield a tendency to process the message was specified as being multiplicative. Therefore, the manipulation in a factorial design of the constructs comprising the tendency to process the message and the subsequent measurement of belief change would be expected to yield significantly positive two- and three-way interaction effects. These effects should be concentrated in the bilinear and trilinear components of the model, respectively (Anderson, 1970; Shanteau and Anderson, 1972). That is, only the bilinear and trilinear components of the interactions should be significant; all residual interaction effects should be nonsignificant.

Empirical research could be designed to test the separate and interactive effects of the constructs represented in the model. The research would employ a message which is logically believable and of sufficient duration to permit variation in comprehension. The attainment of the effects suggested here would provide support for the proposed model as a determinant of belief change.

SUPPORT FOR THE MODEL

Prior and Indirect Evidence

We shall turn now to a consideration of research, which although directed at other issues, may be interpreted as providing findings consistent with the proposed tendency to process information as a determinant of information processing intensity and belief change.

Perhaps the clearest indicant of the tendency to process a message (at least insofar as it relates to message exposure) is provided by research on selective exposure to information. The research paradigm typically employed in this area manipulates both subjects' commitment to a course of action and the usefulness of information on some topic (e.g., Canon, 1964; Freedman, 1965; Lowe and Steiner, 1968; Brock, Albert, and Becker, 1970). Subjects are then either given the opportunity to process or state their desire for a number of alternative messages (or message titles). The messages generally vary in terms of their supportiveness and in terms of their information providing (or uncertainty resolving) qualities. The typical finding is that messages likely to provide information beneficial in coping with an impending task or lending greater clarity to an uncertain situation are preferred to those which are unlikely to provide such information. This preference for the former type of message is frequently obtained even when it deviates from the subject's own past behavior.

Canon (1964) found that subjects about to engage in a debate preferred messages taking the opposite position from their own more strongly ($p < 0.01$) than subjects about to present their own position. Freedman (1965), in a replication of this study, found that more useful information was preferred to less useful information regardless of whether it was consonant with or dissonant from the subject's prior position.[3] Lowe and Steiner (1968) found that people whose decisions were reversible showed a greater preference for comparable information about the decision alternatives and for total information than did people whose prior decisions were irreversible ($p < 0.05$). Brock, Albert, and Becker (1970) found that information describing the likely effects on the subjects of their own past behavior (i.e., side effects of ingested drugs) was preferred to information unrelated to the effects of their past behavior (i.e., side effects of a drug which was not ingested) when that information was not already familiar to them ($p < 0.05$).

Sears and Freedman (1965) exposed subjects to summaries of a trial and then presented to one group a message which they identified as providing new information. They presented to a second group a message which they identified as providing old information. In fact, both groups were presented with the same message. They found that more opinion change occurred in the group which was told they would be exposed to new information than occurred in the group told they would be exposed to old information ($p < 0.05$). This greater effectiveness of expected new information held regardless of whether it was consonant or dissonant with the subjects' initial votes. It occurred even though the groups did not differ significantly with regard to their elapsed reading time. The finding is particularly germane to the position taken here that, given the need for information, the expected value of the message should determine not only the message to which a subject will

---

[3]Information about the opposition was assumed more useful for those about to debate while supportive information was assumed to be more useful for those about to present their own views.

attend but also the amount of opinon change resulting from exposure to that message.

It has been suggested in reviews of the selective exposure literature that the message will be preferred which is perceived as having most utility (e.g., Sears and Freedman, 1967; McGuire, 1968; Sears, 1968). However, treatments employed in this research suggest the operation of a more complex motivational construct (such as the tendency to process the message) as a mediator of exposure and subsequent belief change. Utility in this context seems to include a manipulated state of need for information as well as learned associations with and evaluations of the alternative message types available. If an individual is about to refute the arguments of the opposition on some issue (e.g., Canon, 1964; Freedman, 1965), he would be likely to have an aroused need for information on that topic. Similarly, messages which are believed to provide new information would be likely to be more highly valued than messages believed to provide old information. These factors should lead to more intense information processing and, given logically believable messages, greater belief change.

CONCLUSION

The model presented here represents an attempt to conceptualize the determinants of information-processing intensity in terms of more basic motivational theory. The substantiation of the link between message processing and theories of behavior should enhance the present understanding of the communication process by providing a theoretical framework within which message processing intensity and belief change may be jointly accounted for.

If its role as a mediator of belief change is verified, this theoretical model has the potential of pulling together and making more meaningful many of the seemingly discrepant and isolated findings in the communications literature.

If research supports the validity of the model, its use by practitioners offers the potential of improving the effectiveness of their communication efforts. This may be accomplished by directing attention toward the variables which the model suggests are determinants of processing intensity and belief change. For instance, it follows from the motivational model that communications will be most effective if they reach the target audience when the audience's *need* for that type of information is aroused. Hence, programs may be inaugurated with the objective of enhancing the level of this arousal, for example, by making the recipient's lack of information about a decision more salient. Greater effort could also be made to reach the intended audience at the time when they would most likely be in this aroused state (i.e., when in the process of making the decision).

If the validity of the model is supported, efforts could be made to enhance the perceived *value* of the message and the perceived *expectancy* that processing the message will lead to exposure to relevant information. Thus, the message could be varied in an attempt to increase the levels of these attributes and in this way the level of the resultant tendency as well. Among the variations which would seem to be beneficial in achieving these ends would be variations in message source, message context and message content.

REFERENCES

Anderson, Norman H. (1970), "Functional Measurement and Psychophysical Judgment," *Psychological Review,* 77, 153–70.

Atkinson, J. W. (1964), *An Introduction to Motivation,* New York: Van Nostrand Reinhold.

Atkinson, J. W., and Feather, N. T. (1966), *A Theory of Achievement Motivation,* New York: John Wiley and Sons.

Berlyne, D. E. (1960), *Conflict, Arousal and Curiosity,* New York: McGraw-Hill.

Berlyne, D. E. (1965), *Structure and Direction in Thinking,* New York: John Wiley and Sons.

Bolles, R. C. (1972), "Reinforcement, Expectancy and Learning," *Psychological Review,* 79, 394–409.

Brock, R. C.; Albert, S. M.; and Becker, L. A. (1970), "Familiarity, Utility and Supportiveness as Determinants of Information Receptivity," *Journal of Personality and Social Psychology,* 14, 292–301.

Canon, L. R. (1964), "Self-Confidence and Selective Exposure to Information," in *Conflict, Decision and Dissonance,* L. Festinger, ed., Stanford, Calif.: Stanford University Press.

Freedman, J. L. (1965), "Confidence, Utility, and Selective Exposure: A Partial Replication," *Journal of Personality and Social Psychology,* 2, 778–80.

Hilgard, E. R., and Bower, G. H. (1966), *Theories of Learning,* (3rd ed.) New York: Appleton-Century-Crofts.

Krugman, H. E. (1965), "The Impact of Television Advertising: Learning Without Involvement," *Public Opinion Quarterly,* 29, 349–56.

Lowe, R. H., and Steiner, I.D. (1968), "Some Effects of Reversibility and Consequences of Decisions on Post-Decision Information Preferences," *Journal of Personality and Social Psychology,* 8, 172–79.

MacCorquodale, K., and Meehl, P. E. (1954), "Edward C. Tolman," in W. K. Estes, L. Koch, L. MacCorquodale, P. E. Meehl, C. G. Mueller, R., W. N. Schoenfeld, and W. S. Verplanck, eds., *Modern Learning Theory,* New York: Appleton-Century-Crofts.

McGuire, W. J. (1968), "Selective Exposure: A Summing Up," in R. P. Abelson, E. Aronson, W. J. McGuire, T. N. Newcomb, M. J. Rosenberg, and P. H. Tannenbaum, eds., *Theories of Cognitive Consistency: A Sourcebook,* Chicago: Rand McNally.

Newell, A.; Shaw, J. C.; and Simon, H. A. (1958), "Elements of a Theory of Human Problem-Solving," *Psychological Review,* 65, 151–66.

Norman, D. A. (1968), "Toward a Theory of Memory and Attention," *Psychological Review,* 75, 522–36.

Reitman, W. R. (1965), *Cognition and Thought,* New York: John Wiley and Sons.

Schroder, H. M.; Driver, M. J.; and Streufert, S., (1967), *Human Information Processing,* New York: Holt, Rinehart and Winston.

Sears, D. O. (1968), "The Paradox of DeFacto Selective Exposure Without Preferences for Supportive Information," in R. P. Abelson, E. Aronson, W. J. McGuire, T. N. Newcomb, M. J. Rosenberg, and P. H. Tannenbaum, eds., *Theories of Cognitive Consistency: A Sourcebook,* Chicago: Rand McNally.

Sears, D. O., and Freedman, J. L. (1965), "Effects of Expected Familiarity with Arguments Upon Opinion Change and Selective Exposure," *Journal of Personality and Social Psychology,* 2, 420–26.

Sears, D. O., and Freedman, J. L. (1967), "Selective Exposure to Information: A Critical Review," *Public Opinion Quarterly,* 31, 194–213.

Shanteau, J., and Anderson, N. H. (1972), "Integration Theory Applied to Judgments of the Value of Information," *Journal of Experimental Psychology,* 92, 266–75.

Tolman, E. C. (1932), *Purposive Behavior in Animals and Man,* New York: Century.

Tolman, E. C. (1949), "The Nature and Functioning of Wants," *Psychological Review,* 56, 357–69.

Tolman, E. C. (1951), "A Psychological Model," in T. Parsons and E. A. Shils, eds., *Toward a General Theory of Action,* Cambridge, Mass.: Harvard University Press.

Tolman, E. C. (1959), "Principles of Purposive Behavior," in S. Koch, ed., *Psychology: A Study of Science,* New York: McGraw-Hill.

Weiner, B. (1972), *Theories of Motivation: From Mechanism to Cognition,* Chicago: Markham Press.

SECTION 10

PERSONALITY

Personality is not only something which we often speak of in our everyday lives, but it is also a topic of interest to consumer researchers. Many researchers have tried to determine the relationship between a consumer's personality and that person's consumer behavior. That is, since personality reflects consistent responses to the world, it was believed that personality traits could account for consistent consumer behaviors across product types. For example, if a person is extremely concerned about other people's reactions to what he or she does, then we could hypothesize that the person would actively seek the advice of others before purchasing new items and would respond favorably to advertising appeals based on social approval.

Researchers have tried to discover if in fact people purchase items which reflect their personalities and consider these purchases in ways consistent with their personalities. However, we could also make a case for the possibility that consumers may purchase items which reflect their *desired* personalities rather than their actual personalities. Or, people may purchase certain items that serve as stimuli for developing a personality which is consistent with the item. Thus, a very daring and popular young man may purchase a racy sports car. This would fit his personality. On the other hand, a rather shy, quiet young man may purchase the same type of car in the hopes that others will think of him as more daring and popular.

So what is the relationship between consumer behavior and personality? This is the question which is addressed in the three articles in this section.

"PERSONALITY AND CONSUMER BEHAVIOR: A REVIEW" AND "PERSONALITY AND CONSUMER BEHAVIOR: ONE MORE TIME"

There are so many studies of the relationship between personality and consumer behavior that it is almost unthinkable to try to count them all. Even more difficult would be an attempt to review the findings of even a substantial portion of these studies. Yet this is exactly what is done in the following two articles: the first written by Kassarjian in 1971, and the second written by Kassarjian and Sheffet in 1975. In spite of the cumbersome nature of the task, these two articles do an excellent job of reviewing extant studies by placing similar work together into categories that describe different approaches.

Each of the two articles reviews almost 100 studies of the relationship between various personality concepts and consumer behavior. Readers can easily become swamped if they try to remember the results of each of these 200 studies. Instead, the point of the two articles is to give a general idea of the strength of personality as a predictor of consumer behavior.

The first article states that the results of these 100 studies are "equivocal." That is, some studies find a relationship between some personality concepts and some behaviors of consumers, whereas other studies find no relationship between the two. The problem is that no one seemed to know why these differing results were obtained. In this first article, Kassarjian discusses *why* the results are equivocal. This, rather than the review section, is the most important section of the article. Kassarjian describes why it should almost be expected, given the nature of the studies, that results would often seem inconsistent with each other. He offers several suggestions for ways in which researchers could change the design of their research to enable them to better study the relationship between personality and consumer research.

The second article, written about five years later and published in 1975, reviews developments since the publication of the first article. Again, almost 100 studies are reviewed. Sadly, there is almost no change in the way in which most of these studies were conducted. They are laden with many of the problems described in the first article. As Kassarjian states, there is substantial contribution to breadth since so many studies were published, but they produced no change in the depth of knowledge about the relationship between personality and consumer behavior. Kassarjian and Sheffet give more suggestions about how to improve the quality of personality research done with regard to consumer behavior.

Probably the most useful way to read these two articles is to take notes while reading. Notes can be taken in list form using three major headings:

(1) Approaches to the study of personality in consumer behavior;
(2) Why results are equivocal (i.e., problems with extant research);
(3) Suggestions for improving personality research in consumer behavior.

Using these headings will help the reader focus on the broader issues and not become swamped with the results and findings of the 200 studies of the relationship between personality and consumer behavior.

"RISK- AND PERSONALITY-RELATED DIMENSIONS OF STORE CHOICE"

One personality concept which has received considerable attention in the consumer behavior literature is self-confidence. The Dash, et al. article explores the relationship between self-confidence and store choice. Specifically, patronage of two types of stores is studied—department stores and specialty stores. To make the data more comparable, the study is limited to one type of purchase, that of audio equipment.

Figure 1 in the article shows some of the hypothesized relationships explored in the research. However, several other relationships are examined. The data are also analyzed to determine the relationship between generalized self-confidence and product-specific self-confidence and the relationship between self-confidence and perceived product risk. Thus, the research explored hypotheses which were developed and had reasonable intuitive and empirical support prior to conducting the investigation. The research is not a "fishing expedition" (as criticized in the two previous Kassarjian articles) where a battery of personality instruments are administered in the hopes that some of them will prove statistically significant when related to particular purchase behaviors.

The measures used in the Dash, et al. article deserve some comment as they have some strengths which might not otherwise be noticed. Two measures of self-confidence (generalized and product-specific) were used. There were no *a priori* grounds for believing that the two would be strongly correlated, so both measures were used. In such cases it is a wise research practice to use multiple measures of similar concepts. After the data are collected, the relationship between the different measures can be determined. This is called determining convergent validity, which is the extent to which two different measures of the same basic concept produce similar results. In the research conducted by Dash, et al., the two measures were found to have a statistically significant positive relationship.

A second measurement strength of the Dash, et al. research is the combination of two components to determine perceived product risk. Unlike the case of an attempt to establish convergent validity, the two components of perceived risk measure *different variables.* The basic equation used is:

perceived product risk = uncertainty about product satisfaction multiplied by the consequences or the seriousness of unsatisfactory performance

It is fortunate that the researchers chose to measure these two components separately, because each of the two types of shoppers (department store vs.

specialty store) were found to be different on the two components. The findings are shown below. This shows that the two groups are different on each component, as well as in their overall perceived product risk score. In addition, each group has counterbalancing scores on the two dimensions. Thus, the perceived product risk differences are more complex than the overall score reflects.

Types of Shoppers

Perceived Product Risk Components		Department Store	Specialty Store
	Uncertainty	Not Certain	Very Certain
	Consequences	Less Serious	Very Serious
	Overall Risk	Higher	Lower

A final measurement strength of the Dash, et al. study is the use of a valid measure of the criterion variable. In studying the relationship between certain variables and consumer behavior, researchers often do not measure actual behavior. Instead, they may only find out what someone *says* they would do (behavioral intention), what someone says they actually did (self-reported behavior), or only note how someone reacts in a simulated situation (experimental response). All of these have imperfections as measures of behavior, but for a number of reasons, including convenience and control, they are often used. The Dash, et al. study, however, found respondents who had been named by the store as purchasing audio equipment there. This use of a measure of actual behavior makes the strategy implications more reliable.

PERSONALITY AND CONSUMER BEHAVIOR: A REVIEW

HAROLD H. KASSARJIAN

One of the more engrossing concepts in the study of consumer behavior is that of personality. Purchasing behavior, media choice, innovation, segmentation, fear, social influence, product choice, opinion leadership, risk taking, attitude change, and almost anything else one can think of have been linked to personality. The purpose of this article is to review the literature on consumer behavior and organize its contributions around the theoretical stems from which it grows.

Unfortunately, analysts do not agree on any general definition of the term "personality,"[1] except to somehow tie it to the concept of consistent responses to the world of stimuli surrounding the individual. Man does tend to be consistent in coping with his environment. Since individuals do react fairly consistently in a variety of environmental situations, these generalized patterns of response or modes of coping with the world can be called personality.

PSYCHOANALYTIC THEORY

The psychoanalytic theories and philosophies of Freud have influenced not only psychology but also literature, social science, and medicine, as well as marketing. Freud stressed the unconscious nature of personality and motivation and said that much, if not all, behavior is related to the stresses within the personality system. The personality's three interacting sets of forces, the id, ego, and superego, interact to produce behavior.

According to Freudian theory, the id is the source of all driving psychic energy, but its unre-

---

[1]Hall and Lindzey, in attempting to deal with the dozens of approaches that exist in the literature, frustratingly submit that *personality is defined by the particular concepts which are part of the theory of personality employed by the observer.* Because this article reviews marketing literature rather than psychological literature, the various theories are not described in detail. For a very brief description of several theories and a bibliographic listing of primary sources and references, as well as examples of about a dozen well known volumes on the general topic, see Hall and Lindzey (1969); Hilgard and Bower (1966).

Harold H. Kassarjian, "Personality and Consumer Behavior: A Review," *Journal of Marketing Research,* Vol. 8, November, 1971, pp. 409–18.

strained impulses cannot be expressed without running afoul of society's values. The superego is the internal representative of the traditional values and can be conceptualized as the moral arm of personality. The manner in which the ego guides the libidinal energies of the id and the moralistic demands of the superego accounts for the rich variety of personalities, interests, motives, attitudes, and behavior patterns of people. The tools of the ego are defenses such as rationalization, projection, identification, and repression; its goals are integrated action.

Freud further believed that the child passes through various stages of development—the oral, anal, phallic, and genital periods—that determine the dynamics of his personality. The degree of tension, frustration, and love at these stages leads to his adult personality and behavior.

The influence of Freud and psychoanalytic theory cannot be overestimated. Most of the greatest names in psychiatry and psychology have been followers, disciples, or critics of Freud, much as many good marketing research studies have been criticisms of motivation researchers or experiments applying scientific procedures to motivation research. The work of Sidney Levy, Burleigh Gardner and Lee Rainwater, some of the projects of Martineau, and the proprietary studies of Social Research, Inc., are in the latter tradition. Although today the critics of psychoanalytic applications to consumer behavior far outweigh the adherents, Freud and his critics have contributed much to advances in marketing theory.

SOCIAL THEORISTS

In his lifetime, several members of Freud's inner ring became disillusioned with his insistence on the biological basis of personality and began to develop their own views and their own followers. Alfred Adler, for example, felt that the basic drive of man is not the channelization of the libido, but rather a striving for superiority. The basic aim of life, he reasoned, is to overcome feelings of inferiority imposed during childhood. Occupations and spouses are selected, homes purchased, and automobiles owned in the effort to perfect the self and feel less inferior to others.

Eric Fromm stressed man's loneliness in society and his seeking of love, brotherliness, and security. The search for satisfying human relationships is of central focus to behavior and motivations.

Karen Horney, also one of the neo-Freudian social theorists, reacted against theories of the biological libido, as did Adler, but felt that childhood insecurities stemming from parent-child relationships create basic anxieties and that the personality is developed as the individual learns to cope with his anxieties.

Although these and other neo-Freudians have influenced the work of motivation researchers, they have had minimal impact on research on consumer behavior. However, much of their theorizing can be seen in advertising today, which exploits the striving for superiority and the needs for love, security, and escape from loneliness to sell toothpaste, deodorants, cigarettes, and even detergents.

The only research in consumer behavior based directly on a neo-Freudian approach is Cohen's psychological test that purports to measure Horney's three basic orientations toward coping with anxiety—the compliant, aggressive, and detached types (Cohen, 1967; Cohen, 1968). Cohen found that compliant types prefer brand names and use more mouthwash and toilet soaps; aggressive types tend to use a razor rather than an electric shaver, use more cologne and after-shave lotion, and buy Old Spice deodorant and Van Heusen shirts; and detached types seem to be least aware of brands. Cohen, however, admitted to picking and choosing from his data, and although the published results are by no means conclusive, his work does indicate that the Horney typology may have some relevance to marketing. Several follow-up studies using his instruments are unpublished to date.

STIMULUS-RESPONSE THEORIES

The stimulus-response or learning theory approach to personality presents perhaps the most elegant view, with a respected history of research and laboratory experimentation supporting it. Its origins are in the work of Pavlov, Thorndike, Skinner, Spence, Hull, and the Institute of Human Relations at Yale University. Although the various theorists differ among themselves, there is agreement that the link between stimulus and response is persistent and relatively stable. Personality is seen as a conglomerate of habitual responses acquired over time to specific and generalized cues. The bulk of theorizing and empirical research has been concerned with specifying conditions under which habits are formed, changed, replaced, or broken.

A drive leads to a response to a particular stimulus, and if the response is reinforced or rewarded, a particular habit is learned. Unrewarded and inappropriate responses are extinguished or eliminated. Complex behavior such as a consumer decision process is learned in a similar manner.

According to Dollard and Miller, a drive is a stimulus strong enough to impel activity; it energizes behavior but, by itself, does not direct it. Any stimulus may become a drive if it reaches sufficient intensity (Hall and Lindzey, 1969). Some stimuli are linked to the physiological processes necessary for the survival of the individual, and others are secondary or acquired. With the concepts of cues, drives responses, and reinforcement, complex motives such as the need for achievement or self-esteem are learned in the same manner as brand preference, racism, attitudes towards big business, purchasing habits, or dislike of canned spinach.

Marketing is replete with examples of the influence of learning theory. However, very few personality studies have used this theoretical orientation.

The reason for the lack of impact is probably that personality tests and measuring instruments using this theoretical base do not exist. Until such instruments are developed there will be little use of these theories in relating consumer behavior to personality, irrespective of their completeness and extreme relevance.

TRAIT AND FACTOR THEORIES

As learning theory approaches to personality have evolved from the tough-minded empirical experimentation of the animal laboratories, factor theories have evolved from the quantitative sophistication of statistical techniques and computer technology. The core of these theories is that personality is composed of a set of traits or factors, some general and others specific to a particular situation or test. In constructing a personality instrument, the theorist typically begins with a wide array of behavioral measures, mostly responses to test items, and with statistical techniques distills factors which are then defined as the personality variables.

For one large group of personality instruments the researcher begins with the intent to measure certain variables, for example, need for achievement or aggressiveness. Large samples of subjects predetermined as aggressive or not aggressive (say, by ratings from teachers and employers) are given the instrument. Each item is statistically analyzed to see if it discriminates aggressive from nonaggressive subjects. By a series of such distilling measures and additional validation and reliability studies, an instrument is produced which measures traits the researcher originally was attempting to gauge. Several of these variables are often embodied in, for example, a single 200-item instrument.

A second type of personality instrument is created not with theoretically predetermined variables in mind, but rather to identify a few items (by factor analysis) which account for a significant portion of the variance. Subjects are given questionnaires, ratings, or tests on a wide variety of topics, and test items are grouped in the factor analysis by how well they measure the same statistical factor. The meaning of a particular factor is thus empirically determined and a label arbitrarily attached to it that hopefully best describes what the researcher presumes the particular subset of items measures. Further reliability and validation measures lead to creation of a test instrument with several variables that supposedly account for the diversity and complexity of behavior. The theoretical structure is statistical and the variables are empirically determined and creatively named or labeled.

The concept of traits, factors, or variables that can be quantitatively measured has led to virtually hundreds of personality scales and dozens of studies in consumer behavior. Instruments of this type are discussed below.

Gordon Personal Profile

This instrument purports to measure ascendency, responsibility, emotional stability, and sociability. Tucker and Painter (1961) found significant correlations between use of headache remedies, vitamins, mouthwash, alcoholic drinks, automobiles, chewing gum, and the acceptance of new fashions and one or more of these four personality variables. The correlations ranged from .27 to .46, accounting for perhaps 10% of the variance.

Kernan (1968) used decision theory in an empirical test of the relationship between decision behavior and personality. He added the Gordon Personal Inventory to measure cautiousness, original thinking, personal relations, and vigor. Pearsonian and multiple correlations indicated few significant relationships, but canonical correlation between sets of personality variables and decision behavior gave a coefficient of association of .77, significant at the .10 level. Cluster analysis then showed that behavior is consistent with personality profiles within clusters. Kernan's results, like those of Tucker and Painter (1961) show interesting relationships but are by no means startling.

Edwards Personal Preference Schedule

The EPPS has been used in about two dozen studies or rebuttals in consumer behavior from a trait and factor theory approach. The purpose of the instrument was to develop a factor-analyzed, paper-and-pencil, objective instrument to measure the psychoanalytically-oriented needs or themes developed by Henry Murray. Its popularity in consumer behavior can be traced to Evans' landmark study (1959), in which he could find no differences between Ford and Chevrolet owners to an extent that would allow for prediction. He was, however, able to account for about 10% of the variance. Criticism of Evans' study and conclusions came from many fronts and on many grounds (Jacoby, 1969; Marcus, 1965; Martineau, 1959; Murphy, 1963; Steiner, 1961; Winick, 1961). Rejoinders were written (Evans, 1961; 1962; 1964; Evans and Roberts, 1963), and finally Evans replicated the study (1968). Using Evans' original data, Kuehn then concluded that predictive ability can be improved if one computes a discriminant function based on the two needs displaying the largest initial predictive ability (1963). Kuehn improved Evans' results by using dominance scores minus affiliation scores. However, the psychological significance of dominance minus affiliation has escaped me for five years. Nevertheless, the controversy over Evans' study is in the very finest tradition of the physical and social sciences, with argument and counterargument, rejoinder and replication, until the facts begin to emerge, something very seldom seen in marketing and consumer behavior research. The final conclusion that seems to trickle through is that personality does account for some variance but not enough to give much solace to personality researchers in marketing.

Along other lines, Koponen used the EPPS scale with data collected on 9,000 persons in the J. Walter Thompson panel (1960). His results indicate that cigarette smoking is positively related to sex dominance, aggression, and achievement needs among males and negatively related to order and compliance needs. Further, he found differences between filter and nonfilter smokers and found that these differences were made more pronounced by heavy smoking. In addition, there seemed to be a relationship between personality variables and readership of three unnamed magazines.

Massy, Frank, and Lodahl used the same data in a study of the purchase of coffee, tea, and beer (1968). Their conclusion was that personality accounted for a very small percentage of the variance. In fact, personality plus socioeconomic variables accounted for only 5% to 10% of the variance in purchases.

In a sophisticated study, Claycamp presented the EPPS to 174 subjects who held savings accounts in banks or savings and loan associations (1965). His results indicate that personality variables predict better than demographic variables whether an individual is a customer of a bank or a savings and loan association. These results contradict those of Evans, who concluded that socioeconomic variables are more effective than personality as measured by the same instrument. Using personality variables alone, Claycamp correctly classified 72% of the subjects.

Brody and Cunningham reanalyzed Koponen's data employing techinques like those of Claycamp and Massy, Frank, and Lodahl with similar results (1968) accounting for about 3% of the variance. Further, these results are similar to those from the Advertising Research Foundation's study on toilet paper (1964) in which 5% to 10% of the variance was accounted for by personality and other variables. Brody and Cunningham argued that the weak relationships may have been caused by an inadequate theoretical framework. Theirs consisted of three categories: perceived performance risk—the extent to which different brands perform differently in important ways; specific self-confidence—how certain the consumer is that a brand performs as he expects; and perceived social risk—the extent to which he thinks he will be judged on the basis of his brand decision. The authors concluded that "when trying to discriminate the brand choice of people most likely to have perceived-high performance risk and to have high specific self-confidence, personality variables were very useful" [1968, p. 56]. For people who

were 100% brand loyal, 8 personality variables explained 32% of the variance. As the minimum purchase of the favorite brand dropped from 100% to 40%, the explained variance fell to 13%.

Thurstone Temperament Schedule

This is another factor-analyzed instrument. Westfall, in a well known study that is often interpreted as a replication of Evans' study, compared personalities of automobile owners and could find no differences between brands (1962). He further found no differences between compact and standard car owners on the Thurstone variables. However, personality characteristics did differ between owners of convertibles and standard models.

Using the same instrument, Kamen showed a relationship between the number of people who had no opinion on foods to be rated and the number of items they left unanswered on the Thurstone scale. Using a specially created questionnaire, he concluded that the dimension of "no opinion" is not related to food preference (1964). Proneness to have an opinion does not seem to be a general trait, but rather is dependent on the content area.

California Personality Inventory

This is the newest paper-and-pencil test to be used extensively. Robertson and Myers (1969)—see also (1970) and Bruce and Witt (1970)—developed measures for innovativeness and opinion leadership in the areas of food, clothing, and appliances. A multiple stepwise regression with 18 traits on the CPI indicated poor R^2's; the portion of variance accounted for was 4% for clothing, 5% for food, and 23% for appliances. The study tends to support the several dozen previous studies on innovation and opinion leadership that show a minimal relationship between personality variables and behavior toward new products. Several studies indicate that gregariousness and venturesomeness are relevant to opinion leadership. Two studies using personality inventories have found a relationship between innovation and personality, while three others could find none. Other traits, such as informal and formal social participation, cosmopolitanism, and perceived risk, are related to innovative behavior in about half a dozen studies, while an additional half a dozen studies show no differences. These studies are reviewed in Robertson (1971).

A very recent study by Boone attempted to relate the variables on the California Personality Inventory to the consumer innovator on the topic of a community antenna television system (1970). His results indicate significant differences between innovators and followers on 10 of 18 scales. Unfortunately, the statistical techniques were quite different from those employed by Robertson and Myers, so it is not possible to determine whether or not the two studies are in basic agreement.

Finally, Vitz and Johnston, using the masculinity scale of both the CPI and the Minnesota Multiphasic Personality Inventory, hypothesized that the more masculine a smoker's personality, the more masculine the image of his regular brand of cigarettes (1965). The correlations were low but statistically significant, and the authors concluded that the results moderately support product preference as a predictable interaction between the consumer's personality and the product's image.

THEORIES OF SELF AND SELF-CONCEPT

Relationships of product image and self-image have been studied quite thoroughly by the motivation researchers, particularly Levy (1959) and Gardner (1955). The theoretical base for this work, I presume, rests in the writings and philosophies of Carl Rogers, William James, and Abraham Maslow and the symbolic interactionism proposed by Susan Langer and others.

The core of these views is that the individual has a real- and an ideal-self. This *me* or *self* is "the sum total of all that a man can call his—his body, traits, and abilities; his material possessions; his family, friends, and enemies; his vocations and avocations and much else" [Hall and Lindzey (1957), first edition, p. 467]. It includes evaluations and definitions of one's self and may be reflected in much of his actions, including his evaluations and purchase of products and services. The belief is that individuals perceive products that they own, would like to own, or do not want to own in terms of symbolic meaning to themselves and to others. Congruence between the symbolic image of a product (e.g., a .38 caliber is aggressive and masculine, a Lincoln automobile is extravagant and wealthy) and a consumer's self-image implies greater probability of positive evaluation, preference, or ownership of that product or brand. For example, Jacobson and Kossoff studied self-perception and attitudes toward small cars (1963). Individuals who perceived themselves as "cautious conservatives" were more likely to favor small cars as a practical and economic convenience. Another self-classified group of "confident explorers" preferred large cars, which they saw as a means of expressing their ability to control the environment.

Birdwell, using the semantic differential, tested the hypotheses that: (1) an automobile owner's perception of his car is essentially congruent with his perception of himself and (2) the average perception of a specific car type and brand is different for owners of different sorts of cars (Birdwell, 1964; 1968a; 1968b; see also Evans, 1968). The hypotheses were confirmed with varying degrees of strength. However, this does not imply that products have personalities and that a consumer purchases those brands whose images are congruent with his self-concept; Birdwell's study did not test causality. It could very well be that only after a product is purchased does the owner begin to perceive it as an extension of his own personality.

Grubb (1965) and Grubb and Grathwohl (1967) found that consumers' different self-perceptions are associated with varying patterns of consumer behavior. They claimed that self-concept is a meaningful mode of market segmentation. Grubb found that beer drinkers perceived themselves as more confident, social, extroverted, forward, sophisticated, impulsive, and temperamental than their non-beer-drinking brethren. However, the comparison of self-concept and beer brand profiles revealed inconclusive results; drinkers and nondrinkers perceived brands similarly.

In a follow-up study of Pontiac and Volkswagen owners, Grubb and Hupp indicated that owners of one brand of automobile perceive themselves as similar to others who own the same brand and significantly different from owners of the other brand (1968). Sommers indicated by the use of a Q-sort of products that subjects are reliably able to describe themselves and others by products rather than adjectives, say on a semantic differential or adjective checklist (Sommers, 1963 and 1964). That is, individuals are able to answer the questions, "What kind of a person am I?" and "What kind of a person is he?" by Q-sorting products.

Dolich further tested the congruence relationship between self-images and product brands and concluded that there is a greater similarity between one's self-concept and images of his most preferred brands than images of least preferred brands (Dolich, 1969). Dolich claimed that favored brands are consistent with and reinforce self-concept.

Finally, Hamm (1967) and Hamm and Cundiff (1969) related product perception to what they call self-actualization, that is, the discrepancy between the self and ideal-self. Those with a small discrepancy were called low self-actualizers, a definition which does not seem consistent with Maslow's work on the hierarchy of needs. High self-actualizers decribe themselves in terms of products differently from low self-actualizers, and in turn perceive products differently. For both groups, some products such as a house, dress, automatic dishwasher, and art prints tend to represent an ideal-self, wife, or mother, while others such as cigarettes, TV dinners, or a mop do not.

LIFE STYLE

An integration of the richness of motivation research studies and the tough-mindedness and statistical sophistication of computer technology has led to another type of research involving personality, variously called psychographic or life-style research. The life-style concept is based on distinctive or characteristic modes of living of segments of a society (Lazer, 1963). The technique divides the total market into segments based on interests, values, opinions, personality characteristics, attitudes, and demographic variables using techniques of cluster analysis, factor analysis, and canonical correlation. Wells dubbed the methodology "backward segmentation" because it groups people by behavioral characteristics before seeking correlates (Wells, 1968). Pessemier and Tigert reported that some preliminary relationships were found between the factor analyzed clusters of people and market behavior (Pessemier, 1967). (Similar results were reported in Bass, Tigert, and Lonsdale, 1968; Lessig and Tollefson, 1971; Pessemier and Tigert, 1966; Tigert, 1969; Wells, in press; Wilkie, 1970; and Wilson, 1966.)

Generally, the relationship of the attitude-interest-personality clusters, when correlated with actual buyer behavior, indicates once again that 10% or less of the variance is accounted for. Yet quite properly the proponents of the technique claim that very rich data are available in the analyses for the researcher and practitioner interested in consumer behavior.

MISCELLANEOUS OTHER APPROACHES

The overall results of other studies with other points of view are quite similar. Some researchers interpret their results as insignificant while others interpret similarly minimal relationships as significant, depending on the degree of statistical sophistication and the statistical tools used.

Social Character

In the usual pattern of applying psychological and sociological concepts to marketing and consumer behavior, several researchers have turned their attention to Riesman's theories, which group human beings into three types of social character: tradition-directed, inner-directed, and other-directed. A society manifests one type predominantly, according to its particular phase of development.

Riesman by no means intended his typology to be interpreted as a personality schema, yet in the consumer behavior literature social character has been grouped with personality, and hence the material is included in this review.

A society of tradition-directed people, seldom encountered in the United States today, is characterized by general slowness of change, a dependence on kin, low social mobility, and a tight web of values. Inner-directed people are most often found in a rapidly changing, industrialized society with division of labor, high social mobility, and less security; these persons must turn to inner values for guidance. In contrast, other-directed persons depend upon those around them to give direction to their actions. The other-directed society is industrialized to the point that its orientation shifts from production to consumption. Thus success in the other-directed society is not through production and hard work but rather through one's ability to be liked by others, develop charm or "personality," and manipulate other people. The contemporary United States is considered by Riesman to be almost exclusively populated by the latter two social character types and is rapidly moving towards an other-directed orientation.

Dornbusch and Hickman content analyzed consumer goods advertising over the past decades and noted a clear trend from inner- to other-direction (Dornbusch and Hickman, 1959). Kassarjian (1962) and Centers (1962) have shown that youths are significantly more other-directed and that those foreign-born or reared in small towns tend to be inner-directed.

Gruen found no relationship between preference for new or old products and inner other-direction (Gruen, 1960). Arndt (1967, 1968) and Barban, Sandage, Kassarjian, and Kassarjian (1970) could find little relationship between innovation and social character; Donnelly, however, has shown a relationship between housewives' acceptance of innovations and social character, with the inner-directed being slightly more innovative (Donnelly, 1970). Linton and Graham indicated that inner-directed persons are less easily persuaded than other-directed persons (Linton and Graham, 1959). Centers and Horowitz found that other-directed individuals were more susceptible to social influence in an experimental setting than were inner-directed subjects (Centers and Horowitz, 1963). Kassarjian found that subjects expressed a preference for appeals based on their particular social character type. There was minimal evidence for differential exposure to various mass media between the two Riesman types (Kassarjian, 1965).

In a similar study, Woodside found no relationship between consumer products and social character, although he did find a minimal relationship between advertising appeals and inner other-direction (Woodside, 1969).

Finally, Kassarjian and Kassarjian found a relationship between social character and Allport's scale of values as well as vocational interests but could find no relationship between inner other-direction and personality variables as measured by the MMPI (Kassarjian and Kassarjian, 1966a; 1966b). Once again, the results follow the same pattern: a few studies find and a few do not find meaningful relationships between consumer behavior and other measures.

Personality and Persuasibility

To complete a review on the relationship between personality and consumer behavior, the wide body of research findings relating personality to persuasibility and attitude change must be included. In addition to the dozens of studies carried out under Carl Hovland, (e.g., Hovland and Janis, 1959), there are many relating personality characteristics to conformity, attitude change, fear appeals, and opinions on various topics; see (Lehmann, 1970). The consumer behavior literature studies by Cox and Bauer (1964), Bell (1967, 1968), Carey (1963), and Barach (1967, 1969) tied self-confidence to persuasibility in the purchase of goods. These studies indicated a curvilinear relationship between generalized self-confidence and persuasibility and between specific self-confidence and persuasibility. Venkatesan's results, however, throw some doubt on these findings (Venkatesan, 1968). In a recent reanalysis and review of much of this literature, Shuchman and Perry found contradictory data and felt these were inconsequential. The authors claim that neither generalized nor specific self-confidence appears to be an important determinant of persuasibility in marketing (Shuchman and Perry, 1969). Bauer, in turn, has found fault with the Shuchman and Perry reanalysis (Bauer, 1970).

SUMMARY AND CONCLUSIONS

A review of these dozens of studies and papers can be summarized in the single word, *equivocal*. A few studies indicate a strong relationship between personality and aspects of consumer behavior, a few indicate no relationship, and the great majority indicate that if correlations do exist they are so weak as to be questionable or perhaps meaningless. Several reasons can be postulated to account for these discrepancies. Perhaps the major one is based on the validity of the particular personality measuring instruments used: a typically "good" instrument has a test-retest reliability of about .80 and a split-half reliability of about .90. Validity coefficients range at most from .40 to about .70; that is, when correlated against a criterion variable, the instrument typically accounts for about 20% to 40% of the variance. Too often the marketing researcher is just plain disinterested in reliability and validity criteria. *Tests validated for*

specific uses on specific populations, such as college students, or as part of mental hospital intake batteries are applied to available subjects in the general population. The results may indicate that 10% of the variance is accounted for; this is then interpreted as a weak relationship and personality is rejected as a determinent of purchase. The consumer researcher too often expects more from an instrument than it was orginally intended to furnish.

An additional problem for the marketing researcher is the conditions under which the test instrument is given. The instrument is often presented in the classroom or on the doorstep, rather than in the office of a psychometrician, psychotherapist, or vocational counselor. As Wells has pointed out (Wells, 1966, p. 188):

> The measurements we take may come from some housewife sitting in a bathrobe at her kitchen table, trying to figure out what it is she is supposed to say in answering a questionnaire. Too often, she is not telling us about herself as she really is, but instead is telling us about herself as she thinks she is or wants us to think she is.

To compound the error, consumer researchers often forget that the strength of a correlation is limited by the reliability of the measures being correlated. Not only the personality test but also the criterion itself may be unreliable under these conditions, as Wells has pointed out. Often the criterion used in these studies is the consumer's own account of her purchasing behavior. More often than not, these data are far more unreliable than we may wish to admit.

Adaptation of Instruments
Much too often, in order to adjust test items to fit specific demands, changes are made in the instrument. Items are taken out of context of the total instrument, words are changed, items are arbitrarily discarded, and the test is often shortened drastically. This adjustment would undoubtedly horrify the original developer of the instrument, and the disregard for the validity of the modified

instrument should horrify the rest of us. Just how much damage is done when a measure of self-confidence or extroversion is adapted, revised, and restructured is simply not known, but it would not be a serious exaggeration to claim it is considerable. And, most unfortunately, from time to time even the name of the variable is changed to fit the needs of the researcher. For example, Cohen has pointed out that in the Koponen study male smokers scored higher than average on self-depreciation and association, variables not included in the Edwards instrument. The researcher was apparently using the abasement and affiliation scales (Cohen, 1968). Such changes may or may not be proper, and although they may not necessarily violate scientific canons, they certainly do not help reduce the confusion in attempting to sort out what little we know about the relationships of personality to consumer behavior.

Psychological Instruments in Marketing Research

A second reason for discrepancies in the literature is that instruments originally intended to measure gross personality characteristics such as sociability, emotional stability, introversion, or neuroticism have been used to make predictions of the chosen brand of toothpaste or cigarettes. The variables that lead to the assassination of a president, confinement in a mental hospital, or suicide may not be identical to those that lead to the purchase of a washing machine, a pair of shoes, or chewing gum. *Clearly, if unequivocal results are to emerge, consumer behavior researchers must develop their own definitions and design their own instruments to measure the personality variables that go into the purchase decision rather than using tools designed as part of a medical model to measure schizophrenia or mental stability.*

Development of definitions and instruments can perhaps be handled in two ways. One will require some brilliant theorizing as to what variables do relate to the consumer decision process. If neuroticism and sociability are not the relevant

personality variables, then perhaps new terms such as risk aversion, status seeking, and conspicuous consumption will emerge. Personality variables that in fact are relevant to the consumer model need to be theorized and tests developed and validated.

Another approach to developing such instruments might be that of the factor theorists. Dozens of items measuring behavior, opinions, purchases, feelings, or attitudes can be factor analyzed in the search for general and specific factors that in turn can be validated against the marketing behavior of the individual.

Only with marketing-oriented instruments will we be able to determine just what part personality variables play in the consumer decision process and, further, if they can be generalized across product and service classes or must be product-specific instruments. At that stage, questions of the relevancy of these criteria for market segmentation, shifting demand curves, or creating and sustaining promotional and advertising campaigns can be asked.

Hypotheses

A third reason for the lackluster results in the personality and consumer behavior literature is that *many studies have been conducted by a shotgun approach with no specific hypotheses or theoretical justification.* Typically a convenient, available, easily scored, and easy-to-administer personality inventory is selected and administered along with questionnaires on purchase data and preferences. The lack of proper scientific method and hypothesis generation is supposedly justified by the often-used disclaimer that the study is exploratory. As Jacoby has pointed out (Jacoby, 1971, p. 244):

> Careful examination reveals that, in most cases, no *a priori* thought is directed to *how*, or especially *why*, personality should or should not be related to that aspect of consumer behavior being studied. Moreover, the few studies which do report statistically significant findings usually do so on the basis of

post-hoc "picking and choosing" out of large data arrays.

Statistical techniques are applied and anything that turns up looking halfway interesting furnishes the basis for the discussion section (Jacoby, 1969).

An excellent example of the shotgun approach to science, albeit a more sophisticated one than most, is Evans' original study examining personality differences between Ford and Chevrolet owners. Jacoby, in an excellent and most thoughtful paper, noted that Evans began his study with specific hypotheses culled from the literature and folklore pertaining to personality differences to be expected between Ford and Chevrolet owners (Jacoby, 1969). He then presented the EPPS to subjects, measuring 11 variables, 5 of which seemed to be measuring the variables in question; the remaining 6 were irrelevant to the hypotheses with no a priori basis for expecting differences. If predictions were to have been made on these six scales, Jacoby says, they should have been ones of *no* difference. Using one-tailed tests of significance, since the directions also should have been hypothesized, 3 of the 5 key variables were significant at the .05 level and none of the remaining 6 were significant. In short, Evans' data could have been interpreted such that 9 of the 11 scales were "significant" according to prediction. Jacoby's interpretation leads to a conclusion quite different from Evans', that there are no personality differences between Ford and Chevrolet owners. Also, with a priori predictions, Jacoby did not have to pick and choose from his data, as Kuehn was forced to do in showing a relationship between "dominance minus affiliation" scores and car ownership (Kuehn, 1963).

Finally, personality researchers and researchers in other aspects of marketing seem to need simple variables which can be somehow applied in the marketplace. We seem to feel that the only function of science and research is to predict rather than to understand, to persuade rather than to appreciate. Social scientists can fully accept that personality variables are related to suicide or crime, to assassinations, racial prejudice, attitudes towards the USSR, or the selection of a spouse. They do not get upset that personality is not the only relevant variable or that the portion of the explained variance is merely 20% or 10% or 5%. Yet personality researchers in consumer behavior much too often ignore the many interrelated influences on the consumer decision process, ranging from price and packaging to availability, advertising, group influences, learned responses, and preferences of family members, in addition to personality. *To expect the influence of personality variables to account for a large portion of the variance is most certainly asking too much.* What is amazing is not that there are many studies that show no correlation between consumer behavior and personality, but rather that there are any studies at all with positive results. That 5% or 10% or any portion of the variance can be accounted for by personality variables measured on ill-chosen and inadequate instruments is most remarkable, indeed!

REFERENCES

Are There Consumer Types? (1964), New York: Advertising Research Foundation.

Arndt, Johan (1967), "The Role of Product-Related Conversations in the Diffusion of a New Product," *Journal of Marketing Research,* 4, 291–95.

——— (1968), "Profiling Consumer Innovators," in Johan Arndt, ed., *Insights into Consumer Behavior,* Boston: Allyn and Bacon, 71–83.

Barach, Jeffrey A. (1967), "Self-Confidence and Reactions to Television Commercials," in Donald F. Cox, ed., *Risk Taking and Information Handling in Consumer Behavior,* Boston: Division of Research,

Graduate School of Business, Harvard University, 428–41.

_____ (1969), "Advertising Effectiveness and Risk in the Consumer Decision Process," *Journal of Marketing Research,* 6, 314–20.

Barban, Arnold N.; Sandage, C. H.; Kassarjian, Waltraud M.; and Kassarjian, Harold H. (1970), "A Study of Riesman's Inner-Other-Directedness Among Farmers," *Rural Sociology,* 35, 232–43.

Bass, Frank M.; Tigert, Douglas J.; and Lonsdale, Ronald T. (1968), "Market Segmentation: Group Versus Individual Behavior," *Journal of Marketing Research,* 5, 264–70.

Bauer, Raymond A. (1970), "Self-Confidence and Persuasibility: One More Time," *Journal of Marketing Research,* 7, 256–58.

Bell, Gerald D. (1968), "Persuasibility and Buyer Remorse Among Automobile Purchasers," in Montrose S. Sommers and Jerome B. Kernan, eds., *Consumer Behavior,* Austin: Bureau of Business Research, The University of Texas, 77–102.

_____ (1967), "Self-Confidence and Persuasion in Car Buying," *Journal of Marketing Research,* 4, 46–52.

Birdwell, Al E. (1964), "Influence of Image Congruence on Consumer Choice," *Proceedings,* Winter Conference, American Marketing Association, 290–303.

_____ (1968a), "A Study of the Influence of Image Congruence on Consumer Choice," *Journal of Business,* 41, 76–88.

_____ (1968b), "Automobiles and Self-Imagery: Reply," *Journal of Business,* 41, 486–87.

Boone, Louis E. (1970), "The Search for the Consumer Innovator," *Journal of Business,* 43, 135–40.

Brody, Robert P., and Cunningham, Scott M. (1968), "Personality Variables and the Consumer Decision Process," *Journal of Marketing Research,* 5, 50–57.

Bruce, Grady D., and Witt, Robert E. (1970), "Personality Correlates of Innovative Buying Behavior," *Journal of Marketing Research,* 7, 259–60.

Carey, James W. (1963), "Personality Correlates of Persuasibility," *Proceedings,* Winter Conference, American Marketing Association, 30–43.

Centers, Richard (September, 1962), "An Examination of the Riesman Social Character Typology: A Metropolitan Survey," *Sociometry* 25, 231–40.

Centers, Richard, and Horowitz, Miriam (1963), "Social Character and Conformity," *Journal of Social Psychology,* 60, 343–49.

Claycamp, Henry J. (1965), "Characteristics of Owners of Thrift Deposits in Commercial Banks and Savings and Loan Associations," *Journal of Marketing Research,* 2, 163–70.

Cohen, Joel B. (1967), "An Interpersonal Orientation to the Study of Consumer Behavior," *Journal of Marketing Research,* 4, 270–78.

_____ (1968), "Toward an Interpersonal Theory of Consumer Behavior," *California Management Review,* 10, 73–80.

Cox, Donald F. and Bauer, Raymond A. (1964), "Self-Confidence and Persuasibility in Women," *Public Opinion Quarterly,* 28, 453–66.

Dolich, Ira J. (1969), "Congruence Relationships Between Self Images and Product Brands," *Journal of Marketing Research,* 6, 80–4.

Donnelly, James H., Jr. (1970), "Social Character and Acceptance of New Products," *Journal of Marketing Research,* 6, 80–4.

Dornbush, Sanford M., and Lauren C. Hickman (December, 1959), "Other-Directedness in Consumer Goods Advertising: A Test of Riesman's Historical Theory," *Social Forces,* 38, 99–102.

Evans, Franklin B. (1959), "Psychological and Objective Factors in the Prediction of Brand Choice," *Journal of Business,* 32, 340–69.

_____ (1961), "Reply: You Still Can't Tell a Ford Owner From a Chevrolet Owner," *Journal of Business,* 34, 67–73.

_____ (1962), "Correlates of Automobile Shopping Behavior," *Journal of Marketing,* 26, 74–77.

_____ (1964), "True Correlates of Automobile Shopping Behavior," *Journal of Marketing,* 28, 65–66.

_____ (1968), "Ford Versus Chevrolet: Park Forest Revisited," *Journal of Business,* 41, 445–59.

_____ (1968), "Automobiles and Self-Imagery: Comment," *Journal of Business,* 41, 484–85.

_____, and Roberts, Harry V. (April, 1963), "Fords, Chevrolets, and the Problem of Discrimination," *Journal of Business,* 36, 242–49.

Gardner, Burleigh B., and Levy, Sidney J. (March-April, 1955), "The Product and the Brand," *Harvard Business Review,* 33, 33–39.

Grubb, Edward L. (1965), "Consumer Perception of 'Self Concept' and Its Relationship to Brand Choice of

Selected Product Types," *Proceedings,* Winter Conference, American Marketing Association, 419–22.

———, and Grathwohl, Harrison L. (October, 1967), "Consumer Self-Concept, Symbolism and Market Behavior: A Theoretical Approach," *Journal of Marketing,* 31, 22–27.

———, and Hupp, Gregg (February, 1968), "Perception of Self, Generalized Stereotypes, and Brand Selection," *Journal of Marketing Research,* 5, 58–63.

Gruen, Walter (December, 1960), "Preference for New Products and Its Relationship to Different Measures of Conformity," *Journal of Applied Psychology,* 44, 361–66.

Hall, Calvin S., and Lindzey, Gardner (1957), *Theories of Personality,* 1st ed.; 2nd ed., 1969, New York: John Wiley & Sons.

Hamm, B. Curtis (1967), "A Study of the Differences Between Self-Actualizing Scores and Product Perceptions Among Female Consumers," *Proceedings,* Winter Conference, American Marketing Association, 275–76.

———, and Cundiff, Edward W. (November, 1969), "Self-Actualization and Product Perception," *Journal of Marketing Research,* 6, 470–72.

Hilgard, Ernest R., and Bower, Gordon H. (1966), *Theories of Learning,* 3rd ed., New York: Appleton-Century-Crofts.

Hovland, Carl I., and Janis, Irving L., eds. (1959), *Personality and Persuasibility,* New Haven, Conn.: Yale University Press.

Jacobson, Eugene, and Kossoff, Jerome (August, 1963), "Self-Percept and Consumer Attitudes Toward Small Cars," *Journal of Applied Psychology,* 47, 242–45.

Jacoby, Jacob (1969), "Personality and Consumer Behavior: How Not to Find Relationships," *Purdue Papers in Consumer Psychology,* No. 102, Purdue University.

——— (May, 1971), "Personality and Innovation Proneness," *Journal of Marketing Research,* 8, 244–247.

Kamen, Joseph M. (September, 1964), "Personality and Food Preferences," *Journal of Advertising Research,* 4, 29–32.

Kassarjian, Harold H. (May, 1965), "Social Character and Differential Preference for Mass Communication," *Journal of Marketing Research,* 2, 146–53.

———and Kassarjian, Waltraud M. (June, 1966a), "Personality Correlates of Inner- and Other-Direction," *Journal of Social Psychology,* 70, 281–85.

——— and ——— (January, 1966b), "Occupational Interests, Social Values and Social Character," *Journal of Counseling Psychology,* 12, 48–54.

Kassarjian, Waltraud M. (September, 1962), "A Study of Riesman's Theory of Social Character," *Sociometry,* 25, 213–30.

Kernan, Jerome (May, 1968), "Choice Criteria, Decision Behavior, and Personality," *Journal of Marketing Research,* 5, 155–64.

Koponen, Arthur (September, 1960), "Personality Characteristics of Purchasers," *Journal of Advertising Research,* 1, 6–12.

Kuehn, Alfred A. (April, 1963), "A Demonstration of a Relationship Between Psychological Factors and Brand Choice," *Journal of Business,* 36, 237–41.

Lazer, William (1963), "Life Style Concepts and Marketing," *Proceedings,* Winter Conference, American Marketing Association, 130–39.

Lehmann, Stanley (May, 1970), "Personality and Compliance: A Study of Anxiety and Self-Esteem in Opinion and Behavior Change," *Journal of Personality and Social Psychology,* 15, 76–86.

Lessig, V. Parker, and Tollefson, John O. (November, 1971), "Market Segmentation Through Numerical Taxonomy," *Journal of Marketing Research,* 8, 480–87.

Levy, Sidney J. (July-August, 1959), "Symbols for Sale," *Harvard Business Review,* 37, 117–24.

Linton, Harriet, and Graham, Elaine (1959), "Personality Correlates of Persuasibility," in Hovland, Carl I. and Janis, Irving L., eds., *Personality and Persuasibility,* New Haven: Yale University Press, 69–101.

Marcus, Alan S. (October, 1965), "Obtaining Group Measures from Personality Test Scores: Auto Brand Choice Predicted from the Edwards Personal Preference Schedule," *Psychological Reports,* 17, 523–31.

Martineau, Pierre (December 21, 1959), "Letter to the Editor," *Advertising Age,* 30, 76.

Massy, William F.; Frank, Ronald E.; and Lodahl, Thomas M. (1968), *Purchasing Behavior and Personal Attributes,* Philadelphia: University of Pennsylvania Press.

Murphy, Joseph R. (October, 1963), "Questionable

Correlates of Automobile Shopping Behavior," *Journal of Marketing,* 27, 71–72.

Pessemier, Edgar A., and Tigert, Douglas J. (1966), "Personality, Activity and Attitude Predictors of Consumer Behavior," *Proceedings,* World Congress, American Marketing Association, 332–47.

———— (1967), "Socio-Economic Status of the Family and Housewife Personality, Life Style and Opinion Factors," Paper No. 197, Institute for Research on the Behavioral, Economic and Management Sciences, Purdue University.

Robertson, Thomas S. (1971), *Innovation and the Consumer,* New York: Holt, Rinehart, and Winston.

———— and Myers, James H. (May, 1969), "Personality Correlates of Opinion Leadership and Innovative Buying Behavior," *Journal of Marketing Research,* 6, 164–68.

———— (May, 1970), "Personality Correlates of Innovative Buying Behavior: A Reply," *Journal of Marketing Research,* 7, 260–61.

Shuchman, Abe, and Perry, Michael (May, 1969), "Self-Confidence and Persuasibility in Marketing: A Reappraisal," *Journal of Marketing Research,* 6, 146–54.

Sommers, Montrose S. (1963), "Product Symbolism and the Perception of Social Strata," *Proceedings,* Winter Conference, American Marketing Association, 200–16.

———— (Fall, 1964), "The Use of Product Symbolism to Differentiate Social Strata," *University of Houston Business Review,* 11, 1–102.

Steiner, Gary A. (January, 1961), "Notes on Franklin B. Evans' 'Psychological and Objective Factors in the Prediction of Brand Choice,'" *Journal of Business,* 34, 57–60.

Tigert, Douglas J. (1969), "A Psychological Profile of Magazine Audiences: An Investigation of a Media's Climate," paper presented at the American Marketing Association Consumer Behavior Workshop.

Tucker, William T., and Painter, John (October, 1961), "Personality and Product Use," *Journal of Applied Psychology,* 45, 325–29.

Venkatesan, M. (March, 1968), "Personality and Persuasibility in Consumer Decision Making," *Journal of Advertising Research,* 8, 39–45.

Vitz, Paul C., and Johnston, Donald (June, 1965), "Masculinity of Smokers and the Masculinity of Cigarette Images," *Journal of Applied Psychology,* 49, 155–59.

Wells, William D. (1966), "General Personality Tests and Consumer Behavior," in Joseph Newman, ed., *On Knowing the Consumer,* New York: John Wiley & Sons, 187–89.

———— (1968), "Backward Segmentation," in Johan Arndt, ed., *Insights into Consumer Behavior,* Boston: Allyn and Bacon, 85–100.

————, and Tigert, Douglas J. (in press), "Activities, Interests and Opinions," *Journal of Advertising Research.*

Westfall, Ralph (April, 1962), "Psychological Factors in Predicting Product Choice," *Journal of Marketing,* 26, 34–40.

Wilkie, William (1970), "Psychological Descriptors," paper presented at the Fall Conference, American Marketing Association.

Wilson, Clark L. (1966), "Homemaker Living Patterns and Marketplace Behavior—A Psychometric Approach," *Proceedings,* World Congress, American Marketing Association, 305–31.

Winick, Charles (January, 1961), "The Relationships Among Personality Needs, Objective Factors, and Brand Choice: A Reexamination," *Journal of Business,* 34, 61–66.

Woodside, Arch G. (December, 1969), "Social Character, Product Use and Advertising Appeal," *Journal of Advertising Research,* 8, 31–35.

PERSONALITY AND CONSUMER BEHAVIOR: ONE MORE TIME

**HAROLD H. KASSARJIAN
AND
MARY JANE SHEFFET**

Harold J. Kassarjian and Mary Jane Sheffet, "Personality and Consumer Behavior: One More Time," *AMA 1975 Combined Proceedings,* Series No. 37, pp. 197–201.

By late 1969 some one hundred studies were available in the marketing literature relating personality variables to consumer behavior. A review of these studies (Jacoby, 1971; Kassarjian, 1971; and Wells and Beard, 1973) can be summarized by the single word, "equivocal." The purpose of this paper is to enumerate what has happened to the field in the ensuing half decade. The previous quarter century had produced some one hundred studies. The outpouring of recent research has accumulated an additional one hundred studies in the last five years, not including working papers, privately distributed pre-prints and unpublished proprietary studies.

No major obvious changes have been discernible although some new fads in researchable variables have emerged. For example, one no longer finds the topic of motivation research from a psychoanalytic point of view in the literature. The only true attempt to use a projective technique to be found in the published literature is a replication of the classic Mason Haire Shopping List study by Webster and Von Pechman (1970) which interestingly, yielded significantly different results from the original paper. Instant coffee users are no longer perceived as psychologically different from drip grind users.

The use of the traditionally available paper and pencil psychological inventories is still quite popular. Donnelly and Ivancevich (1974) in turn found a weak but positive relationship between inner other-direction and innovator characteristics. Perry (1973) tied in anxiety, the Eysenck variables, and heredity to product choice concluding that consumption was genetically influenced. He claimed that this genetic relationship has application to primary demand but not product choice.

Rokeach's dogmatism as a variable appeared in some half a dozen studies (Anderson and Cunningham, 1972; Blake, Perloff, and Zenhausern, 1973; Darden and Reynolds, 1972; Joyce, 1972; Michman, 1971; and Peters and Ford, 1972) correlating the variable to risk, innovation and adoption, generally with weak but significant results.

Open-mindedness seems to be positively related to risk taking and willingness to innovate.

Several new instruments appeared for the first time in consumer type studies. Morris and Cundiff (1971) and Vavra and Winn (1971) turned their attention to anxiety and the Taylor Manifest Anxiety Scale, and Hawkins (1972) used the State-Trait Anxiety Inventory. The mixed results generally indicate that low anxiety is related to acceptance of more threatening material such as males' acceptance of feminine products. Peters and Ford (1972) used the California Test of Personality and could find no personality difference between women who buy and do not buy from door-to-door salesmen.

The most widely used instrument new to consumer behavior is the Jackson Personality Research Form. Wilson, et al., (1971) correlated these scores with segmentation variables, Fry (1971) and Ahmed (1972) with cigarette smoking, Kinnear and Taylor (1972; 1974) with ecological products, Worthing, et al., (1973) with a variety of consumer products, and Matthews, et al., (1971) with perceived risk.

Self-confidence had been heavily examined prior to 1969. Its fascination to researchers has not diminished. Studies by Bither and Wright (1973), Barach (1969; 1972) and Ostlund (1969; 1971; 1972) have since appeared. Work in self-concept continues to appear in some eleven studies (American Market Research Bureau, 1972; Dolich and Shilling, 1971; French and Flaschner, 1971; Green, Maheshwari and Rao, 1969; Grubb and Stern, 1971; Hughes and Guerrero, 1971; Joyce, 1972; Landon, 1974; Martin, 1973; Mason and Mayer, 1970; and Ross, 1971) in the struggle to explain purchase behavior by measuring the ideal self and actual self concept.

Perhaps the most dramatic change in the field has been the influence of studies using life style, AIO, or psychographics as they are alternatively termed. These factor analyzed scales have been applied to media exposure (King and Tigert, 1971; and Michaels, 1972), credit card usage (Plummer, 1971b), advertising (Plummer, 1971a), creativity (Winter and Russell, 1973), opinion leadership and innovation (Tigert and Arnold, 1971), and market segmentation (Bushman, 1971; Hustad and Pessemier, 1971a; 1971b; and Ziff, 1971). Discussion articles of the methodology (Reynolds and Darden, 1972; Wells, 1972; Wind, 1971; and Ziff, 1972) as well as reliability and validity studies (Bruno and Pessemier, 1972; and Tigert, 1969) are now available among many others. No topic in our memory has produced as many unpublished papers, university working papers, and private pre-prints as has life style research. Interestingly, the impact has not been as great as the sheer weight of publications might suggest, although psychographics certainly has become a buzz word in industry.

On overview, the conclusions from published research studies over the past five years remain quite similar to those drawn in 1969. The additional studies have generally made little contribution to the depth of our knowledge, although its breadth has certainly been expanded. The correlation or relationship between personality test scores and consumer behavior variables such as product choice, media exposure, innovation, segmentation, etc., are weak at best and thus of little value in prediction. The reasons for such poor predictions have been discussed by Jacoby (1971), Wells and Beard (1973) and Kassarjian (1971), and all agree that personality is a critical variable in the explanation of the purchasing process. The critical question is why do we insist on considering personality, by itself, a salient variable when the data are at best equivocal?

Nakanishi, in a most insightful paper (1972) presented at the 1972 meetings of the Association for Consumer Research, has suggested that the low explanatory power of personality characteristics may have stemmed, in part, from naive conceptualizations of the relationship between personality and consumer behavior often held by researchers in the field. It is obvious that simple linear statistics such as variance analysis, chi square and t-tests are insufficient. For example, canonical correlations have been used by Sparks and Tucker (1971), Bither and Dolich (1972), Alpert (1971) and Darden and Reynolds (1974) with more complex results and somewhat more variance statistically explained. Unfortunately, this adding of additional variables still involves a static view of the consumer. Personality is perhaps better conceived of as a dynamic concept which is not constant over a variety of situations. Rather, personality is a consistency in the manner the individual adjusts to change over time and over situations. Nakanishi writes it is perhaps "more correct to conceive of personality as a moderator variable whose function is to moderate the effects of environmental change in the individual's behavior. This dynamic concept of personality has not been taken seriously in personality research."

Nakanishi seems to be suggesting that what we need is data somewhat analogous to a combination of cross-sectional and times series analysis. The studies conducted to date are of the cross-sectional variety correlating test inventory variables with consumption variables over subjects. And yet, as Wells (1973) points out, a single personality trait may lead to a variety of behaviors. For instance compulsiveness can lead to extremely orderly behavior or expulsive disorderly behavior depending on the situation. On the other hand, several personality traits may lead to a single response, again depending on the situation. Correlating a single trait with a single behavior is bound to be frustrating.

Hence, according to Nakanishi, the relevant variables include personality traits, response and behavior patterns, moderator variables, situations and individuals. Furthermore, for some of these variables it is essential that measurements be taken over time. That is, as we sample individuals, traits and responses, we should also take samplings of situations over time.

If one can generalize from Nakanishi, the low explanatory power of each of these variables stems from naive conceptualizations of the relationships between the variable and the actions of the consumer in the marketplace.

Trained as we have been by psychoanalytic logic, simplistic beliefs emerging from stimulus-response psychology, and basic Aristotelian modes of thought, we insist on retaining the belief that, "The stimulus possesses an adhesion with certain reactions (Lewin, 1935)." This adhesion is regarded as the cause of the event, and somehow, there are mechanically rigid connections or associations between a stimulus and a response. The purchase of canned peas is somehow related to a specific personality variable, a specific type of perceived risk, or to a set of attributions. The belief is that once the mathematical relationship of this mechanically rigid connection is uncovered, the variance will be accounted for and a statistical error term will no longer exist. Hence, if the Edwards schedule does not account for the variance, perhaps the Jackson Inventory will, and if not, there are still Fishbein attitude models, reference groups, and measures of the level of involvement upon which to fall back.

The conception that the individual must be perceived as a dynamic whole has not yet been internalized by the modern-day consumer researcher. We ought not to be concerned with rigid connections, but rather with temporally extended whole individuals. In short, further traditional research attempting to connect the purchase of canned peas with a personality variable using cross-sectional data is bound to fail. What is missing are the interaction effects of that personality variable with other personality characteristics as well as the interaction effects accounted for by needs, motives, moods, memories, attitudes, beliefs, opinions, perceptions, values, etc. in addition to the situation or field. As Tucker (1967) has already suggested, our theories must begin with the study of the whole individual in a purchase act, at a point in time. In short, every specific instance of behavior must be viewed as the result of the interaction and integration of a variety of influences or forces impinging upon the person. The description of behavior cannot concentrate exclusively on one or another of the variables involved. Only after the analysis examines the situation as a whole is it possible to turn to the specific elements and the interactions among the elements (Kassarjian, 1973). Unfortunately a simple methodology for research of this sort has not yet emerged. We do not necessarily advocate a return to the extensive study of a single individual such as the psychoanalytic methodology employed by Freud, or the environmental probability of Egon Brunswick. But, greater awareness of views espoused by Tolman, Freud, Brunswick, Lewin, and other great minds in the social sciences and philosophy might help point out the location of the light at the end of the tunnel.

Only when we can explain the behavior of a single individual in a variety of situations over time can we grasp the idea that there are, in fact, interactions between personality, attitudes, perceived risk, and the psychological field or situa-tion. Once the concept of an interaction effect has been internalized, we can turn from an examination of the whole to analyses of the parts. The proper question then would be, "All other things being equal, what is the relationship between a specific personality variable and a specific act?" The problem with the literature as it exists today is that "all other things are not equal" and yet we continue to express dismay, surprise, or pleasure that personality measures, or attitude measures, or what have you, only account for 5% of the variance. As has already been expressed (Kassarjian, 1971), "What is amazing is not that there are many studies that show no correlation between consumer behavior and personality, but rather that there are any studies at all with positive results. That 5% or 10% or any portion of the variance can be accounted for by personality variables (taken out of context and studies independently of other cognitive or physical variables) . . . is most remarkable, indeed!"

REFERENCES

Ahmed, S. A. (October, 1972), "Prediction of Cigarette Consumption Level with Personality and Socioeconomic Variables," *Journal of Applied Psychology,* 56, 437–38.

Alpert, Mark I. (1971), "A Canonical Analysis of Personality and the Determinants of Automobile Choice," *Combined Proceedings,* American Marketing Association, 312–16.

—— (February, 1972), "Personality and The Determinants of Product Choice," *Journal of Marketing Research,* 5, 89–92.

American Market Research Bureau (May, 1972), "Measuring Self-Concept," unpublished working paper.

—— (1971), *Attitude Research Reaches New Heights,* Chicago: American Marketing Association.

Anderson, W. T., and Cunningham, William H. (February, 1972), "Gauging Foreign Product Promotion," *Journal of Advertising Research,* 12, 29–44.

Barach, Jeffrey A. (1969), "Self-Confidence, Risk Handling, and Mass Communications," *Proceedings,* Fall Conference, American Marketing Association, 323–29.

—— (1972), "Self Confidence and Four Types of Persuasive Situations," *Combined Proceedings,* American Marketing Association, 418–22.

Bither, Stewart W., and Dolich, Ira J. (1972), "Personality as a Determinant Factor in Store Choice," *Proceedings,* Association for Consumer Research, 9–19.

——, and Wright, Peter L. (May, 1973), "The Self Confidence–Advertising Response Relationship: A Function of Situational Distraction," *Journal of Marketing Research,* 10, 146–52.

Blake, Brian; Perloff, Robert; and Heslin, Richard (November, 1970), "Dogmatism and Acceptance of New Products," *Journal of Marketing Research,* 7, 483–86.

Blake, Brian; Perloff, Robert; Zenhausern, Robert and Heslin, Richard (October 1973), "The Effect of Intolerance of Ambiguity Upon Product Perceptions," *Journal of Applied Psychology,* 58, 239–243.

Bruno, Albert V., and Pessemier, Edgar A. (1972), "An

Empirical Investigation of the Validity of Selected Attitude and Activity Measures," *Proceedings,* Association for Consumer Research, 456–73.

Bushman, F. Anthony (1971), "Market Segmentation Via Attitudes and Life Style," *Combined Proceedings,* American Marketing Association, 594–99.

Cohen, Joel B., and Golden, Ellen (February, 1972), "Informational Social Influence and Product Evaluation," *Journal of Applied Psychology,* 50, 54–59.

Darden, William R., and Reynolds, Fred D. (August, 1972), "Predicting Opinion Leadership for Men's Apparel Fashions," *Journal of Marketing Research,* 9, 324–28.

———— (February, 1974), "Backward Profiling of Male Innovators," *Journal of Marketing Research,* 11, 79–85.

Dolich, Ira J., and Shilling, Ned (January, 1971), "A Critical Evaluation of 'The Problem of Self-Concept in Store Image Studies,'" *Journal of Marketing,* 35, 71–73.

Donnelly, James H., Jr., and Ivancevich, John M. (August, 1974), "A Methodology for Identifying Innovator Characteristics of New Brand Purchasers," *Journal of Marketing Research,* 11, 331–34.

French, Warren A., and Flaschner, Alan B. (1971), "Levels of Actualization as Matched against Life Style Evaluation of Products," *Combined Proceedings,* American Marketing Association, 358–62.

Fry, Joseph N. (August, 1971), "Personality Variables and Cigarette Brand Choice," *Journal of Marketing Research,* 8, 298–304.

Gardner, David M. (1972), "An Exploratory Investigation of Achievement Motivation Effects on Consumer Behavior," *Proceedings,* Association for Consumer Research, 20–33.

Green, Paul E.; Maheshwari, Arun; and Rao, V. R. (1969), "Self Concept and Brand Preference: An Empirical Application of Multidimensional Scaling," *Journal of the Marketing Research Society,* 11, 343–60.

Greeno, Daniel W.; Sommers, Montrose S.; and Kernan, Jerome B. (February, 1973), "Personality and Implicit Behavior Patterns," *Journal of Marketing Research,* 10, 63–69.

Grubb, Edward L., and Stern, Bruce L. (August, 1971), "Self-Concept and Significant Other," *Journal of Marketing Research,* 8, 382–85.

Hawkins, Del I. (July, n1972), "Reported Cognitive Dissonance and Anxiety: Some Additional Findings," *Journal of Marketing,* 36, 63–66.

Horton, Raymond L. (August, 1974), "The Edwards Personal Preference Schedule and Consumer Personality Research," *Journal of Marketing Research,* 11, 333–37.

Hughes, G. David, and Guerrero, Jose L. (February, 1971), "Automobile Self-Congruity Models Reexamined," *Journal of Marketing Research,* 8, 125–27.

————; Juhasz, Joseph B.; and Contino, Bruno (October, 1973), "The Influence of Personality on the Bargaining Process," *Journal of Business,* The University of Chicago, 46, 593–603.

Hustad, Thomas P., and Pessemier, Edgar A. (1971a), "Industry's Use of Life Style Analysis: Segmenting Consumer Markets with Activity and Attitude Measures," *Combined Proceedings,* American Marketing Association, 296–301.

———— (1971b), "Segmenting Consumer Markets with Activity and Attitude Measures," unpublished working paper, Purdue University.

Jacoby, Jacob (1971), "Multiple-Indicant Approach for Studying New Product Adopters," *Journal of Applied Psychology,* 55, 384–88.

Joyce, Timothy (1972), "Personality Classification of Consumers," unpublished paper presented at 1972 Annual Meetings, American Psychological Association.

Kassarjian, Harold H. (November, 1971), "Personality and Consumer Behavior: A Review," *Journal of Marketing Research,* 8, 409–18.

———— (1973), "Field Theory in Consumer Behavior," in Scott Ward and Thomas S. Robertson, eds., *Consumer Behavior: Theoretical Sources,* Englewood Cliffs, N. J.: Prentice-Hall, Inc. 118–40.

Kegerreis, Robert J., and Engel, James F. (1969), "The Innovative Consumer: Characteristics of the Earliest Adopters of a New Automotive Service," *Proceedings,* American Marketing Association, 357–61.

King, Charles W., and Tigert, Douglas J., eds. (1971), *Attitude Research Reaches New Heights,* Chicago: American Marketing Association.

Kinnear, Thomas C.; Taylor, James R.; and Ahmed, Sadrudin A. (1972), "Socioeconomic and Personality Characteristics as They Relate to Ecologically Constructive Purchasing Behavior," *Proceedings,* Association for Consumer Research, 34–60.

————, (April, 1974), "Ecologically Concerned Consumers: Who Are They?," *Journal of Marketing, 38,* 20–24.

Landon, E. Laird, Jr. (1972), "A Sex-Role Explanation of Purchase Intention Differences of Consumers Who are High and Low in Need Achievement," *Proceedings,* Association for Consumer Research, 1–8.

———— (September, 1974), "Self Concept, Ideal Self Concept, and Consumer Purchase Intentions," *Journal of Consumer Research,* 1, 44–51.

Lewin, Kurt (1935), *A Dynamic Theory of Personality,* New York: McGraw-Hill, 43–65.

Martin, Warren S. (1973), *Personality and Product Symbolism,* Austin, Texas: Bureau of Business Research, Graduate School of Business, University of Texas.

Mason, Joseph Barry, and Mayer, Morris L. (April, 1970), "The Problem of The Self-Concept in Store Image Studies," *Journal of Marketing,* 34, 67–69.

Mathews, H. Lee; Slocum, John W. Jr.; and Woodside, Arch G. (1971), "Perceived Risk, Individual Differences, and Shopping Orientations," *Proceedings,* Association for Consumer Research, 299–306.

Michaels, Peter W. (1972), "Life Style and Magazine Exposure," *Combined Proceedings,* American Marketing Association, 324–31.

Michman, Ronald D. (1971), "Market Segmentation Strategies: Pitfalls and Potentials," *Combined Proceedings,* American Marketing Association, 322–26.

Morris, George P. and Cundiff, Edward W. (August, 1971), "Acceptance by Males of Feminine Products," *Journal of Marketing Research,* 8, 372–374.

Nakanishi, Massao (1972), "Personality and Consumer Behavior: Extentions," *Proceedings,* Association for Consumer Research, 61–65.

Nicely, Roy E. (1972), "E, I-O and CAD Correlations," unpublished working paper, Virginia Polytechnic Institute and State University, 1972.

Ostlund, Lyman E. (1969), "The Role of Product Perceptions in Innovative Behavior," *Proceedings,* Fall Conference, American Marketing Association, 259–66.

———— (1971), "The Interaction of Self Confidence Variables in the Context of Innovative Behavior," *Proceedings,* Association for Consumer Research, 351–57.

———— (April, 1972), "Identifying Early Buyers," *Journal of Advertising Research,* 12, 25–30.

Perry, Arnon (November, 1973), "Heredity, Personality Traits, Product Attitude and Product Consumption—An Exploratory Study," *Journal of Marketing Research,* 10, 376–79.

Peters, William H., and Ford, Neil M. (January, 1972), "A Profile of Urban Inhome Shoppers: The Other Half," *Journal of Marketing,* 36, 62–64.

Peterson, Robert A. (June, 1972), "Psychographics and Media Exposure," *Journal of Advertising Research,* 12, 17–20.

Plummer, Joseph T. (1971a), "Life Style and Advertising: Case Studies," *Combined Proceedings,* American Marketing Association, 290–95.

———— (April, 1971b), "Life Style Patterns and Commercial Bank Credit Card Usage," *Journal of Marketing,* 35, 35–41.

Reynolds, Fred D., and Darden, William R. (1972), "An Operational Construction of Life Style," *Proceedings,* Association for Consumer Research, 475–89.

Ross, Ivan (January, 1971), "Self Concept and Brand Preference," *The Journal of Business,* The University of Chicago, 44, 38–50.

Sparks, David L., and Tucker, W. T. (February, 1971), "A Multivariate Analysis of Personality and Product Use," *Journal of Marketing Research,* 8, 67–70.

Tigert, Douglas J. (1969), "Psychographics: A Test-Retest Reliability Analysis," *Proceedings,* Fall Conference, American Marketing Association, 310–15.

————, and Arnold, Stephen J. (1971), "Profiling Self-Designated Opinion Leaders and Self-Designated Innovators Through Life and Style Research," *Proceedings,* Association for Consumer Research, 425–45.

Tucker, William T. (1967), *Foundations of a Theory of Consumer Behavior,* New York: Holt, Rinehart and Winston, Inc.

Vavra, Terry G., and Winn, Paul R. (1971), "Fear Appeals in Advertising: An Investigation of the Influence of Order, Anxiety and Involvement," *Combined Proceedings,* American Marketing Association, 444–49.

Webster, Frederick E. Jr., and Von Pechmann, Frederick (April, 1970), "A Replication of the 'Shopping List' Study," *Journal of Marketing,* 34, 61–63.

Wells, William D. (1972), "Seven Questions About Lifestyle and Psychographics," *Combined Proceedings,* American Marketing Association, 462–65.

————, and Beard, Arthur D. (1973), "Personality and Consumer Behavior," in Scott Ward and Thomas S. Robertson, eds., *Consumer Behavior: Theoretical*

Sources, Englewood Cliffs, N. J.: Prentice-Hall, 141–99.

Wilson, David T.; Mathews, H. Lee; and Sweeney, Timothy W. (1971), "Industrial Buyer Segmentation: A Psychographic Approach," *Combined Proceedings,* American Marketing Association, 327–31.

Wind, Jerry (1971), "Life Style Analysis: A New Approach," *Combined Proceedings,* American Marketing Association, 302–5.

Winter, Edward, and Russell, John T. (1973), "Psychographics and Creativity," *Journal of Advertising,* 2, 32–35.

Wiseman, Frederick (April, 1971), "A Segmentation Analysis on Automobile Buyers During the New Model Year Transition Period," *Journal of Marketing,* 35, 42–49.

Worthing, Parker M.; Venkatesan, M; and Smith, Steve, "A Modified Approach to the Exploration of Personality and Product Use," *Combined Proceedings,* American Marketing Association, 363–67.

―――― (April, 1973), "Personality and Product Use Revisited: An Exploration with the Personality Research Form," *Journal of Applied Psychology,* 57, 179–83.

Ziff, Ruth (April, 1971), "Psychographics for Market Segmentation," *Journal of Advertising Research,* 11, 3–9.

―――― (1972), "Closing The Consumer-Advertising Gap Through Psychographics," *Combined Proceedings,* American Marketing Association, 457–61.

RISK- AND PERSONALITY-RELATED DIMENSIONS OF STORE CHOICE

**JOSEPH F. DASH,
LEON G. SCHIFFMAN,
AND
CONRAD BERENSON**

A review of the retail and general marketing literature suggests that most studies dealing with store choice have focused on store image, and that the majority of these studies compared competing department stores in terms of store attributes, such as price of merchandise, convenience of store location, and expertise of store personnel (Martineau, 1958; Arons, 1961; Rich, 1963; Rich and Portis, 1963; 1964). While store image research is of considerable merit, it does not generally answer such questions as: "What psychological factors account for store choice?" "Do different types of stores fulfill unique risk-related needs for consumers of a particular class of merchandise?" and "Why do some shoppers purchase from one type of retailer, while others purchase similar merchandise from another type of retail establishment?"

To examine these questions, the present research was designed to investigate how self-confidence, perceived product risk, and product importance—three risk-perception variables— affected store choice for two groups of shoppers: those who purchased audio equipment from a specialty store and those who purchased similar products from a department store. It was anticipated that the findings would add a new dimension to the work that has already been reported and synthesized on product choice decisions, thereby giving retailers and other marketers a richer understanding of shopping behavior (Engel, Kollat, and Blackwell, 1973; Hansen, 1972; Howard and Sheth, 1959).

BACKGROUND LITERATURE

This study of the interrelationship between risk-perception and store choice is an extension of the benchmark product and persuasive communication research reported in the 1960s (Cox, 1967), which was succeeded by a stream of empirical follow-up studies that have supported the contribution of risk-perception variables as predictors of product choice behavior (Bettman, 1973; Dean,

Source: Joseph F. Dash, Leon G. Schiffman, and Conrad Berenson, "Risk- and Personality-Related Dimensions of Store Choice," *Journal of Marketing,* Vol. 40, January, 1976, pp. 32–39.

Engel, and Talarzyk, 1972; Donnelly and Etzel, 1973; Ostlund, 1969; Popielarz, 1967; Woodside, 1972). The selection here of self-confidence (both generalized and product-specific), perceived product risk, and product importance is largely consistent with this consumer risk-taking research tradition (Barach, 1969; Taylor, 1974).

However, relatively little research has been published that directly ties the three risk-perception variables selected for examination with shopping or store choice behavior.

A RISK-PERCEPTION–STORE CHOICE PARADIGM

A simple paradigm (Figure 1) shows the three risk-perception variables as they were hypothesized to influence the store choice process. Starting with the broadest personality-type variable, generalized self-confidence, it was expected that an individual's evaluation of his abilities and his impression of how others feel about him would affect his store choice process. Specifically, the first hypothesis was that those

shoppers who purchased audio equipment from a specialty store would have more generalized self-confidence than those who purchased similar merchandise from a department store.

As a companion self-confidence variable, product-specific self-confidence was designed to measure the degree to which the two groups of shoppers judged that they could adequately evaluate the quality of audio equipment. It was anticipated that the specialty store's wider assortment of merchandise and exclusive emphasis on audio equipment would be attractive to those shoppers who are particularly confident of their ability to evaluate such an intensive variety of merchandise. Therefore, the second hypothesis was that those who purchased from the specialty store would possess more product-specific self-confidence than those who purchased from the department store.

The third risk-perception variable, perceived product risk, was designed to estimate the extent to which the two groups of shoppers were uncertain about their audio equipment purchases. The study adapted and used the basic perceived risk

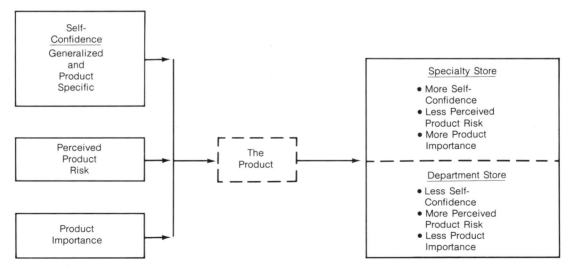

Figure 1 Risk-Perception–Store Choice Paradigm

measurement approach first suggested by Cunningham, which employed two risk components: *uncertainty,* "the probability that a given event will occur"; and *consequences,* "the cost to the consumer should the event occur." (Cunningham, 1967). It was expected that those shoppers who were attracted to a specialty store would perceive that there is less risk involved in an audio equipment purchase and would be better able to deal with the intensity of the merchandise assortment. On the other hand, it was felt that those who bought their audio equipment from a department store would view such a decision as more risky and would, therefore, find the smaller, potentially less confusing selection within the department store to be more appropriate. In keeping with this rationale, the third hypothesis examined was that specialty store customers would perceive less product risk than department store customers.

Finally, product importance was included because this variable has been used in a risk-perception context, and because it was expected to influence store choice behavior. It was anticipated that the specialty store's wider selection of merchandise would be particularly appealing to that type of customer who considered his interest in audio equipment to be important. Therefore, the fourth hypothesis was that specialty store customers would consider the product area to be more important than department store customers.

It is noteworthy that the three risk-perception variables are depicted in Figure 1 as passing through a broken-line box, entitled "The Product," rather than being linked directly to store choice. This intermediate step was included to suggest that the selection of the type of store from which a product is purchased depends on the consumer's perception of the product category. To account for the influence of the product category, the three risk-perception variables were operationally defined in terms of audio equipment rather than in terms of the type of store shopped (specialty store or department store). The operational definition of each of the variables is provided in Table 1.

METHOD

Participating Retail Chains

The assistance of two competing California retail chains, an audio equipment specialty retailer and a major department store, made this study possible. The specialty chain offers an extensive choice of major domestic and foreign brands of audio equipment in each of its locations. The specialty chain's concentration on audio equipment and its wide assortment is underscored by the exclusion of such traditionally related products as television sets. In contrast, in each of its locations the department store chain provides a limited line of audio equipment as part of its major appliance department. The clear-cut differences in breadth of audio equipment sold by these two types of retailers and the fact that each chain had stores located in the same competitive trading areas provided an appropriate "retail climate" for this study.

The Customer Sample

The study was conducted in the winter of 1972. The names and addresses of potential respondents were obtained from cash and credit sales records maintained by the two retail organizations. The final list of 772 customers (468 specialty store customers and 304 department store customers) was restricted to: (1) those who purchased during the most recent two-month period, thereby assuring a large enough sample of qualified customers and adequate respondent recall; and (2) those who purchased audio equipment that cost *no less* than $100, from among the following product categories—tuners, amplifiers, receivers, compacts, consoles, speakers, record players, changers, tape players, or earphones. This second condition insured that customers who merely purchased such low-dollar-valued items as needles and tape head cleaners would be excluded. Finally, as an inducement, an LP disc with a real retail value between $3 and $4 was sent to all respondents who participated in the study.

A total of 459 questionnaires were secured by

Table 1 Measurement of risk-perception variables

Variables	Measurement
Self-Confidence	
Generalized self-confidence[a]	Do you ever feel bothered about what other people think of you? (Choice: three-point scale ranging from "very often" to "almost never.")
	Excluding audio equipment, how do you feel about your abilities in general? (Choice: four-point scale ranging from "very confident" to "almost never confident.")
Product-specific self-confidence[b]	Just before your recent purchase of some audio equipment, how would you have rated your ability to judge the quality of audio equipment? (Choice: six-point scale anchored at the end points with "little ability" and "considerable ability.")
	Just before your recent purchase of some audio equipment, how confident were you in your ability to make a good choice when you recently purchased some audio equipment? (Choice: six-point scale anchored at the end points with "little confidence" and "considerable confidence.")
Perceived Product Risk[c]	
Uncertainty component	Purchasing any kind of audio equipment is, to many people, complicated by the many brands and conflicting performance claims stated by each manufacturer. Before your recent audio equipment purchase, how certain were you that your particular choice would prove to be satisfactory? (Choice: three-point scale ranging from "I was very certain" to "I was not certain.")
Consequence component	How serious would it be if the audio equipment you recently bought proved to give unsatisfactory performance? (Choice: three-point scale ranging from "It would be very serious" to "It would be annoying but not serious.")
Product Importance[d]	Compared to other things or subjects that interest you, how important to you is your audio equipment? (Choice: six-point scale anchored at the end points by "little importance" and "considerable importance.")

[a]The questions and scoring approach used to determine respondents' generalized self-confidence scores are a modification of those used by Scott M. Cunningham, "The Major Dimensions of Perceived Risk," in *Risk Taking and Information Handling in Consumer Behavior,* Donald F. Cox, ed., Boston: Grad. School of Business, Harvard University, 1967, p. 104.
[b]The questions and scoring approach used to determine respondents' product-specific self-confidence scores are a modification of those used by Cunningham, same reference as note (a) above, pp. 104–105; and Gerald D. Bell, "Self-Confidence, Persuasibility, and Cognitive Dissonance Among Automobile Buyers," in *Risk Taking and Information Handling in Consumer Behavior,* Donald F. Cox, ed., Boston: Grad. School of Business, Harvard University, 1967, p. 448.
[c]The questions and scoring approach used to measure the uncertainty and consequence components of perceived product risk are modifications of those first used by Cunningham, same reference as note (a) above, pp. 84–86.
[d]The question used to measure product importance is a modification of the one used by Schiffman, "Perceived Risk in New Product Trial by Elderly Consumers," *Journal of Marketing Research,* Vol. 9 (February 1972), p. 107.

an initial mail questionnaire or a follow-up WATS-line telephone interview designed to reach late respondents. Of this total, 25 questionnaires were excluded because of insufficient data or because a screening question established that the audio equipment purchase was a gift for someone other than the respondent or a member of his immediate household. As with purchases under $100, such gift purchases were disqualified because of the desire to maintain a uniform level of personal involvement and because it seemed unlikely that such respondents would be able to adequately answer a number of highly personal questions, such as the perceived product risk questions. The final data base consisted of 424 questionnaires (267 from specialty store shoppers and 157 from department store shoppers), a usable response rate of 55%.

FINDINGS

To determine if the specialty store shoppers and the department store shoppers differed significantly in terms of the four hypotheses set out above, the chi-square statistic was calculated. Following standard procedure, it was pre-established that if a particular chi-square value differed from chance at .05 or less, the hypothesized relationship would be accepted.

Shoppers' Self-Confidence

Table 2 presents the research findings relating the degree of generalized self-confidence and the type of store shopped. In support of the first hypothesis, the data indicate that the specialty store shoppers were significantly more self-confident than the department store shoppers. The second portion of Table 2, which examines the relationship between product-specific self-confidence and type of store shopped, supports the second hypothesis; that is, the specialty store shoppers were significantly more confident in their ability to cope with their planned audio equipment purchase than the department store shoppers.

In his study of automobile buyer behavior, Bell reported that "the higher one's generalized self-confidence the higher is his specific self-confidence" (Bell, 1967). A pooling of the two shopper groups permitted an examination of the interrelationship between these two types of self-confidence. The results of this analysis revealed a significant positive relationship between generalized and product-specific self-confidence, thereby supporting Bell's earlier findings.

Table 2 Store choice and self-confidence

Variables	Specialty Store	Department Store	Total
Level of generalized self-confidence			
Low	5%	12%	7%
Medium	40	43	42
High	55	45	51
Total	100%	100%	100%
Base	(260)	(158)	(418)
$\chi^2 = 7.0$; $p < .05$; 2 d.f.			
Level of product-specific self-confidence			
Low	14%	36%	23%
Medium	42	51	45
High	44	13	32
Total	100%	100%	100%
Base	(262)	(157)	(419)
$\chi^2 = 52.9$; $p < .001$; 2 d.f.			

Perceived Product Risk

Table 3 compares the specialty store respondents and the department store respondents in terms of the amount of risk they perceived to be inherent in the audio equipment purchase decision. Supporting the third hypothesis, the data reveal that members of the specialty store shopping group were significantly more likely than members of the department store group to perceive *less* risk in an audio equipment purchase decision.

A look at the data for the two underlying components of perceived risk (also presented in Table 3) reveals an interesting pattern. The results pertaining to the uncertainty component indicate that members of the specialty store group were "very certain" that their product choice would prove to be satisfactory, whereas members of the department store group were largely "not certain" that their product choice would prove to be satisfactory. This difference is in keeping with the specialty store shoppers' lower overall level of perceived risk.

Table 3 Store choice and perceived product risk

Variables	Specialty Store	Department Store	Total
Level of overall perceived risk:			
Low	23%	12%	19%
Medium	45	31	40
High	32	57	41
Total	100%	100%	100%
Base	(263)	(157)	(420)
$\chi^2 = 27.8$; p < .001; 2 d.f.			
Uncertainty component:			
Not certain	7%	43%	20%
Somewhat certain	45	39	43
Very certain	48	18	37
Total	100%	100%	100%
Base	(267)	(155)	(422)
$\chi^2 = 88.1$; p < .001; 2 d.f.			
Consequences component:			
Annoying but not serious	11%	10%	10%
Somewhat serious	27	37	31
Very serious	62	53	59
Total	100%	100%	100%
Base	(267)	(157)	(424)
$\chi^2 = 4.8$; p < .10; 2 d.f.			

The consequence component, on the other hand, "suggests" (this relationship is significant at p < .10) that the specialty store shoppers were more, rather than less, likely to consider an error in product selection to be "very serious." This finding implies that the specialty store shoppers' lower overall risk scores are largely a function of their greater perceived certainty, and that their high "seriousness" or consequence scores are distracting from their lower overall scores. It is also true that while the department store shoppers tended to perceive more risk (because of their

greater uncertainty), their lower perceived consequence scores reduced what might have been a higher overall level of perceived risk.

Again, by pooling the data for the two groups of shoppers, it was possible to examine the interrelationship between perceived product risk and generalized and product-specific self-confidence. This analysis indicated a significant inverse relationship between the level of perceived risk and the two self-confidence variables; that is, the greater a shopper's self-confidence (either generalized or product-specific), the less his perceived risk, and vice versa. These results confirm the Hisrich, et al. study of shopping-related risk, which also found perceived risk and the two self-confidence variables to function as reciprocals (Hisrich, et al., 1972).

Product Importance

Consistent with the fourth stated hypotheses, Table 4 shows that the specialty store customers considered audio equipment to be of greater personal importance than did their department store counterparts. That consumers would find expensive and infrequently purchased items like audio equipment to be important is not surprising. What is significant, however, is that the customers who purchased such merchandise in different types of

Table 4 Store choice and product importance

Variable	Specialty store	Department store	Total
Level of perceived product importance			
Low	3%	31%	14%
Medium	30	43	34
High	67	26	52
Total	100%	100%	100%
Base	(262)	(157)	(419)
$\chi^2 = 89.6$; p < .001; 2 d.f.			

retail outlets would differ on the degree of importance they attached to such products.

It is also noteworthy that the greater importance the specialty store shoppers attributed to their audio equipment is in keeping with the results for the other risk-perception variables, particularly the consequence component of perceived product risk. These results suggested that the specialty store customers would consider an error in the selection of audio equipment to be more serious than the department store shoppers would (Table 3).

SUMMARY

The basic store choice research design used in the present study provided an opportunity to compare two distinctly *different* shopping groups: those who purchased audio equipment from a specialty store and those who purchased from a department store. This design departs from previous studies, which have tended to examine store attributes of the "image mix" of competing department stores.

As hypothesized, the results showed that the specialty store customers were more self-confident (both generalized and product-specific), perceived less risk, and considered the product area to be of greater importance than did those who shopped for similar items in a department store.

An examination of the underlying uncertainty component of perceived product risk revealed that the specialty store shoppers were more certain than the department store shoppers that their product choice would prove satisfactory. However, the consequence component suggests that the specialty store shoppers considered an error in product selection to be more serious than did members of the department store group.

For the researcher, these results demonstrate the wisdom of examining the underlying dimensions of perceived risk rather than relying on the overall risk scores. For the retail executive, they suggest that while specialty store customers are

likely to be more certain about their capacity to make the correct decision, if this self-evaluation were proved to be incorrect by a defective or otherwise unsatisfactory product, they would consider such an outcome to be particularly serious. In contrast, department store customers, who were considerably more likely to be less certain about their ability to make a correct decision, were a little less likely to consider a decision that led to the purchase of a product that proved less than satisfactory to be "very serious." As discussed in the next section, these insights have relevance for establishing appropriate risk-reduction strategies.

The study also indicated that the two self-confidence variables are positively related and are reciprocals of perceived product risk. Therefore, if future research confirms these results, it might be advantageous to eliminate one of the two self-confidence variables (either generalized or product-specific) and/or use either self-confidence or perceived product risk.

STRATEGY IMPLICATIONS

For department store management, the higher level of perceived risk and the lower level of self-confidence experienced by their durable goods customers (as compared to customers of specialty stores) suggests that department stores should attempt to reduce uncertainty through in-store pre-purchase customer services and through promotional campaigns that emphasize the assistance that the store provides its customers. More specifically, department stores should attempt to reduce shoppers' perceived risk and build their self-confidence by giving major attention to the fact that their stores carry well-known major brands, as it is likely that department store customers are seeking a minimum of technical and potentially confusing information and embarrassing interchanges. Therefore, by carrying a limited line of easily recognized, well-respected brands, the department store is catering to the needs of this type of shopper.

In addition to concentrating on major brands, the department store should promote the availability of courteous product selection assistance, the financial convenience of its credit programs, free-trial, and/or money-back guarantees (Roselius, 1971). Also the availability of prompt and reliable service should be brought to the attention of potential customers. Most importantly, department stores should continuously emphasize "customer satisfaction" and their willingness to stand by their products.

In contrast, specialty stores should take advantage of the fact that they generally carry a much wider variety of audio equipment and accessory merchandise and that they employ a more expert sales force than would be found in competing department stores (or discounters). For the discerning person who is the most likely potential customer for the specialty store, the ability to choose from among a more complete offering of merchandise and the opportunity to discuss with a professionally trained sales force the nuances that may exist between various brands or models would seem to be two closely related benefits worthy of exploitation as part of such a store's promotional strategy.

The present research also indicated that the specialty store customer is likely to be more sensitive to any potentially negative consequences of his purchase decision, such as a poorly functioning piece of audio equipment. Therefore, it would seem desirable for such stores to emphasize a lenient exchange policy and their capacity to perform quick and effective repairs on even the most complex audio equipment. The specialty store should also consider the possible advantages of establishing and promoting a liberal trade-in policy—to draw into the store those consumers who are already active audio equipment enthusiasts and who may be ripe for more sophisticated equipment.

REFERENCES

Arndt, Johan (August, 1967), "Role of Product-Related Conversations in the Diffusion of a New Product," *Journal of Marketing Research,* 4, 291–95.

Arons, Leon (Fall, 1961), "Does Television Viewing Influence Store Image and Shopping Frequency?" *Journal of Retailing,* 37, 1–13.

Barach, Jeffrey A. (1969), "Self Confidence, Risk Handling, and Mass Communication," *Proceedings,* Fall Conference of the American Marketing Association, Chicago, 323–29.

Bell, Gerald D. (1967), "Self-Confidence, Persuasibility, and Cognitive Dissonance Among Automobile Buyers," in *Risk Taking and Information Handling in Consumer Behavior,* Donald F. Cox, ed., Boston: Graduate School of Business Administration, Harvard University. 452.

Bettman, James R. (May, 1973), "Perceived Risk and Its Components: A Model and Empirical Test," *Journal of Marketing Research,* 10, 184–90.

Cox, Donald F., ed. (1967), *Risk Taking and Information Handling in Consumer Behavior,* Boston: Graduate School of Business Administration, Harvard University.

Cunningham, Scott M. (1967), "The Major Dimensions of Perceived Risk," in *Risk Taking and Information Handling in Consumer Behavior,* Donald F. Cox, ed., Boston: Graduate School of Business Administration, Harvard University, 84–86.

Dean, Michael L.; Engel, James F.; and Talarzyk, W. Wayne (April, 1972), "The Influence of Package Copy Claims on Consumer Product Evaluation," *Journal of Marketing,* 36, 34–39.

Donnelly, James H., and Etzel, Michael J. (August, 1973), "Degree of Product Newness and Early Trial," *Journal of Marketing Research,* 10, 295–300.

Engel, James F.; Kollat David T.; and Blackwell, Roger D. (1973), *Consumer Behavior,* 2nd ed., New York: Holt, Rinehart and Winston.

Hanson, Flemming (1972), *Consumer Choice Behavior: A Cognitive Theory,* New York: The Free Press.

Hisrich, Robert D.; Dornoff, Ronald J.; and Kernan,

Jerome B. (November, 1972), ''Perceived Risk in Store Selection,'' *Journal of Marketing Research,* 7, 364–69.

Howard, John A., and Sheth, Jagdish, N. (1959), *The Theory of Buyer Behavior,* New York: John Wiley and Sons.

Martineau, Pierre (January-February, 1958), ''The Personality of the Retail Store,'' *Harvard Business Review,* 36, 47–55.

Ostlund, Lyman E. (1969), ''The Role of Product Perceptions in Innovative Behavior,'' *Proceedings,* Fall Conference of the American Marketing Association, Chicago, 259–66.

Popielarz, Donald T. (November, 1967), ''An Exploration of Perceived Risk and Willingness to Try New Products,'' *Journal of Marketing Research,* 4, 368–72.

Rich, Stuart U. (1963), *Shopping Behavior of Department Store Customers,* Boston: Graduate School of Business Administration, Harvard University.

———— and Portis, Bernard (March-April, 1963), ''Clues for Action from Shoppers Preferences,'' *Harvard Business Review,* 41, 132–49.

———— (April, 1964), ''The Imageries of Department Stores,'' *Journal of Marketing,* 28, 10–15.

Roselius, Ted (January, 1971), ''Consumer Ranking of Risk Reduction Methods,'' *Journal of Marketing,* 35, pp. 56–61.

Schiffman, Leon G. (February, 1972), ''Perceived Risk in New Product Trial by Elderly Consumers,'' *Journal of Marketing Research,* 9, 106–8.

Spencer, Homer E.; Engel, James F.; and Blackwell, Roger D. (August, 1970), ''Perceived Risk in Mail-Order and Retail Store Buying,'' *Journal of Marketing Research,* 7, 364–69.

Taylor, James W. (April, 1974), ''The Role of Risk in Consumer Behavior,'' *Journal of Marketing,* 38, 54–60.

Woodside, Arch G. (May, 1972), ''Informal Group Influence on Risk Taking,'' *Journal of Marketing Research,* 9, 223–25.

SECTION 11

LEARNING AND INFORMATION PROCESSING

Each section of this reader discusses a particular influence on consumer behavior. Yet unless some kind of information about a particular product or service reaches and is processed by the consumer, none of these influences can have an effect. Information processing is the sequence of mental activities that a person goes through in becoming aware of and either remembering or forgetting some information. The information which is processed may or may not correspond to the message which was intended. Thus, information processing is the end result of the communication process.

The information which is processed in a consumer setting can be of several types. Marketers provide some information through advertisements. Additional information can be found in a store on product labels. Some information may be obtained from friends or acquaintances who have tried the product. Other information is available in government pamphlets and consumer magazines. These latter sources may even encourage consumers to actively seek and compare information available from any of the above sources. Finally, legislation may be enacted which requires that certain information be available.

Yet all of this information must be processed in some way by consumers for it to affect the choices which they make. Before we can suggest that providing additional information will improve consumers' satisfaction with the choices they make, we must understand how and when information processing and learning occur. The three articles in this section provide a base for this understanding.

"ISSUES IN DESIGNING CONSUMER INFORMATION ENVIRONMENTS"

Very frequently references are made to the differences between the "ivory towers" of university scholars' research and the problems of "the real world." However, practitioners in many fields are finding that they can use the results of academic research to help them understand and solve actual problems. The Bettman article does exactly this—it shows how public policy could be formulated based on existing research.

In this article, Bettman does essentially two things: (1) he reviews research on human information processing by briefly discussing attention, memory, and processing of alternatives; and (2) he demonstrates how these research findings could be used to design a nutritional information program. It is not so important that the reader remember all of the details of the proposed trade regulation rule or exactly what alternative program is suggested by Bettman. Instead, the two main insights which can be gained by reading the article include (1) having an exposure to a brief, yet understandable and interesting review of information-processing research, and (2) seeing the process by which research results can be translated into suggested action with regard to a particular situation. In terms of its importance as a goal, learning about the specifics of the proposed trade regulation rule and Bettman's suggested alternative would be much less important. Thus, the key point is that existing research can be used to help policy makers understand *how* to give information about products to consumers.

Considerable attention is given in the article to the distinction between processing by brands and processing by attributes. The following chart may be useful in clarifying this distinction. Imagine for the product class toothpaste a chart containing twelve bits of information.

		Price	*Fluoride Content*	*ADA approval*
			Dimensions or attributes	
Alternatives or	Aim	1	2	3
brands of	Crest	4	5	6
toothpaste	Gleem	7	8	9
	Pepsodent	10	11	12

The numbers in the cells are merely tags for discussion purposes. In an actual information display, the cells would be filled in with the correct bits of information. Processing by brands involves looking at how the first brand rates on each dimension, and then proceeding with each remaining brand. (Thus, the processing sequence would be bits 1, 2, and 3, then bits 4, 5, and 6, . . .) Processing by attributes involves looking at how each brand rates on the first dimension, and then proceeding with each remaining attribute. (Thus, the processing sequence would be bits 1, 4, 7, and 10, then bits 2, 5, 8, and 11, . . .) Therefore, in processing by brands one goes row by row, and in processing by attributes one goes column by column.

Bettman introduces several concepts which are essential to understanding his evaluation of the proposed trade regulation rule. These are introduced so quickly in the review section that they can be easily missed. These concepts are listed here to help the reader make note of them when they are introduced. Concepts introduced include: attention, selectivity, intensity, enduring dispositions, momentary dispositions, short-term sensory storage, short-term memory, long-term memory, chunk, rehearsal, processing by attribute or dimension, and processing by brand or alternatives.

The particular case to which these information processing concepts are applied is nutritional information. However, they can be applied equally well in other contexts. It may be useful to consider how these same concepts could be applied to the design of an information environment concerning life insurance policies or the services and fees of different attorneys. In addition, these concepts can be used to redesign existing legislation concerning interest rate disclosures (Truth-in-Lending) and EPA gasoline mileage ratings on new automobiles.

"THREE LEARNING THEORY TRADITIONS AND THEIR APPLICATION IN MARKETING"

Even within a subarea of consumer behavior there are often several different approaches or theory traditions, each of which has its merits and its weaknesses. Learning is an area which is no different in this respect. The Ray and Webb article reviews three different learning theory traditions which are used in the study of consumer behavior.

The main purpose of the Ray and Webb article is not to decide which of these three is "best" or "most comprehensive." Instead, the point is to discuss in which situations each of them seems to occur. Thus, each of the traditions occurs in certain situations.

Much attention is given to the cognitive, affective, and conative or behavioral components of individual change. The cognitive component involves learning and mental perception of the object. The affective component includes positive or negative feelings about the object. The conative component involves action tendencies or behavioral intentions toward the object. Thus, in responding to microwave ovens, someone might have heard that the ovens were fast (cognitive), but feel afraid of the possibility of radiation (affective), and therefore not plan to purchase one (conative).

Three hierarchy-of-effects models are presented which correspond to the three learning theory traditions. These are hierarchy models because one stage occurs before the next one can begin. Thus, each of these models contains a different ordering of the three components. General indications are given about the types of situations in which one would expect to find each of the three hierarchies. It has been left to the reader to come up with specific situations in which these hierarchies could be expected to occur.

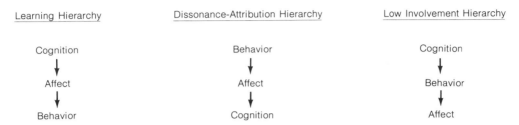

Learning Hierarchy	Dissonance-Attribution Hierarchy	Low Involvement Hierarchy
Cognition	Behavior	Cognition
↓	↓	↓
Affect	Affect	Behavior
↓	↓	↓
Behavior	Cognition	Affect

"CHILDREN'S SOCIAL LEARNING FROM TELEVISION ADVERTISING: RESEARCH EVIDENCE ON OBSERVATIONAL MODELING OF PRODUCT CONSUMPTION"

One of the current social problems which is widely and frequently discussed is the impact of television on children. The paper by Atkin uses some of the conceptual material on learning to examine how, what, and when children will learn from television advertising.

The first section of the paper highlights the concepts from learning theory which are used. In this section, Atkin describes Bandura's four stages or subprocesses of modeling. These are: (1) attention, (2) retention, (3) motoric reproduction, and (4) reinforcement and motivation. Most of the studies described in the second section of the article investigated the effect of some communication strategy (e.g., repetition or perceived source-recipient similarity) on one or more of these subprocesses.

There are several comments which should be made concerning the reported studies. Two kinds of studies are reported—experimental studies and survey investigations. In the experimental studies, children's actual responses to various kinds of advertisements are recorded in a laboratory situation. In the survey investigations, the children are asked to describe what their actual behavior is when they watch television at home. Although self-report measures are in many cases quite accurate, it is not clear if children in grades four through seven can accurately answer questions about how often they watch specific ads. This is not to say that the self-report measures are inaccurate; rather, these measures should be relied upon with caution. Differences in the two types of data collection rather than actual differences in the children's behavior may account for the differences in the findings of the experimental and survey studies of the impact of public service advertisements on inhibiting littering behavior by the children.

In attempting to translate the reported research findings into action implications, the reader should try to answer three questions. What recommendation would you make to a children's toy manufacturer with regard to future television advertising? What recommendations would you make to a legislative group establishing guidelines for advertising on Saturday morning children's programs if their goal is to ensure that children are not "tricked into wanting products?" What suggestions would you make to the producer of a children's public television program to ensure that the educational messages of the program reach the children and are remembered and used by them?

ISSUES IN DESIGNING CONSUMER INFORMATION ENVIRONMENTS

JAMES R. BETTMAN

Consumer research has shown a great deal of concern with public policy issues in the past few years (Wilkie and Gardner, 1974; Jacoby, Speller, and Kohn, 1974a, 1974b; Wilkie, 1974; Ross, 1974). One area of particular interest has been the design of information environments[1] for consumers (Jacoby, 1974; Wilkie, 1975), which provide the right information in the "right" manner so that consumers can make "better" decisions. The purpose of this paper is to discuss some major issues in this design process. The first major set of issues considered is the information processing demands which an information environment imposes on decision makers, relative to their processing capabilities and limitations. A second set, considered more briefly, concerns empirical evaluation of consumer information environments.

Because it is easier to discuss both sets of issues within the context of a particular example, we will consider the design of a system for presenting nutritional information in food advertising—the preliminary staff proposal of the Federal Trade Commission (FTC) for affirmative disclosure of nutrient information in food advertising (Federal Trade Commission, 1974). Although this proposal is clearly preliminary, is yet to be discussed in hearings, and could be varied substantially by the FTC, it is useful as a fairly concrete example of a consumer information environment. That is, the proposal, as outlined below, specifies the specific type of information to be presented to consumers, the amount of information to be disclosed, the mode of presentation, and so forth.

The next section briefly outlines this proposal. An overview of some research relevant to basic human information processing capabilities is then presented. The proposed system is evaluated

[1]The term "information environment" denotes the entire array of product-related data available to the consumer. Some important characteristics of information environments are type of information available, amount of information available, modes of presentation, and modes of organization of information.

Source: James R. Bettman, "Issues in Designing Consumer Information Environments," *Journal of Consumer Research,* Vol. 2, December, 1975, pp. 169–77.

using the research findings reviewed, and implications for the design of a system for provision of nutritional information are presented. Finally, the second set of issues on empirical evaluation of consumer information environments is discussed.

THE FEDERAL TRADE COMMISSION PROPOSAL

The FTC proposal is lengthy, so only a very brief summary of the most salient points is provided here. We will concentrate only upon the proposals for foods with nutrient labels. For more details concerning foods without nutrient labels see the proposed trade regulation rule and staff statement (Federal Trade Commission, 1974). The proposals outlined below are taken from the staff statement.

For television commercials for foods with nutrient labels, there are two cases: commercials whose length is 30 seconds or less and those whose length is greater than 30 seconds. For commercials less than 30 seconds in length, there are two main options. In the first option, the video portion of the commercial must present, for a minimum of six seconds, the names and percentage of the U.S. RDA (Recommended Dietary Allowance) for at least four of the following eight nutrients (protein, vitamin A, vitamin C, thiamine, riboflavin, niacin, calcium and iron) if they are present in a serving in an amount of 10 percent of the U.S. RDA or more. If there are less than four such nutrients, each must be presented. In addition, the number of calories per serving must be presented. If this option is taken and no nutrient is present in a serving at the 10 percent of U.S. RDA amount, a simultaneous audio and video statement of this fact must be made. The second option is to disclose the nutrition information required to appear on the nutrient label on the package for that food for a minimum of 15 seconds. Finally, for either option the audio portion of the commercial must state "Read the food label for more nutrition information" (Federal Trade Commission, 1974,

p. 39860). The proposals for commercials greater than 30 seconds in length follow the same pattern, with the time required for disclosure in the first option increased to 12 seconds. The other times and specifications are the same.

For print advertisements (with some exclusions), each nutrient and its percentage (including zero percent) of the U.S. RDA per serving as well as the calories per serving must be shown, or the nutrient information required on the food label must be shown. For radio advertisements, billboards, and some other display advertisements, the consumer is again directed to the food label.

RESEARCH ON HUMAN INFORMATION PROCESSING

The research cited below falls into three main categories: attention, memory functioning and parameters, and processing of alternatives. In each of these cases, only a brief sampling of research can be presented; a detailed review of each area is not attempted. Only that research thought to be most relevant to the FTC proposal is presented.

Attention
Attention as a cognitive phenomenon has become a central topic in experimental psychology within the last two decades. Attention has two major aspects: selectivity and intensity. Some stimuli are selected and singled out for processing, while others are ignored. Attention also refers to the intensity of the effort expended upon activities. Kahneman (1973) considers attention to be synonymous with a fixed capacity to perform mental work. He then considers issues relating to how this capacity is allocated in performing cognitive activities, particularly memory and processing. Norman (1969), in the context of models of memory, suggests that attention in memory tasks may be equated to rehearsal of material. Under both conceptions, therefore, memory functioning is intimately related to attention.

Kahneman (1973) discusses two major determinants of how attention is allocated: enduring dispositions and momentary intentions. Enduring dispositions refer to relatively involuntary rules of attention, and are perhaps best captured in Berlyne's (1960) notion of collative properties of stimuli: novelty, complexity, surprisingness. In general, attention is directed if there is a mismatch between stimuli and expectations.[2] Momentary intentions refer to voluntary and often goal directed factors: look for information about product X, listen for a particular commercial, and so on.

Memory Functioning and Parameters

Most current models of memory postulate a three part memory structure: a short-term sensory storage, where information enters through the sense organs and decays very rapidly; a short-term memory (STM), to which some subset of the sensory input is transferred; and a long-term memory (LTM) to which information is transferred from short-term memory (Greeno and Bjork, 1973). Transfer of material from short-term to long-term memory is thought to require rehearsal of the material in STM.

The famous paper by Miller (1956) first formulated the hypothesis of a limited size for STM. In specifying this limit, Miller also introduced the concept of a chunk of information, an organized and meaningful information structure. In effect a *chunk* is an organized cognitive structure that can grow as relevant information is integrated into it, a "configuration that is familiar to the subject and can be recognized by him" (Newell and Simon, 1972, pp. 780–1). The limit on the size of the STM store was found to be roughly seven chunks. The actual amount of material stored in STM could be increased by facilitating the formation of

larger chunks. Simon (1974) summarizes research on relative size of chunks for prose, nonsense syllables, words, digits, and chess pieces. McLean and Gregg (1967) also studied preferred chunk sizes in a rote learning experiment, and found subjects used chunks of three to four letters.

Attention is important in memory processes because it affects the rehearsal needed to transfer material from short-term to long-term memory. In fact, the effective size of STM seems to be reduced from its normal capacity of seven chunks to no more than two or three if a task requiring additional attention is undertaken at the same time as rehearsal (Newell and Simon, 1972; Waugh and Norman, 1965). The importance of attention to memory is accommodated by Kahneman's (1973) notion of attention as capacity. Allocation of capacity away from rehearsal to another task will effectively limit the number of items which can be rehearsed. If attention is devoted to processing a stimulus and it is rehearsed, research on memory speeds shows that from five to ten seconds are required to rehearse one chunk of information and fixate it in long-term memory (Newell and Simon, 1972, pp. 793–96; Simon, 1969, pp. 35–42; Bugleski, 1962). If material is not rehearsed in this way, it is lost from short-term memory and forgotten within roughly thirty seconds. The mechanism for loss from short-term memory is as yet unresolved; decay (Atkinson and Shiffrin, 1968) and displacement (Waugh and Norman, 1965) have both been supported.

One final set of findings relating to memory coding is relevant. A series of research studies examined whether encoding and memorization of properties of objects are easier if all the dimensional values of an object are presented (object coding), or if all the values for the set of objects under study on a particular dimension are presented at one time (dimension coding). Haber (1964) used a brief presentation (1/10 second) of cards portraying stimuli which varied along three dimensions. Some subjects were instructed to use an object coding method, while others were in-

---

[2]Research on involuntary rules of attention has often found a nonmonotonic relationship between collative properties and attention. That is, attention may be maximized by moderately complex stimuli, for example, and may be low for stimuli which are very simple or very complex (Kahneman, 1973).

structed to use dimension coding. Haber found that dimension coders were slower and less accurate in recalling unemphasized dimensions. Lappin (1967) used different stimuli, again with three dimensions, and did not instruct his subjects on coding schemes. Rather, he tested recall by objects and by dimensions. He found better recall for the three dimensions of each object than for the same dimension over three objects. Finally, Montague and Lappin (1966) found, in a replication of Haber's (1964) experiment, that object coding was faster than dimension coding. However, they did not find differences in accuracy, contrary to Haber's results.

Processing of Alternatives

A great deal of research has been directed to the study of how humans simplify the choice tasks facing them. Simon (1957) suggested that man is only "intendedly" rational, since his capacities are limited. He proposed that humans satisfice, or find an alternative that is good enough, rather than maximize. Since that time, several researchers have supported the notion that *choice* among alternatives is simplified if processing is organized by *attribute* or *dimension*.[3] That is, it is easier to *compare* alternatives on one attribute, then move to the next attribute, and so forth (this contrasts with the greater ease of *coding* and recall if processing is organized by alternative, as outlined above).

Tversky (1969) developed an additive difference model of choice between two alternatives which postulates within-attribute processing. In this model, the alternatives are compared directly on each dimension. The contribution of this comparison for each dimension to an overall evaluation is then summed for all dimensions. Payne

(1976) suggests how this model could be extended to the multi-alternative case. Tversky argues that intradimensional evaluations are easier than interdimensional ones, because the alternatives can be compared using the same units (since the same dimension is utilized). Tversky thus argues that evaluating each alternative one at a time and comparing these overall evaluations is more difficult than evaluating all alternatives on a dimension and eventually combining over dimensions, since processing by dimensions (attributes) requires only half as many interdimensional evaluations as processing by alternatives. Tversky (1969) also states that processing by dimensions can lead to dropping dimensions from the analysis if all alternatives are seen as equivalent for those dimensions. Finally, Tversky (1972) also proposed another model for processing by dimensions, the elimination by aspects model. In this model, dimensions are selected probabilistically (with probability of selection proportional to the weight attached to a dimension). Alternatives are examined for the selected dimension, and those without a satisfactory value on the dimension are eliminated. A new dimension is then selected and the process continues until a single alternative remains.

Some empirical work has examined whether subjects process by alternative or by dimension. Russo and Dosher (1975) report research in which subjects were asked to choose between two alternatives, each having three attributes. Subjects were found to process by attribute, first comparing alternatives within attributes and then combining over attributes. The study also showed that subjects had a difficult time using more than two dimensions. With two attributes, subjects need only evaluate the relative differences on the two attributes. For three or more, the tradeoffs become much more difficult. However, careful studies on individual differences are needed here to ascertain more precisely the numbers of attributes which can be handled. Some individuals may be able to handle complex displays with many attributes.

[3]The terminology in choice experiments varies greatly. In the psychological literature the terms object and dimension are often used, whereas in consumer research the terms brand and attribute are common. In this paper, for convenience the terms are used interchangeably, particularly dimension and attribute, although some researchers have argued that this is inappropriate (Wright, 1973).

Russo and Rosen (1975) examined choices among six used cars, each having three attributes. The alternatives were presented as verbal descriptions on a cathode ray tube, and subjects' sequences of eye movements were examined. The findings showed that subjects used paired comparisons to evaluate brands, thus breaking the task down to a pair-wise choice task. Their findings did not support the elimination procedure hypothesized in Tversky's (1972) elimination by aspects model.

Payne (1976) and Bettman and Jacoby (1975) examined directly how subjects acquire information. Thus there is evidence that a majority of subjects prefer to process by attributes. In summary, both on theoretical and empirical grounds, it can be argued that facilitation of processing by attributes can help to simplify choice processes.

AN INFORMATION PROCESSING ANALYSIS OF THE PROPOSAL

The analysis below for simplicity will be confined mainly to the case of a 30 second television commercial. The issues considered remain relevant for the other television commercial cases, although some details may change (For a related discussion, see Jacoby, 1974).[4]

The point of view of this author is that it is *crucial* for consumers to have access to nutritional information. The issue is *not* one of whether or not nutritional information should be presented. It *can* and *should be* presented. The issue is rather one of how to present the information most effectively so that consumers can process and use it, if they so desire. Thus, the remarks below about the specific FTC proposal *do not imply* that nutritional information should not be provided. They simply question the proposed mechanisms.

The information environment design embodied in the proposal implies that a consumer attends to the commercial, processes and remembers the information presented, and retrieves it later for use in the purchase situation. Repetitions and over-time effects of the commercial would presumably increase the consumer's ability to remember and use the information. There are other possible effects of the proposal than the learning of nutrient information. For example, there may be motivational effects, in that consumers may be more motivated to look for and use nutrient information in the store. Consumers might also examine nutrient information on products in their cupboards after seeing a commercial. That is, a proposal whose main purpose is to guarantee availability of information may serve to stimulate awareness as well.

As noted above, the consumer must attend to the commercial to take in the nutritional information and to store in memory the presented material. Under the present proposal, it is possible for the nutrient information to be displayed with no simultaneous related audio portion (unless there are no nutrients present at 10 percent of the U.S. RDA). This may not be sufficient to engage the consumer's attention: an audio portion may be necessary. An audio emphasis on nutritional information might be initially incongruous, given current food advertising, and attract attention. Otherwise, a preliminary appeal to nutritional needs and the importance of the ensuing nutrient information might be necessary to direct momentary intentions. The proposal as stated assumes consumers will attend (a variant of the pervasive rational man assumption); cognitive psychology holds that man has limited capacity and allocates it carefully. Attention (or allocation of capacity) must therefore be developed.

[4]For print advertisements, the task is easier on consumers, since length of exposure can be controlled, so the full amount of information might conceivably be assimilated. Alternately, the centralized in-store display or some portion of it could be presented in the ad. Although the print advertisement could provide a much better display from an information processing standpoint, it still seems worthwhile to limit the ad to a role of directing consumers to the in-store display. If the information is presented in the advertisement, then attention and memory are still involved, which could be inefficient. However, the information processing constraints on print advertisements are far less than those on television commercials.

The analysis of attention has been presented strictly from the point of view of a program where there are no external forces leading to increased consumer attention. This may be too restricted a view. There would undoubtedly be a great deal of television and newspaper publicity surrounding any nutrient information program which would increase attention and interest. Also, there presumably already exist segments which have a high degree of interest in nutritional information. Finally, over time some consumers may become more attentive to the information presented even if they do not attend to the first few commercials to which they are exposed. Thus, individual differences become an important aspect to be considered. For some consumers, attention may already exist; it may not always have to be developed. The relative size of this already attentive segment, an empirical research question, then becomes important in formulating designs for information provision. The larger this segment, the less the need to be concerned about strategies to develop attention.

The proposal makes severe demands upon consumers' memory mechanisms. Under the first option, nutrient information is available for six seconds for possibly five to nine pieces of information (at least four nutrients plus calories). Under the second option, as many as nine pieces of information would be shown for 15 seconds. The research on speeds of transfer from short-term to long-term memory reported above shows that such a presentation would probably overtax memory. That is, the time available would allow memorization of only one or two chunks at best, recalling that five to ten second times for fixation of one chunk are derived from verbal learning studies, with subjects motivated to perform well and paying careful attention. In addition, the distractions inherent if only the video portion were nutrient information could easily cause reductions in short-term memory capacity. As noted in the review above, anything which takes attention away from rehearsal effectively reduces short-term memory capacity. The assumption of full attention

to the commercial seems unlikely. Thus, it seems highly improbable that the consumer can take in and remember the information presented, because of limitations in processing ability. This does not include any possible negative effects of information overload on comprehension of the information (Jacoby, Speller, and Kohn, 1974a, 1974b; Wilkie, 1974; Russo, 1974).

The analysis above makes the presentation of nutrient information seem a formidable task indeed. However, there may be mitigating factors which must also be considered. Given that a chunk is an organized cognitive structure, there will be some range of individual differences in the initial content of these structures. Some consumers may have quite complex structures into which nutrient information could be assimilated fairly readily. Repeated exposure might also facilitate learning. The point is that there are several issues involved, including individual differences and over time effects, which are researchable.

The FTC is concerned not only with brand information but also that consumers be able to evaluate entire product classes relative to their personal nutritional standards. In fact, these product-product choices may be more important than brand selection. If consumers have learned acceptable level thresholds for various nutrients, it is possible that they could evaluate product classes under the FTC proposal. If so, then a satisfactory-not satisfactory judgment for a product class might be possible under the FTC proposal since commercials are seen for several brands within a class. However, this depends upon the existence of learned thresholds or acceptable level cutoff points, which consumers may or may not possess. The number of consumers who possess such thresholds could be determined through empirical research. If consumers wished to find products which meet a certain standard, at least 50 percent of the U.S. RDA for vitamin C, for example, then the nutrient information in a commercial could be fairly easily processed to "flag" products meeting this standard. Thus, the whole question of the goals motivating consumers' information processing is a crucial question for empirical research, as individual differences with respect to such goals would affect the evaluation criteria used for proposals for information provision.

The analysis just presented is for a single presentation. However, commercials can be repeated over time. Repetition of the commercials might increase the amount remembered. The significant question would be how repetition affects formation of chunks.

One might argue that the consumer need not remember the information presented, that most of it is, after all, available in the store on the package labels. The commercial can serve to make the consumer aware of nutrient information and lead him or her to examine it in the store. Storage of nutrient information and retrieval in the store are not required. This may be true; however, as discussed below, if all the commercial does is get the consumers to read labels in the store, then the information presented is not really used and a simpler disclosure could be used in the commercial, with the actual information presented in the store.

Ability of consumers to process the information presented in making brand comparisons is also important. The typical presentation of nutritional information under the proposed system, however ingenious it might be, would be by *brand*. Unfortunately, as argued above, it is cognitively easier for humans to make brand comparisons by *attribute*; that is, it is easier to compare the brands under consideration on one attribute, then move on to the next attribute, and so on (Russo, 1975; Tversky, 1969, 1972; Payne, 1976; Bettman and Jacoby, 1975). Processing by attributes directly provides comparative and relative information, and gives a context for judgment. Seeing figures for each brand in isolation means that memory must be utilized to provide the relative information. The context must be created from memory rather than being readily available. Note that this also argues for presenting several attributes at once rather than one attribute at a time. Again,

one might argue that comparisons are made in the store, not in one's head. If that is true, presenting the information in the commercial seems at best inefficient. It may also lead to a more focused search in the store, as a consumer would usually compare only a relatively small number of brands based upon his evaluation of them in memory. This limitation on processing effort is usually a necessary device; methods for expanding the range of alternatives which can be processed are discussed below.

Hidden in the above arguments is a conflict in processing systems. Memory coding, as discussed earlier, is easier if information is presented by brand (Haber, 1964; Lappin, 1967; Montague and Lappin, 1966). However, making brand comparisons is facilitated by presenting information by attribute. This incompatibility within the human information processing system has implications for the design of consumer information environments which we will now discuss.

IMPLICATIONS FOR DESIGN OF CONSUMER INFORMATION ENVIRONMENTS

The above analysis outlines properties of human information processing which imply that the proposed nutritional information program may present obstacles to learning of nutrient information by consumers. Obstacles could perhaps be eased by modifying aspects of the proposal. For example, a format might be developed which provided coded information on nutrients for a brand relative to *other brands* in that class, as well as relative to U.S. RDA requirements. The information relative to other brands would facilitate processing by attributes and brand comparisons. Information relative to the U.S. RDA is also necessary, because the FTC is concerned with the consumer's ability to evaluate a *product class* relative to reasonable nutritional standards, not only with ability to compare brands within a product class. Also, ingenious ways might be found to help consumers organize the nutrient information presented into larger chunks in memory. However, other system designs which more directly attack the issues raised might be more effective. A brief example of such a design is presented below; the issues raised by such a design are then discussed. The alternative design is not intended to be a specific proposal; rather, it is an example of a class of designs which would attempt to facilitate consumer processing. In this alternative design, the commercials *would not attempt* actually to present the nutritional information, due to the probability that consumers simply could not handle the input. Instead, the commercial would emphasize the benefits of nutritional information and direct consumers to an in-store display of this information. Thus, the commercial would direct consumers to a specific mechanism for examining nutrient information.

The core of the approach is the nature of the in-store display. The basic idea for the display was first outlined by Russo, Krieser, and Miyashita (1975) and expanded by Russo (1975). The display would be mounted on the store shelf and would present, for an *entire product class,* a listing of all brands and sizes with summary nutrient information for each brand. Two or three summary attributes would need to be used (if possible to develop) because of the limitations in consumers' ability to combine many attributes into an overall rating documented above (Russo and Rosen, 1975). It is important to understand *why* this system works so that the principles can be applied to other systems. The system appears to work because it handles most of the information processing constraints raised above. First, the system removes the memory demands from the limited time exposure commercial. The commercial provides only one simple directive input. Second, the system partially *decouples* the memory system from the processing system, hence removing a good deal of the memory-processing incongruity discussed above. Since the list is available in the store, there is no need to store a lot in memory. Third, the centralized display, perhaps arranged

with columns for each attribute, greatly facilitates processing by attribute.[5] Fourth, by building summary attributes the consumer is aided in chunking the information for processing. Fifth, the centralized list perhaps makes more brands available for processing, since search may not be guided by evaluations in memory to as great an extent. Also, processing is facilitated by the list, so that more alternatives can be examined without undue effort. Finally, such a list would also facilitate making evaluations of an entire product class relative to other product classes, by making it very clear how well all the brands in that class meet nutritional standards. Evaluation of a product class from such a list would be much easier than attempting to examine each brand individually so that a conclusion about the product class could be drawn.

This example, of course, raises many issues of costs and of implementation. Would store traffic patterns be disrupted by consumers attempting to read the lists? Would stores be responsible for developing the list, perhaps with an allowance from manufacturers for doing so? Would this hurt small grocery retailers, since costs of developing such lists would be higher for them, given less automated operations? How would local brands be handled? Could "summary" attributes ever be developed, given different consumer preferences and the substantial technological and nutritional problems involved? How would changes in brand formulations be handled? Would such a system work as effectively for product-product comparisons as for brand-brand comparisons?

The questions above emphasize the complex array of issues raised by the alternative design proposed. However, it is important to emphasize

---

[5]Processing by attribute can be done with the typical store display, certainly. However, the process of looking from one package to another becomes tedious, particularly for more than two alternatives. A standard revision strategy of comparing two alternatives at a time and retaining the best for the next comparison could also be used (Russo and Rosen, 1975), but this also seems like it would entail a great deal of effort.

at this point that it is *not* the purpose of this paper to give a definitive design. The important point is not the details of the specific proposal, but the *system* of considering information processing issues and attempting to develop designs which are congruent with those issues. Thus, the purpose of the example is to point out one alternative direction a design might take, given human processing limitations. Other alternatives should clearly be considered. The point of this paper is that alternatives should be considered and processing issues must be important criteria in evaluating designs.

The example outlined above presents some alternative directions for provision of information to consumers. As noted, implementation of such alternative directions in a detailed system raises many issues, some of which would need to be resolved empirically. Thus, research would presumably be undertaken before any such design would be adopted or implemented. Some major issues that arise in research intended to evaluate consumer information environments are briefly discussed below. Again, for the sake of clarity, the context is the nutritional information example used thus far.

EMPIRICAL EVALUATION OF CONSUMER INFORMATION ENVIRONMENTS

The two problems which are most significant in empirical evaluation of consumer information environments, and in fact upon the design of the information environments themselves, are choice of appropriate criterion variables and issues of sampling.

Attempting to evaluate empirically the effects of a particular proposal for a consumer information environment immediately raises the difficult problem of an appropriate criterion for evaluation. The basic issue is whether the intent of an information environment is "processing" or "policy" norma-

tive.[6] A system is said to be "processing" normative if it is intended only that consumers should be aided in perceiving and processing the appropriate information, but there is no commitment to how or even if consumers use such information. Usage is a subjective individual consumer decision, and the system does not try to direct that decision other than by providing information in a fashion facilitating processing. A system is "policy" normative if the intent, based upon some notions of rational behavior, is that information be used in a particular manner, if there is a policy or goal of "educating" the consumer to make "better" purchase decisions. The policy maker desires a specific outcome or set of outcomes in the "policy" normative case; in the "processing" normative system the policy maker desires only that information can be handled relatively easily. Outcomes are left to consumer preferences. Consumer research as a discipline has not yet effectively dealt with such normative issues. The basic question is the extent of consumer sovereignty, whether consumers should ultimately decide or whether policies should attempt to direct consumers in specific ways.

The appropriate criteria for evaluating system effectiveness differ greatly, depending upon the normative intent. For a "processing" normative system of nutritional information provision, for example, an appropriate criterion measure seems to be simply how readily the consumer can determine which products are more nutritious. Whether or not the consumer chooses the more nutritious products is of no concern in a processing normative system, so recall and knowledge become important criteria.[7]

---

[6]This distinction is a difficult one; both orientations could be seen as types of policy. Perhaps a continuum, rather than a dichotomy, is appropriate.

[7]Jacoby, Speller, and Kohn (1974a, 1974b) attempted to devise a more complex measure of subjective satisfaction based on ideas from multiple attribute attitude models. However, this approach probably raised more questions than it answered (Wilkie, 1974; Russo, 1974). The arguments above imply that the complexity of this criterion is

For a "policy" normative system, it is necessary that consumers be persuaded that the information presented is important for making choices and should be used. Criteria would then be, for a nutritional program, whether consumers felt an increased need to incorporate nutritional information into their decisions, whether nutritional foods were in fact purchased more under such a system, and so on. Attitudes and behavior become much more important, rather than the relatively cognitive measures (such as awareness, recall, and knowledge) for a "processing" normative system.

A second crucial issue in evaluating information environments is sampling. For controversial proposals, where court action is likely, samples should be representative of the total population. Legal and research orientations may conflict over what constitutes an acceptable sample. However, in addition, there is an obligation to study special populations as well, particularly if the system is to be "policy" normative. For nutritional information, this would entail ensuring that adequate

samples of those groups suffering to the greatest extent from poor nutrition are included: the poor, the elderly, families with many children, and so forth. This will make sampling more difficult, but the groups especially at risk must be examined carefully. The specific locus of the system's influence must be considered, as well as its total extent. A system might be evaluated poorly if none of the groups at special risk were affected, even if other groups were.

The information processing and evaluation issues above are presented as examples of concerns which need to be addressed in designing and judging proposals for consumer information environments. The purpose has been to raise as many issues as possible, and to urge that these issues be considered in the design process. It has become clear in the course of this effort that special attention must be paid to the broad issues of multiple system goals, individual differences in consumers, and over time effects, as well as to the specific information processing and evaluation concerns considered. It is hoped that exposure of these issues will stimulate research and thinking needed for resolution of the important policy and implementation questions that will arise.

---

unnecessary in a truly "processing" normative system, and it does not capture the essence of a "policy" normative approach.

REFERENCES

Atkinson, R. C., and Shiffrin, Richard M. (1968), "Human Memory: A Proposed System and Its Control Processes," in K. W. Spence and J. T. Spence, eds., *The Psychology of Learning and Motivation,* New York: Academic Press, 89–195.

Berlyne, D. E. (1960), *Conflict, Arousal, and Curiosity,* New York: McGraw-Hill.

Bettman, James R., and Jacoby, Jacob (1975), "Patterns of Processing in Consumer Information Acquisition," in B. B. Anderson, ed., *Advances in Consumer Research,* Vol. III, Association for Consumer Research.

Bugelski, B. R. (1962), "Presentation Time, Total Time, and Mediation of Paired-Assoccate Learning," *Journal of Experimental Psychology,* 63, 409–12.

Federal Trade Commission (November 11, 1974), "Food Advertising: Proposed Trade Regulation Rule and Staff Statement," *Federal Register,* 39, 39842–62.

Greeno, James G., and Bjork, Robert A. (1973), "Mathematical Learning Theory and the New 'Mental Forestry'," *Annual Review of Psychology,* 24, 81–116.

Haber, Ralph N. (November, 1964), "Effects of Coding Strategy on Perceptual Memory," *Journal of Experimental Psychology,* 68, 357–62.

Jacoby, Jacob, (1974), "Consumer Reaction to Information Displays: Packaging and Advertising," in Salvatore F. Divita, ed., *Advertising and Public Interest,* Chicago: American Marketing Association, 101–18.

————; Speller, Donald E.; and Kohn, Carol A. (February, 1974a), "Brand Choice Behavior as a Function of Information Load," *Journal of Marketing Research,* 11, 63–69.

————(1974b) "Brand Choice Behavior as a Function of Information Load: Replication and Extension," *Journal of Consumer Research,* 1, 33–42.

Kahneman, Daniel (1973), *Attention and Effort,* Englewood Cliffs, N.J.: Prentice-Hall.

Lappin, Joseph S. (November, 1967), "Attention in the Identification of Stimuli in Complex Visual Dsiplays," *Journal of Experimental Psychology,* 75, 231–28.

McLean, R. S. and Gregg, L. W. (August, 1967), "Effects of Induced Chunking on Temporal Aspects of Serial Recitation," *Journal of Experimental Psychology,* 74, 455–59.

Miller, George A. (1956), "The Magical Number Seven, Plus or Minus Two: Some Limits on Our Capacity for Processing Information," *Psychological Review,* 63, 81–97.

Montague, William S., and Lappin, Joseph S. (November, 1966), "Effects of Coding Strategy on Perceptual Memory," *Journal of Experimental Psychology,* 72, 777–79.

Newell, Allen, and Simon, Herbert A. (1972), *Human Problem Solving,* Englewood Clifs, N.J.: Prentice-Hall.

Norman, Donald A. (1969), *Memory and Attention: An Introduction to Human Information Processing,* New York: John Wiley and Sons.

Payne, John W. (1976), "Task Complexity and Contingent Processing in Decision Making: An Information Search and Protocol Analysis," *Organizational Behavior and Human Performance,* forthcoming.

Ross, Ivan (1974), "Applications of Consumer Information to Public Policy Decisions," in Jagdish N. Sheth and Peter L. Wright, eds., *Marketing Analysis for Societal Problems,* Urbana, Ill.: University of Illinois.

Russo, J. Edward (1975), "An Information Processing Analysis of Point-of-Purchase Decisions," *Proceedings,* Fall Conference of the American Marketing Association.

————(December, 1974), "More Information is Better: A Reevaluation of Jacoby, Speller, and Kohn," *Journal of Consumer Research,* 1, 68–72.

————, and Dosher, Barbara A. (1975), "Dimensional Evaluation: A Heuristic for Binary Choice," Unpublished working paper, University of California, San Diego.

————; Krieser, Gene; and Miyashita, Sally (April, 1975), "An Effective Display of Unit Price Information," *Journal of Marketing,* 39, 11–19.

————, and Rosen, Larry, D. (May, 1975), "An Eye Fixation Analysis of Multi-Alternative Choice," *Memory and Cognition,* 3, 267–76.

Simon, Herbert A. (1957), *Models of Man,* New York: John Wiley and Sons.

————(1969), *The Sciences of the Artificial,* Cambridge, Mass.: MIT Press.

————(February 8, 1974), "How Big is a Chunk?" *Science,* 183, 482–88.

Tversky, Amos (July, 1972), "Elimination by Aspects: A Theory of Choice," *Psychological Review,* 79, 281–99.

————(January, 1969), "Intransitivity of Preferences," *Psychological Review,* 76, 31–48.

Waugh, Nancy C., and Norman, Donald A. (1965), "Primary Memory," *Psychological Review,* 72, 89–104.

Wilkie, Willaim L. (November, 1974), "Analysis of Effects of Information Load," *Journal of Marketing Research,* 11, 462–66.

————(1975), *Assessment of Consumer Information Processing Research in Relation to Public Policy Needs,* Washington, D.C.: United States Government Printing Office, in press.

————, and Gardner, David M. (January, 1974), "The Role of Marketing Research in Public Policy Decision Making," *Journal of Marketing,* 38, 38–47.

Wright, Peter L. (1973), "A Common Vocabulary for Research on Cognitive Structure," Working Paper 93, College of Commerce and Business Administration, University of Illinois at Urbana-Champaign.

THREE LEARNING THEORY TRADITIONS AND THEIR APPLICATION IN MARKETING

MICHAEL L. RAY
AND
PETER H. WEBB

Source: Michael L. Ray and Peter H. Webb, "Three Learning Theory Traditions and Their Application in Marketing," *1974 Combined Proceedings,* American Marketing Association, Ronald C. Curhan, ed., pp. 100–103.

Learning has a bad name in marketing and consumer research. Researchers who see themselves as avant-garde consider learning theory to be mechanistic, simple-minded and old-fashioned. Sessions related to learning theory are carefully titled "learning processes." The key words today are cognition, attribution, perceptual mapping, decision nets, information processing and attitude (although even that is getting a bit old hat). What place does learning, particularly learning theory, have in this picture?

Our argument here is that learning research and learning theory are basic to all research and theoretical speculation in consumer behavior. Every one of the "in" words mentioned above grew out of work in learning theory. Like the Frenchman who learned he was speaking prose all his life, consumer and marketing researchers are constantly using learning research and theory ideas without knowing it. One purpose of this paper is to sharpen their awareness of where and how learning theory comes into consumer research—and how they might better use it when it does.

Our basic notion here is that there are three traditions of learning theory. Each of these traditions has a contribution to make to marketing and consumer research. Each is most appropriate in certain consumer situations. By knowing the potential contribution and appropriate marketing situations for each theoretical tradition, managers and researchers can draw on an extensive body of literature and develop new ideas for dealing with marketing problems.

The three traditions are the contiguity-connectionist, reinforcement, and cognitive-perceptual. Each is first described briefly, so that their actual and potential contributions can be seen. Then one thorough application of the three traditions—to the marketing communication hierarchy of effects controversy—is described. Finally, some of our own data is presented to demonstrate the operation of the traditions in the hierarchy area.

THE CONTIGUITY-CONNECTIONIST TRADITION

The first of three traditions is also the simplest: the contiguity-connectionist one. The roots of this tradition come from the Russian physiologist Pavlov (who first demonstrated classical conditioning), British associationism, and the American "father of behaviorism," Watson, a popularizer who spent the later part of his career with the J. Walter Thompson Advertising Agency.

The most important idea in contiguity-connectionist theory is that of contiguity itself. The idea that all that is necessary for learning to take place is repeated contiguity of stimulus and response.

The American psychologist Guthrie (1952) expressed the contiguity idea in this way: "A combination of stimuli which has accompanied a movement will on its recurrence tend to be followed by that movement." And although he said that in 1952, Guthrie's statement will remind many consumer researchers of Zajonc's idea of the "effects of mere exposure" (1968), of many of the postulates of attribution (Kelley, 1967) and self-perception (Bem, 1972) theories, and of the heavy value placed on information without reinforcement in many consumer information processing theories (Hughes and Ray, 1974).

The key aspect of the contiguity-connectionist position is that there is no need for reinforcement, that connections are formed on the basis of repeated contiguity. In fact, in Guthrie's theory there isn't even the need for repetition. His is an all-or-none learning idea. Repetition has effect only in terms of an increasingly changed stimulus field.

In addition to the applications mentioned above, marketing research is indebted to the contiguity position in terms of mathematical learning theory, which has been heavily applied to studies of brand loyalty, new product introduction models, and brand switching. Despite the fact that learning theory is seen as deterministic, the mathematical learning theories which come from the contiguity-connectionist position are at the heart of stochastic models of consumer behavior, which are hardly deterministic.

THE REINFORCEMENT TRADITION

Now if we switch to the second tradition, we find something quite different from simple rote learning. This second tradition centers on reinforcement. Its roots are from the psychologist Thorndike and his "law of effect," Skinner and his schedules of reinforcement which have led to suggestions for the design of cultures, and, most importantly for the present discussion, the Hull-Spence hypothetic-deductive approach to learning theory.

Hull attempted to develop a full-blown theoretical system complete with postulates and theorems stated in algebraic terms (Hull, 1943; 1952; 1940). Because he was so precise, he also opened himself to much criticism. Little of his theory is used today in learning research, but the basic structure of his system, as shown in Figure 1, will be quite familiar to consumer researchers.

Basically, the reinforcement tradition has evolved to the idea that there are four basic determinants of a tendency to respond: habit, past magnitude of reward, drive, and stimulus intensity. Explanation of learning has to do with determining the importance and combination of these intervening variables.

Consumer researchers should recognize these four components in terms of the levels of the typical hierarchy-of-effects concept, the cognitive-affective-conative parts of attitude structure, or even the components of utility theory.

Reinforcement theorists have been so flexible in their attempts at completeness that they have subsumed many of the concepts of the other two theoretical streams. It is because of this flexibility that this type of learning theory has been the basis of more deterministic attempts to describe consumer behavior (e.g., Amstutz, 1967; Howard, 1965; Howard and Sheth, 1969).

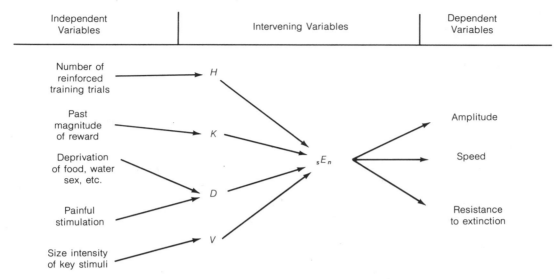

Figure 1   A Schematic Representation of Hull's Basic System

THE COGNITIVE-PERCEPTUAL TRADITION

The third tradition is one that has always challenged the other two—to the point that many people forget that it is a learning theory tradition. This is the cognitive-perceptual tradition. It is based on ideas from the perceptual, view-of-the-world, insight-based Gestalt psychology and Lewin's field theory. It became more relevant to learning with the neo-Gestalt "new look" psychology of the 50s (Bruner, 1951; Postman, 1951).

But perhaps the earliest and best example of cognitive learning theories is Tolman's "purposive behaviorism" (Tolman, 1932). Tolman was concerned with the molar purposes of the individual as he saw them. The view-of-the-world was and is important in cognitive theories. The more modern versions are dissonance (Festinger, 1957; 1964), attribution (Kelley, 1967) and self-perception theories (Bem, 1972). Because much of consumer behavior is meaningful and has purpose, these cognitive theories have been quite important.

The cognitive learning terms and ideas permeate consumer research. Tolman's term "cognitive map" is only a short jump away from "perceptual map." His "sign-gestalt-expectation" term was abbreviated to 'sign-expectancy'' in an interesting discussion by Myers and Reynolds (Kelley, 1967) of product, price and brand perception studies in consumer behavior. Emphasis in consumer behavior has shifted from cognitive learning (similar to rote learning of the connectionist tradition) (e.g., Greenwald, 1968; Leavitt, 1968; Wright, 1974).

AN APPLICATION EXAMPLE: MARKETING COMMUNICATION HIERARCHIES

To summarize thus far, it might be said that there are three learning traditions: one emphasizing simple connections, another complex reinforcement structures, and a third the individual's cognitive view-of-the-world. Each has a particular place in marketing. For instance, when we consider brand choice, it is clear that the connectionist thinking is at the base of stochastic brand loyalty studies of strings of purchases from consumer panels. Reinforcement structures are behind the more complex idea of brand attitude. And cognitive thinking is supportive of brand perception research.

In the brand choice area, as in others, the real value of the learning traditions is when they can be brought together. This is being done in the brand area where brand loyalty studies are being used to determine segments, and brand attitude and perception research provides suggestions for strategies against those segments.

A more detailed example we would like to offer here has to do with the hierarchy-of-effects controversy, which is all too familiar in advertising and marketing communication. Stated simply, the controversy is over the order of certain mental states as affected by a communication campaign. Does learning precede attitude which precedes behavior in stair-step fashion? Or is there some other pattern? The answers to such questions are quite crucial, because of the need to set communications objectives that will be meaningful in terms of planning and control.

The learning theories' answer to these key questions is quite valuable. The answer is that there are three different hierarchy relations in different situations. These situations are clearly definable because of what we know from learning research. And the hierarchy analysis provides quite clear suggestions for planning.

The three different hierarchy relations seem to be as follows:

(1) *The Learning Hierarchy.* This is the standard hierarchy offered in marketing in which cognition (learning) is said to precede affect which then leads to conation (behavior or intention). This comes most directly from the *reinforcement tradition* in which, as in Hull, clear relationships are posited between intervening variables.

(2) *The Dissonance-Attribution Hierarchy.* This is exactly the reverse of the learning hierarchy. Here a behavior is made first, then this

leads to attitude change which affects future cognitive change through selective mechanisms. This can be recognized as the post-purchase pattern of response predicted by dissonance theory. Again, this hierarchy appears to be supported by the *cognitive tradition* in learning theory.

(3) *The Low Involvement Hierarchy.* First proposed by Krugman (1965) to explain the effects of television advertising, this hierarchy assumes minimum cognitive shifts after repetition and low perceptual defense. Once these simple connections are made, behavior can occur given the appropriate circumstances. And, on the basis of experience, attitude or affect might change. This cognitive-conative-affect chain is straight *connectionist tradition,* because the first link is made on the basis of simple contiguity.

Now that these hierarchies have been identified, when and where are they most likely to occur? Again, the learning theory traditions lead toward an answer, which is supported by extensive consumer analysis.

The Standard Learning Hierarchy (Reinforcement Tradition) seems to occur when buyers are involved, alternative products are clearly differentiated, mass media promotion is important and the product is in the early stages of the product life cycle.

The Dissonance-Attribution Hierarchy (Cognitive Tradition)—with purchasing action first—seems to occur when buyers are involved, products are similar, personal selling is more important and the product is in the early maturity stage of its life cycle.

The Low Involvement Hierarchy is most likely to occur when involvement is low, products are seen as similar, broadcast media are important, and the product is in late maturity.

SOME RESEARCH RESULTS

The hierarchy notions have been tested in a series of laboratory studies of repetition effect which are reported in detail elsewhere (Ray, 1973; 1974). A few of the findings will be presented here to demonstrate how learning theory predictions can be shown in the laboratory.

The predictions for the laboratory repetition results follow quite directly from the hierarchies. For the Learning Hierarchy, learning responses should be affected most by repetition, then attitude measures and least affected would be behavioral measures. For the Dissonance-Attribution Hierarchy, the order of repetition effect would be roughly the opposite of the Learning Hierarchy one. And for the Low Involvement Hierarchy, learning measures should be affected most, followed by the effect on behavioral measures. Attitudinal response should be late in coming.

The last or Low Involvement Hierarchy has been most often found in the ten laboratory repetition studies. An example from a study by Sawyer (1971) is shown in Figure 2. As can be seen, the Low Involvement Hierarchy is demonstrated with a significant effect ($p < .001$) on the learning-recall measure and the two conative measures of purchase intention ($p < .05$) and coupon return ($p < .10$), while there was no significant effect on attitude.

In some of the studies both the Learning and Low Involvement Hierarchies are found. An example is shown in Figure 3 with results from a study of political advertising effect by Rothschild (Ray, 1974). Here something like the Learning Hierarchy was demonstrated for the high involvement Presidential race. Steadily decreasing repetition results are demonstrated across recall, connections (an attitude measure) and voting intention. For the lower involvement State Assembly race, however, the Low Involvement Hierarchy was demonstrated.

These results are typical. It should be noted that the Dissonance-Attribution Hierarchy is seldom

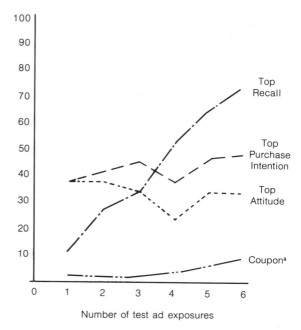

[a]120 observations per exposure condition
Source: (Sawyer, 1971, p. 165).

Figure 2 Effects of Repetition on Comparative Measures

found. This is less due to the quality of the theoretical tradition than it is to the lack of appropriate laboratory manipulation.

CONCLUSION

The three learning theory traditions are much more relevant than is typically realized. With proper analysis they can be applied to marketing problems. With proper method they can be demonstrated empirically.

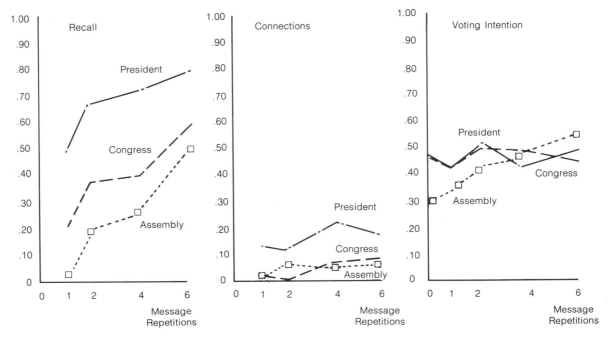

Source: (Ray, 1974). N per message repetitions—exposure condition ranged from 25–31.

Figure 3   Hierarchy Effects Across Various Political Contests

REFERENCES

Amstuz, A. E. (1967), *Computer Simulation of Competitive Market Response,* Cambridge, Mass: MIT Press.

Bem, D. J. (1972), "Self-Perception Theory," in L. Berkowitz, ed., *Advances in Experimental Social Psychology;* Vol. 6, New York: Academic Press, 2–62.

Bruner, J. S. (1951), "Personality Dynamics and the Process of Perceiving," in R. S. Blake and G. V. Ramsey, eds., *Perception, An Approach to Personality,* New York: Ronald Press, 121–49.

Festinger, L. (1957), *A Theory of Cognitive Dissonance,* Evanston, Ill.: Row-Peterson.

———— (1964), "Behavioral Support for Opinion Change," *Public Opinion Quarterly,* 28, 404–17.

Greenwald, A. G. (1968), "Cognitive Learning, Cognitive Response to Persuasion, and Attitude Change," in A. G. Greenwald, T. C. Brock, and T. M. Ostrom,

eds., *Psychological Foundations of Attitudes,* New York: Academic Press, 147–70.

Guthrie, E. R. (1952), *The Psychology of Learning,* rev. ed., New York: Harper & Row.

Howard, J. A. (1965), *Marketing Theory,* Boston: Allyn and Bacon.

————, and Sheth, Jagdish N. (1969), *The Theory of Buyer Behavior,* New York: John Wiley.

Hughes, G. D., and Ray, M. L., eds. (1974), *Buyer-Consumer Information Processing,* Chapel Hill, N.C.: University of North Carolina Press.

Hull, C. L. (1943), *Principles of Behavior,* New York: Appleton-Century-Crofts.

———— (1952), *A Behavior System: An Introduction to Behavior Theory Concerning the Individual Organism,* New Haven, Conn.: Yale University Press.

————, et al. (1940), *Mathematico-Deductive Theory*

of Rote Learning, New Haven, Conn.: Yale University Press.

Kelley, H. H. (1967), "Attribution Theory in Social Psychology," in D. Levine, ed., *Nebraska Symposium on Motivation,* Vol. 15, Lincoln, Neb.: University of Nebraska Press.

Krugman, H. E. (1965), "The Impact of Television Advertising: Learning without Involvement," *Public Opinion Quarterly,* 29, 349–56.

Leavitt, C. (September, 1968), "Response Structure: A Determinant of Recall," *Journal of Advertising Research,* 8, 3–8.

Postman, L. (1951), "Toward a General Theory of Cognition," in J. H. Rohrer and M. Sherif, eds., *Psychology at the Crossroads,* New York: Harper & Row, 242–72.

Ray, M. L. (1973), "Psychological Theories and Interpretations of Learning," in S. Ward and T. S. Robertson, eds., *Consumer Behavior: Theoretical Sourcebook,* Englewood Cliffs, N. J.: Prentice-Hall.

——— (1974), "Marketing Communication and the Hierarchy of Effects," in P. Clarke, ed., *New Models of Communication,* Beverly Hills, Calif.: Sage.

Sawyer, A. G. (1971), "A Laboratory Experimental Investigation of the Effects of Repetition of Advertising," unpublished doctoral dissertation, Stanford University.

Tolman, E. C. (1932), *Purposive Behavior in Animals and Men,* New York: Appleton-Century-Crofts.

Wright, P. L. (1974), "On the Direct Monitoring of Cognitive Response to Advertising," in G. D. Hughes and M. L. Ray, eds., *Buyer-Consumer Information Processing,* Chapel Hill, N. C.: University of North Carolina Press.

Zajonc, R. B. (1968), "Attitudinal Effects of Mere Exposure," *Journal of Personality and Social Psychology,* monograph supplement, 9.

CHILDREN'S SOCIAL LEARNING FROM TELEVISION ADVERTISING: RESEARCH EVIDENCE ON OBSERVATIONAL MODELING OF PRODUCT CONSUMPTION

CHARLES K. ATKIN

Source: Charles K. Atkin, "Children's Social Learning from Television Advertising: Research Evidence on Observational Modeling of Product Consumption," in Beverlee B. Anderson, ed., *Advances in Consumer Research,* Vol. 3, 1976, pp. 513–519.

SOCIAL LEARNING THEORY

Gerwirtz (1969) defines social learning as a category of learning involving stimuli provided by people. There are two basic social learning processes that influence behavior: direct *instrumental training,* where a teacher explicitly attempts to shape responses via differential reinforcement, and *imitation,* where an observer matches responses to discriminative cues provided by responses of a model. The latter process occurs without direct tuition and comprises the vast majority of a child's socialization.

Although traditional learning theories portray behavior as a function of experiential reinforcements, Bandura contends that "virtually all learning phenomena resulting from direct experiences can occur on a vicarious basis through observation of other people's behavior and its consequences for them." This enables man to acquire behavior by example without tedious trial and error practice; similarly, behavioral inhibitions can be induced by observing punishment of others for their actions. There is an important cognitive component in this approach, as people symbolically represent and process external influences for later guidance in performance (Bandura, 1962, 1965, 1969, 1971a, 1973, 1976b; Bandura and Walters, 1963; Bandura, Ross, and Ross, 1963a, 1963b.).

In Bandura's view "most of the behaviors that people display are learned, either deliberately or inadvertently, through the influence of example." The reasons for this are that dangerous mistakes can be avoided by observing competent models who demonstrate proper modes of response, that complex behaviors such as language can only be learned through example, and that novel response patterns can be acquired more efficiently through observational means.

He proposes four subprocesses that govern modeling. A distinction is drawn between acquisition (learning) and actual performance of the behavior. An observed response becomes acquired when stimuli merely elicit mental representations of the behavior; overt performance is primarily determined by reinforcements experienced by the model and the observer.

The initial process is *attention,* where the observer is exposed to the modeling stimuli. Acquisition of matching behavior at the sensory registration level occurs when the observer attends to, recognizes, and differentiates the distinctive features of the model's behavior. Attention is selectively determined by several sets of factors, including opportunity for encounter with direct or mediated models, the relevance, competence, distinctiveness, power, and attractiveness of these models, and the observer's sensory capacities, arousal level, motivations, and reinforcement history. Bandura feels that televised models are so intrinsically interesting that they are highly effective in attracting attention.

Retention processes are crucial because delayed imitation outside of the model's presence requires symbolic representation in memory. This mental representation process involves coding of both images and verbal symbols of observed events.

Motoric reproduction processes are the third component of modeling. The observer must possess the requisite skills for physically executing the behavioral pattern.

Finally, *reinforcement and motivational processes* determine whether the learned behavior will be activated into overt expression. Positive incentives facilitate translation from mental acquisition to behavioral performance of matching actions. In particular, observed reinforcement contingencies provide the crucial instigational cues.

Bandura notes that the anticipation of reinforcement also influences the attentional and retentional processes; observers are more attentive to actions of effective models, and they are more likely to code utilitarian model responses. However, such incentives are facilitative rather than necessary conditions; indeed, attention may be attracted by physical means: "One does not have to be reinforced, for example, to hear compelling sounds or to look at prominent visual displays." In one study Bandura, Grusec and Menlove (1966)

found the same level of imitative acquisition from television stimuli regardless of advance notification that correct modeling would be rewarded.

Bandura identifies several types of modeling functions. *Observational learning* is the transmission of information about ways of organizing component responses into new patterns of behavior. Observers acquire novel response patterns by watching the performances of others via physical demonstrations, pictorial representation, or verbal description. While adults rely on verbal modeling as the preferred mode of response guidance, children who have not developed adequate language skills are more dependent on visual depictions. The varied symbolic modeling portrayals on television constitute an extremely important influence, since children "rarely have to be compelled to watch television, whereas verbal characterizations of the same activities would fail to hold their attention for long. One might also expect observers who lack conceptual skills to benefit less from verbal modeling than from behavioral demonstrations."

The second function involves strengthening or weakening of *inhibitions* that govern the expression of previously learned responses. The observation of reinforcement to a model helps determine how behavioral restraints are modified; vicariously punished responses tend to inhibit expressions of similar behavior, while normally prohibited responses that are rewarded (or merely ignored or not noticed) reduce inhibitory constraints.

Response facilitation is the third major function. This modeling enhancement process occurs when the model performs a socially sanctioned behavior which serves as an external reminder eliciting performance of existing responses in the same general class. Facilitation is distinguished from observational learning in that new behaviors are not acquired, and from inhibition/disinhibition in that these types of behavior are not normally subject to internal or external restraint.

Bandura briefly mentions a fourth function, *stimulus enhancement,* where the observer's attention is directed to the objects employed by the model. Consequently, the observer may be more likely to use these objects, although not necessarily in a directly imitative fashion.

Modeling stimuli are not equally influential in evoking the exemplified behavior. The attributes of the social model combine with the model's reinforcement contingencies to determine impact. Models who are perceived to have high competence, expertise, power, celebrity standing or socio-economic status are overtly imitated to a considerably greater degree, compared to models lacking these qualities. Impact of properties such as age, sex, and ethnic status is more likely to vary according to the observer's characteristics, since perceived similarity to the model is an influential factor. The potency of the dimensions is explainable in terms of the predictably reinforcing outcomes associated with imitation of respected or successful models; copying actions of models who have attained status is more likely to be rewarded. Of course, a mass medium such as television often confers status on individuals who appear in messages, since the audience perceives that those dealt with in the media are important. Status also tends to be attributed to models as a result of their response consequences; a model assumes greater valuation and emulative qualities when positively rather than negatively reinforced. In addition, source generalization processes tend to extend a model's prestige to unrelated domains of behavior and to other models similar to the respected one. The role of similarity is partly due to the expectation that people who possess similar characteristics share many common experiences and outcomes. Berkowitz (1962) observes that the degree of similarity between the circumstances portrayed and the observer's own situation facilitates effects in the same manner.

Observed reinforcement contingencies affect behavior in the same way as directly experienced reinforcers. Bandura argues that vicarious reinforcement is more effective in acquisitional learning, while direct reinforcement is more influential in motivating performance of behavior. A particularly interesting problem is the interactive effect of direct and vicarious reinforcers. Observed consequences provide reference standards for determining whether attained outcomes are judged as positive or negative, as in the phenomena of relative deprivation: "Through social comparison processes, observation of other people's response outcomes can drastically alter the effectiveness of direct reinforcements."

APPLICATIONS

The remainder of this paper will present recent empirical evidence pertaining to vicarious modeling, drawn from data collected in a three-year research program by Atkin (1975). In each section, research findings will be linked to relevant components of social learning theory. First, the stimulus characteristics of children's commercials are examined in terms of effectiveness potential, based on social learning ideas. Then, evidence of actual advertising impact is presented in this theoretical context.

Dimensions of Advertising Stimuli
The nature of the portrayal of product consumption and consequences in commercial messages has significant implications for child modeling of advertising stimuli. A number of content dimensions relating to social learning theory were described in an analysis of all 470 commercials aired on the three television networks on two comparable Saturday mornings in 1972 and 1973. In general, these ads portrayed one or more models in the act of consuming a food product or playing with a toy product and enjoying positive reinforcement as a consequence of this response. The presentation of findings is organized according to the stimulus control and reinforcement control functions, which affect attentional, retentional, and motivational processes.

Stimulus control. The structural elements of advertising presentations contribute to the viewer's attention and retention: ads are placed within and between popular entertainment programs where children have a high opportunity to encounter the messages, and the frequent repetition of specific commercials increases the likelihood of attending and retaining the material. The intermittent repetition is particularly important because younger viewers have a limited capacity for storing an infrequently presented message until the appropriate time for action; since most ads are oriented toward response facilitation effects, repeating the basic message within and across Saturday mornings serves as a key reminder to display previously learned consumption behaviors. The findings showed an average of 20 ads per hour in these two years, and an ad was presented an average of 1.4 times per morning.

The repetition factor is also apparent within commercials. Almost every commercial mentioned the brand name more than once, with almost one-fourth of the ads featuring five or more repetitions. On the average, the name of the brand was verbally mentioned 3.7 times per 30-second message. Retention can also be stimulated by the use of catchy slogans and jingles. More than two-fifths of the ads employed these devices, with musical jingles predominating over verbalized slogans by a five-to-one margin.

Several other attention-getting aspects of advertising stimuli were documented: a humorous tone of presentation was used in almost three-fifths of the ads, and four-fifths of the commercials featured special effects techniques, typically close-ups of the product. Certainly the various model characteristics and reinforcement portrayals described below also induce greater attention.

Almost all ads depicted human characters, and the roles satisfied both the competence/authority and similarity strategies for eliciting that modeling. Nine-tenths portrayed child models, which large segments of the child audience are likely to perceive as similar to themselves. Although few commercials presented adults alone, more than one-fourth had a mixture of children and adults; most adults occupied a parental role. Furthermore, celebrity models were used in one of every twenty ads. Aside from age of characters, a racial analysis showed that about one-fifth of the commercials presented non-white minority persons, almost always in combination with whites.

Another important facet of the stimulus is the explicitness of the behavioral portrayal. Almost nine-tenths of the ads visually illustrated the product in use at some point, typically showing a child playing with a toy or eating a food product. About three-fourths of all commercials relied solely on live-action portrayals, while the rest were split evenly between animated-only presentations and use of the two techniques in combination.

Reinforcement control. The content analysis also attempted to assess the types of rewards attained by models, although this requires a subjective evaluation. Only a handful of commercials did not portray explicit enjoyment or benefit experienced from consuming the product. Almost three-fifths of the ads were judged to show high satisfaction, with verbal and/or nonverbal display of strong liking for the product; the remainder were rated in the moderate satisfaction category. Higher levels of satisfaction were depicted much more often in food ads than in toy ads. Among the rewards associated with product consumption, the feeling of fun was emphasized in two-thirds of the advertisements, particularly ads for foods. Two other categories were frequently found in toy ads: feelings of power and feelings of being grown-up. Finally, the commercials were rated in terms of peer appeals linked to product consumption. Increased status with peers was demonstrated in very few commercials, but more than half of the ads were classified as containing affiliative appeals since the model(s) and product were shown in a social setting with other children present.

The previously cited data that most adults appearing in ads occupied a parental role with respect to child models has important reinforcement implications. Such authority figures either directly approve of the child model's consumption or implicitly endorse it with their mere presence; this might indicate to the viewer that he will similarly be rewarded (or at least not punished) for consuming the product.

The presentation of such reinforcements in commercials contributes to the cognitive and behavioral impact of the message. Attention and retention are heightened by the enticing display of personal and social satisfaction derived from playing with a particular toy or eating a certain cereal or candy. Most significantly, these elements of the advertisement serve as a motivating incentive to perform the consumption behavior and to implement any necessary pre-consumption actions such as requesting purchase of the product.

Attention to Advertising

The initial requisite condition for successful behavioral modeling is securing attention of the target audience. Data from both experimental and survey studies show that commercials attract an attentive reaction from children.

In the experimental research, 500 preschool and grade school students were unobtrusively monitored as they watched a videotaped cartoon in which seven commercials were embedded. Groups of four children were seated in front of a television while a hidden camera recorded their eye contact with the televised presentation. Averaging across the seven 30-second ads, the mean amount of eye contact was 25 seconds. Older children (8–10 years old) paid slightly closer attention than younger children (3–7 years old), by about a 2-second margin.

One of the manipulations in this experiment was the structural formatting of the commercials into a single cluster of seven ads versus conventionally dispersed sets of three or fewer ads. Attention level was actually slightly higher in the clustered condition, regardless of age. Moreover, there was no significant tendency for relative deterioration of attention from earlier to later ads within the cluster. While these findings underline the attention-drawing power of television ads, it must be noted that the generalizability is somewhat limited by the artificial nature of the laboratory setting.

These experimental data are complemented by survey evidence from a sample of 775 children in the fourth through seventh grades. A questionnaire displayed pictures and/or verbal summary descriptions of 26 specific commercials and PSAs representing a wide variety of products and ideas aimed at both child and adult audiences. Respondents were asked to report level of exposure to each along a four-step scale, with the standard question: "When this commercial comes on TV, how much do you watch it?" Averaging across all messages, 17% selected the "always" category, 24% indicated "usually," 40% said "sometimes," and 19% marked "never." The fourth and fifth graders attended slightly more closely than the sixth and seventh graders. By type of message, attention was reported to be highest for PSAs (53% in top two attention categories), followed by candy ads (50%), hygiene ads (41%), cereal ads (39%), shoe ads (38%), toy ads (33%), and medicine ads (25%). Of course, the particular examples of ads selected for each type of product may not be representative, but the overall findings are likely to be typical.

Observational Learning Effects

Observational learning is defined as the acquisition (and performance) of novel forms of behavior. In the case of television advertising, the criterion of "new" response can be met with any of several conditions including: a type of consumption with which the child is not familiar because of limited opportunity for direct observation or experience (i.e., using hygiene products such as deodorants and acne cream, ingesting proprietary medicines such as sleeping pills and laxatives, wearing undergarments, or drinking alcohol), or a distinctive new version of a familiar type of consumption (i.e., playing with a unique style of toy, or eating an innovative brand of dessert). Several sets of data are relevant to observational learning:

Point-it-out. One unique behavior that has been emphasized in a well-known anti-pollution PSA is to point-it-out when polluting or littering is encountered. A series of models distinctively use their fingers to identify various offenders and perhaps to stimulate them to stop polluting. Since children would be unlikely to perform this response without observing the PSA stimulus, it is a prime example of observational learning. In survey questionnaires distributed to 775 older children, one question asked how often they reminded litterers to stop their littering; amount of exposure to this and another anti-littering message was also measured. More than two-thirds of the respondents indicated that they had ever attempted to stop offenders from littering; 25% of the heavier viewers vs. 14% of the lighter viewers reported that they did this frequently. The partial correlation between exposure and reminding others to stop littering was + .19 with the demographic factors controlled. It appears that the novel act of harrassing litterers is effectively taught by televised PSA s.

Model characteristics. Among the stimulus control variables studied in the social learning literature, much attention has focused on model attributes such as sex, age, and race. The racial identity of the advertising model was examined in one of the experiments of the project.

Previous research yields conflicting results. Neely, Heckel and Leichtman (1973) found that young black children imitated a televised white model more than a black model in toy selection. However, Barry and Hansen (1973) reported that young black children were much more likely than whites to express preference for a cereal brand promoted in a TV commercial featuring a black model than an alternative brand advertised without a black model.

In the present experiment, the race of models was manipulated in a specially produced commercial for an unfamiliar toy product. The ad presented a pair of either white actors or black actors playing with and enjoying the toy; all other message elements were held constant.

Half of the sample of 500 preschool and elementary school children viewed each condition. There were no major differences in observed reactions while viewing, in terms of attention, irritation, enjoyment, and verbalizations. In a post-viewing play situation, subjects were offered an opportunity to play with either the advertised toy or an alternative toy. For white subjects, there were no differences in selection between the white-model and black-model treatments; black subjects more often chose the advertised toy in the white-model condition by a clear 14% margin. These findings indicate that black children are somewhat more likely to imitate novel responses of racially dissimilar advertising models.

Inhibitory/Disinhibitory Effects
In addition to teaching new responses, commercials may modify inhibitory restraints governing performance of existing behavioral patterns. Although previous television applications of this component of social learning theory have generally dealt with clearly proscribed forms of behavior such as aggression, the advertising derivations pertain to disinhibition of more mildly prohibited behavioral expression involving minor violations of personal standards or social norms, including: counter-normative types of product consumption (i.e., unconventional definition of appropriate product users or situations for product usage, such as girls playing with electric trains or late-evening snacking with breakfast cereal), and atypical amounts of product consumption (i.e., candy eating beyond normal limits).

Since commercial advertising seldom attempts to restrain behaviors by presenting negative reinforcement of product consumption, inhibitory applications are rare. However, some public service campaigns seek to inhibit the display of generally non-sanctioned forms of behavior such as littering, smoking, drug-taking and car-riding without buckled seat belts. While the goal may not be total prohibition, PSAs often endeavor to restrict the frequency or situational conditions for performing such behaviors.

The research project included evidence dealing with both disinhibition and inhibition of acquisition and performance, following from the examples listed above.

Recreational sex role socialization. Modeling influences may serve to teach non-traditional forms of play through advertising. To test the impact of a counter-stereotypical use of a toy racing car set by female models, two versions of a standard toy commercial were filmed: one portrayed two young boys playing with the racing cars, while the other presented the same actions acted by two young girls. Half of a sample of 400 second through fifth graders viewed each version, which was inserted into a cartoon program on video tape. On a post-viewing questionnaire, the manipulation check disclosed an interesting finding: just two-fifths of the subjects exposed to the female-model condition recognized that they were girls. The dependent variables were the perceived appropriateness of girls playing with racing cars and personal desire to play with the toy. There were no significant main effects between the two experimental treatments. However, examination of the subgroup that correctly perceived the sex of the female models showed substantial differences in the expected direction: this subgroup was almost twice as likely to feel that girls should play with racing cars, and they were slightly more likely to indicate that they would like to play with cars (although they did not express a greater intention to actually ask parents to buy the expensive toy). However, these latter findings may be partially due to self-selection of more attitudinally favorable

subjects into the accurately perceiving subgroup. The pattern of results did not differ according to the sex of the subgroup.

Candy consumption disinhibition. Since almost all children eat candy products at least occasionally, moderate consumption is hardly a novel or proscribed pattern of behavior. Nevertheless, Saturday morning candy commercials repeatedly portray models happily consuming a variety of these candies, often with the additional reinforcement of tacit adult approval. Extensive exposure to these modeling stimuli may suggest to the child that excessive candy eating is acceptable behavior, even though interpersonal messages and intrapersonal judgment typically serve to restrain candy intake. Thus, commercials may cause a reduced level of personal guilt or fear of social disapproval for excessive consumption of candy; this effect should be reflected in greater amounts of candy bars eaten by the child. Since inhibitions probably do not pertain to any particular brand of candy, such an effect should be generalized to consumption of all brands regardless of the frequency that each is advertised on television.

In a questionnaire survey of 506 fourth through seventh graders, exposure to candy advertising was indexed by a generalized candy attention item and two measures dealing with specific ads, multiplied by the amount of viewing time on Saturday mornings. Children were also asked to report how often they ate seven brands of candy bars, including three that were frequently advertised and four that were lightly advertised on Saturday mornings. Exposure correlated $+.29$ with an index of eating heavily promoted brands, and the partial controlling for demographics was $+.25$. Consumption of lightly advertised brands was associated with exposure to the same degree. A separate item measuring number of candy bars consumed per week yielded a weaker partial correlation of $+.10$ with the exposure index. Thus, there is fairly strong evidence that exposure and consumption are functionally related (although the direction of causality is not unambiguous) and that advertising effects tend to be generalized to nonadvertised brand consumption, lending support to the disinhibition explanation.

PSAs and inhibitions. Social learning theorists argue that young people learn to avoid dangerous mistakes by observing the negative consequences incurred by models who don't follow recommended practices, such as buckling seat belts or restricting smoking, rather than learning by direct experience with punishing outcomes. Theoretically, an effective modeling message should graphically display a model performing the illicit behavior and then suffering injury, illness, or death. Public service announcements typically tone down the explicitness of the harmful consequences, but generally follow this basic approach. Two cases are seat belt and anti-smoking campaigns, which display such negative reinforcement as hospitalization, loss of affection, or physical disability.

The questionnaires administered to 775 older children contained items dealing with seat belt buckling behavior and intention not to smoke, along with level of exposure to corresponding public service messages.

Controlling for contaminating demographic variables, there was a negligible +.06 partial correlation between seat belt PSA exposure and frequency of using seat belts; the partial correlation between exposure to anti-smoking PSA exposure and intention not to adopt cigarette smoking was −.11, however. It appears that these PSAs have no positive impact in increasing inhibitions against smoking or riding without seat belts, probably due to the extensive amount of interpersonal influence on these behaviors from parents, teachers, and peers.

One particular pervasive public service campaign has sought to restrain littering behavior. The negative consequences of this type of action are qualitatively different from the previous examples, since the harmful outcomes are aesthetic or social

rather than physical. PSAs typically portray littering responses followed by portrayals of a polluted environment, social disapproval to the model, or a saddened Indian. In the survey, exposure to this type of message was associated +.05 with frequency of proper disposal of litter, with demographic factors controlled.

An experimental test examined the impact of the crying Indian spot on actual littering behavior under controlled conditions. Half of the sample of 500 subjects in the previously discussed experiment viewed this anti-littering message during an entertainment program, while the other half were exposed to an unrelated message. After the viewing session, all subjects were offered a piece of wrapped candy and their disposal of the wrapper was unobtrusively observed by the experimental assistants. The children who viewed the littering announcement were significantly less likely to litter the experimental room than the non-exposed Ss. Among viewers, 25% put the wrapper in the waste basket and 2% threw it on the floor; 19% of the non-exposed Ss disposed of the wrapper in the basket and 11% littered the floor. The others kept it on themselves or left it on the table. The younger children were clearly most influenced. While the experiment demonstrates at least a temporary inhibitory effect, the survey findings show that the influence is not strong in the naturalistic setting.

Response Facilitation Effects

The response facilitation function is highly relevant to modeling of advertising stimuli. Most product consumption in commercials is acceptable, everyday behavior encumbered by minimal restrictions. The same holds for certain socially desirable practices promoted in public service announcements. For instance, children have established habitual patterns of behavior regarding cereal eating, toy playing, and in most instances, litter disposal and seat belt buckling. They have typically experienced direct positive reinforcement for such actions, but performance may not be salient at any given moment. In such cases, advertising might serve as a discriminative cue instigating previously learned behaviors; the ads temporarily remind the child to perform the particular activity. These eliciting cues typically contain a positive rather than negative motivational component. In particular, commercial messages seldom depict the unfavorable consequences of not using the product (except in preliminary scenes before the product is consumed, as in medicine and hygiene ads); the primary modeling sequence is the demonstrated use of the product followed by rewarding outcomes.

An important aspect of this process concerns stimulus and response generalization from a given message. Does advertising motivate consumption of any brand within a product class, or is the effect restricted to the specific brand presented in the commercial? For instance, an ad for one exotically flavored pre-sweetened cereal may trigger eating of similar sugary cereal brands, or the generalization gradient may further carry over to non-sweetened cereals. This generalization process might be expected with children for two basic reasons: the brand-unique cues in a given ad might be perceived as peripheral to the more central modeled sequence of preparing and eating a bowl of cereal (or playing a board game or using a hair shampoo), and the overall message environment or numerous competing cereal brands (or game brands or shampoo brands) may produce a cumulative impression of "eating cereal" (or "playing games" or "using shampoo") rather than learning substantive and symbolic distinctions between brands X, Y, and Z. From a visual modeling perspective, the basic theme is consumption behavior; there are often no unique features of specific brands that models can act out (except listening to snap/crackle/pop). Of course, some models may be more influential exemplars, and there may be non-modeling aspects such as nutritional value, taste qualities, and attractive brand symbols. These other factors should create a tendency for children to more frequently con-

sume heavily advertised brands—but a substantial generalization to consumption of less advertised brands should also be expected.

This notion was tested in a survey investigation of cereal advertising and consumption, where 506 children in the fourth through seventh grades reported on their exposure to cereal ads (indexed by the product of five specific and general attention items times amount of Saturday television viewing) and their patterns of cereal eating. A consumption index for eight heavily advertised cereal brands correlated $+.41$ with the exposure index; when grade, sex, status and school performance were controlled, the partial correlation remained strong at $+.37$. As anticipated, the association between exposure and consumption of five lightly advertised brands was positive but less strong, with a raw correlation of $+.27$ and a fourth-order partial of $+.24$.

Since response facilitation might be counteracted by parental influences restricting the amount of cereal eating, the questionnaire also measured whether parents imposed general snacking rule limitations or allowed children to eat whatever foods they pleased. The conditional correlations showed a substantial interaction: in homes with no rules, the correlation between exposure and overall cereal consumption was $+.51$, while the correlation was only $+.27$ for children reporting parental restrictions.

While it is possible for children to model cereal eating with the cereals available in the home, imitation is to some extent contingent on the intervening variable of persuading parents to purchase cereals in the supermarket. The motivation to imitate may indirectly produce request behavior as a means to physically acquiring the product (advertising codes discourage modeling stimuli of the product acquisition behavioral sequence of asking parents to buy, which would be a much more effective response facilitation strategy). The survey showed that exposure to cereal advertising was correlated $+.32$ with frequency of requesting cereal purchases, with a partial correlation of

+.27. Of course, it should be recognized that each of the relationships reported in this section may be due to reverse causation, as children who often request or eat cereals are motivated to watch TV commercials for cereals. Since a major portion of the exposure variable involves mere amount of time viewing Saturday morning programming, it seems unlikely that a large part of the association could be explained by selective seeking rather than message effects.

Analysis of path coefficients among exposure, requests, consumption and demographic variables indicated that the impact of cereal advertising on advertised brand eating occurs both directly and indirectly via requests. The linkage from exposure to requests was +.27, and from requests to consumption was +.26; the direct path coefficient from exposure to consumption was +.30.

In the case of public service announcements, modeling effects have been primarily interpreted as observational learning and inhibitory processes. For frequently expressed sanctioned behaviors such as seat buckling and proper disposal of trash, an alternative approach emphasizing positive reinforcement can be utilized. Many learning theorists believe that reward is more effective than punishment in shaping behavior. The positive facilitation strategy would be to portray the recommended practices paired with rewarding consequences, such as safe arrival, good health, social approval, self-satisfaction, or a clean environment. Since few PSAs use this approach, the data from this investigation do not provide a good test for these ideas; however, the research of Leibert, Sprafkin and Poulos (1975) suggests that it can be effective.

Stimulus Object Enhancement Effects

Bandura suggests that stimulus enhancement processes direct the observer's attention to objects utilized by the model and produce greater use of the objects beyond demonstrated circumstances. This notion can be applied to evidence on medicine advertising effects gathered in a survey of 256 fifth, sixth and seventh grade students. The analyses showed that exposure to advertisements of headache remedies was slightly associated with the child's self-prescription of the number of aspirin that they should take to relieve a cold; the partial correlation was +.06, with 16% more of the heavy medicine ad viewers than light ad viewers suggesting a dosage of two or more aspirin. On the other hand, there was no difference according to exposure on an item asking the children if it's acceptable to take aspirin if they're not really sick. This evidence provides very limited indications that an enhancement of advertised objects can occur for a significant behavior such as medicine taking.

REFERENCES

Atkin, C. (1975), "The Effects of Television Advertising on Children," final report submitted to Office of Child Development.

   #1 First Year Experimental Evidence (June, 1975).

   #2 Second Year Experimental Evidence (June, 1975).

   #3 Exploring the Relationship Between Television Viewing and Language Development (June, 1975).

   #4 Attitudes of Industry Executives, Government Officials and Consumer Critics Toward Children's Advertising (June, 1975).

   #5 Content Analysis of Children's Television Commercials (June, 1975).

   #6 Survey of Pre-Adolescent's Responses to Television Commercials (July, 1975).

   #7 Parent-Child Communication in Supermarket Breakfast Cereal Selection (October, 1975).

Bandura, A. (1962), "Social Learning Through Imitation," in M. Jones, ed., *Nebraska Symposium on Motivation,* Lincoln: University of Nebraska Press, 211–74.

Bandura, A. (1965), "Vicarious Processes: A Case of No-Trial Learning," in L. Berkowitz, ed., *Advances in Experimental Social Psychology,* Vol. 2, New York: Academic Press, 1–55.

Bandura, A. (1969), "Social-Learning Theory of Identificatory Processes," in D. Goslin, ed., *Handbook of Socialization Theory and Research,* Chicago: Rand-McNally, 213–62.

Bandura, A., ed. (1971a), *Psychological Modeling: Conflicting Theories,* Chicago: Aldine-Atherton.

Bandura, A. (1971b), *Social Learning Theory,* New York: General Learning Press.

Bandura, A. (1973), *Aggression: A Social Learning Analysis,* Englewood Cliffs, N. J.: Prentice-Hall.

Bandura, A.; Grusec, J.; and Menlove, F. (1966), "Observational Learning as a Function of Symbolization and Incentive Set," *Child Development,* 37, 499–506.

Bandura, A.; Ross, D.; and Ross, S. (1963a), "Imitation of Film-Mediated Aggressive Models," *Journal of Abnormal and Social Psychology,* 66, 3–11.

Bandura, A.; Ross, D.; and Ross, S. (1963b), "Vicarious Reinforcement and Imitative Learning," *Journal of Abnormal and Social Psychology,* 67, 601–7.

Bandura, A., and Walters, R. (1963), *Social Learning and Personality Development,* New York: Holt, Rinehart and Winston.

Barry, T., and Hansen, R. (1973), "How Race Affects Children's TV Commercials," *Journal of Advertising Research,* 13, 63–67.

Berkowitz, L. (1962), *Aggression: A Social Psychological Analysis,* New York: McGraw-Hill.

Gewirtz, J. (1969), "Mechanisms of Social Learning," in D. Goslin, ed., *Handbook of Socialization Theory and Research,* Chicago: Rand-McNally, 57–212.

Liebert, R.; Sprafkin, J.; and Poulos, R. (1975), "Selling Cooperation to Children," in W. Hale, ed., *Proceedings,* New York: Advertising Research Foundation.

Neely, J.; Heckel, R.; and Liechtman, H. (1973), "The Effect of Race of Model and Response Consequences to the Model on Imitation in Children," *Social Psychology,* 89, 225–31.

SECTION 12

CONSUMER PROTECTION

Consumerism is a national social movement which is concerned with five basic consumer rights. Each of these rights is sometimes violated as consumers enter into transactions with for-profit and not-for-profit organizations. The five rights are:

1. *The right to safety.* This involves protection against physically harmful goods and services.
2. *The right to be informed.* This right suggests that consumers should be provided with relevant information that is easily understood and easily obtained. Consumers should not be deliberately misled or confused.
3. *The right to choose.* Consumers should not be forced to purchase in a monopolistic situation. Consumers have the right to benefit from the advantages accruing to consumers from a competitive market.
4. *The right to be heard.* Consumer interests should be represented in the development of corporate marketing policy, in the development of policy by not-for-profit agencies such as hospitals, and in the development of government policy.
5. *The right to high quality.* Consumers have the right not simply to an absence of physical harm and deception, but also to the best array of products and services provided in the best manner possible, given reasonable constraints organizations face if they are to survive and to continue to serve the consumer.

There are several issues relating to consumer protection and the various parties involved with or affected by consumer protection issues.[1] One issue focuses on which groups should legitimately be involved in buyer-seller relationships and how they should be involved. Should trade associations, community action groups, states' attorney generals, and the Federal Trade Commission be involved? If so, how should any one of these groups be involved? A second issue concerns the criteria for evaluating consumers' opinions of an organization's marketing practices, including product offerings. Are consumers' perceptions inherently better or worse or much different than those of the legal staff of a government agency? A third issue addresses product information. What type of information should be provided? By whom? Just how much information is it fair to require a vendor to make available (in some way)? An important issue is whether or not regulatory efforts may fail or even backfire. Can a regulation create a false sense of protection among consumers? May the implementation be conducted in a way which actually contradicts the intention of the regulations?

Different assumptions are often made about the nature of consumer problems. This leads to different types of regulatory actions or practices. One set of assumptions emphasizes consumer characteristics as a cause of difficulty. That is, some consumers experience problems because they lack the educational ability to process product information. A response to this problem entails providing special counseling services to consumers and consumer education programs. Another common assumption is that the main problems consumers face, especially those who are elderly, poor, and immobile, is that they do not have any real choice. They must rely on mail order catalogs and stores that provide home delivery. The remedial action this assumption implies is that mail order firms, door-to-door salespeople and others who are used frequently by disadvantaged groups should be regulated carefully. Another assumption is that the problem is with particular kinds of merchants who may be found in any location and in any type of business establishment. Since these merchants cannot be readily located or identified, it becomes necessary to regulate the kind of practices they commonly use.[2]

As might be expected, the entire issue of consumerism is fraught with conflict. The different parties involved—government, business, consumer advocacy groups, and consumers—differ considerably in terms of what they perceive the problems to be and what they perceive appropriate solutions to be. Moreover, there are very different perspectives among the various parties about the effectiveness of different approaches and different legislation and regulations. The reader should keep this in mind when reading the papers selected for this section.

[1]Lawrence P. Feldman, *Consumer Protection: Problems and Prospects,* St. Paul, Minn.: West Publishing Co., 1976, p. 6.
[2]Alan R. Andreasen, *The Disadvantaged Consumer,* New York: The Free Press, 1975.

"NUTRITION LABELING FOR CANNED GOODS: A STUDY OF CONSUMER RESPONSE"

The consumerism movement has led to many changes and additions to legislation. In particular, many industries are now required by law to disclose various kinds of product information to consumers. The requirement of nutrition and ingredient labeling of food products is one example. Since this information must be given to consumers, consumer researchers have devoted considerable attention to the problems of determining which formats of presentation are most useful for consumers.

The Asam and Bucklin article compares four different nutrition labeling formats with regard to their effect on two criterion variables. The two dependent variables are product perception and relative product preference. Product perceptions were measured on scales of taste, tenderness, wholesomeness, liking, and "good buy." Product preference was measured by having respondents rank four brands in the order of their desirability. Although this measure does give a relative ranking of the four brands, it does not give an absolute measure of the desirability of each brand. For instance, the two respondents may be alike in the way they rank the four brands similarly (Brand A, 1st; B, 2nd; C, 3rd; and D, 4th). But the first person may still have no desire to purchase even the top-rated brand. The second person might under certain circumstances consider buying any of the four brands, but prefer Brand A when given a choice among the four brands. Thus, the ratings give relative preferences, but not absolute preferences.

The Latin Square research design which is used in the Asam and Bucklin article may be unfamiliar to some readers, so it will be briefly described here. Table 1 in the article lists the four levels of nutrition information. These are the predictor variables. Since there are two other variables with which these levels can be mixed, a way must be found to discover the isolated effect of the predictor variables. These two other variables are brand/price and store. The research design must, therefore, combine each level of nutrition information with each brand/price and in each store. These 16 combinations are shown in Figure 1 in the article. Any particular respondent sees only four brands, each of which has one of the four levels of information. Thus, each respondent saw the combinations shown in one column of Figure 1. The effect of any particular level of nutrition information is derived by combining the responses to that level of information on each of the four brands in each of the four stores (e.g., for level III, private brand 1 in store A, private brand 2 in store B, major brand 1 in store C, and major brand 2 in store D are combined).

"AN EFFECTIVE DISPLAY OF UNIT PRICE INFORMATION"

Much of the research on the use by consumers of required information disclosures is based on work in the area of information processing. The Russo,

Krieser, and Miyashita article is based in this tradition. A useful distinction is made between available information and processible information. Merely posting information, such as unit prices, makes it available. Yet, this is a far cry from assuring that the information is processible. Russo, et al. recognize that humans as information processors have limits on the amount and types of information chunks which they can handle. To be processible, information must be presented in a format which makes human cognitive processes possible.

The two types of information formats which are compared are (1) individual product tags attached to shelf facings listing regular price and unit price, and (2) a single list of the regular price and unit price of all brands. Unobtrusive measures of behavior are used by determining sales of various products in response to the two different types of information display.

The most interesting finding of the Russo, et al. study is that within product categories there are subcategories within which consumers will search for the product with the lowest unit price. However, they will not switch to a product in a different subcategory in order to obtain a lower unit price. Therefore, not all products within a product category are in price competition. These results could easily be translated into managerial strategies based on market segmentation.

"HOW WILL CONSUMER EDUCATION AFFECT CONSUMER BEHAVIOR?"

The first two articles in this section report on empirical studies which examined how consumers responded to two types of consumer information. The Bloom paper is somewhat different from these two articles. Bloom discusses how consumer education programs may affect the behavior of consumers in the future. The terms *consumer education* and *consumer education program* are defined in the paper, so we will not define them here.

It is important to note one point made by Bloom in the beginning of his paper. He describes the economic and environmental conditions which have made the situation ripe for consumer education programs to grow. It is worth considering what might happen to these programs and to consumer behavior if severe inflationary trends were stopped and energy shortages were solved through the discovery of alternative energy sources.

More importantly, however, the reader should consider what the action implications of the seven hypotheses are. That is, if these hypotheses are true, what action should a marketing manager take? What should a public policymaker do? In other words, how will these changes in consumer behavior affect the strategies used by managers and policymakers?

NUTRITION LABELING FOR CANNED GOODS: A STUDY OF CONSUMER RESPONSE

EDWARD H. ASAM
AND
LOUIS P. BUCKLIN

Source: Edward H. Asam and Louis P. Bucklin, "Nutrition Labeling for Canned Goods: A Study of Consumer Response," *Journal of Marketing,* Vol. 37, April, 1973, pp. 32–37.

Although federally established grades for many food products have existed for some time, nutrition values have not typically been built into the standards despite knowledge of widespread dietary deficiencies (Schoenfeld, 1970, pp. 2399–2400). For basic canned goods—with which this study is concerned—grading has been based upon color, uniformity, blemishes, clearness of the liquid, and, in some instances, toughness and flavor. The amount of vitamins, proteins, fats, carbohydrates, and even calories has historically been ignored. Nor has such information been voluntarily placed on cans by the packers.

However, with the publication of the Department of Health, Education, and Welfare, "Proposed Criteria for Food Label Information Panel," in the March, 1972 *Federal Register* (pp. 6493–6497), the absence of such information appears to be at an end. The proposal calls for an information panel on each food label; food manufacturers would furnish statistics on the amount of vitamins, proteins, fats, carbohydrates, and calories contained in the contents of the package. Although the proposal contains numerous controversial elements, two are of specific interest. The first is the voluntary nature of the requirements, and the second is the so-called 80-80 rule.

The voluntary aspect of the proposal is that it requests all food manufacturers to place this information on the label. Officials of the Food and Drug Administration believe that existing law does not make mandatory regulations possible in this area. They noted that such legislation may be in the offing, although Senator Schweiker of Pennsylvania, author of such a bill, suggested that "legislation may not be needed if the nutritional labeling standards set by your industry are good enough" (*Food Chemical News,* 1972, p. 38).

The 80-80 rule calls for a program in which 80% of the units in a given lot would equal or exceed the nutrient levels stated on an information panel while none of the remaining units would fall below 80% of these values.

The findings of this study relate to the question of the type of labeling rule to be employed and to the voluntary nature of a nutrient labeling policy for canned goods. Specifically, the authors were interested in whether nutritional labels with average industry values would be "good enough." Would they be noted by consumers and affect their choices in any way? If consumers were largely indifferent to this information, then there would be scant pressure from the market to cause firms to provide such data on a voluntary basis. Such a result would suggest that new legislation establishing mandatory labeling would be required to make this information uniformly available and that other regulatory approaches, possibly encompassing the 80-80 rule, should be considered so as to make nutrition play a greater role in consumer decision processes.

RESEARCH DESIGN

Resources to conduct an extended study of actual purchases were, unfortunately, not available. Consequently, although questionnaires were employed to develop the data, the experimenters wished to avoid securing biased information from consumers who were believed to have a yea-say response bias on issues of this type. Therefore, a quasi-laboratory research design was used, based upon Cardozo's proposal that ". . . marketers may be able to maximize customers' evaluation of (positive and accurate) information . . ." (Cardozo, 1964, p. 286).

Cardozo used a laboratory shopping environment and examined the relationship between customer effort and product quality ratings. He concluded that the examination of useful information by buyers led to a higher evaluation of the product purchased compared with circumstances where limited information was provided. He noted, however, that where too much information was provided, and product selection becomes complex, buyers skim or reject the messages. Cardozo surmised that this led to the same low levels of product evaluation that would exist if no information were provided (1964, pp. 286-287). Thus, it was hypothesized that if consumers perceive nutrition labels as useful in making purchase decisions, they will rate brands carrying such information more favorably than brands that do not provide this information.

Brands of canned peas were selected for study because they are a widely used product. The researchers were aware of no major factors that might create extraordinarily different perceptions of one brand versus another. Shopper perceptions were obtained by interviewing patrons outside the supermarkets in which they were about to shop.

The effect of nutrition labels upon shopper attitude was ascertained by varying the degree of nutritional information contained on the label of the can. As shown in Table 1, the minimal description provided a simple promotional statement certifying quality. At a slightly higher level, a listing of the major nutrient components, and the extent to which the product was high or low in them, was provided. The third treatment divulged the major nutrients in the canned peas and the amounts by appropriate unit. The last description listed all nutritional components, including trace materials.

To disguise the research interest in nutrition, the information panels were attached to cans of peas bearing four different brand names and prices. Two were brands of major packers and were priced the highest. Two unknown names were selected to represent the private-brand element of the market. These brands were priced a few pennies below the national brands. Simulated rather than actual private brand names were used to avoid possible confounding of test results with the supermarket location in which the interviews were conducted. For example, an unknown bias might accrue to the rating of A&P's brand among shoppers who regularly visit this chain. Four locations adjacent to different supermarket chains were employed, and 50 shoppers were interviewed in each, for a total sample size of 200 subjects.

Table 1 Variations in nutritional information provided on labels of canned peas

Level I	Sweet and succulent Picked at their prime A tasty part of any meal		Ingredients: whole medium peas, sugar, salt, and water
Level II	High in energy High in protein High in iron High in thiamin Low in fat		Ingredients: whole medium peas, sugar, salt, and water
Level III	Each three-ounce serving of these peas contains: Energy value Protein Carbohydrate Fat Moisture	 80 calories 46 grams 15.0 grams 0.4 grams 79 percent	Ingredients: whole medium peas, sugar, salt, and water
Level IV	Each three-ounce serving of these peas contains: Energy value Protein Carbohydrate Fat Moisture Ash	 80 calories 46 grams 15.0 grams 0.4 grams 79 percent 1.0 grams	Plus: Calcium–25 mg., Phosphorus–67 mg., Iron–1.7 mg., Sodium–206 mg., Potassium–96 mg., Vitamin A–469 units, Thiamin–0.1 mg., Riboflavin–0.06 mg., Niacin–1.0 mg., Ascorbic acid–8 mg., Magnesium–25 mg. Ingredients: whole medium peas, sugar, salt and water

Source: Bernice K. Watt and Annabel L. Merrill, *Composition of Foods: Raw-Processed-Prepared,* Agriculture Handbook No. 8 (Washington, D.C.: U.S. Department of Agriculture, Agricultural Research Service, Consumer and Food Economics Research Division, December, 1963).

A Latin Square experimental design was used to evaluate the results with respect to the four nutritional labels, four brands, and four store sites. This design is suitable where the effect of a single experimental variable (nutritional labeling in the present case) does not interact with the control variables (brand/price and store/site). Although this was a moot assumption in the present case, no basis could be found to suspect an interaction in the design and the Latin Square was deemed suitable.

The experimental design is shown in Figure 1. Each nutritional level treatment was rotated so that it was associated with every brand, and the order of presenting the brands was similarly varied. Shoppers at any one site saw only one nutritional treatment applied to a given brand. Cell values were the mean responses by 50 shoppers associated with the brand/nutritional level combination.

MEASURES OF MARKET RESPONSE

The dependent variables in this study were shopper perceptions and purchase preferences for the different brands/prices and associated nutrition

Stores

Brand and Price

	A	B	C	D
Private 1 21¢	III	IV	I	II
Private 2 22¢	II	III	IV	I
Major 1 25¢	I	II	III	IV
Major 2 26¢	IV	I	II	III

Figure 1 Experimental Design for Four Levels of Nutritional Information, I–IV on Food Labels

labels. Interest was focused on how shoppers appraised the quality of the brand. It was felt that the concepts of *taste, tenderness,* and *wholesomeness* would tap the various dimensions of quality. Since these were highly specific factors, it was believed that a more general, comprehensive measure would also be useful. The term *liking* was viewed as expressing this more inclusive construct.

Since it was presumed that most canned goods brands possess a high cross elasticity of demand, the term *good buy* was used to measure the role of price. A nine-point scale using bi-polar adjectives was used to assess each brand nutritional level combination on the above dimensions.

Purchase preferences were also measured by having each shopper rank the four brands shown to her (each, of course, with a different nutritional label) in the order that she would buy them if given the opportunity.

RESULTS

In analyzing the data derived from the Latin Square design, the sums of squares for the brands, stores, and treatments were computed. The significance of possible differences in these three variance estimates were evaluated by means of the F-ratio (df. 3, 6). This evaluation revealed that nine of the eighteen independent variables (three for each attitude measure) were significant at the 10% level or better. Of these, four reflected differences in the brand/price variable, three related to the store/site factor, and two were attributable to nutritional labeling. Detailed ANOVA computations are presented in Table 2.

Table 3 shows the results for nutrition labeling in greater detail. Scores found in the first five columns derive from a nine-point scale. Buying preferences were based upon rank, with the least desirable of the four alternatives present given a weight of one. Each number in the table represents the mean score registered for the attribute at a specific level of nutritional information. For example, Level III mean scores are derived from the diagonal cells of the Latin Square matrix of Figure 1.

The table shows that nutritional labeling clearly improved consumer perception of the quality attributes of "wholesomeness" and, to a lesser extent, "tender." Some nutritional information effects on the ratings of other attributes appear likely, although these were not statistically significant. A rather consistent pattern exists throughout the table. The Level II information appears to have the smallest effect, whereas higher evaluations were associated with Levels III and IV which provided relatively detailed nutritional information. Interestingly, responses to Level I, which employed only promotional terms such as "sweet and succulent," were comparable, in most instances, to those of Level IV.

CONCLUSIONS

Although these results must be interpreted with caution, their implications appear to be as follows:

(1) Vague nutrition labels which state the presence of elements in loose terms, such as high and low, are not apt to have any effect upon consumer choice patterns.

Table 2 ANOVA results for test scores of selected consumer attitudes toward different nutrition information, brand/price and store/location

Attribute	Source effect	df.	Sum of squares	Mean square	F-ratio
Tender	Nutrition	3	0.7595	0.2532	5.90*
	Brand/Price	3	1.8429	0.6143	14.32*
	Store/Location	3	1.9301	0.6434	15.00*
	Error	6	0.2575	0.0429	
Wholesome	Nutrition	3	0.5577	0.1859	9.44*
	Brand/Price	3	0.0867	0.0289	1.47
	Store/Location	3	0.8649	0.2883	14.63*
	Error	6	0.1179	0.0197	
Taste	Nutrition	3	0.1449	0.0483	0.89
	Brand/Price	3	0.7209	0.2403	4.43*
	Store/Location	3	0.9673	0.3224	5.95*
	Error	6	0.3252	0.0542	
Liking	Nutrition	3	0.2942	0.0981	1.21
	Brand/Price	3	0.0398	0.0133	0.16
	Store/Location	3	0.0238	0.0079	0.10
	Error	6	0.4882	0.0814	
Good buy	Nutrition	3	0.6957	0.2319	1.68
	Brand/Price	3	14.9181	4.9727	36.09*
	Store/Location	3	0.2875	0.0958	0.70
	Error	6	0.8266	0.1378	
Preference (rank order)	Nutrition	3	0.3418	0.1139	1.41
	Brand/Price	3	1.0778	0.3593	4.46*
	Store/Location	3	0.0	0.0	0.0
	Error	6	0.4836	0.0806	

Critical $F(3, 6)$: alpha $(.10) = 3.29$. Asterisks indicate all F-ratios above this level.

Table 3 Mean scores for attitudes and preference scales for four different levels of nutritional information on can labels

Nutritional treatment	Scale					
	Like	Good buy	Tasty	Tender[a]	Wholesome[a]	Preference
Level I	4.73	4.88	5.05	5.78	4.86	2.47
Level II	4.49	4.38	4.87	5.39	4.90	2.28
Level III	4.63	4.71	4.87	5.65	5.13	2.55
Level IV	4.86	4.91	5.07	5.99	5.32	2.69

[a]F-ratio (df. 3, 6) shows chance of difference among means due to random factors to be .10 or less.

(2) More detailed nutrition labels containing average industry values may be used by some consumers and may affect their perception of product quality and the ordering of preferred items.

(3) Promotional terms used by canners, such as "sweet and succulent," will provide some consumers with a feeling of quality assurance comparable to that of more detailed nutrition labels.

(4) Despite the fact that some consumers might use the labels, promotional efforts by canners are likely to obscure the effect of this use on either industry or individual canner sales volume.

These findings suggest that at least some consumer interests would be served by the provision of a labeling program with detailed information and that it be federally mandated to insure complete compliance.

Additional research must necessarily be aimed at understanding the impact of this information upon general awareness of nutrition and menu choice as opposed to consumer decisions among similar types of canned foods.

This broader concern of menu choice suggests that the focus of further research on nutrition labeling for all products might be advantageously moved from just measuring the extent of consumer shift among similar types of food products. It should, instead, examine the impact of labels upon consumer use of nutrition as a factor in meal planning. In addition, the interaction between nutrition labels and other diet information, e.g., from television "commercials," should be evaluated in order to consider the role of labeling in conjunction with other types of programs that can alter current consumption patterns.

REFERENCES

Cardozo, Richard N. (1964), "Customer Satisfaction: Laboratory Study and Marketing Action," in L. George Smith, ed., *Reflections on Progress in Marketing,* Chicago: American Marketing Association.

Federal Register (1972), "Proposed Criteria for Food Label Information Panel," March, 1972, Vol. 37.

Food Chemical News (1972), "FDA Proposed Compliance Policy for Nutritional Labeling Hit," April 17, 1972.

Schoenfeld, Andrea F. (1970), "Nutrition Report/ FDA's Proposal for Guideline Signals New Approach to U.S. Diet," in *National Journal,* Vol. 2.

AN EFFECTIVE DISPLAY OF UNIT PRICE INFORMATION

J. EDWARD RUSSO,
GENE KRIESER,
AND
SALLY MIYASHITA

Source: J. Edward Russo, Gene Krieser, and Sally Miyashita, "An Effective Display of Unit Price Information," *Journal of Marketing,* Vol 39, April, 1975, pp. 11–19.

Unit pricing is an idea whose time has come. As a means of improving consumers' decisions, the posting of unit price information has already been accepted by many groups. Beginning with Massachusetts in 1970, several states have enacted legislation requiring the posting of unit prices for some products (Isakson and Maurizi, 1973). Many supermarket chains are currently posting unit prices or have experimented with them (Monroe and LaPlaca, 1972). Finally, consumer advocates are campaigning for the wider adoption of unit pricing ("Progress Report on Unit Pricing," *Consumer Reports,* 1971).

The argument for unit pricing is straightforward. First, the posting of unit prices should eliminate any confusion due to price calculation, especially across packages of different sizes. The removal of calculation problems ought, in turn, to encourage meaningful price comparisons and result in more purchases of the most economical items. In spite of the plausibility of this reasoning, and of the broad acceptance of unit pricing, the results of research that measured the effects of unit pricing have been inconclusive. Some studies report high consumer awareness of unit pricing, while others report no change (Isakson and Maurizi, 1973). One purpose of the research reported in this article is to resolve the paradox between the apparent usefulness of unit price information and the failure of unit pricing to change consumer purchasing habits.

THEORY

The theoretical framework used in this research was that of information-processing psychology (Lindsay and Norman, 1972; Newell and Simon, 1972; and Segal and Lachman, 1972). In this framework, the consumer is seen as optimizing his performance in a given "task environment" by processing the available information as effectively as possible. Effectiveness is constrained by such processing limitations as a short-term memory capacity of only five to seven items (Miller, 1956;

and Simon, 1974). For the consumer, the specific task is to choose his most preferred package (i.e., brand/size combination) from those offered on the supermarket shelf.

The paradox of the observed ineffectiveness of unit price information can be resolved by making the distinction between available information and processible information. The posting of unit prices, in any format whatsoever, makes available to the consumer the critical information needed to make price comparisons. It is contended here, however, that mere availability is not sufficient. Before consumers can effectively use unit price information, a convenient, processible display of that information is necessary.

Thus, the central question of this research becomes: How can price information be presented in order to maximize its use by consumers? In an attempt to answer this question, three methods of presenting price information will be considered. First is the traditional method of listing the raw prices on shelf facings, separately for each brand/size. Second is the addition of unit prices to the shelf tags. Currently, this is the predominant method of displaying unit price information. The third method is a single, organized list of all raw prices and their corresponding unit prices.

Raw Prices

The traditional price display is an information-processing nightmare. The difficulty for consumers of effectively using only raw prices that are displayed on separate shelf tags has been demonstrated in several studies (Nelson, 1969; Friedman, 1966; Grant, 1969; and Houston, 1972). In each of these studies consumers were asked to select the single most economical package for each of several products. These shoppers had unlimited time, were highly motivated, could make all the calculations they wished, and typically were college educated. In spite of these extraordinary advantages, the error rates in the five studies ranged from 43% to 54%. These error rates clearly demonstrate that when only raw prices are

displayed a thorough comparison of products on the basis of prices is nearly impossible.

Current Unit Pricing

The posting of unit prices eliminates the most formidable step in making price comparisons, namely, the calculation of a price that is comparable across all sizes. Studies by Gatewood and Perloff (1973) and by Houston (1972) demonstrated that displaying the unit prices on shelf tags significantly decreased the number of errors. In these studies, however, the task was to find the single cheapest package. The question remains whether unit prices displayed in this fashion can be effectively used in everyday shopping situations.

The results of research to date are mixed, with the preponderance of evidence indicating that unit pricing has little or no effect on consumer behavior. A central problem with all these studies is the unreliability of self-reported behavior. Indeed, differences in the observed rates of the reported use of unit pricing may have been largely determined by differences in the interviewing methods (Monroe and LaPlaca, 1972).

The distribution of purchases has been used as a dependent variable in only a few studies. Because the authors believe that a positive effect of unit pricing should be claimed only if a shift in actual purchasing patterns can be demonstrated, these studies are the ones most closely related to the present experiment. Overall, the results have been inconclusive. Two studies have claimed to find no effect of unit pricing (Block, Schooler, and Erickson, 1971–1972; and McCullough and Padberg, 1971), while two others did demonstrate a change in purchasing patterns (Granger and Billson, 1972; and Isakson and Maurizi, 1973). As a whole, therefore, previous research has been equivocal. At best, limited effects of unit pricing have been observed; but more often the posting of unit prices caused no significant purchasing changes.

Several explanations have been offered as to why unit pricing has not more clearly altered consumer purchasing patterns in favor of the lower-priced items. Among the reasons given are the strength of quality and brand loyalty factors, the necessity of high education levels in order to use unit prices, and the method of displaying the unit price information (Monroe and LaPlaca, 1972). The central hypothesis of this research is that only by improving the unit pricing display so as to facilitate the necessary price comparisons will unit price information be used in typical purchasing situations. Such a hypothesis does not discount either the roles of quality and brand loyalty, or the advantage of a high level of education. It does assert, however, that the main reason for the observed failure of unit pricing is not these factors, but rather the unorganized fashion in which the unit price information has been presented.

The Unit Price List

It is proposed here that a single list of all brand/sizes and their unit prices is an effective arrangement of unit price information. This assertion has followed from some recent laboratory studies of decision making. In these studies eye movements were used to expose the normally covert processing of information during a choice task. When choosing the most preferred of several used cars, subjects relied primarily on direct pairwise comparisons (Russo and Rosen, in press). Comparison groups larger than two were not used because of the difficulty of concurrently processing the information from more than two alternatives. Furthermore, the two alternatives being compared were usually spatially proximal, indicating subjects' reluctance to process information from separated parts of the display. In a study presenting only two alternatives at a time, eye movements revealed a dimensional comparison strategy (Russo and Dosher, in preparation). Subjects tended to compare the two alternatives dimension by dimension. These studies suggest two considerations in the design of an optimal display of information for consumers: the facilitation of direct comparisons and the importance of organizing the information by dimension.

These design principles led to the display of price information shown in Figure 1. For a given product, like dishwashing liquids, all unit prices were presented on one summary list. The packages were listed in the order of their unit prices, starting at the top with the lowest unit priced package.

The main hypothesis was that the unit price lists would lead to an increased use of price information and, therefore, to fewer purchases of the higher unit priced packages and more purchases of the cheaper packages. Specifically, the hypothesis tested was that there would be an inverse relationship between the order of the unit prices and the order of the purchasing changes as a result of the use of the unit price lists.

METHOD

Design

The study was conducted over a five-week period during March and April 1973, at a large chain supermarket in a medium-size California city. Because the chain already displayed unit prices, the only comparison possible was between the store's current display method—unit prices on separated shelf tags—and the new list format. A comparison of the organized list against a display of only raw prices was not possible.

The first three weeks of the study were used to estimate a baseline distribution of market shares. The lists of unit prices were then posted, and for the next two weeks the distribution of market shares was again recorded. The market shares were the proportions of units sold for individual brand/sizes out of the total sales. Every week the sales of each brand/size were calculated from the difference in the shelf quantities between the beginning and end of the week and from the store's order book, which showed the number of cases stocked that week.

LIST OF UNIT PRICES

Listed In Order Of
Increasing Price Per Quart

Brand / Size	Price	Unit Price
Par 48 oz	54¢	36.0¢ Per Quart
Par 32 oz	38¢	38.0¢ Per Quart
Sweetheart 32 oz	55¢	55.0¢ Per Quart
Brocade 48 oz	85¢	56.7¢ Per Quart
Sweetheart 22 oz	39¢	56.7¢ Per Quart
Supurb 32 oz	59¢	59.0¢ Per Quart
White Magic 32 oz	59¢	59.0¢ Per Quart
Brocade 32 oz	63¢	63.0¢ Per Quart
Brocade 22 oz	45¢	65.5¢ Per Quart
Supurb 22 oz	45¢	65.5¢ Per Quart
White Magic 32 oz	45¢	65.5¢ Per Quart
Brocade 12 oz	27¢	72.0¢ Per Quart
Supurb 12 oz	29¢	77.3¢ Per Quart
Ivory 32 oz	80¢	80.0¢ Per Quart
Dove 22 oz	56¢	81.5¢ Per Quart
Ivory 22 oz	56¢	81.5¢ Per Quart
Lux 22 oz	56¢	81.5¢ Per Quart
Palmolive 32 oz	85¢	85.0¢ Per Quart
Ivory 12 oz	32¢	85.3¢ Per Quart
Palmolive 22 oz	60¢	87.3¢ Per Quart
Palmolive 12 oz	34¢	90.7¢ Per Quart

Figure 1 An Example of a Unit Price List

Products

Three products were used: dishwashing liquid, (canned) dog food, and facial tissue. The products were chosen to cover a wide range of packaged items. In addition, only product categories that possessed a wide range of unit prices were selected.

The most important criterion in choosing products was homogeneity. The authors sought only product categories that did not have large qualitative differences among the products. Product homogeneity was critical in this study, because differences in attributes within a particular product category could significantly reduce the effect of the unit price information on purchases in that category. Thus, it was essential to eliminate the resistance to purchasing changes that might have been due to product heterogeneity. Only within homogeneous product categories could it be expected that the unit price lists would increase the market shares of the lower priced brand/sizes.

Even over as short a period as five weeks there were some product and price changes. A product change was either the introduction of a new package or the discontinuance of an old one. In either case, that package was excluded from all analyses, along with any other items that were likely to have been affected by the change. When minor price changes (maximum = 17%) occurred, the average price over the time period was used. In only one instance did a price change significantly alter a product's unit price ranking. This product was eliminated from all analyses. There were no special promotions or major changes in advertising within any of the four product classes over the five weeks of the study. Shelf position and total shelf space also remained stable.

Unit Price Lists

A sample list of unit prices is given in Figure 1. Except for a block heading, the lists were typed on plain white paper. They varied from three to four inches wide and six to fifteen inches long. Duplicate lists were photocopies of the original. These lists were placed on the vertical supports of the shelving. Two or three identical lists were strategically located within the shelf area of each of the three products. The lists were updated for price changes once a week.

RESULTS

The market share of each brand/size was computed for both the three-week base period and the two-week test period. To assess the effect of the unit price lists, the percent change in market share was computed for each package. This was the difference between the test and base market shares, divided by the base market share. The main prediction was that the percent change in market share would increase as the unit price decreased, that is, that the order of the unit prices would be the opposite of the order of the percent changes in purchasing. To test this hypothesis, Kendall's rank correlation coefficient, tau, was used. A Kendall's tau combined over all three products was computed by merging the individual rank orders normalized to a 0 to 100 scale.

The value of Kendall's tau over all products was $-.192$ ($p \leq .05$). The unit price lists were, therefore, a significant factor in switching purchases toward the lower unit priced packages. The absolute value of the effect, tau $= .192$, was not large, however, indicating an irregular relation between unit prices and changes in the market shares. There could be two reasons for this. First, there is the natural variability in purchasing patterns due to the brief time period over which data were collected. Second is the failure of product homogeneity over the full range of a product.

The data for the individual product categories are shown in Figures 2, 3, and 4; and the results of the tests of the main hypothesis are given in Table 1. The Kendall's taus were all in the predicted direction but were not significant at the .05 level. An examination of Figures 2, 3, and 4 reveals that each product could have been divided into two subgroups. There was a large subcategory satisfying homogeneity and at least one smaller subgroup of brands that were qualitatively different from the main subcategory. When only the main subcategories were considered, a more regular decrease was observed. The results for each product category studied are discussed below.

Dishwashing Liquids

The results for dishwashing liquids are shown in Figure 2. Over the entire range, Kendall's tau was $-.124$, neither statistically significant nor encouraging. On the other hand, when the prediction was restricted to only the cheaper products, tau rose to $-.444$. This value was statistically significant ($p < .025$). In fact, the more expensive brands, those priced above 80¢/qt. also exhibited an improved value of tau ($-.360$, $p = .138$). The two subcategories turned out to be the nationally advertised brands and the local, less advertised brands. There was no overlap between the two groups. The results indicated that the consumers of the expensive brands were not induced by the unit price lists to switch into the cheaper subgroup. Within the less expensive subcategory, however, the predicted effect of the unit price list occurred. The consumers of the more expensive local brands switched to cheaper local brands.

There was some question as to whether there might also have been a systematic change within the subcategory of expensive, national brands. Two conditions mitigated against this. First, the range of unit prices was very narrow, providing little inducement to switch. Second, the national, highly advertised brands should have possessed the most brand loyalty and, therefore, the greatest resistance to purchasing changes. Although the changes in market shares were in the right direction (tau $= -.360$), the effect was not significant at the .05 level. A more detailed examination of purchasing changes, however, revealed a clear pattern (see Table 2). When size was held constant, the less expensive brands showed an increase in market share. In contrast, the more expensive brand in each size showed a drop in market share. Consumers seemed to switch to products with lower unit prices, but only within the same size. There was no associated switch to larger

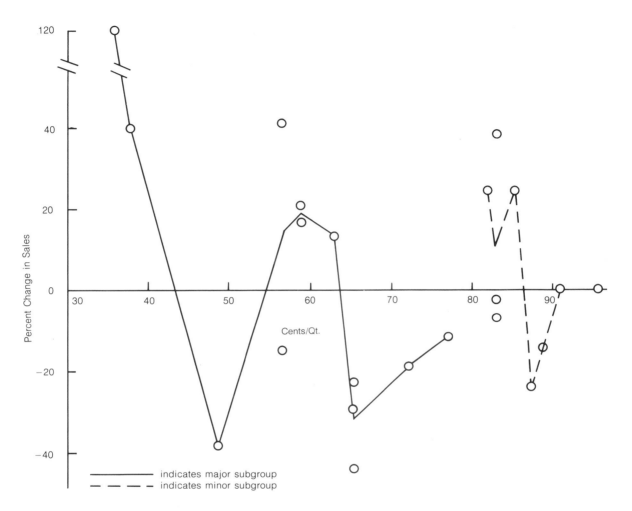

Figure 2 Purchasing Changes for Dishwashing Liquid

sizes, even though the change to lower unit prices corresponded to a trend toward larger sizes for the other products. From this analysis, it was concluded that the data within the subcategory of nationally advertised brands of dishwashing liquid supported the hypothesis that the list of unit prices caused a change toward lower unit priced items. That change occurred, however, only within packages of the same size.

Dog Food

A similar result occurred for dog food (see Figure 3). In this case, it was the most expensive brands that formed the main subcategory and that showed a clear effect of unit price information. For those products priced above 20¢/lb., Kendall's tau was $-.538$ ($p = .005$). All products in this group contained some meat (as well as meat by-products) but no cereal. As unit price decreased,

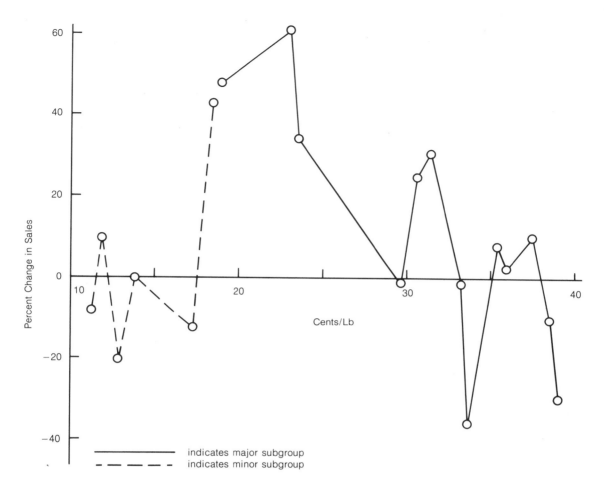

Figure 3 Purchasing Changes for Dog Food

the next three products contained cereal as well as some meat by-products. Finally, the four cheapest brand/sizes contained no meat at all. Apparently, the purchasers of dog foods containing meat were influenced by the list of unit prices to switch to cheaper dog foods with meat, but they could not be induced to change to a brand that contained some or all cereal. The results within the "cereal" subcategory showed no tendency to satisfy the hypothesis. These brands, however, did not form a homogeneous group, because some contained meat while others did not.

Facial Tissue

The data for facial tissue are plotted in Figure 4. Except for the most expensive item, the predicted inverse relationship was nearly perfect. For the least expensive six packages, tau was $-.733$ ($p = .028$). The most expensive item showed no change in market share and doubled the range of

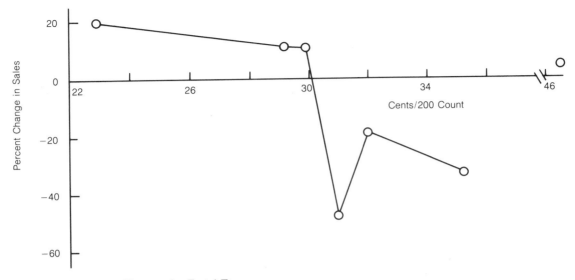

Figure 4 Purchasing Changes for Facial Tissue

unit prices. However, this item differed from all other brand/sizes in the shape of its package. In retrospect, it should not have been included with the regular boxes of facial tissue.

Table 1 Kendall's tau for individual products

Product	Number of brand/sizes	Tau	p
	Full range		
Dishwashing liquid	21	−.124	.225
Dog food	19	−.111	.253
Facial tissue	7	−.524	.068
All products	47	−.192	.034
	Homogeneous subrange		
Dishwashing liquid	13	−.444	.025
Dog food	12	−.485	.015
Facial tissue	6	−.733	.028
All products	31	−.492	<.001

Confirmation of Results

To describe the magnitude of the purchasing changes, the average price per unit of the items actually purchased was computed. These values are shown in Table 3, separately for the base and test periods. These data confirmed the previous results: the mean unit price was lower during the test period for all three products. The savings to

Table 2 Purchase change results for dishwashing liquids, national brands only

Size	Brand	Unit price	% Change
12	A	85.4	+24.2
	B	90.7	− 0.6
22	A,C,D[a]	82.9	+ 5.9
	B	88.8	−15.2
32	A	82.0	+25.2
	B	87.0	−25.5

[a]These three brands all had the same unit prices. The individual sales changes for A, C, and D were +39.9%, −7.5%, and −2.6%, respectively.

consumers ranged from 1.4% for dog food to 2.9% for dishwashing liquid. This statistic, mean unit price of actual purchases, was based on the full product ranges. Larger effects of the unit price lists would have appeared if the restricted ranges had been used.

DISCUSSION

The results supported the hypothesis that an organized list of unit price information would significantly alter consumers' purchasing patterns. It should be remembered that the control group for this study was not a situation where no unit price information was given, but rather the predominant current method for displaying unit prices, namely, individual shelf tags. The only difference between the base and test conditions was the mode of presenting the unit price information. There was no difference in the amount of information available. The results of this study are compatible with the current view in information-processing psychology that specific aspects of the task environment, such as the method of stimulus display, can significantly affect task performance (Lindsay and Norman, 1972; Newell and Simon, 1972; and Segal and Lachman, 1972).

Homogeneous Subcategories
One result whose strength was not fully anticipated was the necessity of confining the tests of the hypothesis to homogeneous subcategories. In canned dog food, a meat versus no meat distinction was observed; and in dishwashing liquids, the nationally advertised brands formed a subcategory separate from the unadvertised, local brands. For both these products, consumers of products in the more expensive subgroup could not be induced to switch to a product in the less expensive subcategory. This can be interpreted as a strong effect of quality, strong enough to nullify the unit price information. Within a subcategory, however, the predicted switching to lower unit priced brands was consistently found. This suggests something

like quality loyalty rather than brand loyalty. In addition, for the nationally advertised dishwashing liquids, the factor of container size was important. Switching seemed to take place primarily to a cheaper brand of the same size.

Cost Considerations
Any benefits to the consumer that result from the posting of lists of unit prices should be measured against the costs involved. The cost of installing and maintaining the current method of displaying unit price information varies widely from store to store (Executive Summary, 1971; Friedman, 1972, pp. 361–369; and *Consumer Reports*, 1971). It is smallest for the large chain store that can efficiently use computers to calculate unit prices and print shelf tags. The Giant Food chain estimates its per store cost as $750 for installation and $100 per year for maintenance (Peterson, 1974, pp. 91–101). Even these modest costs were recouped by the elimination of price-marking errors and by the reduction of stock shortages because of more effective inventory control. The use of unit price lists should increase the costs of the current method only slightly. Furthermore, if the unit price lists were to be substituted for the present display rather than combined with it, the overall cost of providing unit price information might be significantly reduced.

There are several other reasons that favor the adoption of the unit price lists. One is the increase in the market share of house brands, that is, prod-

Table 3 Mean unit prices for the three product categories

Product	Base period	Test period	Units sold per week
Dishwashing liquid	69.5¢/qt.	67.5¢/qt.	342
Dog food	28.0¢/lb.	27.6¢/lb.	2085
Facial tissue	30.2¢/200 count	29.6¢/200 count	617

ucts carrying the store's own label. Since the unit price lists do cause a shift to lower unit priced items, like house brands, supermarkets should derive additional profits from the sale of their own labels. Another advantage of the lists over separate shelf tags is their broader applicability. Lists can be used for products that do not have normal shelving, like frozen foods or stacked items. Finally, there is the customer goodwill that should be generated by a unit price display that results in savings that are clear to the consumer. In this study, a savings of about 2% in the average unit price of items purchased could be attributed to the lists of unit prices.

REFERENCES

"A Study of Consumer Reaction to Unit Pricing and Open Dating in Metropolitan Washington, DC," (1971), Executive Summary (Bethesda: Consumer Research Institute).

Block, Carl; Schooler, Robert; and Erickson, David (Winter 1971–72), "Consumer Reaction to Unit Pricing: An Empirical Study," *Mississippi Valley Journal of Business and Economics,* 7, 36–46.

Executive Summary (1971) "A Study of Consumer Reaction to Unit Pricing and Open Dating in Metropolitan Washington, D.C." Bethesda: Consumer Research Institute.

Friedman, Monroe P. (December, 1966), "Consumer Confusion in the Selection of Supermarket Products," *Journal of Applied Psychology,* 50, pp. 529–534.

———. (1972), "Consumer Responses to Unit Pricing, Open Dating, and Nutrient Labeling," in *Proceedings* of the Third Annual Conference of the Association for Consumer Research, M. Venkatesen, ed, 362–69.

Gatewood, Robert D., and Perloff, Robert (February 1973), "An Experimental Investigation of Three Methods of Providing Weight and Price Information to Consumers," *Journal of Applied Psychology,* 57, 81–85.

Granger, Clive W. J., and Billson, Andrew (August, 1972), "Consumers' Attitudes Toward Package Size and Price," *Journal of Marketing,* 9, 239–48.

Grant, Bess M. (September, 1969), "Truth in Pricing," report to Mayor John V. Lindsey, New York City.

Houston, Michael J. (July, 1972), "The Effect of Unit-Pricing on Choices of Brand and Size in Economic Shopping," *Journal of Marketing,* 36, pp. 51–54.

Isakson, Hans R., and Maurizi, Alex R. (August, 1973), "The Consumer Economics of Unit Pricing," *Journal of Marketing Research,* 10, 277–85.

Lindsay, Peter H., and Norman, Donald A. (Jan. 1972), *Human Information Processing,* New York: Academic Press.

McCullough, T. David, and Padberg, Daniel I. (Jan. 1971), "Unit Pricing in Supermarkets," *Search: Agriculture,* 1, 1–22.

Miller, George A. (March, 1956), "The Magical Number Seven, Plus or Minus Two," *Psychology Review,* 63, 81–97.

Monroe, Kent B., and LaPlaca, Peter J. (July, 1972), "What Are the Benefits of Unit Pricing?" *Journal of Marketing,* 36, 16–22.

Nelson, Helen E. (1962) "Report to the California Consumer Council," discussed in "What's Happened to Truth-in-Packaging?" *Consumer Reports,* January 1969, pp. 40–43.

Newell, Alan, and Simon, Herbert A. (1972), *Human Problem Solving,* Englewood Cliffs, N.J.: Prentice-Hall.

Peterson, Esther (May–June, 1974), "Consumerism as a Retailer's Asset," *Harvard Business Review,* 52, 91–101.

"Progress Report on Unit Pricing" (Feb. 1971), *Consumer Reports,* 84–85.

Russo, J. Edward, and Dosher, Barbara A. (in preparation), "Dimensional Evaluation: A Heuristic for Binary Choice," University of California, San Diego.

———, and Rosen, Larry D. (in press), "An Eye Fixation Analysis of Multi-Alternative Choice," *Memory and Cognition.*

Segal, Erwin M., and Lachman, Roy (January, 1972), "Complex Behavior or Higher Mental Processes: Is There a Paradigm Shift?" *American Psychology,* 27, 46–55.

Simon, Herbert A. (Feb. 8, 1974), "How Big is a Chunk?" *Science,* 482–88.

HOW WILL CONSUMER EDUCATION AFFECT CONSUMER BEHAVIOR?

PAUL N. BLOOM

Source: Paul N. Bloom, "How Will Consumer Education Affect Consumer Behavior?," in Beverlee B. Anderson, ed., *Advances in Consumer Research,* Vol. 3, pp. 208–12.

ABSTRACT

The recent upsurge of interest in consumer education can be expected to lead, in the long-run, to significant changes in consumer behavior. This paper contains a discussion of several hypotheses about how programs of this type could affect consumer behavior.

Interest in consumer education is growing rapidly. Within the last few months, a conference on consumer education has been held at the White House, an Office of Consumers' Education has been established within the Department of Health, Education and Welfare, and courses in consumer education have been made mandatory for all high school students in several states. This growth of interest in consumer education can be attributed to the recent depressed economic situation and, to some extent, the disappointing results achieved by certain consumer *information* programs (see Day and Brandt, 1974; Jacoby, Speller, and Kohn, 1974; Isakson and Maurizi, 1973). Many individuals have come to believe that consumer education programs are needed to help consumers deal with inflation and energy shortages and to teach consumers how to use and benefit from "Truth in Packaging," "Truth in Lending," and "Unit Pricing" disclosures.

A DEFINITION OF CONSUMER EDUCATION

In this paper, consumer education is viewed as *the process by which people learn the workings of the marketplace so that they can improve their ability to act as purchasers or consumers of those products and services they deem most likely to enhance their well-being* (see Willett, 1974; Seitz, 1972, p. 199). Consumer education is therefore treated as being rather different than consumer information—something with which it is often confused. Consumer education is considered to be a learning process which people go through which, of course, cannot be readily observed or heard. Consumer information, on the other hand, is clearly something which *can* be observed or heard.

A consumer education *program* is viewed in this paper as *any organized activity which has as one of its major ultimate goals the advancement of the process of consumer education among some segment of consumers.* This definition permits programs which certain people in the consumer education field might label as consumer information programs—because no teaching in a formal educational environment is taking place—to be viewed as consumer education programs. For example, a program which develops consumer information pieces such as buying guides or curriculum guides for use in high school consumer education courses is considered a consumer education program. Similarly, a program in which advertising messages are designed and distributed that instruct consumers in how to shop for certain categories of products' is considered a consumer education program. Both of these programs are designed to help advance the process of consumer education. However, programs which provide only factual information about specific product offerings, from which consumers can learn little that can be used in a variety of buying situations (e.g., unit pricing or "Truth in Lending" programs), are considered merely consumer information programs.

HYPOTHESIZED CHANGES IN CONSUMER BEHAVIOR

Although many of the current consumer education programs have been in existence for quite some time, there has not been any research reported on how these programs have affected consumer behavior. Clearly, cross-sectional and longitudinal studies should be conducted to try to measure how much various consumer education programs have changed consumer attitudes, preferences, habits, and so on. It should be recognized, however, that research in this area will be filled with many obstacles. It will be difficult to determine whether a change in consumer behavior has been caused by a consumer education program or by other confounding or intervening variables. Moreover, with some programs, it may take long periods of time before program-induced changes in consumer behavior can be detected—the learning process can be very slow.

A group of hypotheses that could be tested when researching the effects of consumer education programs are presented and discussed below. These hypotheses describe the long-run changes that the author expects to occur in the behavior of most consumers as a result of continued exposure to a variety of consumer education programs. In the absence of any past research from which inferences could be drawn, it was necessary to rely upon deductive reasoning to develop these hypotheses.

Hypothesis 1:   Consumers will express their wants and needs to sellers more explicitly and more frequently.

Exposure to consumer education programs should allow consumers to obtain a better understanding of what the marketplace has to offer them in terms of product variations and services. In addition, exposure to consumer education courses which cover areas like "values clarification" or "life adjustment"—such as the course offered at a Portland, Oregon high school in which students simulate real-life adult experiences including getting married, buying a home and car, and getting a divorce ("Divorce Course," 1974)—should help many consumers obtain a better understanding of what they want and need from life and from the marketplace. An improved understanding of both what is available and what is wanted from the marketplace should result in an improved ability among consumers to state explicitly what they want and need to sellers in the form of unsolicited letters, responses to marketing research questions, or other methods of communication. Suggestion letters from consumers should become more helpful to sellers and questionnaire responses of consumers should become less ambiguous. Moreover, consumers should become more likely to communicate their wants and needs to sellers as they learn, through consumer education, more about how consumer feedback can influence the decisions of these sellers. The number of suggestion letters and questionnaire responses received by sellers should increase.

> *Hypothesis 2:* Consumers will seek out and use larger amounts of information to help them make price, quality, and service comparisons before making a purchase.

By teaching consumers where consumer information can be found, how it can be used, and what the benefits are of using it, consumer education programs should tend to lower the perceived costs (in lost time and energy) and increase the perceived benefits of searching for and using consumer information. This, in turn, should lead consumers to seek out and use larger quantities of information from consumer magazines or advertising, unit pricing, open dating, and nutritional content disclosures before making a purchase. Consumers must be expected to "buy" more of a commodity (information) which they perceive to be lower in price and higher in quality than it was previously.

> *Hypothesis 3:* Consumers will make a progressively larger proportion of their purchases from sellers who offer relatively large amounts of easily-acquired information about their products and services.

A seller who provides consumers with a considerable amount of information about his product(s) or service(s) (e.g., ingredients, uses, warranties, unit price, advantages, etc.), through either advertising, label disclosures, or salespersons, will save consumers time and energy that could be lost in searching for this information. If consumers (as a consequence of consumer education) begin to

seek out and use larger amounts of information before making purchases—as hypothesized above—then they should become progressively more appreciative of sellers who can save them information search costs. As consumers develop more favorable attitudes toward information-providing sellers, the likelihood that they will actually prefer these sellers over others will increase. Thus, consumers can be expected to make an increasing proportion of their purchases from information-providing sellers. They will not buy inferior or overpriced products from these sellers, but will buy the products of these sellers with increasing frequency in those cases where all products competing in a market are perceived to have otherwise similar attributes.

> *Hypothesis 4:* Consumers will make a progressively larger proportion of their purchases from sellers who conduct relatively large consumer education programs.

Over time, large numbers of people can be expected to be exposed to consumer education programs. As more people benefit from their experience with these programs, more are likely to become supporters of consumer education. One way these people might show their support for consumer education is by becoming loyal patrons of sellers whose consumer education programs they personally found to be beneficial. Thus, consumers can be expected to make an increasing proportion of their purchases from sellers who conduct relatively large consumer education programs. Evidence that this trend may have already begun can possibly be found in the rapidly improving profit figures of Giant Food, Inc., a firm which is very active in consumer education (Levy, 1975).

> *Hypothesis 5:* Consumers will buy fewer products that are potentially harmful to their own health or to the health of others.

Consumer education programs often teach consumers about nutrition, product safety, health care, and environmental issues. As more people are exposed to these programs, one can expect a decline in the purchase of products which could produce health problems. Consumers will become less likely to buy products such as cigarettes, alcoholic beverages, sugar-laden foods, low-mileage automobiles, or aerosol sprays, and they will become more likely to buy products such as low-cholesterol foods, automobiles with safety and pollution-control features, or dental floss. It should be noted, however, that it will be necessary to reinforce constantly an inclination that might develop among consumers to buy safer, healthier products. If messages about nutrition, product safety, health care, and pollution are not constantly received by consumers, they may forget what they have learned in these areas. For example, many consumers seem to have forgotten what they learned about the dangers of cigarette smoking in the absence of frequent anti-smoking messages. The volume of these messages was reduced significantly following the banning from the broadcast media of cigarette advertising in 1971. Since that time, cigarette sales have increased steadily, reversing several years' decline.

Hypothesis 6: Consumers will more actively seek remedies, redress, or restitution when dissatisfied with a product, service, or marketing practice.

Through exposure to consumer education programs, consumers should learn where to go when they are dissatisfied with an experience they have had in the marketplace. They should learn which agencies, organizations, and individuals can help them if they have been deceived or have found a practice they would like to see discontinued. They should also learn how consumers can achieve highly favorable results by filing complaint letters and lawsuits. This knowledge should lead consumers to become much more active in filing complaints and lawsuits against business firms.

Hypothesis 7: Consumers will become more active participants in the debates over legislation that could affect the workings of the marketplace.

Consumer education programs should teach consumers about the important role that government plays in our economy. They should learn about the laws which exist to protect and help consumers and about the legislative history of these laws. They should discover how important it is, from their point of view, to have their voices heard, along with those of representatives of businesses and government, during debates over legislation that could affect their ability to obtain what they want and need from the marketplace. Consumers should therefore become more active in writing to legislators, lobbying for or against legislation, testifying before legislative committees, and supporting politically-active consumer organizations.

A FEW COMMENTS

The possibility that the changes hypothesized above might occur in the very near future should be recognized. Business firms could respond to a changing consumer population and the changing practices of competing firms by trying to outdo one another in creating progressive, extensive consumer education programs. At the same time, legislators might respond to the increased political activity of consumers by starting and funding new consumer education programs and by requiring consumer education courses for all public school students. The amount of exposure consumers would receive to consumer education programs could therefore increase rapidly, leading to the hypothesized changes in consumer behavior at an earlier point in time.

No matter when they occur, the changes hypothesized above will probably occur more rapidly among middle and upper class consumers, younger consumers, and consumers living in or near large metropolitan areas. These groups are more likely to be exposed to consumer education courses, messages, and materials through school programs, the media, and friends. They are also more likely to learn about the workings of the marketplace at a fast pace. Changes in the behavior of poor, elderly, and rural consumers will probably come much more slowly. Consumer educators will have to do a considerable amount of research to find the best strategies for "marketing" consumer education to these segments.

It should be noted that nothing has been mentioned thus far about the consumer of the future paying less attention to advertising or buying more lower-priced, private-label brands—two results that many people expect from continued exposure to consumer education programs. These changes have not been hypothesized to occur because it seems equally plausible to expect opposite results. Consumers could pay greater attention to advertising as part of their efforts to acquire more information before making purchases. Similarly, consumers could buy less private label brands because of an increased desire to buy familiar, widely-available products about which they have a great deal of favorable information.

Finally, it should be mentioned that if consumer behavior changes in the direction hypothesized above as a consequence of consumer education, it will not necessarily be totally beneficial for consumers. If consumers buy less cigarettes, alcoholic beverages, and low-mileage automobiles, then unemployment could increase. If consumers tie up the courts with lawsuits against sellers, then crime in the streets could increase. And if consumers lobby for more consumer protection legislation, then prices charged by sellers could increase (to cover the cost of compliance with new laws). In short, consumer education might unintentionally hurt the interests of many consumers.

CONCLUSIONS

In the future, consumers will go through a different consumer socialization process than consumers do today. They will spend more time in consumer education classes and will see and hear more consumer education messages. This new socialization process can be expected to produce consumers who will be more willing and able to state what they want and need to sellers and who will also be more willing and able to file complaints and lawsuits against sellers. In addition, this process can be expected to produce consumers who will seek out and use more information before making purchases and who will tend to make an increasing amount of these purchases from sellers who (1) provide large amounts of easily-acquired consumer information, (2) conduct consumer education programs, and (3) offer products that present little danger to the public's health.

Finally, this process can be expected to produce consumers who will fight more actively in the political arena for legislation which serves their interests. All of these hypotheses should be tested by conducting cross-sectional and longitudinal studies of how the many present-day consumer education programs have affected consumer behavior.

REFERENCES

Day, George S., and Brandt, William K. (June, 1974), "Consumer Research and the Evaluation of Information Disclosure Requirement: The Case of Truth in Lending," *Journal of Consumer Research,* 1, 21–32.

"Divorce Course," *Time,* (December 2, 1974), 92.

Isakson, Hans R., and Maurizi, Alex R. (August, 1973), "The Consumer Economics of Unit Pricing," *Journal of Marketing Research,* 10, 277–85.

Jacoby, Jacob; Speller, Donald E.; and Kohn, Carol A. (Februrary, 1974), "Brand Choice Behavior as a Function of Information Load," *Journal of Marketing Research,* 11, 63–9.

Levy, Claudia (June 4, 1975), "Giant's Net Shows Gain over '74," *Washington Post,* D1.

Seitz, Wesley D. (Winter, 1972), "Consumer Education as the Means To Attain Efficient Market Performance," *Journal of Consumer Affairs,* 6, 199–201.

Willett, Sandra L. (June 21, 1974), "Preliminary Statement," A handout prepared for the Panel on Consumer Education of the 1974 meeting of the Education Commission of the States.

INNOVATIONS AND CONSUMER BEHAVIOR

A behavior of fascination to consumer researchers and of great importance to marketers concerns the processes whereby new ideas, products, and services are purchased by individuals and organizations. We shall refer to ideas, products, and services which consumers perceive to be new as *innovations*. In the literature on innovations, buyers are referred to as *adopters*. Five categories of adopters are usually identified. The first category is called *innovators*. Innovators are consumers who are among the first 10 percent of a population to adopt an innovation. The second category includes the *early adopters*. Early adopters are approximately the next 15 percent to adopt after the innovators. The third and fourth categories are the *early* and *late majority* groups, respectively. The early and late majority each represent about 30 percent of the total population. The fifth and last group to adopt an innovation, if ever, includes those called *laggards*. Laggards represent approximately 15 percent of the population. Note that the term *laggard* has a pejorative connotation. It implies there is something wrong with a person who doesn't adopt an innovation until almost everyone else has.

Considerable research exists about the characteristics of the different adopter (or buyer) categories. Some studies have found innovators and early adopters to be younger and to have higher levels of formal education than other adopter categories. Innovative firms have been found to be larger than many other firms in their industries and to send employees to professional meetings more often than less innovative firms. Various research studies are not always in agreement about the traits of the different adopter categories.

For this reason studies about consumer behavior involving innovations should be used more as a source of clues and less as a guideline as to what a specific group of consumers will do with regard to a very specific innovation.

Research findings about the nature of innovative organizations are somewhat more consistent. Innovative organizations are more clearly aware of their needs and spend more staff time trying to understand them. In addition there is usually a strong consensus among members of an innovative organization that action should be taken in response to a need. Members of an innovative organization are less likely to feel threatened by an innovation than members of a much less innovative organization. There is also a greater potential for change in innovative firms or agencies. Potential for change refers to the capacity of an organization to accept and implement change. This capacity may consist of financial ability and the presence of individuals who have the ability to use the innovation appropriately. There is also evidence that members of innovative organizations usually believe they have substantial control over the change process. They feel that to a considerable degree they can influence the selection and implementation of the innovation. Members of less innovative organizations have less of this feeling of control.

The papers included in this section collectively address many of the issues and research findings in the literature on consumer innovativeness.

"APPLYING A PROCESS MODEL OF INNOVATION IN ORGANIZATIONS TO MARKETING SITUATIONS"

In the industrial sector, the marketing of new technologies is an important but difficult undertaking. Yet much of the consumer behavior literature on the adoption of innovations refers only to the adoption processes of ultimate consumers and not to the adoption processes of industrial consumers. The Eveland and Rogers article describes the adoption processes of industrial consumers. In particular, Eveland and Rogers describe these processes by formulating a model. What a model is and what kind of model this is are explained quite well in the article so those ideas will not be described further here.

The Eveland and Rogers article is fairly generalized—that is, it is not limited by context. It may be useful for readers to think of a particular organization and a particular innovation for which the firm would be a potential consumer. The organization can then be characterized using the seven classes of factors listed in the article. If it is unknown how the organization would be characterized using these factors, then conditional statements can be made. For instance, "if the participants were *highly professional,* then the adoption process. . ." Secondly, the five stages of the innovation process can then be understood in the light of the organizational context in which they occur. One can then see the effect of the organizational structure on the process of deciding to adopt an innovation and implement the change.

"A METHODOLOGY FOR IDENTIFYING INNOVATOR CHARACTERISTICS OF NEW BRAND PURCHASERS"

A large part of the work in consumer behavior deals with how consumers react to new products and services. The process which an individual goes through in reacting to a new product or service is called the *adoption process.* The process through which an innovation spreads through the population is called the *diffusion process.* As a new product or service diffuses through the population, different groups of consumers can be identified based on how early or late they are, relative to others, in adopting the innovation.

The five categories of adopters mentioned by Donnelly and Ivancevich in footnote 1 are the names given to these different groups. Their study compares groups of consumers who adopted a product at four time periods to see if there are significant differences between the groups on measures of social character. In addition, adopters are compared with nonadopters to see if there are significant differences between these two groups. These two comparisons were made to determine the relationship between social character and innovativeness.

In the first case, significant differences were found. Innovators are more likely to be inner-directed than are later adopters. As diffusion takes place, adopters in the current period are more likely to be other-directed. In the second comparison, between purchasers of the new product a d purchasers of an established product, only some of the findings are statistically significant. Early purchasers of the innovation are significantly more inner-directed than same-year purchasers of the established brand. However, later adopters of the innovation are not significantly different from established brand purchasers in terms of their social character.

Given these findings, one must ask what action implications can be derived. How can innovations be presented or designed so they will attract other-directed adopters earlier without losing inner-directed individuals who might already become early adopters? The most important question to ask is why these findings were discovered. Why are early adopters more likely to be inner-directed than other-directed? Is this something inherent in inner-direction or is it something inherent in innovations? The question is crucial because it will determine which strategies are possible. If the findings derive from some quality of the innovation itself, perhaps it can be redesigned and/or presented differently. However, if the differences stem from the nature of being inner- or other-directed, the challenge is much greater.

"MULTIPLE-INDICANT APPROACH FOR STUDYING NEW PRODUCT ADOPTERS"

There are two facets of the Jacoby article which make it interesting. First, unlike much work in consumer behavior, a significant relationship is found between a personality variable (i.e., dogmatism) and a consumer behavior (i.e., innovation proneness). It appears that the greater a person's degree of dogmatism, the less will be the person's innovation proneness. This statement makes explicit a continuous relationship between dogmatism and innovation proneness; that is, the relation could be plotted as a linear function:

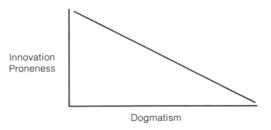

However, this is not the specific finding of the Jacoby article. Jacoby concludes that people in the "high dogmatic" half of the population are likely to be low in innovation proneness, and people in the "low dogmatic" half of the population are likely to be high in innovation proneness. This finding can only be plotted as two points:

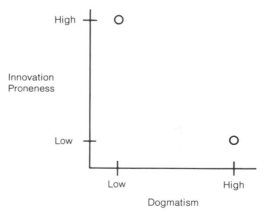

A second interesting point is made in examining whether people are consistently innovative across product categories. This is important because much of the research in consumer behavior examines responses to only one product, but then generalizes these findings to all innovation contexts. The relationship between dogmatism and innovation proneness was found in 11 out of the 15 product categories. If another researcher had conducted this study using only one product category, and that category was one of the four in which no statistically significant relationship was found, the conclusion would have been that no relationship exists. Thus, researchers should use more than one product category, and researchers should be cautious of studies which rely on one product category for obtaining measurements of innovativeness but generalize the results to other product categories.

"THE INNOVATIVE COMMUNICATOR IN THE DIFFUSION PROCESS"

Many of the marketing studies of the diffusion of innovations have studied one of two groups, either early purchasers of new products or opinion leaders who encourage others to purchase new products. Baumgarten's article deals with innovative communicators, or people who are both early users and opinion leaders. The purpose of the article is to see in what ways innovative communicators are different from other people.

Six sets of characteristics are examined to see if they differentiate innovative communicators from others. These six sets are: (1) demographics, (2) media exposure, (3) sociological-social activities, (4) fashion attitudes, (5) psychological self-description, and (6) socio-political attitudes and opinions. Of these, media exposure, sociological-social activities and fashion attitudes were the best distinguishing characteristics, with fashion attitudes providing the single best discrimination between innovative communicators and others. This highlights a well-known fact in studying human behavior: attitudes which are substantively very close to a particular behavior (e.g., attitudes about fashions and fashion communicating behavior) will generally have a stronger relationship than will a more distant attitude and the same behavior (e.g., socio-political attitudes and fashion behavior).

In reading the article it may be helpful for the reader to make a summary chart of the research findings concerning each of the six sets of characteristics.

APPLYING A PROCESS MODEL OF INNOVATION IN ORGANIZATIONS TO MARKETING SITUATIONS

J. D. EVELAND
AND
EVERETT M. ROGERS

In this paper we present the outline of a newly-developed process model of innovation in organizations, and discuss some implications of this model for the development of marketing strategies for new technologies.

WHY MODELS?

One of the major ways in which social science organizes its observations about human behavior is through the development and exploration of what are called models. *Models* are sets of symbols, of concepts abstracted from the real world, which are organized together to represent a problem. Any interaction of concepts can be represented as a model, and models can be as simple or as complex as we wish. By creating models and using them to identify crucial relationships between the key features of individual and social problems, we gain insights into how to deal with these problems. Models are never "true" or "false"—rather, they are simply more or less useful in leading us to these insights, and in suggesting hypotheses for further exploration.

Models are of two general types. The usual kind of model we construct and analyze may be called a *static* model. In a model of this type, we explore relationships between concepts at a single point in time. These models may be causal models, in which we assume that one set of concepts causes another to occur, or simply correlational models, in which we just look at the way in which concepts vary with each other. In either case, what we emphasize are the relationships or structure.

These models are useful for many purposes, but they do not allow us to form many insights about the changes in relationships over time. Problems in which time is a crucial element require us to use *process* models, in which our emphasis is on how the state of concepts at one time affects their state at another time. These models are considerably more difficult to create and interpret than static models, and the statistical methods for assessing their validity are much less developed. Nevertheless, when we are looking at problems in which changes over time are important, process models are essential.

The problem of technological innovation in organizational settings is one such problem. We have recognized for a long time that most changes in technology in both private companies and public agencies take place over considerable periods of time, and that these changes pass through several definite stages. However, most of the analyses of innovation have used static models, primarily because of the advantages of easier data collection and analysis. A number of approaches to process models have been made (for example, Zaltman, et al., 1973), but detailed analysis of innovation processes has received less systematic attention than it deserves.

The model which we propose in this paper was originally developed in the context of public agencies, but we believe that it is equally applicable to private settings and to a wide variety of new technologies. A full report on this model and the data supporting it is contained in Rogers, et al. (1977).

DIMENSIONS OF THE MODEL

Our view of the innovation process is based on a few key propositions:

1. An innovation—*any* innovation—is not a single unitary "thing." Rather, it is made up of many elements, the characteristics of what it is and how it is used. These characteristics are defined by the parties in the process with either more or less specificity at different points in time. *Specificity* in this context is the amount of agreement between two or more people about some characteristic. When people agree, specificity is high. When people are free to hold different opinions, specificity is low. Some innovations by their nature are more specific than others. For example, it is much easier to achieve consensus about a new kind of garbage truck than about a new computer system. In all cases, however, there is some degree of freedom to define either what the innovation is or how it is to be used.

2. The process of innovation is essentially a process of specification carried out within the organization concerned—that is, a process of increasing the specificity of definition of the innovation and its use. It is a process of decision-making. The decisions, however, are not "big" decisions about general strategies of innovation. Rather, they are small decisions, whose effect on the organization is to reduce the ability of individuals to interpret the situation individually and act alone. It is, in short, a process of the formation of an organizational consensus about the innovation and its applications. This process, we believe, passes through several consistent stages in sequence, and each stage is characterized by certain types of decisions which have to be made. This decision-making takes place, at least implicitly, in all cases of organizational innovation.

3. There are two major categories of decisions which have to be made: those relating to the innovation itself (the tool and its shape) and those relating to its application (how it is to be used). No tool has an unambiguous use. For example, a computer may be used to compute, or it can be used as an expensive typewriter. It may be more effective to use it to compute, but that is not its only possible function. Both tool-decisions and use-decisions are made in a specification-sequence. Specification of the tool and specification of its uses are parallel aspects of the innovation process. They generally proceed in a linked fashion, but are subject to differences in pace and speed.

4. The process of innovation is subject to different influences at different points in time. We believe that among these influences there are seven general classes of factors which are particularly important:

   a. The degree of *professionalism* of the participants—that is, the degree to which their attitudes and expectations are shaped by outside professional norms (medicine, law, social work, management, etc.).

   b. The nature of *system support,* or the external sources promoting the innovation (marketers, change agents, etc.).

c. The general *innovativeness* of the organization—that is, its general tendency to look outside itself for solutions to its problems rather than inside.

d. The pattern of *accountability* of the organization—that is, its acceptance of responsibility for achieving and maintaining a certain level of performance in ways influenced by sources outside the organization but commonly accepted within it.

e. The nature of the *resources* available to the organization which might be applied to the innovation.

f. The nature of *communication patterns* within the organization.

g. The nature of the *effectiveness feedback* arrangements within the organization—that is, the mechanisms and criteria used by the organization to determine whether it is doing what it is supposed to be doing.

This list of factors is by no means exclusive; a wide range of other sociological, psychological, and economic factors are clearly related to innovation behavior, and have been included in other models. Our research, however, indicates that factors such as these—internal, closely related to organizational processes—are more important and perhaps more manipulable than others we might have included.

THE STAGES OF INNOVATION PROCESSES

We believe that it is useful to separate the innovation process—that is, the sequence of specification of the details of the innovation—into five general stages, each characterized by a particular range of decisions which must be made in order to create a base for future decisions. These stages are as follows:

1. Agenda-setting: the stage at which general problems of the organization are commonly recognized and defined. Strictly speaking, this process takes place continuously, and is not part of the *innovation* sequence proper but rather a necessary prerequisite for it to begin. However, we include agenda-setting as part of our model to emphasize that without some implicit sense of a problem, of a discrepancy between what *is* and what *should be,* no innovation sequence will begin. The organization's agenda, or list of its problems in priority order, is a major influence on how the shape and use of the innovation are developed. We find that professional expectations (Influence Category A) are most important at this stage, since they shape the sense of organization members as to what problems should be addressed by the organization.

2. Matching: the stage at which a general problem from the agenda and a general idea about a possible "solution" to that problem (an "innovation") are brought together within the organization. Since our model deals only with organizational decision-making, we are not concerned here with the sources of such ideas or how they spread throughout the population—that is a problem of *diffusion.* At the matching stage, it is sufficient that the new idea exist and that it be brought together with a problem in the minds of one or more members of the organization. The new idea may come entirely from inside ("invention") or entirely from outside ("innovation") or may involve some combination of outside ideas with inside modifications ("re-invention"). This latter situation is probably the most common. At this stage, the predominant influences are system support (Influence Category B) and general innovativeness (Influence Category C). These factors influence primarily the organization's awareness of ideas outside its boundaries and the ease with with such ideas can penetrate into the system.

3. Redefining: the stage at which the main characteristics of the innovation are defined in terms relevant to the various members of the different organizational units involved. This stage represents the beginning of specification—that sequence of decisions which reduces the ambiguity of the innovation. Until there is some agreement on those basic characteristics of the innovation among a certain "critical mass" of participants, the subsequent stages cannot be reached. The size of the critical mass obviously varies by innovation and by type of organization. The closer two people are in terms of profession and basic attitudes, the easier it is likely to be for them to agree on a redefinition of the innovation. This stage may take a long time when widely different groups such as, for example, computer programmers and accountants or production managers and planners must be brought together. Accountability (Influence Category D) and resources (Influence Category E) are most important at this stage, since they affect primarily the sharing of perceptions of responsibility and the possibilities for change.

4. Structuring: the stage at which participants engage in joint activity to establish the innovation within the organizational unit which is to be its primary home. More or less of the entire organization may be involved at this stage. It is distinguished by the emergence of recognizable organizational structural and functional arrangements related explicitly to the innovation—for example, an "Office of Systems" and a pattern of regular output reports in the case of a new computer system. Factors of communication (Influence Category F) and feedback (Influence Category G) are predominant at this stage, since they affect how organizational patterns are established and modified within the system.

5. Interconnecting: the stage at which the organizational structure which has been set up around the innovation at the previous stage defines just what its relationships are to the rest of the organization, and those relationships are accepted or modified by the other parts of the system. Like the previous stages, this is also a sequence of specification decisions in which ambiguities and multiple perceptions of the innovation and its structure are gradually reduced to a single mutually-agreed-on version.

This series of five stages represents, we believe, the sequence of decisions through which any innovation process must pass. The decisions may be made explicitly, as an act of the organization or individuals within it, or they may be made implicitly, by simple exclusion or assumption. The activity at one stage cannot really begin until the work at the previous stage is substantially accomplished. Until earlier innovation decisions have been made, there is really no base for making subsequent decisions. The process may move slowly or rapidly; it may even backtrack, as previously unrecognized sources of ambiguity reveal themselves or an already achieved consensus breaks down.

There is a recognizable conclusion to the process, however, at the point where the innovation is no longer thought of by the participants as an "innovation" but rather a natural, normal, "organic" part of the system. Examples of such "institutionalized" innovations might be computerized billing by the oil companies and the cabinet system in American national government. Of course, like any other feature of the organization, institutionalized innovations are liable to be changed through subsequent innovation processes.

It is important to note that each stage involves decisions about both the tool itself and its uses. For those innovations where the shape of the tool is less flexible, less subject to ambiguity, tool-decisions at each stage may be rather simple. Redefining and structuring a tool like a new garbage truck or a plastic-like styrofoam may be relatively easy. However, even for highly rigid innovations, a considerable area of ambiguity is always present in its possible uses. The multitude of different patterns of garbage collection and the myriad uses of styrofoam in packaging and consumer products should make this point clear. It is very rare for there to be an innovative situation where this ambiguity is not present, even if it is not easily clarified or recognized.

To summarize this model—we suggest that there are five basic stages in innovation processes, each characterized by a certain range of decisions which must be made about the tool and its uses. Some influences are more important at one stage than at others. In general, the tendency is to move toward greater specification of the innovation, that is, toward Stage 5, but this process is by no means simple and linear. Table 1 (below) summarizes this model.

USING THE MODEL

As we noted earlier, the value of any model is determined primarily by its utility—that is, the usefulness of the insights which it gives us about the process in question. We believe that this model of the innovation process gives a number of insights which may be particularly helpful to those interested in the marketing of technology, as well as the inherent dynamics of the process itself:

Table 1   Stages in the innovation process

Stage	Decisions about the tool	Decisions about use of the tool	Influence categories
1. Agenda-setting	*	*	a. Professionalism
2. Matching	*	*	b. System support
			c. Innovativeness
3. Redefining	*	*	d. Accountability
			e. Resources
4. Structuring	*	*	f. Communication
			g. Effectiveness feedback
5. Interconnecting	*	*	

*Indicates a specific set of decisions which must be made at this point. The exact nature and content of these decisions varies according to the innovation and the organization concerned.

1. Any person who is promoting new technology has to be aware of the importance of potential problems to his clientele. We have noted that no innovation process begins without an implicit match between some organizational problem and the innovation in question. There is no doubt that in many cases it is the knowledge of the innovation as a possible solution which triggers the recognition of a problem. This does not imply that the problem did not exist until the innovation came along—only that we frequently avoid spending a lot of attention on problems which we cannot do anything about. When it becomes clear that *we can* do something about it, we tend to modify our agenda to make room for it as an active problem. Any salesman or change agent who has an innovation in his "bag of tricks" should be aware of the importance of agendas, and of the necessity of making clear the connection between his innovation and significant organizational problems—taking into account the variable nature of the agenda.

2. The distinction between the specification of the tool and specification of its uses can introduce complications. If we recognize that there is nothing unambiguous about either tool decisions or use decisions and that variations in these specification sequences are both natural and inevitable, we will innovate more effectively and efficiently. Too often salesmen and other change agents forget that the adaptation of their tool through redefining, structuring, and interconnecting is necessary if the innovation is to become truly a part of the organization. We become frustrated when someone does not use a tool in exactly the fashion we envisioned, and view this behavior as something to be resisted. Instead, since it is a necessary part of the innovation process, we would do better to be explicit about this part of the installation process, as, for example, many minicomputer firms have learned to do, and take advantage of adaptation to ensure the best possible match between our tool and the organization's problems.

3. Small decisions are frequently as important or more important than "big" decisions. One of the principal differences between this model and previous models of innovation is the de-emphasis on decisions to "adopt" an innovation and the greater emphasis on the long series of small, limited scale decisions about how the innovation is to be defined and wired into the existing system. Each of these decisions affects only a small part of the whole innovation at any one time. Thus, a salesman or change agent must be aware of how this sequence of decisions is being made, and must understand what parts of his innovation can be changed or modified easily and which parts cannot be changed without altering the essence of the innovation. The more a promoter of an innovation can split it up into pieces suitable for separate attention, separate small-scale innovation, perhaps on a trial basis, the more likely he is to find his innovation accepted. A parallel point is that the opinions and activities of lower-level managers and users of the innovation may in fact be more important than the opinions of top management in shaping how an organization responds to an innovation. This is predictable from our model, which emphasizes small-scale decision-*shaping* rather than large-scale decision-*making;* it is a phenomenon which has often been noted but more often deplored than understood as a normal and functional part of the innovation process. Obviously, then, a salesman or change agent should pay at least as much attention to what is going on relating to his innovation inside the organization as he does to his relationships with top management.

4. Multiple intervention by salesmen and change agents is both a necessity and an opportunity. We have identified five general stages in the innovation process, each with two general types of decisions to be made and innumerable small deci-sions which decisively shape the innovation process. Clearly, a change agent who ends his contact with an organization at the point of "adoption" of the innovation (generally sometime shortly after the matching stage) is likely to find that the ultimate implementation and use of his innovation is rather different from what he had intended. In some cases this does not matter; however, in many cases the experience with the innovation which one organization has may be influential on decisions by the same organization or other organizations to go into the same innovation area again. Change agents who ignore Stages 3–5 in our model are likely to find their *innovations* taking the blame for implementation problems which could have been solved with some systematic attention to these stages by the change agent. Equally important is the necessity to adapt one's intervention to the stage in process; attempts to influence, say, interconnections before the redefining and structuring stages are well along are not likely to be very helpful. The process can be hurried but not short-circuited. Many "horror-stories" about unsuccessful innovation attempts and "resistances to change" are in fact illustrations of attempts to deal with implementation tasks out of sequence. It does not work, and people interested in promoting the use of new technology need to be particularly sensitive to this problem.

As we noted earlier, any social-science model should be capable of generating many different conclusions and hypotheses. In this section, we have identified only a few of the possible lessons which we can draw from the model of the innovation process we define here. We hope that our brief discussion of this model may stimulate the reader to organize some of his own thoughts and observations about innovation, and understand some aspects of the process which might otherwise seem contradictory and nonfunctional.

REFERENCES

Rogers, Everett M.; Evland, John D; and Klepper, Constance (1977). *The Innovation Process in Public Organizations,* a report to the National Science Foundation, Division of Policy Research and Analysis, published by the University of Michigan.

Zaltman, Gerald; Duncan, Robert; and Holbek, Jonny (1973). *Innovations and Organizations,* N.Y.: Wiley-Interscience.

A METHODOLOGY FOR IDENTIFYING INNOVATOR CHARACTERISTICS OF NEW BRAND PURCHASERS

**JAMES H. DONNELLY, JR.
AND
JOHN M. IVANCEVICH**

INTRODUCTION

One aspect of consumer behavior which has recently received particular attention from researchers is the hypothesized relationship between various demographic and behavioral characteristics reportedly possessed by consumer innovators; as a result, we appear to be making progress in identifying differences among the various categories of adopters[1] (Bell, 1964; Blake, Perloff, and Heslin, 1970; Coney, 1972; Donnelly, 1970; Donnelly and Etzel, 1973; Donnelly and Roeth, 1973; Engel, Kergerreis, and Blackwell, 1969; Frank, Massy, and Morrison, 1964; Gruen, 1960; Hayes, 1959; Jacoby, 1971a, 1971b; Harold H. Kassarjian, 1971; Lambert, 1972; Morton, 1967; Ostland, 1969; Popielarz, 1967; Robertson, 1968; Rogers, 1962; Rogers and Stanfield, 1968; Summers, 1972; Uhl, Andrus, and Paulsen, 1970; and White, 1966).

When studying characteristics of innovators, researchers usually compare buyers and nonbuyers of a certain product(s) within a given time period after the product has been introduced or examine willingness to buy in laboratory purchase situations (as is often the case when university researchers use students as subjects). Any differences found between buyers and nonbuyers or between those indicating a willingness to buy and those unwilling to buy are designated as differences between innovators and noninnovators. These conclusions are usually drawn without (1) using a "control" group of purchasers of similar established products for comparison purposes, or (2) comparing the early trier group with later purchasers of the new product.

Not comparing the early trier group with later purchasers of the new product makes it questionable to assume that any differences found are necessarily related to innovativeness since the

Source: James H. Donnelly, Jr., and John M. Ivancevich, "A Methodology for Identifying Innovator Characteristics of New Brand Purchasers," *Journal of Marketing Research,* Vol. 11, August, 1974, pp. 331–34.

[1]Five categories of adopters have been identified: (1) innovators, (2) early adopters, (3) early majority, (4) late majority, and (5) laggards (Popielarz, 1967).

same differences could be found at some later point. For example, finding that early triers of a new product are more venturesome than non-buyers does not necessarily indicate that venture-someness is a characterisitic of the consumer innovator, since future measures could indicate that later buyers of the new product are just as venturesome as the early triers and/or still more venturesome than nonbuyers. If this were the case, venturesomeness would not be related to innovativeness but instead be a constant differ-ence between buyers and nonbuyers of the prod-uct.

RATIONALE

Recently, various writers have begun to stress the need for greater use of longitudinal studies in con-sumer behavior research (Kollat, Engel, and Blackwell, 1970; Zaltman and Stiff, 1973). Since these methods permit multiple measures over time, they can, therefore, be especially powerful in the study of an ongoing process such as the diffu-sion of innovations (Zaltman and Stiff, 1973).

In much of the research in which innovator characteristics have been investigated, the prod-ucts studied were unique new products. However, the majority of new products (or brands) intro-euced annually are often only attempts to alter existing products in order to increase sales or mar-ket share. In studying innovativeness under these conditions, a stronger research design can be used. In the case of new brands, similar existing products are already on the market, and it is there-fore possible to construct a comparison group of purchasers of similar already established products. The use of such a group would enable the re-searcher to determine if the early triers of the new brand possess more of certain characteristics or, better yet, unique characteristics, than buyers of already established similar products (or new ver-sions of similar products where available). Then, comparing purchasers in both groups over time would provide a sound basis for identifying in-novator characteristics for new brand purchasers in addition to making possible more meaningful generalizations concerning differences among the various categories of adopters.

OBJECTIVE

Based on the previous discussion, the objective of this article is to demonstrate a methodology for identifying innovator characteristics of new brand purchasers. Specifically, the study compares the social character of four groups of purchasers of a new model automobile during four different time periods and then compares these purchasers with purchasers of new versions of similar established models during the same four time periods.

The behavioral characteristic "social character" was developed by David Riesman (Riesman, Glazer, and Denny, 1950). Briefly, Riesman's theory is that individuals can be grouped into three types: "tradition-directed," "inner-directed," or "other-directed." A person who is tradition-directed guides himself by membership in a particular class or caste. Riesman believes that there are few, if any, such people in America to-day. Instead, he conceives the social character of the majority of the people in the United States as falling somewhere along a continuum from inner-to other-directed. The inner-directed person relies on his own internal standards and values to guide his behavior; the other-directed person tends to rely on the values of his contemporaries. Thus we can expect an individual's social character to fall somewhere between the two extremes.

RESEARCH DESIGN

Since the research was concerned with the dual variables of social character and innovators, a spe-cial type of new product was sought for which the consequences of its adoption would be of high social significance and the nature of its purchase important. The authors believed that the introduc-tion of the Ford Maverick in April, 1969 would provide them with such a product, since the purchase of a new automobile is a relatively high risk decision in addition to being a highly visible durable good.

The car was introduced in mid-April, 1969. Four groups of Maverick purchasers were included in the study: (1) those who had purchased the car during the first three months after it was introduced (t_1); (2) those who purchased the car during the first three months of the second model year (t_2); (3) those who purchased the car during the first three months of the third model year (t_3); (4) those who purchased the car during the first three months of the fourth model year (t_4). During the first four model years approximately 1 million units were sold making it one of the most successful new model introductions in the company's history.

For comparison purposes, four other groups of automobile purchasers were included in the study. These were new car buyers of already established automobile models who made purchases during the first three months of the same model years (four time periods comparable with the Maverick purchasers). While no existing established model of American car exactly matched the size and price of the Maverick, the comparison group was constructed using purchasers of low-priced American compact cars which were as close to the Maverick as possible on these variables (e.g., Darts, Dusters, and Novas).

New car registrations which are matters of public record were utilized to obtain the names and addresses of new car purchasers. Each subject included in this study was contacted by mail. In the letter they were informed of the nature of the study and asked to participate. They were told that they would be contacted within the next three to five days by a personal interviewer (whose name was provided) who would leave with them a relatively short questionnaire to be completed at their leisure. The interviewer would return within a few days to pick up the completed questionnaire. If they had any questions regarding the nature or

purpose of the study or the questionnaire, they were urged to contact the researchers by telephone. If they did not wish to complete the questionnaire they were asked to inform the interviewer on his return trip. A total of 980 individuals were contacted over the 44 months the study was conducted. Completed questionnaires were obtained from 332 Maverick purchasers and 319 control group purchasers.

Inner- and other-directedness (i.e., social character) was measured by the instrument developed by Kassarjian titled the "I. O. Social Preference Scale," which has been shown to be a reliable and valid instrument (Waltraud Kassarjian, 1962). Examples of 3 of the 36 questions are:

1. I believe:
   a. being able to make friends is a great accomplishment in and of itself;
   b. one should be careful to live up to the prevailing standards of the culture.
2. On the subject of social living
   a. a person should set up his own standards and then live up to them;
   b. one should be careful to live up to the prevailing standards of the culture.
3. I have
   a. a great many friends who are, however, not very intimate friends
   b. few but rather intimate friends.

ANALYSIS

The possible range of total scores for one individual is from 0 to 144. For any single item, scores range from -2 (other-direction) to $+2$ (inner-direction). In order to avoid negative total scores a constant of 72 is added to each score. The lowest score in the other-directed group was 26. The highest score in the inner-directed group was 114. The mean for the group was 72.6. The range of scores and the mean were extremely consistent with previous studies which used the I.O. Social Preference Scale (Donnelly, 1970; Harold H. Kassarjian, 1965; Waltraud Kassarjian, 1962; Woodside, 1968). If an individual scores below 72, he is considered to be other-directed; if he scores above 72, he is considered to be inner-directed (Waltraud Kassarjian, 1962).

The chi-square test has traditionally been used to test the relationship between social character and various dependent variables (Donnelly, 1970; and Woodside, 1968). The use of this test provides a measure of the independence of two sets of classification results. In this case it was used to arrive at the probability levels which distinguish inner- and other-directed results and automobile purchase. The results are shown in Tables 1 and 2.

Table 1 χ^2 probability level of social character of Maverick purchasers over time (N = 332)

Social character	Time period				χ^2 Probability level
	t_1	t_2	t_3	t_4	
Inner-directed	55	45	41	41	
Other-directed	21	39	44	46	<.025

Table 2 χ^2 probability levels of social character and purchase of Maverick and similar established models of automobiles over time (N = 651)

Social character	Purchased Maverick (N = 332)	Purchased similar established brand (N = 319)	χ^2 Probability level
t_1			
Inner-directed	55	38	
Other-directed	21	42	<.01
t_2			
Inner-directed	45	37	
Other-directed	39	41	n.s.[a]
t_3			
Inner-directed	41	37	
Other-directed	44	45	n.s.
t_4			
Inner-directed	41	36	
Other-directed	46	43	n.s.

[a]n.s. = not significant at p. ≤ .05 level of probability.

RESULTS

Examination of Table 1 indicates that over the four time periods under consideration, the social character of Maverick purchasers differed significantly. Specifically, early purchasers of the Maverick were significantly more inner-directed than later purchasers. Note that the buyers became less inner-directed and more other-directed as the product became more widely accepted between t_1 and t_4.

Examination of Table 2 indicates that the social character of the initial purchasers of Mavericks (t_1) differed significantly (more inner-directed) from initial purchasers of new models of similar established brands for the comparable time period. However, as the Maverick became more widely accepted there were no significant differences between the two groups. Table 2 indicates no significant differences in the social character of Maverick purchasers and those purchasing similar established brands during t_2, t_3, and t_4.

DISCUSSION

This study sought to demonstrate a method for identifying innovator characteristics of new brand purchasers. The findings of the study are of interest not only because they provide a sound basis for adding to the existing behavioral profile of the consumer innovator, but also for their implications for future studies of innovators. That is, it should be shown that initial buyers differ from later buyers of the new product and, in the case of new brands, with buyers of similar established brands. In the case of new brands this can only be achieved by studying purchasers of new and established brands over time. The study has also demonstrated the value of longitudinal studies when investigating a process as dynamic as the diffusion of innovations.

REFERENCES

Bell, William E. (1964), "Consumer Innovators: A Market for Newness," *Proceedings,* Winter Conference, American Marketing Association, 85–93.

Blake, Brian; Perloff, Robert; and Heslin, Richard (November 1970), "Dogmatism and Acceptance of New Products," *Journal of Marketing Research, 7,* 483–86.

Campbell, D. T., and Stanley, J. C. (1963), *Experimental and Quasi-Experimental Designs for Research,* Skokie, Ill.: Rand McNally.

Coney, Kenneth A. (November 1972), "Dogmatism and Innovation: A Replication," *Journal of Marketing Research, 9,* 453–55.

Dommermuth, William P. (1967), "The Effects of Behavior Attributes Upon the Acceptance of New Products," *Proceedings,* Southern Marketing Association, 45–49.

Donnelly, James H., Jr. (February 1970), "Social Character and Acceptance of New Products," *Journal of Marketing Research, 7,* 111–13.

———, and Etzel, Michael J. (August 1973), "Degrees of Product Newness and Early Trial," *Journal of Marketing Research, 10,* 295–300.

———, and Roeth, Scott (June 1973), "The Relationship Between Consumers' Category Width and Trial of New Products," *Journal of Applied Psychology, 57,* 335–38.

Engel, James F.; Kergerreis, Robert J.; and Blackwell, Roger D. (July 1969), "Word-of-mouth Communication by the Innovator," *Journal of Marketing, 33,* 15–19.

Frank, Ronald E.; Massy, William F.; and Morrison, Donald G. (1964), "The Determinants of Innovative Behavior with Respect to a Branded, Frequently Purchased Food Product," *Proceedings,* Winter Conference, American Marketing Association, 312–23.

Gruen, Walter (December 1960), "Preference for New Products and Its Relationship to Different Measures of Conformity," *Journal of Applied Psychology, 44,* 351–64.

Hayes, Samuel P. (1959), "The Adoption of New Products: Process and Influence," *Foundation for Research on Human Behavior,* Ann Arbor: University of Michigan Press, 6.

Jacoby, Jacob (May 1971a), "Personality and Innovation Proneness," *Journal of Marketing Research, 8,* 244–47.

——— (August 1971b), "Multiple-Indicant Approach for Studying New Product Adopters," *Journal of Applied Psychology, 55,* 384–88.

Kassarjian, Harold H. (May 1965), "Social Character and Differential Preference for Mass Communication," *Journal of Marketing Research, 2,* 146–53.

——— (November 1971), "Personality and Consumer Behavior: A Review," *Journal of Marketing Research, 8,* 409–18.

Kassarjian, Waltraud (September 1962), "A Study of Riesman's Theory of Social Character," *Sociometry, 25,* 213–30.

Kollat, David T.; Engel, James F.; and Blackwell, Roger D. (August 1970), "Current Problems in Consumer Behavior Research," *Journal of Marketing Research, 7,* 327–32.

Lambert, Zarrel V. (November 1972), "Perceptual Patterns, Information Handling and Innovativeness," *Journal of Marketing Research, 9,* 427–31.

Morton, Patricia Rae (Summer 1967), "Riesman's Theory of Social Character as Applied to Consumer Goods Marketing," *Journalism Quarterly, 44,* 337–40.

Ostland, Lyman E. (1969), "The Role of Product Perceptions in Innovative Behavior," *Proceedings,* Fall Conference, American Marketing Association, 259–66.

Pelz, Donald C., and Andrews, Frank M. (December, 1964), "Detecting Causal Priorities in Panel Study Data," *American Sociological Review, 29,* 836–48.

Popielarz, Donald T. (November 1967), "An Exploration of Perceived Risk and Willingness to Try New Products," *Journal of Marketing Research, 4,* 368–72.

Riesman, David; Glazer, Nathan; and Denny, Reuel (1950), *The Lonely Crowd,* New Haven, Conn.: Yale University Press.

Robertson, Thomas, S. (1968), "Social Factors in Innovative Behavior," in Harold H. Kassarjian and Thomas S. Robertson, eds., *Perspectives in Consumer Behavior,* Glenview, Ill.: Scott, Foresman, 361–72.

Rogers, Everett M. (1962), *Diffusion of Innovations,* New York: The Free Press of Glencoe.

———, and Stanfield, J. David (1968), "Adoption and Diffusion of New Products: Emerging Generalizations and Hypotheses," in Frank M. Bass, Charles W. King, and Edgar A. Pessemier, eds., *Applications of the Sciences in Marketing Management,* New York: John Wiley and Sons, 227–50.

Summers, John O. (January 1972), "Media Exposure Patterns of Consumer Innovators," *Journal of Marketing,* 36, 43–49.

Uhl, Kenneth; Andrus, Roman; and Paulsen, Lance (February 1970), "How are Laggards Different? An Empirical Inquiry," *Journal of Marketing Research,* 7, 51–55.

White, Irving (1966), "The Perception of Value in Products," in Joseph W. Newman, ed., *On Knowing the Consumer,* New York: John Wiley and Sons, 90–106.

Woodside, Arch G. (December 1968), "Social Character, Product Use and Advertising Appeals," *Journal of Advertising Research,* 8, 31–35.

Zaltman, G., and Stiff, R. (1973), "Theories of Diffusion," in Scott Ward and Thomas S. Robertson, eds., *Consumer Behavior: Theoretical Sources,* Englewood Cliffs, N.J.: Prentice-Hall, 416–68.

MULTIPLE-INDICANT APPROACH FOR STUDYING NEW PRODUCT ADOPTERS

JACOB JACOBY

Source: Jacob Jacoby, "Multiple-Indicant Approach for Studying New Product Adopters," *Journal of Applied Psychology,* Vol. 55, August, 1971, pp. 384–88.

The vast majority, perhaps 90% (cf. Rogers & Stanfield, 1968), of the thousands of new products introduced annually end up being rejected by the consumer. Given the high costs involved in the research, development, and introduction of new products, identifying the innovation prone individual (i.e., the consumer most likely to be among the first to try a new product), especially those factors which contribute to his being an innovator, assumes tremendous practical importance. Not only do such individuals provide a toehold for new products, but they also seem to play an integral part in the subsequent diffusion of the innovation through the population at large (cf. Engel, Kegerreis, and Blackwell, 1969; Robertson, 1968; Rogers, 1962; and Zaltman, 1965, p. 31).

Making adequate generalizations requires obtaining several indexes of innovation proneness across a variety of commonly purchased, low priced, necessity-type items. Another desideratum is experimentation based on *a priori* hypotheses. The present study is cast in this mold.

Despite the generally disappointing results of studies trying to link personality to consumer behavior (cf. Engel, Kollat, and Blackwell, 1968, Ch. 8), the construct of dogmatism, as defined by Rokeach (1960) and supported in numerous subsequent investigations (cf. Vacchiano, Strauss, and Hochman, 1969), provides a sound theoretical and empirical basis for making predictions regarding innovation proneness. Consider the relationship of dogmatism to three other variables: anxiety, novelty, and creativity.

According to Rokeach (1960), dogmatism is a generalized mental rigidity factor with individuals aligned along an open- to closed-minded continuum. Highly dogmatic systems represent a cognitive-psychodynamic network of defenses against anxiety; the more persistently anxious or threatened the individual, the more likely he is to manifest a closed mind. This dogmatism-anxiety relationship has been well supported by Rokeach and several others (cf. Vacchiano, et al., 1969). Consider, also, the research (Bauer, 1960; Cox,

1967) which tends to indicate that changing from one brand or product to another usually entails some perceived risk which, for several reasons, increases when one contemplates trying or switching to a new brand or product. Given that perceived risk, in anything other than mild dosages, can be anxiety inducing, high dogmatics should be less likely than low dogmatics to consider innovating.

Based upon both theoretical rationale and empirical evidence, it is predicted that low dogmatics will select significantly more innovations than will high dogmatics.

METHOD

Subjects

The Ss were 60 18–26 year old coeds attending Purdue University during the Fall 1969 Semester. All were volunteers.

Instruments

To obtain an index of innovation proneness, 15 sets of photographs, containing 5 pictures per set, were collected for 15 different product classes. One of the five pictures in each set was of an innovation (as operationally defined above), while the remaining four pictures displayed older or more traditional varieties of the product, either in terms of brand, style, or function.

For example, one product class contained pictures of four women's dress-length coats (i.e., knee length to 5 in. above the knee) and one maxicoat (fashion innovation). Another product class, cigarettes, pictured one pack of Virginia Slims (brand innovation), Kent, Marlboro, Viceroy, and Parliament. A third product class exhibited four regular type pantyhose and one of the lower cut hiplet variety (functional innovation).

The 15 products, classified according to category and type of innovation examined, are presented in Table 1. Across six cosmetic, four clothing, and five miscellaneous products, there were six new brands, five fashion innovations, and four functional innovations.

Table 1 Products and types of innovations investigated

Product	Category	Type of innovation
1. Hair conditioner	Cosmetics	New brand
2. Lipstick	Cosmetics	New brand
3. Hair lightener	Cosmetics	Functional[a]
4. Perfume	Cosmetics	New Brand
5. Blush-on	Cosmetics	Functional[a]
6. Make-up base	Cosmetics	Functional[a]
7. Men's cologne	Miscellaneous	New brand
8. Diamond ring	Miscellaneous	Fashion
9. Beer	Miscellaneous	New brand
10. Luggage	Miscellaneous	Fashion
11. Cigarettes	Miscellaneous	New brand
12. Shoes	Clothing	Fashion
13. Slack outfit	Clothing	Fashion
14. Panty-hose	Clothing	Functional[a]
15. Coat	Clothing	Fashion

[a]Functional = new form of product or method of use (e.g., foam vs. liquid make-up base).

All five pictures in each product set were mounted in a randomized circular array on poster board so that the complete set could be viewed simultaneously. Pictures within each set were matched for size, color versus black-and-white, branded versus unbranded, photograph versus sketch, and container type (e.g., bottle vs. can).

The standard 40-item Form E of the Rokeach Dogmatism scale (Rokeach, 1960) was used to measure dogmatism.

Procedure

The Ss, who were run individually, were instructed to select one out of the five items in each set that they would buy if given the choice. The E continued: "Do not let the colors of the products or brands affect your decision. For example, do not choose a lipstick for the particular shade pictured. Moreover, if you do not use a set of products, buy for someone else." Each S received an innovation score ranging from 0 to 15, depending upon the number of times she selected the innovation contained in each of the product sets.

The 15 sets of pictures were presented in the same order, and each S proceeded at her own pace. The Dogmatism scale was administered upon completion—again with no time limit.

RESULTS

Based upon their dogmatism scores, Ss were split into two groups at the median. Table 2 indicates that the between-group difference in dogmatism scores was significant at beyond the .001 level. As predicted there was a significant overall difference ($t = 10.87$; $p < .01$, one-tailed test) in innovation scores between the two groups.

Product-by-product analysis indicated that the low dogmatics gave more innovation responses than the high dogmatics to 11 out of the 15 product sets. Four of these differences (Products 7, 9, 11, and 12 in Table 1) were significant beyond the .05 level, one-tailed test. The remaining 11 significance tests yielded probability values in excess of .20.

Table 3 provides the analysis of innovative responses according to both type of product and type of innovation. Low dogmatics were considerably more likely ($p < .001$) than high dogmat-

Table 2 Significance of the difference in mean innovation scores of high and low dogmatics

Innovation scores	Low dogmatics[a]	High dogmatics[a]	t
Dogmatism			
$\overline{X}$	118.40	161.13	10.87**
SD	14.53	15.90	
Difference			
$\overline{X}$	3.27	2.17	2.53*
SD	2.03	1.23	

Note.—Dogmatism × Innovation Index: $r = -.32$, $p < .01$.
[a]$n = 30$.
*$p < .01$ (given heterogeneity of variance and using $df = 29$ [cf. Edwards, 1960, p. 108], one-tailed test).
**$p < .001$ (one-tailed test).

Table 3 Frequency of innovative responses by type of product and type of innovation

Type	Low dogmatics	High dogmatics	χ^2
Product			
Cosmetics[a]	31	23	1.19
Clothing[b]	17	11	1.29
Miscellaneous[c]	50	31	4.46*
Innovation			
New brand[a]	48	20	11.53**
Fashion[c]	29	28	.69
Function[b]	21	17	.42

[a]$N = 6$.
[b]$N = 4$.
[c]$N = 5$.
*$p < .05$ (one-tailed test).
**$p < .001$ (one-tailed test).

ics to select new brands of products, especially in the miscellaneous category ($p < .05$).

DISCUSSION

As predicted, low dogmatic individuals tend to make significantly more innovative selections than do high dogmatic individuals. However, the relationship, while significant, does not appear to be exceptionally strong. Only 10% of the variance is accounted for by the correlation between dogmatism and innovation proneness ($r = -.32$). Moreover, the mean low dogmatic innovation score of 3.27 is only .27 above, and the high dogmatic mean only .83 below, the 3.00 value to be expected on a chance basis (1/5 innovations × 15 product sets).

From an applied viewpoint, however, the notion of practical significance is more important than statistical significance or even the size of the relationship. To the extent that marketers and advertisers can capitalize on knowledge regarding the relationship between dogmatism and innovation proneness, and can thereby increase the likelihood of gaining that all-important toehold, the relationship is important. How, then, might this information be applied?

It has been suggested that when introducing new products, "advertisements should emphasize the prestige of owning the item—to appeal specifically to the early adopters" (Zaltman, 1965, p. 52). Given that low dogmatics are more innovative and tend to adopt earlier than high dogmatics, then quite the opposite prediction should be made. In describing the essential differences between high and low dogmatics, Rokeach (1960) states that low dogmatics "act on relevant information from the outside of its own intrinsic merits, unencumbered by irrelevant factors in the situation arising from within the person or from the outside" (p. 57). High dogmatics prefer to rely heavily on the pronouncements of authorities and tend to accept information primarily on the basis of who said it (i.e., the message source), while low dogmatics tend to act based upon their independent evaluation of the information itself (i.e., message content).

Translated into applied terms, this suggests that the marketer-advertiser introducing a new product would be wise to have his advertisements and point-of-purchase displays focus on the product's attributes rather than emphasize irrelevant ego or social factors. As a hypothetical example, advertisers of a cigarette with a new type of filter (ergo, a new product) would do well to stress and describe the filter rather than emphasize people enjoying the cigarette in social situations.

Last, it would appear that a multiple-indicator approach, especially when coupled with theoretically based *a priori* hypotheses, has great promise for the study of innovators. Had a single indicant criterion (i.e., studying the characteristics of innovators based on their responses to only one innovation) been utilized, the predicted significant relationship would have been manifested in only 4 out of 15 instances, and the likelihood of concluding that no relationship existed thereby increased.

REFERENCES

Bauer, R. A. (1960), "Consumer Behavior as Risk-taking," *Proceedings,* American Marketing Association, 389–98.

Cox, D. F., ed., (1967), *Risk Taking and Information Handling in Consumer Behavior,* Boston: Graduate School of Business Administration.

Edwards, A. L. (1960), *Experimental Design in Psychological Research,* New York: Holt, Rinehart and Winston.

Engel, J. F.; Kegerreis, R. J.; and Blackwell, R. D. (1969), "Word of Mouth Communication by the Innovator," *Journal of Marketing,* 33, 15–19.

———; Kollat, D. T.; and Blackwell, R. D. (1968), *Consumer Behavior,* New York: Holt, Rinehart and Winston.

Robertson, T. S. (1968), "Social Factors in Innovation Behavior," in H. H. Kassarjian and T. S. Robertson, eds., *Perspectives in Consumer Behavior,* Glenview, Ill.: Scott, Foresman.

Rogers, E. M. (1962), *Diffusion of Innovations,* Glencoe, Ill.: The Free Press.

———, and Stanfield, J. D. (1968), "Adoption and Diffusion of New Products: Emerging Generalizations and Hypotheses," in F. M. Bass, C. W. King and I. Pessemier, eds., *Applications of the Sciences in Marketing Management,* New York: Wiley.

Rokeach, M. (1960), *The Open and Closed Mind,* New York: Basic Books.

Vacchiano, R. B.; Strauss, P. S.; and Hochman, L. (1969), "The Open and Closed Mind: A Review of Dogmatism, *Psychological Bulletin,* 71, 261–73.

Zaltman, G. (1965), *Marketing: Contributions from the Behavioral Sciences,* New York: Harcourt, Brace and World.

THE INNOVATIVE COMMUNICATOR IN THE DIFFUSION PROCESS

STEVEN A. BAUMGARTEN

Source: Steven A. Baumgarten, "The Innovative Communicator in the Diffusion Process," *Journal of Marketing Research,* Vol. 12, February, 1975, pp. 12–18.

INTRODUCTION

The dynamics of the process by which new ideas, products, and tastes are accepted and then spread through a society has long been of concern to researchers in the social sciences. The emergent large bodies of diffusion research which resulted from this concern have coalesced to form the conceptual framework for the theory of adoption and diffusion of innovations. Within this conceptual framework, expertly summarized by Rogers (1962), empirical marketing research has largely focused upon developing a greater understanding of the characteristics of two key consumer "change agents": (1) the innovator, or early adopter in the life cycle of a new concept or product, who gives the new concept initial physical visibility and functional application; and (2) the opinion leader who presents a "peer group legitimate" evaluation of the new concept and transmits product information and usage experience to the peer group culture.

Fashion is an area where interpersonal communications have been found to be highly important in the diffusion of information (Katz and Lazarsfeld, 1955). Furthermore, the frequent introduction of new clothing styles makes the fashion market a highly desirable arena for diffusion studies focusing upon innovativeness.

This very substantial similarity between the empirically determined characteristics of opinion leaders and early adopters leads to the question of the extent to which opinion leaders *are* early adopters, and vice versa. The research described in this article explores the overlap between fashion opinion leaders and fashion early adopters, and provides some insight into the characteristics of the dual-roled change agent who emerges from that overlap. At this point, it seems desirable to provide this dual-role change agent with a name. Since he is characterized by both early adoption—and hence some degree of *innovativeness*—and by opinion leadership—which is, as usually defined, more a measure of *com-*

municativeness than a true measure of influence—this dual-roled change agent will hereafter be referred to as an *innovative communicator.*

Interestingly, past research findings concerning the characteristics of innovators and early adopters (Coleman, et al., 1966; Rogers, 1962; Wilkening, 1952) have generated a very similar profile to that of opinion leaders.

The broad scope of the research project involved investigation of the process by which men's clothing fashions are adopted and then diffuse through the campus subculture. Since the college campus is often considered to be a barometer of changing values in the younger educated population, understanding more about the process by which campus fashion change occurs can provide valuable information on the expanding 15 billion-dollar-a-year-plus men's fashion market.

RESEARCH METHODOLOGY

Data Collection

The data-collection procedure involved administration of a questionnaire to a stratified random sample of 389 unmarried male undergraduates at Purdue University. In addition to fashion early adoption and opinion leadership, the questionnaire included the following areas: (1) demographics, (2) media exposure, (3) sociological-social activities, (4) fashion attitudes, interests, opinions, and behavior, (5) psychological self-description, and (6) socio-political attitudes and opinions.

The Measure of Opinion Leadership

Measurement of opinion leadership was accomplished using a modification of a six-question self-designating method first used by Rogers (1961), and discussed in Rogers and Catarno (1962). The validity and reliability of this method was demonstrated by Rogers and Catarno, and later used in modified form by Summers (1970). In determining the index score for opinion leadership, a simple unweighted linear combination of the scores for each of the questions was employed. The resultant index is expressed as an integer score ranging from zero through nine.

Based upon the value of their Opinion Leadership Indices, respondents were classified as either low, medium, or high opinion leaders, with 27.7% of the sample being operationally classified as high opinion leaders, representing those whose score was 6 or higher. This compares favorably with the operational classifications in past studies; e.g., Summers (1970) classified the upper 28% of respondents as opinion leaders and Katz and Lazarsfeld (1955) so classified the upper 23%.

The Measure of Early Adoption

It was decided that measurement of early adoption should be based upon *current ownership* of specific "new" styles, an easily recallable behavioral measure. In its simplest form, however, this procedure would require that the researcher subjectively determine which of the many styles extant at a given time are, in fact, "new." In order to avoid the need for this subjective appraisal, it was decided to measure early adoption on a "local" basis wherein the criterion for newness was established by the sample itself. Thus, the measure of local early adoption was based upon the degree to which a respondent had in his wardrobe those styles which, in the aggregate opinion of the entire sample, were increasing in popularity on campus.

Using this criterion the researcher can relatively objectively identify early adopters by determining which respondents *already own* those styles which a large number of people expect to grow in popularity. The measurement procedure has the dual advantage of (1) measuring data which are easily recallable by the respondent, and (2) imposing no requirement that the researcher subjectively determine "newness." Furthermore, by measuring expected popularity growth on a peer group (aggregate sample) basis, the procedure excludes from the early adopter category those persons whose purchases are largely restricted to highly unusual or "kooky" styles. This helps to insure that those respondents identified as early adopters are, in fact, style leaders for the social group under investigation.

The procedure for measuring local early adoption was based upon a series of questions involving suits, sports jackets, slacks, shoes, neckties, and collar styles. Respondents were shown sketches of various styles in each of these six clothing categories and asked to indicate for *each* style: (1) how many such items they currently owned, and (2) whether they thought they would purchase such items during the next six months. The use of sketches removed the confusion the subjects might have had with trade names or inadequate verbal description of these styles.

Aggregate popularity growth was then determined for each style as the ratio of "number of persons who intend to buy" to "number of persons who own at least one." An "early adoption index" was then calculated for each respondent by (1) multiplying the aggregate popularity growth ratio for each style by the number of such styles owned by the respondent, (2) summing across styles *within* each clothing category, (3) normalizing the distribution of scores for *each* of the six clothing categories, and (4) summing the normalized scores of each respondent *across* clothing categories.

The resultant "early adoption index" is thus a measure of the extent to which an individual *currently* owns those styles which, in the aggregate opinion of all respondents, are expected to grow in popularity on campus during the next six months. Based upon the value of this "early adoption index," respondents were then classified as low, medium, or high early adopters. This resulted in 26.3% of the sample being operationally classified as high early adopters, and included those with index scores greater than 2.0.

The Measure of Innovative Communicativeness

As operationally defined in this research, the innovative communicator is a person who is *both* a high early adopter *and* a high opinion leader. With 27.7% and 26.3% of the sample classified as opinion leaders and early adopters, respectively, and assuming independence between these two groups, we would expect that 7.3% (26.3% × 27.7%) of the sample would qualify as *both* opinion leaders and early adopters (i.e., as innovative communicators). In fact, a total of 47 respondents, or 12.1% of the total sample, qualified as innovative communicators (see Table 1). The difference between actual and expected percentage overlap is statistically significant at beyond the .0005 level.

The correlation between innovativeness and early adoption of .34 lends further support to the existence of a strong relationship between early adoption and opinion leadership. [It is interesting to note that these findings are highly consistent with those of Summers' study of opinion leadership-innovativeness overlap (1970)] Summers found the ratio of actual to expected percentage overlap to be 1.8, compared with 1.7 in this study. Furthermore, the correlation between fashion in-

Table 1   Overlap of opinion leadership and early adoption

Degree of opinion leadership	Degree of early adoption			
	Low	Medium	High	Base
Low	54.2%[a]	33.3%	15.7%	(139)
Medium	29.0	41.7	38.2	(142)
High	16.8	25.0	46.1	(108)
Base	100.0% (131)	100.0% (156)	100.0% (102)	

[a]Read: 54.2% of those who scored "low" on degree of early adoption also scored "low" on degree of opinion leadership.

novativeness and fashion opinion leadership among Summers' sample of Indianapolis housewives was .35, compared with .34 in this study.)

RESULTS

Cross-classification analyses with chi-square tests of significance were performed to identify the distinguishing characteristics of innovative communicators versus others. The tabular results display comparisons between percent of innovative communicators with specific attributes and all others with those attributes.

Demographic Characteristics

Only 3 of the 18 demographic characteristics differentiated innovative communicators from others at the .05 level of significance or better (see Table 2). Compared to others, innovative communicators perceived their families to be higher in social class, were more likely to be freshmen and sophomores, and were more likely to be business majors and less likely to be engineering majors.

Among the demographic characteristics which were not significantly related to innovative communicativeness were: family income, age, religion, type of housing lived in, number of siblings, part-time work, father's education, father's occupation, number of past living locations, size of home town, and location of home town. Thus, it was not the case, as is frequently believed, that urban or eastern students were likely to be more innovative or more communicative about fashion.

Sociological Characteristics and Social Activities

Social variables were relatively strong in identifying innovative communicators, who showed a greater propensity to date more frequently, spend more money on each date, and spend more money on nondating social activities (see Table 3). These characteristics are consistent with previous research findings in that opinion leaders have

Table 2   Demographic characteristics: innovative communicators vs. others

Demographic characteristic	Percent of		Level of significance
	Others	Innovative communicators	
Perceived family social class			
Lower or working	11.7[a]	10.6[a]	
Middle	51.5	31.9	$p < .01$[b]
Upper middle or upper	36.8	57.5	
Grade level			
Freshman	26.7	31.9	
Sophomore	26.0	36.2	
Junior	29.5	14.9	$p < 0.1$
Senior	17.8	17.0	
Major subject area			
Earth sciences	7.9	12.8	
Industrial management	14.3	27.7	
Engineering	35.0	14.9	$p < 0.5$
Other	42.8	44.6	
Base	(342)	(47)	

[a]Read: 10.6% of the innovative communicators and 11.7% of all others perceived their families to be members of the lower or working class.
[b]The differences were statistically significant at the .01 level based on χ^2 analysis.

been shown to be more gregarious, cosmopolite, and socially active.

In further support of the innovative communicator's sociability, he was found more likely to be a cigarette smoker (a social habit), and more likely to play golf than others. Although not significant at the .05 level, the innovative communicator is also more likely to play tennis frequently. He does not attend movies, plays or cultural events with any greater frequency than others, but he is more strongly affiliated with the "rock scene," as evidenced by his greater attendance at dances, higher perceived dancing ability, and stronger preference for rock music.

The student innovative communicator is also significantly more concerned with his appearance than are others. He is more likely to think of himself as handsome, and he makes a greater effort to get a suntan early in the season. Casual observa-

Table 3 Social activities and sociological characteristics: innovative communicators vs. others

Sociological characteristic	Percent of		Level of significance
	Others	Innovative communicators	
Sociability			
Low	61.7[a]	27.7[a]	
High	38.3	72.3	p < .0005[b]
Dating frequency			
Once a week or less	76.7	51.2	
More than once a week	23.3	48.8	p < .01
Amount spent per date			
Less than $5.00	62.0	29.8	
$5.00 or more	38.0	70.2	p < .0005
Amount spent socially (other than dates)			
Less than $5.00 per week	65.8	40.4	
$5.00 or more per week	34.2	59.6	p < .001
Cigarette smoking			
Yes	26.3	46.8	
No	73.7	53.2	p < .05
Play golf			
Yes	53.8	72.3	
No	46.2	27.7	p < .05
Number of rock dances attended this year			
One or none	67.5	42.5	
Two or more	32.5	57.5	p < .05
Perceived dancing ability			
Low	47.5	23.5	
High	52.5	76.5	p < .0005
Type of dancing preferred			
None	12.3	0.0	
Nonrock	20.7	6.4	
Rock	67.0	93.6	p < .005
Effort to suntan early			
Yes	52.3	78.7	
No	47.7	21.3	p < .001
Self-perceived handsomeness			
Very	17.5	34.0	
Fairly	70.5	66.0	p < .005
Not particularly	12.0	0.0	
Appearance-consciousness			
Low	39.2	23.4	
Medium	54.1	48.9	p < .0005
High	6.7	27.7	
Base	(342)	(47)	

[a]Read: 27.7% of the innovative communicators and 61.7% of all others scored low on sociability.
[b]The differences were statistically significant at the .0005 level based on χ^2 analysis.

tion of the student subculture leads to the conclusion that sociability, dating, dancing, affiliation with rock music, and appearance-consciousness are all very much a part of the social norms of this group. The fact that innovative communicators exhibit these traits to a much higher degree than others indicates a high degree of norm conformity. This conclusion is also consistent with that expressed by Rogers (1962) who described norm comformity as a characteristic of opinion leaders.

Mass Media Readership

Past research findings have indicated that change agents tend to get their information from more cosmopolite and /or technical sources. Certainly, the innovative communicator demonstrates media readership patterns which are consistent with these past findings. Compared with others, the innovative communicator is substantially more likely to read such cosmopolite sources of information as the *Sunday New York Times* and *New Yorker* magazine, and such "technical" sources of (fashion) information as *Gentlemen's Quarterly* and *Esquire* (see Table 4).

In addition to higher readership of cosmopolite/technical vehicles, however, the innovative communicator also exhibits higher readership of the student newspaper. This characteristic may relate to his greater degree of local sociability, since the student newspaper is, in fact, a prime source of news about the university social scene.

It is further interesting to note that the level of readership of virtually all mass media magazines is substantially higher among innovative communicators than among others. And while it is not surprising to find high readership of *Playboy* among any college student group, the finding that more than 80% of the innovative communicators read every or almost every issue of *Playboy* is substantial, especially when compared with claimed readership by others of only 53.5%.

Perhaps even more interesting than the high level of *Playboy* readership is the finding that more than half of the innovative communicators read three or more of every four issues of *News-*

Table 4 Mass media readership: innovative communicators vs. others

Media	Percent of		Level of significance
	Others	Innovative communicators	
Sunday N.Y. Times			
Never or almost never	89.5[a]	63.8[a]	
At least one in four	10.5	36.2	p < .0005[b]
Purdue Student Newspaper			
Three of four issues or less	49.1	31.9	
Every or almost every issue	50.9	68.1	p< .025
Playboy			
Three of four or less	46.5	19.1	
Every or almost every	53.5	80.9	p < .01
Esquire			
Never or almost never	70.2	40.4	
At least one in four	29.8	59.6	p < .001
Gentlemen's Quarterly			
Never or almost never	90.0	68.5	
At least one in four	9.9	31.5	p < .0005
New Yorker			
Never or almost never	81.6	66.0	
At least one in four	18.4	34.0	p< .05
Sports Illustrated			
Half or less	62.0	34.1	
Three of four or more	38.0	65.9	p < .005
Time			
Half or less	57.9	27.6	
Three of four or more	42.1	72.4	p < .001
Newsweek			
Half or less	74.9	46.9	
Three of four or more	25.1	53.1	p< .0005
Base	(342)	(47)	

[a]Read: 63.8% of the innovative communicators and 89.5% of all others never or almost never read the Sunday New York Times.
[b]The differences were statistically significant at the .0005 level based on χ^2 analysis.

week and *Sports Illustrated,* and that almost three-fourths of the innovative communicators read three or more of every four issues of *Time*.

Fashion Characteristics

Not surprisingly, fashion-oriented variables tended to be the most significant discriminators between innovative communicators and others. On every fashion variable index, the innovative communicator scored higher than the noncommunicator at the .0005 level of significance or better (Table 5). In general, innovative communicators spend more on clothing, know more about clothing styles and brands, and own more different styles than do others. Innovative communicators also are more familiar with and own more cosmetics than others.

These results are consistent with both intuitive expectations and past research. Summers (1970), for example, found that involvement in women's clothing fashions represented the strongest variable set in determining fashion opinion leadership. Greater knowledge of the product category would seem a necessary prerequisite for innovativeness and opinion leadership. Within this context, it also seems probable that greater clothing expenditures help the change agent to keep current.

Psychological Self-Description and Socio-Political Attitudes Factors

Two sections of the questionnaire—the psychological self-description series and the socio-political atitudes series—contained multiple measures of a relatively small number of psychological and attitudinal characteristics. The psychological self-description section involved a series of 119 individual self-description statements. The socio-political attitudes section involved a total of 75 statements oriented toward social and political issues. In both cases, the respondent was required to answer on a five-point Likert scale ranging from "strongly disagree" to "strongly agree."

These two questionnaire sections contain several series of questions which have diverse origins.

Table 5 Fashion characteristics: innovative communicators vs. others

Fashion characteristic	Percent of		Level of significance
	Others	Innovative communicators	
Clothing expenditures			
Low	71.6[a]	31.9[a]	
High	28.4	68.1	p < .0005[b]
Style familiarity			
Low	40.4	6.4	
High	59.6	93.6	p < .0005
Amount paid for clothing items			
Low	42.4	6.4	
High	57.6	93.6	p < .0005
Style variety ownership			
Low	53.3	6.4	
High	46.7	93.6	p < .0005
Brand familiarity			
Low	41.2	10.6	
High	58.8	89.4	p < .005
Cosmetics ownership			
Low	75.4	44.7	
High	24.6	55.3	p< .0005
Cosmetics familiarity			
Low	67.3	36.2	
High	32.7	63.8	p < .001
Base	(342)	(47)	

[a]Read: 31.9% of the innovative communicators and 71.6% of all others scored low on the measure of clothing expenditures.
[b]The differences were statistically significant at the .0005 level based on χ^2 analysis.

The psychological self-description series consists of:

1. Two separate tests which were the products of research performed by Borgatta (1964; 1955), and which were slightly modified to make the questions more pertinent to college students.

2. Two tests previously used by Summers (1970) which were designed to obtain measures of attitudinal dimensions which were not readily available in standard psychological tests, but which were hypothesized to have some relationship to opinion leadership. These tests were modified substantially in order to make them more applicable to a college student sample.

The socio-political attitudes series was generated specifically for this study, in the belief that today's students are strongly societally oriented, and that their attitudes toward a number of social-political issues might prove valuable in predicting opinion leadership and/or innovativeness.

Factor analyses for each of the five tests described above were performed by the principal components method, with orthogonal rotation of vectors using the varimax criterion. The factors thus obtained were subsequently treated as independent variables for cross-classification analysis with chi-square tests of significance. Of the 21 psychological self-description factors, only 4 were statistically significant in differentiating innovative communicators from others (Table 6). Innovative communicators were found to be more impulsive, have lower intellectual interest, be more exhibitionistic and more narcissistic than others.

Among the psychological self-description factors which were *not* significantly associated with innovative communicativeness were: emotionalism, likeability, responsibility, intelligence, assertiveness, leadership, tenseness, aloofness, competitiveness, self-confidence, and individualism. Thus, while some few personality characteristics are significantly associated with innovative communicativeness, innovative communicators do not exhibit a markedly different general personality profile than their peers.

Only two of the seven socio-political attitudes factors significantly differentiated innovative communicators from others. Innovative communicators were found to be more racist and more "student activist"—more positively oriented toward increased student power in the administration of the university. The rationale for these attitudes in their relationship with fashion innovative communication is not clearly evident. However, the innovative communicator's stronger sense of social involvement may help to explain his more liberal attitudes toward student power, in that it was currently "fashionable" to hold such views. In the case of racial attitudes, on the other hand, the

Table 6 Psychological self-description factors and socio-political attitudes factors: innovative communicators vs. others

| | Percent of | | |
Factor	Others	Innovative communicators	Level of significance
Psychological factors:			
Depressive/self-depreciating			
Low	49.1[a]	63.8[a]	Not Significant[b]
High	50.9	36.2	(p < .10)
Impulsiveness			
Low	53.8	34.0	
High	46.2	66.0	p< .025
Intellectual interest			
Low	45.3	66.0	
High	54.7	34.0	p < .01
Exhibitionism			
Low	50.0	29.8	
High	50.0	70.2	p < .01
Narcissism			
Low	54.1	14.9	
High	45.9	85.1	p < .0005
Risk propensity			
Low	53.8	40.4	Not Significant
High	46.2	59.6	(p < .10)
Socio-political factors:			
Sexual liberalism			
Low	48.8	38.3	
High	51.2	61.7	Not Significant
Student activism			
Low	54.1	25.5	
High	45.9	74.5	p < .0005
Racism			
Low	55.6	29.8	
High	44.4	70.2	p < .001
Base	(342)	(47)	

[a]Read: 63.8% of the innovative communicators and 49.1% of all others scored low on the psychological factor "Depressive/self depreciating."
[b]The differences were *not* significant at the .05 level (but were significant at the .10 level) based on χ^2 analysis.

current national trend generally dictates increased liberalism. Simple explanations of the relationship between racism and innovative communicativeness do not readily come to mind, and more com-plex explanations involve substantial conjecture. The very significant statistical difference on this factor, however, would seem to indicate that the relationship between innovative communicativeness and racism is more than just an artifact of the data.

SUMMARY

A general summary profile of the campus fashion innovative communicator is that of a freshman or sophomore who is very active socially, narcissistic, highly appearance-conscious, and strongly at-tuned to the rock culture. He reads more of the popular mass media, especially *Playboy, Time, Newsweek,* and *Sports Illustrated.* He is, of course, highly involved with the fashion scene, and spends more on clothing, knows more about fashion, and owns more different styles than do others. He is more exhibitionistic, more impulsive, and more limited in intellectual interest than other students. He is strongly oriented toward more stu-dent power on campus (although this result may be temporally related to the then-popularity of the student cause) and, inexplicably, significantly more racist than other students.

IMPLICATIONS

While the results of this research provide a profile of the innovative communicator which may be useful in understanding more about his general characteristics, it should also be noted that the specific findings may have substantial practical import in directing communications more effec-tively at him. Thus, media readership characteris-tics indicate that *Playboy* is the most widely read mass magazine and *Playboy* may, as many fash-ion advertisers apparently already believe, be a prime vehicle for fashion advertising. But readership of *Newsweek, Time,* and *Sports Illus-trated* is also quite substantial, and any of these magazines represent a lower-cost alternative to advertising in *Playboy*. Furthermore, ads placed in *Time, Sports Illustrated,* and *Newsweek* may tend to attract more attention since large numbers of fashion advertisers do not habitually advertise in these vehicles.

The high readership level of the campus newspaper would imply that it is a prime (low-cost) media vehicle for local retailers. Interestingly, at the time of this study, most local clothing retailers only rarely advertised in the student newspaper. The very high social involvement of the innovative communicator implies that social activities are of central importance to him. This result would suggest that the fashion marketer orient his advertising to the social conditions of the target market segment, and that the social value of the advertised product be stressed in the ad copy as well as the illustration. The innovative communicator's highly narcissistic orientation may imply a need for the fashion marketer to emphasize the appearance-enhancing value of his product, again, in both copy and illustration.

Finally, it should be noted that one of the networks by which the innovative communicator disseminates information is verbal in nature. His sociability, along with respect of his peers, enables him to function as an influential in a particular context. This would imply that communicable information content should be a prime ingredient of any message directed at the innovative communicator by fashion marketers. Details regarding styling, tailoring, fabric, social appropriateness, value, retail locational availability, and price, among others, may therefore be highly desirable inclusions in advertisements. The traditional clothing advertisement showing a mannequinish model wearing the advertised item, against a neutral background, and published in the traditional media vehicles, may not be effective in reaching today's youthful change agent.

REFERENCES

Borgatta, Edgar F. (February, 1964), "A Very Short Test of Personality: The Behavioral Self-rating (BSR) Form," *Psychological Reports,* 14, 275–85.

———— (July–August, 1955), "A Short Test of Personality: The S-indent Form," *Journal of Education Research,* 58, 452–56.

Coleman, James S.; Katz, Elihu; and Menzel, Herbert (1966), *Medical Innovation: A Diffusion Study,* Indianapolis: Bobbs-Merrill.

Katz, Elihu, and Lazarsfeld, Paul J. (1955), *Personal Influence,* Glencoe: Free Press.

Rogers, Everett M. (1961), *Characteristics of Agricultural Innovators and Other Adopter Categories,* Agricultural Experiment Station Research Bulletin 882, Wooster; Ohio.

———— (1962), *Diffusion of Innovations,* New York: Free Press.

————, and Catarno, David G. (Fall, 1962), "Methods of Measuring Opinion Leadership," *Public Opinion Quarterly,* 26, 435–41.

Summers, John O. (May, 1970), "The Identity of Women's Clothing Fashion Opinion Leaders," *Journal of Marketing Research,* 7, 178–85.

———— (August, 1971), "Generalized Change Agents and Innovativeness," *Journal of Marketing Research,* 8, 313–16.

Wilkening, Eugene A. (September, 1952), "Informed Leaders and Innovativeness in Farm Practices," *Rural Sociology,* 17, 272–75.

CONSUMER RESEARCH

Throughout this book articles that report the results of research have been included to indicate what is known about consumer behavior. In this section we will turn to descriptions of how research can and should be conducted. When we hear someone describe a particularly interesting or unusual piece of gossip, we often ask, "How did you find that out?" or "Who told you that?" Similarly in reading reports of the findings of consumer research, it is just as important to ask, "How did the researchers find this out?" as it is to ask, "What did they discover?"

Only if the research meets certain standards can we believe that the results are true. It is only possible to determine if these standards were met if the description of how the research was conducted is read carefully. Good research must meet the standards of nonbias, validity, reliability, and sampling and data collection which are appropriate for the research questions being addressed. These standards are described in the four articles in this section.

But first we must ask why research is necessary at all in consumer behavior. The primary reason is that there is much that is not known about the subject. We might speculate as to what makes consumers behave as they do, but only research which is carried out scientifically can provide information that is valid, reliable, and judged as to the probability that it reflects the true state of things. Second, there are many new areas related to consumer behavior which have only recently drawn the attention of consumer behavior researchers. These include public policy topics such as the utilization of information by consumers, and not-for-profit organizations, such as health clinics and universities, which are discovering that they can learn more about their interaction with their users through consumer behavior research. Finally, but not least in importance, is the need to constantly monitor changes in consumer behavior in order to be able to modify marketing strategies accordingly.

"CONSUMER RESEARCH: TELLING IT LIKE IT IS"

This is a written version of what was originally presented as a luncheon speech at the 1976 Association for Consumer Research Conference. This speech contains many excellent points with regard to consumer research which are all too often ignored when research is conducted and used.

First, the interdisciplinary and transdisciplinary aspects of consumer behavior are noted. The study of consumer behavior is interdisciplinary because concepts and methods from several academic disciplines are relevant. Yet, as Jacoby notes, consumer behavior itself is transdisciplinary; it exists regardless of who studies it. Jacoby gives a definition of consumer behavior that is quite comprehensive, including acquisition, consumption, and disposition activities.

In his speech, Jacoby discusses several terms which may need further explanation. The first of these is the distinction between applied and basic research. Research can be differentiated on the basis of its purpose. Research which is conducted in order to provide an answer to a specific problem encountered by someone is *applied research*. An example in marketing would be research conducted by an advertising agency to see which of three house paint ads produced higher recall after one week. *Basic research* is research conducted to answer general questions which may or may not turn out to be relevant to particular problems encountered by others. For example, a curious professor may conduct a research project to find out what attributions consumers make following experiences with technological innovations. As Jacoby states, the two types of research lie on a continuum rather than being dichotomous.

A second term discussed by Jacoby which needs elaboration is *theory*. There is probably more confusion about what a theory is than about any other term used in this book. In everyday language there are several uses of the term which do not have the same meaning as the meaning implied here. For example, in discussing some event, we frequently hear someone say, "I have a theory about why it happened. It's because..." Usually this means that the speaker will make some speculations about why the event might have occurred. In this sense, theory is used to mean uncertain, unproven armchair speculations. This is not what theory means in the scientific sense. Another example of everyday usage occurs in classrooms, where we frequently hear someone say, "Let's stop being so theoretical; let's get back to the real world and be practical for a moment." In this sense, theory is used to mean abstract thoughts which are unrelated to daily life. Yet, using the scientific meaning of the word, many have said that there is nothing as practical as a good theory.

So theory is not uncertain speculation and it is not irrelevant ideas. But what *is* theory? A theory is built in steps: concepts are combined to produce propositions, and propositions with similar concepts are combined to produce a theory. Therefore, what does Jacoby mean when he says little theory is used in consumer research? He means that measurements of many concepts are taken (e.g., giving consumers 160-question personality inventories) and then statistical tests are used to see if there is a significant relationship between any of them. Yet no prior thought is given to how or why certain relationships might be expected to exist. Thus, the research sequence should be: (1) construct hypotheses about expected relationships and their direction, (2) gather data, (3) analyze data to see if hypotheses are supported, and then (4) report results.

Jacoby also places great emphasis on the importance of research validity. He puts data validity before statistical significance or complexity of analytical technique. He defines and discusses five types of validity: face validity, predictive validity, cross validity, construct validity, and convergent validity.

"RESEARCH METHODS IN CONSUMER BEHAVIOR"

Many methods are discussed in the Cipkala paper. Most of the terms are defined and explained in the paper. For introductory purposes, a brief outline of the methods discussed is presented here. This outline can be used by the reader as a guide for points to look for in reading the paper.

In addition, readers should use this outline and the paper as a way to check their understanding of consumer behavior research methods. Before reading anything, think of five different questions which could be answered by conducting research (e.g., "What is the relationship between social class and early adoption propensity?"). Then decide which of the methods discussed in the Cipkala paper could possibly be used to answer each of these questions. Which methods are best or most appropriate for each of the questions? Why?

Outline of research methods

I. Secondary Data Collection
II. Primary Data Collection
    A. Surveys
        1. Means of conducting
            a. Personal interview
            b. Mail questionnaire
            c. Telephone interview

2. Objectives
   a. Disguised
   b. Nondisguised
3. Sequence of questions
   a. Structured
   b. Nonstructured
B. Observation
   1. Personalness
      a. Personal
      b. Mechanical
   2. Reactivity
      a. Reactive
      b. Nonreactive
C. Experimentation
   1. Where conducted
      a. Laboratory
      b. Field
   2. Validity
      a. Internal
      b. External
   3. Design
      a. After-only
      b. Before-after
      c. Before-after with control
      d. Four group–six study (Solomon four group)
      e. After-only with control
      f. Panel
      g. Factorial
      h. Latin Square

"CONTENT ANALYSIS IN CONSUMER RESEARCH"

The article by Harold H. Kassarjian discusses a research methodology relatively new to marketing although it is common in other fields such as journalism and political science. This research methodology is called *content analysis.* Content analysis is the study of the message itself independently of what the source or the receiver perceives to have been the message.

The research methodology has considerable potential for consumer research. Kassarjian cites several instances where it has been used in consumer behavior research and where it could be used. Its range of uses is limited only by the imagination of the researcher.

Three necessary characteristics of content analysis are discussed. One characteristic is *objectivity.* This is often accomplished by having other researchers analyze the material and seeing whether the results they come up with are consistent with those of the original researchers. Another characteristic is that rules about what to analyze and what not to analyze should be formulated clearly and used systematically. This, then, is the characteristic of *systematization*. The third characteristic is *quantification*. This means that the categories of content be scored so that statistical techniques can be applied to aid in the interpretation of observations being made about the contents of a communication.

Kassarjian also discusses the units of measurement used in content analysis. The most common units are words, themes, characters, space and size of communications. After studying the Kassarjian article, the reader will find it interesting to do a content analysis of various advertisements for a given product, say beer or cigarettes. It is quite likely that the reader will develop a very different sense of the advertising message. It is important to remember that not all themes or messages that exist in a communication and that can be uncovered by content analysis are deliberately put there. Communicators themselves are not always aware of the various messages they are actually sending. Thus, they may not be totally aware of all the messages consumers are actually receiving.

"ETHICS IN MARKETING RESEARCH: THEIR PRACTICAL RELEVANCE"

Not only are research ethics an important consideration from a moral and philosophic point of view, but they are also important for the researcher to consider. The main point of the Tybout and Zaltman article is that ethics are necessary to ensure high quality research.

The authors discuss three basic rights of the research subject or respondent. These are the right to choose, the right to safety, and the right to be informed. They discuss the components of each right, practical considerations resulting from it (e.g., how the data may be affected by undermining or adhering to the respondents' rights), and possible solutions.

As an exercise, the reader may wish to look back over several of the papers in this book in order to see if there is any indication that ethical questions were considered or dealt with properly in the reported research. If these questions were not considered or dealt with properly, the reader can use the Tybout and Zaltman article as a basis for formulating a set of questions and suggestions which might be presented to the researchers.

CONSUMER RESEARCH: TELLING IT LIKE IT IS

JACOB JACOBY

DEFINING CONSUMER BEHAVIOR

Let me begin by defining what I mean by the terms "consumer research" and "consumer behavior." I prefer to view consumer behavior as being independent of any disciplinary orientation. To me, it is a fundamental form of human behavior; it simply exists. Moreover, it will continue to exist regardless of whether or not any discipline makes it the subject of formal inquiry. As I define it (cf. Jacoby, 1975, 1976a, 1976b), *consumer behavior* is the acquisition, consumption, and disposition of goods, services, time, and ideas by decision making units (e.g., individuals, families, firms, etc.)[1] As such, it represents three broad classes of behaviors (namely, acquisition, consumption and disposition) directed toward aspects of the environment.

Consumer behavior encompasses much more than just *buying* products and/or services. For example, acquisition can occur in a wide variety of ways, not all of which involve purchasing and the exchange of money.

Borrowing the neighbor's rake—a form of temporary acquisition which does not involve the exchange of money—can also be considered a form of consumer behavior. One could even argue that the chimpanzee who works for tokens and then exchanges them either for a banana or an opportunity to look through a window into another room is also engaging in consumer behavior (cf. Cowles, 1937; Wolfe, 1936).

Quite clearly, many would end their definition of consumer behavior at this point. The most often cited models of consumer behavior (cf. Engel, Kollat, and Blackwell, 1968, 1973; Howard and Sheth, 1969; Nicosia, 1966; Hansen, 1972) focus predominantly on pre-purchase acquisition, they barely mention or discuss actual consumption (i.e., the decisions and behaviors involved in actu-

Source: Jacob Jacoby, "Telling It Like It Is," in Beverlee B. Anderson, ed., *Advances in Consumer Research,* Vol. 3, 1976, pp. 1–11.

[1]"Behavior" is used here in a general sense to include both overt behavior and related cognitive behavior which may occur prior to, during, and subsequent to overt behavioral acts.

ally using or consuming the product) and completely ignore disposition. However, consumer behavior also includes these other basic categories of human behavior. Like acquisition, consumption and disposition are both complex decision processes having many facets. Among other things, consumption may be immediate, delayed, or extended through time, and the object of consumption may be entirely consumed (e.g., a cookie) or may remain in complete or partial form after consumption has ceased (e.g., a candy bar wrapper, an old shirt, an auto which is beyond repair). In the latter event, the consumer eventually becomes involved in a decision-making and behavioral process regarding whether to throw the object away, give it away, sell it, rent it, convert it to another purpose, etc. Often, the acquisition, consumption, or disposition of one item requires the acquisition, consumption, or disposition of another item (e.g., buying a car usually requires that we purchase auto insurance, using a car requires that we purchase gasoline, selling a car usually requires that a new vehicle be acquired, or a new mode of transportation be employed). Thus, consumer behavior often assumes complex overlays of multiple decision making and choice behavior regarding acquisition, consumption, and disposition.

Consumer research, then, is simply research addressed to studying any aspect of consumer behavior. It is not necessarily applied, although it could be and often is. However, it is important to note the growing tendency to consider the study of consumer behavior as a worthy endeavor in its own right (cf. Jacoby, 1969a; Sheth, 1972). In other words, there are also ''basic'' as well as ''applied'' consumer researchers. Having now made a distinction between these traditional orientations to research, let me say that the distinction is more arbitrary and artificial than real. Where there are differences between the two, they are more in degree rather than in kind. Applied research almost invariably utilizes basic research concepts and is often concerned with being able to use the obtained information at later points in time

(i.e., generalizing). Accordingly, I believe that the issues I am about to raise regarding consumer research are just as relevant for people who call themselves applied as for those who have a more basic orientation.

PROBLEMS IN CONSUMER RESEARCH

It is all too apparent that *much too large a proportion of the contemporary consumer research literature is not worth the paper it is printed on or the time it takes to read it.* Unless we begin to take corrective action soon, we will all drown in a mass of meaningless junk! Let me document this assertion by considering five broad categories of problems: our *theories* (and comprehensive models), our research *methods*, our research *measures,* our *statistical techniques,* and our *subject matter.*[2]

Consumer Behavior Theories, Models, and Concepts

The past decade has witnessed an increasing amount of attention devoted to the development, presentation, and discussion of relatively comprehensive theories and models of consumer behavior (Andreasen, 1965; Nicosia, 1966; Engel,

---

[2]Let me shout it at the outset: MEA CULPA! I have committed many of the sins that I am about to describe. No doubt, I will continue to commit at least some of them long after this address is published and forgotten. There is no one of us without guilt. However, we have to begin casting stones about and break our false idols lest our collective guilt suffocate the periodic airing of our sins and, in doing so, also suffocate the impetus to improve.

I would also like to note at this point that naming names and citing specific articles as illustrations of the problems I am iterating would probably serve few, if any, positive ends. The interested reader has only to examine the articles in our leading journals to find numerous examples of what I mean. On the other hand, and because they may serve a guidance function for some, I have named names and cited specific articles in order to illustrate positive examples addressed to the issue under consideration. It should be noted, however, that citing an article as being positive in one respect usually does not mean that it is void of other deficiencies.

Finally, some of the positively cited articles will be my own. I beg the reader's forebearance for the human tendency to be most familiar with and cite one's own work.

Kollat, and Blackwell, 1968, 1973; Howard and Sheth, 1969: Hansen, 1972; Markin, 1974). However, Kollat, et al. (1972, p. 577) noted that; "These models have had little influence on consumer behavior research during the last five years. Indeed, it is rare to find a published study that has utilized, been based on, or even influenced by, any of the models identified above." Unfortunately, not much has changed since then.

Look Ma—No Theory. Despite the availability of theory and the necessity for theory in any scientific endeavor seeking to extend understanding via empirical research, the impetus and rationale underlying much consumer behavior research seems to rest on little more than the availability of easy-to-use measuring instruments, the existence of more or less willing subject populations, the convenience of the computer, and/or the almost toy-like nature of sophisticated quantitative techniques. Little reliance is placed on theory either to suggest which variables and aspects of consumer behavior are of greatest importance and in need of research, or as a foundation around which to organize and integrate findings. It is still true that nothing is so practical as a good theory. However, while most of us talk a good game about the value and need for theory, it is clear that we would rather be caught dead than using theory.

The *Post Hoc*, Atheoretic, Shotgun Approach to Conducting Consumer Research. A fundamental problem relating to the neglect of theory and theoretically derived concepts is that the researcher increases the likelihood that he will fail to understand his own data and/or be able to meaningfully interpret and integrate his findings with findings obtained by others. In a set of unpublished working papers now six years old (Jacoby, 1969a, 1969b; as well as in a subsequent empirical investigation, Jacoby, 1971), I referred to the problem as "the atheoretical shotgun approach" and tried to illustrate its nature by considering empirical attempts to relate personality

variables to consumer behavior. Reaching back into ancient history, the most frequently quoted and paraphrased passage from these papers is as follows:

Investigators usually take a general, broad coverage personality inventory and a list of brands, products, or product categories, and attempt to correlate subjects' responses on the inventory with statements of product use or preference. Careful examination reveals that, in most cases, the investigators have operated without the benefit of theory and with no a priori thought directed to *how*, or especially *why*, personality should or should not be related to that aspect of consumer behavior being studied. Statistical techniques, usually simple correlation or variants thereof, are applied and anything that turns up looking halfway interesting furnishes the basis for the Discussion section. Skill at post-diction and post hoc interpretation has been demonstrated, but little real understanding has resulted.

These papers went on to advocate and illustrate why it was necessary for consumer researchers to use theoretically derived hypotheses for specifying variables and relationships in advance. That is, they called on consumer researchers: (1) to make predictions of differences and *no* differences, (2) to explain the reasons underlying these predictions, and (3) to do both prior to conducting their research.

Although considered in the context of relating personality variables to consumer behavior, these working papers also made it clear that almost every aspect of consumer research reflected the atheoretic shotgun approach, particularly when it came to utilizing concepts borrowed from the behavioral sciences. In a word, the problem was pandemic. Yet despite the fact that this passage was later liberally quoted and re-emphasized by such influential writers as Engel, Kollat, and Blackwell (1973, p. 653–53; Kollat, Engel, and Blackwell, 1972, p. 576–77) and Kassarjian (in his frequently cited review of personality research, 1971, p. 416), the impact of these calls for greater reliance on theory and less shotgunning in consumer research has been negligible. Most consumer researchers are still pulling shotgun triggers in the dark.

Concepts Misplaced, or Whoops! Did you Happen to See Where my Concept Went?

Even in those instances where consumer researchers seem to be sincerely interested in conducting research based upon a firm conceptual foundation, they sometimes manage to misplace their concepts when it gets down to the nittygritty. For example, the author of one recent article states: ". . . it is imperative that our definition of deception in advertising recognize the interaction of the advertisement with the accumulated beliefs and experience of the consumer." Two paragraphs later he provides a definition which *ignores* his imperative. He then goes on to propose plans for detecting deception which completely disregard the fact that deception may occur as a function of the prior beliefs of the consumer and not as a function of the ad (or ad campaign) in question.

Another equally frustrating example is provided by those who define brand loyalty as a hypothetical construct predicated upon the cognitive dynamics of the consumer—and then proceed to base their measure of brand loyalty solely on the buyer's overt behavior. The consumer behavior literature contains an abundance of similar examples of our inability to have our measures of concepts correspond to these concepts.

The "Theory of the Month" Club.

Interestingly, however, the failure to use and test existing theories and comprehensive models of consumer behavior has not discouraged some of us from proposing new theories and comprehensive models, thereby providing us with a different kind of problem. Several of our most respected colleagues seem to belong to a sort of "theory of the month" club which somehow requires that they burst forth with new theories periodically and rarely, if ever, bother to provide any original empirical data collected specifically in an attempt to support their theory. Perhaps those with a new theory or model should treat it like a new product: either stand behind it and give it the support it needs (i.e., test it and refine it as necessary)—or take the damn thing off the market!

Single Shot vs. Programmatic Research.

Another theory-related problem evidenced in the contemporary consumer behavior literature is the widespread failure to engage in programmatic research. Judging from the literature published since the inception of ACR, there are fewer than a dozen individuals who have conducted five or more separate investigations in a systematic and sequential fashion which were addressed to providing incremental knowledge regarding the same broad issue. Instead, what we have is a tradition of single shot studies conducted by what one scholar has termed "Zeitgeisters-Shysters" (Denenberg, 1969).

Rarely, however, have single shot investigations answered all questions that need to be answered or made definitive contributions on any subjects of importance. Yet many consumer researchers seem to be operating under the illusory and mistaken belief that they are capable of yielding payout of substance and duration. I am not advocating that we do *only* programmatic research. Having engaged in enough single shot studies myself (e.g., Kyner, Jacoby, and Chestnut, 1975), I full well appreciate the allure, excitement and challenge often inherent in single shot studies and the potential that such studies *sometimes* have for providing resolution to an applied problem of immediate concern. I also recognize that it is difficult to caution someone in the depth of an infatuation not to be beguiled. However, if we are to deserve the label "serious researcher" and make contributions of substance, it is necessary that a greater proportion of our efforts be programmatic.

Consumer Research Methods

Verbal Report vs. Actual Behavior.

By far, the most prevalent approach to gathering data in

consumer research involves eliciting verbal reports from subjects either via an interview or through the use of a self-administered questionnaire. Typically, these verbal reports assess either (1) recall of past events and behavior, (2) current psychological states (including attitudes, preferences, beliefs, statements of intentions to behave and likely reactions to hypothetical events), and/or (3) socio-demographic data. Of the 44 empirical studies in the published Proceedings of last year's conference (Schlinger, 1975), 39 (or 87%) are based principally or entirely on verbal report data collected from respondents. Similarly, of the 36 empirical studies found in the first six issues of the *Journal of Consumer Research,* 31 (more than 85%) were based primarily or solely on verbal report data. Even if the verbal reports were the best of possible methods, the following observation by Platt (1964, p. 251) would still remain true: "Beware the man of one method or one instrument . . . he tends to become method-oriented rather than problem-oriented." However, the verbal report is probably not the best of all possible methods. Given the numerous sources of bias in verbal reports and the known and all-too-often demonstrated discrepancy between what people say they do and what they actually do, it is nothing short of amazing that we persist in our slavish reliance on verbal reports as the mainstay of our research.

For the greater part, the problem inherent in the ubiquitous verbal report approach can be organized into one of three broad categories; interviewer error, respondent error, and instrument error. We will here disregard consideration of interviewer errors, since more than 75% of the verbal report studies (or two-thirds of our published empirical effort) are based upon the self-administered questionnaires.

Respondent Error in Verbal Reports. It is exceedingly important to note that verbal report data are predicated upon many untested and, in some cases, invalid assumptions. Many of these are in regard to the respondent. As examples, consider the following assumptions inherent in attempts to elicit recall of factual information: (1) Prior learning (and rehearsal) of the information has actually taken place; that is, something exists in memory to be recalled. (2) Once information is stored in memory, it remains there in accurate and unmodified form. (3) Said information remains equally accessible through time. (4) There are no respondent differences in ability to recall which should be controlled or accounted for. (5) Soliciting a verbal report is a non-reactive act; that is, asking questions of respondents is unlikely to have any impact on them and on their responses.

Analogous assumptions exist with respect to assessing psychological states via verbal reports (e.g., regarding attitudes, preferences, intentions, etc.). For example, in a paper published eight years ago—which I believe should be required reading for all consumer researchers—Leo Bogart noted that the simple act of asking the respondent a question often "forces the crystallization and expression of opinions where [previously] there were no more than chaotic swirls of thought" (1967, p. 335). It should be noted that the assumptions which underlie the use of verbal reports are invalid. The reader is asked to perseverate regarding the ramifications of this fact.

Instrument Error in Verbal Reports. If these problems are sobering, consider the fact that our paper and pencil instruments (either self-administered questionnaires or interview schedules) often contribute *as much or more* error than do our interviewers or our respondents. In general, *most* of our questionnaires and interview schedules are terrible and tend to impair rather than assist us in our efforts to collect valid data. More often than not, we provide respondents with questionnaires which, from their perspective, are ambiguous, intimidating, confusing, and incomprehensible. But questions and questionnaires are easy to prepare, right? Wrong! Preparing a self-administered questionnaire is one of the most difficult steps in the entire research process. Unfortunately, it is commonly the most neglected step. Formulating questions and developing the questionnaire seems like such a simple thing to do that we are usually lulled into a false sense of security. Everyone is assumed to be an expert here. Yet many of us never become aware of the literally hundreds of details that should be attended to in constructing questionnaires (cf. Erdos, 1970; Payne, 1951; Kornhauser and Sheatsley, 1959; Selltiz, Jahoda, Deutsch, and Cook, 1959). We simply assume that because *we* know what we mean by our questions and *we* comprehend the lay-out and organization of our instrument, data collected using such an instrument are naturally valid. If the data are not valid, then the error is obviously a function of the respondent, not a function of our instrument. The result is that we are often left with what in computer parlance is referred to as GIGO, that is, garbage in–garbage out. In most instances, we ourselves are hardly even cognizant of the fact that this has occurred.

Please don't misinterpret what I am saying. I am NOT suggesting that we do away with verbal reports and self-administered questionnaires. This aproach to gathering data is a valid and vital part of our methodological armamentarium. However, if we are to continue placing such great reliance on it, the least we ought to do is clean it up. Too many of us are caught up in the excitement and challenge of research and ignore the basics. One of the things I am *most emphatically* calling for is that we get down to these basics to learn how to formulate questions and structure questionnaires. I care not that a finding is significant, or that the ultimate in statistical analytical techniques have been applied, if the data collection instrument generated invalid data at the outset. Relative to other aspects of conducting research, more time must be devoted to developing and polishing our

verbal report instruments. Perhaps if journal editors found it important to require publication of the instrument (or at least the critical questions used), it would stimulate improvement in this area.

Verbal Reports vs. Actual Behavior: Continued. But do we actually have to place slavish reliance on the verbal report? Certainly not! One alternative is to devote less time to studying what people *say they do* and spend more time examining what it is that they actually *do do*. In other words, we must begin to place greater emphasis on studying behavior, relative to the amount of effort we place on studying verbal reports regarding behavior. There have been several recent developments in this regard. Let me simply note that the verbal report and behavioral approaches each have their unique advantages and disadvantages. The optimal procedure would probably involve some combination of both (cf. Wright, 1974). Such an approach is most likely to provide us with a better fix on and deeper understanding of our findings.

Consumer Behavior: A Dynamic Process Studied with Static Methods. In addition to the necessity of cleaning up our verbal reports and developing greater attention to alternative approaches, we also need to begin studying consumer behavior (which includes consumer decision making) in terms of the dynamic process that it is. Virtually all consumer researchers tend to consider consumer behavior as a dynamic, decision making, behavioral process. Yet probably 99+% of all consumer research conducted to date examines consumer decision making and behavior via static, *post hoc* methods. Instead of being captured and studied, the dynamic nature of consumer decision making and behavior is squelched and the richness of the process ignored.

Roosters Cause the Sun to Rise. Another methodological issue I would briefly like to mention is the necessity for greater reliance on the experimental method, particularly in those instances where cause-effect assertions are made or alluded to. Examination of our literaure reveals a surprising number of instances in which causation is implied or directly claimed on the basis of simple correlation. It bears repeating that no matter how highly correlated the rooster's crow is to the sun rising, the rooster does not cause the sun to rise.

More and Richer Dependent and Independent Variables.   A final set of methodological issues I would like to raise at this point—in part, because they are related to the issue of measurement (particularly validity) to which I will turn next—concerns the need for research: (1) which incorporates measures of a variety of dependent variables, (2) which explores the combined and perhaps interacting impact of a variety of independent variables, and (3) which moves away from using single measures of the same dependent variable. With respect to the former, it is often possible to measure a variety of *different* dependent variables at little additional cost (e.g., accuracy, decision time, and subjective states, in Jacoby, Speller, and Berning, 1974). Unfortunately, opportunities for substantially enhancing understanding through the inclusion of a variety of dependent variables are generally ignored. Equally important, we live in a complex, multivariate world. Studying the impact of one or two variables in isolation would seem to be relatively artificial and inconsequential. In other words, we also need more research which examines the impact of a variety of factors impinging in concert.

It is also all too often true that conclusions are accepted on the basis of a single measure of our dependent variable. The costs involved in incorporating a second or third measure of that *same* variable are usually negligible, particularly when considered in terms of the increased confidence we could have in both our findings and concepts if we routinely used a variety of indices and found

that all (or substantially all) provided the same pattern of results (e.g., Jacoby and Kyner, 1973). This second issue (namely, using multiple measures of the same variable) relates more to the validity of our measures than to our methods, and is elaborated upon below.

Consumer Research Measures and Indices: Our Bewildering Array of Definitions.
Another problem which Kollat, Blackwell, and Engel (1972) referred to is the "bewildering array of definitions" that we have for many of our central constructs. As one example, at least 40 different and distinct measures of brand loyalty have been employed in the 300 studies comprising the brand loyalty literature (cf. Jacoby and Chestnut, 1975). Virtually no attempt has been made to weed out the poor measures and identify the good ones. Almost everyone has his own preferred measure and seems to blithely and naively assume that findings from one investigation can easily be compared and integrated with findings from investigations which use other definitions. The same horrendous state of affairs exists with respect to many of our other core concepts and constructs. There are at least four different categories of "innovator" definitions (cf. Kohn and Jacoby, 1973; Robertson, 1971) and three different categories of "opinion leadership" definitions (i.e., self-designating, sociometric, and key informant). Each one of these categories can be and usually is broken out into several specific forms of operationalizations. As examples, Rogers and Catarno (1962), King and Summers (1970) and Jacoby (1972) all provide different operationalizations of self-designating opinion leadership.

More incredible than the sheer number of our measures is the ease with which they are proposed and the uncritical manner in which they are accepted as meaningful indicants. In point of fact, most of our measures are only measures because someone *says* that they are, not because they have been shown to satisfy the standard measurement criteria of validity, reliability, and sensitivity.

Wanted, Desperately: Validity.   A core problem in this regard is the issue of validity. Just how valid are our measures? Hardly anyone seems to be interested in finding out. Like our theories and comprehensive models, once proposed, our measures seem to take on an almost sacred and inviolate existence all their own. They are rarely, if ever, examined or questioned. Several basic types of validity exist, although often described with somewhat varying terminology (e.g., American Psychological Association, 1966; Angelmar, Zaltman, and Pinson, 1972; Cronbach, 1960; Heeler and Ray, 1972; Nunnally, 1973). The psychometrician, Nunnally, in a highly readable and almost layman-like presentation of the subject, writes of three basic types of validity: content validity (which is generally irrelevant in consumer research), predictive validity, and construct validity. Face validity is a fourth, non-psychometric variety and refers to whether a measure *looks like* it is measuring what it is supposed to be measuring. Examination of the core[3] consumer behavior journals *(Journal of Consumer Research, Journal of Marketing Research, Journal of Marketing, Journal of Applied Psychology, Public Opinion Quarterly, Journal of Consumer Affairs, and Journal of Advertising Research)* and conference proceedings (of the Association for Consumer Research, American Marketing Association, and the American Psychological Association's Division of Consumer Psychology) since 1970—a body of literature consisting of approximately 1000 published articles—reveals the following with respect to validity.

Face Validity.   First, there are numerous examples of face validity. The measures being

[3]As considered from my biased perspective, i.e., "as I sees it."

used almost always look like they are measuring that which they are supposed to be measuring. However, the overwhelming majority of studies go no further, i.e., provide no empirical support. In other words, face validity is often used as a substitute for construct validity.

Predictive Validity.   There are also a sizable number of studies which suggest the existence of predictive validity, that is, the measure in question seems to correlate with measures of other variables as predicted. Unfortunately, many investigators do not seem to recognize that predictive validity provides little, if any, understanding of the reasons for the relationship. One can have a predictive validity coefficient of .99 and still not know why or what it means—other than the fact that the scores on one measure are highly predictive of scores on a second measure. Indeed, the relationship may even be meaningless.

However, there is one type of predictive validity which receives all too little attention, and that is cross-validity. "Whereas predictive validity is concerned with a single sample, cross validity requires that the *effectiveness* of the predictor composite be tested on a *separate* independent sample from the *same* population" (Raju, Bhagat, and Sheth, 1975, p. 407). It should be obvious that unless we can cross-validate our findings, we may really have no findings at all. Again, examination of the consumer behavior literature reveals few attempts at cross-validation (Kaplan, Szybillo, and Jacoby, 1974; Raju, Bhagat, and Sheth, 1975; Speller, 1973; Wilson, Mathews, and Harvey, 1975).

Construct Validity: A Necessity for Science.   From the perspective of science, the most necessary type of validity to establish is construct validity. Examination of the recently published literature indicates that less than 2% of our productivity has been directed toward determining construct validity. A large part of the problem lies in the fact that scientific research is a game played by creating measures and then applying them directly to reality. Although guided by some implicit conceptualization of what it is he is trying to measure, the consumer researcher rarely makes his implicit concepts sufficiently explicit or uses them as a basis for developing operational measures. Yet virtually all contemporary scholars of science generally agree that the concept must precede the measure (e.g., Massaro, 1975, p. 23; Plutchik, 1968, p. 45; Selltiz, et al., 1959, p. 146–47).

It is not my intention to get into a lengthy discussion of the nature of scientific research.[4] I simply wish to point out that many of our measures are developed at the whim of a researcher with nary a thought given to whether or not it is meaningfully related to an explicit conceptual statement of the phenomenon or variable in question. In most instances, our concepts have no identity apart from the instrument or procedures used to measure them. As a result, it is actually impossible to evaluate our measures. "To be able to judge the relative value of measurements or of operations requires criteria beyond the operations themselves. If a concept is nothing but an operation, how can we talk about being mistaken or about making errors?" (Plutchik, 1968, p. 47). In other words, clearly articulated concepts (i.e., abstractions regarding reality) must intervene between reality and the measurement of reality.

Probably the most efficient means for establishing construct validity is the Campbell and Fiske (1959) multi-method × multi-trait approach. Despite the fact that numerous articles refer to this approach as something that could or should be applied, considerably less than 1% of our published literature has actually employed this approach for systematically exploring construct validity (Davis, 1971; Jacoby, 1974; Silk, 1971). Yet if we cannot demonstrate that our concepts are valid, how can we continue to act as if the findings based upon measures of these concepts are valid?

As Campbell and Fiske (1959, p. 100) note: "Before one can test the relationship between a specific trait and other traits, one must have confidence in one's measure of that trait."

Convergent Validity. One basic and relatively easy to establish component of construct validity is convergent validity. This refers to the degree to which attempts to measure the same concept using two or more different measures yield the same results. Even if there are few full-scale construct validity investigations available, it seems reasonable to expect that we should find many studies to demonstrate convergent validity. After all, and as noted above, many of our core constructs are characterized by numerous and varied operationalizations. Surely, there have been many investigations which have used two or more measures of these constructs, thereby permitting us to examine convergent validity. Examination of the literature reveals that such is not the case. Somewhat incredibly, only two (out of 300) published studies exist which administered three or more brand loyalty measures concurrently to the same group of subjects, thereby permitting an examination of how these measures interrelated. Our other core constructs fare equally poorly. Data that are available often indicate that different measures of the same construct provide different results (e.g., Kohn and Jacoby, 1973). Given that we cannot demonstrate adequate convergent validity, it should be screamingly obvious that we have no basis for comparing findings from different studies and making generalizations using such a data base. What we urgently need is more widespread use of multiple measures so that we can begin the relatively simple job of assessing convergent validity. We are being strangled by our bad measures. Let's identify and get rid of them.

Reliability. Another fundamental problem with consumer behavior measures is that data regarding their reliability, particularly test-retest reliability, are rarely provided. As an illustration, only a single

---

[4]The interested reader is referred to Chapter 4 in Jacoby and Chestnut (1975) for an extended discussion of these issues.

study appears in the entire 300 item brand loyalty literature which measures the test-retest reliability of a set of brand loyalty measures. A similar state of affairs exists with respect to indices of other core constructs. In particular, consider the case of the test-retest reliability of recall data. In the entire literature on the use of recall data in advertising—and I suspect that this takes into account several thousand studies—only two *published* articles can be found which provide data on the test-retest reliability of recall data (Clancy and Kweskin, 1971: Young, 1972). Alarmingly, one of these authors (Young, 1972, p. 7) notes that results obtained in ten retests were the same as those in the initial test *in only 50% of the cases.* Assuming we were ill and actually had a body temperature of 103° Farenheit, how many of us would feel comfortable using a thermometer if, with no actual change in our body temperature, this thermometer gave us readings of 97.0°, 100.6°, 98.6°, and 104.4°, all within the space of one 15-minute period. Yet we persistently employ indices of unknown reliability to study consumer purchase decisions and behavior. More sobering, we often develop expensive nationwide promotional strategies and wide-ranging public policies based upon findings derived from using such indices. Obviously, reliability should not only be a concern in Ph.D. dissertations and M.S. theses.

Open Publication Tradition.   Let me digress for a moment—because this seems to be as good a point as any—to briefly touch upon my use of and stress upon the words "published literature." No doubt, work has been conducted by and for industry which addresses many of these fundamental issues. Much of this work is of high quality. Rarely, however, are the findings from these investigations permitted to enter the published literature. Although there are several reasons for this, a dominant reason is that industry is phobic. Firms are afraid that by permitting such data to be published, they will be giving up trade secrets and competitive advantages. I submit that, in the long run, industry probably has more to gain than lose by permitting this material to surface. No single firm has the resources necessary to make progress along all, or even a sizable proportion of the important research fronts. Contributing to the basic fund of knowledge would yield dividends to all.

Replication.   There is a strong necessity for us to replicate our findings using different subject populations, test products, etc. The name of the game is confidence in our findings.

Measurement Based on House-of-Cards Assumptions.   Another problem which makes its appearance in the literature with alarming frequency is the tendency to have one's measures (or proposed measures) rest upon an intertwined series of untested and sometimes unverifiable assumptions so that the measures used are sometimes 5 or even 15 steps removed from the phenomenon of interest.

Interpreting data collection via such measures of measurement systems represents a form of specious logic. In such cases, if a single one of the many assumptions is rendered invalid, the entire measurement system must necessarily come cascading downward. However, perhaps there is a positive side to this problem in that it indicates consumer researchers are at least beginning to recognize that their measurements are predicated upon basic assumptions. Stating these assumptions in clear and explicit detail is a necessary and important step before meaningful progress can be made.

The Folly of Single Indicants.   A final measurement problem I would like to note is perhaps most easily illustrated by posing the following question: "How many of us would feel comfortable having our intelligence assessed on the basis of our response to a single question?" Believe it or not, that's exactly the kind of thing we do in consumer research. As examples, brand loyalty is often measured by the response to a single question. The same is true with respect to virtually all of our other core constructs. Just a few months ago I came across an exceedingly expensive, large scale, multinational study of consumer information seeking which assessed opinion leadership on the basis of each subject's response to a single question. Examination of our literature reveals hundreds of instances in which responses to a single question suffice to establish the person's level on the variable of interest and then serves as the basis for extensive analysis and entire articles.

Just as is true of such constructs as personality and intelligence, most core concepts in consumer research (e.g., opinion leadership, brand loyalty, innovation proneness, shopping proneness, etc.) are multifaceted and complex. Intelligence and personality are generally measured through the use of a battery of different test items and methods. Even single personality traits are typically assessed by 30 or 40 item inventories. Given the complexity of our subject matter, what makes us think that we can use responses to single items (or even to two or three items) as measures of these constructs, then relate these scores to a host of other variables, arrive at conclusions based upon such an investigation, and get away with calling what we have done "science?"

Statistics in Consumer Research

Let me now turn to a consideration of the manner in which we use statistics to analyze our data. In general, this is the area where we have the fewest number of problems and, in recent years, probably the greatest number of advances. However, as I sees it, we still do have three major problems which I will call "number crunching," "using calipers to measure melting marshmallows," and "static state statistics."

Number Crunching. I have finally reached the point where I am no longer automatically impressed by the use of high-powered and sophisticated statistics. Why? Because too often the use of these statistics appears *not* to be accompanied by the use of another high-powered and sophisticated tool, namely the brain. For example, what does it really mean when the fourteenth canonical root is highly significant and shows that a set of predictors including size of house, purchase frequency of cake mix, and number of times you brush your teeth per day is related to age of oldest child living at home, laundry detergent preference, and frequency of extra-marital relations? Given the penchant that some have for coming up with brilliant interpretations of such findings, let me hasten to add that my question was simply rhetorical. Of course, this particular mindless application of high-powered statistics is only a way-out example—or is it? A critical examination of the recent consumer research literature will reveal many more instances of such mindless and mindblowing applications.

Multilayered Madness. In its most sophisticated (a word which, it should be remembered, derives from sophism) form, number crunching involves the multilayering of statistical techniques so that the output from one analysis provides the input for the next analysis. Sometimes, this statistical version of musical chairs involves five to ten different techniques used in series. Again, given the nature of the data collected in the first place, what does the final output actually mean?

Measuring Giant Icebergs in Millimeters and Using Calipers to Measure Melting Marshmallows. Perhaps what is most surprising about this number crunching is the fact that the data being crunched are usually exceedingly crude and coarse to begin with. As already noted, the large majority of our data are collected using the self-administered questionnaire. Yet many consumer researchers don't have the foggiest idea about what the basic do's and don'ts are when it comes to questionnaire construction. Consider also the fact that the realiability and validity of the data we collect are often assumed, not demonstrated. Finally also consider the fact that trying to measure diffuse, complex, and *dynamic* variables such as personality, attitudes, motives, brand loyalty, information seeking, etc. may be like trying to measure melting marshmallows with vernier calipers.

In other words, what are we doing working three and four digits to the right of the decimal point? What kind of phenomena, measures, and data do we really have that we are being so precise in our statistical analysis? I submit that our statistical methods are already too sophisticated for the kinds of data we collect. What we need are substantial developments in both our methodology (particularly in regard to questionnaire constuction) and in the psychometric quality of our measures (particularly in regard to validity and reliability) before use of the high-powered statistics can be justified in many of the instances where they are now being routinely applied.

Static State Statistics. There is one area, however, in which our statistics can use some improving. By and large, most of our statistics are appropriate only for use with data which are collected using our traditional cross-sectional, static methodologies. However, just as we have a need for the further development of dynamic methodologies, we need the development of statistics for analyzing data collected using such methods. That is, we need statistics which do not force dynamic process data to be reduced to static state representations. To a certain extent, trend analysis and cross-lagged correlations can and have been used in this manner. However, our repertoire of statistical techniques for handling dynamic data needs to be expanded, either by borrowing from disciplines accustomed to dealing with dynamic data, or through the creative efforts of statisticians working within the consumer research domain.

Consumer Research Subject Matter

A final set of consumer research problems I would like to touch upon concerns our subject matter.

Systematically Exploring the Varieties of Acquisition. To begin with, most definitions of consumer behavior tend to shackle us by confining our attention to the purchase of products and services. Aside from the fact that purchase can itself take a variety of forms (e.g., buying at list price, bargaining, bidding at auction), purchase is but one form of acquisition. There are many others. Receiving something as a gift, or in trade, or on a loan basis are three such examples. Each of these can have important economic, sociological, and psychological dynamics and consequences different from purchase. For example, on an aggregate level, if one million more Americans this year than last suddenly decided to borrow their neighbor's rake to handle their fall leaf problems, the impact on the rake industry could be enormous. For that matter, what are the dynamics underlying being a borrower or being a lender? What are the dynamics underlying giving or receiving a gift (cf. Hart, 1974; Weigl, 1975)? Hardly any published data exist regarding these facets of acquisition. Obviously, one thing we must do is systematically explore the realm of consumer acquisition decisions and behavior.

Putting Consumption Back into Consumer Behavior. Although considerable work has been done on consumption, particularly by the home economists, this fact is not adequately reflected in the predominant theories and textbooks of consumer behavior. The work dealing with consumption itself must be given greater salience and more tightly integrated with the existing consumer behavior literature.

And What About Disposition? The third major facet of consumer behavior, namely disposition, appears to have been completely neglected. This unfortunate state of affairs should be rectified for at least four reasons. First, from a purely scholarly perspective, disposition decisions deserve to be studied in their own right. The scientific approach requires that we study all aspects of a phenomenon, not just part of it. This is particularly important in this instance, since many disposition decisions have significant economic consequences for both the individual and society. Some disposition decisions (e.g., when and how to properly dispose of unused or outdated prescription drugs) may even have important health and safety ramifications. Second, on more practical grounds, much consumer behavior seems to be cyclical and a variety of marketing implications would most likely be forthcoming from an understanding of the disposition subprocess. Third, we are entering an age of relative scarcity in which we can no longer afford the luxury of squandering our natural resources. Understanding consumer disposition decisions and behavior is a necessary (and perhaps even logically prerequisite) element in any conservationist orientation. Finally, the study of consumer disposition could conceivably provide us with new "unobtrusive" (cf. Webb, Campbell, Schwartz, and Sechrest, 1966) macro indicators—both leading and trailing—of economic trends and the state of consumer attitudes and expectations. An empirical and taxonomic start toward exploring consumer disposition has recently been made (Jacoby, Berning, and Dietvorst, 1975).

Consumption and Production. Not only does the definition of consumer behavior have to be expanded and its various facets studied, but the relationship between consumption and production should be explored. As implied by the "leaf rake" example above, consumption and production are integrally related. Studies are needed which examine this interrelationship by considering both domains simultaneously.

Addressing Important Social Issues.   Much of our subject matter is obviously a function of the pressing social issues which confront us. Or is it? Probably the most significant and potentially overwhelming problem that we as a nation—and, indeed, the entire world—have ever confronted is the emerging energy crisis. This problem dwarfs

the Viet Nam war in its heyday, the Arab-Israeli situation, our economic stability, misleading advertising, nutrition labeling, and any other problem you can think of. These other problems are all pimples compared to the rogue elephant that is the emerging energy crisis. Yet the total contribution on this subject appearing in the consumer literature is fewer than five empirical and non-empirical papers. Even in those subject areas where we have supposedly been devoting attention, our record is not much better. Regardless of quality, how much empirical work, as opposed to rhetoric, has actually been addressed to the issues of consumer behavior and the elderly, product safety, deceptive and misleading advertising, nutritional labeling, etc., etc.? In general, far fewer than ten published studies exist on each of these topics. As Cohen noted, we need to stop toying with the trivial and start addressing that which is significant.

EXHORTATION

This compendium (summarized for students in Table 1) is by no means an exhaustive iteration of all of the problems in and confronting consumer research. Among others, I have not touched upon the widespread tendency to overgeneralize from our results, our relative inattention to cross-cultural comparisons, and the numerous avoidable or controllable problems which crop up in regard to the use of experimental designs in our research (cf. Campbell and Stanley, 1963; Rosenthal and Rosnow, 1969). The compendium does, however, cover what I view to be the most frequently occurring and severe problems which confront us.

Most of these have been previously discussed in print by one or more of us within the consumer research community. The problems are serious and bear periodic repeating. Some are easier to attend to than others. Hopefully, sensitization will produce awareness which, in turn, will provide the impetus for change.

Quite clearly, I think it's important to know what we don't know—important so that we don't de-

Table 1 An incomplete compendium of major problems in consumer research[1]

Theories, models, and concepts	*Measures*

Theory unused
  as a basis for guiding research
    —lack of *a priori* specification of variables
    —lack of *a priori* specification of relationships
    —reliance on shotgunning
  as a basis for integrating research
  as a basis for generating from research
Theory noted, then ignored
  in going from concept to measurement
  in interpreting data obtained
Theory proliferation
  untested "theory of the month" club contributions
  Zeitgeisting (single-shot vs. programmatic research;
    see Denenberg's 1969 index)
	Our operational definitions: a bewildering array
	Validity
	  predictive validity
	    —cross-validation
	  construct validity—essential and missing
	    —full test (e.g., multimethod × multitrait approach)
	    —convergent validity—relatively easy but generally ignored
	Reliability
	  test-retest reliability
	Replication
	Measurement based on house-of-cards assumptions
	The folly of single indicants

Methods	*Statistics*

Verbal reports: underlying assumptions and problems
  respondent error
    —in assessing prior events via recall
    —in assessing current or anticipated psychological
      states
  instrument error: our soft vulnerable underbelly
    errors too numerous to cite individually
    —must return to the basics
Slavish reliance on the verbal report
  failure to develop and utilize alternatives
Consumer behavior as a static vs. dynamic process
Correlation ≠ causation
  necessity for greater reliance on experimental method
Our dependent and independent variables
  need to simultaneously employ a variety of dependent variables
  need to simultaneously explore a variety of independent variables
  need to simultaneously utilize several indicants of the same dependent variable
	Number-crunching
	  multilayered number-crunching
	Measuring giant icebergs in millimeters
	  measuring melting marshmallows with vernier calipers
	Static-state statistics
	
	Content
	Systematically exploring acquisition
	Integrating consumption into consumer research
	What about disposition?
	Consumption and production
	Addressing important issues
	  the emerging energy crisis
	  everything else

[1] "as I sees it."

lude ourselves and others about the *quality* of our research and validity of our findings as providing sound bases upon which to make decisions of consequence. It is also important to recognize that we are in the midst of a consumer research information explosion and unless we take corrective action soon, we stand to become immersed in a quagmire from which it is already becoming increasingly difficult to extricate ourselves. Perhaps one of the things we most need to learn is that we must stop letting our existing methods and tools dictate and shackle our research. They are no substitute for using our heads. The brain is still the most important tool we have and its use should *precede* more than succeed the collection of data.

Because I have chosen to focus on our problems, the tone of this address has been rather negative. However, I would like to conclude on what I believe is a very legitimate positive note. Almost every one of the problems noted provides us with numerous opportunities to make meaningful contributions. Simply establishing the validity of a single one of our core constructs and shucking off our poor measures of this construct will require

a substantial effort. Consider, also, the need to develop a process technology (incorporating appropriate process methods and statistics) for examining consumer behavior in terms of the dynamic, ongoing phenomenon that it is. As another example, we have need for reviews which not only summarize, but also *critically* evaluate the empirical evidence bearing on the adequacy of our concepts and measures. Numerous other opportunities become apparent from a consideration of our problems.

It is important to periodically take stock of where we are. However, it is probably more important that we give more than just lip service to these issues; we must begin doing something about them. The time is already overdue.

REFERENCES

American Psychological Association (1966), *Standards for Educational and Psychological Tests and Manuals,* Washington: American Psychological Association.

Andreasen, Alan R. (1965), "Attitudes and Consumer Behavior: A Decision Model," in L. Preston, ed., *New Research in Marketing,* Berkeley, Calif.: Institute of Business and Economic Research, University of California, 1–16.

Angelmar, Reinhard; Zaltman, Gerald; and Pinson, Christian (1972), "An Examination of Concept Validity," in M. Venkatesan, ed., *Proceedings of the Third Annual Conference of the Association for Consumer Research,* 586–93.

Bogart, Leo (Fall, 1967), "No Opinion, Don't Know, and Maybe No Answer," *Public Opinion Quarterly,* 31, 331–45.

Campbell, Donald T., and Fiske, Donald W. (1959), "Convergent and Discriminant Validation by the Multitrait-Multimethod Matrix," *Psychological Bulletin,* 56, 81–105.

Campbell, Donald T., and Stanley, Julian C. (1963), *Experimental and Quasi-Experimental Designs for Research,* Chicago: Rand McNally.

Clancy, Kevin J., and Kweskin, David M. (April, 1971), "T.V. Commercial Recall Correlates," *Journal of Advertising Research,* 11, 18–20.

Cowles, John T. (1937), "Food Tokens as Incentives for Learning by Chimpanzees," *Comparative Psychological Monographs,* 5, 4.

Cronbach, Lee J. (1960), *Essentials of Psychological Testing,* 2nd ed., New York: Harper & Bros.

Davis, Harry L. (August, 1971), "Measurement of Husband-Wife Influence in Consumer Purchase Decisions," *Journal of Marketing Research,* 8, 305–12.

Denenberg, Victor, H. (June, 1969), "Prolixities A. Zeitgeister, B.S. M.S., PhONY," *Psychology Today,* 3, 50.

Engel, James F.; Kollat, David T.; and Blackwell, Roger D. (1968), *Consumer Behavior,* New York: Holt, Rinehart & Winston.

Engel, James F.; Kollat, David T.; and Blackwell, Roger D. (1973), *Consumer Behavior,* 2nd ed., New York: Holt, Rinehart & Winston.

Erdos, Paul L. (1970), *Professional Mail Surveys,* New York: McGraw-Hill.

Hansen, Flemming (1972), *Consumer Choice Behavior: A Cognitive Theory,* New York: Free Press.

Hart, Edward W., Jr. (1974), "Consumer Risk-Taking for Self and for Spouse," unpublished Ph.D. Dissertation, Purdue University.

Heeler, Roger M., and Ray, Michael L. (November, 1972), "Measure Validation in Marketing," *Journal of Marketing Research,* 9, 361–70.

Howard, John A., and Sheth, Jagdish N. (1969), *The Theory of Buyer Behavior,* New York; Wiley.

Jacoby, Jacob (1969a), "Toward Defining Consumer Psychology: One Psychologist's Views," *Purdue Papers in Consumer Psychology,* No. 101, 1969, Paper presented at the 77th Annual Convention of the American Psychological Association, Washington, D.C.

Jacoby, Jacob (1969b), "Personality and Consumer Behavior: How *NOT* to Find Relationships," *Purdue Papers in Consumer Psychology,* No. 102.

Jacoby, Jacob (May, 1971), "Personality and Innovation Proneness," *Journal of Marketing Research,* 8, 244–47.

Jacoby, Jacob, (1972) "Opinion Leadership and Innovativeness: Overlap and Validity," in M. Venkatesan, ed., *Proceedings of the Third Annual Conference of the Association for Consumer Research,* 632–49.

Jacoby, Jacob (Spring, 1974), "The Construct Validity of Opinion Leadership," *Public Opinion Quarterly,* 38, 81–89.

Jacoby, Jacob (October, 1975), "Consumer Psychology as a Social Psychological Sphere of Action," *American Psychologist,* 30, 977–87.

Jacoby, Jacob (1967a), "Consumer and Industrial Psychology: Prospects for Theory Corroboration and Mutual Contribution," in M.D. Dunnette, ed., *The Handbook of Industrial and Organizational Psychology,'* Chicago: Rand McNally.

Jacoby, Jacob (1976b), "Consumer Psychology: An Octennium," in P. Mussen and M. Rosenzweig, eds., *Annual Review of Psychology,* 27, 331–58.

Jacoby, Jacob; Berning, Carol K.; and Dietvorst, Thomas (1975), "What About Disposition?" *Purdue Papers in Consumer Psychology,* No. 152.

Jacoby, Jacob, and Chestnut, Robert W. (1975), "Brand Loyalty Measurement: A Critical Review," monograph submitted for publication.

Jacoby, Jacob, and Kyner, David B. (February, 1973), "Brand Loyalty vs. Repeat Purchasing Behavior," *Journal of Marketing Research,* 10, 1–9.

Jacoby, Jacob; Speller, Donald E.; and Berning, Carol Kohn (June, 1974), "Brand Choice Behavior as a Function of Information Load: Replication and Extension," *Journal of Consumer Research,* 1, 33–42.

Kaplan, Leon, B.; Szybillo, George J.; and Jacoby, Jacob (June 1974), "Components of Perceived Risk in Product Purchase: A Cross-Validation," *Journal of Applied Psychology,* 59, 287–91.

Kassarjian, Harold H. (November, 1971), "Personality and Consumer Behavior: A Review," *Journal of Marketing Research,* 8, 409–18.

King, Charles W., and Summers, John O. (February, 1970), "Overlap of Opinion Leadership Across Consumer Product Categories," *Journal of Marketing Research,* 7, 43–50.

Kohn, Carol A., and Jacoby, Jacob (2, 1973), "Operationally Defining the Consumer Innovator," *Proceedings, 81st Annual Convention of the American Psychological Association,* 8, 837–38.

Kollat, David, T.; Blackwell, Roger, D.; and Engel, James F. (1972), "The Current Status of Consumer Behavior Research: Development During the 1968–1972 Period," in M. Venkatesan, ed., *Proceedings of the Third Annual Conference of the Association for Consumer Research,* 576–85.

Kornhauser, Arthur, and Sheatsley, Paul B. (1959), "Questionnaire Construction and Interview Procedure," in C. Selltiz, M. Jahoda, M. Deutsch, and S. W. Cook, eds., *Research Methods in Social Relations,* New York: Henry Holt & Co., 546–87.

Kyner, David B.; Jacoby, Jacob; and Chestnut, Robert W. (1975), "Dissonance Resolution by Grade School Consumers," in B. B. Anderson, ed., *Advances in Consumer Research,* Vol. 3, (Proceedings of the Sixth Annual Conference of the Association of Consumer Research).

Markin, Ron J. (1974), *Consumer Behavior: A Cognitive Orientation,* New York: McMillan Publishing Co.

Massaro, Dominic W. (1975), *Experimental Psychology and Information Processing,* Chicago: Rand McNally.

Nicosia, Francesco (1966), *Consumer Decision Processes,* Englewood Cliffs, N.J.: Prentice-Hall.

Nunnally, Jum C. (1973), *Psychometric Theory,* New York: McGraw-Hill.

Payne, Stanley L. (1951), *The Art of Asking Questions,* Princeton, N.J.: Princeton University Press.

Platt, John R. (1964) "Strong Inference," *Science,* 146, 347–53.

Plutchik, Robert (1968), *Foundations of Experimental Research,* New York: Harper & Row.

Raju, P. S.; Bhagat, Rabi S.; and Sheth, Jagdish (1975), "Predictive Validation and Cross-Validation of the Fishbein, Rosenberg, and Sheth Models of Attitudes," in M. J. Schlinger, ed., *Advances in Con-*

sumer Research, Vol. 2, Proceedings of the Fifth Annual Conference of the Association for Consumer Research, Chicago: University of Illinois, 405–25.

Robertson, Thomas S. (1971), *Innovative Behavior and Communication,* New York: Holt, Rinehart & Winston.

Rogers, Everett M., and Cartano, David G. (1962), "Methods of Measuring Opinion Leadership," *Public Opinion Quarterly,* 26, 435–41.

Rosenthal, Robert, and Rosnow, Ralph L., eds. (1969), *Artifact in Behavioral Research,* New York: Academic Press.

Schlinger, Mary Jane, ed., (1975), *Advances in Consumer Research: Vol. 2,* Proceedings of the Association for Consumer Research, Chicago: University of Illinois.

Selltiz, Claire; Jahoda, Marie; Deutsch, Morton; and Cook, Stuart W. (1959), *Research Methods in Social Relations,* New York: Henry Holt & Co.

Sheth, Jagdish N. (1972), "The Future of Buyer Behavior Theory," in M. Venkatesan, ed., *Proceedings of the Third Annual Conference of the Association for Consumer Research,* 562–75.

Silk, Alvin J. (Fall, 1971), "Response Set and the Measurement of Self-Designated Opinion Leadership," *Public Opinion Quarterly,* 35, 383–97.

Speller, Donald E. (2, 1973), "Attitudes and Intentions as Predictors of Purchase: A Cross-Validation," *Proceedings, 81st Annual Convention of the American Psychological Association,* 8, 825–26.

Webb, Eugene J.; Campbell, Donald T.; Schwartz, Richard D.; and Sechrest, Lee (1966), *Unobtrusive Measures: Non-Reactive Research in the Social Sciences,* Chicago: Rand McNally.

Weigl, Karl (1975), "Perceived Risk and Information Search in a Gift Buying Situation," unpublished M.S. thesis, Purdue University.

Wilson, David T.; Mathews, Lee H.; and Harvey, James W. (March, 1975), "An Empirical Test of the Fishbein Behavioral Intention Model," *Journal of Consumer Research,* 2, 39–48.

Wolfe, John B. (1936), "Effectiveness of Token-Rewards for Chimpanzees," *Comparative Psychological Monographs,* 5, 12.

Wright, Peter L. (1974), "Research Orientations for Analyzing Consumer Judgement Processes," in S. Ward and P. L. Wright, eds., *Advances in Consumer Research,* Vol. 1, Urbana, Illinois; Association for Consumer Research, 268–79.

Young, Shirley (February, 1972), "Copy Testing Without Magic Numbers," *Journal of Advertising Research,* 12, 3–12.

RESEARCH METHODS IN CONSUMER BEHAVIOR

JOHN CIPKALA

INTRODUCTION

To put the notion of research methods in consumer behavior in proper perspective, it is important to clarify the terms research and methods. Webster's New Collegiate Dictionary defines research as "an investigation aimed at the discovery and interpretation of facts, revision of accepted theories or laws in the light of new factors, or practiced application of such new or revised theories or laws." For example, one common goal of any discipline is expanding its knowledge base. Researchers often begin by examining the present state of knowledge in a particular area and then follow with empirical studies to test hypotheses about some aspect of the relevant theory. If the research is sound, the results from the empirical studies will not only advance the knowledge in the discipline, but also will generate further research in related areas. Thus, there seems to be little doubt that research is vital to understanding more about any discipline.

Methods in consumer behavior are the means of gathering data. For example, "methods include such procedures as the making of observations and measurements, performing experiments, building models and theories, or providing explanations and making predictions" (Miller, 1970, p. 65).

The research process can be divided into seven steps:

(1) a definition of the problem and/or research objectives;
(2) the construction of a theoretical framework;
(3) the development of hypotheses;
(4) the selection and execution of a research design;
(5) the analysis and interpretation of results;
(6) a written report; and
(7) research utilization.

The role of methods in consumer behavior research is in research design. Research design includes the plan, structure, and strategy of investigation to obtain answers to research questions. The plan is the overall scheme of the research and

423

includes an outline of what the researcher will do from formulating the hypotheses and their operational implications to the final analysis of the task. The structure of the research is more specific. It is the outline of the relationships among the variables. Strategy is also more specific than the plan of the investigation. It includes the methods to be used to gather and analyze the data. Thus, strategy determines how the research will be tackled (Kerlinger, 1973, p. 300).

There are two types of data: primary data and secondary data. Secondary data are data already existing, having been originally collected for some purpose other than the project at hand. Examples of secondary data are the data found in government publications, libraries, and the results from other studies in consumer behavior. Primary data, in contrast, are original data collected specifically for the current research project, such as when a researcher stands in a supermarket and observes whether people use shopping lists and also in what order they go to the various departments. Of course, secondary data sources always ought to be exhausted before gathering primary data. The emphasis in this chapter will be upon the collection of primary data, since most studies in consumer behavior research require a significant collection of primary data. The remainder of this chapter will discuss the major methods of gathering primary data, some of the common statistics employed, and, finally, some conclusions about the state of research methods in consumer behavior.

METHODS OF GATHERING PRIMARY DATA[1]

There are three principal methods of gathering primary data: survey, observation, and experimentation. Normally, not all three methods are used in the same project. The choice of

[1]For a more comprehensive discussion of the basic methods of gathering primary data, see Zaltman and Burger (1978).

methods will depend largely upon the availability of time, money, and personnel. However, to increase the validity of the data, sometimes more than one method for gathering data is used.

Survey

A survey is a study of a population by selecting and studying samples chosen from the population. The purpose of many surveys is simply to provide someone with information. The information may be descriptive (e.g., how families of different sizes spend their income), or explanatory (e.g., determining how and why attitudes toward education influence voting behavior on a school bond issue).

The instrument for collecting data in surveys is the interview or questionnaire. An interview is an interpersonal contact between an interviewer and a respondent in order to obtain answers pertinent to some research problem. Surveys may be conducted on a personal face-to-face basis, over the telephone, or by mail. The instrument may be structured or nonstructured; that is, the questions, their sequence and wording, may or may not be fixed. These different types of instruments can be evaluated on the following criteria: (1) flexibility, (2) amount of information to be obtained, (3) accuracy of information, (4) speed, (5) cost, and (6) administration.

The personal interview is a face-to-face contact between an interviewer and a respondent. This interviewing may be conducted in a number of settings, such as the home of the respondent, the office of the respondent or of the interviewer, in the street, or virtually any meeting place. The personal interview may be on either an individual basis or in a group. Group interviews are called focus group interviews when the interviewer focuses attention upon a given experience and its effects.

Personal interviews are probably the most flexible of all interviews. The interviewer is able to alter the form, content, and order of questioning in order to probe deeper or ask unplanned questions. More information is usually possible relative to the telephone or mail interview. Virtually every subject lends itself to personal interviewing. In addition to probing, the interviewer may also obtain supplementary information by observing, for example, the respondent's standard of living, home, and neighborhood, Finally, a statistically sound sample is ordinarily more easily obtainable with personal interviewing than with the telephone or mail interview. However, there is also the accompanying problem of interviewer bias. If, for example, the interviewer does not always ask a particular question in the same way, respondents will get different stimuli which will produce additional variations in their responses.

The other major limitations of personal interviewing are its relatively high cost and the difficulties of administration. Not only is personal interviewing expensive, but it is also time consuming. Lastly, personal interviewing requires much administration since interviewers must be selected, trained, and supervised.[2]

Surveys conducted by mail involve mailing a list of questions to potential respondents and having them return the completed form by mail. Unlike the personal interview, there is no interviewer bias since the manner in which questions are posed is uniform. Mail interviewing also lends itself to wide geographic coverage at a rather low cost, particularly because there are virtually no expenses beyond the cost of stamps, paper, and envelopes. Also, since respondents may answer the questions in their leisure time, responses can be more carefully thought out. Because respondents remain anonymous, they will probably give true answers since they do not feel any need to impress the interviewer or feel embarrassed. Finally, it is easier to reach some groups by mail than by the personal interview or telephone.

Mail surveys offer little flexibility since there can be no probing or observing for supplemental information. Also, not much information can be ob-

tained because questions must be few and simple in order to increase the probability of return. Another problem of interviewing by mail is the rather slow return time. Leisure time allows the respondent to wait a week or two (or even a couple of months) before responding. In many cases, the respondent doesn't even answer, creating the problem of sample representativeness (often referred to as nonrespondent bias). If those people who did not respond would have responded differently from those who did respond, then generalizing the results from the sample to the population would be incorrect. Another major problem with mail interviewing is the compilation of a good mailing list, especially in broad-scale surveys. Mailing lists for baby shoes, for example, can be very good since newspapers print the names of newborns and their parents daily. A mailing list for cable television subscribers is probably more difficult to obtain.

The telephone survey includes interviews conducted over the telephone. It is more flexible than the mail survey, but less flexible than the personal interview. Telephone interviewers can clarify questions and probe beyond basic questions, but obtaining supplementary information by observation is impossible. Similarly, more information can be obtained by telephone interviewing than by mail interviewing, but less than by personal interviewing. Telephone interviewers can probe to obtain more information, but only on a limited basis because respondents normally do not want to talk by phone for more than just a few minutes. Because of the timeliness of telephone interviewing, the information obtained can be very accurate. For example, suppose a telephone interviewer were to call a person's home and ask whether the person is watching television and, if so, which television show and who the sponsor is. The response given is surely more accurate than, say, the answer to a mail interviewer who asks the ques-

---

[2]For a more complete listing of the advantages and disadvantages of personal interviewing, see Miller (1970, pp. 86–88).

[3]For a more complete listing of the advantages and disadvantages of mail interviewing, see Miller (1970, pp. 76–77).

tions: which television program did you watch last Tuesday at 8:30 p.m. and who was the sponsor? Telephone interviewing is also relatively inexpensive. Despite long-distance phone calling, costs can be kept at a low level since there are no travel expenses and only a few interviewers from a central location are required.

Although only a few interviewers are required and although wide geographic coverage is feasible, there remains one major limitation to the telephone survey. It is virtually impossible to get a very good cross-section of the population. Some people do not have phones, some have unlisted numbers, some are not at home when the interviewer calls, and others simply refuse to respond. Table 1 summarizes the advantages and disadvantages of these three types of surveys.

In all three types of surveys, someone fills out a questionnaire. In a mail survey the respondent reads questions and then writes down the answers. In personal and telephone interviews the interviewer asks the questions (either from memory or from a piece of paper). The respondent gives verbal answers, and the interviewer writes them down (either immediately or later). The questionnaire is the interview schedule, a formal list of questions used to conduct a survey. The importance of the questionnaire and the difficulty of designing it cannot be overemphasized. Payne (1951) devotes an entire book to the preparation of questionnaires. In addition, Moser and Kalton contend that "No survey can be better than its questionnaire, a cliche which expresses the truth that no matter how efficient the sample design or sophisticated the analysis, ambiguous questions will produce noncomparable answers, leading questions biased answers, and vague questions vague answers. Design of the questionnaire must begin at the start of the planning stages and will not end until the pilot surveys are completed" (1972, p. 308).

One procedure for questionnaire construction is set forth by Boyd and Westfall (1972, pp. 288–316). First, it is necessary to determine what information is needed to answer the research questions. Second, what type of survey should be used—personal interview, mail, or telephone? Next, the questionnaire designer must determine the content and necessity of each question and try to determine whether the respondents can and will answer it. Is the question necessary? Are several questions needed instead of one? One of the biggest mistakes in questionnaire design is to throw in a hodgepodge of questions because "they might turn up something interesting." Fourth, the type of question to use must be determined—open-ended, multiple choice, etc. Fifth, the wording of the questionnaire must be decided. It is imperative at this step to define the issue, to use simple words, to avoid ambiguous and leading questions, and to decide whether to use an objective or subjective question, a positive or negative question. The sixth step is deciding on the sequence of questions. Opening questions must win the interest of the respondent. Difficult questions usually should be saved for the body or end of the questionnaire. After respondents have answered a number of questions, they are apt to be more at ease with the interviewing process and will be less likely to balk at personal questions such as those relating to income and knowledge. It is also important to consider the influence of succeeding questions. If mentioning the sponsor of the survey would bias the answers, then any questions suggesting the sponsor ought to be left at the end of the questionnaire. Finally, questions ought to follow one another in a logical order—that is, an order which is logical to the respondent! Seventh, the questionnaire designer must determine the physical form, layout, and method of reproduction. For mail surveys, cover letters stating the nature and purpose of the survey are often very useful in gaining the cooperation of respondents. Questionnaires may be legal, letter, or postcard size. Questions should not be crowded together on a page, and sufficient space must be provided for answering the questions. The next step is to prepare a preliminary draft and pretest it under field conditions. No matter how hard the researcher tries, it seems inevitable that something

Table 1 Advantages and Disadvantages of Three Survey Types

Criteria	Type of Survey		
	Personal Interview	Mail Survey	Telephone Interview
1. Flexibility	Most flexible; much probing possible	Little flexibility; no probing possible	Medium amount of flexibility
2. Amount of information obtained	Much information can be obtained	Can only have a few simple questions	Medium amount of information
3. Accuracy of information	Depends on specific questions—can be high or low	Fairly high if anonymous	Depends on specific questions—can be high or low
4. Speed	Time consuming to conduct	Slow return time	Medium amount of time required
5. Cost	High	Low	Medium
6. Administration	Difficult; requires much supervision	No interviewers required; questionnaire must be easily understood	Requires some supervision

has been left out, is not necessary, or is ambiguous. Lastly, the questionnaire must be revised and a final draft prepared.

Questionnaire studies can also be classified by disguise and structure, depending upon, respectively, whether the objectives are clear to the respondent and whether a prescribed sequence of questions is followed (Boyd and Westfall, 1972, pp. 136–143). Using these two bases for classification, four types of questionnaire studies can be identified as shown in figure at right.

Most questionnaire studies are structured-nondisguised (Type A). The objectives of the questionnaire are made clear to the respondent. A formal list of questions is asked directly and in a predetermined sequence. Answers are frequently limited to a list of alternatives. The structured-nondisguised questionnaire is speedy, it permits an easy tabulation of the data, and it is reliable,

since interviewer bias is at a minimum. However, it is also rather inflexible, since probing is not possible.

The nonstructured-nondisguised questionnaire (Type B) is used for the purpose of allowing the respondent to talk freely about some subject of interest. It employs the psychoanalytic technique of depth interviewing, a technique where the interviewer tries to put respondents at ease and en-

	Structured	Nonstructured
Nondisguised	A	B
Disguised	C	D

courage them to express any ideas they have about the subject. For example, a fixed list of direct questions dealing with motives seldom generates useful answers. People often cannot articulate their motives or, if they can, may be embarrassed to do so. For example, the family that bought a new Cadillac as a status symbol may respond in direct questioning that the car is really very economical in the long run. The nonstructured-nondisguised questionnaire therefore attempts to ask questions in such a way that status considerations, for instance, may be mentioned. With nonstructured-nondisguised questionnaires, there is the major problem concerning the validity and reliability of the interviewer's interpretations. Different interviewers may interpret the same information quite differently.

In order to circumvent the problems of socially acceptable responses, false answers, or answers which cannot be articulated, disguised methods of gathering data are used (Types C and D). Projective techniques, where individuals reflect themselves in interpreting a situation, are commonly used for this purpose. Three common projective techniques are word associations, sentence completion, and story telling. In word association, a series of words is read one at a time to the respondent who, in turn, says the first thing that comes to his or her mind. Sentence completion, as the term suggests, requires the respondent to complete an incomplete sentence. In story telling, the respondent is shown a picture and is then asked to tell a story about it.

Structured-disguised questioning (Type C) has many of the characteristics discussed above. The questioning is speedy, the answers are easy to tabulate, and there is less chance for interviewer bias; however, the questioning is less flexible and is limited to the collection of factual information. An illustration of the structured-disguised type of questioning might be a test for political party preferences. Psychological theory posits that an individual's knowledge, perception, and memory are conditioned by attitudes. Therefore, it would be reasonable to expect that Democrats listen to more speeches by other Democrats than by Republicans and, thus, Democrats have more information about Democratic candidates than about Republican candidates. A straightforward question, such as "Are you a Republican or a Democrat?" might get a biased answer. Instead, a simple test of information about the candidates would probably better distinguish Republicans from Democrats.

Observation

The survey method of gathering primary data is rather inexpensive, speedy, and versatile enough to apply to almost all types of problems. When people are unwilling or unable to respond or when the questioning process influences the results (for example, giving socially acceptable answers or saying what the interviewer wants to hear), the observation method of gathering primary data can be used. In the observation method, data is collected by observing some action of the respondent rather than asking for information. The underlying premise is that the person is unaware of being observed and, hence, will behave in the usual manner, or if aware of being observed, at least over time can only behave in his or her ordinary manner.

Observation studies can be classified according to two dimensions: personalness and reactivity. This classification scheme may be diagrammed as follows:

Reactivity

		Nonreactive	Reactive
	Personal	Personal Nonreactive	Personal Reactive
Personalness	Mechanical	Mechanical Nonreactive	Mechanical Reactive

Each cell is discussed below.

In personal nonreactive (unobtrusive) observation, information is obtained by a researcher without any interaction with the respondent. Numerous examples have been cited (Webb, et al., 1966) from the literature in consumer behavior research. One investigator measured the level of whiskey consumption in a tavern which was officially "dry" by counting empty bottles in trash cans. The degree of fear induced by a ghost-story-telling session was measured by noting the shrinking diameter of a circle of seated children. Finally, to determine where their customers came from, store owners have recorded license numbers of cars in the parking lot and then traced the addresses of the owners through the license bureau.

The personal reactive observation method obtains information by a researcher interacting with the respondent. The interaction may be simple and direct. For example, "in an effort to find ways of improving the service in a retail store, an observer may mingle with the customers in the store and look for activities that suggest service problems" (Boyd and Westfall, 1972, p. 162).

The interaction may also be contrived, such as an observer posing as a customer and bargaining with the salesperson over price in order to test the salesperson's selling abilities. An interesting contrived observation is the lost letter technique. To measure the relative interest in a political candidate in different geographical areas, a researcher may stamp and address fifty letters to:

Educators for President Jimmy Carter
c/o John Dobson
136 Market Street
Pittsburgh, Pennsylvania 15216

By dropping these letters on the sidewalk on various streets (i.e., "losing" them before they were placed in the mailbox), and also by "losing" in the same areas another set of fifty letters with the same address except for the first line, the observer could then determine the proportion of letters returned from both the experimental and control groups in each area.

Another type of personal reactive research is participant observation. Here the observer joins in the life of the group being studied. The participant-observer watches what happens to the members and how they behave. This type of researcher also engages in conversations with them to find out their reactions to, and interpretations of, the events that have occurred. The observer's task is to take on a position in which he or she can get a complete and unbiased picture of the life of the group. If the observer can become so accepted as part of the group that its members forget about being observed, he or she will naturally get a more authentic picture of its behavior (McCall and Simmons, 1969).

Mechanical observations use a piece of apparatus to do the recording. The recording apparatus may be either reactive or nonreactive with the respondent. A very common use of mechanical observation is the A. C. Nielsen Company audiometer which is attached to the TV set or radio to identify which channel is being watched or listened to. Two-way mirrors are nonreactive mechanical observation, since there is no interaction with the person being observed. Tape recorders and cameras may be either reactive or nonreactive, depending upon the physical feasibility and the purposes of the research. When the respondent speaks into a tape recorder, the research is said to be nonreactive. However, if the tape recorder asks questions, then it is reactive.

The observation method has several merits. First, information is often obtained in a natural rather than an artificial setting. It can be highly accurate, since it removes any conjecture about what the respondent does in a given situation. With the ease of mechanical devices, more detailed and permanent information is possible. A major drawback, however, can be observer bias (analogous to interviewer bias in the survey method). Finally, it can be very expensive, since at times there may be simply nothing to observe.

Experimentation

Experimentation is a research process in which one or more variables are manipulated under conditions that permit the collection of data which shows the effects of these variables. The underlying premise of experimentation is that small-scale experiments will furnish valuable information in designing or testing a large-scale consumer behavior program.

The basic structure of experimentation is quite simple. First, a hypothesis is formulated: "if X, then Y." For example, if advertising, X, is used, more sales, Y, will be generated. Next, depending upon the purpose of the experiment, X is either manipulated or measured. Then Y is observed to see if there is a concomitant variation as a result of the variation in X. If there is, then there is evidence of the validity of the hypothesis. Finally, to achieve control of both the extraneous variables[4] and the experimental variables, the experimenter will randomly assign subjects to groups and will actively manipulate X.

Experiments can be conducted either in the laboratory or in the field. The laboratory experiment is a research study in which the variance of all or nearly all of the extraneous variables is kept at a minimum. This control is achieved by isolating the experiment in a physical setting apart from the routine of ordinary living and by manipulating one or more experimental variables under rigorously specified conditions. An illustration of a lab experiment might be an artificial store setup, in, say, a hotel ballroom where food shoppers are asked to go through the artificial store and select products *as if* they were on a regular shopping trip. If prices are varied and if actual selections are comparable to purchases in a real store setting, then the price which generated the greatest sales, for example, can be determined.

A field experiment is a research study conducted in an everyday setting in which one or more experimental variables are manipulated under as carefully controlled conditions as possible. The contrast between the laboratory experiment and field experiment is not precise—often the differences are matters of degree. Where the laboratory experiment has a maximum of control, most field studies are conducted with less control, a factor that is often a serious limitation to the experiment. However, this limitation of control in field experiments is sometimes compensated for by the natural settings which permit consumers to behave in their normal manner. The artificiality of laboratory experiments, in contrast, often allows consumers to behave differently than normal which, consequently, can invalidate the results of the experiment.

Two very serious issues in experimentation are internal and external validity. Internal validity asks the question: "Did the experimental variable in fact make a difference in the experiment?" It may be that the extraneous variables, instead of the experimental variables, were the source of the experimental outcomes. There are seven major factors which can jeopardize internal validity.[5] If not controlled, these factors will invalidate the results. They are as follows:

1. History. Events specific to the experiment can occur between the first and second measurement of the experimental variable. For example, attitudes and preferences toward a particular product may change over time, perhaps as the result of television advertising or news articles. More consumers may purchase a domestic automobile after a price decrease than before the price change, not because of the price decrease

---

[4]An extraneous variable is a variable which has an effect on the experimental outcome which confounds the effect of the experimental variable. See the following discussion of factors jeopardizing internal and external validity.

[5]For a very comprehensive treatment, see Campbell and Stanley (1963).

itself, but rather because there was strong sentiment not to buy foreign products.

2. Maturation.

Like history, maturation is a function of time. However, instead of events specific to the experiment occurring, maturation is concerned with general types of events occurring, particularly the biological and psychological processes of the respondent (such as growing older, hungrier, wiser, more tired, and more bored). Though a consumer's last car was a sports car, he may not purchase another one because he is older and feels it doesn't fit his image, regardless of price, styling, and the like.

3. Testing.

Testing refers to the effect of a pretest. If a group of food shoppers were asked to report on a weekly basis the grocery items they purchased and the amount spent, they may in time become very concerned about being thrifty, and also very conscious about what specific brands they purchase. As a result, they may alter their normal purchasing behavior. Thus, pretests can influence future behavior and thereby confound the effects of the experimental variable.

4. Instrumentation.

It is possible that over the duration of the experiment the calibration of the measuring device or the way observers score responses may change. At one point, consumers may be designated as brand loyal if they purchase the same brand three times successively. Later, the same experimenter or even a different experimenter may categorize a consumer as being brand loyal if four out of five purchases were of the same brand.

5. Statistical regression.

Due to chance, low scorers on a pretest may score higher on a post-test when, in fact, no real change has taken place as a result of the experimental variable. Such a phenomenon occurs because there is no *perfect* relationship between the pretest and post-test.

6. Selection.

The effect of the experimental variable may be confounded by the way respondents are selected for an experiment. For example, if a researcher advertises in a newspaper that subjects are being recruited for some research on product dissatisfaction and that participating subjects will receive $5, there may be bias in the sample which results. The researcher is likely to get subjects who want $5 (and, therefore, may not value their time very highly) and subjects who are particularly interested in product dissatisfaction (maybe they have had an unusually bad experience).

7. Mortality.

Differences other than the experimental effects can arise because people drop out of the experiment. It is extremely unlikely that replacements will be exactly equivalent to those who left and, in many cases, replacements are not even recruited. In experimentally testing a group of consumers for packaging preferences, preferences may be overstated if those who dropped out of the experiment didn't like the packaging.

External validity is a second major issue in experimentation. It is concerned with how the experimental results can be generalized to other populations and settings. There are four major factors which can jeopardize external validity.[6]

1. The interaction of testing and the experimental variable.

A pretest might increase or decrease the respondent's sensitivity to the experimental variable. Therefore, the results obtained from the pretested population will probably not be representative of the effects of the experimental variable for the nonpretested population.

2. The interaction of selection and the experimental variable.

It is possible that the experimental results are valid only for the specific

[6]For a more comprehensive discussion, see Campbell and Stanley (1963).

population of the experiment. This possibility becomes more tenable as subjects become harder to find.

3. The interaction of experimental arrangements.

A common reason for not being able to generalize experimental results is the artificiality of the experimental setting (such as the hotel ballroom acting as a mock-up supermarket) and subjects' knowledge that they are participating in a experiment. When subjects know they are play-acting, being observed, and acting as guinea pigs, they may be less likely to behave as they usually do.

4. The interaction of multiple experimental variables.

Where many experimental variables are used on the same subject, the effects of each experimental treatment[7] become difficult to erase. The subject probably remembers previous actions and responses and, consequently, it may be impossible to isolate the effects of the current stimuli from the previous experimental stimuli.

Experiments may be designed in many ways, depending upon the nature and purpose of the research. Some of the major experimental designs are discussed below. The notation of Campbell and Stanley (1963) is used where

X_i represents the ith treatment of the experimental variable;

O_i represents the ith observation or measurement;

R represents a random assignment of subjects to treatments;

X and O in the same row represent a treatment and observation of the same subject;

E represents the effect of the experimental variable.

Time sequence is represented horizontally.

---

[7] An experimental treatment is a specific manipulation of the experimental variable.

A very simple design is the "after only" ("one shot") design, diagrammed as

$$X \quad O$$
$$E = O.$$

First, a treatment of the experimental variable is applied to a group of subjects and then an observation or measurement is made. Studies having such designs can be of little scientific value because of the total absence of control. The experimenter cannot be sure what the effect of the experimental variable is because there is nothing with which to compare it. The design does not allow the experimenter to know whether or not subjects not receiving the treatment behave exactly as those who did receive the treatment. "After only" designs therefore are usually limited to exploratory studies, where the purpose is only to generate hypotheses and ideas for testing.

A second design is the "before-after" ("one group pretest post-test") design. It is denoted as

$$O_1 X O_2$$
$$E = O_2 - O_1$$

In this design, an observation or measurement is made both before and after a specific treatment is applied to the subjects. Though often judged as better than the "after-only" design, the "before-after" design still has many problems of internal validity, namely history, maturation, testing, instrumentation, and statistical regression. Also, the experimenter still cannot be sure whether or not subjects not exposed to the experimental variable might also show the change reflected by the difference between the two observations.

The "before-after with control" ("pretest post-test control group") design eliminates many of the above problems. It is a very common design in consumer behavior research and is diagrammed as:

$$R \, O_1 X O_2$$
$$R \, O_3 \quad O_4$$
$$E = (O_2 - O_1) - (O_4 - O_3).$$

In addition to observations or measurements before and after the experimental treatment is applied, this design also permits a comparison of those subjects who received the treatments with those who did not. The experimental group (those subjects who receive the treatments) and the control group (those subjects who do not receive the treatments) are selected in such a way that they are as similar as possible. Matching subjects on such characteristics as age, sex, income, and attitudes is one method of achieving similarity of groups, but this method is difficult to apply, since it is usually impossible to find two groups or even two people who are exactly alike. An alternative and more feasible method of achieving similarity of groups is randomization. By randomly assigning all subjects to the experimental and control groups, it is presumed that there will be a similar distribution of subject types in each group. This principle of randomization also minimizes the effect of selection as a confounding factor to determining the effect of the experimental variable. However, the mortality factor still remains.

The "four group–six study" ("Solomon four group") design can be diagrammed as:

$$R\ O_1\ X\ O_2$$
$$R\ O_3\quad O_4$$
$$R\quad X\ O_5$$
$$R\qquad O_6$$
$$E = [(O_2 - O_1) + O_5] - [(O_4 - O_3) + O_6].$$

This design is a combination of the previous designs: the top half of this design is equivalent to the "before-after with control group" design; the third row is simply the "after-only" design; and the last row is just an observation or measurement of a fourth group of subjects at the same time that O_2, O_4, and O_5 are obtained. The "four group–six study" design is ideal for experiments in which data are collected from individuals in such a way that they realize it is being done—it eliminates the testing effect. Unfortunately, this design has little practical value. Since six observations are re-

quired, the difficulty of obtaining a large number of subjects and the time and expense involved often makes this design impractical for many consumer behavior studies. However, it can serve as an ideal against which to compare other proposed designs.

In some of the designs presented, pretests were used. Suppose that pretests are not possible or feasible because of such reasons as time, money, and availability of subjects. In some cases, the "after-only with control" design, diagrammed

$$R\ X\ O_1$$
$$R\quad O_2$$
$$E = O_2 - O_1$$

may be used. Again, the experimental and control groups are selected in a way, such as by randomization, to be as alike as possible. The experimental effect then is simply the difference between the two observations or measurements.

A variation of the "before-after" design is the "panel" design. One type of panel design appears as:

$$O_1\ O_2\ X_1\ O_3\ X_2\ O_4\ O_5\ X_3\ O_6$$

The treatment effect of, say, X_2 would be computed as:

$$E\ (\text{treatment } X_2) = O_4 - O_3.$$

A sample of subjects is recruited and information is obtained from the members continuously or at intervals over a period of time. The members of the panel typically are asked to record in a diary their purchasing behavior relevant to the experiment. The drawback to panel designs, however, is that the experimenter must select the sample such that it is representative of the population and that the subjects properly, honestly, and conscientiously record entries in their diary.

Factorial designs, unlike the above designs, permit the experimenter to test two or more experimental variables at the same time. This design allows the determination of not only the main effects of each experimental variable, but also of the interactions between variables. A factorial design, for example, might be used to determine the proper concentration of sugar and carbonation in soft drinks. Suppose there are four levels of carbonation and three levels of sugar, as below:

		Carbonation			
		1	2	3	4
	1	a	b	c	d
Sugar	2	e	f	g	h
	3	i	j	k	l

If the experimenter were to test each combination of carbonation and sugar on the same group of subjects, then the best combination could be determined by simply observing the highest score on some scaled measure of likes and preferences (or the greatest sales if each of the twelve types were actually sold in the marketplace under similar conditions).

Unfortunately, many tests are required for such experiments. A Latin Square design can economize on the number of studies necessary, although at the expense of larger errors. Suppose an experimenter wanted to test the effects of three variables, such as the effects of packaging, test city, and price, as shown below:

		Packaging			
		1	2	3	4
	1	A	B	C	D
Test	2	B	A	D	C
city	3	C	D	A	B
	4	D	C	B	A

This arrangement has the same number of levels (four) for each variable and may be viewed as sixteen "after-only" designs. The four different prices are represented by the letters A, B, C, and D. Each price is tested once and only once with each of the test cities and with each of the different types of packaging.[8] The sum of the sales associated with all four of any one letter, i.e., one specific price, could be compared with the total sales associated with all four of any other letter to determine which price to charge. However, if there were an interaction between test city and packaging (such as one city being out of stock of one of the packaging types due to a delivery strike), then the results from this design could not be generalized to other test cities and packaging types. In order to generalize the results, there must not be any interactions among the variables. Thus, the savings in fewer test cells (sixteen instead of sixty-four with the usual factorial design) can result in confounding the effect of price with an interaction effect of test city and packaging.

The experimental method, in summary, has its strength and weaknesses. Its principal strength is the ability to determine cause and effect, often in very realistic and natural settings. Unfortunately, however, it also frequently requires much time, money, and administration, especially in selecting subjects and controlling for extraneous variables.

SUMMARY

Researchers in consumer behavior have an arsenal of methods and techniques available to them. To use these methods and techniques effectively and efficiently, it is important that the researcher clearly understand their assumptions, purposes, and limitations. New techniques will undoubtedly evolve in the future, but probably the most significant advances in research methods in consumer behavior over the short run will come from new applications of existing methods. As researchers become more familiar with methods and techniques, they will become better able to apply the proper mix of techniques which is necessary to plan, design, analyze, and interpret solutions to research problems.

---

[8]Note, however, that each price is not tested with each of the possible test city–packaging levels. For example, the fourth test city and the second type of packaging receive only one price treatment, C.

REFERENCES

Boyd, Harper W., Jr., and Westfall, Ralph (1972), *Marketing Research: Test and Class,* Homewood, Ill.: Irwin.

Campbell, Donald T., and Stanley, Julian C. (1963), *Experimental and Quasi-Experimental Designs for Research,* Chicago: Rand McNally.

Kerlinger, Fred N. (1973) *Foundations of Behavioral Research,* New York: Holt, Rinehart and Winston.

McCall, George J., and Simmons, I. L., eds. (1969), *Issues in Participant Observation,* Reading, Mass.: Addison-Wesley.

Miller, Delbert C. (1970), *Handbook of Research Design and Social Measurement,* New York: David McKay Co.

Moser, C. A., and Kalton, G. (1972), *Survey Methods in Social Investigation,* New York: Basic Books.

Payne, Stanley L. (1951), *The Art of Asking Questions,* Princeton, N.J.: Princeton University Press.

Webb, Eugene J., et al. (1966), *Unobtrusive Measures: Nonreactive Research in the Social Sciences,* Chicago: Rand McNally.

Zaltman, Gerald, and Burger, Philip C. (1975), *Marketing Research: Fundamentals and Dynamics,* 2nd ed., Hinsdale, Ill: Dryden Press.

CONTENT ANALYSIS IN CONSUMER RESEARCH

HAROLD H. KASSARJIAN

Source: Harold H. Kassarjian, "Content Analysis in Consumer Research," *Journal of Consumer Research,* Vol. 4, June, 1977, p. 8–18.

In 1953, more than two decades ago, Cartwright wrote:

When one stops to think of it, it is really surprising how much of the subject matter of social psychology is in the form of verbal behavior. The formation and transmission of group standards, values, attitudes, and skills are accomplished largely by means of verbal communication. Education in the schools, in the home, in the business, in the neighborhood, and through the mass media is brought about by the transmission of information and by the exercise of controls which are largely mediated through written or spoken words. If one is concerned with problems of social organization, the situation is similar. Supervision, management, coordination, and the exertion of influence are principally matters of verbal interaction. Social and political conflicts, although often stemming from divergent economic interests and power, cannot be fully understood without studying the words employed in the interaction of conflicting groups, and the process of mediation consists largely of talking things out. The work of the world, and its entertainment too, is in no small measure mediated by verbal and other symbolic behavior. (Cartwright, 1953, p. 422)

Surprising or not, there is no doubt that much of the subject matter of the social sciences including consumer studies is in the form of verbal and symbolic behavior. The exchange process in the marketplace and the communication of the values of the exchange depends upon the written or spoken word. And yet, research on communications content, the "systematic description of these phenomena," has not been accorded much attention in consumer research although first introduced to the field two decades ago by Ferber and Wales (1958).

Although not independent, the study of content variables is approached apart from the study of the communicator or the audience. The signs and symbols (Mead, 1934; Morris, 1946) are the units of analysis rather than the intent of the communicator or the actions of the interpreter. Of interest is what was said, the properties of the stimuli, rather than what the communicator claims he said or the interpreter perceived to have been said. Much of consumer research has concentrated on the characteristics, opinions, or behavior of the interpreter of communications messages or on the characteristics of the communicator. Content analysis is the study of the message itself, and not the communicator or the audience. It is the study of the stimulus field (Fearing, 1953). The purpose of this paper is to present and discuss some of the issues in content analysis methodology and, tangentially, to review the studies carried out in consumer research using the technique.

DEFINITIONS OF CONTENT ANALYSIS

Content analysis, although relatively new to consumer research as a formal methodology, is not new to political science, journalism, social psychology, communications research, or political propaganda analysis. The literature in these fields is replete with detailed studies and definitions. For example:

—Content analysis is a research technique for the objective, systematic, and quantitative description of the manifest content of communication. (Berelson, 1952, p. 55)

—Latent content as well as manifest content may be examined by content analysis, a series of judgments or descriptions made under specifically defined conditions by judges trained in the use of objectively defined criteria. (Fearing, 1954)

—The term "content analysis" is used here to mean the scientific analysis of communications messages. . . . The method is, broadly speaking, the "scientific method," and while being catholic in nature, it requires that the analysis be rigorous and systematic. (Barcus, 1959, as cited in Holsti, 1969, p. 3)

—Content analysis is a phase of information-processing in which communications content is transformed through objective and systematic application of categorization rules into data that can be summarized and compared. (Paisley, 1969, p. 133)

—Content analysis is a systematic technique for analyzing message content and message handling—it is a tool for observing and analyzing the overt communication behavior of selected communicators. (Budd, Thorp, and Donohew, 1967, p. 2)

—Content analysis, while certainly a method of analysis, is more than that. It is . . . a method of observation. Instead of observing people's behavior directly, or asking them to respond to scales, or interviewing them, the investigator takes the communications that people have produced and asks questions of the communications. (Kerlinger, 1964, p. 544)

—Content analysis will not tell us whether a given work is good literature; it will tell us whether the style is varied. It will not tell us whether a paper is subversive; it will tell us if the contents change with party line. It will not tell us how to convince the Russians; it will tell us what are the most frequent themes of Soviet propaganda. (Lasswell, Lerner, and Pool, 1952, p. 45)

These researchers and others agree that the distinguishing characteristics of content analysis are that it must be *objective, systematic,* and *quantitative.*

Objectivity

The requirement of objectivity stipulates that the categories of analysis be defined so precisely that different analysts may apply them to the same body of content and secure the same results (Berelson, 1952).

Each step in the research process must be carried out on the basis of explicitly formulated rules and procedures. Even the simplest and most mechanical forms of content analysis require the investigator to use his judgment in making decisions about his data. What categories should be used? What criteria are to be used to decide that a content unit (word, theme, story, picture, etc.) should be placed in one category rather than another? From these data what was the reasoning that led to one inference rather than alternative ones? According to Holsti (1968), objectivity implies that all decisions are guided by an explicit set of rules that minimize—although probably never quite eliminate—the possibility that the findings reflect the analyst's subjective predispositions rather than the content of the documents under analysis. Thus one test of objectivity is: Can other analysts, following identical procedures with the same set of data, arrive at similar conclusions?

This requirement of objectivity gives scientific standing to content analysis and differentiates it from literary criticism. A newspaper reporter studying Soviet press coverage of an event, a politician carefully listening to the speeches of his opponent, or a TV critic discussing coverage on American television of the same event cannot be classified as employing the scientific method. Their results may be penetrating, sensitive, shallow, accurate, literary, or biased, but not scientific. For what is lacking is replicability, reliability, or what Berelson has chosen to call objectivity.

In the great majority of studies in the consumer behavior literature where some form of content analysis has been carried out, the objectivity requirement has seldom been met. Typically, the author has analyzed the communications material himself with no expressed concern about the reliability of the analysis or controls for selective perceptions and biased predispositions.

Systematization

Systematization means that the inclusion and exclusion of communications content or analysis categories are done according to consistently applied rules (Holsti, 1969). This requirement is meant to eliminate partial or biased analysis in which only those elements in the content which fit the analyst's thesis are selected. The requirement clearly eliminates analysis in which only materials supporting the investigator's hypotheses are admitted as evidence.

The second meaning of "system" is that analysis must be designed to secure data relevant to a scientific problem or hypothesis (Berelson, 1952). The findings must have theoretical relevance and be generalizable. Purely descriptive information about content unrelated to other attributes is of little value. Thus, a tabulation simply reporting the number of periodicals acquired by a librarian would not represent a content analysis study unless the results were used for a trend of comparative analysis or for some other generalization. Stated somewhat differently:

> A datum about communications content is meaningless until it is related to at least one other datum. The link between these is represented by some form of theory. Thus all content analysis is concerned with comparison, the type of comparison being dictated by the investigator's theory (Holsti, 1969, p. 5).

Quantification

This requirement is perhaps the most distinctive feature of content analysis. Quantification of judgments distinguishes content analysis from ordinary critical reading. A measurement of the extent of emphasis or omission of any given analytic category is what content analysis is all about. Although early researchers equated quantification with strict frequency count (Leites and Pool, 1942, as cited in Lasswell, Leites, and Associates, 1949; Janis, 1943) and the assignment of numerical values (Kaplan and Goldsen, 1949), this demand is perhaps too strict and unnecessary (Kracauer, 1952). Berelson (1952) feels that the quantification requirement can take the form of quantitative words like more, always, increases, or often. What is implied by the quantification requirement is that the data be amenable to statistical methods not only for precise and parsimonious summary of findings but also for interpretation and inference. Whether the statistical method involved requires parametric or nonparametric data or nominal, ordinal, or interval scales is not relevant.

THE USE OF CONTENT ANALYSIS

To summarize, content analysis is a scientific, objective, systematic, quantitative, and generalizable description of communications content. In consumer behavior and marketing, content analysis has been used to study the following questions:

—What are the changing values in society as reflected in the analysis of mass periodical fiction (Johns-Heine and Gerth, 1949)? Is the Riesman hypothesis about increasing other-directedness of American society supported by changing content of consumer goods advertising (Dornbush and Hickman, 1959)?

—What are the product and company images of selected consumer goods as reflected in the mass media (Stone, Dunphy and Bernstein, 1966; Woodside, 1972)?

—What are the advertising appeals that are used for nontechnical graduates in a college newspaper (Ybarra, 1970)? Do recruiting appeals for technical and managerial positions in newspaper advertisements differ in their inner- and other-directedness (Makinson and Welge, 1970)?

—What are the content characteristics of bestselling novels and can literary success be predicted by analyzing content variables (Harvey, 1953)?

—Which of several decision-choice models (compensatory, lexicographic, risk, etc.) are used by magazine and television advertisers (Wright and Barbour, 1975)?

—Are minority Americans presented in a prejudicial fashion in magazine fiction (Berelson and Salter, 1946)? Have minorities on television gone through successive stages from nonrecognition to ridicule to respect as suggested by social science theory (De Fleur, 1964)?

—Does the portrayal of blacks differ between television, magazine, and television advertisers (Wright and Barbour, 1975)?

—What is the frequency of appearance and roles of blacks and other minorities in the mass media (Shuey, King, and Griffith, 1953; Boyenton, 1965; Cox, 1969; Kassarjian, 1969, 1976; Dominick and Greenberg, 1970; Ferguson, 1970; Roberts, 1970; Wanderer, 1970; Geizer, 1971; Greenberg and Kahn, 1971; Bush, et al., 1974, 1977; Hair, et al., 1977)?

—What is the portrayed image and role of women in the mass media (Courtney and Lockeretz, 1971; Wagner and Banos, 1973; Venkatesan and Losco, 1975; Belakaoui and Belkaoui, 1976)?

—How are women, blacks, foreigners, and conservatives depicted in comic strips (Spiegelman, Terwilliger, and Fearing, 1952, 1953)?

—What is the information content found in television advertising (Resnik and Stern, 1977)? Is comparison advertising leading to misleading, dysfunctional, and ambiguous messages on television (Shimp, 1975)?

—What is the ease of readability of various marketing, advertising, and consumer research journals, including *The Journal of Consumer Research* (Lacho, Stearns, and Villere, 1975)?[1]

Naturally, a wide range of other problems can be studied by content analysis ranging from measures of bias in newscasting and news reporting to differences between communications in the stylistic use of verbs, nouns, adjectives, and adverbs. According to Holsti (1969), content analysis is likely to be especially appropriate for at least three general classes of research problems which may occur in virtually all disciplines and areas of inquiry.

First, it may prove useful when data accessibility is a problem and the researcher's data are limited to documentary evidence (e.g., the social and organizational structure of Soviet prisons, McDonough, 1975) or under conditions when subjects can no longer be easily located (e.g., "Public Opinion in Colonial America," Merritt, 1963). Moreover, content analysis may also function as a supplementary source of data or as an unobtrusive measure (Webb, et al., 1966; Webb

---

[1] Using the Flesch index based on average sentence length and number of syllables per 100 words, the *Journal of Consumer Research* in 1974 ranked the most difficult to read among the 11 journals studied. The readability scores were lower (harder to read) than the *Journal of Advertising Research, Journal of Marketing,* and *Journal of Marketing Research,* among others.

and Roberts, 1969). For example, in a study of public attitudes and voting intentions, researchers at Stanford University have used not only survey data involving interviews and questionnaires, but also carried out content analyses of "letters to the editor" (Roberts, Sikorski, and Paisley, 1967), political bumper stickers, graffiti, and defaced political posters.

Such multiple indicants for hypothesis testing add a dimension of validity seldom found in consumer behavior research. In other cases, content analysis as an unobtrusive measure may be necessary when direct observation might alter the behavior pattern of the subjects, such as in "love" and "changing courtship patterns" (Carey, 1968; Horton, 1957; Webb and Roberts, 1969).

Second, some form of content analysis is necessary when the subject's own language and mode of expression are crucial to the investigation. Analysis of information processing protocols, responses to projective tests, or subtle inferences to be found in in-depth interviews or focus groups are examples.

Finally, content analysis can be particularly helpful when objective systematic evaluation of material is needed that is much too voluminous for a single investigator. In studies of newspapers, movies, radio, literature, Soviet propaganda, Voice of America themes, or the role of women in magazine literature, the volume of material may well exceed the investigator's ability to undertake the research himself, no matter how unbiased or aware of his own selective perception he may be. Under conditions in which the training of assistants, systematic sampling of stimuli, and interjudge reliability become critical, the formal methods of scientific content analysis become indispensable.

Nevertheless, content analysis is not relevant to all research. It can rarely be used to determine the truth of an advertising claim, or to evaluate the aesthetic qualities of a TV program. Content analysis cannot determine whether or not Ban antiperspirant in fact "keeps you 20% drier," or whether Farrah Fawcett-Majors will be perceived as "incredibly beautiful." Also, it might be foolish to use content analysis to determine whether the *New York Times* supported Humphrey or Nixon in 1968 when methods other than content analysis could be used more efficiently (Holsti, 1969). However, if we wished to determine at this late date whether the *Berliner Zeitung* supported the rise of Hitlerism in the 1920s or whether the rise of Hitler could have been predicted from the themes found in German motion pictures (Kracauer, 1947), content analysis might well be necessary.

The procedures involved in the methodology consist of selecting from the available population of documents to be studied, a reasonably sized sample for study. The second step would be to determine the unit of measurement, whether it be the specific word, an overall theme, or simply the existence or nonexistence of some event or claim. Then the procedures call for the training of judges for categorization of the content according to predetermined rules, and finally statistical treatment and analysis of data.

SAMPLING

For most content analysis studies, the immense task of analyzing existing documents begins with sampling procedures. Suppose one were to study the role of women in network television prime-time advertising during 1977. One can quickly imagine the enormous number of ads that would have to be analyzed. Further, if the research question were something like, "A comparison of local and network television advertising presentations of the role of women in society," the number of ads to be processed would have to be increased many fold. If, in addition, one were also interested in differences over time, regional or geographic differences, or comparisons between prime-time and daytime television, the need for sampling and careful definition of the universe, rather than analysis of the entire population, becomes painfully evident.

Fortunately, researchers in the fields of marketing and communications as well as in consumer research are acquainted with sampling procedures. Most of us have been trained in drawing samples from populations of consumers, or people in general. Although drawing a sample of documents may pose some unique problems, the concerns of the research are no different. Needed is a sample of manageable size, randomly drawn, that is representative of the defined universe such that generalizations are possible. The sample, rather than consisting of consumers, voters, or subscribers, is composed of comic strips, magazine advertisements, daily newspapers, or scripts of radio commercials.

Other than simple random or interval sampling, sophisticated procedures such as cluster sampling and multistage sampling may be appropriate. The problems in determining what size sample to use are similar to determining sample size in other aspects of consumer research.

UNITS OF MEASUREMENT

Content analysis calls for the qualification of elements in the communication stimuli. An element or subdivision of the content may range from large to small. Thus a content analysis could determine the extent of support or opposition on a controversial issue found in local newspapers. The analysis could examine the amount of space devoted to the topic or the number of articles, a sampling of the paragraphs or sentences in the articles, or even selected key words or terms. Such subdivisions are the units of analysis.[2]

[2]Perhaps the finest presentation of this material is to be found in Berelson (1952). Most authors in the field of content analysis have based their presentations on Berelson in discussion of the units of content analysis. This paper continues in that tradition.

Word

The smallest unit generally used is the word. According to Berelson, content analysis can be done on the basis of a single letter as the unit in cryptoanalysis and the breaking of international codes. Such activity, however, is usually beyond the scope of consumer research. The word as a unit is identical with what Lasswell (1952) calls a symbol and may include word compounds, e.g., phrases, as well as single words. In this type of research one might study the relative occurrence of key symbols or value-laden terms such as religious, sexual, supernatural, democratic, social, friendly, clean, sparkling, and so on, until the content has been systematically examined relevant to the hypotheses of the study. Readability studies (Flesch, 1951) have used the word unit in content analysis. Typically, such studies construct readability formulas on the basis of personal references, prepositional phrases, different hard words, words with prefixes and suffixes, etc. (Berelson, 1952).

Theme

The next larger unit is the theme, a single assertion about a subject. The theme is among the most useful units of content analysis because issues, values, beliefs, and attitudes are usually discussed in this form. However, it is also the most difficult unit of analysis. For example, the sentence, "These clandestine Soviet actions on the imprisoned island of Cuba will not be tolerated by the American people," contains assertions about three nations. The coder must be able to reduce this sentence into its component themes before they may be placed in the proper categories (Holsti, 1968).

Perhaps the best known thematic analysis in consumer behavior was made of the content of Kate Smith's broadcast on the marathon bond drive during World War II. After 18 hours of hourly and half-hourly spot announcements from fifteen seconds to one minute each in length, Kate Smith managed to sell 39 million dollars worth of

War Bonds through the CBS radio network. The content of her appeals was analyzed by themes—those of sacrifice, participation, competition, facilitation, and familial and personal appeals appearing most often (Merton, 1946).

Character

Use of the fictional or historical character as the recording unit is often employed in the studies of fiction, drama, movies, radio, and other forms of entertainment material. In a well-known study involving the appeals of the radio daytime serial or soap opera, Arnheim (1944) used the characters as the unit of analysis. A fascinating study on ethnic characteristics of heroes and "bad guys" in Sunday comics, using the character as the unit of analysis, can be found in Spiegelman, Terwilliger, and Fearing (1953).

Item

The item is the whole natural unit employed by producers of symbolic material. It may be the entire speech, radio program, letter to the editor, editorial, or news story. This unit is often too gross for most research according to Holsti (1969), but Berelson (1952) presents two dozen studies in which the unit of analysis was the item—motion pictures, musical compositions, paintings, cartoons, and jokes. Most consumer behavior studies previously mentioned as using content analysis have used the item as the unit of analysis. For example, the studies on the role of blacks or the role of women in American advertising have used the entire advertisement for various aspects of the analysis.

Space-and-Time Measures

Some studies have classified content by physical divisions, such as the column inch (newspapers), the line or paragraph, the minute (radio and TV), or the foot (films). Almost *every* conceivable space-time measure has been used.

In a given study, different units will sometimes be employed to test each of several hypotheses.

Thus the item (total ad) may be the unit of analysis to examine the frequency of the use of blacks in magazine advertising. A space-time measure may be employed to determine the relative size of "black" ads as compared to "white" ads. The theme may be utilized in analyzing the values presented by the communicator, and a word count used as a measure of emphasis.

CATEGORIES OF ANALYSIS

Content analysis calls for the categorization of the various elements in the occupations of the characters in the novel, the frequency of occurrence of incompetent females in detergent advertisements, or the proportion of racially integrated advertisements in general circulation magazines.

Content analysis is no better than its categories, since they reflect the formulated thinking, the hypotheses, and the purpose of the study. The categories are, in essence, the conceptual scheme of the research design. For example, Wayne (1956) attempted to compare the values expressed in the content of two major family magazines, one in the United States *(Life Magazine)* and the other in Soviet Russia *(Ogonek).* His purpose was to shed light on the different underlying value systems of these two powerful and contending nations.

Life and *Ogonek* were the leading general circulation weekly pictorial magazines that appealed to most members of the family. The universe was restricted to pictures and pertinent captions, if necessary, rather than the text. Hence, the purpose was a study of American and Soviet themes and values, as depicted in pictures presented in thirteen randomly selected issues of both magazines in the year 1948. A further limitation was imposed on the sample by excluding from the analysis all pictures lacking human action.

The categories selected for the study of values were an adapted version of Spranger's value categories from his *Types of Men* (1928). The definition of the categories emerged from Spranger's treatise. For example, in order to come under the *theoretical* category, a picture had to show an activity connected with the search for truth. Thus a photo showing scientists at work might be so classified. A photograph of engineers and technicians laboring in their laboratories to increase harvest in the Ukraine or the American prairie might be categorized as *economic* (utilitarian) value. The results indicated a greater incidence of economic and aesthetic values in the Soviet magazine and greater emphasis on religious and social values in the United States. There were no differences between the two countries on theoretical or political (power) values.

In this particular study, the judges were to classify each picture into one of several polynary categories (e.g., economic, theoretical, religious, social, political, and aesthetic). Other researchers have used a binary method of classification. In one phase of their study, Spiegelman, Terwilliger, and Fearing (1952) wished to examine the situations in which comic strip adventures occurred. The authors arranged the categories in a series of dichotomous decisions to be made by each judge. Is the action on Earth or in interstellar space? If on Earth, is it in the United States or is it foreign? If in the United States, is it historical or contemporary? If contemporary, is it rural or urban?

Whether the categories should be binary or polynary has been studied (Schutz, 1952, 1958) with the conclusion that the polynary approach generally results in better reliability figures but only for the more difficult decisions.

Consumer researchers, experienced in questionnaire construction and in developing coding categories for open-ended questions, will find similar problems and procedures in creating content analysis categories. In the former case the respondent presents his opinion. The function of the interviewer or the coder-editor is to convert the verbal statement into a classificatory scheme. In the latter case, a highly trained judge, following explicitly stated rules, selects the categories that best describe the content.

Direction

The problem of direction is probably one of the most frustrating issues facing the researcher because it is one area in which the element of subjectivity is difficult to control and impossible to eliminate entirely (Budd, Thorp, and Donohew, 1967). Direction refers to the pro or con treatment of the subject matter. Basically, it asks the question: Is the communication for or against the particular subject, or neutral? In the literature various synonyms have been used for pro and con, presumably reflecting differences in the specific materials analyzed: indulgence-deprivation, approval-disapproval, favorable-unfavorable, positive-negative, for-against, and optimistic-pessimistic. Obviously, content analyses can be most productive when it is able to show direction—or the lack of it. "Although direction is a commonly recognized characteristic of communications content, it is not always easily analyzed in an objective fashion. Many textual passages are not clearly pro or con or neutral; the borderline is often indistinct" (Berelson, 1952, p. 150).[3]

To exemplify the issues and problems in selecting the units of measurement and the categories of analysis one can consider the following paragraph:

> I'd like to see all trade barriers down after the war. Raw goods should be shared where they're needed. It's money and raw goods and poor living that caused most of this war. We should see that Germany gets its fair share this time or we'll have another war. Russia is fighting for her way of life just like we are for ours. England is fighting along with us and Russia to protect the people against fascism—to be free, not slaves. Churchill and Roosevelt and Stalin are great men. They know how the people feel. We can't stay on our side of the pond anymore. The union's taught me that. (Cartwright, 1953, p. 435)

Literally dozens of variables or attributes can be found in this passage. To list a few: number of

---

[3]The rather elaborate rules that have been devised for classifying direction are beyond the scope of this paper. The interested reader should turn to Budd, Thorp, and Donohew (1967), Janis and Fadner (1949), and references therein.

words, percentage of personal pronouns, attitude toward free trade, perceived cause of war, degree of confidence in the Allies, degree of confidence in leaders, attractive traits of leaders, attitude toward isolationism, evidence of previous isolationism, source of influence on attitudes, implied values, inclusiveness of cognitive structures, and degree of approval of war aims. Once the variables under study have been determined, say confidence in leaders, the variable under scrutiny must be broken down into categories, such as unqualified confidence in leaders, qualified confidence, balanced, qualified mistrust, unqualified mistrust, not classifiable (Cartwright 1953). Obviously, not only are many other attributes or variables possible depending on the hypotheses of the study, but many other schemes for categorization are also possible.

THE PROBLEM OF RELIABILITY

Since the researcher's subjectivity must be minimized to obtain a systematic, objective description of the communications content, the issue of reliability becomes paramount. Reliability, or reproducibility, is one of the distinguishing characteristics of content analysis as contrasted with other techniques of describing communications content—the work of a literary critic, the commentary of a newspaper reporter, or the opinions of a layman. "The importance of reliability rests on the assurance it provides that the data obtained are independent of the measuring event, instrument, or person" (Kaplan and Goldsen, 1949).

Category Reliability
This important measure of reliability depends upon the analyst's ability to formulate categories and present to competent judges definitions of the categories so they will agree on which items of a certain population belong in a category and which do not. If this aim cannot be achieved (and the other sources of disagreement are controlled), the understanding of the category as specified is not yet sufficiently clear for scientific usage (Schutz, 1958, p. 512).

In the Kassarjian study on the role of blacks in magazine advertising (1969, 1976), one of the categories consisted of racial composition of the characters in the advertisement. The categories consisted of *all black* characters, *all caucasian* characters, *integrated peer* (in which both black and white characters are peers), *integrated non-peer, separate pictures* (panel ad in which the characters do not appear in the same scene), and *don't know*. The reliability of this category was nearly 100%, that is, judges did not disagree about whether ads contained all black models, all white, or both in a peer or nonpeer relationship.

Perusal of ads that contained both black and white characters in a nonpeer relationship indicated that one seldom saw a white shoeshine boy with a black patron or a black supervisor giving orders to a white employee. A category was then created called the authority relationship. The author was interested in finding the frequency of ads in which the black model had a superior role to the white. Although the meaning of this category was clearly described, defined, and redefined, and the judges trained and retrained, reasonable levels of reliability could not be established.

In many ads the judges could not agree on which character had the superior role. For example, one ad contained white patrons in an exclusive restaurant sitting at a table with expensive linen and silver service. A black waiter with a haughty patronizing glare was waiting for orders. Some judges claimed the white patrons were in the superior role, giving orders to the black waiter. Other judges claimed the intimidating waiter was clearly in the superior role and that the patrons were pretty well at his mercy. After fruitless effort to reach agreement, the category was discarded with the explanation that superior and inferior roles in interpersonal relationships between white and black could not be scientifically defined in that study.

Interjudge Reliability
Interjudge reliability is the percentage of agreement between several judges processing the same

communications material. It is the degree of consistency between coders applying the same set of categories to the same content.

A commonly used measure of reliability is the ratio of coding agreements to the total number of coding decisions. Thus, if in a particular study two judges make a total of 1,000 decisions each, and agree on 930 of them and disagree on 70, the coefficient of reliability would be 93 percent. If more than two judges are involved, the typically reported figure is the percent agreement between each pair of judges. The average interjudge agreement can be presented as a composite reliability score. A second approach to a composite score would be to take a ratio of all coding agreements to the total number of coding decisions made by all judges.[4]

Generally, the reported reliabilities in the literature are extremely high. Berelson (1952) claims the range is between 66 and 95 percent with a concentration at about 90 percent. It is my belief that researchers can be quite satisfied with coefficients of reliability above 85 percent. Studies with reported reliabilities of less than 80 percent should be treated with suspicion.

Fortunately, there is a reasonable likelihood of underestimation of reliability in many studies, arising from the measurement of reliability on detailed categories for reporting purposes (Berelson, 1952). For example, in the Kassarjian study of the role of blacks in advertisements, the greatest disagreement emerged from two or three variables. One of these was the judgment whether the advertisement was a photograph of an actual scene, a drawing, or cartoon. Judges had difficulty discriminating between a drawing and a cartoon. Nevertheless, the coefficient of reliability was 91.8 percent. In reporting the data these two categories were combined, as were others that caused difficulty in discrimination. As in most studies reported in the literature, a new or net reliability figure based on the combined categories was not tabulated.

As can be seen in this example, if the categories are narrowed and simplified, and the decisions for the judges made quite simplistic, reliability can be increased, but at a price. "Reliability is a necessary condition for valid inquiry, but paradoxically, the cost of some steps taken to increase reliability may be a reduction in validity" (Holsti, 1969). In formulating research designs, analysts have often been forced to strike some balance between reliability and the relevance of categories and units. Obviously, the reliability coefficient cannot be the sole criterion for the quality of a study.

VALIDITY

Validity is defined as the extent to which an instrument measures what it purports to measure. Any time an inference is made from the results of an instrument, questionnaire, scale, or other tool, questions of reliability and validity should be paramount. In the field of content analysis, choice of categories and content units enhances or diminishes the likelihood of valid inferences.

The methodological literature abounds in references to validation procedures, ranging from content validity to predictive, concurrent, and construct validity measurements (Technical Recommendations, 1954) to the multiple indicant approaches of Webb, et al. (1966), Webb and Roberts (1969), and Roberts, Sikorski, and Paisley (1969).

Unfortunately, the few content analysis studies that exist in the consumer research literature have completely ignored measures of validity. Perhaps the best that can be expected at this stage of development of content analysis in consumer research is that after close examination of the units

---

[4]Using for a reliability index the percentage of judgments on which coders agree out of the total number of judgments has been criticized by Scott (1955). By chance alone, agreement should increase as the number of categories decreases. One would expect better agreement on a two-category variable or scale than on a five-category variable. To correct for this, Bennett, Alpert, and Goldstein (1954) and Scott (1955) have presented new reliability indices. However, the literature continues to follow the more conventional approaches to reporting reliability figures, and hence technical details of the Scott approach will not be discussed in this paper.

of measurement, categories, sampling procedures, and results, the instruments appear valid using some form of content validation or face validity. Over time one could expect that with repetition of studies and multiple measures of similar hypotheses from several points of view with multiple tools, differing coding schemes, and varied sources of communications content, reasonable measures of validity may emerge in the consumer behavior literature. In the development of categories and other features of the methodology, researchers in the future might build into the study design measures of predictive, concurrent, and construct validity.

THE COMPUTER

Often content analysis involves an enormity of dull clerical processing of data, and yet requires highly trained sensitive coders. Doubtlessly, reliability, accuracy, validity, and the ability to make inferences and generalize from the data suffer if bored coders do not carry out their tasks accurately.

In this day and age, when tasks require repetitive and tedious behavior, the natural solution is to turn to machines. Also in content analysis numerous attempts have been made to turn to the computer. The involvement has gone beyond simple tabulations of frequencies and data manipulation to having the computer do the actual coding. The machine can be used in any task for which unambiguous instructions can be prepared.

The greatest use of computers has been in those studies that require a word count or symbol count. Computers can count words at high speeds and with perfect reliability. Numerous programs exist which convert written passages, novels, or entire languages into several hundred categories. The analyst's task consists of little more than keypunching the entire text on computer cards. The output serves as the basis for subsequent analysis and hypothesis testing.[5]

---

[5] Readers interested in the technical detail can turn to the several papers in Gerbner, et al. (1969), Stone, et al. (1966),

The General Inquirer and Dictionaries

Perhaps the most sophisiticated use of computers in content analysis has emerged as part of the General Inquirer System. In the late 1950s, several investigators began working on the problems of automatic syntax analysis and synthesis, mechanical translation from one language to another, storage and retrieval of large amounts of text information, indexing, and the design of question and answer systems (Stone, et al., 1966). From this work at MIT a set of computer procedures for processing "natural text" emerged; procedures that locate, count, and tabulate text characteristics.

The core of each General Inquirer System of content analysis is a dictionary in which each word is defined with one or more "tags" representing categories as ordinarily used in content analysis. The text to be analyzed is punched on computer cards, usually with some prior editing to separate complex sentences or thought sequences. The computer will then process the text into root words and tags or categories. Themes can also be processed, and programs have been prepared to deal with homographs (words with different meanings but identical spelling, e.g., "bear in mind that a male circus bear cannot bear a cub"). In short, the General Inquirer program can do much that human processors had to handle in the past.[6]

In recent years as advanced versions of the General Inquirer have emerged, the potential for computer-based research has become even more appealing. Studies in consumer research, however, have not yet been logically amenable to computer technology. In many cases published consumer research has tended to use television advertisements measured live off the airwaves or magazine advertisements in which the picture was

---

and references to actual studies using computer output presented in Budd, Thorp, and Donohew (1967) and Holsti (1968, 1969). A paper by Starkweather and Decker (1964) may be particularly helpful.

[6] Technical details are available in Dunphy, et al. (1965); Hunt, et al. (1965); Stone, et al. (1962, 1965, 1966); and the several papers in Gerbner, et al. (1969).

critical to the study. Computers are not yet programmed to deal with nonverbal communications material such as a picture. In other instances, even where the unit of measurement is the sentence, theme, or word, the use of computers may not be practical. The available dictionaries, root words, and tags may not be appropriate, but of greater concern should be the fact that preparation of the study for computer mechanization may well not be worth the effort involved. It is probably still easier to do it by hand, especially since bright graduate students with tolerance for clerical detail are not yet in short supply.

CONCLUSION

Bernard Berelson, one of the earliest researchers in content analysis, in another place and at another time, has written the following conclusion to one of his papers. It fits this paper, in this place, and at this time just as well:

> This, then, is content analysis....How the contributions of content analysis measure up against those of other methods in social science research is difficult if not impossible to say. Because of the relative availability of the raw material, many sins have been committed in the name of content analysis simply because something else was harder or more inconvenient to do. At the same time, however, the method has produced a number of useful studies which combine original ideas with sound, careful documentation. This is, of course, the heart of the matter.
>
> In content analysis, as anywhere in social research, it is important to start in the right way. Simply going on a fishing expedition through some common communication material is almost certain to be unrewarding. Unless there is a sensible, or clever, or sound, or revealing, or unusual, or important notion underlying the analysis, it is not worth going through the rigor of the procedure, especially when it is so arduous and so costly of effort (Berelson, 1954, p. 518).

In consumer research, content analysis offers no new magical qualities. In fact, it demands that the researcher, rather than merely describing his

impression of documents, be excruciatingly systematic, objective, and quantitative. Yet, the methodology does open new avenues for research, ranging from studies on the themes and appeals found in mass media to studies of deception in advertising.

The methodology allows for the reliable, valid, and quantitative answers to questions such as the following:

1. Have recent consumer-oriented actions such as the affirmative disclosure program of the FTC been effective in changing the content of advertising? Has comparative advertising led to greater information being communicated to the consumer?

2. Do certain advertisers (or agencies) engage in the use of certain types of themes, appeals, claims, or deceptive practices more than other advertisers or agencies? What is their apparent intent? Who is their apparent audience?

3. Do themes and appeals found in television (or other media) differ from country to country? How do the press releases disseminated by the Exxon corporation in the United States, Israel, and the Arab countries differ? Do the themes, informational content, or questionable practices found in the advertising of multinational corporations differ from country to country?

4. Do certain newscasters (newsmagazines, newspapers) use more liberal (conservative) symbols and demonstrate more bias than other newscasters? Is editorial support for a political candidate also reflected in biased news sections?

5. In what ways do the rhetoric, articles, speeches, and books that emerged in the consumerism wave of the 1960s differ from the two earlier waves? Did the themes and appeals greatly change over the years?

6. What is the image of big business (government, universities) as reflected in advertising, television programs, radio disc jockey jokes, or magazine fiction?

7. What values are disseminated by comic strips such as Doonesbury, Peanuts, Mary Worth, Little Orphan Annie, Dick Tracy, Andy Capp, etc.? Has the portrayal of minorities, foreigners, liberals, women, children, or scientists changed in the past decades?

8. What values are reflected in the graffiti found in subway stations, buses, men's and women's toilets, various ghettos, or various countries? Can assumptions about the tensions, values, and concerns of a people be made by using unobtrusive measures such as analysis of graffiti, bumper stickers, jokes, or jargon?

9. What are the stylistic, content, and readability differences between media such as *True Confessions* and the *New Yorker*, between public service, local and network television, between consumerists and apologists for industry, or between textbooks, journals, or trade publications?

Further, using content analysis, one can make assumptions about readership of magazines no longer in existence, such as the *Saturday Evening Post*, or gather data about the apparent readership of an existing magazine without approaching subscribers. Analysis of historical documents could lead to conclusions about public opinion, consumer values, or buyer beliefs in an earlier era. Content analysis has been and can be used to prove authorship of particular documents, such as the Federalist Papers. The effect of public policy, as for example, advertising substantiation and new trade rules emerging from governmental agencies, can be tested for effectiveness. The extent of industry's "newly found" social responsibility can be examined.

In short, the methodology can be most useful whenever documentary evidence is available. Its limits are perhaps the limits of the ingenuity and creativity of the consumer researcher. That it has not yet been extensively used in studies of consumer behavior is really rather remarkable considering our proclivity to use varied methodologies and varied approaches to consumer issues.

REFERENCES

Arnheim, R. (1944, "The World of the Daytime Serial," in P. F. Lazarsfeld and F. N. Stanton, eds., *Radio Research: 1942–1943,* New York: Duell, Sloan, and Pearce, 34–85.

Belkaoui, A., and Belkaoui, J. M. (1976), "A Comparative Analysis of the Roles Portrayed by Women in Print Advertisements: 1958, 1970, 1972," *Journal of Marketing Research* 13, 168–72.

Bennett, E. M.; Alpert, R.; and Goldstein, A. C. (1954), "Communications Through Limited Response Questioning," *Public Opinion Quarterly,* 18, 303–6.

Berelson, B. (1952), *Content Analysis in Communications Research,* Glencoe, Ill.: The Free Press.

———(1954), "Content Analysis," in G. Lindzey, ed., *Handbook of Social Psychology: Theory and Method,* Vol. 1, Cambridge, Mass.: Addison-Wesley, 488–522.

———, and Salter, P. J. (1946), "Majority and Minority Americans: An Analysis of Magazine Fiction," *Public Opinion Quarterly,* 10, 168–90.

Boyenton, W. H. (1965), "The Negro Turns to Advertising," *Journalism Quarterly,* 42, 227–35.

Budd, R. W.; Thorp, R. K.; and Donohew, L. (1967), *Content Analysis of Communications,* New York: Macmillan.

Bush, R. F.; Solomon, P. J.; and Hair, J. F., Jr. (1974), "A Content Analysis of the Portrayal of Black Models in Television Advertising," *Proceedings,* American Marketing Association, 427–30.

———; Solomon, P. J.; and Hair, J. F., Jr. (1977), "There Are More Blacks in TV Commercials," *Journal of Advertising Research,* 17, 21–5.

Carey, J. T. (1968), "Changing Courtship Patterns in the Popular Song," *American Journal of Sociology,* 74, 720–31.

Cartwright, D. P. (1953), "Analysis of Qualitative Material,'' in L. Festinger and D. Katz, eds., *Research Methods in the Behavioral Sciences,* New York: Holt, Rinehart & Winston, 421–70.

Courtney, A. E., and Lockeretz, S. W. (1971), ''An Analysis of the Roles Portrayed by Women in Magazine Advertisements,'' *Journal of Marketing Research,* 8, 92–95.

Cox, K. K. (1969–1970), ''Changes in Stereotyping of Negroes and Whites in Magazine Advertisements,'' *Public Opinion Quarterly,* 33, 603–6.

———— (1970), ''An Audit of Integrated Advertisements in Television, Magazines, and Newspapers,'' paper presented at the meeting of the Western Psychological Association, Los Angeles.

DeFleur, M. L. (1964), ''Occupational Roles as Portrayed on Television,'' *Public Opinion Quarterly,* 28, 57–74.

Dominick, J. R., and Greenberg, B. S. (1970), ''Three Seasons of Blacks on Television,'' *Journal of Advertising Research,* 10, 21–27.

Dornbush, S. M., and Hickman, L. C. (1959), ''Other-Directedness in Consumer-Goods Advertising: A Test of Riesman's Historical Theory,'' *Social Forces,* 38, 389–94.

Dunphy, D. C.; Stone, P. J.; and Smith, M. S. (1965), ''The General Inquirer: Further Developments in a Computer System for Content Analysis of Verbal Data in the Social Sciences,'' *Behavioral Science,* 10, 468–80.

Fearing, F. (1953), ''Towards a Psychological Theory of Human Communication,'' *Journal of Personality,* 22, 71–88.

———— (1954), ''Human Communication,'' unpublished manuscript, Dept. of Psychology, University of California, Los Angeles.

Ferber, R., and Wales, H. G., eds. (1958), *Motivation and Market Behavior,* Homewood, Ill.: Irwin.

Fergurson, R. D., Jr. (1970), ''The Role of Blacks in Magazine and Television Advertising,'' unpublished Master's thesis, Boston University.

Flesch, R. (1951), *How to Test Readability,* New York: Harper.

Geizer, R. (1971), ''Advertising in Ebony: 1960 and 1969,'' *Journalism Quarterly,* 48, 131–34.

Gerbner, G.; Holsti, O. R.; Krippendorff, K.; Paisley, W. J.; and Stone, P. J., eds. (1969), *The Analysis of Communications Content: Developments in Scientific Theories and Computer Techniques,* New York: Wiley.

Greenberg, B. S., and Kahn, S. (1971), ''Blacks in *Playboy* Cartoons,'' *Journalism Quarterly,* 48, 557–60.

Hair, J. F., Jr.; Solomon, P. J.; and Bush, R. F., (1977), ''A Factor Analytic Study of Black Models in Television Commercials,''*Journal of Business,* 50, 208–15.

Harvey, J. (1953), ''The Content Characteristics of Best-Selling Novels,'' *Public Opinion Quarterly,* 17, 91–114.

Holsti, O. R. (1968), ''Content Analysis,'' in G. Lindzey and E. Aronson, eds., *The Handbook of Social Psychology, Vol. 2,* Reading, Mass.: Addison-Wesley.

———— (1969), *Content Analysis for the Social Sciences and Humanities,* Reading, Mass.: Addison-Wesley.

Horton, D. (1957), ''The Dialogue of Courtship in Popular Songs,'' *American Journal of Sociology,* 62, 569–78.

Hunt, E. B.; Kreuter, J.; and Stone, P. J. (1965), *Experiments in Induction,* New York: Academic Press.

Janis, I. L. (1943), ''Meaning and the Study of Symbolic Behavior,'' *Psychiatry,* 6, 425–39.

————, and Fadner, R. (1949), ''The Coefficient of Imbalance,'' in H. D. Lasswell, N. Leites, and Associates, eds., *Language of Politics: Studies in Quantitative Semantics,* New York: George Steward, 153–69.

Johns-Heine, P., and Garth, H. H. (1949), ''Values in Mass Periodical Fiction, 1921–1940'', *Public Opinion Quarterly,* 13, 105–13.

Kaplan, A., and Goldsen, J. M. (1949), ''The Reliability of Content Analysis Categories,'' in H. D. Lasswell, N. Leites, and Associates, eds., *Language of Politics: Studies in Quantitative Semantics,* New York: George Steward, 83–112.

Kassarjian, H. H. (1969), ''The Negro and American Advertising: 1946–1965,'' *Journal of Marketing Research,* 6, 29–39.

———— (1976), ''Some Evidence on the Changing Image of Black People,'' in B. F. Bobo and A. E. Osborne, eds., *Emerging Issues in Black Economic Development,* Lexington: Heath-Lexington, 167–87.

Kerlinger, F. H. (1964) *Foundations of Behavioral Research: Educational and Psychological Inquiry,* New York: Holt, Rinehart & Winston.

Kracauer, S. (1947), *From Caligari to Hitler: A Psychological History of the German Film.* Princeton, N. J.: Princeton University Press.

———— (1952), ''The Challenge of Qualitative Content Analysis,'' *Public Opinion Quarterly,* 16, 631–42.

Lacho, K. J.; Stearns, G. K.; and Villere, M. F. (1975), "An Analysis of the Readability of Marketing Journals," *Combined Proceedings,* American Marketing Association, 489–97.

Lasswell, H. D.; Lerner, D.; and De Sola Pool, I. (1952), *The Comparative Study of Symbols,* Stanford, Calif.: Stanford University Press.

———, Leites, N., and Associates, eds. (1949), *Language of Politics: Studies in Quantitative Semantics,* New York: George Steward.

Makinson, J., and Welge, B. (1970), *The Content Analysis of Recruitment Appeals,* unpublished term paper, Graduate School of Business Administration, University of California, Los Angeles.

McDonough, J. J. (1975), "One Day in the Life of Ivan Denisovich: A Study of the Structural Requisites of Organization," *Human Relations,* 28, 295–328.

Mead, G. H. (1934), *Mind, Self, and Society,* Chicago: University of Chicago Press.

Merritt, R. L. (1963), "Public Opinion in Colonial America: Content Analyzing the Colonial Press," *Public Opinion Quarterly,* 27, 365–71.

Merton, R. K. (1946), *Mass Persuasion: The Social Psychology of a War Bond Drive,* New York: Harper.

Morris, C. (1946), *Signs, Language and Behavior,* Englewood Cliffs: Prentice-Hall.

Paisley, W. J. (1969), "Studying Style as Deviation from Encoding Norms," in G. Gerbner, et al., eds., *The Analysis of Communications Content: Developments in Scientific Theories and Computer Techniques,* New York: Wiley, 133–46.

Resnik, A., and Stern, B. L. (1977), "An Analysis of Information Content in Television Advertising," *Journal of Marketing,* 41, 50–53.

Roberts, C. (1970–1971), "The Portrayal of Blacks on Network Television," *Journal of Broadcasting,* 15, 45–53.

Roberts, D. F.; Sikorski, L. A.; and Paisley, W. J. (1969), "Letters in Mass Magazines as Outcroppings of Public Concern," *Journalism Quarterly,* 46, 743–52.

Schutz, W. C. (1952), "Reliability, Ambiguity and Content Analysis," *Psychological Review,* 59, 119–29.

——— (1958), "On Categorizing Qualitative Data in Content Analysis," *Public Opinion Quarterly,* 22, 503–15.

Scott, W. A. (1955), "Reliability of Content Analysis: The Case of Nominal Scale Coding," *Public Opinion Quarterly,* 19, 321–25.

Shimp, T. (1975), "Comparison Advertising in National Television Commercials," *Combined Proceedings,* American Marketing Association, 504–8.

Shuey, A. M.; King, M.; and Griffith, B. (1953), "Stereotyping of Negroes and Whites: An Analysis of Magazine Pictures," *Public Opinion Quarterly,* 17, 281–87.

Spiegelman, M.; Terwilliger, C.; and Fearing, F. (1952), "The Content of Comic Strips: A Study of a Mass Medium of Communication," *Journal of Social Psychology,* 36, 37–57.

———; Terwilliger, C.; and Fearing, F. (1953), "The Content of Comics: Goals and Means to Goals of Comic Strip Characters," *Journal of Social Psychology,* 37, 189–203.

Spranger, E. (1928), *Types of Men,* Translated by P. J. W. Pigors, Halle, East Germany: Max Niemeyer Verlag.

Starkweather, J. A., and Decker, J. B. (1964), "Computer Analysis of Interview Content," *Psychological Reports,* 15, 875–82.

Stone, P. J.; Bales, R. F.; Namenwirth, J. Z.; and Ogilvie, D. M. (1962), "The General Inquirer: A Computer System for Content Analysis and Retrieval Based on the Sentence as a Unit of Information," *Behavioral Science,* 7, 484–94.

———; Dunphy, D. C.; and Bernstein, A. (1965), "Content Analysis Applications at Simulmatics," *American Behavioral Scientist,* 8, 23–28.

———; Dunphy, D. C.; and Bernstein, A. (1966), "The Analysis of Product Image," in P. J. Stone, et al., eds., *The General Inquirer: A Computer Approach to Content Analysis,* Cambridge, Mass.: The MIT Press.

———; Dunphy, D. C.; Smith, M. S.; Ogilvie, D. M., and Associates, eds. (1966), *The General Inquirer: A Computer Approach to Content Analysis,* Cambridge, Mass.: The MIT Press.

"Technical Recommendations for Psychological Tests and Diagnostic Techniques," (1954), *Psychological Bulletin,* Suppl., 201–38.

Venkatesan, M., and Losco, J. (1975), "Women in Magazine Ads: 1959–1971," *Journal of Advertising Research,* 5, 49–54.

Wagner, L. C., and Banos, J. B. (1973), "A Women's Place: A Follow-up Analysis of the Roles Portrayed by Women in Magazine Advertisements," *Journal of Marketing Research,* 10, 213–14.

Wanderer, Aviva (1970), "The Negro Image in Television Advertising—1970,'' University of California, Los Angeles.

Wayne, I. (1956), ''American and Soviet Themes and Values: A Content Analysis of Pictures in Popular Magazines,'' *Public Opinion Quarterly,* 21, 314–20.

Webb, E. J.; Campbell, D. T.; Schwartz, R. D.; and Sechrest, L. (1966), *Unobtrusive Measures: Non-Reactive Research in the Social Sciences,* Chicago: Rand McNally.

———, and Roberts, K. H. (1969), ''Unconventional Uses of Content Analysis in Social Science,'' in G. Bergner, et al., eds., *The Analysis of Communications Content: Development in Scientific Theories and Computer Techniques,* New York: Wiley, 319–32.

Woodside, A. G. (1972), ''A Shopping List Experiment of Beer Brand Images,'' *Journal of Applied Psychology,* 56, 512–13.

Wright, P., and Barbour, F. (1975), ''The Relevance of Decision Process Models in Structuring Persuasive Messages,'' *Communications Research,* 2, 246–59.

Ybarra, F. M. (1970), ''Advertising to the Nontechnical Graduate in a College Newspaper,'' unpublished Master's thesis, Graduate School of Business Administration, University of California, Berkeley.

ETHICS IN MARKETING RESEARCH: THEIR PRACTICAL RELEVANCE

ALICE M. TYBOUT AND GERALD ZALTMAN

Source: Alice M. Tybout and Gerald Zaltman, "Ethics in Marketing Research: Their Practical Relevance," *Journal of Marketing Research,* Vol. 11, November, 1974, pp. 357–68.

INTRODUCTION

The significance of ethical issues in marketing is fostered by several emerging trends. First, the development of a broadened concept of marketing has expanded the domain of marketing research to incorporate areas such as education, family planning, and municipal government. Investigations in these substantive areas require that marketers respect their prevailing ethics. Second, researchers' increased concern with explanation as well as prediction has led to greater use of experimentation as a research tool. The use of experimentation raises ethical issues in marketing that were previously more relevant to psychologists, sociologists, and anthropologists. Moreover, since the sheer quantity of marketing research is expanding, ethical issues are encountered with greater frequency. Not only do these trends raise numerous moral questions, but also the manner in which these issues are resolved may have a significant influence on the quality of marketing research data.

Few ethical guidelines are currently available to the marketing researcher. The AMA has adopted a marketing research code of ethics. Unfortunately, this code focuses on the researcher-client relationship and is most relevant to survey techniques which historically constituted the predominant marketing research paradigm. The code neglects issues that emerge in researcher-subject relationships which are particularly salient in experiments.

Central to this article is the contention that *an understanding of ethical issues involved in marketing research is essential for producing quality research.* The quality of data, whether survey or experimental, in the traditional or broad domain, may be adversely affected unless ethical considerations are recognized and contended with. The purpose of this article is to discuss basic subjects' rights and the effects that violation of these rights may have on the quality of data and consequently on clients and the researcher's colleagues. The basic rights of subjects may be con-

Table 1 Codes of ethics

Subjects' rights	AMA	MRS	APA	ASA	POR
A. Right to choose					
1. Awareness of right		X	X		
2. Sufficient information to choose		X	X		
3. Opportunity to choose		X	X		
B. Right to safety					
1. Protection of anonymity	X	X	X	X	X
2. Freedom from stress		X	X	X	
3. Freedom from deception		X	X	X	
C. Right to be informed					
1. Debriefing			X		
2. Dissemination of data	X			X	X

AMA—American Marketing Association
MRS—Market Research Society
APA—American Psychological Association
ASA—American Sociological Association
POR—American Association for Public Opinion Research

ceived as being analogous to the rights specified for consumers: the right to choose, the right to safety, the right to be informed, and the right to be heard. Although these rights are not mutually exclusive, they provide a convenient framework for analyzing ethical issues. The following questions will be addressed in the discussion of each right: How may subjects' rights be violated? How may subjects' rights conflict with clients' and/or professions' rights? What are the practical implications of violation of subjects' rights and potential data distortion? A summary statement of each of these issues is presented in Table 2.

THE RIGHT TO CHOOSE

Most investigators assume that subjects have the freedom to choose whether or not they will participate. The researcher may reason that since subjects have agreed to participate he is relieved of any obligation to protect them. This rationale is not unlike the "caveat emptor" philosophy which prevailed in marketing prior to World War II. However, subjects' right to choose may be vio-

lated in three ways; (1) subjects may be unaware of their right to refuse; (2) subjects may lack sufficient knowledge to make an informed choice; and (3) subjects may not be given the opportunity to choose.

The right to refuse may be undermined in several ways: (1) subjects may not be cognizant of their right to refuse and, (2) subjects who are aware of their right to refuse may experience such external pressure from the investigator and peers that it is difficult for them to freely exercise this right. For example, poorly educated respondents are usually neither aware of the right to refuse nor prepared to exercise it. Alternatively, subjects recruited from church or social groups are often induced to participate by offering donations to the group's treasury or favorite charity for each member participating. The high response rates typically received are undoubtedly attributable to group pressure.

Kelman (1972) suggests that the subject may fail to exercise his right to refuse because he believes that he lacks both the capacity and right to question research procedures. In essence, the re-

Table 2 Summary of ethical questions for market researchers

Subjects' rights	Possible results of violation of rights	Research questions[a]
A. The right to choose		
1. Awareness of right	1. Feelings of forced compliance, biased data	1. How do responses from subjects who perceive participation in research to be purely voluntary differ from those of subjects who feel coerced?
2. Adequate information for an informed choice	2. May violate the client's desire for anonymity, may enable subjects to enact subject role	2. Does knowledge of the research client distort subjects' responses? What, if any, subject roles are enacted when subjects are given full information prior to participation? What alternatives to complete disclosure of information prior to subjects' participation are available? How effective are these methods in gaining unbiased data and protecting subjects?
3. Opportunity to make a choice	3. Subjects may avoid environments where this right is violated	3. If subjects suspect that unobtrusive measures of their behavior are being taken, how is their behavior affected? Do subjects avoid environments where they suspect unobtrusive measures are taken?
B. The right to safety		
1. Protection of anonymity	1. Biased data, refusal to participate in future research	1. How does the degree of anonymity affect subjects' responses? How does violation of promised anonymity affect subjects' willingness to participate in future research?
2. Subject stress	2. Biased data, refusal to participate in future research	2. How does the degree of subject stress affect subjects' responses? How do stressful studies affect subjects' willingness to participate in future research? Can debriefing effectively relieve subject stress?
3. Deception of subjects	3. Biased data, refusal to participate in future research	3. How does deception influence subjects' responses? Under what conditions is deception essential? What effects does deception have on subjects? How does deception influence subjects' willingness to participate in future research? What alternatives to deception are available and under what conditions can they be employed? What are the implications of using deception on the client's and profession's image? Can debriefing relieve the negative effects of deception? Can complete disclosure produce valid results when the subject believes he will gain by cooperating with the researcher?
C. The right to be informed		
1. Debriefing	1. Unrelieved stress, feelings of being used, refusal to participate in future research	1. How does debriefing affect subjects' responses in future research? Do subjects believe they gain from debriefing? Conversely, does lack of debriefing make subjects feel used and less willing to participate in future research? Does debriefing perpetuate or reduce marketers' image as manipulators of human behavior?
2. Dissemination of data	2. Subjects may feel that they gain nothing from and are exploited by participating in research and consequently may distort their response and decline to participate in future research	2. Do subjects want access to research findings? Would giving participants access to research findings increase their willingness to cooperate? Under what conditions would dissemination of research findings to subjects reduce a client's competitive advantage?

[a]While some solutions or answers to these questions have been suggested throughout the paper, more research particularly in a marketing context, is needed.

spondent attributes expert and legitimate power (French and Raven, 1959) to the researcher. The investigator is perceived as knowledgeable about research techniques and their implementation and the subject suspends judgment, placing unquestioning trust in the investigator. An individual who perceives such a power disadvantage is likely to unwittingly submit himself to potentially damaging psychological or physical manipulations. Poorly educated individuals and children are likely victims of such a power disadvantage and consequently may require special attention.

Galliher (1973) has recently suggested the following revision in the American Sociological Association Code of Ethics which would recognize subjects' differential needs for protection and information to insure that they have an opportunity to exercise their rights.

> Every person is entitled to equal privacy and dignity of treatment as a private citizen. However, equal protection may require unequal treatment of different types of subjects. More elaborate warnings and explanations may be required in dealing with economic and racial minorities and others who are poorly educated and are more (sic) likely to be ignorant of the research process than with other citizens (p. 97).

Similar protection for special groups of subjects may be warranted in marketing research.

Subjects who are aware of and exercise their right to refuse may nevertheless lack sufficient knowledge to make an informed choice. Consent to interviews and experiments is often obtained on the basis of little or no information about what participation entails. This is particularly true when deception is part of the research procedure. Several Codes of Ethics (American Psychological Association [APA], American Sociological Association [ASA] suggest that under conditions of incomplete disclosure prior to participation, subjects may be protected by informing them that they have the right to withdraw from the study at any time. However, once the subject has given his consent he may find it difficult later to withdraw or refuse to answer when personal or sensitive questions are asked. The interview or experiment is a social situation where previous assent effectively prevents the participant from terminating the relationship. Marketers are not only well aware of this pressure on the subject, but often capitalize on it by placing highly personal questions at the end of the interview or experiment.

Finally, subjects may be deprived of their opportunity to exercise the right to choose. Psychological techniques, such as projective tests, and unobtrusive measures may be utilized to circumvent the need for subjects' consent. These techniques may reveal information which subjects would withhold under normal circumstances.

Researchers often contend that unobtrusive measures taken in settings where the individual could reasonably expect his behavior to be observed raise little ethical question. However, the Codes of Ethics of the APA, ASA, and MRS all specifically address unobtrusive measures as a serious violation of the individual's right to refuse. The Market Research Society specifically outlines procedures to be employed when collecting unobtrusive data: (1) special precautions must be taken to insure the anonymity of the individuals observed, and (2) immediately after the data are collected the individual must be informed of the observation, given an opportunity to view the data, and if he so desires, have the data deleted or destroyed. Similar protective procedures may be warranted in the AMA Code of Ethics.

Furthermore, unobtrusive measures are often taken in nonpublic places. An interviewer in a respondent's home may note style preference in home furnishings, type of kitchen appliance, books apparently read, and the like. Alternatively, the experimental subjects may not be informed that his actions will be monitored through a one-way mirror, or that what appears to be another subject is actually a stooge observing and reporting the subject's behavior. All these actions constitute violations of the subject's right to choose and place the researcher in an ethically untenable position.

Practical Considerations

Clearly, violation of the right to choose is objectionable because it infringes upon the individual's right to freedom of choice. More practically, the failure to make research participants aware of their right to choose may introduce artifacts into the data. Subjects who would like to leave an experiment or interview but feel obligated to continue may become anxious or antagonistic toward the researcher.[1] As a result, they may give brief and speeded responses. Similarly, subjects who suspect that their right to choose is being circumvented through the use of unobtrusive measures such as one-way mirrors in stores may become self-conscious and behave abnormally or avoid the environment being monitored. In their study comparing responses from coerced and volunteer subjects, Cox and Sipprelle conclude:

> . . . the practice of using coercion, however mild and disguised, to secure research subjects should come under scrutiny as a possible error in the design, conduct, and generality of the research (1971, p. 728).

Additional research is needed to determine *how* and *under what conditions* responses from subjects who perceive participation to be purely voluntary differ from those who feel coerced.

To preserve subjects' right to choose it has been suggested that the researcher inform the participant of all features of the research which might reasonably influence his willingness to participate (American Psychological Association Code of Ethics). Implicit in the subject's right to know *all* relevant information is his right to know who the research sponsor is and how the research data will be used. Subjects may object to participating in research sponsored by certain firms or supplying information to be used in improving advertising persuasiveness. However, clients may strongly object to releasing such information arguing that they have a right to anonymity. The client may desire that the nature of the research remain confidential

to avoid quickened competitive reaction and its attendant financial losses. Further, the client may argue that knowledge of the research sponsor, probable uses of data, and all aspects of the research procedure prior to data collection may distort subjects' responses by evoking one of the commonly discussed subjects' roles (i.e., the good, faithful, apprehensive, or negativistic subject) and thereby lower the value of the research.

Nevertheless, clients should recognize that under some circumstances knowledge of the research sponsor may actually improve data quality. For example, if the firm is viewed as subscribing to the modern marketing concept, the respondent may view the research process as an opportunity to communicate his interests and needs to a firm concerned with better serving him. This is consistent with Jourard's (1972) assertion that the veracity of an individual's responses is heightened when he believes a gain will result from doing so.

Possible Solutions

At the outset of a project the researcher and client must agree on disclosure or withholding of relevant information. When releasing all relevant information prior to subjects' participation is likely to bias the results, a variety of procedures may be instituted to insure subjects' right to choose. For example, Holmes and Bennett (1974) suggest an informed consent procedure which initially entails providing the subjects with an introduction to experimentation where it is mentioned that deception is sometimes essential to produce valid results. Subjects are then told the general nature of the particular experiment including what they will be asked to do, and are informed that they may withdraw from the study at any time; only after the data have been gathered will they be informed of all the aspects of the research. At this point subjects are allowed to withdraw their data if they do desire. Holmes and Bennett empirically support the efficacy of their procedure by demonstrating that the data obtained are similar whether or not participants are forewarned about deception.

---

[1] A thought provoking open letter from a subject to experimenters appears in Kelman, (1972).

An alternative approach to insuring respondents' right to choose involves anticipating their consent rate (Berscheid, et al., 1973). A sample drawn from the subject population is informed of the purpose and procedure of a proposed experiment. After subjects have familiarized themselves with the description, they state how willing they would be to participate in the experiment. Consent rates for the population can then be derived from the data. Refusal by a significant portion of subjects indicates that the experiment should be redesigned and retested. To test the predictive validity of their procedure, Berscheid, et al. (1973) compared consent rates of subjects reading the Milgram experiment procedure to ones actually participating in Ring, et al.'s (1970) version of the Milgram experiment. Estimates obtained by the informed consent procedure were conservative; they tended to overestimate the refusal rate by approximately 10%. However, the conservative bias may be attributed to the possibility that the Milgram procedure was more severe than that of Ring, et al. (1970).

The anticipating informed consent procedure offers a method for protecting subjects from harmful or unpleasant experiences. At the same time it mitigates the distortion likely to result from full disclosure of all relevant information prior to participation. When this procedure is used, full disclosure and an opportunity for subjects to withdraw their data can be incorporated into the debriefing session.

RIGHT TO SAFETY

Research respondents have a right to safety or freedom from psychological and physical harm. Although marketing researchers rarely conduct investigations likely to result in physical harm (i.e., studies employing electrical shocks or drugs), their investigations may inflict psychological harm which is even more detrimental. Violation of promised anonymity, stressful situations, and deception all may be psychologically damaging.

Each of these three potentially harmful procedures will be discussed, their practical implications specified, and possible solutions presented.

Protection of Anonymity

The AMA Marketing Research Code of Ethics specifies that respondents in research have the right to protection of anonymity if it has been agreed to by the researcher. Further, any information given shall be held in confidence and used only for research purposes. However, violations of promised anonymity frequently occur.

Responses to sensitive questions, those of age, income, religion, and political affiliation, are often collected by market researchers promising confidentiality. Yet these researchers frequently rely upon the honesty and moral will of their employees to keep this promise. In research offices, uncoded questionnaires containing confidential data often lie in full view of employees and visitors. Furthermore, the researcher may forward uncoded questionnaires to clients, assuming that the client can be trusted to protect the subject's anonymity. These data may actually be used to develop sales appeals employed by the company salesmen when calling on respondents.

Some researchers strive to give the impression of anonymity where none exists. The pretext of an unsigned mail questionnaire is all too often violated by placing codes in the stapling, binding area, or under the stamp, or by systematic misspelling of return addresses (Boruch, 1971; Manniche and Hayes, 1975; Sawyer and Schecter, 1968). These practices are not only unethical but as will be discussed below, they may actually bias the research data.

Practical Implications

Over time, promises of anonymity may be regarded suspiciously by subjects. As a result they may refuse to respond to personal or controversial questions or, more drastically, refuse to participate in research. Individuals who do participate may respond less than candidly to sensitive questions.

Either reaction distorts data. Additionally, disregard for subjects' promised anonymity may generate ill will toward the researcher's sponsor and profession.

King (1970) has investigated the effect of anonymity on questionnaire returns and responses to sensitive questions (drug usage) and found that the anonymous questionnaire yielded higher returns and higher admission of drug usage than openly coded questionnaires. However, this difference was not significant at the .05 level. More empirical investigations are needed to determine the extent and manner in which subjects' responses to questions vary according to the perceived confidentiality of responses.

Possible Solutions

Several methods which protect the anonymity of the respondent are currently available. Elaborate "link" systems may guard subject anonymity in confidential longitudinal studies (Astin and Boruch, 1970). The implementation and explanation of such a system may reassure subjects that their data will remain confidential and thus encourage them to respond candidly.[2] Researchers conducting short-term studies can protect subjects by assigning them identifying numbers and destroying the original identifying data.

An alternate approach for insuring anonymity when responding to sensitive or potentially embarrassing questions is the "randomized response technique" (Greenberg et al., 1971; Warner, 1965). This procedure allows the respondent to reply to a question selected at random from two or more questions without the interviewer knowing which question he is responding to. Statistical procedures are later used on the aggregate responses from a sample to separate the distributions of responses to the alternative questions. Although this technique guarantees anonymity, its application is limited. It is cumbersome to administer and only provides aggregate data. However, tests of the technique indicate that it does improve response rates and response accuracy (Greenberg, et al., 1971) thereby attesting to the effect of perceived anonymity on data quality.

Subject Stress

Research procedures may induce stress and anxiety without offering relief. Stress may be an unintended consequence of the research procedures such as deception, asking questions the respondent cannot answer, or providing the respondent with unpleasant information about himself. Alternatively, stress may be intentionally induced as a motivating device in simulations or experiments.

When an individual is asked either factual or opinion questions he is unable to answer he may blame himself. The very fact that he is asked such questions implies he should know the appropriate response. Furthermore, an individual participating in a study may discover unpleasant facts about himself. He may find that the three unmarked cans of beer which he stated tasted quite different were, in fact, all the same brand. In turn, this discovery might lead the subject to doubt his competence as a shopper. Occasionally experimenters find it necessary to induce stress in subjects intentionally. This may occur in simulation games where the researcher wishes to produce behaviors which are assumed to be caused by stress in the real world (i.e., competition, high achievement drive, or conflict).

Practical Implications

Subjects' stress has several practical implications for marketers. First, subjects who find research settings stressful may avoid participating in research. Ultimately only those individuals with a high tolerance for stress are likely to serve as research participants. The sample bias induced would limit the

---

[2]This reassurance may be of particular importance in view of recent court rulings that require reporters to divulge confidential souces of information. Under the broadened concept of marketing, researchers investigating sensitive social issues may be called upon to do the same.

generalizability of the research results. Second, subjects' stress may result in contrived responses. Subjects may feel compelled to create responses to questions they are unable to answer, or may experience evaluation apprehension (Rosenberg, 1965) and distort their responses to insure favorable self-presentation. Finally, experimenters who intentionally induce stress to produce behaviors such as competition may fail to reproduce the real-life behavior. In fact, the naturally occurring behavior may not be generated by stress; rather, stress may be a consequence of the behavior.

Possible Solutions

Researchers can protect subjects from stress by pretesting the level of stress, employing procedures which limit the stress evoked, or relieving the stress which does occur. Both pretesting of manipulations and use of anticipating informed consent procedures may be used to assess the level of stress inherent in a study. Investigations judged to induce an excessive amount of stress should be revised. In addition, when designing a study the researcher can make an effort to avoid potentially stressful procedures such as deception (alternatives to deception will be discussed in the next section). Stress may also result when the subject feels that his actions, attitudes, or intelligence are being judged by the researcher. Disclaimers such as "there are no correct responses, we are merely interested in your opinion" may relieve some stress and improve the data. Although it is preferable to minimize stress, in some investigations the induction of stress will be deemed essential. Under these circumstances the researcher may use the debriefing session to reassure subjects and allay any fears or misgivings they might have.

Deception of Subjects

Deception in research investigations is perhaps the most frequently discussed ethical issue. Attention has focused on deception as a result of its potentially damaging consequences: violation of the subjects' right to make an informed choice regarding participation, violation of the investigator-subject trust relationship, and possible psychological harm to the subject. Additionally, the prevalence of deception in social psychological research increases the incidence of these damaging consequences.

Deception is a common practice in marketing research as in many other research contexts. The brand names of products that the subject is to compare may be falsified; the identity of the research client may be misrepresented; and elaborate cover stories may be generated to hide the research hypothesis. The effect of deception will be assessed, its practical implications presented, and alternatives to deception suggested.

Subjects may be deceived in ways which are either potentially harmful or which present little danger of harm (Kelman, 1967). Deception is potentially harmful in that it prevents the subject from making a rational choice as to whether or not he wishes to participate in a study. Furthermore, it may trick the subject into revealing more than he contracted for. As mentioned previously, deception may result in psychological stress by providing the subject with potentially disturbing insights. A subject may discover he is easily swayed by persuasive appeals or in a more extreme case such as Milgram's obedience study (1963), he may find that he lacks the courage to resist commands by the researcher to perform destructive behaviors.

In addition to potentially harmful effects of deception there are other effects which may not be viewed as harmful in the conventional sense. It can be argued that the mere use of deception violates the researcher-subject trust relationship. Although deception is an integral part of life (i.e., individuals often maintain fronts in their interpersonal relationships to mask undesirable traits; Goffman, 1959), the researcher-subject relationship involves a certain degree of trust not necessarily present in many other interpersonal relationships. The subject places his safety in the experimenter's hands. Violation of this trust can result in a breakdown of the researcher-subject relationship.

Practical Implications

Deception may have several implications for the quality of data: its use may bias data, contaminate the subject pool, and result in public outcry. Experimental evidence addressing the effect of deception on research data is equivocal. Evidence can be marshaled to support both contentions that the *use* and the *absence* of deception biases research results. The rationale underlying the use of deception is that the subjects' awareness of the research hypothesis will influence their behavior by allowing them to choose which subject role they will enact: the good or helpful subject who tries to confirm the experimenter's hypothesis (Orne, 1962), the negative subject who tries to disconfirm the hypothesis (Masling, 1966), or the apprehensive subject who tries to present himself favorably to the experimenter (Rosenberg, 1965). Furthermore, the particular subject role which is enacted may vary across situations and persons. Enactment of rules such as the ones above makes research results uninterpretable.

Several studies lend support to the argument that nonnaivete biases result. Glinski, Glinski, and Slatin (1970) found that nonnaive subjects exhibited significantly less conformity than naive subjects in an Asch-type conformity experiment. Resnick and Schwartz (1973) conducted a verbal learning experiment in which subjects were either deceived (nonethical condition) or not deceived (ethical condition) about the true purpose of the experiment. In the nonethical condition significant conditioning was found in a positive direction (similar to previous findings), however, in the ethical condition findings were exactly the opposite. Furthermore, Resnick and Schwartz (1973) report that they experienced extreme difficulty in obtaining subjects for the ethical condition. They conclude that participants enjoy an element of non-disclosure and are bored when informed of all aspects of the research. What subjects may in fact be enjoying is outwitting the experimenter by playing the "guess the deception" game.

Although lack of deception may alter findings, so may the use of deception. Subjects who have been previously deceived and debriefed or who have learned of deception through textbooks, journals, and friends are likely to be suspicious of research procedures. Suspicion of deception may lead the subject to search for cues to the true purpose of the experiment regardless of whether or not deception is used in the particular experiment. Evidence for the prevalence of suspicion is given by findings that subjects in ethical (nondeception) studies are often unwilling to believe that deception is not being employed (Argyris, 1968; Resnick and Schwartz, 1973).

Irrespective of whether or not the subject is able to uncover the true hypothesis, he may formulate a hypothesis about the experiment and react accordingly (i.e., may enact one of the subject roles). Cook, et al., (1970) conducted a series of attitude change experiments which varied the frequency of previous deceptions and debriefings and observed what subject role was enacted by subjects with a longer experimental history. They reported that merely learning of deception did not have a significant effect. However, prior experience of deception did have the effect of biasing data away from what might presumably be seen as the experimenter's hypothesis (negativistic subject role). Moreover, the finding that suspicion interacts with experimental performance has been confirmed by other investigators (Silverman, et al., 1970; Stricker, et al., 1968; Stricker, et al., 1969). Thus, there appears to be some indication that in certain situations past deception may lead to enactment of subject roles and biased experimental results.

In summary, both the use and absence of deception may affect research results. As long as deception is a popular research tool, subjects are likely to be suspicious of all experimental situations and this suspicion may affect their experimental performance. The absence of deception affords the subject the opportunity to select which subject role he will employ and thereby confounds results. However, Jourard (1972) and Argyris (1968) suggest that if the subject believes he will gain by providing accurate data he will probably do so. Thus, deception may be unnecessary if the research is designed to benefit the subject by helping him expand his alternatives through a better understanding of himself and by allowing the researching firm to better understand his needs.

Further investigation of the effects of deception is needed. Whenever deception is employed, its efficacy should be probed in the debriefing session. Gergen (1973) calls for research to determine both the ethical effects (i.e., harm to subjects) and biasing effects of deception. Marketers have a special interest in such research (particularly biasing effects) as costly decisions may be based on results from research employing deception.

The researcher's decision as to whether or not he will use deception also has several implications for his profession. As indicated above, deception may lead to contamination of the subject pool and distortion of results in colleagues' studies. Further, the use of deception may result in researchers being cut off from the subject pool by public opinion or legal restraints. The growing strength of the consumer movement and its accompanying legal restraints are all too familiar to the marketer. Abuse of individuals as subjects in marketing research seems a likely target for consumer complaint. In fact, some congressional hearings on the use of children as subjects in marketing research have already been held as the result of public demand. If for no other reason than the protection of marketing research from severe regulation, marketers should proceed cautiously in their use of deception. Furthermore, research should be conducted to determine the effect of deception on data and its effects on subjects. In the future, legislators and the general public may call upon marketing researchers employing deception to present em-

pirical support for its use and an analysis of its effects on subjects.

Possible Solutions

Undoubtedly there may be some topics which cannot be researched without the use of deception. Nevertheless, deception should be used only when other alternatives have been exhausted and potential harm to the subjects is minimal (Holmes and Bennett, 1974). In this section several alternatives which have been considered and seem applicable to marketing research—role playing, forewarning, and anticipating informed consent —will be discussed.

Role Playing. In lieu of deception, role playing has been endorsed by several well-known psychologists (Kelman, 1967; Ring, 1967). Role playing offers a potential solution to the ethical and methodological deficits of deception by:

> ...drawing on subject's active participation and involvement in the proceeding and encouraging him to cooperate in making the experiment a success, not by giving the results he thinks the experimenter wants, but by conscientiously taking the roles and carrying out the tasks the experimenter assigns him (Greenberg, 1967, p. 9).

Although in the Inter-Nation Simulation Procedure role playing has been found to generate a high level of involvement and elicit real-life quality motivations (Guetzkow, et al., 1963), support for it as an alternative to deception is limited. Greenberg (1967) was able to replicate Schachter's (1959) experiment on anxiety and affiliation by asking subjects to imagine they were actually subjects in an experiment and giving them a description of the procedure. However, he was forced to partition subjects on the basis of perceived rather than manipulated anxiety indicating that subjects were unable to take the roles they were assigned. In a comparison of the results of a deception versus role-playing experiment, Willis and Willis (1970) found that the role-playing subjects were able to replicate the obvious main effect exhibited by the deceived subjects but not a more subtle interaction. Similarly, Holmes and Bennet (1974) found role-playing subjects able to replicate the self-reports of deceived subjects but not their pulse and respiration rates.

Role playing has come under strong attack from Freedman (1969) who contends that it merely provides information about how people think they would behave rather than how they actually behave. This contention is supported by Horowitz and Rothchild's (1970) finding that in an Asch-type conformity study prebriefed role-playing subjects exhibited significantly less conformity than either forewarned (to be discussed) or deceived subjects. Further, Miller's (1972) review of the role-playing literature supports Freedman's arguments and adds that role playing equates behavioral or outcome similarity with causal similarity. Even when role playing and deception provide the same outcomes, it cannot be concluded that the outcomes are the result of the same process. Therefore, general statements about the utility of role playing cannot be made and a deception group will always be necessary for comparison. If this argument holds, role playing will not decrease the need for deception.

Forewarning. Willis and Willis (1970) have suggested a variant on the role-playing alternative in which subjects are merely informed that all facets of the experiment cannot be revealed prior to their participation. The explanation of deceptions, which is included in role playing, is eliminated and subjects receive the treatment in the same manner as deceived subjects.

Horowitz and Rothchild (1970) report a direct comparison between deception, forewarning, and role playing. Their results indicate that forewarned and deceived subjects yielded comparable results and further that forewarned subjects were less suspicious than either deceived or role-playing subjects. Holmes and Bennet (1974) report analogous findings. These findings are of particular significance since, as mentioned previously,

suspiciousness can lead to distortion of results. The preliminary results suggest that forewarning may avoid some of the same pitfalls of deception without forfeiting the experimental realism of manipulation. Forewarning aids in preserving the experimenter-subject trust relationship and the subject's self-esteem. Mere forewarning may not be sufficient protection for subjects in a high-involvement, stressful experiment such as Milgram's obedience study; however, it may provide sufficient protection in the majority of marketing studies. Like role playing, forewarning may be subject to criticism on the grounds of equating outcome similarity with causal similarity. Forewarned subjects may assume good or faithful subject roles as a function of the demand characteristics present in the situation. Clearly, further research on the effectiveness of forewarning is needed.

Simulations are similar to forewarning. The subject is aware that the situation is artificial and yet he may play an active, involving role in the situation; thus his behavior is real rather than role playing. Simulation has not been investigated as an alternative to deception to date. However, it offers interesting possibilities in situations where deception in the real world would be highly unethical.

Anticipating informed consent. Anticipating informed consent, a technique elaborated on under the right to choose, may also be used to protect subjects from offensive deception. This technique may be used to screen experiments and then actual subjects in the experiment could be merely forewarned. This combination of techniques could go a long way to protect subjects and the reputation of the profession. Further, employing this technique would help reduce suspicion and thereby benefit the client and profession by increasing the quality of the results.

Alternatives to deceptions have been discussed; however, there may be occasions where the use of deception is necessary. When deception is used, debriefing is often viewed as a method of countering the potentially harmful effects of deception as well as a method of repaying the subject for his participation in the study. While debriefing should be included in any research procedure to fulfill subjects' right to be informed, research investigating its ability to counteract the adverse effects of deception is equivocal.

Holmes and Bennett (1974) found that debriefing was successful in removing subjects' stress brought on by deceiving subjects about possible electric shocks. However, Walster, et al. (1972) investigated the ability of debriefing to remove the effect of false feedback on subjects and found that it was not immediately effective. They conclude that aftereffects may be complex and unpredictable, varying with the individual. The difference between these two deception studies lies in the type of deception. In one case subjects were deceived about something external to themselves (shocks), while in the other the deception involved feedback about their own performance and personality. It may be more difficult to remove the adverse effects of deception about oneself than about external events. In such instances the deception cannot be clearly displayed to be false and the subject may continue to harbor self-doubts. This would suggest that deception which provides the individual with false information about himself may be particularly harmful and difficult to counteract.

RIGHT TO BE INFORMED

Research subjects have a right to be informed of all aspects of the research. The importance of providing subjects with complete, accurate information regarding a research project has been discussed under subjects' right to choose. Furthermore, under the right to safety, deception was criticized because it distorts the information given to subjects. However, in instances where complete knowledge is likely to bias data, information may be withheld until data collection is completed. Debriefing following the investigation may be used to

provide subjects with complete information about the study's purpose and procedure and to relieve any stress resulting from deception or other procedures. Furthermore, debriefing makes the research a more equitable relationship by providing subjects with a learning experience. Finally, subjects have a right to be informed of the research findings. Informing subjects of the findings not only increases the knowledge subjects gain but also protects subjects from having those findings used against them (Guskin and Chesler, 1973; Warwick and Kelman, 1973). In this section subjects' rights to debriefing and to be informed of research findings are discussed.

Debriefing

Debriefing is an element of research procedure which has been neglected in marketing research. Marketing research textbooks and researchers publishing in marketing journals rarely make mention of it. While it is likely that marketing researchers do employ some form of debriefing, the procedure warrants more attention than it has received in the marketing literature to date.

Debriefing has been suggested as one method of counteracting and minimizing the negative effects of deception of stress (Kelman, 1967). It can also be argued that subjects should gain in some positive manner from their participation in research. Debriefing converts the research experience into a learning experience for subjects. For these reasons it seems imperative that all research sessions conclude with a thorough debriefing of subjects.

The importance of careful debriefing cannot be overemphasized. Abrupt debriefing which bluntly informs the subject he has been ''had'' can be more destructive than no debriefing. Proper debriefing allows the subject to save face by uncovering the truth for himself. The experimenter should begin by asking the subject if he has any questions or if he found any part of the experiment odd, confusing, or disturbing. This question provides a check on the subject's suspiciousness and the effectiveness of manipulations. The experimenter continues to provide the subject cues to the deception until the subject states that he believes there was more to the experiment than met the eye. At this time the purpose and procedure of the experiment is revealed.

During debriefing the experimenter should evince his own discomfort at having deceived the subject. He should also explain why deception was necessary to test the hypothesis. Finally, the subject should be sworn to secrecy, stressing the damage which could result if later subjects were told about the deception. Encouragingly, it has been found that few subjects break the faith even under great pressure from friends (Aronson, 1966). (A good discussion of debriefing appears in Aronson and Carlsmith, 1962.)

Although debriefing is most often discussed in reference to laboratory experiments, it is also applicable in field experiments or surveys where deception is used. However, in longitudinal studies such as panel studies the question of when to debrief may be problematic. Debriefing after each wave of data collection may bias subsequent results by providing the subjects with information about the experimenter's hypothesis. This contention is supported by Cook, et al.'s (1970) and Brock and Becker's (1966) findings that subjects who had been debriefed following a deception experiment and were then subjects in another, similar, deception experiment tended to yield biased data relative to naive controls. However, this result only occurred when the second experiment was similar to the debriefed experiment and when both experiments were conducted in rapid succession. Under such conditions it would seem wise to delay debriefing until all data collection is complete. In the case of panel studies, delayed debriefing is unlikely to harm subjects since little deception occurs (i.e., subjects are merely asked to record their purchases over time).

Practical Implications

Debriefing is an important research tool. It helps to relieve any discomfort that the study may have

caused subjects and it makes the study a learning experience for participants. In the absence of such feedback the individual may feel that he is being used, say, to design advertisements whose sole purpose is to manipulate his behavior. A negativistic attitude may develop and cause subjects to distort responses purposefully in future research. Other individuals may simply decline to participate in research reasoning, "Why should I *help* marketers manipulate my behavior?"

Although debriefing is desirable, it may be opposed when the research sponsor is in a highly competitive industry. For such clients disclosure of research purposes and procedure may eliminate any competitive advantage the research might provide, and thereby eliminate the motivation to conduct research. Furthermore, it can be argued that debriefing may make subjects wise to deception and thereby contaminate the subject pool. However, as reported earlier, debriefing was only found to have a significant effect in subsequent deception experiments when the test experiment was clearly *similar* to the debriefed one (Brock and Becker, 1966; Cook, et al., 1970). In light of subjects' rights the answer to such a problem would seem to be eliminating deception, not debriefing.

On the other hand debriefing provides some benefits to the researcher, his client, and profession. It provides an opportunity to evaluate the effectiveness of the deception and manipulations. Subjects may be probed regarding the degree to which their behavior in the experimental situation differs from that in the real world. Such discussion may generate additional data and suggest ways of improving the study. Subjects' aid can be enlisted in improving the experiment. Finally, debriefing may stimulate the subjects' interest in the marketing profession and its research.

Dissemination of Research Findings

Included in the subjects' right to be informed is their right to be informed of research results. This right increases in importance as market researchers broaden their scope into social problem areas where the research sponsor may actually be seeking support and strategies for his oppression and exploitation of research subjects (i.e., sponsor: federal government, subjects: Black; Guskin and Chesler, 1973). This knowledge is essential if subjects are to protect themselves from the research sponsor. Jourard states:

> If psychologists reveal knowledge of "determiners" of human conduct to people other than the ones from whom they obtained this understanding, and if they conceal this knowledge from its source, the volunteer subjects (who have offered themselves up to the scientist's look), they put the recipients of the knowledge in a privileged position. They grant them an opportunity to manipulate men without their knowledge or consent . . . (1972, p. 7).

Moreover, the researcher must prevent research users from drawing false conclusions about the data by acknowledging factors which may have influenced data—biased sampling or wording, and inadequate operationalization of concepts.

Practical Implications

The view that subjects are entitled to access to research results is a radical departure from the traditional perspective that the client is the sole owner of the data. Clients' desire for a competitive advantage is likely to preclude dissemination of data to subjects. However, there is little incentive for subjects to spend their time providing data to which they have no access and which may be used against their interests. In the future, withholding data from research participants is an issue which may be adopted by consumerists and legislation may eventually force such dissemination. Until the time when such dissemination is required, clients will be reluctant to risk their competitive advantage by disseminating data to subjects. However, clients might discover that to adopt a "subject-orientation" may itself provide a competitive advantage not unlike that enjoyed by firms adopting a "consumer-orientation." Benefits might include more accurate data.

CONCLUSION

This article focuses on the practical implications of violation of subjects' rights. Table 2 summarizes the rights of subjects, practical implications of these rights, and questions they raise for marketing researchers. Implicit in the discussion of subjects' rights to this point is a basic subject right: the right to be heard. Consumers' right to be heard is recognized as an integral part of the modern marketing concept. For firms adhering to this concept, marketing research is a way of operationalizing this consumer right. Research provides the consumer an opportunity to communicate his needs and desires to firms concerned with improving consumer satisfaction. However, as indicated in Table 2, the accuracy of data generated in research may be influenced by the researcher's violation of subjects' rights to choose, to safety, and to be informed. When these rights are violated and results biased, all parties lose. Subjects lose an opportunity to communicate clearly and researchers and clients may draw false conclusions resulting in costly marketing errors.

If subjects' rights are continually violated, they may exercise their right to be heard in the form of protest against abusive researchers. Protests may involve boycotting marketing research or lobbying for legislation restricting marketing researchers. There are several indicators that subjects' protests may be forthcoming. Recently William R. Simmons, head of W. R. Simmons and Associates, Research, Inc. stated, "People are refusing to take part in our surveys to a greater extent than ever before" (*Business Week,* 1973, p. 216). Moreover, Robert Choate, head of the Council on Children Media and Merchandising, has called for regulations of marketing researchers' use of children as subjects. For these reasons, marketing researchers should turn their attention and research efforts in the direction of answering the ethical questions raised here.

REFERENCES

Argyris, Chris (September, 1968), "Some Unintended Consequences of Rigorous Research," *Psychological Bulletin,* 70, 185–97.

Aronson, Elliot (August, 1966), "Avoidance of Inter-subject Communication," *Psychological Reports, 19,* 238.

———, and Carlsmith, J. Merrill (1962), "Experimentation in Social Psychology," in G. Lindzey and Elliot Aronson, eds., *The Handbook of Social Psychology,* 2nd ed. Reading, Mass.: Addison-Wesley, 1–79.

Astin, Alexander, and Boruch, Robert R. (November, 1970), "A Link System for Assuring Confidentiality of Research Data in Longitudinal Studies," *American Education Research Journal,* 7, 615–24.

Berscheid, Ellen; Baron, Robert S.; Dernier, Marshall; and Libman, Mark (October, 1973), "Anticipating Informed Consent," *American Psychologist,* 7, 913–25.

Boruch, Robert F. (May, 1971), "Maintaining Confidentiality of Data in Educational Research: A Systemic Analysis," *American Psychologist,* 26, 412–30.

Brock, Timothy C., and Becker, Lee Alan (May, 1966) "Debriefing and Susceptibility to Subsequent Experimental Manipulations," *Journal of Experimental Social Psychology,* 2, 314–23.

Business Week (September 15, 1973), "The Public Clams Up on Survey Takers," 216–20.

Cook, Thomas D.; Bean, James R.; Carter, Bobby J.; Frey, Robert; Krovietz, Martin L.; and Reisman, S. R. (March, 1970), "Demand Characteristics and Three Conceptions of the Frequently Deceived Subject," *Journal of Personality and Social Psychology,* 14, 185–94.

Cox, D. E., and Sipprelle, C. N. (August, 1971), "Coercion in Participation as a Research Subject," *American Psychologist,* 26, 726–31.

Freedman, Jonathan L. (October, 1969), "Role Playing: Psychology by Consensus," *Journal of Personality and Social Psychology,* 13, 107–14.

French, John R. P., and Raven, Bertram H. (1959), "The Bases of Social Power," in Dorwin Cartwright ed., *Studies in Social Power,* Ann Arbor: University of Michigan Press, 160–67.

Galliher, John F. (August, 1973), "The Protection of Human Subjects: A Rexamination of The Professional Code of Ethics," *The American Sociologist,* 8, 93–100.

Gergen, Kenneth J. (October, 1973), "The Codefication of Research Ethics," *The American Sociologist,* 8, 93–100.

Glinski, Richard J.; Glinski, Bernice C.; and Slatin, Gerald T. (March, 1970), "Nonnaivety Contamination in Conformity Experiments: Sources, Effects, and Implications for Control," *Journal of Personality and Social Psychology,* 16, 478–85.

Goffman, Irving (1959), *The Presentation of Self in Everyday Life,* New York: Doubleday.

Greenberg, Bernard G.; Kuebler, Roy R., Jr.; Abernathy, James R.; and Horvitz, D. G. (June, 1971), "Application of the Randomized Response Technique for Obtaining Quantitative Data," *Journal of the American Statistical Association,* 66, 243–50.

Greenberg, Martin S. (February, 1967), "Role Playing: An Alternative to Deception," *Journal of Personality and Social Psychology,* 7, 152–57.

Guetzkow, H.; Alger, C. F.; Brody, R. A.; Noll, R. C.; and Snyder, R. C. (1963), *Simulation in International Relations,* Englewood Cliffs, N.J.: Prentice-Hall.

Guskin, Alan E., and Chesler, Mark A. (1973), "The Partisan Diagnosis of Social Problems," in Gerald Zaltman, ed., *Processes and Phenomena of Social Change,* New York: Wiley-Interscience.

Holmes, David S., and Bennett, David H. (March, 1974), "Experiments to Answer Questions Raised by the Use of Deception in Psychological Research: I. Role Playing as an Alternative to Deception; II. Effectiveness of Debriefing after a Deception; III. Effects of Informed Consent on Deception," *Journal of Personality and Social Psychology,* 29, 358–67.

Horowitz, Irwin A., and Rothchild, Bertram H. (March, 1970), "Conformity as a Function of Deception and Role Playing," *Journal of Personality and Social Psychology,* 14, 224–26.

Jourard, Sidney M. (1972), "A Humanistic Revolution in Psychology," in Arthur G. Miller, ed., *The Social Psychology of Psychological Research,* New York: Free Press, 6–13.

———(1972), "Experimenter-Subject Dialogue: A Paradigm for a Humanistic Science of Psychology," in Arthur G. Miller, ed., *The Social Psychology of Psychological Research,* New York: Free Press, 14–24.

Kelman, Herbert (January, 1967), "Humane Use of Human Subjects: The Problem of Deception in Social

Psychological Research," *Psychological Bulletin, 67,* 1–11.

———(November, 1972), "The Rights of the Subject in Psychological Research," *American Psychologist,* 27, 989–1016.

King, Francis W. (October, 1970), "Anonymous versus Identifiable Questionnaire in Drug Usage Surveys," *American Psychologist,* 25, 982–85.

Manniche, E., and Hayes, D. P. (Winter, 1957), "Respondent Anonymity and Data Matching," *Public Opinion Quarterly,* 21, 384–88.

Masling, John (1966), "Role-related Behavior of the Subject and Psychologist and Its Effects upon Psychological Data," *Proceedings,* Nebraska Symposium on Motivation, 67–103.

Milgram, Stanley (1963), "Behavioral Study of Obedience," *Journal of Abnormal and Social Psychology,* 67, 371–78.

Miller, Arthur G. (July, 1972), "Role Playing: An Alternative to Deception," *American Psychologist,* 27, 623–36.

Orne, Martin T. (November, 1962), "On the Social Psychology of the Psychological Experience: With Particular Emphasis to Demand Characteristics and Their Implications," *American Psychologist,* 17, 776–83.

Resnick, Jerome H., and Schwartz, Thomas (February, 1973), "Ethical Standards as An Independent Variable in Psychological Research," *American Psychologist,* 134–39.

Ring, Kenneth (February, 1967), "Experimental Social Psychology: Some Other Questions about Some Frivolous Values," *Journal of Experimental Social Psychology,* 3, 113–23.

——— ; Wallston, Kenneth; and Corey, Michael (January, 1970), "Mode of Debriefing as a Factor Affecting Subjective Reaction to a Milgram-type Obedience Experiment: An Ethical Inquiry," *Representative Research in Social Psychology,* 1, 28–42.

Rosenberg, Milton J. (January, 1965), "When Disso-

nance Fails: On Eliminating Evaluation Apprehension from Attitude Measurement," *Journal of Personality and Social Psychology,* 1, 28–42.

Sawyer, Jack, and Schecter, Howard (November, 1968), "Computers, Privacy, and the National Data Center: The Responsibility of Social Scientists," *American Psychologist,* 23, 810–18.

Schachter, Stanley (1959), *The Psychology of Application,* Stanford, Calif.: Stanford University Press.

Silverman, Irwin; Shulman, Arthur; and Wiesenthal, David (March, 1970), "Effects of Deceiving and Debriefing Psychological Subjects on Performance in Later Experiments," *Journal of Personality and Social Psychology,* 14, 203–12.

Stricker, Lawrence J.; Messick, Samuel; and Jackson, Douglas N. (December, 1968), "Desirability Judgments and Self-reports as Preditors of Social Behavior," *Journal of Experimental Research in Personality,* 3, 151–67.

———(May, 1969), "Evaluating Deception in Psychological Research," *Psychological Bulletin,* 71, 343–51.

Walster, Elaine; Berscheid, Ellen; Abrahams, Darcy; and Aronson, Vera (1972), "Effectiveness of Debriefing Following Deception Experiments," in Arthur G. Miller, ed., *The Social Psychology of Psychological Research,* New York: Free Press, 209–24.

Warner, Stanley L. (1965), "Randomized Response: A Survey Technique for Eliminating Evasive Answer Bias," *Journal of the American Statistical Association,* 60, 63–69

Warwick, Donald P., and Kelman, Herbert C. (1973), "Ethical Issues in Social Intervention," in Gerald Zaltman, ed., *Processes and Phenomena of Social Change,* New York: Wiley-Interscience.

Willis, Richard H., and Willis, Yolanda A. (July, 1970), "Role Playing Versus Deception: An Experimental Comparison," *Journal of Personality and Social Psychology,* 16, 472–77.

INDEX